P9-CAO-138

The Mainstream of Civilization

To 1500

Fourth Edition

Harcourt Brace Jovanovich, Publishers

San Diego / New York / Chicago / Washington, D.C. / Atlanta
London / Sydney / Toronto

JOSEPH R. STRAYER
Princeton University

HANS W. GATZKE
Yale University

The Mainstream of Civilization

To 1500

Fourth Edition

The Mainstream of Civilization *To 1500*
Fourth Edition

Cover: Mask of Tutankhamon. Photo © Lee Boltin. Background design adapted from Egyptian hieroglyphics on sarcophagus of the high priest Aho, Saïte Dynasty, Musée du Louvre, Paris. Photo Alinari-Scala from Art Resource.
Maps by Jean Paul Tremblay

ISBN: 0-15-551575-6

Library of Congress Catalog Card Number: 83-81467

Printed in the United States of America

Source of Illustrations on pages v–vi constitutes a continuation of the copyright page.

Source of Illustrations

Chapter 1

2: Photography by Egyptian Museum, The Metropolitan Museum of Art
4: American Museum of Natural History
5: Jericho Excavation Fund
6: Reproduced by Courtesy of the Trustees of the British Museum
7: Hirmer Fotoarchiv, Munich
8: Nelson-Atkins Museum of Art, Kansas City, Missouri (Nelson Fund)
11: *l* Trans World Airlines Photo; *b* Photo Almasy
12: *t* The Egyptian Museum in Cairo; *b* HBJ Collection
13: *t* Society of Antiquaries of London; *m* Reproduced by Courtesy of the Trustees of the British Museum; *b* Ashmolean Museum, Oxford
16: The Egyptian Museum in Cairo
19: Hassia, Paris
21: Reproduced by Courtesy of the Trustees of the British Museum
22: Courtesy of the Oriental Institute, University of Chicago
24: The Metropolitan Museum of Art, Fletcher Fund, 1954

Chapter 2

27: Katherine Young
28: Staatliche Museen zu Berlin
31: The Metropolitan Museum of Art Purchase, 1947, Joseph Pulitzer Bequest
32: The Metropolitan Museum of Art, Rogers Fund, 1914
34: American School of Classical Studies at Athens: Agora Excavations
35: National Archaeological Museum, Athens
36: Deutsches Archäologisches Institut, Rome
37: *t* Acropolis Museum, Athens; *b* Sparta Museum, Greece
40: Numismatic Museum of Athens TAP Service
41: *t* American School of Classical Studies at Athens: Agora Excavation; *b* Reproduced by Courtesy of the Trustees of the British Museum
42: The Metropolitan Museum of Art, Fletcher Fund, 1927
43: E. M. Stresow-Czakó
44: Phot. Bibl. nat. Paris
45: Museum of Fine Arts, Boston, H. L. Pierce Fund
46: Reproduced by Courtesy of the Trustees of the British Museum
48: Alinari/Editorial Photocolor Archives
49: Phot. Bibl. nat. Paris
51: The Mansell Collection
52: The Metropolitan Museum of Art, Rogers Fund, 1909

Chapter 3

56: Alinari/Editorial Photocolor Archives
58: Alinari/Editorial Photocolor Archives
59: *both* Deutsches Archäologisches Institut, Rome
61: Alinari/Editorial Photocolor Archives
63: Alinari/Editorial Photocolor Archives
64: Courtesy of The American Numismatic Society, New York
66: Alinari/Editorial Photocolor Archives
68: *l, r, m* Alinari/Editorial Photocolor Archives; *b* Staatliche Antikensammlungen und Glyptotek, Munich
69: Phot. Bibl. nat. Paris
70: Staatliche Antikensammlungen und Glyptothek, Munich
71: Ny Carlsberg Glyptotek, Copenhagen
73: Musée du Louvre, Paris
74: Musée du Louvre, Paris
75: H. Roger-Viollet

Chapter 4

78: John G. Ross, Photo Researchers
80: Courtesy of The American Numismatic Society, New York
82: HBJ Collection
83: Museum of Fine Arts, Boston, H. L. Pierce Fund
84: *t* Courtesy of The American Numismatic Society, New York; *b* Alinari/Editorial Photocolor Archives
85: Alinari/Editorial Photocolor Archives
86: *both* Alinari/Editorial Photocolor Archives
87: HBJ Collection
88: Deutsches Archäologisches Institut, Rome
89: Culver Pictures
91: Alinari/Editorial Photocolor Archives
92: *t* Alinari/Editorial Photocolor Archives; *b* Ny Carlsberg Glyptotek, Copenhagen
93: Alinari/Editorial Photocolor Archives
94: Museo Nazionale, Naples
96: Alinari/Editorial Photocolor Archives
99: Deutsches Archäologisches Institut, Rome

Chapter 5

102: Alinari/Editorial Photocolor Archives
104: John Johnston
105: The Brooklyn Museum, Charles Edwin Wilbour Fund
107: Alinari/Editorial Photocolor Archives
109: *t* Alinari/Editorial Photocolor Archives; *b* Musée Romain, Switzerland/Mme. Guiley-Lagache
110: The Metropolitan Museum of Art. Gift of J. Pierpont Morgan, 1917
112: Kunthistorisches Museum, Vienna
114: Giraudon
115: Kunthistorisches Museum, Vienna
116: Giraudon
118: Courtesy of The American Numismatic Society, New York
120: Alinari/Editorial Photocolor Archives

Chapter 6

123: Archaeological Survey of India, New Delhi
124: From Zimmer, Heinrich, *The Art of Indian Asia: Its Mythology and Transformations,* ed. Joseph Campbell,

Bollingen Series XXXIX, Vol. 2. Copyright © 1955, 1960 by Princeton University Press. Reproduced by permission of Princeton University Press

125: Raghubir Singh, Woodfin Camp and Associates
130: Courtesy of the Smithsonian Institution, Freer Gallery of Art, Washington, D.C.
131: Archaeological Survey of India, New Delhi
132: *t* United Nations; *b* Courtesy of the Smithsonian Institution, Freer Gallery of Art, Washington, D.C.
134: *t* From Chiang Yee's *Chinese Calligraphy: An Introduction to its Aesthetic and Technique,* 3rd Ed., Revised and Enlarged, Copyright © 1973 by the President and Fellows of Harvard College; *b* Reproduced by Courtesy of the Trustees of the British Museum
138: Courtesy of the Consulate General of the People's Republic of China
140: Richard C. Rudolph Collection, Los Angeles

Chapter 7

142: Museo Nazionale, Florence
145: *t* Deutsches Archäologisches Institut, Rome; *b* Rheinisches Landesmuseum, Bonn
146: Rheinisches Landesmuseum, Trier
147: *t* The Metropolitan Museum of Art, Purchase, 1895
149: Phot. Bibl. nat. Paris
150: Biblioteca Nazionale, Naples
151: The Bettmann Archive
152: *b* Staatsbibliothek, Bamberg; *t* Reproduced by Courtesy of the Trustees of the British Museum
153: Crown Copyright. Victoria and Albert Museum, London
154: Phot. Bibl. nat. Paris
155: Deutsches Archäologisches Institut, Rome

Chapter 8

158: Erich Lessing, Magnum Photos, Inc.
160: Courtesy of the Dumbarton Oaks Collection, Washington, D.C.
162: Alinari/Editorial Photocolor Archives
163: Alinari/Editorial Photocolor Archives
164: Reproduced by Courtesy of the Trustees of the British Museum
166: The Bettmann Archive
167: *t* The Metropolitan Museum of Art, The Cloisters Collection, 1966; *b* The Metropolitan Museum of Art, Gift of J. Pierpont Morgan, 1917
169: Aramco Photo
171: Courtesy of the Smithsonian Institution, Freer Gallery of Art, Washington, D.C.
173: *t* Courtesy of The American Numismatic Society, New York; *b* The Metropolitan Museum of Art. Bequest of Edward C. Moore, 1891
174: Karen Collidge

Chapter 9

178: Foto Ann Münchow, Aachen
180: Historical Pictures Service, Inc., Chicago
183: Stadtbibliothek, Schaffhausen
185: Millet-Connaisance des Arts, Louvre, Paris
186: *t* Reproduced by Courtesy of the Trustees of the British Museum; *b* Österreichische Nationalbibliothek, Vienna
188: New York Public Library. Astor, Lenox, and Tilden Foundations
190: *t* Swedish Information Service; *b* Antikvarisk-Topografiska archivet, Stockholm
191: Phot. Bibl. nat. Paris
194: *l* Foto Hinz, Basel; *tr* The Bettmann Archive; *br* Abbey Archives/ Scala/Editorial Photocolor Archives
197: The Metropolitan Museum of Art, Gift of George Blumenthal, 1941
198: Bayerische Staatsbibliothek, Munich
201: Reproduced by permission of the British Library

Chapter 10

205: Giraudon
207: *both* The Bettmann Archive
208: Bodleian Library, Oxford ms. Douce 118, fol. 55r
211: *t* Giraudon; *b* The Phaidon Picture Archive, from *The Bayeux Tapestry* published by the Phaidon Press, Ltd., Oxford, England
212: The Phaidon Picture Archive
214: HBJ Collection
215: The Granger Collection, New York
216: Foto Biblioteca Vaticana, Rome
218: Archives Photographiques, Paris
219: Bibliothèque Municipal, Dijon
220: *l* Simone Roubier; *m, r* F. S. Lincoln
221: *l* F. S. Lincoln; *r* Simone Roubier

Chapter 11

228: French Cultural Services
231: Ets J. E. Bulloz
232: Simone Roubier
234: Reproduced by permission of the British Library
237: *t* The Bettmann Archive; *b* Giraudon
241: The Bettmann Archive
243: Museo di Roma
244: Foto Biblioteca Vaticana, Rome
246: Culver Pictures
248: Alinari/Editorial Photocolor Archives

Chapter 12

252: Master and Fellows of Corpus Christi College, Cambridge
254: All Courtesy of The American Numismatic Society, New York, except second from top, Ashmolean Museum, Oxford
255: H. Roger-Viollet
256: Reproduced by permission of the British Library Board
258: By Courtesy of the Dean and Chapter of Westminster
259: The Bettmann Archive
261: Foto Biblioteca Vaticana, Rome
262: Alinari/Editorial Photocolor Archives
265: Reproduced by permission of the British Library
267: Reproduced by permission of the British Library
268: By permission of The British Library
271: Alinari/Editorial Photocolor Archives

Chapter 13

274: Reproduced by permission of The British Library Board
277: *both* The Bettmann Archive
279: Foto Biblioteca Vaticana, Rome
283: By Courtesy of the Dean and Chapter of Westminster
284: Phot. Bibl. nat. Paris/Roger-Jean Segalat
285: Giraudon
286: Masters of the Bench of the Inner Temple, London
289: Musée d'Art et d'Histoire, Geneva
291: Courtesy of the Trustees, National Gallery, London
293: *t* New York Public Library, Astor, Lenox and Tilden Foundations; *b* Rare Books and Manuscripts Division, New York Public Library, Astor, Lenox and Tilden Foundations
294: The Bettmann Archive
295: The Bettmann Archive

Chapter 14

298: A. y R. Mas (Arxiu Mas), Barcelona
300: Courtesy of the Dumbarton Oaks Collection, Washington, D.C.
301: Reproduced by permission of the British Library
303: The Metropolitan Museum of Art, Rogers Fund, 1913
305: Giraudon
309: Phot. Bibl. nat. Paris
310: Novosti Press Agency, London
312: From Michael Prawdin's *The Mongol Empire,* George Allen & Unwin, Hemel Hempstead, England
313: Historical Pictures Service, Chicago
315: Novosti Press Agency, London
317: Topkapi Palace Museum Library, *Treasures of Turkey* © by Editions d'Art Albert Skira S.A. Geneva

Preface

It requires a certain amount of courage to attempt to write a history of civilization in one volume. Once the task has been accomplished, however, it is easier to do it a second, third, and even a fourth time. As before, we have deliberately omitted certain details so that we could discuss as fully as possible the basic characteristics of each civilization and of different periods in the history of each civilization. We have tried to emphasize connections and interrelations—the ways in which politics, economics, art, scholarship, and religion all influence one another. We have tried to capture the flavor of each age—the unique combination of beliefs, activities, and institutions that distinguishes one society from another. In choosing the illustrations and the inserts in the text we have tried to give some idea of the diverse and ever-changing ways in which people have looked at and lived in their world. Finally, we have tried to consider the most difficult of all historical questions—the nature of and the reasons for change in human communities. Why and how do new institutions, new activities, new ideas rise and flourish? Why do they fade away? There are no easy answers to these problems; all we can do is suggest lines of inquiry that the reader may wish to pursue.

Obviously, it is easier to assess the characteristics and achievements of earlier periods than those of the age in which we live. The English Revolution of the seventeenth century ended long ago; the communist revolutions of the twentieth century continue to develop in unpredictable ways. Obviously also, it is more important to know details about the nature and background of problems that are still with us than details about problems that have been solved (at least partially). For these reasons the book broadens as it reaches the nineteenth century. More information is provided and more events are described in the hope that the reader will better understand the present state of the world.

We trust that no one will passively accept our interpretations or believe that our book is an adequate summary of human history. Our work is only an introduction, an attempt to persuade the reader to think deeply about history and to study it in detail. We are convinced that historical-mindedness is a necessity of human life. Consciously or unconsciously, we all base our estimates of the future on our knowledge of the past. It is important, then, that our knowledge of the past be as accurate and as deep as possible.

We remember with gratitude the contribution of the late Professor E. Harris Harbison to the first edition. He left us a framework that has been useful in subsequent revisions. We have also found the contribution of our former collaborator, Professor Edwin L. Dunbaugh, to be helpful in our work.

We owe special thanks to Conrad Schirokauer, City College of the City University of New York, for his contribution of Chapters 6 and 15.

The authors are greatly indebted to the following historians, who critically read *The Mainstream of Civilization* and made many valuable comments and suggestions: Bernard Bacharch, University of Minnesota; Shiva Bajpai, California State University at Northridge; Stanley Chodorow, University of California at San Diego; Tony Grafton, Princeton University; Frank Kidner, San Francisco State University; Ronald P. Legon, University of Illinois; David Luft, University of California at San Diego; Edward Malefacis, Columbia University; Don McLarney, Highland Community College; M. Gwyn Morgan, University of Texas at Austin; Frederick Murphy, Western Kentucky University; Kenneth Pennington, Syracuse University; and William Sewell, Jr., University of Arizona.

J. R. S.
H. W. G.

Foreword *The Study of History*

Consciously or unconsciously, all of us are historians. We can plan for the future only because we remember the past. We can add to our knowledge only because we do not lose memory of former experiences. Everyone, from the peasant to the scholar, tries to meet new situations by discovering familiar elements that make it possible to evoke analogies with the past. An individual who has lost his memory, who has forgotten his own history, is helpless until he has recovered his past or has slowly built up a new past to which he can refer.

What is true of individuals is also true of societies. No community can survive and no institution can function without constant reference to past experience. We are ruled by precedents fully as much as by formal laws, which is to say that we are ruled by memories of the past. It is the memory of common experiences that unites individuals into communities, and it is the memory of his own experiences that makes a child into an adult. Some of the memories may not be happy ones, but in reacting against them we are still linked to the past that produced them.

If everyone is his own historian, if individuals and societies necessarily draw on their memories of the past in order to deal with the present, then what is the need for formal, scholarly history? Isn't it enough to remember only the history that serves our immediate needs?

It is not enough, for two reasons. Human memory is fallible; individuals and societies forget many things that might be useful in solving their problems. This is why we have written records (which are a kind of formal history); this is why illiterate peoples try to preserve their customs and traditions through repeated oral recitations by the elders of the tribe. Second, the more complicated a society becomes, the narrower the range of individual experience in proportion to the total of possible experiences. A peasant living in a medieval village shared most of the experiences of his neighbors, and village custom gave solutions of a sort even to rare and unusual problems. No one living in an urbanized society shares many of the experiences of his neighbors, let alone the experiences of the millions of people throughout the world with whom he is connected by political and economic ties. No one can sum up the past experiences of his society, and of the societies with which his own interacts, with a few customary formulas; and yet these past experiences place a heavy burden on the present. In facing any problem, we look for familiar elements; if these are lacking, we feel fearful and helpless. Knowledge of history increases the chance of finding something familiar in a new and difficult situation.

Certain card games show how this process works at an elementary level. There is almost no chance that one distribution of cards will be repeated in a subsequent deal in bridge. Yet a person who has played several thousand hands of bridge should be able to make intelligent decisions and predictions even though every deal presents a new situation. He should be able to use his high cards and long suits effectively; he should be able to make some shrewd guesses about the location of cards in other hands. Not every experienced player will develop these skills. Some people are unable to generalize from their past experiences, and others cannot see analogies between the present and the past. But, generally speaking, an experienced player will make better use of his cards than a person who has played only ten hands. There is such a thing as a sense of the realities and possibilities of social activity, which can be developed from a knowledge of history.

At the very least, the past has left us the problems that we are trying to solve and the patterns of living that we are seeking to modify. At the most, we may find in the past suggestions for understanding and coping with the present. It is the historian's task to study the behavior of man in the past, to uncover facts, sort them, mass and link them, and so provide connections between past and present.

At the same time the historian must avoid certain pitfalls along the way. Connections with the past cannot be broken, but they can be misrepresented or misunderstood. Primitive peoples have little sense of chronology; they are apt to stir all their memories into a timeless brew of legend. At a more sophisticated level, the past has been used as a means of justifying present values and power structures. Many writers, from ancient times down to the present, have found historical examples to prove that their people were specially favored by the gods, that their state was founded and strengthened by heroes of superhuman ability, that virtue and wisdom (as defined by the author) have always brought success, while folly and vice have led to disaster. "History is philosophy teaching by example," said an ancient Greek (Dionysius of Halicarnassus), and it was more important for the examples to be edifying than for them to be true.

But it is not difficult to avoid deliberate distortions of the past. What *is* difficult is to avoid distortions caused by the incompleteness of our knowledge of the past. Many human activities have left few traces, especially in written records. For example, for thousands of years agriculture has been the chief occupation of the human race, but there are still serious gaps in our knowledge of the history of agriculture. "The short and simple annals of the poor" are short because information is scanty. If we had better information we would probably find that the life of a poor man in any period was anything but simple; it must have been filled with an unending series of nagging problems. In general, we know more about political history than social history, more about the privileged few than the unprivileged masses, more about the history of art than the history of technology, more about the ideas of philosophers and religious leaders than the beliefs of the common people.

Historians have become more skillful in recent years in finding material that gives a better-balanced picture of the past. Archeology reveals not only the palaces of kings, but the homes of ordinary people with their tools, their toys, their cooking utensils, and even fragments of their food. Gods and heroes may dominate the great works of art, but the common folk going about their ordinary business are there too—on Greek vases, Roman tombs, and portals of Gothic cathedrals. Discoveries of hoards of coins reveal unexpected trade relations. Aerial photography can bring out traces of ancient methods of plowing land and dividing fields. Even the written records, which have been studied for centuries, contain hitherto unused facts about such things as family life, migrations, and changes in economic patterns. There are still many holes in the record, but there is no reason to complain about lack of material.

The historian's greatest difficulty is not in discovering facts, but in deciding what facts can be ignored, or merely sampled, or clumped together in a single generalization. No one could master all the facts in yesterday's issue of the *New York Times,* and there are files of newspapers that run back to the eighteenth century. No one could master all the facts brought out in a single session of the Supreme Court, and the records of American courts and of the English courts from which they were derived go back to the twelfth century. To deal with the overwhelming mass of facts, historians have to arrange them, link them together, establish meaningful sequences of causes and effects.

The massing and linking of facts is not only essential, if history is to rise above the level of a catalogue; it is also inevitable, since it is the way the human mind deals with past experience. We do not recall every word we have exchanged when we decide that a certain person is a good friend. We do not remember every paragraph we have read when we decide that we like a certain book. But, while the process of massing and linking is essential and inevitable, this operation is the point of greatest danger in any kind of historical thinking. Consciously or unconsciously, one can mass facts to produce a misleading impression, even though each individual fact is true. Any governmental system can be made to appear obnoxious by discussing only the cases in which there is clear evidence of corruption or oppresion. Any society can be wreathed in a golden haze by dwelling only on its accomplishments in art, literature, and scholarship. Individuals and communities can become convinced that the whole world is conspiring against them if they remember only the occasions when they were treated unjustly. The nature of the sources themselves may cause distortion. For example, it is very easy to find material on political life in the city of Rome during the first century of the Roman Empire. It is difficult to collect evidence on provincial government or on social and economic development. The natural tendency is to overemphasize court intrigues and to pay little attention to such topics as economic growth or the spread of Latin culture throughout the West.

There is no easy way to overcome these problems, but an understanding of the principle of interconnectedness will help. No one is a purely political or economic or ideological being, and societies are composed of such varied human beings. Historians must look for the ways in which these (and other) forces interact. For example, the kind of food men eat can affect their whole social structure: a society dependent on olive oil for its fats will differ in many ways from one that depends on animal products such as lard, butter, and cheese. Religion can have an influence on trade: medieval churchmen aided the growth of Mediterranean commerce by importing silk for their vestments, incense for their ceremonies, and precious stones for their altar vessels and relic boxes. Trade in turn can influence the development of a religion: often it has been the merchant who prepared the way for the missionary. Ideas, technologies, institutions, social patterns, shifts in consumer preferences interact in complicated and bewildering ways. For example, increased use of easily washable cotton clothing in modern Europe improved personal hygiene and thus may have reduced death rates and contributed to growth of population. At the same time, increased demand for cotton encouraged the extension of slavery in the United States and thus was one of the causes of the Civil War.

Full realization of the connections among all human activities should lead to three conclusions. First, there are multiple causes for every event; single explanations for change are almost always wrong. Second, change in any one part of the social pattern may affect any other part of the pattern. Finally, the connections lead back into the past, and therefore the past influences the present.

The relationship between continuity and change is an interaction that the historian must watch with special care. All societies change, and yet all societies retain some connection with the past. The most "traditional" society is less traditional than it realizes; the most "modern" society is more influenced by tradition than it would like to believe. The Anglo-Saxons, theoretically bound by immemorial custom, invented the office of sheriff about the year 1000 A.D. The Americans, theoretically free to create an entirely new political structure, have preserved the office of sheriff with many of its original powers. Conquests and revolutions do not break all the connections with the past. Even where there has apparently been a complete break, the roots of a society may again grow down into its past. Roman law practically vanished from the West after the fifth century A.D.; it reappeared as a powerful force in the thirteenth century.

If there were no continuity, there would be no use in studying history, since nothing in the past would have any bearing on what is done today. If there were no change, there would be no history; a few years of practical experience would teach anyone all he needed to know about human behavior in society at any time and in any place. But, in the world as it is, the forces that would make for change are modified and even distorted by habit and custom, the forces that make for continuity are weakened and limited by new desires and new ideas. It is of some importance to understand where, why, and to what degree the desire for change prevails.

It is easy to see multiple, interlocking activities and rapid rates of change in the modern world. It is less easy to get a sense of the complexity and capacity for change of premodern and non-European societies, which is why the history of such societies often seems flat and uninteresting. The European Middle Ages are summed up as an "Age of Faith"; the history of much of Asia is dismissed with talk of the "unchanging Orient." Yet the Middle Ages were also a period of state building, economic growth, and technological invention—activities that have influenced the modern world fully as much as the Christian Church. The "unchanging Orient" produced all the great world religions, and each of these religions was a powerful force for change. Moreover, there are advantages in studying societies that are less complex and in which rates of change are less rapid than in our own. It is easier to observe and to draw conclusions about human behavior when the number of variables is small and changes do not come so fast that their effects are blurred.

A good historian, then, will try to give adequate attention to a wide variety of human activities, to discuss the interactions among these activities, and to trace the connections between past and present. But these principles cannot be applied mechanically. A writer who is careful to give an exactly equal amount of space to politics, economics, religion, the arts, and scholarship will probably not produce an adequate description of a society. The importance and even the identity of each of these activities varies with time and place. Religion had more influence on Indian than on Chinese society. Economics and politics merge in primitive societies, such as that of the early Germans. It is probably true that the vast majority of the world's scientists were born in the twentieth century; this could not be said of theologians. Thus the impact of scholarship on early societies is different from its impact on modern societies. To understand such variations and transformations, the historian must be more than a meticulous scholar. He must develop a feel for the period he is writing about, a sense of how people lived and worked and thought. It takes time and experience to acquire this feeling for the past, but once it has been acquired historians can give reasonably accurate, and occasionally penetrating, descriptions of earlier societies.

It is this understanding of the development of human society that gives history its chief value. History, even at its worst, gives us the comforting and necessary feeling that there are some familiar elements in a changing world and that there is some hope of understanding the changes that do occur. History at its best gives us a chance of reacting sensibly to problems as they arise. It does not guarantee the correctness of our responses, but it should improve the quality of our judgment. Good judgment about human behavior in society is badly needed today.

A Note on the Paperbound Editions

This volume is one of a number of variant printings of the Fourth Edition of *The Mainstream of Civilization.* It is not a revised or condensed text. Many users of the Third Edition found the various paperbound versions of that edition useful because the variant printings made it possible for them to fit the text into their own patterns of teaching and scheduling. In the Fourth Edition, the publishers have continued the practice of preparing separate paperbound volumes. Users may choose the volume that best corresponds to the chronological period covered by their courses. The variants are:

1. A two-volume edition

   The first volume (Chapters 1 through 21) starts with the beginnings of western civilization in the ancient Middle East and continues to the eighteenth century. The second volume (Chapters 20 through 35) begins with the seventeenth century and carries the account forward to the present day.

2. A three-volume edition

   The first volume (Chapters 1 through 14) starts with the beginnings of western civilization in the ancient Middle East and continues to the end of the Middle Ages. The second volume (Chapters 13 through 23) begins with the late Middle Ages and ends with Napoleon. The third volume (Chapters 23 through 35) begins with the French Revolution and Napoleon and carries the account forward to the present day.

3. *Since 1500* (one volume)

   Since 1500 (Chapters 16 through 35), after a Prologue that summarizes events to the year 1500, begins with the Renaissance and carries the account forward to the present day.

In all the variant printings, the pagination, index, illustrations, maps (except for the color maps in the three-volume printing), and other related materials from the one-volume version are retained. The difference between the one-volume and the other versions of this book is a difference only in form.

Contents

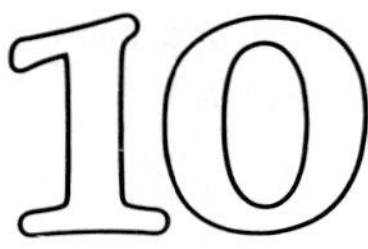

14

List of Maps

Introduction

This is a history of civilization, with emphasis on the civilization developed by the peoples of Europe. Like all histories, it must be selective. Incomplete as our record of the past is, it is still too full to permit discussion in a single book of all civilizations or even of all events in the history of one civilization. The principles that have guided our selection of topics may be indicated by a definition of our subject. We must answer two questions: What is civilization, and what has been the role of western civilization in creating the conditions that we find in the world today?

Civilization is derived from the Latin word for city, *civitas.* There is reason to emphasize this derivation, for every great civilization has had great cities, and the basic characteristics of civilization are easiest to observe in cities. Civilization is first of all *cooperation*—men working together to satisfy their material and spiritual needs. It requires *organization*—as soon as several people start working together there must be some sort of social, political, or economic pattern to regulate their activity. It encourages *specialization*—as soon as several people begin to cooperate in an organized way there are obvious advantages in dividing the work so that no one man has to do everything for himself. The character of a particular civilization is determined by the type and degree of the organization and specialization of that civilization. Ten thousand Greeks living in a small city-state could accomplish much more than ten thousand Indians scattered through the forests of North America. A few hundred men specializing in science have done more to change our civilization in the last few centuries than millions of artisans working through past ages. Intensive organization and specialization can produce spectacular results, and they can also create spectacular problems.

Civilization requires faith in certain ideals and values as well as skill in organization and techniques. The immediate and direct advantages of organization and specialization are not very apparent to most people. Organization sets limits on personal freedom, and specialization makes a man dependent on other men who may not be wholly trustworthy. In the long run the advantages are greater than the disadvantages, but farseeing, enlightened self-interest is a very rare human quality, probably rarer than altruism. And if men hesitate to give up present benefits for advantages in their own future, they will be even more hesitant if the advantages are to be gained only by their descendants. There is always resistance to increasing the scale and scope of organization; there is usually resistance to new types of specialization. This resistance can be overcome only by belief that there is something more important than the individual—a religion that emphasizes cooperation, a divinely appointed ruler or ruling class, a nation that has become almost a divinity, a theory of society that has taken on the aspects of a religion. There is a close connection between the dominant beliefs of a people and the kind of civilization it creates.

This history of civilization examines, more than anything else, how and why people have worked together. It is concerned with political history because the political record helps us to understand why people have been more successful at some times than at others in organizing on a large scale, and why some types of organization have proved more effective than others. It is concerned with economic and social history because economic and social organization has a direct effect on both political organization and the type and degree of specialization. It is concerned with the history of ideas and their manifestations in art and literature because organization and specialization are possible only within a framework of accepted beliefs. The interactions among political organizations, economic institutions, and dominant beliefs determine the character and development of a civilization.

Western civilization is only one, and by no means the oldest, of the civilizations that has left a historical record. The earliest civilizations touched Europe and the West only slightly; they centered in the river valleys of Egypt, the Near East, and China. Only with the appearance of the Greek city-states after 1000 B.C. can we see the beginnings of a civilization that belongs to the same family as our own. The Greeks drew heavily on the older civilizations of their neighbors, but they reorganized their borrowed materials and added significant elements to them. Ideas and forms of organization that have remained important in western civilization for over twenty-five hundred years first appear in ancient Greece. The Romans followed the Greeks as the dominant people in the Mediterranean basin. Like the Greeks, they borrowed from their predecessors, rearranged the old materials in new ways, and added ideas of their own, especially in government and law. Roman civilization is the direct ancestor of the civilization of modern European countries. There has never been a time, from the first conquests of the Roman Republic down to the present, when Roman law and Roman political ideas were not being discussed in some parts of the Continent.

Yet, while there is unbroken continuity between the civilization of the Greeks and the Romans and that of the modern West, it is well to remember that continuity is not identity. Much has been added—for example, the ideas brought in by Christianity—and much has been changed. Greco-Roman civilization was neither western nor European; it was Mediterranean. It was most highly developed on the eastern shores of the Mediterranean, and it was greatly influenced by the Orient. France and Spain were colonial outposts that contributed little to Greco-Roman civilization; Germany, Scandinavia, and the Slavic countries were outside the limits of the civilized Mediterranean world.

This Mediterranean civilization ran into trouble in the fourth and fifth centuries A.D. The economic organization proved unsatisfactory, and loyalty to the political organization weakened. As the Roman Empire slowly crumbled, the unity of the Mediterranean basin was destroyed, never to be restored. The southern and eastern shores became part of an Arab empire, part of the non-European Moslem civilization. A remnant of the old Roman Empire, centering around Constantinople, became the Byzantine Empire. This empire developed its own civilization—Christian in belief, Greek in language, but strongly influenced by the East in organization. Byzantine civilization made a great impression on the Slavic peoples of eastern Europe and had some influence on the Latin and Germanic peoples of the West. But it was never fully integrated with the civilization that grew up in western Europe. The western Europeans thought of the Byzantines as remote and somewhat untrustworthy relatives, who might hand out valuable gifts from time to time but who were too eccentric to live with. This attitude, in turn, has made it difficult to integrate eastern and western Europe, since the eastern countries borrowed much more from Byzantium than did those of the West.

With the Arab and Byzantine empires developing separate civilizations, the western European remnant of the old Mediterranean world was thrown back on its own resources. These were at first not very great. Western Europe saved only a fragment of its Roman inheritance, and this Roman inheritance was itself only a fragment of the old Mediterranean civilization. Moreover, the Germanic peoples of northern and central Europe, who had never been included in the Mediterranean world, were for a time dominant in western Europe. They brought in some new ideas and institutions, but they were backward in both political and economic organization. They were slow in assimilating the fragments of Roman civilization that remained, and even slower in developing effective types of organization. In the same way, the Christian religion, which eventually had great influence on European civilization, was only slowly absorbed by the half-barbarized Latins and the half-civilized Germans. For six centuries Europeans struggled with the problems of assimilating the Roman inheritance, integrating Latin and Germanic peoples, and implementing the basic ideas of Christianity. Only when this triple task was done did western Europe at last achieve an independent and consistent civilization. Only then could it profit from its contacts with the more highly developed civilizations of the Arab and Byzantine worlds.

Once it was established as a separate and viable entity, western Europe civilization developed rapidly. Many of our basic institutions and ideas, such as universities and representative assemblies, were worked out in the twelfth and thirteenth centuries. But this western European civilization was confined to a very small area. Its center was in the north, in a triangle bounded by Paris, Cologne, and London. The peripheral countries—Spain, Ireland, Norway, Sweden, Poland, Bohemia, and Italy—did not share in all the manifestations of this civilization, though they accepted its basic ideas. And beyond these countries the influence of western European civilization dropped off sharply. It had little effect on the Moslem world and none whatever on the peoples of Africa and Asia who lived beyond the limits of Moslem influence. It had some impact on Byzantium, but not enough to erase the differences that separated Byzantium from the West. There were some contacts with Russia, but the Russians were probably more influenced by the Byzantines. And the Mongol conquest of the thirteenth century weakened the ties that the Russians had with the West and forced them to face east for two centuries.

Meanwhile, another group of civilizations had developed in the Far East, in India, China, and Japan. Each had its own characteristic values—religious in India, secular and political in China, military in Japan. All three tended to become somewhat self-satisfied and isolated; neither India nor China, for example, was as interested in foreign voyages in the sixteenth century as it had been earlier. In all three the economic system was still based largely on village agriculture. Finally, in spite of promising beginnings, none of the Far Eastern civilizations had developed a strong scientific tradition. These characteristics put the Far Eastern countries at a disadvantage in dealing with Europeans, who were deeply interested in strange lands and peoples, were beginning to develop an economy based on machine production, and were just about to make their first important scientific discoveries.

The great voyages of exploration and the great mechanical inventions, both of which began in the fifteenth century, enabled western European civilization to emerge from its narrow corner and to spread throughout the world. Eastern Europe gradually accepted much of the civilization of the West, though the process was never complete. Three new continents—North America, South America, and Australia—were occupied by Europeans, and a fourth, Africa, was dominated by them. Asia, with its old civilizations and its dense population, was not so easily overrun, but even Asia was profoundly influenced by the European impact. Thus, for the first time, all the peoples of the world were brought into contact with a single civilization. The results of this great experiment are only beginning to be apparent.

There is some justification, then, for the conventional division of history into Ancient, Medieval, and Modern. Ancient history deals with the period in which some of the basic elements of western civilization were developed and passed on to later peoples. But ancient history must be focused on the Near East and the Mediterranean, not on Europe. It must give greater weight to Greece, Asia Minor, Syria, Mesopotamia, and Egypt than to Gaul, Britain, or Germany. Medieval history deals with the period in which a distinct western European civilization appeared. But this civilization was confined to a small part of the European peninsula, and it had little influence outside that area. During the

Middle Ages each great region of the world had its own civilization, and no one civilization was able greatly to modify another. Modern history deals not only with the rapid development of western European civilization in its old homeland but also with relations between that civilization and the rest of the world.

This growth and diffusion of western civilization has gone so far that we have perhaps entered a fourth period in its history. This period is marked by the appearance of distinct types of western civilization in the different areas occupied by Europeans, and, even more, by the revitalization of other civilizations following their contact with the West. Both the appearance of different types of western civilization and the revival of old civilizations are stimulating factors; they should help to prevent ossification and decay. Unfortunately, a stimulus can also be an irritant, and the reactions among competing civilizations may lead to efforts for mutual destruction rather than for mutual instruction.

The history of civilization begins in obscurity and ends with a question mark. Yet past experience is our only guide in solving present and future problems, and knowledge of our history may help us answer the great question with which we are faced today, that of the survival of civilization in any form.

The Mainstream of Civilization

To 1500

Fourth Edition

1 The Ancient Middle East to *ca.* 500 B.C.

Human beings have long been interested in their past. But for most peoples the remote past has been very difficult to recover. A few undated monuments, confused mixtures of ancient utensils and ornaments, groups of often contradictory legends were all that was available. As recently as two hundred years ago—or about the time of the American Revolution—western scholars knew almost no history before that of the classical age of Greece (*ca.* 500 B.C.). True, there was some understanding of the historical passages of the Hebrew scriptures, and some awareness that the colossal monuments along the Nile were the remnants of a very early Egyptian civilization. But little attention was given to these evidences of the existence of preclassical societies.

Just at this time, however, the excavations at Pompeii began, and the discoveries made there gave a tremendous impetus to the development of the science of archeology. During the past two centuries it has become clear that thousands of years before the Greeks there were highly developed civilizations in many parts of the Old World. About the year 1800, archeologists and historians began to reconstruct the long and fascinating history of ancient Egypt. More recently, in the nineteenth and twentieth centuries, they uncovered many other civilizations—notably in Mesopotamia, in India, and on the island of Crete—whose existence had not been known before.

Although great cities long unknown have been unearthed and whole libraries and archives discovered, the pace of new excavations continues unabated. Historians of the preclassical civilizations must be constantly prepared to revise their interpretations in the light of new evidence.

PREHISTORY TO *ca.* 3500 B.C.

Human beings, or something akin to human beings, have inhabited the earth for at least 4 million years and perhaps more. All but the last 5500 years of this span is regarded as prehistory, since it antedates the invention of writing. A vast sweep of human prehistory from about 4 million to 15,000 B.C. is known as the Old Stone Age because of the primitive pebble and stone tools used by humanlike animals and by humans throughout this era. During the Old Stone Age several species of humanlike creatures appeared

Opposite: The gold-plated inner coffin of the pharaoh Tutankhamon (*ca.* 1340 B.C.).

Origins of Manlike Animals *ca.* 2,000,000 B.C. | Appearance of *Homo sapiens* (Cro-Magnon Man) *ca.* 40,000 | Invention of Agriculture *ca.* 10,000 | Emergence of Civilization *ca.* 3500 B.C. | **20th Century**

Old Stone Age | New Stone Age | Era of Civilization

B.C. | A.D.

Art of the Old Stone Age:

Harpoon

Dart thrower of reindeer antler

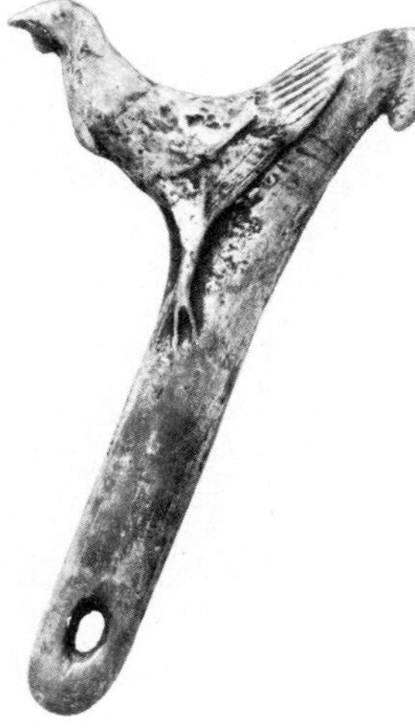

Baton de commandement of reindeer antler, showing wild horses

and disappeared. It was not until about 40,000 B.C. (a relatively recent date in prehistory) that Cro-Magnon man, the species from which all modern people are descended, first wandered into Europe, though we cannot know where or for how long this species may have existed before that time.

The New Stone Age ca. *10,000–3500 B.C.*

It took more than 2 million years to advance from the first crude pebble tools of the Old Stone Age to the precisely made, ground and polished tools characteristic of the New Stone Age. But in the relatively short span of about seven thousand years, there were two basic changes in the human way of life: the introduction of agriculture shortly before 10,000 B.C. and the emergence of early city-states sometime around 3500 B.C. The first step seems to have been connected with the drastic changes in climate between about 17,000 and 12,000 B.C. that followed the last of the four great Ice Ages and the subsequent melting of the glaciers that had covered much of the Northern Hemisphere. More people survived when the climate became more favorable, but it was difficult for the larger population to feed itself simply by hunting and gathering wild fruit and seeds. It took a long time to develop domesticated animals and plants, but when this had been achieved there was a second burst of population growth. With more food, more people could specialize in work that did not have a direct connection with agriculture or herding, and these people could live in the clustered settlements that became cities.

Around 1700 B.C. the largest concentrations of human life seem to have existed in a wide belt embracing southern Europe and northern Africa, and extending eastward through Palestine, Syria, Mesopotamia, and Persia to the Indus River and Yellow River valleys. There were gaps in this belt, however, where there was not much contact between the inhabitants of these regions. As a result, different types of populations developed (e.g., the Chinese in the Yellow River region). These lands abounded in the animal life on which people fed. But as the glaciers gradually retreated northward, the rainfall decreased, and much of the land became dry. The melting glaciers left behind great river systems which ran through fertile valleys better suited to plant than to animal life. The animals either migrated northward or died out. Man's response was the invention of agriculture—the domestication of plants and animals. Recent historians of agriculture have suggested that the first attempt to plant and harvest grain took place somewhere between Palestine and the upper Tigris-Euphrates Valley about 10,000 B.C. Over the next eight thousand years, the knowledge of farming, and later of animal breeding, spread throughout the areas of human habitation, though many primitive peoples in the hills and hinterlands continued to live only by hunting and food gathering, as some isolated tribes still do today.

As hunters, men had moved about as freely as the animals on which they preyed and as widely as the plants they foraged. Each small band tended to follow a regular circuit and returned again and again to favorite camping places, but no permanent dwellings were erected. As farmers, men had to settle down, at least temporarily. The oldest, more or less permanent constructed habitations that have been uncovered by archeologists date from about 10,000 B.C. These dwellings (as opposed to caves and hunting camps) appeared approximately the same time as the introduction of agriculture.

Little is known about life in these early villages, but we can make certain assumptions. With larger numbers of people living and working together, life became more complex. Crafts developed—the making of cloth from flax and from wool, the working of leather, the manufacture of pottery, and, much later, the smelting and shaping of metals. No one family could produce all these goods, and not every man or woman could work at a craft and still raise enough food for a family. Some means of exchanging goods and services had to be devised. Permanent settlements had to be protected against animals, roving plunderers, and the ravages of nature. In short, even in a small village, some organization was needed, and regular patterns of behavior had to be worked out to guide people in their relations with one another. These patterns gradually hardened into fixed customs, which replaced long, drawn-out arguments and violence in settling disagreements. A chieftain and a council of advisers were needed to enforce these

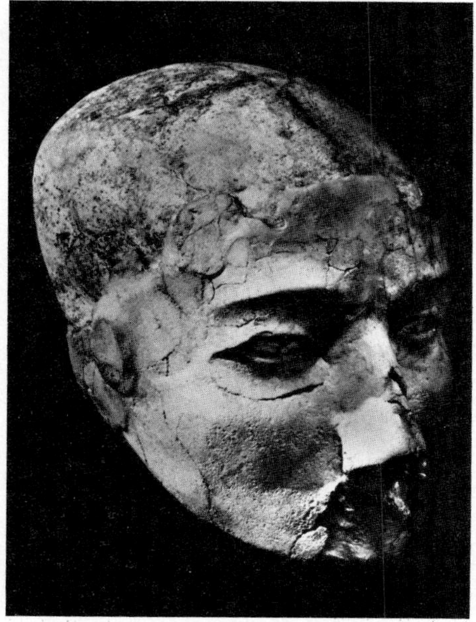

Human skull from the ruins of Jericho (*ca.* 7000 B.C.). The inhabitants of this city developed the art of "portraiture" by modeling the features in plaster and inlaying the eyes with shell in an attempt to reconstruct the face of the dead man.

THE ANCIENT MIDDLE EAST

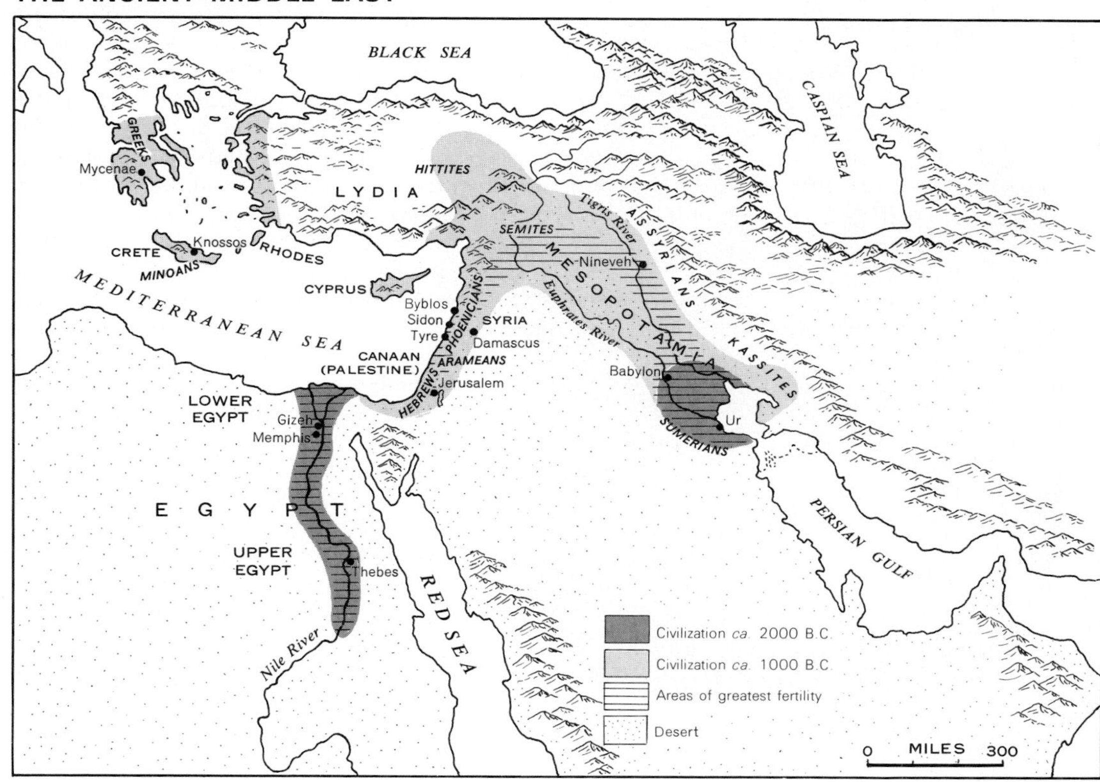

customs and to maintain order; this was the basis of village government. It was also necessary for the chieftain to organize the villagers when there was fighting with hostile neighbors or with wandering raiders, and to intercede for his people with spirits they might have offended. Living in villages and cooperating under village leaders, men gained better protection against human and natural enemies, a more regular supply of food, and a more ordered life. This was, in short, the first step toward civilization.

EARLY CIVILIZATIONS *ca.* 3500–1500 B.C.

With improved food supply and better protection, the number of humans continued to increase rapidly. But at the same time the lands they inhabited continued to dry up. Once again, men found that they would have to develop new techniques if they were to survive. In time it became obvious that a larger and more regular food supply could be obtained by cultivating the fertile soil in the valleys of large rivers. But the low-lying lands near the larger rivers provided a far from satisfactory environment. The river banks were too marshy to build on. The steaming swamps along the rivers bred disease. And the floods that came every spring were often strong enough to sweep away whole villages. As men began to make their homes along the rivers, they had to learn to drain the swamps, control the floodwaters, and irrigate the higher land away from the river beds. To carry out such projects on a large scale, they had to organize into larger communities, accept more complex and more authoritarian forms of government, and acquire greater technical skills than they had had before. It was in valleys of the Tigris-Euphrates, Nile, Indus, and Yellow rivers that the first cities and the first civilizations appeared. Since a city was helpless without controlling the surrounding agricultural lands, it had to extend its authority over a wider and wider area and become a city-state.

A Babylonian boundary stone (*ca.* thirteenth to tenth century B.C.), showing an example of cuneiform writing.

Mesopotamia

The earliest evidences of civilization were found in Mesopotamia (Greek for "between the rivers"), the valley of the Tigris and Euphrates rivers, in what is now Iraq. This civilization began about 3000 B.C. when a people known as the Sumerians established city-states in the area bounded by the lower courses of the two rivers. It is still not known where the Sumerians came from. Some historians believe that they migrated into the region from much older agricultural villages in the hilly country further up the valley. More likely, they came to Mesopotamia from somewhere else—perhaps by sea, as their own myths suggest.

The Sumerian cities were united in a loose league. They shared a culture, they spoke a common language, and they worshiped the same gods. A typical Sumerian city-state consisted of the city proper and as much of the surrounding population as the city walls could accommodate in times of crisis. The focal point of each city was a great platform raised above the surrounding residential areas. On it were erected the places of worship, including ultimately the many-storied temples (ziggurats) that became the typical form of Babylonian monumental architecture.

Writing, in the strict sense of the term, was first invented and employed in Mesopotamia about 3100 B.C. New finds suggest that writing may have been preceded by counting. If many objects had to be enumerated, small clay counters could be used to represent them. For a more permanent and more quickly recognizable record, the counters could be impressed in lumps of clay, using different patterns of impressions to represent different numbers. Tallies of this kind have been found from Syria to Iran. If pieces of clay could mean twelve or sixty or six hundred, then they could be marked in other patterns to convey other ideas. The first attempts to write words appear in southern Mesopotamia.

If the Sumerians did not actually originate this writing, they very soon took it over to represent their language. Most of the earliest examples of Sumerian writing are records concerned with trade throughout Mesopotamia. But school texts appeared almost at once as a means of educating specialists in the new technique. Literary texts and historical records followed in due course. The Sumerians wrote by pressing split reeds on wet clay that was then baked until it was hard. Originally quasi-pictographic, Sumerian writing soon lost all resemblance to pictograms and developed the characteristic symbols called cuneiform (from the Latin word for "wedge-shaped").

The advantages of civilization could not be contained within the confines of the Sumerian city-states. Extensive trade with other peoples spread the ideas and organization of the Sumerian cities throughout the Middle East. By about 2500 B.C., cities on the Sumerian model had spread from the Tigris-Euphrates Valley to Syria and Palestine on the eastern coast of the Mediterranean—the so-called Fertile Crescent. A recent and startling example of the spread of cities is the discovery of the ruins of Ebla, a thriving city-state in northern Syria at this time. There were also trade routes that led from lower Mesopotamia to the Indus Valley.

The people of the newer cities in the Fertile Crescent were not Sumerian but Semitic. The Semites, a number of different peoples speaking similar languages, seem to have originated in the Arabian Peninsula, where they had been nomads who lived by breeding animals. As they recognized the superior attractions of the urbanized area of the Fertile Crescent, Semites moved in several waves into Palestine, Syria, and the parts of Mesopotamia north of the Sumerians. By about 2300 B.C. the old Sumerian cities were merely the core of a much larger civilization that embraced the entire Fertile Crescent and whose population was primarily Semitic.

A Semitic warrior named Sargon (*ca.* 2300 B.C.) was the first to unite the city-states of Mesopotamia into a single em-

Ziggurat at Ur (*ca.* 2250 B.C.).

Hammurabi (*ca.* 1765 B.C.).

pire, though the union survived him by little more than a century. There followed an era of about 150 years when the Sumerians again controlled Mesopotamia. But about 2000 B.C. the valley was conquered by a newly arrived Semitic people called the Amorites ("westerners"). Under the Amorites the Sumerian Empire at first dissolved into a number of small kingdoms. But in time the city-state of Babylon, under its greatest ruler, Hammurabi (*ca.* 1792–50 B.C.), briefly reunified the entire valley under a single empire.

After Hammurabi's death, Babylon lost its supremacy, and Mesopotamia was again divided into a number of small states. The situation was complicated by the appearance of the Kassites, a people of unknown origin. Babylon itself fell to the Kassites soon after 1600 B.C., and southern Mesopotamia was ruled by the Kassites for more than four hundred years. Little is known about this period; what evidence we have suggests a rather stagnant, if peaceful, civilization. Upper Mesopotamia had a more eventful existence, but Babylonia did not resume its primary role in the development of Mesopotamian civilization until the seventh century B.C.

The economy of the pre-Kassite Babylonian civilization was based on commerce as well as agriculture. There was so much buying and leasing and trading that the Babylonians, earlier than most other peoples, developed a system of commercial law. Over the centuries, many Babylonian rulers attempted to collect the laws of the various cities and collate them into a single legal code. The most extensive and comprehensive of them was the Code of Hammurabi.

Babylonian laws seem harsh today. Some offenses called for the loss of the tongue or a hand. Many were punishable by death. But the Babylonian codes were no harsher than those of many European states of the eighteenth century and were certainly less disruptive of social order than personal attempts at vengeance. The very creation of written laws, impossible before there were governments strong enough to enforce them, was a major advance toward justice and order.

The Babylonians produced the first known mathematics. They handled rather complicated problems in arithmetic and geometry; they also had some understanding of algebra. Babylonian numbers were ordered on multiples of sixty (unlike our own, which are ordered on multiples of ten), and such Mesopotamian units of measure as the sixty-minute hour and the 360-degree circle are still in use.

The Babylonians also became interested in astronomy. There were the obvious regularities in the apparent movements of the sun and the moon, from which the concepts of a year, a month, and a week developed. There were the far less obvious regularities in the movements of the planets, which Babylonian astronomers also observed. We may wonder if the concept of laws of nature, from which all science derives, would ever have developed if early astronomers had not studied and tabulated the motions of the heavenly bodies. There are more regularities in heaven than on earth.

Although urban life brought many advantages and a higher level of living for part of the population, no region in Mesopotamia enjoyed long periods of peace and prosperity. The rival states were frequently at war, and often whole cities were razed to the ground. Devastating floods and plagues swept through the lands. These uncertainties were especially shocking because they afflicted so many people at the same time. This may be why the Babylonians took a gloomy view of life, seeing their gods as selfish beings who paid little heed to men except to deliver an occasional blow, apparently out of sheer caprice. Babylonian religion was roughly like a business arrangement: the Babylonians believed that if they performed certain ceremonies the gods would leave them in peace. There was a great deal of magic and very little emphasis on morality in their religious observances. To appease the gods, it was more important to know the right prayers and the appropriate sacrifices than it was to lead an upright life. This does not mean that there was no code of ethics, simply that it was not the business of the gods to enforce it. Yet these same people set very high standards in their business dealings with one another. And the great myths of this period, such as

ca. 3100 B.C.	ca. 2700	ca. 2150	ca. 2050	ca. 1650	ca. 1550	ca. 1100	ca. 650	525
Proto-Dynastic	Old Kingdom	1st intermediate period	Middle Kingdom	2nd intermediate period	New Kingdom	3rd intermediate period	Saïte Dynasty	

Gilgamesh, anticipated some of the themes and moral issues of the Old Testament.

The Emergence of Egyptian Civilization

During the same era in which the Mesopotamian city-states were battling the elements, one another, and a succession of foreign invaders, another civilization appeared, matured, and flourished in relative serenity only nine hundred miles away, in Egypt. The Nile Valley, seat of the ancient Egyptian civilization, extends about six hundred miles into Africa, although in Upper (southern) Egypt the fertile belt along the river is rarely more than ten miles wide. The Delta in Lower (northern) Egypt forms a large triangle that widens steadily until it reaches the sea, but much of the land in the Delta is swampy because the Nile splits into many branches. Primitive agricultural communities appeared along the Nile as early as 5000 B.C. when a variety of peoples, including both Blacks and Semites, sought refuge there from the encroaching deserts. About 4000 B.C. these communities began to consolidate into a series of small kingdoms, and by 3000 B.C. the entire Nile Valley had been united under a single monarch.

The civilization that began to appear in Egypt shortly before 3000 B.C. may have received an initial stimulus from Mesopotamia. But Egypt, unlike Mesopotamia, was rapidly united under a single political and economic system, and Egyptian civilization matured more rapidly than that of Mesopotamia. Once established, Egyptian civilization endured as a separate and clearly indentifiable entity until Egypt was absorbed by the Persian Empire in 525 B.C.—a span of 2500 years, as long a period as that from 525 B.C. to the present.

Egypt had many advantages over Mesopotamia, most of them derived from the peculiar nature and position of the Nile Valley. The flooding of the Tigris and Euphrates rivers was irregular and unpredictable. Sometimes there was not enough water to irrigate the crops; at other times heavy floods might wipe out a whole year's harvest. But the Nile flooded every year at the same time and rose to very nearly the same level, and Egyptian life could be geared to the rhythmic regularity of the river. Also, the Mesopotamian plain was open to invasion from all sides, and the frequent incursion of new peoples helped to keep the region divided into warring states. The Nile Valley was exposed to invasion only at its northern and southern extremities. Attackers from the north had to cross the Sinai desert; those from the south had to follow the long, narrow valley of the upper Nile. Thus invasions were less frequent than in Mesopotamia, and when they did occur they could be dealt with easily by a unified military effort.

Thus it was relatively easy and obviously useful for the small kingdoms along the Nile to consolidate into the large states of Upper (southern) and Lower (northern) Egypt. Some sort of struggle obviously preceded the unification of the "Two Lands" (as ancient Egypt was named by its contemporaries), but it occurred so early that only traces of it remain in religious legends. During almost all its history, ancient Egypt was ruled by kings who wore the double crown of the North and the South.

The long expanse of ancient Egyptian history can be divided into four eras, each preceded by a period of transition that began with internal weakness and ended with national consolidation and expansion. Thus the first four centuries of proto-dynastic unification (*ca.* 3100–2700 B.C.) were followed by the Old Kingdom (or the Pyramid Age) from about 2700 to 2150 B.C. Collapse of central power (*ca.* 2150–2050 B.C.) was rapidly reversed by the rise of the Middle Kingdom (*ca.* 2050–1650 B.C.). This era

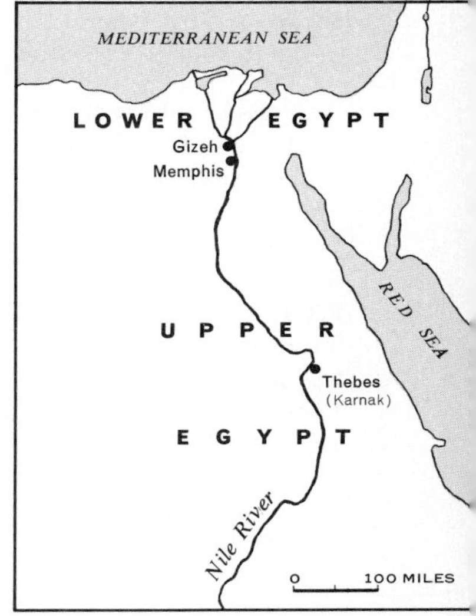

ended with another weakening of central authority and the conquest of Egypt by the Hyksos (*ca.* 1650–1550 B.C.). The expulsion of the Hyksos led to the period of Egypt's greatest expansion under the New Kingdom (*ca.* 1550–1100 B.C.). The next decline was longer (*ca.* 1100–650 B.C.), and the brief revival under the Saïte dynasty (*ca.* 650–525 B.C.) was only a pale reflection of former glories. The Persian conquest of 525 B.C. ended the independence of ancient Egypt.

The Old Kingdom and Middle Kingdom in Egypt ca. *2700–1550 B.C.*

The era of the Old Kingdom in Egypt was one of the most dynamic periods in human history. Within three or four centuries after civilization first appeared in the Nile Valley, some of the most notable achievements of the Egyptian civilization had already been realized: the erection of a strong monarchy and a complex bureaucracy capable of maintaining peace and order throughout the country; the introduction of hieroglyphics, a system of writing that, like cuneiform, used both word signs and syllable signs, but that, unlike cuneiform, retained its original pictographic form; the development of sufficient engineering skill to erect large stone structures (including the pyramids) for the first time in history; and the invention of a calendar so accurate that, with minor modifications, it is still in use.

The most important factor in the rapid progress of Egyptian civilization was that all the abundant agricultural resources and ample manpower of the Nile Valley were controlled by a single divine and absolute ruler, known to us, from the Hebrew scriptures, as the pharaoh. The Egyptians believed that the land belonged to the gods. They were grateful to the gods for the gifts of water and grain, and they were beholden to them for the use of the land. They worshiped their pharaoh as one of their gods and as the earthly representative of all the gods, a status accorded to very few Mesopotamian kings. With this unquestioning loyalty of their subjects, the powerful pharaohs of the Old Kingdom were able to administer Egypt almost as a private estate. Agents of the pharaoh—using their calendars to predict the regular rise and fall of the Nile—told the Egyptian peasants when and where to plant their seed and when to harvest their crops. Such a planned economy ensured a maximum yield, and much of the profit was used to enrich and strengthen the government.

As in most ancient societies, Egyptian peasants accepted their humble status, viewing the authority of the pharaoh as necessary to their well-being. Unlike the Mesopotamians, who feared the caprice and ill will of many of their deities, the Egyptians thought of their gods—including the pharaoh—as well disposed toward men.

Because the Egyptians buried their dead on the fringes of the desert, in places that were never cultivated, thousands of their tombs have survived. From the contents of these tombs we can get a

Egyptian Religion

Fourteenth century B.C.

Morality and the Last Judgment in the Book of the Dead.

Hail to you, ye gods. . . . Behold, I came to you without sin, without evil, without wrong. . . . I gave bread to the hungry, water to the thirsty, clothing to the naked, and a ferry to him without a boat. I made divine offerings for the gods and food offerings for the dead. Save me! Protect me!

◇ ◇ ◇

Monotheism in the hymn to the sun god (Aton). This was written during the brief period when King Akhnaton (1375–1358 B.C.) was trying to establish the cult of a single sun god.

How manifold are thy works!
They are hidden before men.
O sole God, beside whom is no other,
Thou didst create the earth according to thy heart. . .
Thou didst make the distant sky in order to rise therein,
In order to behold all that thou hast made
While thou wast yet alone.
Shining in thy form as living Aton,
Dawning, glittering, going afar and returning.
Thou makest millions of forms
Through thyself alone.

From James H. Breasted, *The Dawn of Conscience* (New York: Scribner's, 1934), pp. 259, 284–85.

Ramses II, ruler of the Egyptian Empire at its height, built this temple to Amon at Karnak. Below is a colossal statue of Ramses at Karnak. At his knees is his queen, Nefertari.

clearer view of Egyptian religious beliefs than of those of other ancient peoples. It is evident that the Egyptians were tremendously interested in the afterlife and that they devoted much of their energy and wealth to assure survival in the next world. Other peoples believed that the soul might linger in some shady nether world, but the Egyptians were convinced that man participated in the same life-death-rebirth cycle they observed in nature. In Egypt's clear, dry air, dead bodies did not decompose; they turned brown and brittle like the grain stalks. Thus it seemed natural to the Egyptians that if the soul of a man—like the seed of a plant—could be preserved through the human equivalent of a "dry" season, he would be restored to life in another world when the time came for his rebirth.

The Egyptians gave considerable attention to the problem of providing the soul with a suitable place to reside when the body died. In the era of the Old Kingdom, the Egyptians apparently believed that only the pharaoh's soul had to be preserved and that he would take care of the rest of his subjects in the afterworld. It was to provide an elaborate palace for their afterlives that some of the earlier pharaohs built the pyramids between about 2700 and 2200 B.C. In later eras more individualistic views prevailed and even people of moderate means built tombs for themselves, furnished with texts to guide them to the next world and with provisions for the journey.

The pyramids are only the most impressive examples of the remarkable engineering skill of the ancient Egyptians. The concentration of wealth and manpower under a single strong government made it possible for the Egyptians to build many magnificent temples, tombs, and statues on a scale that could be rivaled only in the greatest states of Mesopotamia. Although even the Egyptians did not attempt to build anything as large as the pyramids after the era of the Old Kingdom, structures like the temple at Karnak, built in the era of the New Kingdom, are still awe-inspiring in their size and artistic perfection. The pharaohs, who were gods, built like gods; their temples dominated space just as

Ceremonial axe of victory over the Hyksos showing the pharaoh Ahmose smiting an enemy.

their statues dominated representations of ordinary men.

Egypt's first long period of peaceful development, under the Old Kingdom, ended about 2150 B.C. when a series of weak pharaohs permitted the government to fall into the hands of powerful local administrators. Without centralized supervision, Egypt experienced an era of local famines and civil wars. After a century of turmoil, the country was reunited under the Middle Kingdom (*ca.* 2050–1650 B.C.). But toward the end of this era, Egypt again experienced a time of troubles, caused largely by foreign invaders. The invaders were known as the Hyksos, and their origin is still not exactly clear. They were probably a Semitic people (perhaps Amorites) whose kinsmen had already conquered the eastern arm of the Fertile Crescent. Aided by their horse-drawn chariots, they gained control of Egypt and then established themselves strongly in the Delta. Elsewhere they were weaker, and they were unable to govern all Egypt for more than a century. Native armies began to push them back, and by about 1550 B.C. the Hyksos had been expelled from Egypt.

It was perhaps no accident that Mesopotamia was overrun by the Kassites at just about the same time that the Hyksos attacked Egypt. Growth of population created pressures for expansion, and new military techniques, such as the horse-drawn chariot, and improvements in metallurgy (which led to stronger and sharper weapons) facilitated conquest. But Egypt recovered much more rapidly from the Hyksos domination than Mesopotamia did from the Kassite conquests.

Cretan fresco of court ladies seated around a pillar shrine at a public festival, from the palace at Knossos.

Crete

The island of Crete stretches for more than 150 miles across the entrance to the Aegean Sea. The Greeks preserved legends about a great King Minos of Crete who was so powerful that even the city of Athens had to send him an annual tribute. But since the sandy soil of Crete has barely been able to sustain its small population throughout historical times, no one was inclined to take the legend of a powerful kingdom on the island very seriously. Then in 1900 Arthur Evans, an English archeologist, dug into a mound on the northern coast of Crete and uncovered a magnificent palace, the size of a small city, which he assumed to be Knossos, the ancient capital of King Minos.

In addition to the palace at Knossos, Evans and his successors discovered many other sites. They were able to show that a civilization, separate from those of Egypt and Mesopotamia, had flourished on the island from about 2000 to 1400 B.C. This civilization had a style of its own, not monumental like the Egyptian nor stolid like the Mesopotamian, but delicate and cheerful, made for human beings and not for gods. It also appears that women had a more important role in this society than in any other contemporary culture. Evans called this civilization the Minoan after the legendary King Minos. During this era the Minoans seem to have prospered not by farming, but by dominating the trade of the Aegean and the eastern Mediterranean.

The archeologists found that the Minoan civilization must have succumbed to some great catastrophe, for virtually every settlement they discovered showed evidence of violent destruction dating from about 1480 B.C. The palace at Knossos was rebuilt after the catastrophe, but Evans concluded that it was occupied by a people other than its original inhabitants. His main proof was that in the palace he discovered examples of tablets inscribed with two distinct scripts. One of them, which he called Linear Script A, was used throughout the island during the whole era of the Minoan civilization. The second, Linear Script B, was used only at Knossos and only after the rebuilding of the palace.

Many questions still remain unanswered: Who were the Minoan people? Where did they come from, and how did their civilization originate? What was their society like? What form of government did they have? What great disaster overtook Crete about 1480 B.C.? And who were the people who occupied the palace at Knossos after that time?

Two recent discoveries provide some clues to these questions. In 1952 an Englishman named Michael Ventris showed that Linear Script B was actually an old way of writing Greek, which means that the people who occupied the palace after its original destruction were probably Greeks. Then in 1966 a group of American oceanographers discovered a thick layer of volcanic ash at the bottom of the eastern Mediterranean. They were able to demonstrate that around 1480 B.C., on an island about one hundred miles north of Crete, there had been a volcanic eruption four times more violent than any ever recorded. The eruption was followed by enormous tidal waves. Such a disaster could well account for the destruction of Knossos and other sites on Crete at about that time.

Linear Script A has not yet been conclusively deciphered; until it is, most of the story of the Minoan civilization must remain a mystery. But with the few clues now available we can attempt a reconstruction, however hypothetical, of Minoan history.

Archeological evidence indicates that the first civilized settlers on Crete arrived from Asia Minor some time after 3000 B.C., that they were at least partly Semitic, and that they had already learned some of the elements of civilization from Mesopotamia. Commerce began early in the eastern Mediterranean but the traders were not always peaceful. Crete was ideally situated for controlling the commerce between Mesopotamia or Egypt and the more primitive peoples on the shores of Europe. Thus it has been assumed that the Minoan civilization that emerged was based on trade and on the domination of some of Crete's weaker neighbors.

The greater part of Minoan trade was apparently with the villages located around the Aegean Sea. The populations of these settlements began to increase rapidly after about 2000 B.C. when the Greeks, migrating south from central Europe, began to settle in the lands around the Aegean (see p. 28). Minoan trade increased proportionately, so that the height of Minoan prosperity, and of Minoan civilization, came after 2000 B.C.

In time the Greeks created a civilization of their own, known as the Mycenaean civilization, which owed a good deal to the Minoan example (see p. 29). By 1500 B.C. Greek traders were competing with the Minoans in the markets of the Aegean and also in Syria and Egypt.

Greeks apparently occupied the palace at Knossos after the Minoan civilization had been weakened by disaster about 1480 B.C. They probably attempted to dominate the island and to take over its commerce. About 1400 B.C. the palace was again destroyed, possibly as a result of a revolt of the Minoans against their Greek rulers. At any rate the Minoan civilization declined rapidly after this time. By about 1200 B.C. it had virtually disappeared, and Crete was nothing more than a backwater of Greek civilization.

Above is a seal stone impression of the earliest form of Minoan writing, from which Linear A developed. Below is a Linear A tablet. At bottom is a Linear B tablet.

The Indo-Europeans

The Greeks were but one of several peoples known collectively as Indo-Europeans. The term *Indo-European,* like the term *Semitic,* does not refer to a race of related peoples. Rather it describes a mixture of peoples speaking similar languages. Their ancestors may have come from various parts of the earth, but at some stage in their histories—the stage in which their languages took form—they apparently lived close to one another. For this reason, their cultures as well as their languages developed certain common characteristics.

Shortly before they first appear in history—about 2000 B.C.—the Indo-European peoples seem to have been concentrated somewhere north of the Black Sea between the Danube and the Volga rivers. From this center, as their numbers grew, they spread out in all directions. In the era between about 2000 and 1000 B.C. several waves of Indo-European peoples migrated southward toward the Mediterranean. The westernmost branch—consisting of several separate tribes (including the Latins)—crossed the Alps and settled in Italy.

We have already seen that the Greeks, whose language was similar to Latin, settled in the Aegean area at about the same time that the western tribes settled in Italy. Still further east were the Hittites, who ruled an empire in Asia Minor from about 1800 to 1200 B.C. The Hittites were among the first people to use horses and iron weapons in combat and were one of the most feared military powers of their time. The easternmost branch of the Indo-Europeans settled in Persia, and then in northern India, also in the same era.

By 1000 B.C. Indo-European peoples had occupied all of the continent of Europe. It is from their languages that most tongues spoken in the western world today are derived, including the Romance languages (such as Italian, Spanish, and French), the Germanic languages (such as English, German, and Dutch), the Celtic languages (such as Gaelic and Welsh), and the Slavic languages (such as Russian, Polish, and Czech). The Persian and Indic languages spoken in Asia are also of Indo-European origin.

The Spread of Civilization

Before 2000 B.C. civilization was still not very widespread even in the Middle East, where Egypt, Mesopotamia, and Crete were fairly close and had some contacts with one another. There was a civilization in the Indus Valley that traded with Mesopotamia and a somewhat isolated civilization in the Yellow River Valley of China (see p. 133). The rest of the Eastern Hemisphere was still inhabited by peoples who had not gone much beyond the village level of organization. But the wealth and skills of Egypt, Mesopotamia, and Crete impressed their neighbors and encouraged them to build more complex societies. By 2000 B.C. Mesopotamian civilization, the most dynamic because of its active trade beyond its own frontiers, had spread westward throughout the Fertile Crescent to include Syria and Palestine as well as the Mesopotamian valley. It became almost contiguous with Egypt. On the east, the Iranians (the inhabitants of what became Persia and is now Iran) had acquired a great deal of technical knowledge from their neighbors and were beginning to develop a civilization of their own. The Iranians living in the region between the Tigris and the Indus valleys naturally had contacts with India as well.

By about 1500 B.C. the Greeks and the Hittites were also building cities, organizing states, and engaging in wide-ranging trading ventures. Thus a civilized world extended without a break from the Aegean Sea to the Persian Gulf. With the influx of new peoples and the steady increase in the populations of the older centers, the number of people in this civilized area was probably four or five times greater in 1500 B.C. than it had been in 2000 B.C. Trade increased proportionately, and with it the general standard of living. In the prosperous period between about 1500 and 1200 B.C., the leading power of the ancient world was Egypt. The Minoan civilization disappeared shortly after 1500 B.C., and much of the Mesopotamian world was still controlled by less advanced northern peoples.

THE NEW KINGDOM IN EGYPT *ca.* 1550–1100 B.C.

Egypt was freed from foreign domination about 1560 B.C. when an Egyptian nobleman named Ahmose led a successful revolt against the Hyksos rulers and established himself as pharaoh of all Egypt. The reign of Ahmose marked the beginning of the New Kingdom, the most glorious phase of Egypt's long history.

The Egyptian Empire

Ahmose not only expelled the hated Hyksos; he pursued them across the desert to Palestine and Syria. To prevent further invasions, he placed both of these lands under Egyptian protection. Thus for the first time the Egyptians abandoned their centuries-old tradition of isolation and extended their rule to areas beyond their borders. The Egyptian Empire inaugurated by Ahmose later included not only Palestine but also Libya to the west and Nubia to the south.

Under the New Kingdom, Egypt also began to take an active part in the Mediterranean trade that had already enriched the Minoan and Mesopotamian civilizations. After the fall of Crete, Egypt dominated the commerce of the eastern Mediterranean for several centuries.

With tribute from their empire and with commerce to convert their bounteous grain supply into cash, the wealthy and powerful pharaohs of the New Kingdom created the most elaborate architectural monuments in Egyptian history. These pharaohs were no longer content with pyramids for their graves (they were too easily plundered); instead, they carved lavishly decorated tombs out of the sandstone cliffs of the Upper Nile near the new capital at Thebes. The discovery in 1922 of the tomb of Tutankhamon (*ca.* 1340 B.C.)—the only tomb that had not been completely sacked by thieves over the centuries—provided historians with an invaluable source of information on the life and tastes of the upper classes of the New Kingdom.

Akhnaton
ca. *1375–1358 B.C.*

Throughout most of the history of the New Kingdom, Egypt was at war with the

Race

Race and language are not the same. This should be obvious, for not all who speak Arabic are Arabians and not all who speak English are of the White race. . . . A man's hereditary features and the language he speaks depend on two different sets of circumstances. His hereditary anatomy depends upon his remote ancestors, and his language depends upon the speech he heard as a child.

A race does not move forward as a whole. . . . Race is not a touchstone by which civilized people can be separated from uncivilized. . . . The lesson of history is that pre-eminence in cultural achievement has passed from one race to another, from one continent to another; it has embraced not whole "races" but certain fragments of an ethnic group which were for certain historical reasons favorably situated at the moment.

From Ruth Benedict, *Race: Science and Politics* (New York: Viking, 1945), pp. 9, 18.

THE HITTITE AND EGYPTIAN EMPIRES *ca.* 1450 B.C.

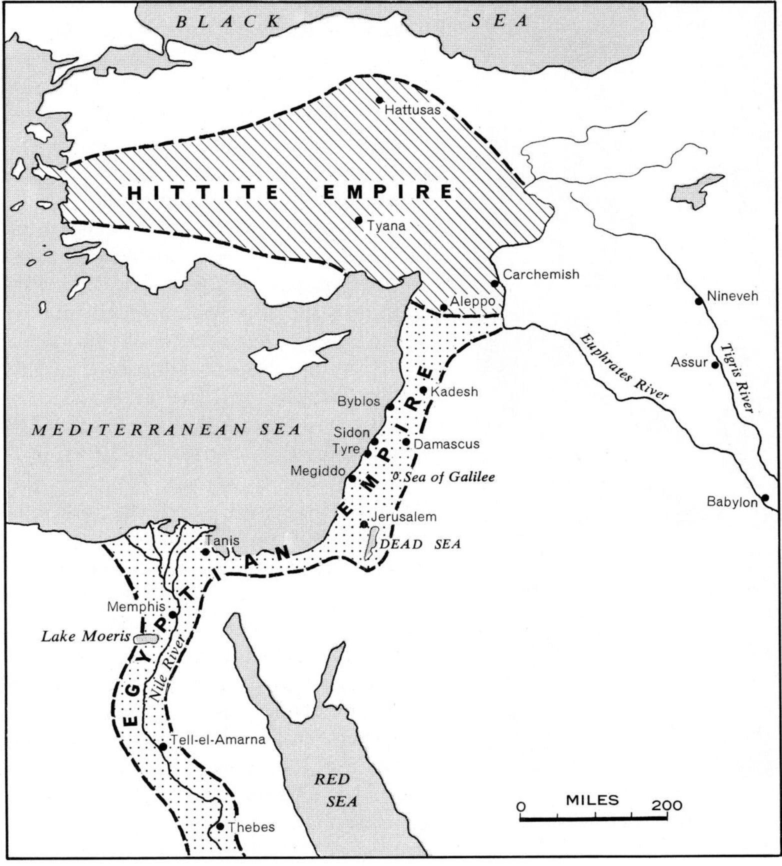

The Tomb of Tutankhamon

The English archeologist Howard Carter writes of the excitement of uncovering the tomb of the pharaoh Tutankhamon in 1922.

Slowly . . . the remains of passage debris that encumbered the lower part of the doorway were removed, until at last we had the whole door clear before us. The decisive moment had arrived. With trembling hands I made a tiny breach in the upper left hand corner. Darkness and blank space, as far as an iron testing-rod could reach, showed that whatever lay beyond was empty, and not filled like the passage we had just cleared. Candle tests were applied as a precaution against possible foul gases, and then, widening the hole a little, I inserted the candle and peered in. . . . At first I could see nothing, . . . but presently, as my eyes grew accustomed to the light, details of the room within emerged slowly from the mist, strange animals, statues, and gold—everywhere the glint of gold.

From Howard Carter and A. C. Mace, *The Tomb of Tut-ankh-Amen* (London: Cassell, 1923), Vol. I, pp. 95–96.

Akhenaton, from a pillar statue in the temple of Aton.

Hittites over the control of Syria and Palestine. Thus most of the pharaohs of the era were warriors. One exception was Akhnaton, who was a religious reformer. Akhnaton tried to superimpose on the ancient and complex religious traditions of Egypt the worship of the Aton, or sun-disk, which he believed to be the supreme and perhaps even the only god. This is the first instance in history of something close to the concept of pure monotheism: the belief in one god. But Akhnaton's religion was never popular in Egypt. The old religious beliefs were deeply ingrained in the thinking of the Egyptian people, and the priests of the old gods, who guarded the formulas for entrance into the afterlife, were far too powerful to be bypassed, even by the pharaoh. As a result, soon after Akhnaton's death the old religion was restored.

Akhnaton was a sensitive man given to writing poetry but little interested in affairs of state. Largely as a result of his negligence, Egypt declined as a military power. Syria was lost to the Hittites, and much of Palestine was overrun by bands of invaders called the Habiru. Akhnaton's immediate successors proved as weak as he, and the dynasty founded by Ahmose ended ignominiously as a consequence of a military coup. Subsequent pharaohs regained some of the territory and prestige that Egypt had lost. A series of protracted wars between Egypt and the Hittites over control of Syria was terminated only about 1275 B.C. by a treaty between Ramses II and the Hittite king. This treaty is famous as one of the first recorded international agreements, but it came too late. Both powers, weakened by their struggle, now had to face new dangers of invasion from the north.

THE ERA OF SMALL KINGDOMS *ca.* 1250–750 B.C.

Between about 1250 and 900 B.C. new Indo-European incursions upset the stability of the ancient world. In the Aegean area the invaders were another wave of Greeks, called Dorians (see p. 30), who nearly destroyed the Mycenaean culture that had flourished since the fall of Crete three centuries earlier. Other Indo-Europeans moved into Asia Minor. They overthrew the Hittite Empire, already weak after its wars with Egypt, and established several smaller kingdoms in its place. Many people of the Aegean area, some of them Greeks, fled from the invaders in fleets of small boats. The "sea-peoples" had been known before, but had been traders rather than raiders. Now they were looking for new homes, and they were quite ready to engage in piracy and plundering along the way. Their attacks on Egyptian shipping and their raids in the Nile Delta contributed to the decline of the New Kingdom and ended Egypt's role as a commercial power.

After the decline of the Hittite and Egyptian empires, no strong power appeared in the Middle East until the rise of the Assyrian Empire about four centuries later. During those centuries several small kingdoms and city-states emerged in the lands at the eastern end of the Mediterranean now occupied by Syria, Lebanon, and Israel. Before about 1200 B.C. these lands had been occupied by a Semitic people known as Canaanites, whose culture was derived from that of Mesopotamia. But Ahmose, as we have seen, had placed this area under Egyptian protection. When Egypt declined as a world power and Egyptian garrisons were withdrawn, the Canaanite cities were left defenseless. In the period between about 1200 and 1000 B.C., the "sea-peoples" attacked them from the Mediterranean, while two new waves of Semitic peoples, first the Hebrews and later the Aramaeans, attacked them from the east and south.

Eventually most of the Canaanite cities succumbed to the invaders. One group of the "sea-peoples," known as the Philistines, established a string of independent city-states along the coast of the Mediterranean. Inland, the Aramaeans settled in what became the kingdom of Syria, with its capital at Damascus. South of Syria were the two smaller Hebrew kingdoms of Israel and Judah, of which more will be said later.

The Phoenicians

The only Canaanite cities to survive the invasions were those along the rocky coast of Syria that were relatively easy to defend. The inhabitants of these cities were a mixture of Canaanites and "sea-peoples" and were known as Phoenicians. When the raids of the "sea-peoples" subsided, Phoenician ships were the first to venture into the Mediterranean. By about 1100 B.C. the Phoenicians had begun to revive the trade routes abandoned by the Minoans and the Egyptians, and for the next three centuries they controlled Mediterranean commerce.

The ancient trade routes from India and the East were still funneling goods into Mesopotamia. From there, the eastern wares, along with local Mesopotamian produce, moved along the Aramaean caravan routes to one of the Phoenician cities. There they were loaded onto small ships bound for Egypt, Asia Minor, North Africa, or even western Europe. Returning ships carried raw materials from the western Mediterranean to the Phoenician cities, where they were fashioned into finished products and sent to the markets of Mesopotamia.

The Phoenicians were better sailors than any other ancient people, even the Greeks. They were the first people from the Middle East to trade and colonize in western Europe. They were also the first on record to venture beyond Gibraltar into the Atlantic, for their ships sailed regularly to Brittany and Cornwall to obtain the tin needed in the manufacture of bronze. Egyptian sources suggest that the Phoenicians may have sailed around Africa, a feat that would not be repeated until the fifteenth century A.D. Some scholars believe that the Phoenicians may even have reached America.

The largest Phoenician city was Tyre. But by far the oldest—dating from before 2000 B.C.—was Byblos, which specialized in the manufacture of writing materials. It was from Byblos that the Greeks took their word for "book"—*biblion*—and it is from *biblion* that we get such English words as *Bible* and *bibliography.* The Phoenicians also helped to refine and to spread the use of the West Semitic system of writing. Written records were essential for their large-scale business operations, and earlier systems of writing were not very useful for men trading all over the known world. Ultimately reduced to only twenty-two letters that could be drawn and recognized without difficulty, the Phoenician alphabet was much easier to use and to understand than either cuneiform or hieroglyphic writing. For the first time in history it was possible for almost anyone to learn to read and write without long years of training. Learning could be more widely diffused, and more men could enter administrative careers. The Phoenician

Typical letters of the alphabet in Phoenician, Greek, and Roman forms. The final Greek letter, omega, is pronounced like the Roman long *o*.

Phoenician	Greek	Roman
𐤀	A	A
𐤁	B	B
𐤂	Γ	G
𐤃	Δ	D
𐤄	E	E
𐤅	[Y]	F
𐤆	Z	Z
𐤇		H
𐤉	I	I
𐤊	K	[K]
𐤋	Λ	L
𐤌	M	M
𐤍	N	N
𐤏	O	O
𐤐	Π	P
𐤒		Q
𐤓	P	R
𐤔	Σ	S
𐤕	T	T
	Y	U,V
	X	X
	Ω	

THE MIDDLE EAST *ca.* 800 B.C.

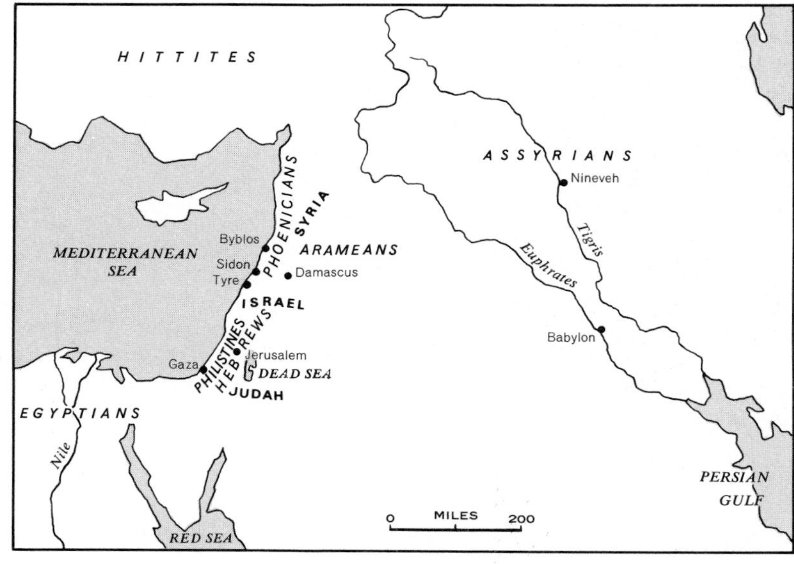

alphabet provided the basis for all three of the major alphabets now in use in the western world: the Hebrew, the Latin (which we use), and the Greek. The Greek alphabet, in turn, is the basis for the Cyrillic alphabet used in Russia and much of eastern Europe. And an Aramaic version of the West Semitic script formed the basis for the writing systems of India. It is curious that so useful a discovery was never duplicated, even by such ingenious people as the Chinese.

Just as the merchants of Europe later brought their civilization to America in their search for new markets and raw materials, the Phoenician traders carried the civilization of the Middle East to the western Mediterranean. They established colonies and trading posts in many places, particularly on the island of Sicily and in North Africa. The largest Phoenician colony was at Carthage, located near the site of modern Tunis. Here the Phoenician settlers were able to make serfs of the natives and to put them to work on large plantations growing agricultural products for the home markets.

The Phoenician cities came under the domination of the Assyrian Empire after about 750 B.C., and declined rapidly thereafter. At that time the leading merchant families emigrated to Carthage, which became the center of the Phoenician world until it was destroyed by the Romans in 146 B.C.

A God of Social Justice

The writings of the prophet Amos contain one of the earliest references (*ca.* 750 B.C.) to Jahweh as a god of social justice.

Hear this, O ye that swallow up the needy,
even to make the poor of the land to fail,
Saying, When will the new moon be gone, that we may sell corn?
and the sabbath, that we may set forth wheat,
making the ephah small, and the shekel great,
and falsifying the balances by deceit?
That we may buy the poor for silver,
and the needy for a pair of shoes;
yea, and sell the refuse of the wheat?

Shall not the land tremble for this,
and every one mourn that dwelleth therein?

From *The Dartmouth Bible,* ed. by Roy B. Chamberlin and Herman Feldman (Boston: Houghton Mifflin, 1961), p. 541.

The Hebrews

Among the peoples of the ancient world, the Hebrews played a relatively unimportant political role. If we were to consider only their significance to their contemporaries, we might dismiss them with a few sentences or perhaps not mention them all. But during the years from about 1200 to 400 B.C. the Hebrews developed a religion that was unique among ancient peoples and that has given their history enormous significance to the modern world. Their religion has helped the Hebrews to maintain their identity, even to the present day, whereas most ancient peoples mixed with one another or with successive waves of conquerors. Moreover, because the ancient Hebrews maintained a detailed record of the evolving relationship between themselves and their God, Jahweh, their scriptures constitute one of the richest original sources for ancient history. The religion developed by the ancient Hebrews provided the basis for three of the major religions of the modern world: Judaism, Christianity, and Islam.

Most of the Hebrew scripture (that part known to Christians as the Old Testament) was written down by many different authors between about 1000 and 150 B.C. It includes rules of law and of religious behavior, legend, history, poetry, prophecy, and apocalyptic visions. But it is given unity by the firm belief in an enduring relationship between God and his people. The first several books recount the stories preserved by the Hebrews about their early history. Although recent archeological discoveries show that many of these stories may well be based on actual historical events (just as archeologists have shown that the poems of Homer are probably based on actual events in early Greek history), there is not enough evidence to reconstruct the history of the Hebrews before about 1000 B.C. with any certainty.

According to their scriptures, all Hebrews were descended from Abraham, who migrated westward from Ur in Mesopotamia when Jahweh promised him and his descendants the land of Canaan (Palestine). Abraham's grandson Jacob (also called Israel) had twelve sons who were believed to be the progenitors of the twelve tribes into which the Hebrews were later divided. Joseph, one of Jacob's sons, was taken to Egypt as a slave but later rose to a high position in the pharaoh's government. His father and his brothers then joined him in Egypt. The second book of the Old Testament, Exodus, explains that a new pharaoh arose who "knew not Joseph," and who reduced the children of Israel (by then a sizable tribe) to slavery. It is in Exodus that we are introduced to Moses, one of the most impressive figures in literature.

Moses was an Israelite who, according to the account in Exodus, was raised by a daughter of the pharaoh. One day when Moses was alone in the wilderness, Jahweh, the God of Abraham, called to him. While Moses listened in awe and terror, Jahweh renewed his Covenant with the children of Israel: to guide and protect them as long as they worshiped him and him only and obeyed his laws. Jahweh then ordered Moses to lead the Israelites back to the land of Palestine. Moses led the Israelites out of Egypt into the Sinai Desert, where they remained for forty years before trying to enter Palestine. During this sojourn in the desert, Jahweh gave Moses the Law, which included the Ten Commandments and a long catalogue of religious, ethical, and juridical regulations.

Two books, Joshua and Judges, give differing accounts of the Hebrew attack on Palestine after the death of Moses. Here we are on somewhat more solid historical ground, since Egyptian records show that the Canaanite cities were attacked by tribes from the desert during the thirteenth century B.C. Archeological evidence also shows that Jericho and several neighboring cities were besieged and destroyed at about that time. The Hebrew conquest was complicated by the more or less simultaneous arrival of the Philistines, who attacked from the sea. For about a century a three-way battle took place among the Hebrews, the Canaanites, and the Philistines.

In the final stages of the conquest of the Canaanites, the Hebrew tribes decided to unite under a king. Samuel, a religious leader, chose Saul (*ca.* 1000 B.C.) as the first king and later designated David (*ca.* 1000–960 B.C.) as Saul's successor. It was King David who completed the conquest of the Canaanites and the Philistines and united the Hebrew people in a kingdom with its capital at Jerusalem. The Philistines were permitted to maintain their independent cities along the Mediterranean coast, but the Canaanites were eventually absorbed by the Hebrews. Since the Canaanites had been exposed to Mesopotamian influence, they may have been the source of the many Mesopotamian elements in the Hebrew culture, such as the story of the Flood.

Solomon (*ca.* 960–930 B.C.), David's son and successor, built an impressive royal palace and a temple to Jahweh in Jerusalem and established commercial

Semite prisoner inscribed on a relief at the temple of Luxor (perhaps dating from the period of Hebrew residence in Egypt).

and diplomatic relations with neighboring states. The Hebrew people, however, whose memory of tribal independence was still fresh, resented Solomon's royal pretensions and high taxes. At Solomon's death the ten northern tribes seceded and established the Kingdom of Israel under another dynasty. From about 930 B.C. on, there were two Hebrew kingdoms: Israel in the north, the larger and more prosperous of the two; and Judah in the south, a smaller agricultural kingdom that remained loyal to the house of David.

According to the Bible, the Hebrew concept of monotheism goes back at least to the time of Moses. But monotheism—the worship of one god—does not necessarily imply that this god is sovereign over the entire earth and is to be worshiped by all peoples. When they first entered Palestine, the Israelites believed that, according to their Covenant, they were to worship only Jahweh and to obey his laws, but that other people might worship other gods. They seem to have conceived of Jahweh as being rather like the gods of other nomadic desert peoples: he protected them from their enemies, he took their side in battles, and he provided them with food and water.

Once the Hebrews had ceased to be desert nomads and had settled down as farmers in Palestine, the worship of a desert god had less meaning for them. Although Jahweh remained the official national god of the Hebrews, many of them turned also to the Baalim, the Canaanite version of the Mesopotamian fertility gods. The conflict between the Baal-worshipers and the defenders of Jahweh produced the first Hebrew prophets, such as Elijah and Elisha. These peripatetic preachers warned that Baal-worship was a breach of the Covenant and would bring the wrath of Jahweh down on all the Hebrew people. The recorded versions of their preaching include some of the most stirring passages in any literature.

The teaching of the prophet Amos

THE ASSYRIAN EMPIRE *ca.* 700 B.C.

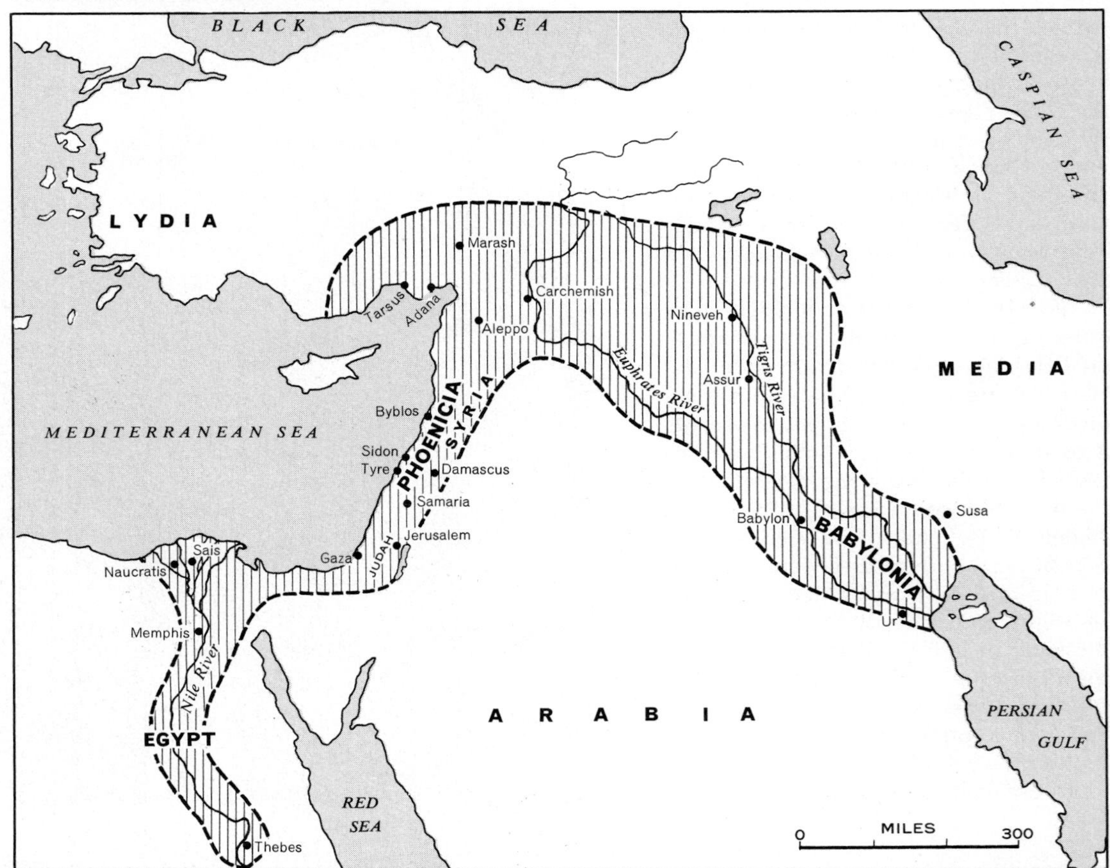

ca. 750 B.C.	626	612	549	539	333 B.C.
Assyrian Empire					
	Chaldean Empire				
			Persian Empire		

(*ca.* 750 B.C.) marks a turning point in the evolution of the Hebrew religion. In powerful measured verse, Amos named the various neighboring peoples known to the Hebrews, listed their sins, and promised that Jahweh would punish them. Although Amos himself may not have realized it, in so preaching he became the first Hebrew teacher—as far as written records show—to speak of Jahweh not merely as the God of the Hebrews but as a god whose law extended to all people.

Amos did not stop, however, after he had listed the sins of Israel's neighbors. He reached a crescendo of fury when he spoke of the sins of the Hebrews themselves. In the time of Amos, many Hebrews were beginning to live in cities and to engage in trade. They were beginning to learn, as the Greeks were learning at the same time, that when a society first turns to a money economy, some men become very rich while others are reduced to poverty or even servitude. The Greeks considered the problem a political matter to be solved through constitutional reforms. For Amos, as for most Hebrews, it was a religious matter. The Hebrews were sinning against Jahweh, he warned, when they "sold the righteous for silver, and the needy for a pair of shoes." Amos gave a new dimension to the worship of Jahweh by stating explicitly something that was already implicit throughout the Law of Moses—namely, that Jahweh was a god of social justice, and that worldly success is not necessarily a sign of goodness. Thus in Amos we find the first clear expression of the concept of ethical monotheism that made the Hebrew religion unique in the ancient world.

The teachings of such later prophets as Hosea, Isaiah, and Jeremiah reflect a continuing evolution in the Hebrew concept of Jahweh. They presented a universal abstract God, who could be reached by his worshipers wherever they were; a God possessed of infinite power and infinite sanctity and infinite love; a God far above the need for the petty sacrifices of the Baal-worshipers; a God whose relationship to his people was that of a loving father.

The repeated warnings of the prophets that Jahweh would punish the Hebrews for their sins were reinforced by the growing danger from the Assyrians to the east. By the eighth century this militaristic people had gained control of most of Mesopotamia and had already begun to threaten the small states along the Mediterranean coast. There could be no doubt in the minds of the Hebrews just what form Jahweh's punishment would take should it ever come.

A NEW AGE OF EMPIRES *ca.* 750–333 B.C.

Such small states as the Phoenician cities and the Hebrew kingdoms had been able to survive only because there were no major powers to threaten them in the period from about 1150 to 750 B.C. Between about 750 and 333 B.C., however, three successive empires dominated the entire Fertile Crescent. These empires brought all the small states of Mesopo-

An alabaster relief showing an Assyrian king on a hunt.

Lydians paying tribute to the Persian emperor Darius I.

tamia, Syria, and Palestine under their control and at times even extended their power over Egypt.

The Assyrian Empire ca. *750–612* B.C.

The first of the new empires was created by the Assyrians, a Semitic people living in the hilly country of the upper Tigris Valley. Located at the northern extreme of the Mesopotamian world, the Assyrians were generally the first to feel the blows of the repeated invasions from the north. They had to become militarily strong in order to survive. In time they built up the most efficient army the ancient world had seen, with long-service professional soldiers and what were probably the first effective cavalry units. About 900 B.C., when barbarian threats from the north temporarily subsided, the Assyrians began to use their army to terrorize and conquer their Mesopotamian neighbors. By about 750 B.C. their empire included the whole Mesopotamian valley. Then in a series of swift and devastating thrusts to the west, they conquered Syria, the Phoenician cities, the Kingdom of Israel, and finally even Egypt.

The Assyrians enforced their rule with cruelty, enslaving and deporting whole peoples and torturing and killing thousands of captives. A large part of the population of Israel, for instance, was either killed or deported, and the land was resettled with people from other parts of the empire. The ten northern Hebrew tribes lost their identity forever. The only Hebrews left were the two tribes of the southern Kingdoms of Judah, which survived as an Assyrian dependency.

Assyrian art (expressed mostly in sculptured reliefs) reflects many of the characteristics of these fierce people. Strong, harsh, and realistic, it abounds in scenes of war, torture, and death. The human figures are somewhat stiff, but no artists have ever surpassed the Assyrians in depicting animals fighting, charging, and writhing in their death agonies.

There were simply not enough Assyrians to garrison a territory stretching from the Nile to the borders of Persia, and the systematic cruelty of the Assyrians made it impossible for them to control conquered peoples except by force of arms. The Babylonians, eager to regain their old supremacy, launched an uprising and were enthusiastically supported by other subject peoples. Nineveh, the Assyrian capital, fell in 612 B.C., and the great Assyrian Empire crumbled overnight.

The Chaldean Empire ca. *626–539* B.C.

After the fall of Assyria, most of Mesopotamia came under the short-lived Chaldean Empire, which had its capital in the ancient city of Babylon. Trying to avoid domination by the Chaldeans, the small Kingdom of Judah joined a coalition led by Egypt. But in 587 B.C. Nebuchadnezzar, the Chaldean king, overran Judah, devastated the land, destroyed Solomon's Temple in Jerusalem, and led the king and several thousand leading citizens back to Babylon as captives. During this "Babylonian Captivity," the Hebrews came to believe that Jahweh had a divine plan for his people that was being worked out through history. At first their fate perplexed them. If Jahweh was the only true God, and if the Hebrews were the only ones to worship him and follow his laws, why had they been subjected to conquest and cruelty at the hands of nonbelievers? The answer was provided by the new prophets of the period of exile, such as Joel. The day would soon come, they believed, when Jahweh would reveal himself to all peoples and institute his rule of righteousness. When that time came, the Hebrews would lead the nonbelievers into the paths of Jahweh. Meanwhile, the Hebrews would have to be educated and purified through suffering. Their numbers would be reduced by conquest and slaughter until only a "saving remnant" of dedicated souls was left to carry out the will of Jahweh.

The Book of Daniel gives a dramatic account of the fall of Babylon in 539 B.C. According to this version, a spectral hand began to write on the wall during a banquet given by the crown prince Belshazzar. Only Daniel, a Jew, was able to interpret the message for Belshazzar and his terrified guests. The Chaldean Empire would fall that night. According to other sources, the handwriting on the wall was unnecessary, for the Persian troops were already at the gates, and the citizens of Babylon, frustrated by the weakness of their rulers, were offering no resistance.

The Persian Empire 549–333 B.C.

The Persians, an Indo-European people, lived in a loose federation with the Medes and other neighbors in the hilly region east of Mesopotamia. They were a tough, pastoral people, good horsemen, led by a military aristocracy. In 549 B.C. Cyrus, a very able military leader, established himself as king. This was the beginning of the great period of Persian expansion. In 543 B.C. Cyrus conquered and annexed all of Asia Minor. With his victory over the Chaldean Empire in 539 B.C., he added Mesopotamia, Syria, Palestine, and the Phoenician cities to his empire. When his son conquered Egypt in 525 B.C., the Persian Empire embraced almost all of the Middle East.

The organization of the Persian Empire was more successful than that of earlier empires, and its value is shown by the fact that the Romans, quite independently, found the same solution to governing a mixture of many peoples. The Persian system combined a large measure of local autonomy with careful

THE PERSIAN EMPIRE *ca.* 500 B.C.

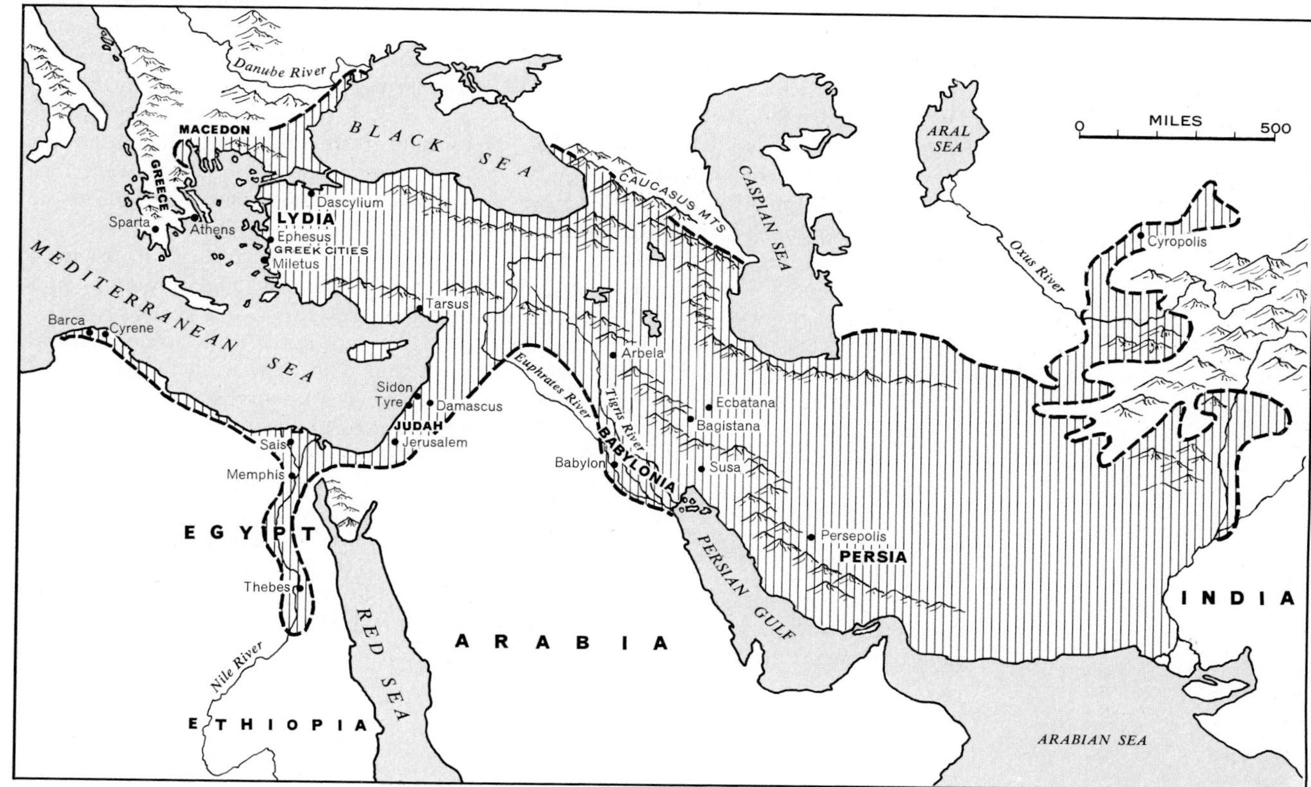

Persian gold cup (fifth century B.C.).

supervision by the central government. Each of the subject peoples was allowed to keep its own customs, its own religion, and often even its own local government. The Hebrews, for instance, were allowed to return to Judah, to reestablish their kingdom, and to rebuild the Temple in Jerusalem. A Persian governor and a Persian garrison were assigned to each of the provinces to maintain order and to supervise the collection of taxes. When faced with rebellion, however, the Persians did not hesitate to take extreme military measures.

One result of the Persian conquests was that Persian religious beliefs left a strong mark on the later religions of the western world. The Persian religion, in its earliest known form, was essentially the deification of natural forces. It gave special prominence to Mithra, the sun god. By the time of the Persian conquests, however, the king and most of the leading families had embraced a newer creed based on the teachings of the prophet Zoroaster. According to Zoroaster there were two gods. Ahura-Mazda, the god of good and light, was engaged in a perpetual struggle with Ahriman, the god of evil and darkness. Humans had free will and could ally themselves with either side. After thousands of years, there would be a final struggle in which good would triumph. Those who had chosen to fight on the side of good would go to paradise (a Persian word); the rest would be consumed in eternal fire. Although Zoroastrianism never spread far beyond Persia, it must be counted as one of the most influential religions of history. Its dualism explained one of religion's most difficult problems: How can a good god permit the existence of evil? Although the belief in two separate gods has never been accepted by Jews or Christians, popular Christian concepts of the Devil in the Middle Ages were not much different from Zoroaster's description of Ahriman. Even more influential on both Christianity and Islam were Zoroaster's teachings about paradise, hell, and the Last Judgment.

The Persians first tasted defeat at the battle of Marathon in 490 B.C. when they failed in their attempt to subdue the Greek city-state of Athens (see pp. 38–40). The reason for Persia's defeat was probably not the superior fighting ability of the Athenians, as Greek historians would have us believe, so much as a combination of weaknesses in the Persian system. The most obvious problem was that of logistics. It was difficult to keep an army healthy and well-supplied when it had to march hundreds of miles to reach an enemy. The Persian government also relied too heavily on the ability of its king. Such a system could succeed only under a man who was both a good administrator and a good general. During the fifth century B.C. the Persian Empire was ruled by a series of men who were neither. Other factors contributed to a general decline of the eastern civilizations under Persian rule. The Persians were not originators or intellectual leaders; they accepted with little change most of the cultures of their subjects. The Persians created favorable conditions for trade and for the exchange of ideas, but they were not themselves great thinkers or traders. High taxes and subjection to a foreign power apparently dampened the initiative of such trading people as the Phoenicians, whose economic activity declined. The Persians never learned to use their manpower efficiently. In fact, under Persian rule opportunities for the ordinary man decreased. He became a peasant, bound to the soil, rather than a free farmer or a free warrior. This change had a bad effect on the army, which became more and more dependent on mercenaries, many of whom were barbarians from areas outside the Persian Empire.

During the fifth century B.C., the most important advances in commerce, philosophy, art, letters, and social organization were not made in the older civilizations that had come under Persian rule. They came from that small part of the eastern world that had escaped Persian domination: the city-states of the Greek peninsula, whose histories will be examined in the next chapter. Greek strength grew as the Persian Empire decayed, until finally, in 333 B.C., the Greek king Alexander defeated the Persian armies and added all of the Persian Empire to his own domains.

Suggestions for Further Reading

Note: Asterisk denotes a book available in paperback edition.

General Several good texts are devoted specifically to ancient history. Among those are W. E. Caldwell and M. F. Gyles, *The Ancient World*, 3rd ed. (1966), and C. G. Starr, *A History of the Ancient World* (1965). W. H. McNeill, *The Rise of the West** (1963), is more successful than most in placing ancient western history in a framework that includes the ancient world as a whole. See also D. B. Nagle, *The Ancient World, a Social and Cultural History** (1979). For a detailed study, see J. B. Bury et al., eds., *The Cambridge Ancient History* (1923–29). The first two volumes have been issued in a paperback edition. Some works on the ancient world before the Greeks are V. G. Childe, *What Happened in History** (1964); H. Frankfort, *The Birth of Civilization in the Near East** (1956); S. Moscoti, *The Face of the Ancient Orient** (1962); and J. Hawkes, *Life in Mesopotamia, the Indus Valley and Egypt* (1973). L. Cottrell, *The Anvil of Civilization** (1957), is shorter but scholarly and informative. Seton Lloyd, *The Art of the Ancient Near East** (1961), is an excellent introduction to the subject.

Archeology and Prehistory There are two works that recount recent archeological discoveries: C. W. Ceram, *Gods, Graves, and Scholars,** rev. ed. (1967), and L. Woolley, *Digging Up the Past** (1940). Ceram is especially helpful in giving references to the work of the great archeologists. R. J. Braidwood, *Prehistoric Men** (1963), and J. Hawkes and L. Woolley, *Prehistory and the Beginnings of Civilization** (1963), are interesting summaries of what is known of human history before the invention of writing.

Mesopotamia A good summary is W. W. Hallo and W. K. Simpson, *The Ancient Near East: A History** (1971). A. L. Oppenheim, *Ancient Mesopotamia* (1964), and H. W. F. Saggs, *The Greatness That Was Babylon* (1962), are detailed surveys of Mesopotamian history. S. Moscoti, *Ancient Semitic Civilizations** (1960), is shorter and includes Syria and Palestine. The two books by S. N. Kramer, *History Begins at Sumer** (1959) and *The Sumerians* (1963), contain excellent source material for the political, social, and religious thinking of the Sumerians, the first people to keep written records. L. Woolley, *Ur of the Chaldees** (1950), is one of many books by a leading authority on Mesopotamian archeology. An interesting description of the Mesopotamian world may be found in G. Contenau, *Everyday Life in Babylon and Assyria* (1954).

Egypt There are two good surveys of ancient Egypt. Of them, A. H. Gardiner, *Egypt of the Pharaohs** (1961), is more factual; J. A. Wilson, *The Culture of Ancient Egypt** (1963), more interpretive. For a study of Egyptian monuments, see either I. E. S. Edwards, *The Pyramids of Egypt,** rev. ed. (1961), or W. S. Smith, *Art and Architecture of Ancient Egypt** (1958). H. Frankfort, *Ancient Egyptian Religion** (1948), largely replaces some of the older standard works on this subject. P. Montet, *Everyday Life in Egypt in the Days of Ramses II* (1958), is a counterpart to Contenau's book on Babylon.

Crete There is no complete and generally accepted history of the Minoan culture, though most of the texts on Greek history mentioned at the end of the next chapter have short surveys. A recent study of the archeological discoveries on Crete is R. W. Hutchinson, *Prehistoric Crete** (1963). L. Cottrell, *The Bull of Minos** (1953), is shorter and more readable.

The Indo-Europeans The best general account is V. G. Childe, *The Aryans: A Study of Indo-European Origins* (1926). O. R. Gurney, *The Hittites** (1952), is a good introduction to the study of the Hittites, and C. W. Ceram, *The Secret of the Hittites* (1956), gives a fascinating account of the archeological expeditions that uncovered the Hittite civilization.

Syria and Palestine Informative studies of the non-Hebrew peoples who inhabited Syria-Palestine can be found in J. Gray, *The Canaanites* (1964); D. Harden, *The Phoenicians* (1962); and R. A. H. Macalister, *The Philistines* (1913). There is such a wealth of material on the ancient Hebrews and their religious evolution that any short list must omit even many standard works. Among the better general histories are W. F. Albright, *The Biblical Period from Abraham to Ezra** (1963); J. Bright, *A History of Israel* (1959); C. H. Gordon, *The Ancient Near East** (1965); A. Lods, *Israel* (1932); and the early chapters of A. L. Sachar, *A History of the Jews** (1966). For a briefer treatment, see E. J. Ehrlich, *A Concise History of Israel** (1965), or H. Orlinsky, *Ancient Israel** (1964).

Assyrians, Chaldeans, and Persians The Assyrians and the Chaldeans are both treated in the general histories of Mesopotamia mentioned above. For studies of the Persians as well as of the diverse peoples they ruled, see either R. N. Frye, *The Heritage of Persia* (1963), or A. T. Olmstead, *A History of the Persian Empire** (1959).

2 Greek Civilization

Even though Persia was weakening when it met its first defeats at the hands of the Greeks, it is still surprising that a few small, loosely allied Greek cities could resist the professional army of a great empire. The Greek success is even more astonishing when we consider that many Greek cities were so afraid of Persia that they took no part in the war. The Greek victories were won by a minority of the Greek people.

The same paradox appears in other Greek achievements. The Greeks were very conscious of their identity, very proud of being Greek, very scornful of the barbarians (anyone who was not Greek) who did not share their culture. They worshiped the same gods, revered the same oracles, spoke what was basically the same language, met and competed with one another at great festivals such as the Olympic Games. Yet Greece was divided into many quarreling states, and most Greeks were peasant farmers who contributed little to and were little influenced by the high culture of the Greek world. That culture was created by a few men living in a few cities scattered around the rim of the Aegean Sea. It was a long time before Greek culture penetrated very far inland; Boeotia, only thirty miles from Athens, was notorious among the Greeks as the home of dull, ignorant, blundering yokels. Greek culture eventually spread throughout the Mediterranean world, but the Golden Age of Greece was a golden age for only a few hundred thousand men.

Geography helps explain the divisions and uneven development of the Greek people. Rocky mountains enclose fertile plains, emerge from the Aegean Sea to form countless islands, and rise again to form the craggy promontories of Asia Minor. The best harbors were usually not near the best farming land. It was in the seaports that new ideas and new patterns of social organization were most likely to emerge, either through contact with other cities or because of the pressure of growing population. The more fertile areas of Greece, such as Thessaly, had fewer outside contacts and were under less pressure to make innovations.

Geography made it easy for many small states to emerge and to survive. But geography alone cannot account for the particularism of ancient Greeks. Equally important were the intensity of political life in the local communities and the fierce competitiveness of the Greek spirit. It was not impossible to unite Greece, but it was far more difficult than it had been to unite Egypt, and the task took many centuries. Meanwhile the Greeks lived in small, independent communities, each of which developed its own pattern of life. Obviously some patterns would be more likely to encourage writers, artists, and philosophers than others. Cities

The Parthenon at Athens.

The earliest representation of Homer, on a fourth-century B.C. coin.

that had an active intellectual and artistic life attracted capable men from other parts of the Greek world. Thus small differences became magnified with the passage of time. Early Athens and early Sparta had a good deal in common, but by the middle of the fifth century B.C. Sparta was a garrison state and Athens was the cultural center of the Greek people.

EARLY GREEK HISTORY TO *ca.* 800 B.C.

The Greeks knew little about their own past and were apt to exaggerate the originality and the rapidity of development of their civilization. Their oldest historical records were the two epic poems of Homer—the *Iliad* and the *Odyssey*. These poems celebrate the siege of Troy by a league of Greek warriors. The siege probably took place about 1250 B.C., and its memory was probably preserved in legend, but Homer (or the two or more poets whose work was ascribed to Homer) did not compose the epics before 750 B.C. and perhaps not until a half century or so later. The Greeks were not very conscious of or concerned by these dates. For them the Homeric poems were their earliest historical record, a guide to right conduct, a foundation for their religion, and the fountainhead of a common culture. The epics were works of timeless value, and Homer's heroes were taken as typical of the early Greek character.

Nineteenth-century European scholars saw little historical value in the Homeric legends, except as evidence about the state of Greek society and religion at some date before the classical period. But a German businessman named Heinrich Schliemann was convinced that there had been a siege of Troy. In 1870 he began to excavate a mound near the Dardanelles in Asia Minor that was the traditional site of Troy. To the astonishment of the scholarly world, he found layer after layer of ancient settlements, one of them a large fortified city that had been destroyed shortly before 1200 B.C., and another older and very rich town that had fallen earlier (1800 B.C.). He assumed that the older city was Homer's Troy; actually, layer 7a (the city that fell about 1250 B.C.) was the one he should have selected. Schliemann then went to Mycenae in southern Greece, the legendary home of the Greek leader Agamemnon, and began a search for the king's palace. Here he found evidence of a surprisingly advanced civilization whose roots went back at least as far as 1800 B.C.

Schliemann's successors found similar sites, and it became evident that this Mycenaean civilization was fairly widespread throughout the Greek peninsula. It seemed probable that the Mycenaeans were early Greeks; the decipherment of Linear Script B in 1952 (see p. 13) strengthened this hypothesis. We know that the Greeks reached the Aegean area about 2000 B.C., that they had contacts with the Minoan civilization, that they traded and raided in the Aegean Sea, and that they finally settled in the Greek peninsula, the Aegean islands, and along the coast of Asia Minor. These early Greeks spoke an Indo-European lan-

The Discovery of Troy

Heinrich Schliemann's discovery of Troy in 1873 helped trigger further archeological expeditions.

He struck into the mound, boldly ripping down walls that to him seemed unimportant. He found weapons and household furnishings, ornaments and vases, overwhelming evidence that a rich city had once occupied the spot. And he found something else as well. . . . Under the ruins of New Ilium he disclosed other ruins, under these still others. The hill was like a tremendous onion, which he proceeded to dismember layer by layer. Each layer seemed to have been inhabited at a different period. Populations had lived and died, cities had been built up only to fall into decay. Sword and fire had raged, one civilization cutting off another, and again and again a city of the living had been raised on a city of the dead.

. . . The question now arose which of these nine cities was the Troy of Homer, of the heroes and the epic war. . . .

Schliemann dug and searched. In the second and third levels from the bottom he found traces of fire, the remains of massive walls, and the ruins of a gigantic gate. He was sure that these walls had once enclosed the palace of Priam. . . .

From C. W. Ceram, *Gods, Graves, and Scholars,* rev. ed. (New York: Knopf, 1967), pp. 36–37.

guage, knew the use of bronze, and were strong enough and numerous enough to conquer and assimilate the earlier inhabitants of the region.

The Mycenaean Civilization ca. *1650–1150* B.C.

By about 1600 B.C., or soon thereafter, this early Greek, or Mycenaean, civilization had reached a fairly advanced state. As was to be the case for centuries, there were many small independent political units, each one based on a strongly fortified citadel and ruled by a king and his band of warriors. The Greek city of later centuries did not exist then, but a fairly large merchant class traded throughout the Aegean and with Crete. There was certainly some competition (perhaps violent) with the Minoans for trade, but there must have been periods of peaceful cooperation as well. The great palaces of Mycenae, Tiryns, and Pylos show Minoan influence, and the enormous wealth of the rulers of Mycenae must have come largely from trade.

The Mycenaean Greeks may have contributed to the downfall of Minoan Crete about 1480 B.C.; certainly the Greeks attempted to profit from the disaster. As we have seen in Chapter 1, Greeks probably took over and rebuilt the palace at Knossos; they also must have hoped to take over Minoan trade routes. If so, they were disappointed. It was Egypt under the militant pharaohs of the New Kingdom that became the dominant commercial power of the eastern Mediterranean. The Mycenaeans continued to trade in the Aegean and eastern Mediterranean, and began to penetrate the Black Sea. This may have stirred up rivalry with Troy, which was well placed to block the entrance to the Straits, though the legendary wealth of Troy could also have been a cause of conflict. If there ever was a Trojan War, which some scholars doubt, it would have taken place after the fall of Crete and before

THE AEGEAN WORLD *ca.* 1500–146 B.C.

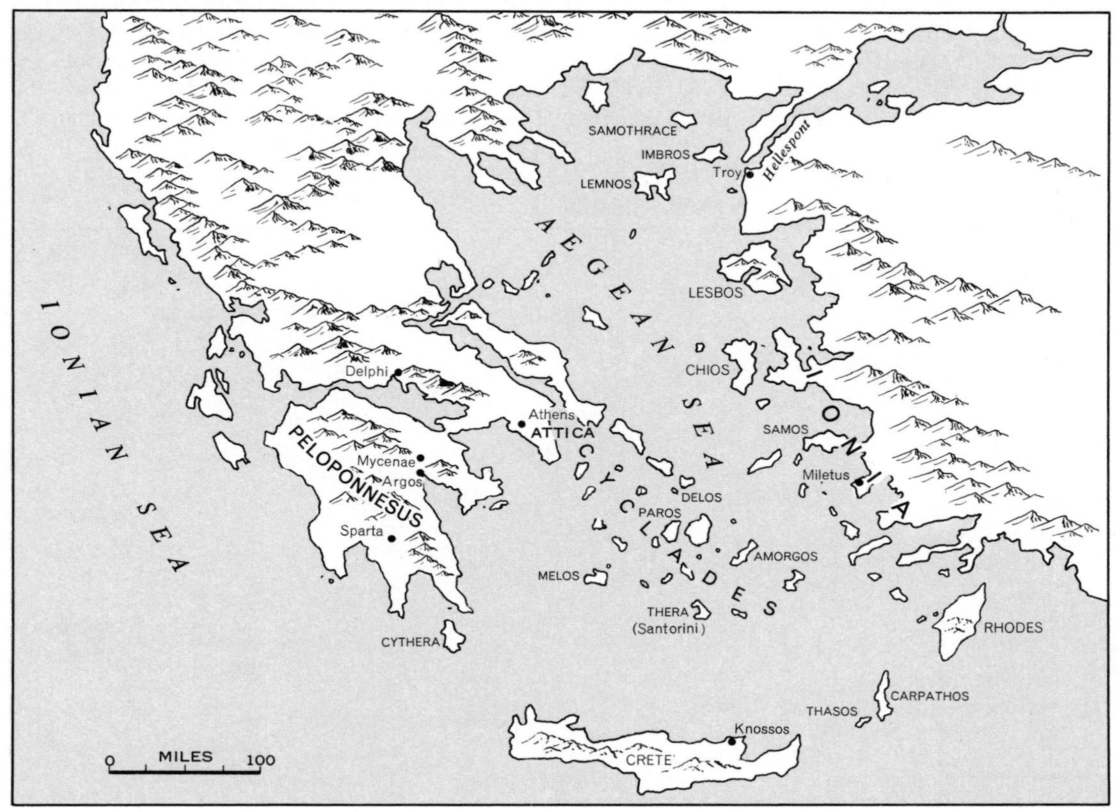

the collapse of the Mycenaean civilization—that is, very near the traditional date of 1250 B.C.

The Greek Dark Ages ca. *1150–800* B.C.

The Mycenaean world was wracked by a series of violent attacks from unknown invaders soon after 1200 B.C. Royal palaces were burned, towns destroyed, and kingdoms overthrown. A few places escaped with little damage, notably Athens, and many Mycenaean Greeks were able to flee to islands in the Aegean or to Greek settlements in Asia Minor. Nevertheless, the Mycenaean ruling class was wiped out and with it Mycenaean art and the Mycenaean system of writing.

The last and fatal blow to the Mycenaean civilization was struck by a Greek-speaking people, the Dorians. The Dorians may have completed the destruction of the fragments of Mycenaean civilization that had survived the attacks of the earlier invaders; certainly they did nothing to rebuild the old way of life. They were a rustic people who had had little contact with the civilizations of the eastern Mediterranean; their communities were composed of small farmers dominated by groups of warriors. The Dorians were especially numerous in the Peloponnesus, the old center of Mycenaean civilization. As a result, memories of the past faded, especially since there were no written records to preserve old traditions and to report the activities of the new ruling class. Very little is known about Greece during the "Dark Ages" that followed the Dorian invasions.

THE GREEK WORLD *ca.* 800–500 B.C.

More information is available about the Greek world after 800 B.C., and especially about the Greeks of Ionia along the western coast of Asia Minor. It is evident that an economic revival had occurred and that a number of trading cities had emerged. Some commerce must have existed even during the "Dark Ages," and with both Egypt and the Phoenician cities under Assyrian control, the Greeks had a new opportunity to expand their trade routes throughout the eastern Mediterranean. For example, Miletus and eleven other cities had a seaport (Naucratis) in the Nile Delta. Miletus also had a string of trading posts along the shores of the Black Sea where goods from Egypt and western Asia could be sold to the peoples of eastern Europe.

GREEK AND PHOENICIAN COLONIZATION AND TRADE *ca.* 750–550 B.C.

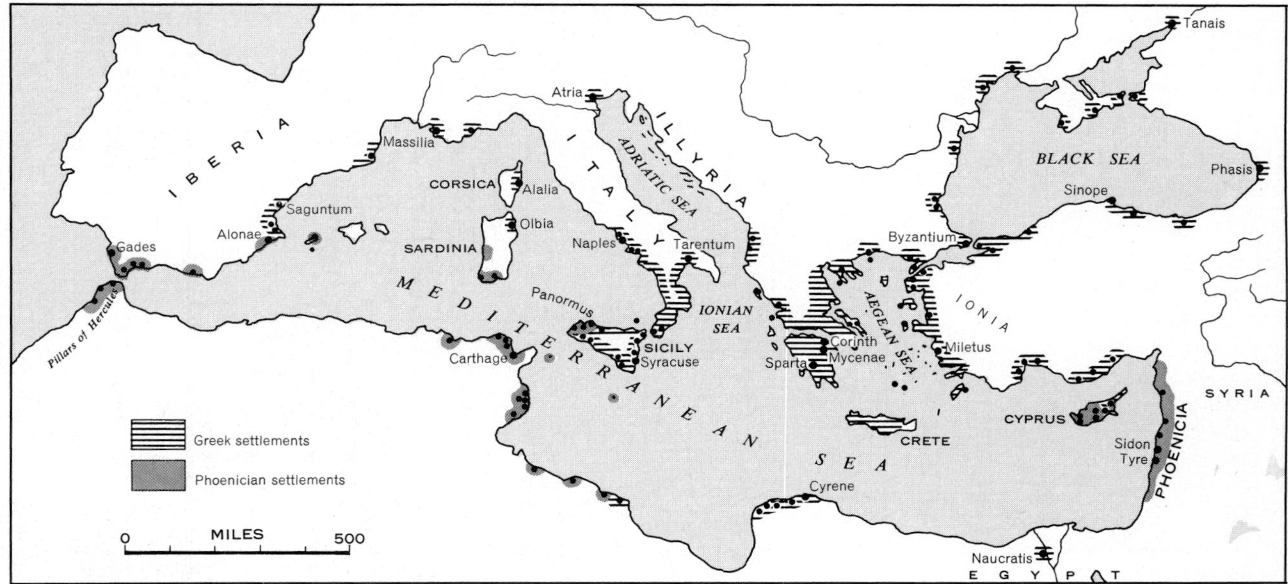

ca. 2000 B.C.	*ca.* 1700	*ca.* 1480	*ca.* 1100	*ca.* 800	*ca.* 600	404	323	146 B.C. Conquest by Rome
Minoan Civilization on Crete			"Dark Ages"	Dominance of City-states of Asia Minor	Dominance of Athens and Sparta	Decline of City-state System and Conquest by Macedon	Hellenistic Era	
Arrival of Greeks	Mycenaean Civilization in Aegean Area							

Trade was greatly stimulated by the invention of coined money, which occurred in Asia Minor (probably in the kingdom of Lydia) in the late seventh century B.C. Gold and silver had long been prized, and the value of other goods had often been expressed in terms of specific weights of these precious metals. But testing, weighing, and cutting a bar of gold or silver was too tedious for ordinary small transactions. It was eventually discovered that the metal could be cut up into many small bits, stamped to show that a ruler guaranteed their weight and fineness, and then used repeatedly for any sort of business. By making it easier to buy and sell goods of all kinds, this discovery increased the volume of trade.

As Greek trade expanded, towns on the western shore of the Aegean (such as Corinth) began to prosper. Population increased, both in Ionia and in the Greek peninsula. The commercial cities became crowded, and few of them controlled enough agricultural land to guarantee an adequate food supply for all their people. Fortunately, the Mediterranean region was still thinly settled, and there were many districts where small native populations could be subdued or displaced by colonists from the Greek shores of the Aegean. Just as the Phoenicians had taken over North Africa, so, from 750 B.C. on, the Greeks took over southern Italy and eastern Sicily; Naples and Syracuse were both founded by Greeks, and other Greek cities in the region were so numerous that the Romans later called southern Italy Magna Graecia, or Great Greece. Other Greek colonies were even more remote, such as Massilia (Marseilles) in southern France, trading posts in Spain, and Tanais on the north shore of the Black Sea. Greek colonies usually maintained cultural and religious ties with their mother-cities, but normally they were fully independent and owed no political or military support to their founders.

Cultural Development

Prosperity, as it often does, encouraged cultural development. It was in Ionia that the Greeks rediscovered the art of writing by adapting the Phoenician alphabet to the Greek language in the eighth century B.C. This discovery encouraged poets to put orally transmitted legends into permanent written form, as was done with the story of the Trojan War. In the same way, the works of lyric poets could now be preserved. Writing spread rapidly throughout the Greek-speaking communities, and, as will be seen, Ionia was not the only region that produced famous poets in the seventh and sixth centuries B.C. Nevertheless, until they lost their independence about 540 B.C., the Ionians remained the intellectual leaders of the Greeks.

Throughout the Greek world there was a rapid development of literature and the arts. Not long after the Homeric epics were written, Hesiod, a small landowner in Boeotia, wrote his long didactic

Scene from a Greek vase (*ca.* 550 B.C.) showing merchants weighing produce. As trade routes multiplied, Greek merchants and wine and oil producers prospered.

poems describing the origins of the gods and the hard life of the farmer. The first famous woman poet was Sappho of Lesbos; the Spartan commander Tyrtaeus composed martial songs to inspire his soldiers. Even the remote and newly colonized cities of Sicily produced their poets. And in Ionia the foundations were being laid for work in philosophy and natural science.

Some remarkable works of art were produced during the seventh and sixth centuries B.C. The Greek temple began to take on its characteristic form—an oblong building framed by pillars with sculptured figures on the lintels and above the columns. Early Greek sculpture owed much to the Egyptians; the figures are stiff and tense, ritualistic rather than realistic. But the Greeks had already learned to depict figures in full profile (which the Egyptians could not or would not do), and they were already showing interest in the beauty of the human figure. Most typical because most common were the vase paintings, which portray lively and realistic pictures of all sorts of human activities.

Greek vase of the late sixth century B.C. depicting a foot race. The vase was awarded to the winner of the foot race contest at the Panathenaic festival in Athens.

Social and Political Change

The rapid growth of trade and population put serious strains on the old political and social system. The *Iliad* and other early Greek writings suggest that a typical Greek community of the "Dark Ages" was ruled by a king or chieftain, who was advised and often contradicted by a council of very independent warriors. The warriors in turn held most of the land and dominated the peasant farmers and herders. The petty kings of the Homeric Age had very little power compared with an Egyptian pharaoh or a Persian emperor, and as time went on they tended to lose what power they had. The community was controlled by the land-holding aristocracy; if the king survived at all it was only because he was needed to perform certain religious rites, or because it was convenient to have a predesignated war-leader ready for sudden emergencies.

In communities with an adequate amount of good land, slow-growing populations, and relatively little commercial activity, this pattern of aristocratic government persisted throughout the period of independent Greek states, for example in Thebes and the rest of Boetia, and in Thessaly. But in the trading cities there was more reason for the aristocracy to break up into factions and for friction between rich and poor. Some of the aristocrats became traders and joined forces with merchants of humbler origin; some continued to draw most of their income from their estates. There could be serious policy differences between those who sought to protect and extend trade routes and those who sought to protect and extend their lands. But even those in the latter group were involved in commerce, since they discovered that there was a market for wine and olive oil throughout the Mediterranean. Only a rich landowner could afford the initial investment needed to start a vineyard or an olive grove and the long delay before a crop could be harvested (ten years or more for olives). The peasants therefore continued to grow grain. But the profits on wine and oil exports could be used to buy cheap grain in Egypt or Sicily, where the soil was more productive. Thus while small farmers and day laborers suffered, landlords, merchants, shipbuilders, and skilled artisans like those who made the great pottery jugs for wine and oil prospered. With grain prices low, peasants fell into debt, and with interest rates running at 16 percent or more, they seldom were able to repay their loans. At best they lost their land and had to join the casual labor force in the city; at worst they and their children were sold into slavery.

The logical outcome of this crisis would have been either a bloody rebellion or the establishment of a society in which a few masters dominated thousands of slaves. But the Greeks had always lived in small, tightly knit communities in which every family had its place and every man was known to most of his fellows. Such communities could not fully accept the depersonalizing effects of a commercial economy based on formal business contracts. If anything, economic growth forced people closer together as villages became cities and as the rural population became more dependent on the urban nucleus. The old sense of mutual responsibility and individual dignity persisted and was reinforced by a growing realization that these emerging city-states must make the best use they could of the limited manpower at their disposal. Enslaving half the population was not a good use of manpower; neither was a rebellion that might have killed off most of those who had military, political, and commercial skills. Most Greek cities avoided both these extremes and gradually satisfied the protests of debt-ridden farmers and laborers by a long drawn-out series of political reforms.

One of the first reactions to social strains was the establishment of tyrannies. A tyrant was usually a colorful politician who gained support by making vague promises of better government so that he could make himself dictator. Most tyrants were aristocrats with considerable political experience; many of them were quite capable rulers. Pisistratus of Athens, for example, greatly strengthened his city, and at the same time preserved its laws. Tyrants usually tried to weaken the landed aristocracy by favoring commercial interests. They also allowed a somewhat larger group of citizens to take part in the political process. For a time they seem to have succeeded in reducing social tensions, but they did not solve the problems of slavery and land reform. Although some tyrants managed to pass their power on to their sons, no tyranny persisted for more than three generations. The Greeks disliked the idea of tyranny, not because the tyrants were evil men (though a few of them were), but because they had seized power illegally and behaved arrogantly. The Greeks could accept class differences, but to the very end they remained suspicious of a single man who tried to dominate his fellow citizens. Thus tyranny did not become accepted as a new and desirable form of monarchy; instead it gained a reputation for oppressiveness that has persisted to the present day.

The seventh and sixth centuries B.C. were an age of tyrants, but they were also an age of lawgivers. The latter were rather more successful than the former. Old customs had to be adapted to new conditions, and the ruling classes gave full support to (and usually chose) men who tried to bring the laws up to date. Early laws were rigid and severe (the word *draconian* is still a memorial to the harsh code of the Athenian Draco), but, even so, fixed rules had advantages over decisions based on obsolete customs or whims of kings or aristocratic councils. And later lawgivers were less severe and were more concerned with the welfare of the poorer part of the population. About 590 B.C., for example, Solon of Athens reduced the burden of debt on small farmers and forbade enslavement for debt. Though he was followed by a tyrant, Solon's laws remained in force and formed the basis for a new constitution at the end of the sixth century. Other cities had similar experiences. In time it became a matter of pride to the Greeks that while other peoples were ruled by the will of kings, the Greeks were ruled by laws, not by men. Every Greek knew the laws of his city; they determined and protected his rights; they bound aristocrats and public officials as well as the poor and private citizens. And because the law was known, it was always possible to consider ways in which it could be changed and reformed.

The City-State

By 500 B.C. most of the tyrannies had ended, and many enduring codes of law had been drafted. The worst of the social crises caused by rapid changes in the economy were over, although many reforms were still needed. The Greeks were ready to try their great political experiment, the establishment of basically secular governments in which power and responsibility were shared by a considerable part of the citizenry. The kings were gone, and religion was becoming a form of civic patriotism. Basic loyalty went to the *polis*—the city-state—and the *polis* was a republic. It might have been controlled by a handful of aristocrats, but it might also have allowed most or all of the citizens to participate in the work of government. Whatever the distribution of power, the peak of Greek civilization was reached during the period in which the city-state, like an early Greek kingdom, controlled only a limited area, usually no more than that of a small American county. Much of the land was devoted to farming, but the center of the *polis* was the city itself with its marketplace, its citadel, and its temples. No city-state had a very large population: with over 250,000 inhabitants, Athens was probably the biggest, but many cities had only ten thousand or so.

This stele informed the Athenians of the Law Against Tyranny in 336 B.C.: "Should anyone, in an attempt at absolute power, rise up against the people or try to overthrow the democracy of Athens—whoever kills him shall be blameless."

The smallness of the population was compensated for by the intensity of communal life. The citizens knew one another better and shared one another's experiences more fully than in any modern city of comparable size. Most activities took place in the open, since Greek houses were small and simple—places to eat and sleep, but not to live. Public and private business was transacted on the streets or on the porches of temples and law courts. Artisans and merchants worked in small shops open to the street. Actors gave their performances in unroofed theaters; teachers met their pupils in public gardens; politicians argued in the public squares. Everyone had a chance to know everything that was going on in the city; there was little privacy and apparently little desire for it.

In such close-knit communities it was easy to judge the character and ability of every citizen. And with such small populations it was essential to make the most of these human resources, especially in time of war. The days when a few aristocratic warriors with horses and chariots could carry the main burden of combat were long since gone. Greek armies were now composed of heavy-armed infantry (*hoplites*) fighting in close formation (the *phalanx*); all but the very poorest citizens were supposed to provide their own weapons and serve in the ranks. And when, as in the case of Athens, it was necessary to man a fleet of warships as well as provide an army, even the poorest citizens were needed for service. They could pull an oar even if they could not afford shields and weapons.

Men who served in the armed forces at their own expense could scarcely be barred from the political activities of the community. In many cities the officials, or a governing council, were elected by a general assembly. The tendency was to increase the power of the general assembly, by admitting more and more citizens (in some cases all citizens), and to increase the number of men eligible for political office. Even at their greatest extent, however, these concessions did not produce pure democracy. The franchise was limited to adult males; women were excluded from political life. Slaves, who were numerous in every Greek city, had no rights, and immigrants from other Greek states, who formed a large part of the population in various trading cities such as Athens, could not vote even after many years of residence because they could not become citizens. Moreover, the aristocratic type of government persisted, with slight modifications, in many states. Overall, however, by the end of the sixth century B.C., a larger percentage of the male citizen population (varying from 100 percent in Athens to 10 percent in Sparta) participated in the political process than in any earlier period.

This increasing participation in politics strengthened the bonds between the citizen and his city. The *polis* was not just an area of land or a group of buildings; it was a way of life that shaped every human activity. As Socrates once put it, the laws and customs of Athens were his parents; they had raised and nurtured him. He was the kind of person he was because he had been born a citizen of Athens. But if the *polis* shaped the lives of its citizens, the citizens also shaped the life of the *polis.* Even in aristocratic states the rulers had to pay some attention to public opinion; elsewhere very little could be done without the approval and active assistance of a considerable part of the body of citizens.

Approval and assistance went far beyond the making and enforcing of laws. The adornment of the city with public buildings, the encouragement of poetry and drama, the support of teachers and scholars all were influenced by public opinion; and all were, to some degree, dependent on the support of the wealthier classes. Peasants and day laborers were probably not greatly interested in art and literature, but men who had a little money and some leisure could argue endlessly about esthetic and intellectual problems. In fact, one of the excuses for slavery was that it made it possible for the citizen to participate fully in the cultural and political life of his city by freeing him from the routine of daily work. Not all citizens took advantage of their opportunities, even in the most enlightened cities, but enough of them did to enable a sophisticated civilization to develop on a very small population base.

This discussion of life in the Greek city-state has focused exclusively on men. But society then was thoroughly male dominated, which may be why there was a considerable amount of homosexuality, especially among the upper classes. The underlying idea was that a being of beauty *and* brains could only be male. Women stayed home, unless they were courtesans or lesbians, as Sappho reputedly was.

Greek Religion

The religion of the Greeks both bound them together and encouraged strong local patriotisms. Some of the Greek gods probably went back to the religion of pre-Greek inhabitants of the Aegean area; some certainly came in with successive waves of invaders; but by Homeric times they had been combined into a family of twelve major gods who lived on Mount Olympus. Zeus was ruler of the gods and wielder of the thunderbolt; his wife, Hera, was goddess of women and marriage. Strangely enough, Ares, the god of war, was not especially honored by the Greeks, in spite of their belligerent spirit.

Each city gave special honor to one divinity, who was its protector and patron. Thus Athena, goddess of wisdom, was greatly revered in Athens, even though this meant giving second place to Poseidon, god of the sea and the chief god of many communities in Attica. Artemis, the twin sister of Apollo, was worshiped at Sparta as the spirit of bravery and courage. Apollo, god of prophecy, was not so closely tied to any one city; people came from all parts of the Greek world to seek guidance from his oracle at Delphi, and his shrine on the island of Delos was a center of religious life for many of the Greek islands. Zeus was also widely worshiped. In their great festivals, such as the Olympic and Isthmian games, the Greeks honored all the gods in competitions to determine who was the best poet, the fastest runner, the ablest playwright, the strongest wrestler. But in their frequent wars, the Greeks expected each god to defend his own city, even to the extent of fighting with the god of the opposing city. Religion gave the Greeks cultural but not political unity.

Greek mythology, especially as reported by Homer (whose works were the Greek equivalent of the Bible), was not very edifying or inspiring. The gods were simply human beings on a large scale. They had great power and were immortal, but they were also quarrelsome, lustful, and prejudiced. They lied to and cheated one another; they interfered in human affairs in unpredictable and whimsical ways; they were completely undisciplined. Zeus had no real control over them (especially when he was off on one of his amorous adventures), and their worshipers could never be sure what would please them. One could only sacrifice and hope for the best.

Educated Greeks tried hard to draw

Athena, goddess of wisdom, protector of the home and the citadel, is shown in this bronze statue in military dress (*ca.* seventh century B.C.).

ca. 2000 B.C.	*ca.* 1700	*ca.* 1480	*ca.* 1100	*ca.* 800	*ca.* 600	404	323	146 B.C.
Minoan Civilization on Crete								
Arrival of Greeks	Mycenaean Civilization in Aegean Area		"Dark Ages"	Dominance of City-states of Asia Minor	Dominance of Athens and Sparta		Hellenistic Era	Conquest by Rome

Decline of City-state System and Conquest by Macedon

Delphi
Thebes
Athens
Corinth
Olympia
Mycenae
MESSENIA
Sparta

some moral lessons from the confused stories of the gods, but with little success. Something could be done with Apollo as the god of reason and light, and Zeus could be reverenced as the Father of all by ignoring the scandalous stories about him. But while the Greeks were reasonably sure that there were supernatural beings, they were not very sure that they knew much about them. The official religious cult was an excuse for festivals and parades, for building temples and carving statues, for writing poems and plays. It furnished an outlet for civic patriotism. The basic problems of the meaning of life and of the right conduct of life had to be solved in other ways.

It is doubtful that the common people had ever been wholly devoted to the Homeric gods, who were the gods of the old aristocracy. The pre-Greek fertility cults, centered on the worship of Demeter, goddess of grain and fertility, and Dionysus, god of wine and ecstasy, remained popular with them. Both involved secret rituals; both gave some promise of immortality. Through ritual and moral purity the initiate could be united to Demeter and be assured of lasting bliss. Through drinking wine mixed with sacrificial blood, the followers of Dionysus could rise from the dead, as their god had done. Often the two fertility cults were combined, and they spread throughout the Greek world. The most famous Greek dramas were written for the annual festivals of Dionysus, one of the great religious events at Athens.

Gorgon from the Temple of Artemis, goddess of the hunt, at Corfu (600 B.C.).

THE PERSIAN WARS 499–479 B.C.

In the last decades of the sixth century B.C. the Greeks were clearly ready for "take-off"; they had the economic, political, and intellectual base on which to build a great civilization. Precisely at this point came the crisis of the Persian Wars. War can ruin a civilization that is fully developed and set in its ways, but it can stimulate a civilization that is still in its early stage of development. Victory over the Persians confirmed the belief of the Greeks in their uniqueness and in their destiny; the wars were followed immediately by the Golden Age of Greece.

Persian power had been a serious threat ever since Cyrus the Great conquered the Ionian cities about 540 B.C. The Greek world was shocked by this calamity, but an effective response to Persian aggression could come only from the mainland of the Greek peninsula. And leadership there had gradually concentrated in two cities, Athens and Sparta. If they could cooperate, Persia might be resisted; if not, the prospects were dim. But cooperation was not easy, for Athens and Sparta stood at the two extremes of the Greek political system.

Sparta

Sparta in the early period of its history was not very different from other Greek states; like them, it took a prominent part in the early development of Greek art and literature. But Sparta was situated in a fertile agricultural region, one that was not greatly concerned with commerce. It sought to make the most of its favorable agricultural position by dominating other grain-producing communities in its neighborhood. About 650 B.C. one of these neighboring communities, Messenia, revolted and almost destroyed the Spartan state. By 600 B.C. the Spartans were victorious, but they had been badly frightened. They decided to turn the entire male population of their *polis* into a standing army and to suppress any activity that might interfere with military efficiency.

When the reorganization had been completed the population of the Spartan state (called Lacedaemon) was divided into three groups. First were the Spartan male citizens (less than ten thousand men), who had all political rights and enjoyed full equality among themselves. Then came the free citizens of the neighboring communities, who could manage their own affairs but who had nothing to say about decisions of the ruling city. Third were the *helots,* serfs who worked the lands of Lacedaemon for the benefit of Spartan citizens.

The citizens paid a high price for their political and economic privileges. At the age of seven they were taken from their homes to be trained for military service. They entered the army at twenty and were allowed to marry then, but they could not live with their wives until they were thirty. They remained liable for military service until they were sixty.

It is easy to see how this sytem created the best-disciplined army in the Greek world and how it enabled Sparta to control most of the Peloponnesus, either directly or through an alliance with other cities known as the Peloponnesian League. It is less easy to understand why other Greeks, even in the liberal-minded and unregimented city of Athens, admired the Spartans so greatly. Bravery, discipline, frugality, scorn of luxury were characteristic of the Spartans, and it may

A procession recorded in marble at the Parthenon (fifth century B.C.). The paraders on their way to the Acropolis carry jars containing sacrificial gifts.

Head of a Spartan warrior believed to be King Leonidas, who commanded the Greek force at Thermopylae (early fifth century B.C.).

be that the many Greeks who lacked these qualities found some satisfaction in seeing them embodied in at least one community. Even so, self-discipline is more attractive than discipline imposed by the state; it seems likely that for most people Spartan success was more impressive than Spartan virtue.

Athens

Athens was more like an Ionian city than most of the other Greek states. Dependent on commerce rather early (sixth century B.C.), the Athenians aimed to suppress or control trade rivals rather than add agricultural regions to their holdings. Athens had one asset that most other cities lacked—the silver mines of Laureium, which by the fifth century B.C. yielded enough to pay for great expenses, such as the building of a fleet.

As we have seen, Athens had its early lawgivers (Draco and Solon) and its sixth-century tyrants. The net result of these experiences had been to increase somewhat the number of citizens eligible to take an active role in government, although the wealthy still retained control. A sharp change came after the last tyrant was overthrown in 510 B.C., when the reformer Cleisthenes put through some basic constitutional reforms. Cleisthenes divided the citizens into ten tribes, so arranged that each tribe was a cross section of the whole population, rich and poor, rural and urban. Fifty citizens chosen by lot from each tribe made up the Council of Five Hundred, which prepared business for the assembly. A general assembly of all citizens passed the laws, as had long been customary. The top civil and military offices were open only to the wealthier citizens, and the old Council of the Areopagus, or council of ex-archons (the highest civil officials), had considerable power for a generation or more after Cleisthenes' reforms. But even these officials were elected by popular vote, and since they were not paid, the poorer citizens had no great desire anyway to become archons or generals or treasurers.

The Athenian constitution thus gave every citizen the right to influence the government and to participate in its activities. Almost every citizen took a passionate interest in politics, education, art, and literature. There were, of course, private interests and political factions; the Athenians could be as shortsighted, selfish, and unreasonable as many modern voters. But for almost a century the Athenian system succeeded in releasing the energy of all citizens and in concentrating a good part of it on the common welfare.

The Defeat of Persia

When the Greek cities of Asia Minor revolted against Persia in 499 B.C., Athens sent a fleet to assist them. After the revolt had been put down, the Persian King Darius dispatched a punitive force by sea to Attica. But this force was repulsed by a small Athenian army at Marathon in 490 B.C. The Persian king, unwilling to let such a humiliation go unpunished, planned a full-scale campaign against the cities of the Greek peninsula. Fortunately for the Greeks, Darius died before he could begin his attack. It was only in 480 B.C. that his successor, Xerxes, and a Persian army of over one hundred thousand men crossed the Dardanelles and marched down the Greek peninsula. Faced with such an overwhelming force, most of the small cities north of Athens declared their neutrality. Athens and the Peloponnesian League were left to defend what remained of Greek civilization from envelopment by the Persian Empire.

The Peloponnesian League formed the basis of the Greek defense against the Persians. The Athenians had hoped for Spartan help at Marathon and were quite ready to form a new league in alliance with the Peloponnesians, although in so doing they were forced to accept the leadership of Sparta. As the Persian forces moved southward, a small Spartan detachment at the head of some six thousand Greeks attempted to hold the pass at Thermopylae, north of Athens, until a decisive naval battle could be fought. This battle, which took place off the coast, was a draw. The Greek forces withdrew to take up new positions at the Isthmus of Corinth and the Bay of Salamis. Meanwhile, the Persians broke through the pass at Thermopylae after the entire Spartan detachment had been

THE PERSIAN WARS 499–479 B.C.

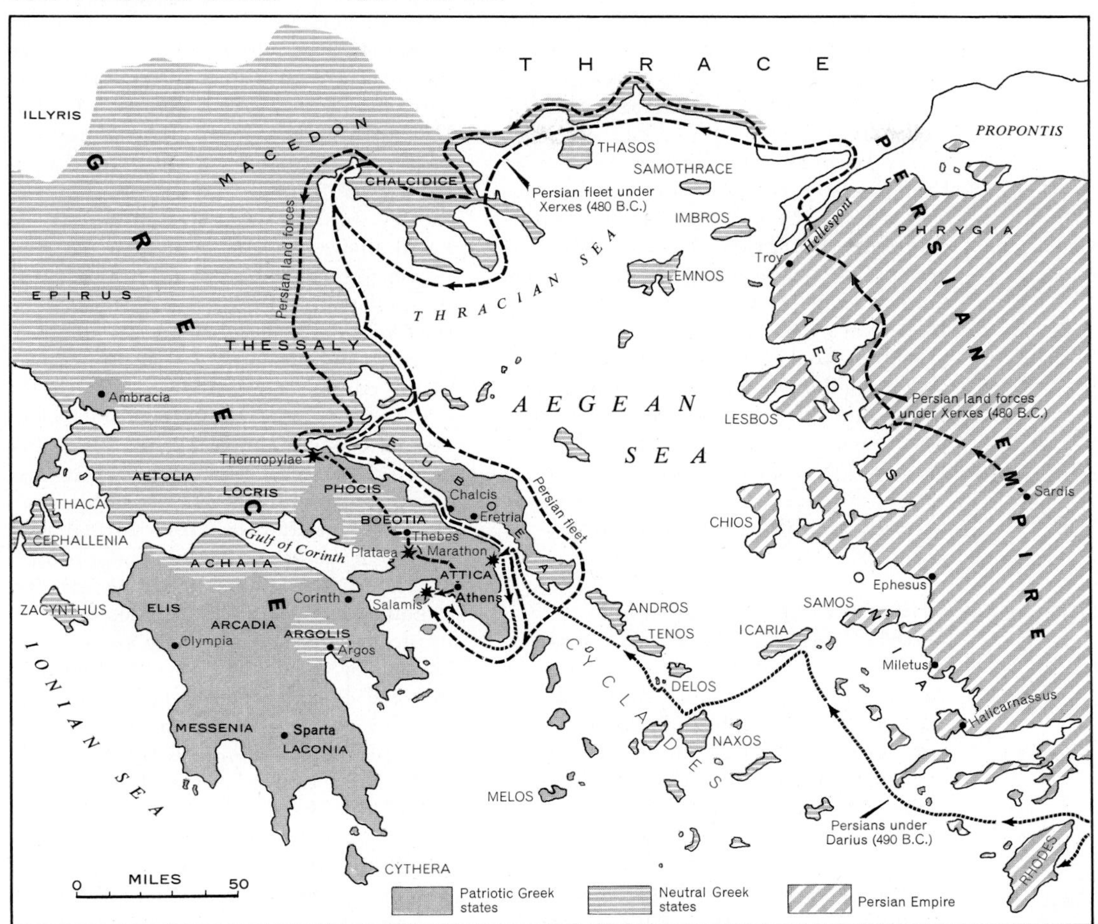

killed trying to defend it. With Thermopylae unguarded, the Persians had an open road into Athens. The Athenian citizens were quickly evacuated to nearby islands, where they watched in horror as the Persians looted and burned their city.

Though the city was destroyed, Athens was not defeated. Before the Persian attack, Themistocles, an ambitious but farsighted politician, had persuaded the Athenian assembly to put all the income of the silver mines into building a fleet far larger than a city the size of Athens would normally require. He realized that, while the Greeks could not expect to defeat the massive Persian armies in battle, the Greek peninsula with its islands and inlets could never be conquered except by sea. Shortly after the Persians occupied Athens, a Greek fleet, at least two-thirds of which was Athenian, met the Persian navy in the Bay of Salamis and destroyed it in a single engagement. Cut off from supplies coming by sea from Asia Minor, the Persians were badly crippled. After a final defeat at Plataea by a Spartan-led force (479 B.C.), they retired permanently from the Greek peninsula. In the same year the Greek fleet virtually wiped out the Persian navy in a battle off the coast of Asia Minor.

The defeat of Persia in 479 B.C. meant that the Greek world remained outside Persian control. Since Persia no longer had a strong navy, the Greek cities of Asia Minor were also able to reassert their independence, though they never regained their former strength. The Persian Empire was not completely defeated, however. For the next century and a half, Persia retained its control over the rest of the eastern Mediterranean—Egypt, Palestine, Syria, most of Asia Minor, and Mesopotamia. And the Persian king was able, at times, to influence Greek politics by siding with one or another group of quarreling states.

The victory over the Persians was to the Greeks what the American Revolution was to the colonists, an inexhaustible source of pride and confidence. A few small states had defeated a great empire. Now the Greeks were more sure than ever that they were destined for greatness, that their way of life was superior to that of all other peoples, that they could succeed in any enterprise they undertook. The century following the Persian Wars was the Golden Age, in which the Greeks made their indelible mark on the history of civilization.

THE AGE OF ATHENIAN DOMINATION, 478–431 B.C.

As soon as the Persians retreated, the Athenians rebuilt their city on an even grander scale. Proud of their city, proud of their democracy, proud of their victory over Persia, and prosperous beyond all expectations, the Athenians of the fifth century B.C. not only dominated the Aegean but created one of the most striking cultural patterns in the history of western civilization.

A four drachma coin from Athens showing Athena and her owl (*ca.* sixth century B.C.).

The Athenian Empire

A basic factor in Athens' rise to power and cultural supremacy was wealth. A century earlier, most of the commerce in and out of the Aegean had gone to Miletus or to one of the other Greek cities of Asia Minor. But as these cities declined during the late sixth century, enterprising Athenian merchants began diverting trade to Athens. After the Persian Wars, the Athenians used their large navy to bring former Milesian trading stations—on the Black Sea and in Syria—under their own control.

In the vast expansion of their sphere of influence, the Athenians took advantage of their position as leaders of the Delian League. This league was an alliance of the Greek maritime cities around the Aegean. Its original purpose was to continue the naval war against Persia until all Persian forces had been driven from the Aegean Sea and all Greek cities had been freed of Persian control. Delegates met first in 478 B.C. on the island of Delos, from which the league took its name. Each member state was to contribute an annual quota of ships or money. Since Sparta was of no use in naval affairs, the Athenians had no rival power to face in the league. And because they contributed by far the largest fleet, the Athenians were given the right to name the admiral and the administrators of the common treasury.

In time, the navy of the Delian League became almost exclusively Athenian. Other members, with only a few exceptions, contributed cash rather than ships. Naturally, the navy of the league was soon being used primarily to protect and even extend the Athenian empire. When one of the member cities resigned in protest, the league's navy appeared in its harbor, besieged the city, and dismantled its fortifications. From that time on, the city was governed by Athens, and the other league members were made to understand that a similar fate awaited other defectors. Finally, in 454 B.C., when the league's treasury was moved from Delos to Athens, it was clear that the league had become an Athenian Empire and that the members were little more than Athenian dependencies. Athens, however, did champion the spread of democracy among the states of the league; one of the penalties of rebellion was the forced acceptance of a democratic constitution.

Although the cities comprising the league had no choice but to remain in it, the other cities of the Greek peninsula became increasingly alarmed at the growth of Athenian power and began to seek closer ties with Sparta and the Peloponnesian League. Between 454 and 431 B.C. most of the cities of the Greek peninsula and around the Aegean became associated with one of the two alliance systems: the Delian League dominated by Athens or the Peloponnesian League dominated by Sparta.

During this time the productive power of Athens was enriched by the influx of thousands of artists, artisans, and merchants from the more sophisti-

Ostraka, or broken pieces of pottery, on which citizens wrote the names of those they wished to ostracize from Athens (*ca.* 470 B.C.). The names on these pieces are Themistocles, who was later recalled, and Cimon.

cated Greek cities of Asia Minor, who saw greater opportunities in Athens than in their home cities. These immigrants, known as *metics* (that is, Greeks who were not Athenians), provided a labor supply for the expanding Athenian economy. And the many artists, poets, and philosophers among them deserve much of the credit for making the fifth century Athens' Golden Age.

Another source of Athenian postwar prosperity was the large number of prisoners of war brought to Athens as slaves. With *metics* to help produce and sell their wares and with slaves to labor in their shops and mines, all but the poorest Athenian citizens could participate fully in the cultural and political life of the city. And with the wealth derived from tribute paid by the Delian League, plus the income from commerce and mining, the life of the Athenian *polis* was remarkably rich and complex.

Politics

The Athenian constitution, by the middle of the fifth century B.C., gave almost equal rights to all citizens; only a few vestiges of aristocratic privilege remained. In fact, in some areas even the privileges of merit were avoided; for example, the members of the Council of Five Hundred were chosen by lot. The general was the only important elected official—a peculiar and, as it turned out, an unfortunate exception. The Greeks called this system "democracy," and many modern writers have echoed the phrase. But in a population of approximately two hundred thousand, there were many more *metics* and slaves than citizens. Neither *metics* nor slaves could vote, nor could the wives and daughters of citizens. Thus only some thirty thousand male citizens (at most, ten percent of the population) had political rights. This was a high proportion, by standards of the ancient world, but it was not what we would call democracy.

The really significant change in the fifth century was not an increase in the number of voters, but an increase in the political power of the lower classes. These men manned the fleet, which was the source of Athenian wealth and power. Leaders of political factions had to seek the favor of the common citizens, and their favor could shift with alarming rapidity. To prevent a revival of tyranny, the Athenians had invented a device known as ostracism: a majority of citizens could vote the exile for ten years of any politician who seemed to be gaining too much power. Many of the ablest leaders of the city were ostracized, including Themistocles, who had built the fleet that preserved the liberty of Athens. The system of government was unwieldy; the general assembly was too large, and the Council of Five Hundred changed its leadership each month. Policy had to be decided in private conferences among politicians and then be "sold" to the citizens. It took an extremely able leader to give consistency to Athenian policy without falling into demagogy on the one hand or self-righteous disdain of public opinion on the other. It is remarkable that several men in the fifth century succeeded in this difficult task and that one man, Pericles, was a powerful politician from 463 to 429 B.C. and (because he was annually reelected to the generalship) the unchallenged leader of Athens for the last fifteen years of this period.

The issues discussed by the people ranged all the way from charges of corruption and excessive ambition to basic

Pericles, from a Roman copy of a Greek bust of the fifth century B.C.

Marble grave relief of a girl with pigeons (*ca.* 450 B.C.).

questions of foreign policy. There were conservatives who feared that the growth of Athenian power was alienating friends of Athens and forcing them to ally with Sparta; there were expansionists who wanted to grab everything in sight. But there were not two organized political parties. The Athenians were too individualistic to fall into rigid political allegiances, and as long as the expansionist policy was successful, the majority did not really want to drop it. Thus Pericles' chief opponent during the early years of his power was Cimon, who had been dubious about extending voting rights to all citizens but who accepted the reforms, and who certainly was not an opponent of expansion. Only when they were faced with the disaster of a losing war did the Athenians think seriously about modifying their basic policies.

Art and Architecture

The destruction of Athens by the Persians meant that the city had to be rebuilt, and the new wealth of Athens allowed it to be rebuilt splendidly. Construction was rather haphazard until Pericles became "boss" of the city and put his friend Phidias, a sculptor, in charge of what might be called city planning. With plenty of money at their disposal from the revenues of the Delian League, Pericles and Phidias were able to attract architects, sculptors, and painters from all over the Greek world. There was nothing at Athens that could not be found in other Greek cities, but there was more of it, and, on the whole, it was better arranged.

Greek art of the fifth century B.C. was an art that had solved its technical problems. Greek architects could construct imposing and well-proportioned buildings; Greek sculptors could represent all the details of the human body with absolute accuracy. It was also an art with definite and limited goals. Greek artists were interested in the finite, not the infinite; they never undertook the hard task of giving concrete form to visions. They idealized life here on earth, not life in a heaven about which they thought little. The ideal man was a demigod, and the god was simply an idealized man. There is little sense of conflict in the Greek art of this period, no antagonism between the real and the ideal. Life in this world at its best could be beautiful and satisfying, and this is what the artists sought to represent.

These characteristics of Greek art are evident in the crowning achievement of the rebuilding of Athens—the temple of the Parthenon,* dedicated to Athena, the patron goddess of the city. The Parthenon did not attempt to impress the beholder through mere size as Egyptian structures had done. Though the Parthenon is almost as large as a football field, its basic qualities are harmony and proportion; it is constructed on a scale that can be measured and understood by the

*The Parthenon served as a place of worship for over two thousand years; it was a temple to Athena, then a Christian church, and finally a mosque. It was almost intact until it was blown up in a minor war three hundred years ago. Today only the outer row of columns is standing, though many of the sculptures were saved.

Pericles on Athens and Sparta

This oration, inserted by the Greek historian Thucydides in his *History of the Peloponnesian War,* does not give Pericles' exact words, but it does express admirably the pride of the Athenians in their city and its form of government.

We are called a democracy, for the administration is in the hands of the many and not of the few. But . . . the claim of excellence is also recognized, and when a citizen is in any way distinguished, he is preferred to the public service, not as a matter of privilege, but as the reward of merit. . . . Our city is thrown open to the world, and we never expel a foreigner or prevent him from seeing or learning anything of which the secret, if revealed to an enemy, might profit him. . . . In the matter of education, whereas the Spartans from early youth are always undergoing laborious exercises which are to make them brave, we live at ease, and yet are equally ready to face the perils which they face. . . . For we are lovers of the beautiful, yet simple in our tastes, and we cultivate the mind without loss of manliness. . . . Such is the city for whose sake these men fought and died; . . . and every one of us who survive should gladly toil on her behalf.

From Pericles' Funeral Oration, in Thucydides, *The History of the Peloponnesian War,* trans. by B. Jowett in Francis R. B. Godolphin, ed., *The Greek Historians* (New York: Random House, 1942), Vol. I, pp. 648–50.

human eye. The Parthenon stands on the crest of the Acropolis, the hill that dominates Athens, but it does not reach toward heaven like a Gothic cathedral. It is the crown of an earthly city, not the gateway to a heavenly one.

The sculpture of the Parthenon, carved by Phidias and his followers, represents the gods as well as the people of the city in their processions, their athletic contests, and their military exercises. Here again, the Greeks did not distinguish between the religious and the secular; or, to put it another way, the noblest and best secular activity was also a religious act.

Drama

Built into the side of the Acropolis sloping away from the city was an outdoor amphitheater dedicated to the god Dionysus. Here, during the two annual festivals of Dionysus, the Athenians attended a series of plays. These plays were not staged for amusement. An important part of the religious festival, they were presented by the city to instruct and purge the citizens before they attended the sacred Dionysian rites.

The Greeks had long celebrated religious festivals with semidramatic performances in which a single speaker told a story to which a chorus offered responses. But during the Golden Age the Athenian dramatists transformed these rituals into full-fledged drama by adding a second and then a third speaker. The stories were not new to the audience. Playwrights used themes drawn from ancient Greek myths to illustrate the religious and ethical problems of the present world. What is right conduct? Can a man avoid the fate decreed him by the gods? What course can an individual take when civic and religious laws conflict? These are some of the questions posed by the great Athenian dramatists of the Golden Age: Aeschylus (525–456 B.C.), Sophocles (496?–406 B.C.), and Euripides (480?–406? B.C.).

Running through all the Greek tragedies is the theme that man must remain in harmony with the universe. The Greeks admired a man who was strong and self-sufficient. But the Greek ideal was "moderation in all things," and—as might be expected in a society where most people knew one another—the Greeks could not tolerate a man who believed that he was superior to other men. Thus the greatest fault was *hybris*, or pride. Specifically, *hybris* meant assuming a role reserved for the gods, par-

The Acropolis at Athens.

Sophocles, popular fifth-century B.C. playwright.

ticularly in taking the life of another human being, even by accident. Thus most Athenian tragedies deal with guilt and expiation—the misfortunes that must come to a man who defies the gods by not accepting the limitations placed on him as a human.

Best known of the plays of Aeschylus are the blood-chilling tales of the *Oresteia* trilogy, which examine the religious aspects of justice through the story of the downfall of the house of Agamemnon. Agamemnon, betrayed by his wife, is avenged by his son, but the son must suffer for assuming the prerogative of the gods in dealing out retribution. In *Oedipus the King,* Sophocles, the most popular playwright of the period, deals with the problem of the man who has unwittingly done wrong. Not knowing who his parents were, Oedipus killed his own father and married his own mother. In his *Antigone,* Sophocles portrays a conflict that is still acute today—the conflict between the demands of the state and the desire of the individual to follow a higher moral law. Creon, King of Thebes, forbids the burial of his nephew, who had been killed in an unsuccessful rebellion. The body must be left to rot in the fields; anyone who touches it will be put to death. Antigone, sister of the victim, defies the king, for no human order can justify breaking the laws of the gods. Creon decrees that Antigone be confined in a rocky vault, and she kills herself. Creon's subsequent remorse is not enough to save him. His son, who had loved Antigone, commits suicide; his wife kills herself in despair. Human pride, which had defied religion, conscience, and family ties in order to strengthen the state, had been punished.

Euripides was the youngest of the three great tragedians of the Golden Age. Unlike his predecessors, he was more interested in human emotions than in the problems of guilt and retribution. His plays were not always well received, for they frequently dealt with unpopular themes. In *Medea,* for instance, Euripides elicits the sympathy of his audience for a half-crazed foreign woman who murders her own children to spite the Greek husband who had abandoned her. And in *The Trojan Women,* presented when Athens was at war and bursting with pride, Euripides made the Athenians watch a play about the inhuman atrocities perpetrated by a people at war and passed off as patriotic acts.

The writers of comedies were at least as popular as the writers of tragedies, and they probably came closer to reflecting the ideas of ordinary citizens. The only fifth-century comedian whose works have survived was Aristophanes (448?–380? B.C.). Many of his plays have been lost, but those that we possess are witty commentaries on the events of his own day. At times he seems to have been seeking the applause of the lowbrows; for example, the philosopher Socrates appears in one of his plays, *The Clouds,* as a ridiculous figure who talks learned nonsense. But Aristophanes had an honest dislike of humbug and pomposity and a sincere aversion to war. One of his most effective plays is *Lysistrata,* an antiwar comedy in which the women of Athens persuade their husbands to make peace by refusing to sleep with them.

History and Philosophy

Sculpture and architecture, tragedy and comedy, reached their peak in the Athens of the fifth century B.C. History and philosophy, which started later, naturally attained their highest level at a later date. The foundations for both disciplines were laid during the period when Athens was rising to greatness, but the most influential books on these subjects were written after the collapse of the Athenian Empire.

Little is known of the first Greek historians; they seem to have been interested chiefly in genealogies and in establishing dates for earlier important events. But with Herodotus of Halicarnassus (*ca.* 480?–420 B.C.), one of the many scholars who visited Athens, we find the historian who is a storyteller and who is interested in the curious differences among the customs of peoples. Herodotus' theme was the war between the Persians and the Greeks, which he saw as the culmination of a long struggle between the culture of the Orient and the culture of Greece. He therefore felt that he should describe the development of all the peoples of the Persian Empire, including the Egyptians and the Babylonians. Herodotus had traveled through these countries and had talked to many well-informed men. He preserved many useful facts, but he himself knew that there were as yet no techniques for separating facts from legends. Even his account of the Persian War is so influenced by national pride that it is not entirely reliable, but it is still exciting reading. It took the tragedy of another great conflict—the Peloponnesian War—to produce the greatest Greek historian, Thucydides (see p. 47).

Philosophy and science had their roots in the learning of Egypt and Babylonia. In both countries there had been accurate astronomical observations, development of basic principles of mathematics, and some speculation about the nature of the physical world. The Greeks of Ionia, who were a gifted people, probably had ideas of their own about such matters, but they were enormously stimulated by the knowledge they received from the older civilizations of the East. By the sixth century B.C. the Ionians were attempting to organize scattered facts and ideas into coherent systems, to discover first principles and general laws, to express the difference between things as they are and things as they seem. They were somewhat too ready to generalize from insufficient data, somewhat inclined to oversimplify complex problems, somewhat too willing to ascribe human values to mere abstractions (for example, "lucky" or mystical numbers, such as seven). But in beginning to develop the idea of laws of nature, in looking behind appearances to reality, in seeing mathematics as a powerful tool for solving problems, the early Greek philosophers laid the foundations for all later scientific thought in the West.

The search for a single first principle was not very successful as long as it was confined to purely physical entities, such as "water" or "fire." But several Greek philosophers, notably Heraclitus and Anaxagoras, reached the idea of a *logos* or a Mind that governed and permeated the world. Pythagoras, an Ionian who migrated to southern Italy, saw the organizing principle in numbers, naturally enough, since he was a distinguished mathematician. The appearance of change also perplexed early philosophers: How can a flowing river remain the same river? Anaxagoras resolved the paradox by arguing that the world was made up of countless tiny particles, unchanging themselves, but constantly rearranging to give the appearance of change. This was a forerunner of the "atomic" theory of Democritus, rejected by most of the Greeks but revived by modern scientists.

Athens attracted scholars just as it did artists. The intellectual climate was stimulating, and the Athenians could afford to hire teachers for their youth and to support distinguished writers. By the fifth century B.C. Athens had become the center for the teaching of philosophy, which it remained for many centuries. With so many men arguing about basic truths, opinions were bound to be voiced that shocked conservative citizens. For example, Anaxagoras was accused of atheism because he taught that the sun was simply a ball of fire and that the earth rotated around it. Since Pericles was a patron of Anaxagoras, charges against the philosopher could be used to discredit the statesman.

Even more annoying to many Athenians were the Sophists (the "Wisdomers"), a group of wandering teachers primarily interested in problems of human reason and behavior. They tried to make students think for themselves by asking questions without giving answers. The naive responses of the students were then demolished by logical arguments, so that eventually (at least in theory) the students would begin to think logically themselves and discard prejudices and outworn dogmas.

Teaching students to think for themselves and opposing time-honored beliefs with logic are always dangerous occupations. The Sophists made things worse by being relativists. "Beauty," said one Sophist, "is in the eye of the beholder." If beauty is relative, so is truth, so is justice. And if justice is relative, why should not a bright young man trained in logic and rhetoric go to the law courts and win bad cases with clever arguments?

This is precisely what the enemies of the Sophists feared. Their concern was not unjustified. The Sophists did develop an excellent technique of logical analysis, used by all succeeding Greek philosophers, but they also developed a number

An actor wearing a mask, in a declamatory pose, is depicted in this bronze statue from the Greco-Roman period.

Socrates, statuette from the Hellenistic period.

of tricks of argument that could bewilder the simple, honest, uneducated man. The Athenians did believe in justice, even if they could not define it logically, and the Sophists offended their civic and religious beliefs. Men of the lower and middle classes, who could not afford to hire tutors for their sons, were also offended by the fact that the Sophists sold "wisdom" for money.

Socrates (469–399 B.C.), one of the few native Athenian philosophers, shared the dislike of many of his fellow citizens for the Sophists. He would not take money for his teaching, and he spent his life trying to prove that the Sophists were wrong by using their own techniques to reach opposite conclusions. He believed that truth, beauty, and justice were eternal and existed independently of man. If an object was beautiful, it would be beautiful whether or not a human being was there to see it. Similarly, if an action was a crime, it was wrong for all people and for all time. Socrates taught that each man was born with an innate knowledge of eternal truth, but that this knowledge became clouded by his experiences in a selfish and materialistic world. To know the truth, a man must clear away the misconceptions acquired in this world and discover the spark of eternal truth that was in his own soul. To make his point, Socrates, like the Sophists, asked apparently simple questions to make people see for themselves where their thinking was unclear or illogical. Although Socrates was beloved by his immediate followers, his methods did not endear him to the populace, most of whom classed him with the Sophists. Aristophanes' mockery of him in *The Clouds* reinforced this belief. And in one of the great ironies of history, this opponent of the Sophists was finally executed on charges that, like the Sophists, he was corrupting the youth of the city (see p. 48).

The Trial of Socrates

Plato, in his dialogue *The Apology,* reported the trial of Socrates. In this passage Socrates explains why he cannot change his ways.

Suppose . . . you said to me "Socrates, we shall disregard Anytus and acquit you, but only on one condition, that you give up . . . philosophizing. If we catch you going on in the same way, you shall be put to death." . . . I should reply, "Gentlemen, . . . I owe a greater obedience to God than to you; and so long as I draw breath and have my faculties, I shall never stop practicing philosophy and exhorting you and elucidating the truth for everyone that I meet." I shall go on saying . . . , "My very good friend, you are an Athenian and belong to a city which is the greatest and most famous in the world for its wisdom and strength. Are you not ashamed that you give your attention to acquiring as much money as possible, . . . and give no attention or thought to truth and understanding and the perfection of your soul? . . . Wealth does not bring goodness, but goodness brings wealth and every other blessing, both to the individual and to the State." Now if I corrupt the young by this message, the message would seem to be harmful. . . . And so, gentlemen, I would say, "You can please yourselves . . . whether you acquit me or not; you know that I am not going to alter my conduct, not even if I have to die a hundred deaths."

From Plato, *The Last Days of Socrates,* trans. by Hugh Tredennick (Baltimore: Penguin Books, 1959), pp. 61–62.

THE PELOPONNESIAN WAR 431–404 B.C.

The Peloponnesian War was viewed by its historian, Thucydides, as a Greek tragedy that was acted out in history. It was caused by *hybris*—the ambition of Athens and of Sparta, the desire of politicians for renown, the deliberate renouncement of justice and reason. It was an evil that endured when it could soon have been stopped. It ended with the humiliation of one "actor" and the realization by the other that victory had created only new troubles. One might easily see in this tragedy the downfall of classical Greece.

Such a view is, of course, a gross exaggeration. Life is less logical and less coherent than a classical tragedy. Actually, some of the greatest achievements of Greek culture came during and after the war—the plays of Euripides and Aristophanes, the philosophy of Plato and Aristotle. While the war weakened many Greek city-states, especially Athens and Sparta, the Greek world of competing city-states had always been insecure. It could endure only so long as no great power existed to threaten it. Once the decaying Persian Empire was replaced by new and powerful kingdoms, the Greek cities, strong or weak, could exist only on sufferance. The Peloponnesian War simply underlined a fact that had long been apparent: the Greeks could not unite into a single state. If they could not unite, they were doomed to lose their independence.

The ostensible causes of the war were quarrels between Athens and Corinth over the colonies of Corcyra and Poteidaea and the decision of Athens to exclude the merchants of Megara (an ally of Sparta) from Athenian markets. These acts seemed to prove Athen's intention to dominate trade with southern Italy, an increasingly important source of grain for the densely populated Greek peninsula. They also seemed one more proof of the dangers of Athenian imperialism. It was under these circumstances that Sparta and the Peloponnesian League, as champions of the independence of the smaller cities, declared war in 431 B.C.

Pericles' war plan was to abandon the Athenian rural areas, concentrate the population inside the city walls, and rely on his navy to harass the enemy and keep open the sea lanes. Since Sparta had no navy, Athens could be sure of an adequate supply of imported food and thus could hold out indefinitely. But in the second year of the war a plague broke out in Athens, killing a considerable part of the population, including Pericles himself. No one could really take his place. The loss of Pericles, the shock of plague, and the strains of war caused political disarray, uncertain leadership, and inconsistent policies. The Athenians did well enough in the early fighting, and Sparta made peace in 421 B.C. But ambitious politicians seeking to gain power by a victorious war reopened the conflict, and from that point it was all downhill. The Athenians took greater and greater risks, such as their disastrous attempt to conquer Syracuse from 415 to 413 B.C., and in the end their naval power was completely destroyed. In 404 B.C. they surrendered to Sparta.

For a brief period Sparta dominated the Greek world. The Spartans put Athens under the control of a brutal oligarchy and tried to set up similar governments in other enemy states. This was standard practice; alliances among Greek states were often based on similarities in their social/constitutional structures, and if those similarities did not exist they were imposed by the stronger partner. But Sparta also was suffering from the effects of the war, and political dissension at home weakened its power abroad. Athens soon threw off the harsh government imposed by Sparta and reverted to its old political system. (One might note that the trial of Socrates [399 B.C.] took place during this period of crisis. The Athenians might have been less suspicious of new ideas if they had not been struggling to preserve their old institutions.) Other cities followed the Athenian example. Although Sparta struggled for several decades to maintain its hegemony, its army, never very large, steadily dwindled in a series of losing battles. By 370 B.C. Sparta had become so weak that it could not even defend the Peloponnesus.

As we mentioned earlier, the great war between Athens and Sparta produced a great historian, Thucydides (*ca.* 460–400 B.C.). An Athenian general who had been deprived of his command, Thucydides very early began to collect material for a history of the conflict. He wanted to be absolutely accurate, to write only from his own experience or from the testimony of eyewitnesses. But even more, he wanted to describe the behavior of politicians and states in terms that would have meaning for all future generations. In his own words, his history was to be "an everlasting possession." He succeeded in this high endeavor as few other historians have. The Funeral Speech that he ascribed to Pericles describes what a democratic community can be at its best. The Melian dialogue shows Athens descending to naked imperialism in dealing with a small city. This dialogue portrays so accurately the behavior of a conscienceless conqueror that it was reprinted without changing a word to describe Hitler's takeover of Czechoslovakia in 1938.

GREECE IN THE FOURTH CENTURY B.C.

The Peloponnesian War and the subsequent struggles against Spartan hegemony created a confused political situation in which there was no real center of

Plato (426–347 B.C.), Socrates' pupil.

Aristotle (384–322 B.C.), pupil of Plato and organizer of Greek thought.

power in the Greek world. The king of Persia interfered again in Greek affairs and established a loose and intermittent control over the Greek cities of Asia Minor. Athens rebuilt its naval empire, but it was a much weaker one than that of the fifth century. Syracuse dominated the Greeks of Sicily and Italy, but it could not intervene in the Aegean area. None of these states had a political future; in the end the great power of the Near and Middle East was to be the half-Greek, almost unknown, Kingdom of Macedon.

Plato and Aristotle

Political confusion did not destroy Greek culture; it simply gave the Greeks something more to talk about. The greatest Greek orators were men of the fourth century. They urged the Greeks, eloquently but vainly, to forget their petty quarrels and to unite against common enemies. More lasting than oratory, however, was the work of the philosophers who taught at Athens, the city that had been, and was long to remain, the center of Greek culture.

The beginning was not auspicious. The citizens of Athens, humiliated by their defeat, looked for a scapegoat and picked on the philosopher Socrates. Some of his pupils had been leaders in the unfortunate expeditions that crippled Athenian naval power; moreover, in his persistent questioning, Socrates had challenged many accepted dogmas. He was accused of sacrilege (he believed in "eternal truth" rather than in the gods of the city) and of corrupting the youth. He was arrested in 399 B.C. and condemned to death by a narrow vote of a citizen's court. He could easily have escaped from his prison (which is probably what the authorities wanted him to do), but he refused to renounce his city or to disobey its laws. He died bravely, even cheerfully, and set an example for all his successors.

His memory lived on in his devoted students, and especially in Plato (426–347 B.C.). Most of what we know of Socrates comes from Plato's Dialogues, and Plato's own work was founded on that of his teacher. He took Socrates' concept of the eternal good and expanded it into a more complex philosophy of his own. According to Plato, the only reality was the world of "ideas," where all things had existence in an abstract and perfect form. In the world of ideas the perfect "house" or "table" existed forever as a concept, not as a material object. Here on earth we have but poor and temporary copies of these things. Earthly houses are not true houses. They are but wood or stone that men have tried to shape into a copy of the true and eternal house; they can burn, blow apart, or deteriorate. The real house—in the world of ideas—can never change or deteriorate. The same, according to Plato, is true of "beauty" and "justice." True justice can exist only in the world of ideas; man may come closer to true justice by contemplating this ideal, but his efforts will always be subject to error. Plato thus provided a solution to the paradox posed by the teaching of Heraclitus, who said that all things were constantly changing, and the teaching of Parmenides, who held that change was impossible and therefore illusory. According to Plato, change was a characteristic only of the physical world. In the world of ideas, all things remain eternally the same.

Like almost all Greeks, Plato believed that the city-state was the best form of political organization and that the character of the citizen was determined by the laws of the city. For him, the constitution of the state to its citizens was what the soul was to an individual: a good constitution produced good men. Plato was an intellectual aristocrat; he disliked Athenian democracy and doubted that the poor and half-educated lower classes could ever be virtuous unless they were controlled by an intellectual elite. His plan for an ideal city-state in the *Republic* showed a clear preference for the Spartan rather than the Athenian example. Each individual's life was to be carefully regulated from birth for the benefit of the whole community. Justice, of course, must be the basis of society, but justice belongs to the eternal world of ideas. It can be understood only by the most intelligent and most carefully educated citizens. Thus the heart of the *Republic* is the description of the training of the "philosopher-kings," who would rule and lead all other citizens to the good life.

Aristotle (384–322 B.C.), Plato's most famous pupil, was the great organizer of Greek thought. By his time the Greeks had accumulated a large amount of information and were trying to arrange it in meaningful order. Aristotle provided a powerful tool for classifying and deriving general propositions from scattered facts. This tool was logic, which he distilled from the somewhat erratic arguments of the Sophists. Aristotle developed rigorous, consistent, and intellectually honest rules of logic and thus gave western thinkers an instrument that could be used for intellectual exploration of any field. Aristotle wrote treatises on everything from biology through political theory to poetics, and he supplied the vocabulary and the basic ideas that were used for centuries in almost every field of learning.

Aristotle was less of an idealist than Plato and was more concerned with observing actual facts. For example, he studied the constitutions of hundreds of Greek cities and came to the conclusion that pure monarchy, pure aristocracy, and pure democracy were equally excellent concepts in and of themselves, but were apt to degenerate; democracy, for example, easily falls into dictatorship. Thus the most stable government is a mixed government, in which a strong executive, an aristocratic council, and a democratic assembly balance one another. This idea still influences western society. But Aristotle applied it only to the city-state, in spite of the fact that in his later years the Kingdom of Macedon had gained control of almost all the Greek cities.

Aristotle, unlike Plato, did not believe that ideas were independent entities. He believed in the value of general propositions, but he felt that they grew out of concrete experiences. And in his distinction between Form and Matter he stimulated thought about developmental processes in the universe. Thus the sculptor imposes Form on the Matter of a piece of clay; the Matter of the acorn contains within it the Form of an oak.

Aristotle's logic was not entirely free from flaws; it depended a little too much on words with overtones that went beyond pure description. Yet western theology, law, mathematics, and science were all marked in their formative periods by strict applications of Aristotelian logic. Aristotle tended to generalize too rapidly, and difficulties in taking exact measurements vitiated some of his facts. These weaknesses were especially apparent in his works on the physical sciences; some of his guesses were helpful, but some, such as his theory of motion, were stumbling blocks for centuries. Even at his worst, however, Aristotle posed fundamental problems. For centuries western scholars began their work with a study of his books.

Greek coin bearing the likeness of King Philip, conqueror of Athens.

The Rise of Macedon

During the fourth century most of the cities of the Greek peninsula came under the domination of the Kingdom of Macedon. Macedon was a country of peasants ruled by crude, hard-living warriors who formed a loose federation under a king. Its culture was not much above the level of that described in the *Iliad.* These primitive people posed no threat to the Greeks in earlier periods. The Persian and Peloponnesian wars, however, brought the Macedonians into closer contact with the Greeks of the South. These contacts resulted in the Macedonians' rapid progress. During the fourth century, when the Greek city-states were weak, the remarkable King Philip (359–336 B.C.) managed to organize the Macedonian warriors into a powerful and unified fighting force. Once his control of Macedon was secure, Philip began to extend his control over the city-states of the Greek peninsula. Once again, as during the Persian threat more than a century earlier, there was a great debate among the Greek city-states on how best to meet the danger. Demosthenes of Athens, the most famous orator of the golden age of Greek oratory, vainly warned his countrymen of the danger from Macedon, and urged them to unite. But, as so often before, the Greek cities were unable to support any single policy. Many, in fact, looked on Philip as a liberator from the domination of the more powerful Greek cities. Enough cities resisted to provoke a war with Macedon, but they could not cooperate to the extent of presenting a unified defense. As a result, Philip defeated the coalition of Greek city-states in 338 B.C. and turned the Greek peninsula into a Macedonian protectorate. Individual cities remained independent in theory, but they could not oppose Philip's will.

Alexander the Great 336–323 B.C.

Two years later, before Philip could complete his project by reconquering the Greek cities of Asia Minor from Persia, he was assassinated. He was succeeded by his twenty-year-old son, Alexander (336–323 B.C.). Conceited, overbearing, undisciplined, and wildly temperamental, Alexander was also brilliant and could display a mesmerizing charm. He was idolized by his soldiers—no small factor in his military success—and even among his enemies he became a legend in his own short lifetime.

Before his death, Philip had planned to unify the Greeks and rally them to his banner by leading a combined Greek army in a war of revenge against the Persians. Determined to carry out his father's plan, Alexander crossed the Hellespont with a Greek army in 334 B.C. and soon proved himself one of the most successful military strategists in history. At the very beginning of his campaign, he won a decisive battle against a Persian force in Asia Minor. The following year he moved eastward into Syria, where he met and routed an army under the Persian king himself. In 332 B.C. Alexander invaded Egypt. After conquering the country, he took two momentous steps. He founded the city of Alexandria, which soon became the leading seaport of the eastern Mediterranean and a center of Greek scholarship. And he visited the ancient oracle of Amon at Siwah in the Libyan desert, where the priests greeted him as the son of the god. Egypt, at least, had long been ruled by a god-king, and Alexander may have intended to adopt this model as a basis for his position both in Egypt and elsewhere. In Greece an official proclamation of Alexander's divinity was eventually issued; how much of an impression this made is uncertain. Some of the Greeks, at least, may have persuaded themselves that Alexander was the son of Zeus (whom they identified with Amon) and therefore their rightful ruler. In any case, the precedent set by Alexander was followed by his successors. Even the hard-headed Romans eventually accepted the idea that their emperor was divine and found it helpful to force conquered peoples to accept it too.

From a military point of view the rest was easy. Alexander proclaimed himself king of Persia, defeated the last Persian

ALEXANDER'S EMPIRE 336–323 B.C.

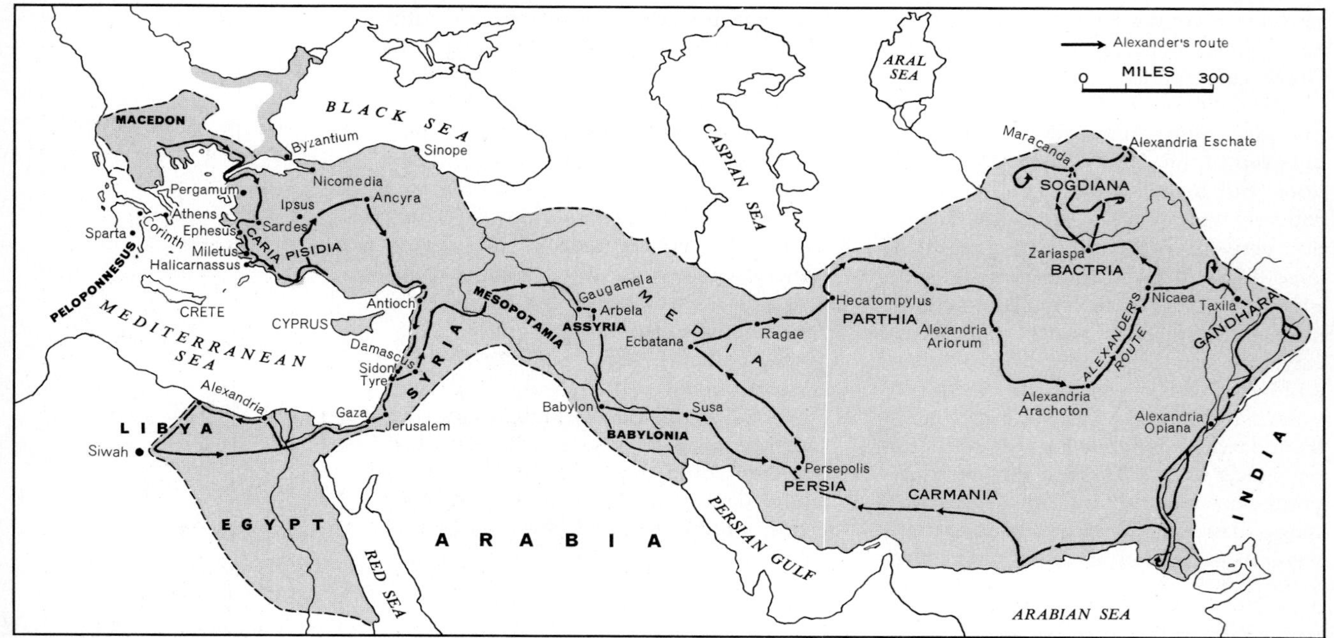

army without difficulty, and took his troops on a wild march north to Turkestan, south into the Indus Valley, and back to Babylon. The real problem was political, not military. How could this vast empire, inhabited by such different peoples, be made into a unit? Alexander apparently hoped to use Greek culture to control Asian manpower. Greek colonies were founded everywhere, even in western India; Greeks were encouraged to marry Asian women; and Greek was to be the common language of all the upper classes. Alexander died of fever in 323 B.C., at the age of thirty-three, before he could see how his plan worked. The amazing thing is that even without his guiding hand, even during the bitter quarrels among his successors, his plan did work. For eight hundred years Greek culture was the dominant and unifying culture of the Middle East.

THE HELLENISTIC ERA 323–*ca.* 30 B.C.

Alexander's sudden death meant that he had had no time to consolidate his empire or to arrange for an orderly succession. His Macedonian generals fought among themselves for his conquests. Ptolemy took Egypt immediately, and Seleucus eventually gained control of most of the old Persian Empire, which became known as the Seleucid Empire. Matters could not be arranged so neatly in the old Greek heartland. Antigonus became king of Macedon and protector of the city-states of the Greek peninsula. But he could not hold Asia Minor, where many of the cities were united in the Kingdom of Pergamum and where the island of Rhodes became an independent naval power. And as time went on, Macedon's control over the southern Balkans and the Greek peninsula steadily diminished.

Political disunity, however, did not interfere with Alexander's vision of a commonwealth of peoples united by Greek culture. All the successor states were dominated by Greeks and by natives who imitated the Greek way of life. Of course the peasants and much of the urban population of the Middle East held fast to their native cultures and native languages. But scholars, administrators, and businessmen all used Greek and were guided, to some degree, by Greek ideas and customs. This era, in which the Middle East was permeated by Greek

Idealized statue of Alexander, probably the work of an artist of Pergamum in Asia Minor.

THE PARTITIONING OF ALEXANDER'S EMPIRE *ca.* 300 B.C.

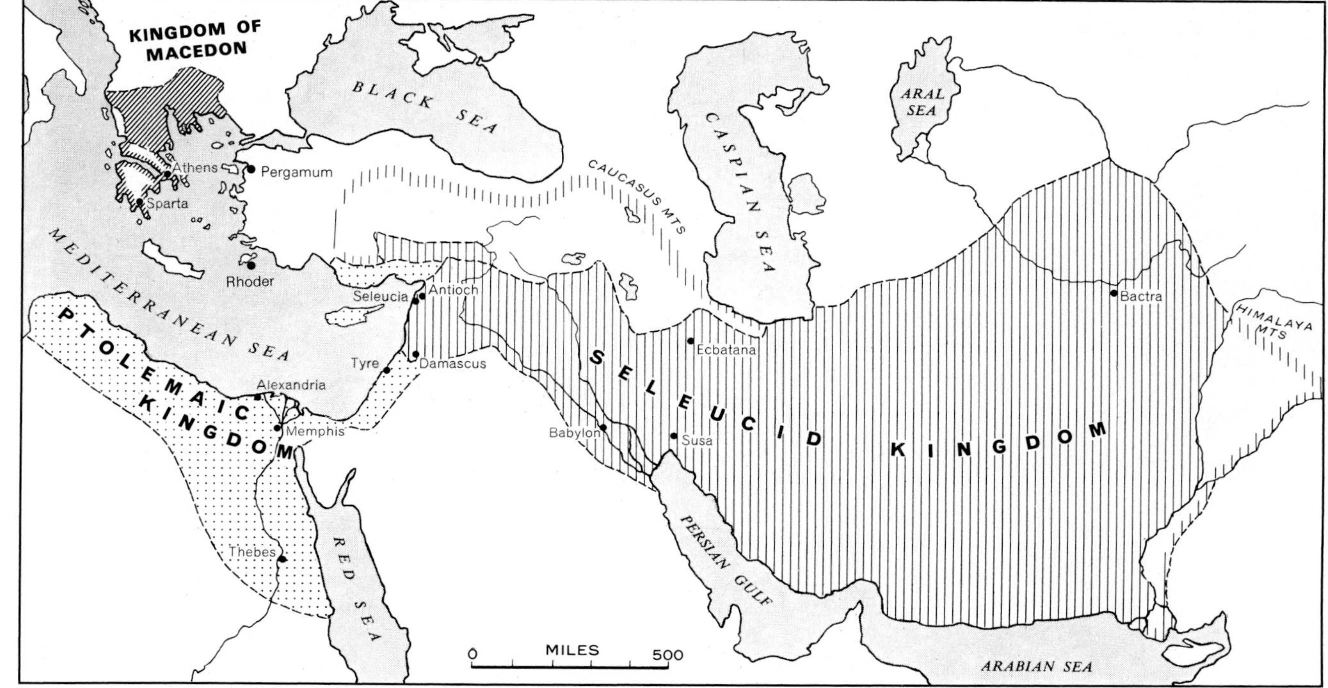

549 B.C. | 338 323 | ca. 30 B.C.

Persian Empire
Independent Greek City-states
Hellenistic Era
Rise and Dominance of Macedon

influence is known as the Hellenistic period.* It ended politically in 30 B.C., when Rome annexed Egypt, the last nominally independent Hellenistic state. But the cultural unity of the Middle East lasted far longer; it was broken only after the Moslems conquered Syria and Egypt in the seventh century A.D., but even then not completely.

Hellenistic culture flourished, especially in Egypt. Alexandria, the capital of the Ptolemies, had a population of about one million. Athens and its suburbs, at the peak of Athenian strength, had had about two hundred thousand. Alexandria profited from the boom in international trade that was one of the great unifying forces of the Hellenistic period. Into its harbor came ships from all parts of the Mediterranean; its caravans crowded the routes that led to Syria, Mesopotamia, and the Red Sea ports that traded with India. The ruling family encouraged the arts and sciences, and Alexandria imported ideas as well as merchandise. Next to the palace of the Ptolemies was a magnificent temple to the Muses (called the Museum) for the study of the arts and sciences, and next to the Museum was a remarkable library. These facilities attracted scholars from all parts of the Hellenistic world and helped make Alexandria the only Greek city that could rival Athens as a cultural center. But Alexandria was more than a Greek city. Native Egyptians made up most of the laboring class, and in its streets one might hear almost any language of the ancient world. There were more Jews in Alexandria than in Jerusalem; it was in Alexandria that the Old Testament was translated into Greek. This Greek version was proof that even the Jews, a most preclusive people, had been Hellenized, and it was the Greek version that was used by early Christian scholars.

Alexandria was by far the largest Hellenistic city, but Antioch, the capital of the Seleucid Empire, was also a great trade center. Rhodes and Pergamum prospered as transshipment points for goods headed for the Aegean and Black Seas. Pergamum also attracted a group of very able artists. Dozens of other Hellenistic cities took part in commercial, intellectual, and artistic activity of the period.

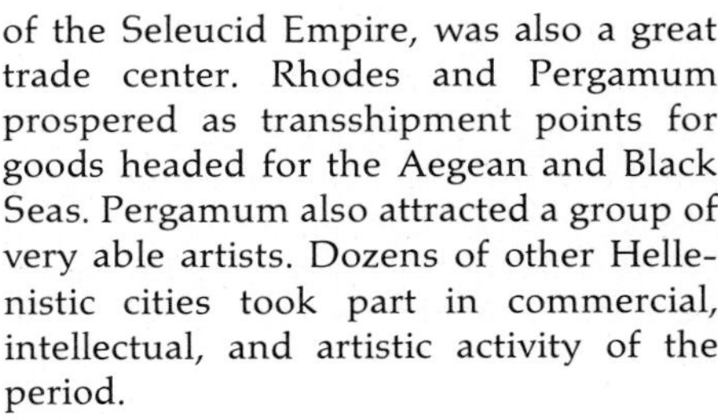

Old Peasant Woman. Sculpture from the Hellenistic era is more emotional and realistic than art of the fifth century B.C.

Art and Literature

Hellenistic art naturally differed from that of the fifth century; it had lost the serenity and self-confidence of the work of Phidias. It was more emotional and at times almost too emotional in depicting pain and suffering. Occasionally it sought to impress by mere size, as in the statue that stood astride the harbor of Rhodes or the Mausoleum at Halicarnassus. But at its best it created works that are still impressive. The Winged Victory of Samothrace, the Venus of Milo, and the Dying Gaul of Pergamum are probably better known than the statues of the Parthenon.

Hellenistic art turned more and more toward realism as time went on. Paintings, mosaics, and statues in this style are not great art, but they are remarkably helpful to the historian. They show men and women as they were, and life as it was lived.

The literature of the period is not as well known. Theocritus was a lyric poet of merit; unfortunately, so many followers imitated his pastoral settings that his originality has been forgotten. Apollonius wrote an epic in the Homeric style, and he too might be better remembered if so many later poets had not done the same thing. Certainly the writer whose influence has lasted longest was Menander. Although his comedies lack the bite of Aristophanes, his plots have amused audiences for two thousand years. Picked up by the Romans and passed down to Shakespeare, they still inspire modern musical comedies.

*The Greeks called themselves Hellenes; *Hellenistic* means "Greek-like."

Science

Many scholars would say that the most striking achievements of the Hellenistic age were in science. Hellenistic scientists performed some remarkable experiments and developed theories that foreshadowed the discoveries of the sixteenth and seventeenth centuries. But science did not have the same significance in the Hellenistic world that it has in ours. It was only an aspect of philosophy, a speculative pastime with little effect on ordinary life. Herophilus came very close to a theory of the circulation of the blood, but his work did little to change the practice of medicine. Aristarchus of Samos developed a theory of a solar system with planets revolving about the sun, but most people, even scholars, clung to the belief that the earth was the center of the universe. Eratosthenes made an estimate of the circumference of the earth that was very nearly correct, but it was centuries before anyone acted on this proof that the world was not impossibly large and that a voyage from Europe to the Far East would not take an impossible length of time. On the whole, Hellenistic science was not incorporated into the intellectual tradition of the Mediterranean world. Men reverted to the older doctrines of Aristotle, which remained the standard explanations of natural phenomena throughout the Roman and much of the medieval period. The first to take up the work of the Hellenistic scientists were Moslem scholars, and their writings did not reach western Europe until the thirteenth century A.D.

The most important exception to this rule was mathematics. Even practical-minded people could see the value of geometry, and Euclid (*ca.* 300 B.C.), who built scattered propositions about geometry into a coherent system, has been studied from his day to our own. Archimedes of Syracuse (278?–212 B.C.) worked out basic problems concerning mass and motion; he also perfected the theory of machines, such as the compound pulley. Again, there was a practical side to this work: missile-throwing machines built on his principles nearly defeated a Roman attack on Syracuse. This was remembered, but his more theoretical work was long neglected. In Europe the works of Archimedes were not studied until the thirteenth century, but their revival began a scientific revolution that has continued into the present.

Philosophy and Religion

Hellenistic philosophy and religion reflected the great problem of the age: What part could an individual play in a society in which individual effort seemed useless? In a small city-state of the fifth century the individual had an important role in his community; he could find meaning and purpose in his life and work. But in the great kingdoms of the Hellenistic world and in the huge cities that were the centers of Hellenistic culture, what could one man do? Would his greatest efforts have any impact on his society? Because of this problem, the three most popular schools of philosophy of the period emphasized private virtues and self-discipline, not participation in public life. The Stoics, whose influence lasted longest, believed in a universal law, which bound all men. Since all men were subject to this law, all men were brothers. Everyone from slave to king must do his duty in the position in which he found himself. Power and wealth, human desires and affections, were dangerous distractions. Public office was not to be sought, though it might be one's duty to accept it. The ideal existence was that of the private citizen, unaffected by external events. The Epicureans went even further. The wise man sought pleasure, but real pleasure came from right conduct, serenity of mind, and moderation in all things. Political ambition and pursuit of wealth caused more pain than they were worth, and the wise man avoided strong attachments to family, friends, or country. The Cynics doubted the possibility of any true knowledge and saw no sense in trying to save a world sunk in hopeless ignorance. Thus the wise man should not worry about wealth and power; he should find peace of mind by withdrawing from worldly concerns.

The philosophers spoke mainly to the middle and upper classes. The mass of the population sought spiritual satisfaction in the mystery cults, with their exotic ceremonies and mystic symbolism. With the active cross-fertilization of culture made possible by trade, new religions traveled from one part of the Hellenistic world to another, and all borrowed concepts and ceremonies from one another. Especially popular were the Dionysian rituals from the Greek cities, Isis worship from Egypt, and the cult of the Great Mother from Asia Minor. Most of these cults offered their initiates a ceremonial purification from earthly sins, the comforts of a personal and loving god or goddess, a mystic community that gave each member a sense of security and personal worth, and a promise of eternity for the soul. The cults did not try to reform the world any more than the philosophies did; they helped the initiates to forget their miseries by giving hope that they would be compensated for present sufferings in a future life.

The Fall of the Hellenistic States

The Hellenistic states were never very strong militarily; and they were further weakened by wars and rebellions. For example, the Seleucid Empire soon lost Bactria and Persia, and in 167 B.C. the Jews, led by the Maccabees, regained their independence. It was easy for Rome, which became the dominant state in the Mediterranean by 200 B.C., to take advantage of quarrels among the fragmented states of the Hellenistic world and to annex them one by one. Rome had effective control of the region by 146 B.C.; with the seizure of Egypt in 30 B.C., it had acquired all of Alexander's empire, except Persia. But the Romans admired Hellenistic culture and, as far as they could, spread it to the West in Latin forms. Greek remained the language of the upper classes in the East, and Athens and Alexandria were the cultural centers of the Roman Empire. In a sense, the Hellenistic culture never ended, though its sphere of influence began to shrink after 500 A.D. It gradually and imperceptibly changed into Byzantine culture, and Byzantine culture ended only after the fall of Constantinople in 1453 A.D.

Suggestions for Further Reading

Note: Asterisk denotes a book available in paperback edition.

General J. B. Bury, *A History of Greece,* remains the most thorough history of the ancient Greeks. Originally published in 1901, it is now available in a revised edition by R. Meiggs (1975). G. W. Botsford and C. A. Robinson, *Hellenic History,* 5th ed., rev. by D. Kagan (1969), the standard text, is also excellent. R. Sealey, *A History of the Greek City States, 700–338 B.C.** (1976), combines a good introductory narrative with detailed discussion of controversial problems. Among the shorter treatments, M. I. Finley, *The Ancient Greeks** (1963), makes an interesting introduction to Greek history. A. R. Burn, *The Pelican History of Greece** (1979), is dry but detailed. A. Andrewes, *The Greeks* (1967), and F. J. Frost, *Greek Society* (1972), are interpretive rather than chronological. A representative selection of historical sources can be found in M. I. Finley, ed., *The Greek Historians** (1959). Complete texts of all the Greek writers are available in Greek and English in the *Loeb Classical Library.*

The Mycenaean Era and the Dark Ages The most thorough study of the Greek world before the Golden Age is C. G. Starr, *Origins of Greek Civilization, 1100–650 B.C.* (1961). For the early period, see A. E. Samuel, *The Mycenaeans in History* (1966). M. I. Finley, *Early Greece** (1970), is an excellent short introduction. There have been several recent studies of the Greek world at the time of the Trojan Wars: C. W. Blegen, *Troy and the Trojans* (1963); M. I. Finley, *World of Odysseus** (1954); and D. L. Page, *History and the Homeric Iliad* (1959). G. S. Kirk, *Homer and the Epic** (1965), is also useful.

The Greek World from 800 to 500 B.C.

A. R. Burn, *The Lyric Age of Greece* (1960), presents a detailed and factual history of the politics and literature of this era. The Greek cities of Ionia and of Sicily and Italy respectively are studied in J. M. Cook, *Greeks in Ionia and the East* (1962), and A. G. Woodhead, *Greeks in the West* (1962). On Greek colonization in general, see J. Boardman, *The Greeks Overseas** (1964). F. de Coulanges, *Ancient City** (1956), is the classic study of the development of the city-state. H. Michell, *Sparta** (1952), helps explain the evolution of Sparta's unique institutions. On political change, see W. G. Forrest, *Emergence of Greek Democracy** (1966), and A. Andrewes, *The Greek Tyrants** (1965).

The Fifth Century

Recent studies of the Persian Wars include A. R. Burn, *Persia and the Greeks* (1962), and C. Hignett, *Xerxes' Invasion of Greece* (1963). For the political history of Athens in the Golden Age, see A. E. Zimmern, *The Greek Commonwealth** (1956), considered the classic work on the subject, or one of the excellent shorter treatments, such as A. R. Burn, *Pericles and Athens** (1962); C. A. Robinson, *Athens in the Age of Pericles** (1959); V. Ehrenberg, *From Solon to Socrates** (1968); and W. R. Connor, *The New Politicians of Athens* (1971). H. Michell, *Sparta** (1952), deals with Sparta in the same period. A discussion of Athenian economics may be found in H. Michell, *The Economics of Ancient Greece,* 2nd ed. (1963), or W. S. Ferguson, *Greek Imperialism* (1913). However, the best discussion is in M. I. Finley, *The Ancient Economy** (1973). A comprehensive study of the Peloponnesian War is B. W. Henderson, *The Great War Between Athens and Sparta* (1927). See also D. Kagan, *The Origins of the Peloponnesian War* (1969). Difficult, but thorough, is R. Meiggs, *The Athenian Empire* (1972).

Art, Literature, and Drama

Excellent introductions to Greek art are J. Boardman, *Greek Art** (1964); G. M. A. Richter, *A Handbook of Greek Art** (1974); and T. B. L. Webster, *Greek Art and Literature** (1939). G. Murray, *The Literature of Ancient Greece* (1956), is standard. Most thorough is A. Lesky, *A History of Greek Literature* (1966). Among the many studies of Greek drama, H. D. F. Kitto, *Greek Tragedy** (1954), and D. L. Page, *History of Greek Tragedy** (1951), are particularly well-written introductions. For history, see T. S. Brown, *The Greek Historians** (1973).

Greek Religion

A good account is M. Nilsson, *A History of Greek Religion,* 2nd ed. (1949). R. Graves, *The Greek Myth** (1961), presents a new and exciting version of Greek mythology. Two excellent studies of Greek religious beliefs and practices are W. K. C. Guthrie, *The Greeks and Their Gods** (1950), and M. Hadas and M. Smith, *Heroes and Gods* (1965). E. R. Dodds, *The Greeks and the Irrational** (1951), examines Greek religion in the era before and during the Golden Age, and F. C. Grant, *Hellenistic Religions* (1953), covers the era after the Golden Age.

Science and Philosophy

The best introductions to Greek philosophy are to be found in general works on the history of philosophy. One of the best is F. Copleston, *A History of Philosophy,* Vol. I (1946). W. Jaeger, *Paidaea* (1944–45), is a remarkable book. The most useful recent summaries of Greek philosophy are W. K. C. Guthrie, *The Greek Philosophers from Thales to Aristotle** (1950), and B. Snell, *Discovery of the Mind: The Greek Origins of European Thought** (1953). G. S. Kirk and J. E. Raven, *Presocratic Philosophers** (1957), and F. M. Cornford, *Before and After Socrates* (1932), both have well-written accounts of the philosophers of the Milesian school. There are many excellent scholarly studies of Socrates, Plato, and Aristotle; for the interested student, A. E. Taylor, *Socrates** (1933); G. M. A. Grube, *Plato's Thought** (1935); and W. Jaeger, *Aristotle** (1962), are recommended. For the later period, see A. A. Long, *Hellenistic Philosophy* (1974).

Alexander the Great and the Hellenistic Era

The chief source for the career of Alexander the Great is the Anabasis of Alexander* by Flavius Arrian, a Greek historian. The famous Greek biographer Plutarch wrote a Life of Alexander,* of which there are many editions. Two scholarly but readable modern studies of Alexander are A. R. Burn, *Alexander the Great and the Hellenistic World** (1947), and U. Wilcken, *Alexander the Great** (1932). Beautifully written and well illustrated is P. Green, *Alexander the Great* (1970).

No writer on the Hellenistic era has successfully disentangled himself from the complexities of the politics of the period. For the reader who has learned the art of selectivity in studying political and diplomatic history, however, there are several useful and interesting works. The two standard works on the period are M. Cary, *A History of the Greek World from 323 to 146 B.C.* (1932), and M. I. Rostovtzeff, *Social and Economic History of the Hellenistic World* (1941). W. W. Tarn and G. T. Griffith, *Hellenistic Civilization** (1952), is shorter but thorough. M. Hadas, *Hellenistic Culture: Fusion and Diffusion* (1959), emphasizes the effect of Hellenistic culture on the Jews.

3 Rome and the Unification of the Mediterranean World

Rome succeeded in unifying the ancient world, a feat that neither Darius the Persian, nor Alexander of Macedon had accomplished. It is true that Persia never came under Roman rule, but Rome held North Africa and Western Europe, lands far larger than those that remained under Persian rule. In the days of Darius and Alexander, Rome would have seemed a very unlikely candidate for this role. It was a small city without a good harbor and not much given to commerce; it controlled only a part of the Italian peninsula; its inhabitants were, from a Greek point of view, uneducated, unsophisticated barbarians. Even in the western Mediterranean there were cities that were richer, that possessed a higher culture, and that seemed as strong as Rome. The eastern cities and kingdoms were even more advanced. The rise of Rome has puzzled historians in all ages. The Greek Polybius, who witnessed the crucial period of Roman expansion and was the first to ask what made the expansion possible, gave an answer framed largely in terms of politics. Rome conquered because it had a good constitution, knew how to keep the loyalty of its allies, and played the game of international politics with tenacity and ruthless determination. This is not a complete explanation, but it contains enough of the truth to warrant giving more attention to Roman politics than to the politics of earlier empires.

Linguistically the Romans and their Italic allies were closely related to the Greeks. Both were branches of the Indo-European-speaking peoples who had moved toward the Mediterranean from the interior of Europe in the period after 2000 B.C. But the Romans, unlike the Greeks, were far removed from eastern civilizations, and the geography of the Italian peninsula did not encourage long-distance commerce. There were few good natural harbors on either coast; those that did exist, such as Naples, were soon occupied by Greek colonists. However, there was more good farmland in the Italian than in the Greek peninsula; for a long time expansion was inland rather than overseas. Rome and its Italic neighbors thus tended to resemble the Greek communities that were based on control of agricultural land rather than those based on control of trade routes. Roman interests and values were rural in nature and remained so long after Rome became the center of an empire. In this respect, Rome was very similar to Sparta.

The Italian peninsula, though a clearly delimited geographic entity, was never difficult to invade. When the ancestors of the Romans arrived about 2000 B.C., Italy was occupied by a mixture of peoples in many small states. While these groups were gradually assimilated by the Romans, other invaders continued to try to conquer or to settle in Italy. It was not entirely hypocritical when the Romans claimed that some of their wars were forced on them by the continual influx of aggressive newcomers.

THE ITALIAN PENINSULA TO *ca.* 500 B.C.

By 1000 B.C. most of Italy was held by tribes that spoke Latin or one of the related Indo-European dialects. Soon after 800 B.C., however, two new peoples appeared in Italy: the Greeks, who settled to the south of Rome, and the Etruscans, who settled to the north. Both built walled cities and subdued neighboring Italic tribes; both were active in Mediterranean commerce and brought Italy into closer contact with eastern civilization.

The Etruscans

The Etruscans had a more immediate impact on the Romans and their Latin neighbors than did the Greeks. Unfortunately their origins have not yet been discovered, and most of their surviving inscriptions and writings have not yet been deciphered. Their civilization at its birth seems to have combined a language and certain religious practices from Asia Minor with forms of burial and art native to their center of development in Italy. Out of the mixture the Etruscans evolved an independent and highly sophisticated culture of their own. Their art was as remarkable as that of the Greeks, and sometimes more powerful. Their religion, especially their devices for forecasting the future, long influenced the Romans and other peoples of Italy. As middlemen in trade between the Greek world and

Opposite: The lid of a bronze container from Praeneste, in Latium (fourth century B.C.). The handle represents two warriors carrying a slain comrade.

Detail from an Etruscan sarcophagus (mid-sixth century B.C.). The deceased couple is shown reclining on a couch, pouring libations as if at their own funeral banquet.

the peoples of central Europe, as producers of iron, and as workers in bronze and gold and terra cotta, the Etruscans became very wealthy. Wealth supported their high civilization and enabled them to dominate Italy from the Po Valley down into Campania, the fertile plain around the Bay of Naples. The peak of Etruscan power and culture (roughly 600–500 B.C.) overlapped the Golden Age of Athens (600–400 B.C.). And like the Athenians, they were to be subjugated by a semibarbarous neighboring state.

The Origins of Rome

In 600 B.C. Rome was only the largest of several fortified villages in the surrounding plain of Latium. According to Roman legend, the city was founded by the twins Romulus and Remus in 753 B.C. The site had been occupied on and off long before that date, but archeology suggests that the first permanent settlement was established in the eighth century B.C., perhaps to strengthen local defenses against the Etruscans.

The early government of Rome resembled that of the Greek states of the eighth and early seventh centuries B.C. A king ruled with the help and advice of a council of leading citizens (the Senate). Major decisions, such as a declaration of war, had to be ratified by an assembly composed of all male citizens old enough for military service.

Within this society, wealth was very unevenly distributed, and the wealthy controlled religion, law, and politics. By the end of the period of the kings and perhaps earlier, a formal split had developed between an upper stratum, called patrician, and the rest of the population, called plebeian. Almost all members of the Senate were patricians, and only patricians could hold public office. A few plebeians were well-to-do members of the establishment, but most of them were small landholders, tenant farmers on patrician estates, and artisans and shopkeepers. There must have been some inhabitants who were not citizens such as slaves and foreign merchants, but little is known about them in the early period.

Rome came under Etruscan control around 600 B.C., when an Etruscan aristocrat managed to get himself accepted as king. He and his Etruscan successors raised Rome from a citadel and small market town to a city. Greek and Etruscan merchants frequented the town, and the Romans acquired some understanding of the culture and institutions of the civilized world. Cultural benefits, however, seldom make a people grateful for foreign domination, and the Romans were no exception to this rule. About 509 B.C. (this traditional date is as good as any) a group of Roman patricians (led, however, by L. Brutus, a plebeian) drove out the Etruscan king and proclaimed Rome an independent republic.

Rome then went through a stage very like that of the Greek cities a few centuries earlier: aristocracy replaced monarchy. All power passed into the hands of the patricians, and these Roman aristocrats were much more careful than their Greek counterparts to make sure that power could never again be concentrated in the hands of a single man. All administrative functions were performed by committees of at least two men, whose term of office, with few exceptions, was limited to one year. Thus the supreme executive authority was given to two consuls, who served both as chief magistrates and as commanders of the army. In times of crisis a single man could be named dictator with absolute authority, but his power lasted only for the duration of the emergency, and in no case for more than six months.

This was a republic, not a democracy. If one man could not rule, neither could the multitude. The Senate, however, was the real political power in Rome. In the assembly, citizens voted by classes based on their wealth, and they could elect only patricians for public office. These officials served for only one year and were always influenced by the wishes of the Senate, a body that included all former officials. It was hard for anyone to disregard the advice of such a wealthy, experienced, and prestigious group of men.

TERRITORIAL EXPANSION AND POLITICAL REFORM *ca.* 500–265 B.C.

The early Roman constitution might have produced complete chaos, with its division of power among short-term officials, an assembly, and a Senate, and with flagrant discrimination against a majority of its citizens. But Rome was saved by the political skill of the patricians, who knew how to make concessions that did not undermine their economic and political influence, and by the realization of the lower classes that internal struggles might have upset a basically sound economy and invited foreign conquest. One may wonder whether there would have been so much good sense and so much patriotism if the very life of the community had not been constantly threatened by outside enemies during the first two centuries of the Republic. Nevertheless, the Romans behaved better under pressure than most of their contemporaries; neither internal grievances nor external defeats destroyed the coherence and stability of the community. They were cautious in exploiting their victories and, at least in their early years, skillful in gaining the friendship of defeated enemies. These qualities gave them security at home and, by 265 B.C., control of all the Italian peninsula except for the Po Valley.

Threats from outside enemies began almost as soon as the Etruscans had been expelled. Under the Etruscans, Rome had dominated the other cities of Latium, but with Rome independent these Latin cities wanted independence too. United in the Latin League, they challenged Roman domination (*ca.* 496 B.C.) with sufficient success to gain virtual equality. Linguistically and culturally there was no real difference between the Latin cities and Rome. Rome realized that it had other neighbors who were more dangerous than the Latins and that it needed Latin support. The treaties Rome made with the League formed a pattern for Roman relations with other Italian states. Rome and the League recognized that Roman and Latin citizens had equal rights in one another's courts and that all cities were bound to help one another in war. Thus a relatively large Roman–Latin army was created that acquired a large amount of new territory. "Latin" colonies were established on the conquered lands, new and independent cities inhabited both by Romans and by former citizens of the League. These new cities further increased the military strength of the alliance. This relationship was immensely successful until the fourth century B.C., when it began to break down (see p. 61).

Plebeian Activity and Political Reform

The Roman leaders had shown that they could conciliate outside enemies; they soon had the task of conciliating their own citizens. The plebeians formed the bulk of the army, yet they suffered many political and social disabilities. Probably toward the beginning of and certainly later in the fifth century B.C., the plebeians staged a series of sit-down strikes; if they were denied political rights they would not serve in the army. The Romans, like the Athenians in the same period, realized that they needed the full cooperation of all citizens in order to survive. Little by little the plebeians gained most of their demands.

The first concession, and one of the most important, was the election of two (later ten) tribunes to protect the interests of the plebeians. The persons of the tribunes were inviolate; to attack a tribune meant death without trial. A tribune could veto the acts of a consul or any other official, and his veto could not be overridden. Equally important was the fact that the tribunes were elected by an assembly of tribes, not by the old assembly in which citizens were divided into groups based on their wealth. Because the tribes were based on geographical

CITIES OF THE LATIN LEAGUE
ca. 400 B.C.

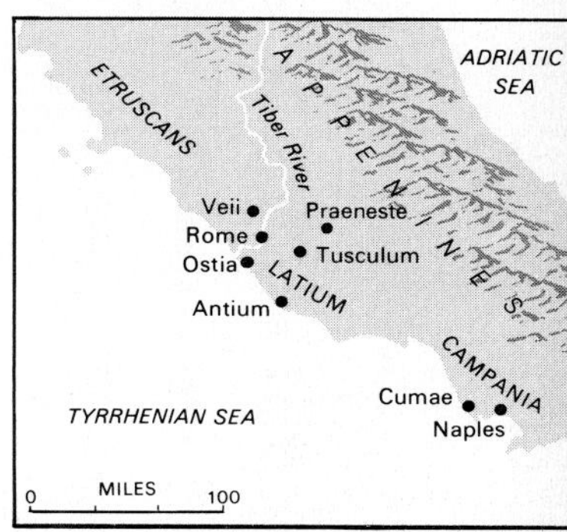

Etruscan kitchen utensils: a water bottle and a spoon.

districts, the patricians could not dominate this assembly. Resolutions passed by the assembly of tribes and approved by the Senate had the force of law. It was always difficult for the Senate to withhold such approval, and eventually the requirement was removed (287 B.C.), but long before that date resolutions of the assembly of tribes had become a normal form of Roman legislation. Consuls and other high officials, however, continued to be elected by the older form of assembly, which was controlled by the wealthier classes.

Like the Greeks, the Roman plebeians wanted written laws to protect them against arbitrary decisions of patrician officials. About 450 B.C. a committee of ten men was appointed to revise and complete the Roman code of law. All power was turned over to this committee, which drew up the basic laws of Rome, the Twelve Tables. It proved somewhat more difficult to get rid of the commission than to establish it, but its work endured even when its members were driven from power. The Twelve Tables were a rather rudimentary set of laws, but through skillful judicial interpretation they satisfied the needs of the Roman people for many generations. They set the tone and marked the beginning of the greatest Roman intellectual achievement, the Roman law.

Finally, the plebeians gradually gained access to all public offices. This took a little longer than the other reforms; it was only in the fourth century B.C. that restrictions on secular offices were removed and only around 300 B.C. that plebeians were admitted to the priesthood. This last concession was more important than it seems, since a priest could block many political acts by declaring that the auspices were unfavorable for certain actions.

Rich plebeians gained the most from these reforms: only they could afford the time and money to play the political game. Officials were unpaid, and a seat in the Senate, which regularly followed the holding of high office, was a time-consuming honor. But the plebeians as a whole seem to have been satisfied by their gains. Their tribunes and tribal assemblies gave them considerable power when crucial political decisions had to be made; invidious legal distinctions had been removed; and theoretically all ca-

Plebeian Reforms

Enslavement for debt was a constant threat to the poorer peasants of the ancient world. In this passage, the Roman historian Livy (59 B.C.–17 A.D.) shows how the plebeians gained constitutional safeguards against enslavement for debt by refusing to fight in a time of emergency.

An old man suddenly presented himself in the Forum. . . . Though cruelly changed from what he had once been, he was recognized, and people began to tell each other, compassionately, that he was an old soldier who had once commanded a company and served with distinction. . . . "While I was on service," he said, "during the Sabine War, my crops were ruined by enemy raids, and my cottage was burnt. Everything I had was taken, including my cattle. Then, when I was least able to do so, I was expected to pay taxes, and fell, consequently, into debt. Interest on the borrowed money increased my burden; I lost the land which my father and my grandfather had owned before me, and . . . I was finally seized by my creditor and reduced to slavery. . . ."

The man's story . . . caused a tremendous uproar, which spread swiftly from the Forum through every part of the city. . . .

On top of this highly critical situation came the alarming news . . . that a Volscian army was marching on Rome. . . . For [the plebeians] it seemed like an intervention of providence to crush the pride of the Senate; they went about urging their friends to refuse military service. . . . [One of the consuls then issued] an edict, to the effect that it should be illegal . . . [to] imprison a Roman citizen. . . . As a result of the edict, all "bound" debtors who were present gave their names on the spot, . . . and in the ensuing fight with the Volscians no troops did more distinguished service.

From Livy, *The Early History of Rome,* trans. by Aubrey de Sélincourt (Baltimore: Penguin Books, 1960), pp. 113–16.

reers were open to all citizens. In actual fact, the Roman ruling class did what many ruling classes have done—it drew the ablest plebeians into its own ranks through marriage alliances and, at times, adoption. Thus they became part of a new senatorial artistocracy. After 287 B.C. the ruling class was a mixture of patricians and plebeians, and their cooperation made possible the gradual expansion of Roman power.

Rome's Conquest of Italy

The first real test of the Roman system came about 400 B.C. when the Romans decided to end the Etruscan threat to central Italy. After a long and difficult siege (*ca.* 405–396 B.C.) the Romans captured Veii and pushed the Etruscans back from the region of the Tiber, permanently shifting the balance of power between the two peoples. One reason, however, for Etruscan weakness was that they were also being attacked in the north by a new group of invaders, the Gauls. The Gauls were a branch of the Celts, another one of those Indo-European-speaking peoples who had been striking at the civilizations of the Mediterranean, the Middle East, and India ever since 2000 B.C. By the fifth century B.C. the Celts had occupied what is now Germany, the British Isles, and France, which was then called Gaul from the name of the Celtic group that had settled there. The Gauls then crossed into Italy and drove the Etruscans out of the Po Valley. They moved south rapidly, and only a few years after the fall of Veii they destroyed a Roman army on the Tiber (*ca.* 390 B.C.). Rome was abandoned; only the citadel held out. Fortunately for Rome, this was only a raid, and the Gauls withdrew after sacking the city. Rome barely survived this catastrophe; some of its allies fell away, and expansion almost ended for a generation. But the Romans were tough enough to rebuild their city and their power. By the 360s B.C. they were attacking both the Gauls and the Etruscans, and by about 350 they had annexed southern Etruria. The danger from the north had been greatly lessened.

After 350 B.C. the chief threat to Rome came from other Italic peoples, who, like Rome, were expanding. Interests and boundary claims began to conflict especially in the south and east. Even the Latin allies resented Roman hegemony, and the more distant cities saw no reason to allow Rome to expand indefinitely. Rome, on the other hand, wanted to stop the growth of potential rivals. The situation was complicated by the weakening of the Greek cities of southern Italy. Their trade had declined as a result of wars in Greece and the occupation of western Europe by the Celts, but they were still rich prizes. No Italic people would willingly let one or more of the Greek cities go to a rival. Finally, the partially Hellenized inhabitants of the Balkans were beginning to cross the Adriatic and mix in Italian affairs, a course that reached its peak with the invasions of King Pyrrhus of Epirus in the years after 280 B.C.

The strongest Italic people were the Samnites, who held much of south-central Italy, including most of the fertile plain of Campania. They were in a much better position to take over Greek cities than the Romans, and they could count on the help of many of the other peoples of Italy. But before Rome could fully concentrate on the Samnites, it had to suppress a rebellion of its own allies. The Latin cities had for some time been treated as inferiors and had been exploited as Rome expanded. They now wanted full independence and joined other peoples around Latium in the Great Latin War (*ca.* 340–338). The Romans crushed the coalition, dissolved the Latin League, and instituted a new and harsher system for controlling subject cities. Most of the Latins had to fulfill the duties of Roman citizens, without the vote or the right to hold office. They could gain full citizenship by faithfully serving the Romans, but it took many years to acquire this status. Some municipalities were governed directly from Rome; others retained limited rights of self-government. Rome also retained the system of free, allied cities with full rights of self-government and limited military obligations, but there had to be strong political reasons and a good prospect of faithful cooperation to put a city in this category.

With the Latins under control, the Romans could turn on the Samnites. In a

This head of a statue of Hermes (*ca.* 500 B.C.) was part of a group of terra cotta figures that adorned the roof of a temple of Apollo in Veii. It became a spoil of war when Veii fell to beseiging Romans in 396 B.C.

EARLY ITALY *ca.* 275 B.C.

long series of wars (*ca.* 325–290 B.C.) the Romans finally defeated the Samnites and their allies. It was not an easy task; the Samnites won most of the early battles and, through an alliance with the Etruscans, forced Rome to fight on two fronts. But Rome's superior military organization and tight system of control of subject and allied cities prevailed over the loose Samnite and Etruscan confederacies. After the last Samnite War (298–290 B.C.), there was still a little mopping up to do, but the Romans basically controlled all Italy except for the Gauls in the Po Valley and the Greeks in the south. Some of the Greeks prudently allied themselves with Rome; others, led by Tarentum, called in King Pyrrhus of

Founding of City of Rome ca. 750 B.C.	ca. 600	ca. 400	264	146	27 B.C.
Independent Roman Kingdom	Etruscan Dominance	Rome Conquers Italian Peninsula	Punic Wars	Rome Conquers Entire Mediterranean Area	

Epirus to protect their liberties. Like most of Rome's enemies, Pyrrhus won many battles but lost the war.* By 265 B.C. the Greek cities of the peninsula had accepted Roman domination.

Rome's success in war was due to the remarkable staying power of its army. Roman generals were not infallible, but the Roman military system was unbeatable in the long run. The consuls enforced stern discipline: there was no straggling on the march or wavering on the battlefield; disobedience was punished with death. The basic military unit, the legion of about 4300 men, had great striking power and at the same time great flexibility, for it was divided into smaller units that could maneuver independently. Most important of all was Rome's control over its subject and allied cities. The Romans never accepted defeat, not only because they were courageous, but also because they could always raise new armies. Italy's agricultural lands were far better than those of Greece or Asia Minor, and could support a larger population. Sheer manpower favored Rome; at the time that Alexander was conquering the East with about thirty thousand men, the Romans could deploy an army of about sixty thousand. With this advantage, stubborn perseverance could win more for Rome than brilliant strategy. Even the strongest states of the Mediterranean world could not hold out against the steady pressure that Rome could exert.

ROMAN EXPANSION OVERSEAS, 264–146 B.C.

In acquiring the Greek cities of southern Italy, Rome inherited their struggle with Carthage for the control of Sicily. The resulting "Punic" Wars (Latin *Poenicus*=Phoenician=Carthaginian) tested Rome's staying power even more severely than had the Samnite Wars; several times Rome came close to total defeat. Since Carthage had been the strongest naval power in the Mediterranean, Roman victories over Carthage meant that Rome became dominant on sea as well as on land. This made it easy for Rome to intervene in the eastern Mediterranean, and long before the destruction of Carthage in 146 B.C., Rome had begun to dominate the Hellenistic world.

*In 279 B.C. Pyrrhus gained a victory over the Romans that cost a ruinous loss of his forces. Hence the term *Pyrrhic victory.*

The Punic Wars, 264–146 B.C.

The first war with Carthage started in 264 B.C., only a year after Rome's final conquest of southern Italy, and lasted until 241 B.C. Without a fleet, Rome could not contest Carthaginian control of western Sicily, much less attack the center of Carthaginian power in North Africa. With characteristic confidence in their ability to master any military problem, the Romans built a fleet, and made up for lack of naval experience by constructing ships that would let them profit from their skill in hand-to-hand combat. Grappling irons and movable boarding bridges locked hostile ships together and so enabled the Romans to convert a sea battle into something like a land engagement. Even with these advantages, Rome came close to losing the war. After initial victories, the Romans lost three fleets in succession, not to the enemy but to shipwreck and storm. (The boarding bridge was useful in combat but dangerously top-heavy in bad weather, which may explain some of these losses.) It was all they could do to build a fourth fleet (this time, without boarding bridges); but this one was victorious in a battle off western Sicily. Carthaginian naval superiority was permanently broken, and Carthage surrendered Sicily to the Romans in 241 B.C.

To make up for the loss of Sicily the Carthaginians decided to take over the rich mines and farmlands of Spain. Under the leadership of one of its best generals, Hamilcar Barca, Carthage

Symbol of Sicily, found in Ostia, chief port of Rome. The symbol's three legs correspond to the three points of Sicily.

This third-century B.C. coin bears one of the few known contemporary portraits of Hannibal. The elephant appears on the reverse.

gained control of southern and eastern Spain. This region was soon producing more revenue for Carthage than Sicily ever had. When Hamilcar died he was succeeded as governor of Spain first by his son-in-law and then by his twenty-five-year-old son Hannibal (221 B.C.).

Roman legend has it that Hannibal as a child swore to his father that he would avenge the Sicilian defeat by destroying Rome. For their part, the Romans were clearly annoyed by Carthaginian success in Spain and were furious when Hannibal attacked a city in northeastern Spain allied to Rome. They determined to crush Carthage in Spain as they had in Sicily. But the fighting had scarcely begun in Spain when Hannibal made one of the most daring strategic moves in all history. In 218 B.C. he left Spain, marched through southern Gaul, and crossed the Alps with a large army including fifty war-elephants. Cut off from his supplies, usually outnumbered, Hannibal repeatedly defeated the massive Roman armies sent against him. For fifteen years he ravaged the Italian countryside and on one occasion came close to Rome. In this desperate war, Rome was saved by the loyalty of its allies in Latium, Samnium, and Etruria, who made it impossible for Hannibal to establish himself in central Italy. In the south, through fear or favor, more of the allied and subject municipalities went over to Hannibal, and it looked as if he could maintain himself there indefinitely.

The deadlock was not broken until the Romans were able to send a first-rate general, Scipio Africanus, into the field. Scipio first went to Spain, where an indecisive war had been dragging on for years, and conquered the region for Rome. He then led a Roman army to North Africa and laid siege to Carthage itself. As he had anticipated, the Carthaginians recalled Hannibal, thus ending his Italian adventures. Losses in Italy and Spain had weakened the Carthaginian army; when Scipio met Hannibal at Zama, a few miles from Carthage, he won a decisive victory (202 B.C.). Carthage had to accept a harsh treaty: Spain was ceded to Rome; a heavy war indemnity was levied; and the Carthaginian fleet was limited to ten ships. Carthage had ceased to be a first-rate power.

Rome and the Hellenistic East

Unlike the Roman conquest of Sicily and Spain, it is hard to find a consistent pattern in Roman expansion in the East. Rome wanted to protect her interests there and Roman generals certainly wanted triumphs. Eastern states threatened by their neighbors kept asking for aid, and one Roman intervention led to another until withdrawal became almost impossible. But annexation of these distant lands was long avoided. Rome did not have a definite plan for conquest and expansion; it was difficult to find troops to garrison conquered lands and it was also difficult to keep Roman generals from misusing their power. Again and again, Rome refused to annex defeated states.

As we have seen, the Hellenistic kingdom of Epirus had tried to block Roman expansion in southern Italy, and Macedon gave some assistance to Hannibal when he was operating in the same region. Rome had defeated both kingdoms and in the process had learned a good deal about the richness and the weakness of the Hellenistic world. Because there was no strong state in the area, there was constant bickering among Egypt, the remnant of the Seleucid Empire, the little kingdoms of Asia Minor, Macedon, and leagues of Greek cities. Everyone sought the aid of Rome in their quarrels, but every peace settlement imposed by Rome collapsed. Rome soon found itself hopelessly entangled in a political mess. Roman leaders naturally became exasperated; they could neither keep order in the Hellenistic world nor get out of it.

When the Romans were exasperated they could become brutal. Macedon and Epirus were plundered in 167 B.C.; thousands of their inhabitants were sold as slaves. Growing admiration for Greek culture did not keep the Romans from turning savagely on Greek cities that disobeyed Roman orders. Corinth was destroyed in 146 B.C., and thousands more young men were sent to Italy as slaves. Macedon became a Roman province; Rome controlled the Greek cities, allowing them a good deal of autonomy in internal affairs; Asia Minor became a sort of protectorate. Rome was less interested in ruling Syria and Egypt (the Romans had favored Egypt more consistently than any other Hellenistic state), but Rome made it clear that neither country was to take any initiative without its approval. Most of the Hellenistic world was now in Roman hands.

In 149 B.C. the Romans declared war on Carthage. Carthage had regained some of its wealth but not its military power. Although no threat to Rome, its very existence offended men who remembered stories of the desperate battles against Hannibal. After a long blockade and a six-month siege, Carthage fell in 146 B.C. Every inhabitant was slaughtered or enslaved. The city was destroyed stone by stone, and the lands behind it were made a Roman province. Most of North Africa, however, remained independent under native rulers.

CONSEQUENCES OF EXPANSION

By 146 B.C. Rome controlled Italy, Sicily, Sardinia, Corsica, and parts of Spain and North Africa in the West, and Macedon and Greece in the East. During the next century the gaps in this ring around the Mediterranean were filled in, but the problems of empire existed long before the empire was complete. How could the institutions of a city-state be used to govern the vast territories now ruled by Rome? How could leaders be found who could keep the confidence of the Roman people and gain the obedience of Roman subjects when the ablest politicians could gain wealth and power from conquered provinces outside the control of Roman citizens? How could Rome and Italy adjust to the drastic social and economic changes caused by the growth of large agricultural units, rural indebtedness, commerce, the influx of wealth from plundered enemies and tribute-paying provinces, and the importation of hundreds of thousands of slaves? How could one find a focus of loyalty in an empire that was also a republic, that had no dominant religion, no god-king, not even a chief of state? These were the questions that the Romans struggled with in the last two centuries before Christ. They found only partial answers at best. The resulting dissatisfaction destroyed the Roman Republic with its multiple leadership and led to the creation of an empire with a single head.

Governing the Provinces

One problem could not be postponed—how to govern the provinces. The Romans soon found a workable if not entirely satisfactory solution. Rome had long used former officials as military commanders. For example, Rome had only two consuls, but it might well have four or five theaters of military operations; in that case outgoing consuls (proconsuls) would command some of the armies. Since most provinces had Roman garrisons, it seemed natural to make the military commander (the proconsul) the governor. This was not an ideal solution. Backed up by an army, an unscrupulous governor could easily enrich himself. In fact, in 149 B.C. the Romans had to establish a special court to try corrupt governors. But not all governors were corrupt, and the mere existence of the court shows that there was some feeling against exploiting the provinces. Moreover, since there were repeated rebellions in some provinces, notably in Spain, military governors were needed to hold the Empire together.

The governors usually had very small staffs and left local affairs to the leaders of local communities. A few allied cities had complete autonomy; elsewhere Roman officials could intervene when they felt it necessary or profitable. The inhabitants of the provinces paid regular taxes to Rome, which, added to the money extorted by corrupt officials, imposed a heavy burden on the provincial economies. Earlier rulers, however, had been no less greedy, and Rome did put an end to the wars that had devastated many parts of the Mediterranean world. After the initial shock of conquest and after the penalties for unsuccessful rebellions had been dealt, the provinces seem to have adjusted fairly well to their new situation.

Changes in Religion, Literature, and Art

Closer contacts with the Hellenistic world brought about changes in Roman

ROMAN PLUNDERING 167–146 B.C.

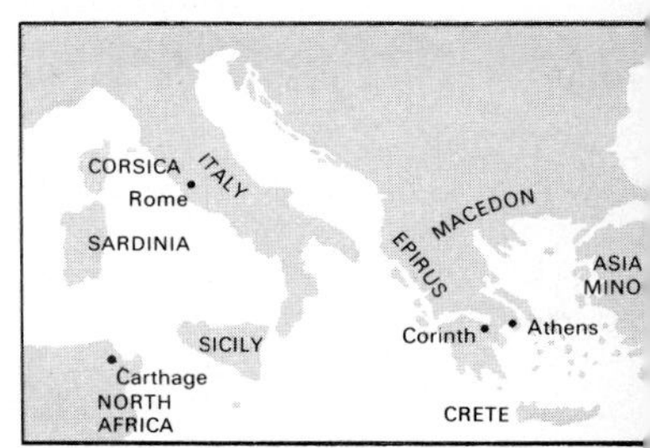

This fresco found in a villa on the outskirts of Pompeii depicts initiation rites of a Dionysian mystery cult, but they are rendered in such a way as to make precise interpretation difficult for the outsider.

art, literature, and religion. Even before the eastern wars, educated Romans had known and been influenced by Greek models, but the sudden arrival of tens of thousands of Greek slaves and hostages in Rome came very close to producing culture shock. Some Romans were horrified at the idea of imitating despised foreigners; they wanted to be more Roman than ever: severe, warlike, unbending lovers of the simple life. Others felt that there was little that was good in the old Roman cultural tradition, and that only the Greek style was worthy of respect. Most Romans, of course, accepted neither of these extreme points of view, but the disagreement ran deep enough to have repercussions in politics. Conservative senators were sure that Greek influence caused political unrest, and this was one of the reasons why they opposed reform movements.

In religion, the Romans identified Greek gods with their own; for example, Zeus was Jupiter and Hera was Juno. Historically, these identifications had a foundation in fact: both sets of gods went back to early Indo-European divinities. But in their Greek form the gods were more human and more wayward than the generally faceless and impersonal gods of Rome. In Rome as in Greece, the official religion had been controlled by the aristocracy, and it was already losing its hold on the masses, but it is probable that the introduction of Greek myths made it seem even less applicable to the needs of the people. In any case, some Romans turned to the mystery religions of the East. During the dark days of the Second Punic War, the Senate itself introduced the Asian cult of Cybele, the Great Mother, in order to bring good fortune to Rome. The cult of Dionysus came in about the same time, even though the Senate disliked its uninhibited ceremonies. But the Oriental religions began to exercise their full influence only after the end of the Republic.

In art, and especially in literature, Greek influence was so great that it is difficult to discover material that does not show some signs of Roman imitation of Greek models. The Romans had certainly written poetry and worked up their tribal myths into a sort of history in the early period of the Republic, but one of the first long poems written in Latin was a translation of the *Odyssey,* and around 200 B.C. Romans writing history used Greek. As was pointed out, an excellent account of Rome's rise to dominance in the Mediterranean was written in Greek by Polybius, one of the Greek hostages held in Rome. Polybius was deeply impressed by Roman power and by the Roman constitution, but he imitated Thucydides rather than Roman historians. Only with Cato's book on early Roman history (*ca.* 168 B.C.) was a solid historical work attempted in Latin. Cato, who was one of the anti-Greek senators, made a deliberate effort to bring Latin prose up to the Greek level.

The Romans thoroughly enjoyed Greek drama, and the first plays given at Rome were written in Greek. Later the playwrights Plautus and Terence satisfied the Roman desire for amusement by writing comedies in Latin based on earlier works by Hellenistic authors. Little is known about early Roman architecture and sculpture, but before 200 B.C. the rough, vigorous native style of these art forms was being influenced by Greek originals. Only in works on law was Greek influence minimal. Rome's mission, as Virgil later saw (see p. 83), was to give law to the lawless. This was the area in which Roman thinkers excelled and in which Rome preserved its cultural identity. Soon after 200 B.C. Romans were writing solid treatises on basic legal texts and their interpretation. By the first century B.C., the Romans also began to produce important books on political theory and philosophy.

Social, Economic, and Political Change

In addition to providing a constant stream of wealth flowing toward Italy, the provinces supplied Rome with cheap labor. Each conquest and each rebellion was followed by the enslavement of a large part of the defeated people. The result of this influx of money and men was to change the nature of the Roman social and economic system. The upper classes could profit from the new opportunities offered by the acquisition of an empire; the lower classes could not. The gap between rich and poor grew steadily wider. And gaps appeared among the rich as well. War was no longer a fight for existence but a hunt for plunder; public office was no longer a burden but a chance to acquire wealth. As a result, competition for magistracies, army commands, and contracts for public works became intense, and factional struggles among the governing class eventually made it incapable of governing.

The upper classes included the senators and the *equites,* or equestrians. The senators belonged to families, both patrician and plebeian, that had held high public office and hence were entitled to seats in the Senate. Most officials, and consequently most senators, came from old senatorial families; only occasionally could a new man break into this privileged group. It cost a good deal of money to campaign for public office, and the profits began coming in only when a man had reached the higher ranks. On the way up, ambitious men often competed for lower offices by providing expensive amusements for the public. By the first century B.C. bribery of voters had become common, and made campaigning even more costly. Moreover, the great noble families felt that they alone were worthy of office; they used all their influence to exclude lesser men.

The equestrians were those who had enough money to provide their own horses for service in the army. As a class, they were less wealthy than the senators although the richer equestrians were better off than the poorer senators. Most equestrians were substantial landowners, but some of them were merchants, bankers, and bidders for public contracts. Custom and law forbade senators to engage in these activities, though they often did so by making secret arrangements with businessmen. On the whole, the interests of the senatorial and equestrian classes coincided fairly closely, but the equestrians preferred profits to politics and as long as their vital interests were not threatened, they let the senators run the government.

A major impetus to social and political change was agricultural change. At the beginning of Roman expansion there was a considerable amount of uncultivated land in Italy. Most of this land, as well as cultivated land confiscated from defeated enemies, fell into the hands of the Roman government. Ordinary citizens, especially those who went out to found colonies in the peninsula, received some of the new lands, but the largest part was leased to the upper classes. They discovered, as rich men in other societies have discovered, that a large estate can be run more efficiently than a small farm, especially when cheap labor is available. The Roman conquests provided them with an almost inexhaustible supply of slaves. Slaves cost little, were cheaper to support, and were at times literally worked to death.

Free peasant farmers found it difficult to compete with plantations using slave labor. Their lives were disrupted by continual calls for military service. They were under pressure to sell out to rich

Scenes from everyday life in first-century Rome. Top left: grain from African colonies is being unloaded. Top right: a Greek slave appears to be tutoring his master and mistress. Above: a goldsmith practices his trade. Below: a stooped farmer takes his produce to market.

men seeking a safe, respected, and profitable investment for their money in land. Around the cities, family farms were bought up for specialized agriculture. In the hills and backlands, ranching, which required an investment that a peasant could not make, displaced subsistence farming. The returning veterans and the displaced peasants seldom found work in the countryside, but drifted to Rome, where work was equally scarce. The city was growing rapidly; it had no major export industry, and most of the poor had no permanent jobs. Some became "clients" of the rich and especially of the senators. Their duties were to run errands, act as bodyguards, applaud speeches, and start riots when it seemed helpful to their boss or to his faction. Others lived on odd jobs and formed a floating vote that could be captured by ambitious politicians.

Thus there were two depressed classes in Roman society: the slaves and the poor freemen. Of the two, the slaves caused the less trouble. The agricultural slaves, who were treated most harshly, were carefully watched, even to the point of being locked in underground dungeons at night. Household slaves, such as the educated Greeks who acted as tutors for rich young Romans, had an easier life. They were often allowed to go into business for themselves and could then buy their freedom, or they might be freed simply because in their long service they had practically become members of the family. Thus the slaves, already divided by race and language, were still further divided by occupation and level of living; it was difficult for them to form an organized resistance. There were remarkably few slave rebellions in the history of the Roman Republic. There were only three really large-scale movements. The slaves rose twice in Sicily, but were crushed by Roman armies. The rebellion of Spartacus in Italy (73–71 B.C.) was more dangerous, but it also failed. Thereafter the brutality of masters and the hopes of slaves lost their edge, and the "peculiar institution" was absorbed into Rome's social structure.

The poor freemen, however, were a constant problem. If they lived in Rome they could vote, and their votes were not always predictable. If they remained on the land as farmers, they were expected to be the backbone of the army, but military requirements were growing, while the number of peasant farmers was decreasing. This particular difficulty was resolved in 107 B.C. by permitting landless men to enlist. Such an action, however, merely intensified the problem: the most discontented part of the citizen body now had military as well as political power. Obviously some form of government intervention was needed to save the small farmers and improve the lot of the proletariat, but in spite of long discussions, the ruling class could never agree on a policy. In the end the poorer classes put their faith in military rather than political solutions. The rival generals whose quarrels destroyed the Republic kept the loyalty of their followers by promises of bonuses and grants of land, not by appeals to political programs.

THE COLLAPSE OF THE REPUBLIC 146–59 B.C.

The Gracchi

Tiberius and Gaius Gracchus were the first members of the senatorial class to realize that something had to be done about the problem of the poorer citizens. But even they did not fully understand the crisis. They thought more in terms of an idealized early republic than in terms of an empire facing a social crisis. They believed in the old Roman virtues of honesty, self-sacrifice, and devotion to the public welfare, which they thought were incarnate in the class of small farmers. They also believed, more realistically, that the army was being weakened by a decline in the peasant population. Finally, they may have felt that their political group could profit from popular support. The Gracchi were members of the highest aristocracy, grandsons of the great Scipio who had conquered Carthage, but while their birth ensured them high office, it did not confer control of policy. As events proved, the Gracchi could never bring many senators to their side; their tragedy was that they could not develop a solid base of political power in any other section of the population.

Tiberius Gracchus was elected tribune in 133 B.C. His first step was to demand that state land virtually owned by rich men with long-term leases should be broken up into small farms. He succeeded in getting the popular assembly to pass a law limiting the amount of public land held by one family, but this action outraged the senators. It not only hurt their interests; it went against an unwritten rule that measures unacceptable to the Senate would not be pushed. The Senate persuaded another tribune to veto the act; Gracchus, in an unprecedented move, had the tribune voted out of office. To make sure that his reform would endure he ran for a second term as tribune, a violation of custom if not of law. This act threatened senatorial domination of the state. If an elected official could hold office indefinitely, all the old checks on popular power were gone. So a group of senators led their clients in a riot in which Gracchus was lynched.

Some ten years later (123 B.C.) Gaius Gracchus, the younger brother of Tiberius, managed to get himself elected tribune in spite of the hostility of many of the senators. Gaius tried to find a wider political base than his brother had, and for a time he had more success. He gained the support of the impoverished proletariat by providing for state distribution of grain at a subsidized price. This law was so necessary and so popular that no succeeding politician dared to repeal it. He tried to win over the equestrians by giving them control of the juries that judged official corruption. This was a sensible move, since the senators (who had furnished the juries before) held all important offices and were not apt to convict one of their own group, while the equestrians had no reason to acquit senators. He continued his brother's policy of land reform and tried to increase the number of small farmers by establishing new colonies.

A coin minted in 137 B.C. celebrates the private ballot. A Roman is shown dropping a stone tablet into a voting urn.

Gaius also saw a danger that Tiberius had ignored, the discontent of the Italian allies, such as the Samnites, who did not have Roman citizenship. These allies had given Rome faithful service during the Punic and the eastern wars, but they were treated as inferiors. Their inhabitants could not vote in Roman elections, and they received few material benefits from Roman victories. Although they faced many of the same social and economic problems that Rome did, no one was worrying about them.

Gaius proposed to give Roman citizenship to the Italian allies. This would have relieved them of some of their financial burdens and gained Gracchus a great deal of good will, but it would have been difficult to transform that good will into votes: a citizen could vote only by going to Rome. It is curious that Rome, with its genius for law, never entertained the principle of representation, by which each community could have participated in political decisions by sending one or two men to a central assembly. They believed, as had the Greeks, that each citizen was entitled to vote personally on issues affecting him. In any case, Gracchus' proposal was not accepted. Senators, equestrians, and lower classes agreed to reject the law, revealing the weakness of Gracchus' support. Gaius defended his legislation during two terms as tribune, but in the end was lynched like his brother. His death sharply increased tension in Italy and laid the foundation for the bitter civil wars of the next generation.

During the second century B.C., Roman leaders seem to have lost the gift for compromise and accommodation that had held the state together during its early history. The stakes in an imperial economy were so high that the upper classes were less willing to share the power that ensured their wealth. Attempts to solve social and economic problems by legal and peaceful means had broken down. A new series of wars, beginning in 107 B.C., was to put still further strains on the Roman system of government and give increasing power to military commanders. Ultimately, decisions would be made and enforced by the generals.

Marius and Sulla

Sulla, dictator of Rome from 82 to 79 B.C.

The military difficulties that led to the downfall of the Republic began with a long and bitter war in western North Africa against a recalcitrant ally. As usual, the Romans made a bad start. They began to win only after they discovered a very capable general in an equestrian from rural Italy named Marius. Elected consul in 107 B.C., Marius ended the African war with a complete victory. It was high time that he did, because a new Indo-European invasion, this time by the Germans, was throwing all of Europe north of the Alps into confusion. Two German tribes appeared in Gaul, raided Spain, and then threatened Italy. After they won several victories over Roman armies, Marius was again called to the rescue. He was reelected consul in 104 B.C., as well as in each of the next four years (103–100 B.C.). Such a series of reelections was unprecedented, but the need to preserve continuity in command was obvious, and there was no real opposition to the break with tradition. Marius justified the confidence placed in him: he annihilated the German armies in two hard-fought battles (102 and 101 B.C.). Thus ended the first, but by no means the last, of the Roman–German wars.

It was during this crisis that the old connection between ownership of land and military service was broken. Marius had to recruit landless men in order to have sufficient forces. Since the state could not pay these men, Marius rewarded them with bounty from the defeated enemies and grants of land in occupied territories. Most of his successors followed this pattern, but while it provided necessary manpower, it introduced two dangers that endured to the end of Roman history. Troops who received their reward from their general were loyal to that general, not to the state. If land or a substantial bonus was the chief reward for service, then enlistment would be most attractive to the poor and disadvantaged. Over the centuries, fewer and fewer Romans or Italians joined the armed forces. Their places were taken first by provincials, and then by barbarians, men who had little understanding of or loyalty to the Roman state.

Marius was in a strong position after his defeat of the Germans, but he had no political program of his own. Some of his associates wanted to revive the Gracchan policy of land reform; Marius turned against them and helped suppress their movement. This equivocal behavior thoroughly discredited Marius, although other leaders proved no wiser. Nothing was done to allay the grievances of the Italian allies, or the discontent of provincial subjects. As a result, two dangerous uprisings occurred almost simultaneously in Italy and in the East.

The so-called Social War (that is, the war with the Italian allies—*socii* in Latin) began in 90 B.C. The Italian cities formed a confederacy, created their own senate, raised an army, and held out against Rome for over two years. Marius defended the north, on the whole successfully, but one of his former officers, Sulla, made an even better record in the south. The Romans realized that they had little to gain by devastating Italy, especially since they needed to free their armies for war in the East. They ended the Social War by offering full citizenship to all Italians who would lay down their arms, an act that could have prevented the civil war had it been adopted earlier.

The eastern uprising was led by Mithridates, king of a small Hellenistic state on the Black Sea, who hoped to create a new Greek empire. Most of the Greek cities, including Athens, gave him enthusiastic support. They were so embittered by Roman bankers, soldiers, and tax collectors that in 88 B.C., when Mithridates gave the signal, they murdered eighty thousand Romans and Italians in the Greek cities of Asia Minor.

No Roman army was immediately available to avenge this massacre, and a bitter struggle broke out over who was to command an expeditionary force. Sulla, consul in 88 B.C., had the best claim, but while he was away from Rome winding up the Social War, Marius obtained the command by a popular vote. Sulla marched on Rome, overturned the vote, and then set out with his army for the East. After three years of hard fighting, he defeated Mithridates and his Greek allies and restored Roman control in Greece and Asia Minor. Sulla demanded an enormous indemnity from his conquered enemies but otherwise was fairly lenient. Mithridates was even allowed to retain his kingdom.

One reason for his leniency was Sulla's eagerness to return to Rome. During his absence opponents had taken over the government and had once more attempted to deprive him of his military command. But when Sulla landed in Italy in 83 B.C. his army of veterans defeated the scattered forces of his opponents one by one. When Sulla took Rome in 82 B.C. he was named dictator for an unlimited period. He proscribed his enemies; that is, he put a price on their heads and confiscated their property. Thousands of "bad citizens," as he called them, were put to death. The property seized from his enemies and from Italian towns that had supported the opposition was distributed among his soldiers. Sulla established colonies throughout Italy and filled them with his adherents.

Although Sulla had full power to revise the Roman constitution, he found no way of overcoming its basic weaknesses. His plan seems to have been to weaken the popular assembly and concentrate power in the Senate, stacked with his own supporters. Once this was done, he retired to his country estate (79 B.C.), where he died the following year. But the new senators were not very different from the old ones; the restrictions on the assembly and the tribunes were gradually removed; and the Roman political system remained inherently unstable.

The New Leaders: Pompey, Crassus, and Cicero

As before, the chief goal of ambitious politicians was to gain the overseas commands that would give them money and control of a loyal army. Danger spots throughout the Roman world offered opportunities for establishing such commands. The East was restless; a bitter opponent of Sulla controlled much of Spain; piracy was rampant in the Mediterranean. The ablest and most popular Roman general was Pompey, who had helped Sulla regain control of Italy in 83 and 82 B.C., but Pompey had some respect for constitutional procedures and some willingness to compromise with his rivals. Thus for almost three decades no one man dominated Rome. Power was held by shifting coalitions of leading politicians, and in a good many cases unaligned majorities in the Senate still had a decisive voice.

Pompey's chief rival was Crassus, a man who had made a fortune in questionable real estate operations. He was not a career general, but he acquired some military reputation when the one really dangerous slave rebellion in Roman history broke out. Led by the gladiator Spartacus, the slaves at first won several victories, but were finally defeated by Crassus in 71 B.C. Pompey meanwhile had been ending a rebellion in Spain, and there was some danger of a collision between the two victorious generals. They settled their differences, however, and both men were elected consul for the year 70 B.C.

Bust of Pompey showing him late in life.

The third political leader to emerge at this time was Cicero, the only civilian with a real following. Cicero gained public favor when he secured the conviction of a spectacularly corrupt Roman provincial governor; his whole career depended on his skill as a lawyer, orator, and writer. Although he came from an equestrian family, it is not remarkable that he was able to enter the Senate—a good many men of similar background did. But the old senatorial families looked down on these "new men," and most of them went no farther. It was only his extraordinary ability that carried Cicero to the highest office, the consulship.

Cicero was more honest than most men in that age of corruption. He tried to avoid violence at a time when most problems were settled by civil war. The Romans had already developed a powerful style of oratory; Cicero perfected this style to the point where one of his speeches could sway the entire Senate. He was *the* orator; century after century every educated man studied his orations. As one who thought deeply about Rome's constitutional problems, he tried to halt the drift toward the concentration of powers in the hands of rival politician-generals. Like many successful politicians, Cicero practiced the art of compromise to a degree that often made him seem indecisive, and he knew enough about Roman politics to find it difficult to commit himself to a single faction. In a pinch, he was apt to favor Pompey, who had some of his own qualities (or defects), but as the crisis in Roman government deepened, both men became unable to control events. Cicero was respected to the end, but he lost most of his political influence.

In 74 B.C. Mithridates again tried to rally the Hellenistic world against Rome, and this time he kept the war going for a decade. Some Roman commanders were incompetent; some conducted brilliant operations; but none of them was able to end the war. This gave Pompey a chance to shine once more. In 66 B.C. the Senate passed a law giving Pompey extraordinary powers (Cicero made a great speech supporting the proposal), which allowed Pompey to end the eastern problem that had plagued Rome since the third century B.C. Mithridates was defeated; parts of Asia Minor and Syria were annexed and the rest put under the control of subject kings. The Jewish kingdom of Palestine was one of these vassal kingdoms. When Pompey returned to Rome in 62 B.C. he had acquired more territory for his country than any previous general.

The Senate gave Pompey a splendid triumphal procession and a cool reception. He had committed Rome to a series of treaties with the eastern kingdoms, and he had promised his soldiers grants of land. The Senate hesitated to ratify these acts, even though Pompey had been given extraconstitutional power to end the war. Pompey was determined to have his promises honored; when the senators refused to satisfy him he had to find ways of putting political pressure on them. The means to do so lay in the person of Gaius Julius Caesar.

THE RISE OF CAESAR 59–44 B.C.

Caesar was a young aristocrat with political ambitions, popularity with the masses—and huge debts. Crassus, who

Electioneering in Rome in the Last Days of the Republic

Quintus Cicero to his brother when the latter was running for consul in 64 B.C.

I have said enough about gaining friends, now I should speak of acquiring popular support. The people like to be called by name, flattered, be courted, receive favors, hear about you, feel that you are working for the public good. . . . You must flatter endlessly; this is wrong and shameful in ordinary life, but necessary in running for office. . . . Be in Rome and in the Forum and ask for support. . . . See that you and your friends give parties, widely and to many voting groups. . . . Make it possible for men to see you at any time, day or night. . . .

Let the voters say and think that you know them well, that you greet them by name, that you are generous and open-handed. . . . If possible accuse your competitors of having a bad reputation for crime, vice or bribery. . . . Remember that this is Rome, a city made up of many peoples, in which plots, lies and all kinds of vices abound. You must suffer much arrogance, many insults, much ill-will and the pride and hatred of many people.

Translated from Dante Nardo, *Il Commentariolum Petitionis* (Padua: Liviana, 1970), pp. 213, 215.

still hoped for power, was aware of his own lack of popularity both in the Senate and with the people, so he decided to back Caesar. By paying off the debts Crassus gained a hold on Caesar; by using Crassus' money Caesar gained an enthusiastic personal following and rapid political advancement. He had a reputation for being unconventional and thus, perhaps, a reformer; those who knew him best realized that he also had a tremendous desire for power. By 60 B.C. he was ready to run for consul.

The First Triumvirate 59–53 B.C.

Caesar found it an easy matter to bring together Crassus and Pompey, who was still furious with the Senate. Pompey's prestige, Crassus' wealth, and Caesar's popular following made an almost unbeatable combination. The three bosses, or First Triumvirate (to give them their more dignified modern appellation), had about the same degree of power that a similar coalition would have today. They could get most of what they wanted for themselves, and some of what they wanted for their followers, but they were far from having absolute power. And they had to threaten the Senate with force in order to get as much as they did.

Caesar's election to the consulship for the year 59 B.C. made the formation of the Triumvirate politically possible and effective. As consul, Caesar saw to it that Pompey's promises were honored, and he distributed land not only to Pompey's veterans, but also to other citizens. Caesar also tried to curb corruption in provincial government by expanding measures taken by Sulla and earlier leaders. He was not entirely successful, but he may have gained some popularity in the provinces.

What Caesar wanted most of all was a military command that would give him a reputation equal to that of Pompey. The one weak link in Rome's control of the Mediterranean was in southern Gaul, where the Romans held only a thin strip of territory linking Italy to Spain. The rest of Gaul was held by Celtic tribes, who were relatively civilized, but who were constantly at war with one another or with Germans pushing in from the East. These wars had a nasty way of spilling over into Roman territory or the territory of Rome's allies. Clearly, it would help Rome if the political situation in Gaul could be stabilized, but it seemed an unrewarding task. Gaul had neither the wealth nor the splendor of the East. Would a victory over a few Celtic tribes be equivalent to Pompey's triumph over the kings of Asia? Nevertheless, in 58 B.C., a proconsular command over Gaul fell to Caesar's lot, for a period of five years, a term later extended to ten. The command included the old Gallic settlements in the Po Valley—a region that was largely Romanized—and Transalpine Gaul, roughly the French Riviera.

It is difficult to say what Caesar's plans were when he first went to Gaul. Certainly he wanted to pacify the tribes living near the Roman frontier and protect the Gauls who seemed friendly to Rome. Probably he wanted to enlarge the Roman province of Transalpine Gaul. But, as often happens in such a situation, one war of pacification led to another, and every time the zone of Roman-protected territory moved northward new enemies appeared. In the end, Caesar conquered all of Gaul and made it a

Bust of Caesar showing him at the time of his assassination.

CAESAR IN GAUL 58–49 B.C.

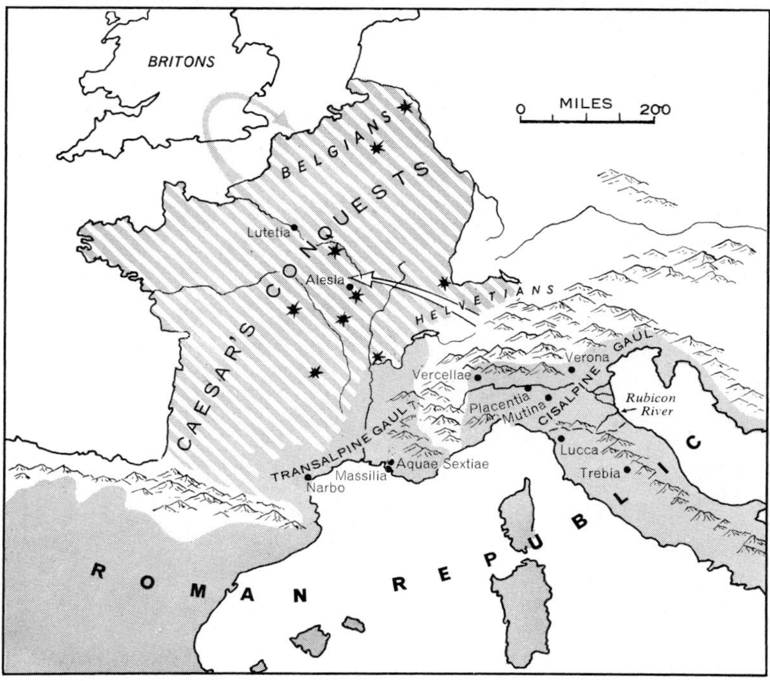

Richly embossed helmet of an aristocratic warrior of Gaul, at the time of Julius Caesar's conquest.

Roman province. As a warning to neighboring peoples, he invaded Britain twice and crossed the Rhine to fight the Germans. Britain was a refuge and staging ground for Gallic enemies, and the Germans had threatened to intervene in Gaul, so Caesar had good reasons for these expeditions. All these accomplishments Caesar described in clear terse style in his *Commentaries on the Gallic War.* Any Roman who read this book would be convinced that Caesar was a great general and a first-rate administrator.

While Caesar was conquering Gaul, Crassus, still seeking a military reputation, led an army against the Parthians, a people who had taken over Persia. His army was cut to pieces, and Crassus himself was killed (53 B.C.). Meanwhile, Caesar and Pompey had begun to drift apart. The First Triumvirate had come to an end.

Caesar and Pompey

Of the two surviving Triumvirs, Pompey in Rome seemed to have the better position. Mob violence in the city had made orderly government impossible; it created such a dangerous situation that in 52 B.C. Pompey was elected sole consul with practically dictatorial powers. He dominated the Roman government; he was hailed as *Princeps,* or First Citizen. Yet he was not secure as long as Caesar commanded an intensely loyal army in Gaul and northern Italy.

Pompey's obvious move was to try to deprive Caesar of his military command, an act that would have ended Caesar's political career and perhaps his life. But Caesar had friends in Rome, and the Senate was afraid of starting a civil war. It tried to arrange a compromise by which both Caesar and Pompey would give up their armies, but Pompey would have been perfectly safe in Rome without an army and Caesar would not. Caesar therefore refused to give up his command. In 49 B.C. the Senate ordered Pompey to march against him.

Caesar's outstanding quality as a general was his ability to make quick decisions and to carry them out rapidly. There was no real army in Italy; Pompey's military supporters were mainly in Spain and Greece. Caesar had to strike at once to avoid being caught in a pincers. He marched his army across the Rubicon, a little river marking the boundary between his province of Cisalpine Gaul and Italy, and thundered down on Rome. Pompey, unable to defend the city, fled to Greece with most of the Senate. Caesar had to spend a year securing his position in the West, which gave Pompey time to build a large and well-trained army. When Caesar followed him to Greece, the fighting at first went in Pompey's favor, but Caesar finally won a decisive victory at Pharsalus in 48 B.C. Although Pompey managed to escape to Egypt, he was murdered there by order of the king. Caesar and his lieutenants spent the next three years overcoming supporters of Pompey in Spain, North Africa, and the East. By 45 B.C. Caesar was master of the Roman state.

Caesar's Rule, 48–44 B.C.

Caesar's rule was too short for us to know what his plans were, and it is likely that he himself was not very sure what was to be done. It was clear that the old constitution had collapsed and that the Roman state must be led by one man. But the Romans still hated the idea of a king, and Caesar had to combine several offices to get the power he needed. He was *imperator* (whence our word *emperor*); that is, he had the *imperium,* the full right of military and civil command. He was dictator for life by vote of the Senate. He enjoyed the privileges and immunity of a tribune. These, and other titles and privileges that he accumulated one by one, made Caesar a king in all but name.

With personal command of the army it was not too difficult to restore order in Rome and in the provinces. Beyond this, Caesar's program was not unlike the programs of Sulla and Pompey, though it was carried out on a larger scale. More land was distributed to veterans, and Roman colonies (in effect, transplanted army divisions that became centers of Roman power in conquered lands) were established in the provinces. The Senate was enlarged again; this time a few provincial leaders were given seats. Caesar, like his predecessors, tried to lessen corruption in provincial administration, but since he did not change the basic system of giving short-term appointments to proconsuls and other ex-officials, he did little to suppress the temptation to loot and run. Although Caesar managed to speed up the Romanization of the western provinces and gained the support of some of the upper classes in Gaul and Spain, the full incorporation of the provincials into Roman society was still a long way in the future. His most lasting reform was to change the Roman calendar, which was based on an unworkable compromise between a lunar and a solar year. By adopting the 365-day Egyptian year, with an extra day every four years, he introduced the system that, with minor changes, is still used.

Many senators saw their careers blocked because they had opposed Caesar; others, who believed in the old Roman tradition of government, were shocked by the unconstitutional accumulation of power in the hands of one man. The result was a widespread conspiracy. When Caesar entered the Senate on the Ides of March (March 15), 44 B.C., the conspirators, led by Brutus and Cassius, stabbed him to death.

The Murder of Caesar

44 B.C.

The *Lives,* written by the Greek historian Plutarch around 100 A.D., supplies valuable information on Greek and Roman history, particularly on the confusing years of the late Republic. As may be seen from this passage, Plutarch's *Lives* served as a source of Shakespeare's play *Julius Caesar.*

When Caesar entered, the senate stood up to show their respect to him, and of Brutus's confederates, some came about his chair and stood behind it. . . . Tillius, laying hold of his robe with both his hands, pulled it down from his neck, which was the signal for the assault. Casca gave him the first cut in the neck. . . . Those who were not privy to the design were astonished, and their horror and amazement at what they saw were so great that they durst not fly nor assist Caesar, nor so much as speak a word. But those who came prepared for the business enclosed him on every side. For it had been agreed that they should each of them make a thrust at him, and flesh themselves with his blood; for which reason Brutus also gave him one stab in the groin. Some say that he fought and resisted all the rest, shifting his body to avoid the blows, and calling out for help, but that when he saw Brutus's sword drawn, he covered his face with his robe and submitted, letting himself fall . . . at the foot of the pedestal on which Pompey's statue stood. . . .

From Plutarch, *The Lives of Noble Grecians and Romans,* trans. by John Dryden, rev. by Arthur Hugh Clough (New York: Modern Library, n.d.), pp. 892–93.

THE SECOND TRIUMVIRATE 43–36 B.C.

Men like Brutus, who represented the interests of the old senatorial class, were convinced that by killing Caesar they could restore the old Republic. But the old system had broken down completely, and the Senate had little popular support. The trouble was that no one else had much support either. Brutus and Cassius left Rome to take up military commands in the East. Mark Antony, who was consul at the time, was loyal to Caesar's memory; he gained the support of the veterans and some of the lower classes by his famous oration at Caesar's funeral. His position was challenged by Octavian, Caesar's grandnephew and adopted son. Octavian, a frail and sickly lad of eighteen, had very little popular support at first. Cicero and other senators, thinking that it was safe to use him against Mark Antony, accepted him as Caesar's true successor. But Octavian, even at that age, was an astute politician and knew where the real power lay. He used his name of Caesar to gain popularity with the people and, more importantly, with the army. When he had gained all he could from the Senate, he switched sides suddenly and joined Antony and Lepidus (another of Caesar's lieutenants). With Caesar's armies be-

Coin commemorating the death of Caesar. One side bears the portrait of Brutus; the other side shows the assassins' daggers, and in-between the cap of liberty.

hind them, the three men formed the Second Triumvirate, and marched on Rome in November of 44 B.C. There the assembly granted them full power for five years.

The first act of the Second Triumvirate was a bloody proscription in which thousands of political opponents were put to death. Cicero, a personal as well as a political enemy of Antony, headed the list. While terrifying the opposition, the Triumvirs divided confiscated lands among veterans and won the support of a new class of landholders. Next, the Triumvirate took its armies across the sea to Macedonia, where they won a quick victory over Brutus and Cassius in 42 B.C.

The three men now divided the Roman world among themselves. Antony had the largest army and controlled both Gaul and the East. Italy was common ground to all three Triumvirs. As neither Octavian nor Lepidus had much military power, Antony paid little attention to his colleagues. In a series of struggles Octavian crushed Lepidus and gradually united Italy behind himself. Lepidus was driven into retirement, but Antony still seemed secure in the East, with its wealth and its tradition of one-man rule.

Antony began to lose support when he became the lover and then the consort of Cleopatra, Queen of Egypt. Although Caesar had also had an affair with Cleopatra, he did not let it interfere with serious business. Antony did: he lived with Cleopatra at the court in Alexandria and rather neglected his other territories. Like many later ill-advised Roman generals, he started a war with the Parthians (who now held Persia). Nothing of any value was gained, and thousands of Roman soldiers were killed, making Antony appear a poor general and un-Roman. By 32 B.C. Octavian felt strong enough to move against Antony. He exaggerated and exploited reports that Antony wanted to give Rome's eastern provinces to Cleopatra's children. Then he secured a decree depriving Antony of

THE EXPANSION OF THE ROMAN REPUBLIC BEYOND ITALY First century B.C.

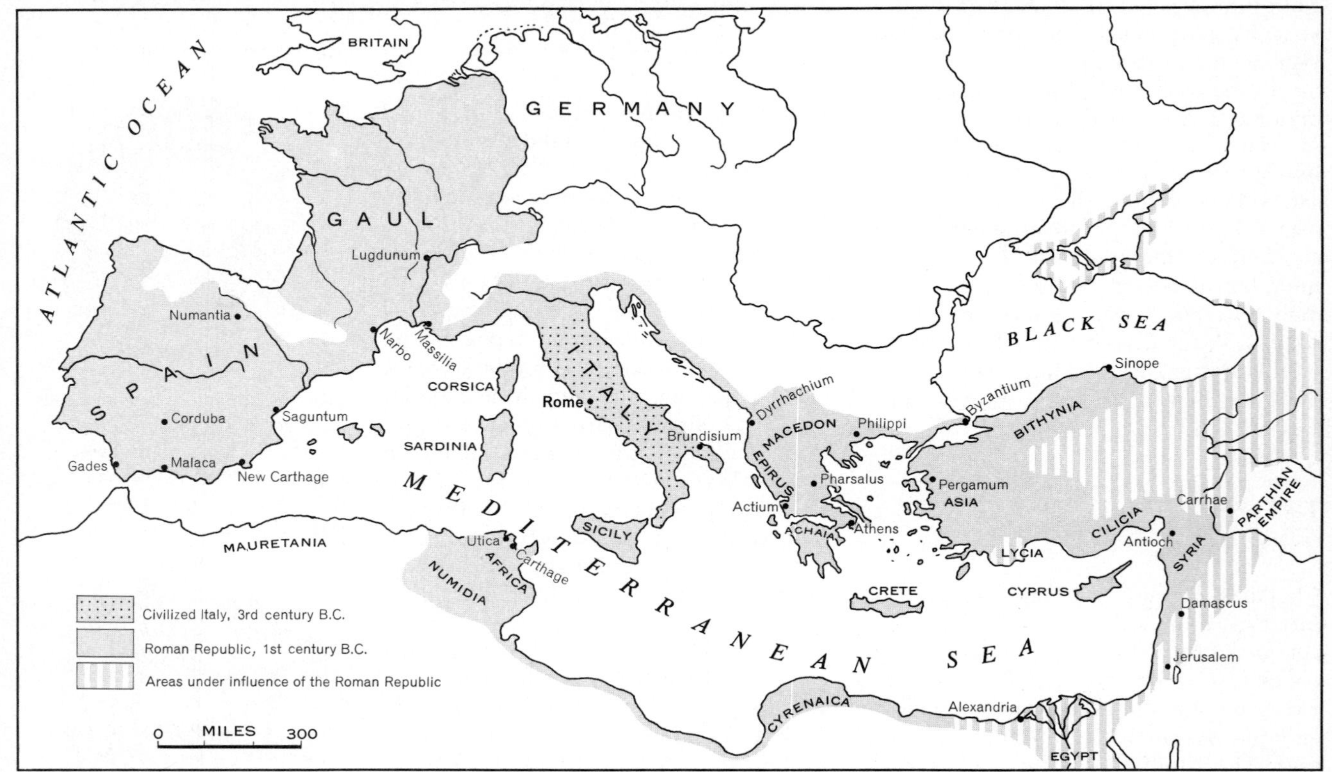

his command. It took some time for each side to marshal its strength, but the two rival forces finally met in the naval battle of Actium in 31 B.C. Octavian's fleet, commanded by his very capable lieutenant, Agrippa, won a decisive victory. Antony fled and later committed suicide; Cleopatra followed his example when she found that she could strike no bargain with Octavian. Egypt was annexed by the victor.

The battle of Actium ended the long period of civil war. Octavian was the master of the Roman world. He proclaimed the restoration of the Republic, but, like Caesar, he occupied all the positions of power. Unlike Caesar, he was able to make his monopoly of power acceptable to the vast majority of citizens and subjects. No military commander opposed him; no politician roused the discontented; no political theorists complained about the break with old traditions. Octavian was to be chief of state for over forty years, and during those years the Roman Empire was born.

Suggestions for Further Reading

Note: Asterisk denotes a book available in paperback edition.

General

The surveys of ancient history mentioned at the end of Chapter 1 have sections on the Roman era. There are also many reliable texts devoted specifically to Rome, of which one of the best is H. H. Scullard, *History of the Roman World from 753 to 146 B.C.*, 3rd ed. (1961). A. E. R. Boak's *A History of Rome to A.D. 565* has been revised by W. G. Sinnigen (1977), and is useful and clear. Shorter but more vivid are M. I. Rostovtzeff, *Rome** (1964), and D. R. Dudley, *The Civilization of Rome** (1962). M. Grant, *The World of Rome** (1964), emphasizes Roman institutions, customs, and attitudes. A very rich sampling of source readings is collected in the first volume of N. Lewis and M. Reinhold, eds., *Roman Civilization** (1951).

Early Italy, Roman Political Evolution, and Roman Expansion

O. J. Brendel, *Etruscan Art** (1978) is first-rate. H. H. Scullard, *The Etruscan Cities and Rome* (1967), and R. Bloch, *The Etruscans* (1958), provide up-to-date accounts of a period still quite obscure and complicated. Bloch carries the story further in his *The Origins of Rome* (1966). On the evolution of Rome's constitution, L. Homo, *Roman Political Institutions** (1929, 1962), needs updating but is still the best. Expansion throughout Italy is described in great detail by E. T. Salmon, *Samnium and the Samnites* (1967) and *Roman Colonization under the Republic* (1969). Two recent works unfold Rome's developing power overseas against Carthage and the Hellenistic states: R. M. Errington, *The Dawn of Empire* (1972), and E. Badian, *Roman Imperialism in the Late Republic* (1968).

The Last Century of the Republic, 146–30 B.C.

There is such a wealth of material on this complex and chaotic century that only a sampling can be mentioned here. Students interested in a detailed account of the period may consult either F. B. Marsh, *History of the Roman World from 146 to 30 B.C.*, 3rd ed. (1961), or H. H. Scullard, *From the Gracchi to Nero: A History of Rome from 133 B.C. to A.D. 68* (1975). L. R. Taylor, *Party Politics in the Age of Caesar** (1949), gives a concise picture of Roman politics in the later years of this era. R. Syme, *The Roman Revolution** (1939), a classic, offers a detailed but exciting account of the social as well as the political changes that accompanied the failure of the Republic and the creation of the Empire. See also R. E. Smith, *The Failure of the Roman Republic* (1955), and J. M. Carter, *The Battle of Actium: The Rise and Triumph of Augustus Caesar* (1970).

For a description of Roman society in the late Republic, see T. Frank, *Life and Literature in the Roman Republic** (1930). The best studies of Cicero are R. E. Smith, *Cicero the Statesman* (1966), and D. Stockton, *Cicero* (1971). F. R. Cowell, *Cicero and the Roman Republic** (1956), combines a short, lively biography of Cicero with a discussion of the politics of the era. There are many excellent biographies of Caesar as well as many that are not. The most valuable is M. Gelzer, *Caesar, Politician and Statesman* (1968). D. Earl, *The Moral and Political Tradition of Rome* (1967), offers striking insights into the culture and psychology of the times.

4 The Early Roman Empire
27 B.C.–284 A.D.

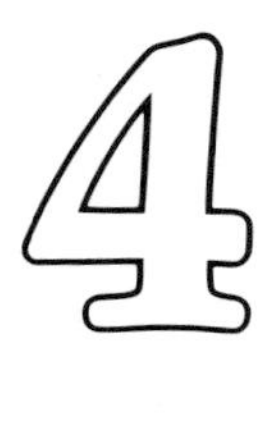

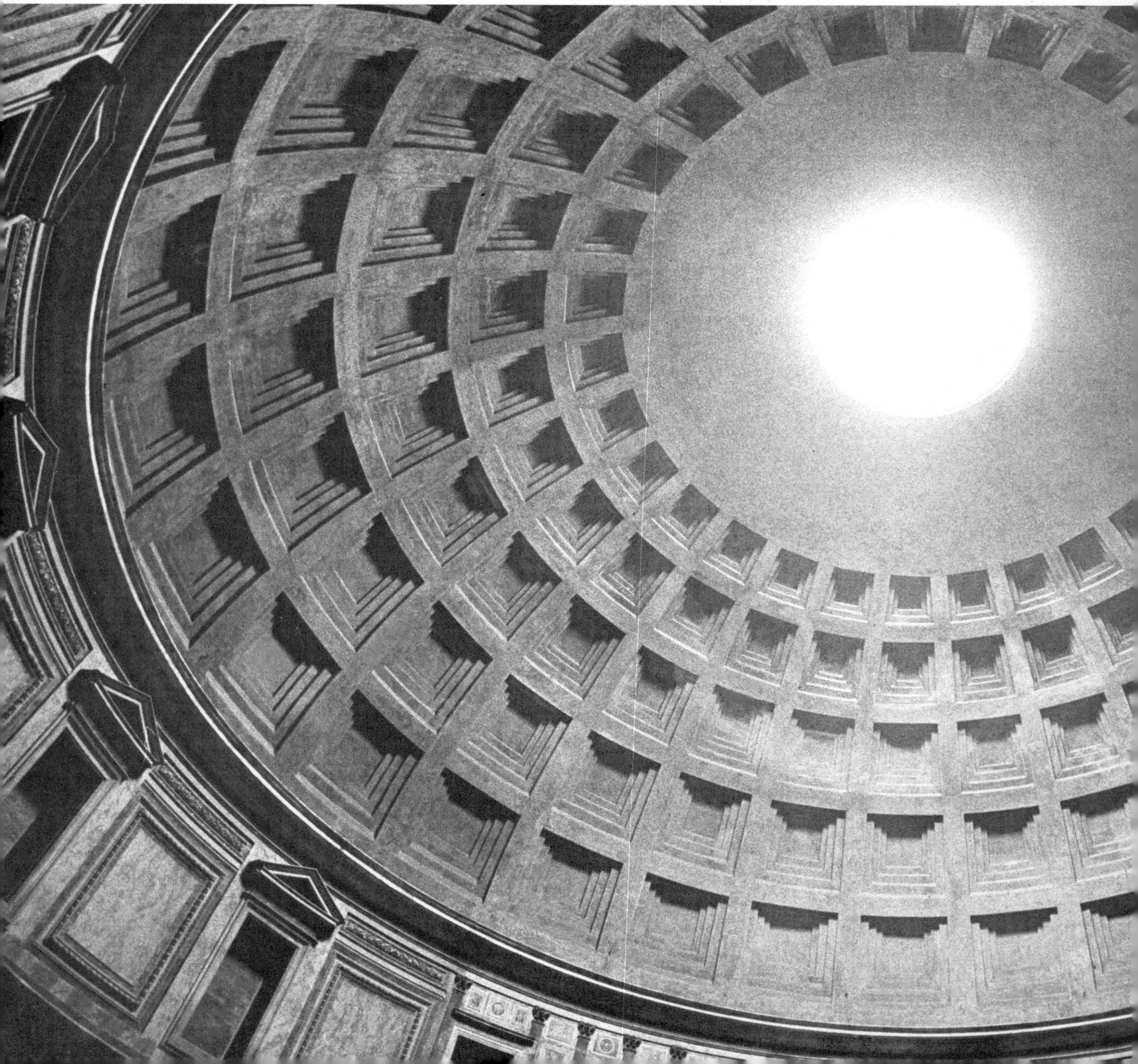

Returning in triumph to Rome after his victory at Actium, Octavian worked carefully and cautiously to solidify his position. He was quite willing to conciliate the upper classes by preserving old institutions. Consuls were elected every year; the Senate, purged of its recalcitrant members and filled with Octavian's supporters, continued to meet; even the popular assembly was summoned from time to time to give formal approval to Octavian's proposals. But no one was deceived by this facade of republican respectability; as far as we can see, no one cared. The common people simply wanted tranquility, and the Senate theoretically kept its old powers. Since Octavian had been given full power to restore order and stability, it seemed sensible to let him make all the important decisions. Like Caesar, he was *imperator,* commander of all the armies. Like Caesar, he had the power and immunities of a tribune, including the right to propose laws. He spoke first in the Senate, thus controlling the flow of business through that body; he had his own staff of officials and advisers. He was not quite a sovereign, since theoretically the Senate or the assembly could have voted him out of power if he had ever lost his ability to control them. But he was more than a political boss, because he was surrounded by an aura of sanctity and infallibility that no boss has ever enjoyed.

Octavian himself preferred to be called "Princeps," or First Citizen, and his government and those of his immediate successors are often called the period of the "Principate." But in 27 B.C. the Senate gave him the title of Augustus. Anyone who was *augustus* was to be looked on with awe and reverence. It was a title that could be used of gods as well as men; it carried overtones of holiness, dignity, wisdom, and authority. Thus, to oppose Augustus was not only politically inexpedient, it was also immoral.

THE PRINCIPATE OF AUGUSTUS 27 B.C.–14 A.D.

Augustus could not have had a very clear concept of the form and extent of imperial authority, since he had only begun the process of developing that authority. But he did have a clear idea of what he wanted to do with his power: there was to be security, a revival of the old Roman virtues, and stability throughout the Roman world.

Theoretically, the Senate was to help Augustus in this task. Rome and Italy would be governed by the Senate and the elected magistrates, and provincial districts that were completely pacified and

The dome of the Pantheon in Rome (*ca.* 125 A.D.), with its oculus at the crown.

27 B.C.	14 A.D.	68	96	180 A.D.
Principate of Augustus	Julio-Claudian Emperors	Flavian Emperors	The "Five Good Emperors"	

needed no armies would be governed by senatorial representatives (proconsuls and the like). Augustus, with permanent proconsular power, had authority over all the provinces in which armies were stationed. Though most of these provinces were backward and poor, they were far more numerous than those that were entrusted to senators. Moreover, Augustus held Egypt, the wealthiest part of the Empire.

In practice, the division of power, while it secured political tranquility, had some weaknesses. To be secure Augustus had to control Rome and Italy. Some senators, unhappy about their reduced role in government, secretly intrigued against the emperor. At the same time, the Senate could not take any initiatives. Augustus formulated the program of the government. Some of his projects, such as a reform of morals and a revival of the old Roman religion, had little effect. The upper classes officially supported the religious revival, since they enjoyed the prestige and income derived from priestly offices, but they remained quite uninhibited in their sexual activities. The rest of the population showed no great interest in official religious activities. Rome was a cosmopolitan city; even Augustus could not make it revert to the idealized social patterns of the early Republic.

In the provinces the old problem of an inadequate and untrained bureaucracy continued to exist. There were few Roman officials in any province, and most of them served only for short periods. No doubt the lieutenants of Augustus who administered his provinces were somewhat more honest than senatorial governors had been in the past. However, imperial provinces had to support a Roman army, while senatorial provinces did not. In general, Augustus would not permit the flagrant maladministration that had recurred in the last century of the Republic, and under his rule provincial grievances were lessened, though not ended.

Augustus issued these coins to proclaim the submission of Egypt and Armenia to Roman power.

Even with these strains, there was no danger that the Roman Empire would fall to pieces. In the first place, there were no longer independent armies, each loyal to its own general. Augustus was commander-in-chief, and his close friend Agrippa was his chief of staff. The army was more or less insulated from the rest of the population, since enlistments were for a period of twenty years. About half of the army was made up of Roman citizens, enrolled in some twenty-five legions of (theoretically) six thousand men each. At the end of their service these men were given plots of land, and occasionally cash bonuses. The rest of the army was made up of provincials who served as auxiliary troops. The legions were usually under full strength, so Augustus had about 250,000 soldiers. This army was completely loyal to him and numerous enough to put down any uprising.

The second factor that made the inadequate Roman administrative system viable was that it actually had very little administrative work to do. In one way or another, most of the details of government were turned over to local authorities. On the fringes of the Empire were semi-independent kingdoms, like that of Herod in Judea, which controlled their own internal affairs. Even more numerous were the city-states, which administered rural districts from an urban center. As long as local aristocracies kept order in these city-states there was relatively little interference from Roman authorities. In fact, the system worked so well that it was transferred to the less developed parts of the Empire. The Gauls, for example, were encouraged to develop cities that could act as administrative centers for each tribe.

The Frontiers

Augustus wanted to round out the holdings of the Empire in order to make his frontiers more defensible. In most places this was done fairly easily. The border with the Parthians was fixed at the Euphrates, thus ending for a time the Parthian wars. It took only a little fighting to establish firm boundaries between Judea and Arabia, Egypt and Ethiopia, and North Africa and the Berber desert tribes.

The one frontier that was never certain and never secure was the frontier with the Germans. The Rhine was not a good boundary. As Caesar had discovered, the Germans frequently pushed across the river into Gaul. The Rhine also made an awkward angle with the Danube, which was a possible frontier against the eastern Germans. It was clearly desirable to push the Germans back from the Rhine to the Elbe, but this advance was checked in 9 A.D. when the German chieftain Arminius (Herman) annihilated three Roman legions. Though Arminius became a national hero for modern Germany, his fellow chieftains killed him soon after his great victory. Augustus did not try to take advantage of this act; Germany was not worth risking another three legions. His stepsons, Tiberius and Drusus, did advance toward the Danube line in what are now Switzerland and Austria, and later in the first century, the middle Rhine and the upper Danube were linked by a fortified wall. But on the whole, little German territory was permanently annexed by Rome.

Augustus acquired a considerable amount of territory in creating defensible boundaries for Rome. The lands he acquired, however, had more strategic than economic value. The conquest of Alpine territory, for example, did not produce the flood of gold and highly skilled slaves that had come from the conquest of Asia Minor. There were no magnificent triumphs, such as those celebrated by Pompey. Except for the island of Britain, which was to be conquered in 43 A.D., and some short-lived conquests in the East, Rome had reached the limits of its expansion.

Augustus' Rule

Augustus had not been very popular as a young man, and the Senate was never entirely happy about his dominant position. But, as in many other cases, the mere length of his reign enhanced his popularity; one could scarcely imagine Rome without Augustus. Moreover, Augustus deliberately tried to build up support for his government. New official positions were created for the equestrians, and the class as a whole profited from an increase in commerce and in

THE GERMAN PROBLEM
First and second centuries B.C.

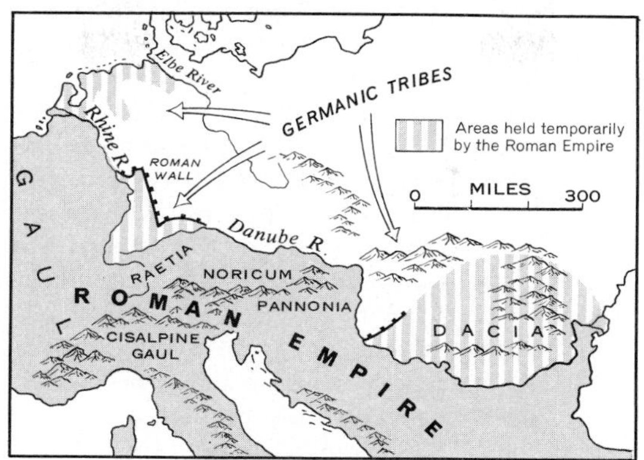

The Deeds of Augustus

This excerpt is from a long epitaph that Augustus composed for himself in his old age, and that was inscribed on brazen columns at Rome and copied in stone in many provincial cities. The only relatively complete copy that has survived is at Ankara (Ancyra). Note how Augustus poses as the preserver of the old Roman Republic.

In my twentieth year, acting upon my own judgment . . . I raised an army by means of which I restored to liberty the Republic which had been oppressed by the tyranny of a faction. . . . Those who killed my father [Julius Caesar], I drove into exile . . . and when they waged war against the Republic I twice defeated them in battle. . . . I have extended the boundaries of all the provinces of the Roman people. . . . I have reduced to a state of peace . . . the lands enclosed by the ocean from Gades [Cadiz] to the mouth of the Elbe. . . . I have added Egypt to the empire of the Roman people. . . . I accepted no office which was contrary to the customs of the country. . . . When I had put an end to the civil wars . . . I transferred the commonwealth from my own power to the authority of the Senate and the Roman people. In return for this favor I was given by decree of the Senate the title Augustus. . . . After that time I excelled all others in dignity, but of power I held no more than those who were my colleagues in any magistracy.

From Augustus, as quoted in *Monumentum Ancyranum: The Deeds of Augustus,* ed. and trans. by William Fairly, *Translations and Reprints* (Philadelphia: University of Pennsylvania Press, 1898), Vol. V, No. 1, pp. 12ff.

financial transactions. The lower classes of Rome were kept quiet by increasing the dole of grain and by lavish public entertainments. The inhabitants of Italy had an opportunity to take part in the establishment of new colonies in the thinly settled western provinces. Non-Roman subjects still bore heavy burdens, but at least their lands were no longer ravaged by civil wars, and Augustus had made some effort to improve provincial administration.

Augustus also tried to build up an all-inclusive patriotism that would override local loyalties. Worship of the "spirit" of Rome became an official cult. To this was added worship of the "genius" of the emperor. This was not quite the same thing as saying that the emperor was a god, but it certainly implied that he was guided and imbued by a divine spirit. Such nice distinctions were not important in the East, where rulers had long been worshiped as gods, but they were essential in Italy, which was definitely hostile to the idea of a god-king.

The Golden Age of Latin Literature

In the last years of the Republic and during the first years of the Empire Latin literature reached its peak. Prose writers dealt mainly with history, political theory, and philosophy. Cicero covered the widest range, writing extensively on ethics and rhetoric as well. His orations and letters were circulated as examples of an elegant and polished style. Caesar's accounts of his wars showed that military communiqués could have both style and political purpose. Sallust (86–34 B.C.) was an enemy of Cicero, and his account of Cicero's consulship is just about as biased as Cicero's defense of his actions. But Sallust was an excellent prose writer and could be a good historian, as he showed in his account of the *Jugurthine War* (a campaign in North Africa). The most influential historian of this period was Livy (59 B.C.–17 A.D.), who summed up the books of earlier writers in a monumental history of Rome. Most of this work has been lost, but enough survives to show that he was chiefly interested in celebrating the piety, civic spirit, and heroism of the early Romans. This was very much in keeping with Augustus' plans for a revival of the old Roman virtues, but Livy's history was more effective than imperial edicts. Livy retold legends splendidly and more than anyone else created the tradition that Roman character was the source of Roman strength, a tradition that has impressed historians for almost two thousand years.

The poets of the late Republic avoided politics. Catullus (87–54 B.C.) wrote graceful lyrics about his love affairs. The greatest poet of the Republic, and perhaps the most original of all Latin authors, was Lucretius (99–55 B.C.). In his *De rerum natura* he expressed his version of the Epicurean philosophy and his view of the universe in verses of remarkable beauty and power. Although he drew many of his ideas from Hellenistic philosophers, the synthesis was his own. But Lucretius was too speculative to appeal to the practical Roman mind; he had little influence and no successors.

The poets of the early Empire, unlike their predecessors, were deeply involved in politics. Virgil and Horace were not wealthy men; they could devote themselves to writing only because they were patronized by the emperor, or rather by one of his chief advisers, Maecenas. As a result, some of their work has an official

Contemporary bust of Cicero, the great orator of the first century B.C.

flavor. Thus when Virgil (70–19 B.C.) wrote his epic, the *Aeneid*, he was careful to include compliments to the imperial family. The poem itself argues that Rome was founded under divine auspices, that its glorious destiny had long been predicted, and that its brilliant success was due to the virtue of its founders. Virgil imitated the Homeric model, but imitation did not keep him from being a great poet; he wrote some of the most effective lines that appear in the literature of any country. His famous phrase—"Rome is to rule through law, to spare the conquered and put down the mighty from their seats,"—sums up Augustus' vision of the Empire.

Horace (65–8 B.C.) wrote official poems for Augustus' religious festivals and celebrated the virtue of the early Romans. But he was much more than an official poet. He was a shrewd and experienced man, a keen observer of human behavior, and a master of summing up his observations in brief and striking verses.

The fate of Ovid (43 B.C.–17 A.D.) shows why it was well to pay some attention to pleasing the emperor. Drawing on Greek mythology for much of his material, Ovid could tell a good story in graceful verse. But there was little morality in his sources, and Ovid did not bother to add any. Since Augustus was trying to restore the old Roman virtues it is not surprising that Ovid was banished from his comfortable life in Rome to a very uncomfortable life on the shores of the Black Sea. His work remained popular, however, and was the chief source of knowledge of Greek mythology during the Middle Ages and the Renaissance.

With the exception of Lucretius, these Latin authors contributed few new ideas to the intellectual tradition of the ancient world. But they did perfect the Latin language by fixing its grammatical rules and by increasing its vocabulary. In their hands Latin became a precise and efficient language. Since much of the world's thinking was to be done in Latin for the next fifteen hundred years, this was no mean achievement. They also introduced eastern ideas to the West in a form in which they could be easily assimilated. Something was lost in the process: Latin was never able to reproduce all the subtle distinctions that could be made in Greek, and the Romans had little interest in Greek scientific work. But by borrowing from the Greeks, and by putting what they borrowed into enduring form, Latin authors laid the foundations for much of the later literature of the West.

Lucretius on Atoms

If you think that basic particles can stand still, and by standing still can beget new motions among things, you are astray and wander far from true reasoning. For since basic particles wander through the void, they must needs all be carried on either by their own weight or by a chance blow from one or other. For when in quick motion they have often met and collided, it follows that they leap apart suddenly in different directions. . . . And to show you more clearly that all the bodies of matter are constantly being tossed about, remember that there is no bottom in the sum of things, and the first bodies have nowhere to rest, since space is without end or limit. . . . Beyond doubt no rest is granted to the first bodies, . . . some after being pressed together then leap back with wide intervals, some again . . . are tossed about within a narrow compass. And those which being held in combination more closely condensed collide and leap back through tiny intervals, . . . these constitute the strong roots of stone and . . . iron and others of this kind. . . . The rest leap far apart and pass far back with long intervals between; these supply thin air for us and the gleaming light of the sun.

From Lucretius, *De rerum natura,* trans. by W. H. D. Rouse (Cambridge, Mass.: Harvard University Press, 1937), Book II, ll. 80–108.

SUCCESSORS TO AUGUSTUS 14–68 A.D.

It was clear long before Augustus died that his system of government would endure. But who was to succeed him? He was not a hereditary monarch, and he had no son. On the other hand, his own career had shown the value of family connections; he owed his position to the fact that he was the grandnephew and adopted son of Caesar. Therefore, Augustus looked around the circle of his relatives and, after a long series of intrigues and premature deaths of possible successors, settled on his stepson Tiberius. He made Tiberius his associate in the tribunician power and in the *imperium,* so that Tiberius had no trouble in taking over the government when the old

Relief of a figure thought to be Horace (fragment of a marble frieze, Greco-Roman period).

A family portrait.
Above: Claudius (*ca.* 50 A.D.).
Right: Agrippina, Claudius' wife, with her child Nero.

emperor died in 14 A.D. But the episode revealed a weakness in the imperial system that was never cured: the absence of a fixed rule of succession and the danger that the title could be seized through intrigue and violence. The Julio-Claudian emperors* (the first four successors of Augustus) all shared these problems.

*These men were all related, by blood or by marriage, to the great Roman families of the Julians and the Claudians

Tiberius (14–37 A.D.) and Caligula (37–41 A.D.)

Tiberius was an able administrator and a good general, but he had been embittered by the fact that Augustus had passed him over repeatedly in his search for a successor. Though he came from one of the most distinguished families in Rome (his father was a Claudian), many senators resented his supremacy and intrigued against him. He made more enemies by weeding out subordinates who seemed dishonest or incompetent. Quarrels in his own family over the succession led to several suspicious deaths. Disgusted with Rome and fearful for his life, Tiberius took refuge on the island of Capri near Naples. This move made it easier for intrigue to flourish in Rome. Suspicious of everyone around him, Tiberius ordered the execution of many officials and senators on charges of treason. There was general relief when he died in 37 A.D.

He was succeeded by his grandnephew, Caligula, who seemed as attractive as Tiberius had been morose. Unfortunately, Caligula was also thought to be insane. His whimsical cruelty and his lack of military sense disgusted the palace guard (the elite corps of the army) and led to a conspiracy in which Caligula was put to death.

Claudius (41–54 A.D.) and Nero (54–68 A.D.)

With the death of Caligula, some senators hoped to abolish the position of emperor and restore the Republic; others squabbled among themselves as to who should be the next emperor. All of them had forgotten that for more than a century real power had rested in the army, and that the army had no great respect for the Senate. While the senators were debating, the palace guard found Caligula's sickly uncle Claudius and proclaimed him emperor.

Claudius turned out to be a more capable ruler than anyone had expected. He initiated the conquest of Britain and gained good will in the provinces by generous grants of Roman citizenship. He started the reorganization of the imperial government by creating four administrative bureaus, each headed by a freedman (usually a liberated Greek slave). Senators still commanded armies and governed provinces and equestrians handled most of the financial affairs of the Empire, but a new imperial bureaucracy was to grow out of Claudius' group of freedmen.

Claudius married his niece Agrippina, an evil and ruthless woman who persuaded him to disinherit his son by an earlier marriage and to give the succession to her own son, Nero. She then poisoned Claudius and took control of the government, along with Nero's tutor, the philosopher Seneca, until Nero decided to take power into his own hands. When he did, he offended most of the leading men of the Empire by his lack of dignity and his cruelty. Nero was self-indulgent and unstable. He believed that he was a great poet and musician, and he traveled about the Empire performing his works. When a disastrous fire almost destroyed Rome in 64, there were rumors, almost certainly not true, that Nero had set the blaze to provide a brilliant background for a recitation of his poetry. Seeking a scapegoat, Nero blamed the fire on Rome's small community of Christians and put many of them to death.

Naturally there were plots against such a man, and naturally Nero imagined plots where none existed. He condemned to death his mother, his old friend Seneca, the poet Lucan, and the brilliant general Corbulo, who had defended the eastern frontier against the Parthians. He executed many senators and confiscated their property. And while he was building up a mountain of resentment against himself, he was paying no attention to the administration or to the army.

This time the legions led the rebellion, not the palace guard. This was a new and ominous development. The guard had been able to agree on one man; the scattered legions could not. Each group advanced the claims of its own general, and the result was the famous "year of the four emperors" (68–69). Nero, easily overthrown, committed suicide; then three army commanders in succession marched on Rome, claimed the imperial title, and promptly lost it to the next aggressor. The commander in the East, Vespasian, was wiser: he consolidated his hold on his own region and waited to see what would happen. When his rivals had killed each other off, Vespasian had no opposition. He gained control of Rome in 69 A.D. and held the imperial title until his death ten years later.

Nero as emperor.

THE EMPIRE AT ITS HEIGHT 69–180 A.D.

Vespasian's rule marked a change in the character of the Empire. His predecessors had all come from the old aristocratic families that had held the highest offices in Rome for the last three centuries. Vespasian was not an aristocrat; he came from a middle-class family (the Flavians) in a small Italian town. He had become emperor through his own efforts, not through family connections and palace intrigues. He knew the provinces better than he knew Rome, and he relied on the Roman or Romanized inhabitants of the provinces more than any of his predecessors had done. He maintained correct relations with the Senate, but the Senate

27 B.C.	14 A.D.	68	96	180 A.D.
Principate of Augustus	Julio-Claudian Emperors	Flavian Emperors	The "Five Good Emperors"	

Vespasian, founder of the Flavian dynasty.

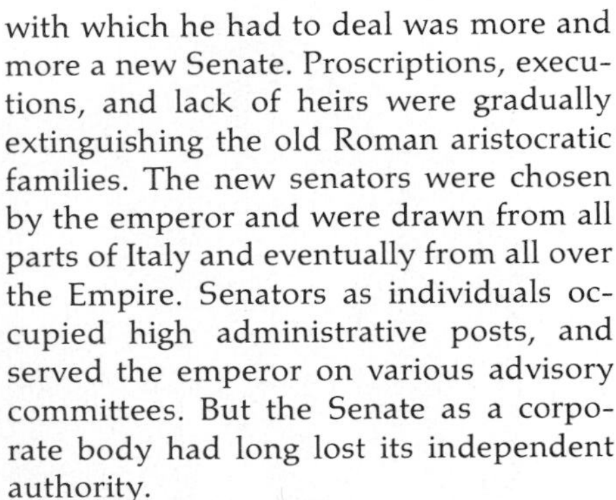

with which he had to deal was more and more a new Senate. Proscriptions, executions, and lack of heirs were gradually extinguishing the old Roman aristocratic families. The new senators were chosen by the emperor and were drawn from all parts of Italy and eventually from all over the Empire. Senators as individuals occupied high administrative posts, and served the emperor on various advisory committees. But the Senate as a corporate body had long lost its independent authority.

These tendencies continued under Vespasian's successors. Most of them had had some administrative or military experience. Most of them came from new families. Most of them knew and were concerned with the provinces—two of them were born of Roman families that had settled in Spain.

The Flavian Emperors 69–96 A.D.

Vespasian was an excellent administrator. The Empire was deeply in debt after Nero's extravagances; Vespian made it solvent by reforming the tax structure and by conducting an empire-wide census. He eliminated the practice of farming taxes (selling the right to collect taxes to corporations of bankers), which had already been cut back by earlier emperors. Procurators appointed by the emperor took over financial administration in the provinces. The vast amounts of land owned by the state or confiscated from alleged traitors were organized to produce maximum revenues. The frontiers of the Empire were strengthened in places where defense was difficult.

Vespasian was succeeded by his two sons, Titus (79–81) and Domitian (81–96). Titus was as capable as his father and, with the financial crisis over, could avoid the unpopularity caused by some of Vespasian's financial practices. Domitian seems to have ruled the provinces well, but he was disliked in Rome. The cult of the Republic was almost dead, but philosophers were now arguing that the "best man" should rule. Domitian did not seem the best man to many of his subordinates, and he grew more autocratic as he grew older. Writers accused him of wishing to be addressed as "lord and god"; whatever the truth of this accusation, he certainly executed a number of men of high rank on flimsy charges. A palace conspiracy was formed, and Domitian was assassinated in 96 A.D. The armies were taken by surprise and made no move, so that for once the Senate was able to act. With the approval of the palace guard, it chose one of its own members, Nerva, as emperor.

Trajan (*ca.* 100 A.D.).

The "Five Good Emperors" 96–180 A.D.

Nerva was an upright and distinguished senator, but he knew that he needed military support. He designated Trajan, commander of the armies on the Rhine, as his successor. With Nerva and Trajan began the era of the "five good emperors," which lasted from 96 to 180 A.D. Gibbon once wrote that this was the happiest period in the history of the human race; certainly it was the most prosperous and least troubled period in the history of the Roman Empire. Because they had no direct heirs, and perhaps because they shared a belief in the rule of "the best man," four emperors in succession passed their power on to adopted sons, and each of the men they chose proved worthy of ruling. The old problem of the succession seemed to be solved; the old jealousy between emperor and Senate almost disappeared; the old distinction between privileged Italy and oppressed provinces was practically eliminated; and the imperial administrative system was greatly improved.

This is not to say that there were no problems or no mistakes on the part of the emperors. The Germans along the lower Danube and the Parthians on the eastern frontier were a constant menace. Trajan (98–117) tried to end this danger by annexing enemy bases. He took Mesopotamia from the Parthians and Dacia (roughly, modern Romania) from the Germans at great cost in both money and lives. Under Trajan the Empire reached its greatest extent, but even Trajan could not hold all of Mesopotamia, and Dacia had to be abandoned a century and a half later.

Hadrian (117–138) was less a soldier and more an administrator. He abandoned what was left of Mesopotamia and strengthened fortifications along the frontiers. One example of these efforts is Hadrian's Wall, much of which is still visible; it was built to protect northern Britain from raids by the inhabitants of Scotland. But Hadrian's real interest was in perfecting the imperial civil service. He continued earlier trends by appointing equestrians instead of freedmen as bureau chiefs, by organizing a regular hierarchy of positions, and by developing a group of career officers who could be advanced from post to post until they reached the highest positions in the government. He kept careful watch over these men and made long trips through the Empire to inspect provincial government. His success may be measured by the fact that the reign of his successor, Antoninus Pius (138–160), was so uneventful that contemporary writers have little to say about it. The reign of Marcus Aurelius (161–180), the last of the "good emperors," was not uneventful, but his problems are discussed in a later section.

The Empire in the Second Century

From the time of Vespasian to the death of Marcus Aurelius, most inhabitants of the Empire could go about their business without fearing invasion and without suffering from misgovernment. The letters exchanged by Trajan and Pliny the Younger, who was a provincial governor in Asia Minor, show the high standards set for administrators and a real concern for the welfare of the governed. Certainly there were some corrupt officials and some cases of undue severity, but on the whole the provincials could at last feel that they were members of the Roman commonwealth, not subjects of a foreign conqueror.

The distinction between senatorial and imperial provinces had become meaningless; all provincial administration was controlled by the imperial bureaucracy. And while that bureaucracy occasionally interfered in local affairs, the city governments still had most of the responsibility for administering their towns and the surrounding countryside. The city-state was the natural unit of local government in the East, and Rome had tried to build similar units in the western provinces. By the middle of the

Inscription from Trajan's column in the Roman forum (*ca.* 114 A.D.) celebrating his victories over the Germans and Dacians: "The Senate and the Roman people to the *imperator* Caesar, son of the deified Nerva, Nerva Trajan Augustus conqueror of the Germans and the Dacians. . . ."

SENATVS·POPVLVSQVE·ROMANVS
IMP·CAESARI·DIVI·NERVAE·F·NERVAE
TRAIANO·AVG·GERM·DACICO·PONTIF
MAXIMO·TRIB·POT·XVII·IMP·VI·COS·VI·P·P
AD·DECLARANDVM·QVANTAE·ALTITVDINIS
MONS·ET·LOCVS·TAN ... IBVS·SIT·EGESTVS

Roman soldier fighting on the Danube frontier (108–109 A.D.).

second century almost all the Empire was divided into these city-states, which proved to be powerful instruments for spreading a common Greek or Latin culture and common loyalties. The Roman city-state was a state in the American, not European, sense; that is, a subordinate, but autonomous, political entity that took care of almost all the needs of the local population. All offices in the cities were reserved for men from the upper classes, who were expected to set an example of good citizenship to the rest of the community. They collected the taxes and made up any deficits in the assigned quota from their own pockets; they erected public buildings and monuments in the Roman style; they supported the official religion of Rome and the emperor. But to become one of these local notables a man had to accept Latin culture in the West and Greek culture in the East. The imperial government did not trust people who clung to old customs and spoke odd languages.

This gradual assimilation of Greco-Roman culture worked better in the West than in the East. The memory of earlier cultures was disappearing in the West, at least among the urban population. In the cities one either learned Latin and adopted Roman customs or one remained isolated from the mainstream of life. In the rural areas the process took longer. It was only in the fourth century A.D. that Gaul and Spain become thoroughly Romanized. In Britain, which was conquered late and lost early, Latin culture never struck deep roots. The East had plenty of time to assimilate Greek culture, but even though Hellenization had been going on since the third century B.C., Egyptian and Syrian traditions persisted. Most business, public and private, was conducted in Greek, but the old Oriental languages did not vanish, as Celtic gradually vanished in Gaul.

The Roman authorities, like the Hellenistic rulers of the earlier centuries, had encouraged assimilation and were reasonably satisfied with the results. Roman citizenship was given to the ruling classes of provincial cities and to provincials who served in the Roman army. By the end of the second century, most men of any standing in provincial society were citizens. When, in 212, the emperor Caracalla extended Roman citizenship to all free men in the Empire, he was only giving legal sanction to an already existing psychological reality.

The Jews

Two groups seemed deliberately to avoid assimilation, the Jews and the Christians. The Jews' concept of Jahweh as the one universal God made it impossible for them to accept the idea that in their devotion to Jahweh they were simply worshiping another manifestation of Zeus-Jupiter. The Jewish scriptures gave them an acute sense of their own identity as a people. To be integrated into Greco-Roman culture was to deny the whole meaning of their history and their special relationship with Jahweh.

Most Jews lived together in Judea. Many, however, lived in Hellenistic cities such as Alexandria. There was some mingling of Greco-Roman and Jewish cultures: the Old Testament was translated into Greek (an important basis for the later Christian version), and some

Romanized citizens were converted to Judaism. But on the whole the Jews remained a people apart. They could not take part in the sacrifices and rituals that demonstrated allegiance to the government. They had to be exempted from the state cults and military service and allowed to live by their own law.

When Rome took over the Hellenistic kingdoms, the special privileges of the Jews were confirmed and Judea was made a client kingdom. But the client kings were not very satisfactory, and after some wavering, Judea was made a Roman province. This action was resisted by the Jews, especially in Galilee, where a group called the Zealots were determined to preserve the Law of Moses (the *Torah*) with the teachings concerning the Law (the *Mishna*) and its interpretations (the *Talmud*) by using terrorist techniques. An open rebellion erupted in 66 A.D. The Jews fought heroically, but the Romans sacked Jerusalem, the capital of Judea, in 70 A.D., destroying the Temple where the Torah was kept and slaying thousands of Jews. Thousands of others were sent into slavery, many of whom were put to work building the Colosseum in Rome.

The final blow came under Hadrian. With the best of intentions, but with less than his usual sensitivity, he tried to rebuild Jerusalem as a Greco-Roman city, with a temple dedicated to Roman gods. Again Judea rebelled, and again the Jews were slaughtered by the thousands. With Judea largely depopulated, the Jewish communities around the Mediterranean became the centers of Jewish culture.

The Beginnings of Christianity

The religion that was eventually accepted by most inhabitants of the Empire was founded in the reigns of Augustus and Tiberius. Jesus of Nazareth was born about 4 B.C.;* his brief period of active teaching and the conversion of the first disciples came during the years from 26 to 30 A.D. Shortly after the birth of Jesus, Augustus had taken direct control of Judea from a client king. Many Jews dreamed of a Messiah who would free them from this foreign rule and prove

*Jesus' birth should, of course, have begun the year 1 A.D. But most Church historians now agree that there are errors in the New Testament dating. In any case, the reckoning of years from the birth of Jesus did not begin until the sixth century, and by that time an error of a few years made no great difference.

Spoils taken by the Romans from the Temple in Jerusalem (detail from the Arch of Titus, Rome, 81 A.D.).

that theirs was the only true religion. When Jesus began teaching, some Jews accepted him as the Messiah, especially since he quoted passages from the prophets that seemed to refer to such a mission. But most of these followers became discouraged when Jesus made it clear that his kingdom was "not of this world," that he was interested in a new view of the relation between God and man, and not in earthly politics. On the other hand, those who really understood his message were convinced that he was the Christ, the Son of God, and that his teaching of the love of God and the brotherhood of man was the most important revelation that the human race had ever received.

The dominant group among the Jews at this time was the sect of the Pharisees, strict upholders of the Jewish Law. They were shocked by Jesus' claim that he bore a new revelation that superseded the Law and even more by his assertion that he was the Son of God. They accused Jesus of blasphemy and denounced him to the Roman governor, Pontius Pilate. Pilate was not very sure what he should do, but Judea was a troubled area, and anyone who stirred up strong popular feelings might be dangerous to Roman authority. So about 30 A.D. Jesus was crucified—a Roman form of execution reserved for criminals of the lowest classes.

Pilate and the Pharisees thought that this was the end of the matter. But the disciples remained faithful, for they were convinced that Jesus had risen from the dead and had repeatedly appeared to his followers. The Resurrection gave them courage and confidence. They began to understand the divine purpose: God had become man and had suffered on earth to redeem the sins of mankind. All who believed in Jesus would be saved by his sacrifice. Strong in their faith, they began to make converts among the Jews of Palestine and Syria. At this time they began to be called Christians.

The new religion was at first only a Jewish sect, ignored by the rest of the

THE ROMAN EMPIRE AT ITS HEIGHT 117 A.D.

world and bitterly opposed by many Jews. At this critical point the conversion of Saul of Tarsus enabled Christianity to broaden its appeal. Saul, though Greek in education and Roman in citizenship, was a fiercely orthodox Jew who felt it was his duty to attack the Christians. In the midst of his campaign he suffered a physical collapse (in the Acts of the Apostles it is said he was blinded); on his recovery he announced his conversion to the faith he had opposed. He took the name of Paul and began preaching Christianity in the cities of Asia Minor and Greece, and eventually in Rome itself.

It was Paul who made Christianity attractive to the non-Jewish inhabitants of the Roman world. He persuaded early Christian leaders that many Jewish ritual practices could be abandoned; one could be a Christian without first having to become a Jew. He also explained Christian doctrine in terms that were understandable to men thinking in terms of Greek philosophy. In his Epistles, he began the work of building a Christian philosophy and theology that could appeal to men of all races.

Meanwhile, other disciples were spreading the faith outside Palestine. Peter, the leader of the group, probably went to Rome; very early tradition holds that he was head of the Roman Church and was martyred there. Other churches were established in Egypt, Asia Minor, Greece, and later in Gaul and in Spain. Stories of the sayings and doings of Jesus were collected and by the end of the first century began to take shape as the Gospels. To these were added the letters and acts of the apostles, and so the body of writings that eventually became the New Testament was formed.

Christianity was a vigorous, active faith at a time when the old state religions were losing their credibility and the mystery cults were not very precise about their doctrines. Its leaders were of humble or, at most, middle-class origins, so its appeal was greatest among the poor and, in the West, among eastern slaves and laborers. There were enough Christians in Rome so that Nero could blame them for the great fire that almost destroyed the city in 64 A.D. During the second century they began to cause problems for the imperial governors. They were persecuted sporadically, most often by local citizens, though the most serious attacks did not come until the third century.

The problem was that, like the Jews, the Christians were a people apart who

This marble relief pictures a small Italian city as it looked in the days of the early Caesars. Blocks of two- and three-story tenements are enclosed by the ancient town wall. At the right, the country villas of the wealthy, with their gardens and colonnades, sprawl across the nearby hillsides.

A gladiator contends with a wild animal (detail from a fourth-century mosaic).

refused to participate in rituals honoring the state and the emperor. Unlike the Jews, they were not protected by ancient privileges. They were not a small ethnic minority; they were infiltrating the Roman and Romanized population. Their religion was an unknown quantity and their exclusiveness made them objects of suspicion. The imperial government did not care for them, but was puzzled about how to handle the problem. Even the "good emperors" could find no satisfactory solution, as a letter from Trajan to Pliny the Younger, governor of Bithynia, demonstrates (see p. 95). Trajan did not want to hunt down Christians, but if they were found, he did want them to renounce their faith by making a sacrifice to the gods of the state religion. Later emperors were less lenient.

Society and Economy

By the time the Empire had reached its greatest extent, Rome had a population close to a million. In the East, only Alexandria was as large, but in both East and West there were some cities of a hundred thousand or more. The rich lived luxuriously in their town houses or suburban villas, but the poor were crowded into tenements that rose to five or six stories. The ground floor was used for small shops; the upper stories were divided into small, dark apartments. Roman engineers knew how to bring water into a city by aqueducts, but to raise it to the upper stories of a tall building was expensive and only the rich could afford it. It is not surprising that most people spent as much time in the street as possible. The emperors had to forbid vehicular traffic in Rome during the day; all deliveries were made at night when the streets were less crowded.

For the Romans, as for the Greeks before them, the existence of public buildings, market squares, and gardens was an absolute necessity. The old Roman Forum was lined with temples and shops; the emperors built several new forums nearby. They also provided the people with arenas for public spectacles. The Colosseum, started by Vespasian and dedicated by Titus, held 50,000 spectators. It was used chiefly for combats between gladiators or between slaves, criminals, and wild beasts. The Circus Maximus, which could seat about 150,000 persons, was the center for chariot racing. There were also elegant public baths, though the largest ones were not built until the third century.

Most of the western cities were like Rome—they had forums, temples, arenas, and baths. The eastern cities, with older traditions, had more individuality. But, as archeological excavation shows, there was enough resemblance among

Greek and Roman merchants traveled freely in the stable world of the first two centuries A.D. Their ships could average more than one hundred miles a day (detail from a sarcophagus from Ostia, *ca.* second or third century A.D.).

the cities so that people traveling through the Empire found themselves at home wherever they went.

The class structure was as rigid as it had been under the Republic. Although few of the old Roman senatorial families had survived the civil wars and the purges of the early emperors, a new senatorial class had replaced them. This class had little political power, but it enjoyed great wealth and held vast estates in Italy and in the provinces. It insisted more than ever on its social supremacy to make up for its loss of authority. The equestrians, as before, were not far behind the senators. Next came the municipal aristocracies. Far below these privileged groups were the country folk (small farmers, tenants, and laborers), and in the cities, shopkeepers, workers, and unemployed freedmen. And at the very bottom, as in the days of the Republic, were the slaves, who worked in chain gangs in mines and on the great Roman estates.

The imperial government increased the rigidity of the class structure in various ways. By the second century the law made a strict distinction between upper and lower classes, not only in officeholding but also in judicial procedure. Only the *humiliores* (the more humble) could be tortured or executed in cruel ways, such as by crucifixion. However, some attempts were made to improve the lot of the slaves: they could not be treated as cruelly as they had been under the Republic, and the freeing of slaves was favored. The very poor could improve their position by enlisting in the army.

Internal peace stimulated commerce, especially in the eastern cities. Greeks, Syrians, and Egyptians brought their wares to western markets in Gaul and in Britain. They also went far beyond the borders of the Empire. There was an active trade with India and indirect trade with China, since Chinese merchants brought their silk to Indian markets. (Some Romans, however, like Pliny the Elder [23–79], were concerned that the export of gold to India and other areas to conduct such trade would cause a gold drain in Rome.) There were also expeditions into central Africa in search of wild animals to stock the arenas, while Germany furnished amber, furs, hides, and slaves.

The Romans were not interested in the invention of labor-saving devices. The crane pictured here required the work of many slaves to operate the treadmill (detail from a tomb relief, first century A.D.).

This prosperity, however, rested on very narrow foundations. The chief occupation of most inhabitants of the Empire remained agriculture, which was not increasing in efficiency; more land was being cultivated, but agricultural techniques were not improving. Some areas were declining in population and wealth. Generally speaking, economic growth in the outlying provinces was matched by decline toward the center of the Empire. For example, when olive trees were planted in Spain and vineyards in Gaul, there was no reason to export oil or wine from Italy or Greece. Agriculture supported the upper classes in luxury and the lower classes at a subsistence level, but it did not produce very much of a surplus for investment.

Industrial production was even less profitable. Famous pottery, for example, was made in Etruria and was widely exported, but this center declined as

A Roman girl with a writing tablet is depicted in this fresco from Pompeii (*ca.* 70 A.D.).

Roman techniques spread to the provinces. When southern Gaul could produce pottery indistinguishable from the best Italian ware, there was no reason to pay the cost of transport from Italy. Roman manufactures were not very complicated—textiles, metalwares, and pottery. It was easy for each region to become relatively self-sufficient in goods for ordinary consumption. Luxury goods were another matter, but producers and traders who dealt in these goods formed a very small part of the population.

The Romans were backward in finding new sources of energy. They never learned how to harness horses so that they could pull heavy loads. As a result, land transport was limited to small, two-wheeled carts, usually drawn by oxen. Although water mills were used to grind grain in places like Rome, elsewhere grain was ground by hand. True, the flow of Mediterranean rivers was irregular, but not all Romans lived on the shores of the Mediterranean. The rainy regions of Gaul had few water mills in Roman times, whereas there were thousands of them in the Middle Ages. In a subsistence economy, with a surplus of manpower (at least until the third century), there was no real need for labor-saving devices. Roman conservatism made innovation even more difficult. They simply did not think in terms of applying scientific theories to practical problems; science was for gentlemen, not mechanics.

Art and Literature of the Silver Age

Roman architecture, like Roman law, expressed the Roman desire for order and stability. It reached its peak at the end of the first and the beginning of the second century, a little earlier than the time of the great jurists of the Empire. It was based on two techniques that had long interested the Romans: the use of concrete as a building material and the use of the round arch as the essential unit of construction. As the quality of concrete improved, architects were no longer confined to rectilinear structures of stone columns and beamed ceilings; they could curve their walls and roof their buildings with vaults and domes. The arch had long been used for bridging rivers and carrying aqueducts across deep valleys; when it came to be used in building, it made possible a whole new variety of forms. A series of arches formed a barrel vault over rooms or passageways; an arch at the end of a large enclosed space could be pierced to admit light; a rotated arch formed a dome. The Romans could construct large and magnificent buildings with these techniques—imperial palaces, baths, and temples like the Pantheon, which was dedicated to all the gods (and is still in use as a Christian church). Unlike the Greeks, who were interested largely in exteriors (the sanctuary of a Greek temple was often a small, dark room), the Romans achieved their most impressive effects in the interiors of their buildings. The heart of the Pantheon was the great circular sanctuary covered by an enormous dome and lit by windows high in the walls and in the center of the dome itself. It gave a feeling of power, order, and authority; it expressed the majesty of the Roman state and the insignificance of the individual.

This new "imperial style" spread throughout the provinces, from Britain to Syria. Every city had its baths, its temples, its arenas (such as the Colosseum in Rome), which were based on a series of arches. This common style was a unifying force and was so perceived at the time. Both the central and local governments spent large sums of money on public buildings, and thought that it was money well spent. And the "imperial style" left an indelible impression on the European mind. Again and again in the centuries that followed the fall of Rome, architects tried to recreate the vast enclosed spaces of the Roman buildings.

Roman wall frescoes tended to be realistic, but at times served merely as decorative, high-class wallpaper. Roman sculpture was also realistic—busts of emperors and famous men, scenes of battles and processions on triumphal arches. (Here the arch was a sign of power and glory; it had no other function.) But the sculptors at times went beyond realism and expressed the inner character of the people they were portraying.

The literature of the late first century and second century A.D.—sometimes called the Silver Age—gave the Latin style its highest polish. Pungent epigrams and pithy sayings mark the work of the leading writers. In poetry Juvenal satirized and Martial (*ca.* 40–102) exemplified the corruption of Roman society. Tacitus (55–118), the greatest of the Roman historians, was also a master of the epigrammatic style. He was strongly prejudiced in favor of the old aristocracy and against the emperors, and he attached too much importance to gossip about intrigues at court. But few historians have written so well or have been so skilled in characterizing their subjects. His description of one of the ephemeral emperors of 68–69 A.D. as a man who in everyone's opinion was qualified to rule if only he hadn't tried it would fit a good many subsequent politicians. We still see the emperors of the first century through Tacitus' eyes.

Other writers of the period have had somewhat less influence. Seneca (*ca.* 4 B.C.–65 A.D.), Nero's tutor and victim, was a Stoic philosopher; he wrote the only Roman tragedies that have survived—very noble and rather bloody (hence their influence on Renaissance drama). Seneca's nephew and fellow victim Lucan (39–65 A.D.) composed the *Pharsalia,* an epic on republican resistance to Caesar, which has some memorable lines. Suetonius (*ca.* 75–110) in his *Lives of the Twelve Caesars* regaled his readers with amusing anecdotes about Julius Caesar and the emperors through Domitian. Josephus (*ca.* 37–100), a Jewish army officer during the rebellion of 66 A.D. who went over to the Roman side, tried to explain the peculiar history and nature of his people in his *Jewish Antiquities.* Finally, the elder Pliny (13–79 A.D.) compiled a *Natural History,* an account of the entire world of nature, full of good stories but not very accurate.

Two promising starts were made at creating the literary form we know as the novel. One was the *Satyricon* by Petronius (d. 65 A.D.), an elegant courtier at the time of Nero. The other was the *Golden Ass* by Apuleius (*ca.* 125–180), who lived in North Africa. Both works bear an extraordinary resemblance to the first novels in modern European languages. Both describe the adventures of heroes whom misfortune dooms to wander among strange, often disreputable, people. But while Petronius and Apuleius had a few successors, the novel never became an established branch of ancient literature.

The younger Pliny (61–113?) was a cultivated gentleman and an honest and conscientious public servant. His *Letters* (modeled somewhat on those of Cicero) are helpful in reflecting the ideas and interests of the upper classes. Pliny's correspondence as governor of Bithynia with the emperor Trajan shows the ex-

Imperial Administration

The letters between the emperor Trajan and Pliny the Younger, his representative in one of the provinces of Asia Minor, suggest that imperial administrators, however severe, were generally more concerned with achieving justice than with following the letter of the law.

PLINY TO TRAJAN

. . . Having never been present at any of the trials of the Christians, I am unacquainted with the method and limits to be observed either in examining or punishing them. Whether any difference is to be made on account of age, or no distinction allowed between the youngest and the adult; whether repentance admits to a pardon, or if a man has been once a Christian it avails him nothing to recant. . . .

In the meanwhile, the method I have observed . . . is this: I interrogated them whether they were Christians; if they confessed it I repeated the question twice again, adding the threat of capital punishment; if they still persevered, I ordered them to be executed.

TRAJAN TO PLINY

The method you have pursued, my dear Pliny, in sifting the cases of those denounced to you as Christians is extremely proper. It is not possible to lay down any general rule which can be applied as the fixed standard in all cases of this nature. No search should be made for these people; when they are denounced and found guilty they must be punished; with the restriction, however, that if the party denies himself to be a Christian, and shall give proof that he is not (that is, by adoring our Gods) he shall be pardoned on the ground of repentance. . . .

From Pliny, *Letters,* trans. by William Melmoth, rev. by W. M. L. Hutchinson, The Loeb Classical Library (Cambridge, Mass.: Harvard University Press, 1953), pp. 401, 407.

The emperor Marcus Aurelius (160–180) entering Rome in triumph (detail from the column of Marcus Aurelius in Rome).

tent of imperial control and some lack of initiative on Pliny's part. Pliny asked Trajan's advice on every difficult question—for example, on how to deal with the Christians—and the emperor seems to have been wearied by all these questions.

The scholarly traditions of the Hellenistic era continued under Roman rule. Athens was still the center for the study of philosophy and Alexandria of science. During the second century the Greek physician Galen wrote his treatises on medicine and Ptolemy his studies in astronomy. Both were regarded as basic texts well into the sixteenth century. Unfortunately, both contained serious errors mixed with useful information. Thus Ptolemy's system made it possible to predict the position of the planets with accuracy, but it was based on a belief that the earth was the center of the solar system.

Plutarch (46?–120) wrote a series of short biographies in Greek—*Parallel Lives of Famous Greeks and Romans.* Plutarch had little primary source material on men such as Pericles or Pompey, but he used, and thus preserved, stories from earlier histories that have since been lost. His biographies are lively reading and are often our only source of information about a good number of episodes in ancient history.

Philosophy and Theology

Hadrian's reign (117–138) marked a turning point in the history of literature, as in many other activities. For writers in Latin, especially, there was a tendency to imitate past masterpieces and to write in a deliberately archaic style. Poetry, history, and oratory never fully recovered from this blight. At the same time, a tremendous amount of intellectual energy was poured into philosophy and theology. The second century was a century of religious searching, and some of the searchers were able to put their beliefs into words that made a lasting impression on Mediterranean and European societies.

It was in the second century that the first Church Fathers, writing in Greek, increased the appeal of Christianity to the educated classes by deriving a theology and a philosophy from Biblical texts. And by the end of the century Neoplatonism was revived more as a religion than a philosophy. Starting with Plato's belief in eternal, incorporeal Ideas (see p. 48), the Neoplatonists developed a system in which God, who was pure Spirit, generated lesser spirits through whom the physical world was created and through whom the human spirit could reach out toward God. In its lower forms, Neoplatonism came close to magic (which was very popular at this time); in its higher forms, it had some influence on Christian philosophy.

During the second century Stoic philosophy was given its highest expression in the writings of the slave Epictetus (60–140) and the emperor Marcus Aurelius (121–180). The careers of these two men illustrate the basic Stoic doctrine: whether slave or emperor, a man must follow the eternal law. But Stoicism appealed mainly to the upper classes. The masses clung to their traditional and regional religions of infinite variety, in which the worship of Zeus or Jupiter jostled Celtic or Semitic cults.

Roman Law

The long period of political stability and the interest of the emperors in good administration made the second century the decisive period in the formulation of Roman law. The Romans, like many other peoples, had started with a few simple rules of law that had been expanded and amended until they covered most of the ordinary problems of Roman citizens. But the Romans also had allied and subject cities, each with its own law. Since inhabitants of different cities often had legal dealings with one another, Roman judges had to discover equitable principles that would be accepted by all reasonable men. Stoic philosophy, which influenced most Roman jurists, helped in this quest. It was easier to discover principles that were valid at all times and in all places if one was first convinced, as the Stoics were, that such principles existed. And as Roman jurists began to formulate these principles in the late Republic and early Empire it seemed reasonable to apply them to all kinds of cases. Rules derived from the common experience of all peoples must be closer to the eternal law of nature than the peculiar and imperfect laws of a single city. Thus the Romans themselves began to prefer the general principles of the law of nations to their own municipal law, which in many respects was out of date.

This process was speeded up in the second century as the emperors began to take increasing responsibility for the administration of justice. The concentration of judicial authority in the hands of the emperor and his appointees naturally led to a greater uniformity in interpreting the law. Able jurists began to produce textbooks that the courts accepted as authoritative. Some emperors, such as Hadrian, asked for official formulations of some parts of the law. This process of putting the law into enduring form continued for many generations; some of the most eminent Roman lawyers wrote in the first half of the third century.

The formulation of Roman law was one of the great achievements of western civilization. It was not perfect—no law is—but it was a great improvement over all earlier legal systems. It was consistent, logical, and complete, and it was based on principles of justice and equity. The Romans themselves described it as "the art of goodness and justice," or "a constant and perpetual will to give every man his due." Roman law did not quite reach this standard; for example, the courts treated the poor much more harshly than the rich, and there were practically no restrictions on the power of the state. These weaknesses were due in part to the fact that the Roman law expounded by the jurists was almost entirely civil law. Criminal law remained crude and harsh and the lower classes were the ones most apt to be accused of criminal offenses. But the majesty of the law impressed even the emperors. They admitted that they should follow the law rather than their own whims, even if they did not always live up to this principle. Roman law, comprehensive and flexible enough to be adapted to any situation, survived all the misfortunes of the Late Empire; Justinian's great compilation in the sixth century (see p. 164) was based largely on the work of Roman jurists of the second and third centuries. Through Justinian's compilation, Roman law has influenced the jurisprudence of every European country, and from Europe this influence spread throughout the world.

Cicero and Ulpian on Justice

Cicero was an able lawyer as well as one of the leading Roman politicians of the first century B.C.

Since reason is given to all men by nature, so right reason is given to them, therefore they are also given law, which is right reason in commanding and forbidding; if law, therefore justice . . . thus a sense of what is right is common to all men.

From Cicero, *De legibus,* I, 33.

Ulpian was one of the great Roman jurists of the early third century A.D. These passages from Ulpian were quoted by Justinian's lawyers at the beginning of the *Digest,* an authoritative treatise on Roman law (see p. 164).

Justice is a constant and perpetual will to give every man his due. The principles of law are these: to live virtuously, not to harm others, to give his due to everyone. Jurisprudence is the knowledge of divine and human things, the science of the just and the unjust.

Law is the art of goodness and justice. By virtue of this we [lawyers] may be called priests, for we cherish justice and we profess knowledge of goodness and equity, separating right from wrong and legal from the illegal. . . .

THE CRISIS OF THE THIRD CENTURY

During the second century the Roman Empire seemed to have found a permanent solution to many of the problems that had long plagued the ancient world. By uniting the peoples living around the Mediterranean into one state the Empire had given peace and security to a vast area. Improvements in imperial administration and the granting of Roman citizenship had almost ended the resentment that subject peoples had felt toward their conquerors. Millions of people shared a culture, at least to the extent of having a common language (Latin in the West and Greek in the East) and a common pattern of social and political organization. They offered a huge market to enterprising businessmen. The third century might have seen an ever more prosperous and powerful Empire. Instead, it witnessed a series of catastrophes from which the Empire never fully recovered.

Political Weakness

One obvious cause of the troubles of the third century was the old problem of the succession. When Marcus Aurelius died in 180 he was succeeded by his son, Commodus, thus breaking the long chain of adoptions that had produced the "good emperors." Commodus was rather like Nero, vain and capricious, although he fancied himself as a gladiator rather than as a poet. When Commodus was assassinated (192 A.D.) the Senate once more tried to name an emperor, but its nominee was swept away, and the army again divided, with each group of legions supporting a rival emperor. The shrewdest of the generals, Septimius Severus, came out on top; he and members of his family ruled from 193 to 235. Their reign resembles the history of Vespasian and his sons, and Septimius Severus, like Vespasian, undertook many major reforms in government; for example, in the system of collecting taxes. But when the last of the Severi was assassinated, the Senate and the army could not agree on a successor; they could find no Nerva, no Trajan. Instead, the army made and unmade emperors with appalling rapidity. Between 235 and 284 there were twenty-six emperors and at least as many unsuccessful pretenders. Many of these emperors were men of real ability, but few of them remained in power for as long as five years. Rulers whose reigns began with a civil war and ended with assassination could do little to solve the problems of the Empire.

Military Weakness

Joined to the problem of the succession were very serious military problems. Trouble had begun early in the reign of Marcus Aurelius, when the Parthians attacked in the East, while Germans pushed across the Danube. It took years of fighting to drive back these enemies, and the peace won by Marcus Aurelius lasted less than a generation. The Germanic peoples, especially the Goths, renewed their attacks on the Rhine-Danube frontier. In the East the Sassanid ruler of Persia overthrew his overlord, the Parthian emperor, and established a revived and militant Persian Empire. The Parthians had been a rather stable force during their last century of power; the Sassanids were far more dangerous. They were fiercely nationalistic and anti-Hellenistic; they resented Roman power and despised Greek culture. The Sassanids plundered the eastern provinces, while the Goths pushed into the Balkans and even built a pirate fleet that disrupted Mediterranean commerce.

The long wars put a severe strain on the finances of the Empire and on the morale of the army. The fighting was desperate, often hopeless. The soldiers tended to magnify the virtues of their own general if he was successful and if he gave them adequate rewards. On the other hand, they were quick to rebel against generals or emperors whom they did not know, especially if they seemed incompetent or cowardly. These soldiers led a hard life; they expected bonuses when they completed a campaign or helped their general to become emperor. If money was not available—and often it was not—there would be a mutiny. But not all third-century emperors were as-

ROMAN MILITARY WEAKNESS
Late second century

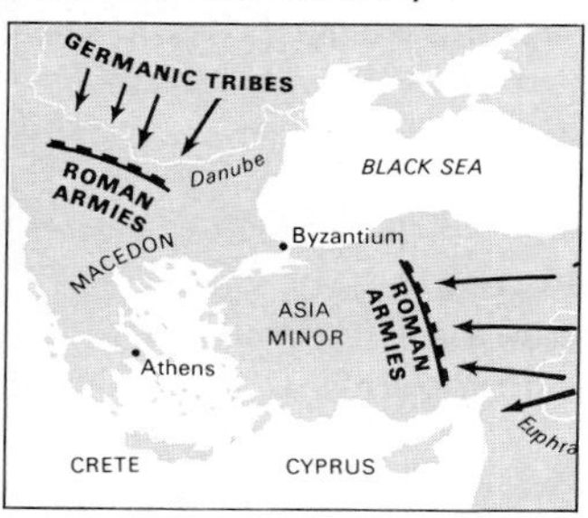

sassinated or executed by their soldiers: a good many fell in battle or died on campaigns. Even if the army had been completely united and loyal, there would have been many short reigns.

Since the largest part of the army was permanently stationed in frontier provinces, recruits came from the poorest and least Romanized groups in the population. These characteristics were accentuated when Marcus Aurelius began the practice of inviting Germans into the Empire, giving them land, and enlisting them in the army to defend the frontier against their fellow tribesmen. Such soldiers probably understood little about the institutions or the values of the Empire. But they do not seem to have been any more irresponsible than the crack troops of the imperial bodyguard, who murdered more emperors than did the provincial soldiers.

More and more the quality of the army determined the character of the Empire. Beginning with Septimius Severus, the Roman state became increasingly militarized. Army officers took over civilian tasks, such as tax collection and some kinds of legal jurisdiction. Italy, which was more closely supervised by the emperor in the third century than it had been before the crisis, had a garrison of regular troops. This militarization was necessary in a period in which the Empire was on the defensive, and military men were not necessarily bad administrators. It was, perhaps, more unfortunate that civilians found it necessary to take on military posts. Two of the greatest Roman jurists, Papinian and Ulpian, became commanders of the palace guard, and—like most men who rose to that dangerous eminence—died in rebellions led by their own troops.

Economic Weakness

Economic as well as military problems forced the emperors to militarize the state. As we have seen, even in the second century there were weaknesses in the Roman economy. In a sense, the Empire had simply lived off the profits made by the conquests of the Republic. Areas annexed after the beginning of the Christian era probably never yielded a profit because of the cost of defense. In the third century this cost rose sharply. Army pay had to be increased, and the size of the armed forces increased. Frontier and civil wars devastated many areas and impoverished others. Mediterranean commerce had reached its peak before the appearance of Gothic pirates on the sea; most economic historians agree that it suffered greatly during the third century and never regained its earlier level. Great landowners, high public officials, and a few dealers in luxury goods still had comfortable incomes, but small farmers and middle-class businessmen found it hard to meet extraordinary expenses, and even harder to accumulate capital for new enterprises. Their situation was aggravated by spectacular waves of inflation. Emperors or candidates for the title paid their troops in debased currency. The great increase in the amount of money in circulation raised prices, and fears of further debasement encouraged wild spending that raised prices even more. No government seriously attacked this problem until the end of the third century, and inflation continued to be a problem well into the fourth century.

Third-century tomb relief showing an affluent banker and two struggling Roman laborers. The Roman economy was weakened by this gap between the wealthy few and the poor masses.

Weakness in Municipal Government

All these forces tended to weaken local governments. In some respects, the early Empire could have been described as a federation of cities, each responsible for the political and economic welfare of the surrounding territory. During the third century these cities lost population and income. General insecurity affected both local and long-distance trade. Cities far from the frontier had to be fortified; even Rome was encircled by walls during the reign of Aurelian (270–275). Municipal government began to break down, since the local aristocracies could no longer afford to hold office. The richest and ablest had been promoted to the Senate, and those who were left were responsible for the collection of taxes; when the central government increased its demands, more and more pressure was put on fewer and poorer city leaders. Coercion, harsh laws, and dictatorial bureaucrats left little initiative or independence for city officials. Exploitation had replaced the benevolent care of the "good emperors."

Weakness in Society

The Empire shrank in on itself during the third century. Physically, it lost some of its outposts, such as Dacia; spiritually, it lost some of its vigor and confidence. The ordinary man had long ceased to have political significance, but even well-to-do citizens now had little influence on policy, either in Rome or in provincial cities. Neither the upper nor the lower classes felt much responsibility for the general welfare: that was the business of the emperor and his officials. In a declining economy there was little that anyone could do to improve his lot or to increase productivity; great increases in wealth came largely from service to or favors from the emperor. Repeated outbreaks of plague, beginning in the reign of Marcus Aurelius and continuing into the second half of the third century, may not have greatly reduced the population, but they certainly weakened morale.

Unable to understand or to influence events in this world, a considerable part of the population looked to the next world for hope and consolation. Emperors tried to use religion, through sacrifices to "the spirit of Rome and the genius" (guiding spirit) of the emperor, to gain popular support, but the policy had little effect. The mystery religions continued to grow. The number of Christians, who refused to make the official sacrifices, increased enough to worry the emperors; the first large-scale persecutions took place in the third century. None of the eastern religions advocated open opposition to the state, although many of them considered that service to the state was unimportant at best, and an obstacle to salvation at worst. The Empire continued to exist, but it had only the passive loyalty of many of its citizens. Those who were galvanized into resistance were often interested in their own districts, not in the Empire as a whole. Thus Gaul had its own emperors for some fourteen years: they defended only Gaul, not the Danube line or the East.

The Establishment of Military Absolutism

Even its most disillusioned inhabitants could not conceive of a world in which the Empire did not exist. They proved wise in their own generation. After 270 the emperors were still short-lived, but they did their job better. Outside invaders were gradually beaten back, and internal rivals for power were

The Empire in Decline

This passage, the musings of a trader as he revisits a provincial city in Switzerland in the third century, is from a modern historical novel.

It was a pleasant town. Demetrius paused to look at the Treasury inside its stone wall, and the villas scattered within shady gardens. Yet each year they were a little more neglected; the temple yard had not been properly swept, a latch was hanging loose from a shutter, the gutter was choked by a dirty mass of what had once been somebody's garland. He wondered why the place had changed so much during the six years since his first visit. Then there had been chariots on the streets, and many wagons, an indefinable sense of the city being alive. Was the Empire too big? Yet it had been larger, and nobody had counted the provinces. Were the young so ungrateful? It seemed to him that there was just the same proportion of honest men and rogues as in his childhood. There was constant talk about invasion; nobody now was certain as to who was emperor of what, but the Treasury still functioned reasonably well, most roads got mended, trade went on, yet he could not deny the change. Something had happened; it was as if a sentry had been asked to keep one watch too many, and his fibre had snapped.

From Bryher, *Roman Wall* (New York: Pantheon, 1954), p. 124.

eliminated, restoring unity and security to the Roman world. Thus, in the end, it was the generals who saved the Empire. They made themselves absolute sovereigns and imposed a strict, almost military, discipline on their subjects. In 284, one victorious general, Diocletian, became emperor and began the reforms that held the Empire together for another century.

Suggestions for Further Reading

Note: Asterisk denotes a book available in paperback edition.

General The texts mentioned at the end of the preceding chapter will also serve as introductions to the era of the Roman Empire. A reader seeking a more detailed discussion of the imperial period should consult M. Cary and H. H. Scullard, *History of Rome,* 3rd ed. (1975). Somewhat shorter is J. Wells and R. H. Barrow, *A Short History of the Roman Empire* (1931). Since this book ends with the death of Marcus Aurelius, one might read H. M. D. Parker, *History of the Roman World from* A.D. *138 to 337* (1935), or M. Grant, *The Climax of Rome* (1968), for the later period. The classic nonpolitical history of the era is M. I. Rostovtzeff, *The Social and Economic History of the Roman Empire,** rev. ed. (1957). Two short studies of the Roman Empire, both extremely well written, are M. P. Charlesworth, *The Roman Empire** (1951), and H. Mattingly, *Roman Imperial Civilization** (1959). An excellent collection of original source material may be found in N. Lewis and M. Reinhold, eds., *Roman Civilization,* Vol. II (1955). M. I. Finley, *The Ancient Economy** (1973) is also excellent.

Government There are two exhaustive studies of the creation of the Roman Empire: F. B. Marsh, *Founding of the Roman Empire* (1927), and M. Hammond, *The Augustan Principate in Theory and Practice* (1933). See also R. Syme, *The Roman Revolution** (1939), and H. T. Prowell, *Rome in the Augustan Age* (1962). A good biography of Augustus is T. R. Holmes, *The Architect of the Roman Empire,* 2 vols. (1928–31), which contains a thorough description of the Empire in the Augustan era. There are many good studies of the individual reigns of the later emperors. V. Scramuzza, *Claudius* (1940), and R. Seager, *Tiberius* (1972), are the best biographies of these two emperors. B. W. Henderson's two lengthy studies, *Life and Principate of the Emperor Nero* (1903) and *Life and Principate of the Emperor Hadrian* (1932), are useful, as is B. H. Warmington, *Nero** (1969). For the second century, see M. Hammond, *The Antonine Monarchy* (1959); B. W. Henderson, *Five Roman Emperors* (1927); and A. Birley, *Marcus Aurelius* (1966) and *Septimius Severus* (1970).

The Provinces, Provincial Administration, and Roman Law For the frontier provinces, see F. Millar, *The Roman Empire and Its Neighbors* (1968). On provincial administration, the most thorough treatment is found in W. T. Arnold, *The Roman System of Administration* (1914). A later, and excellent, survey is G. H. Stevenson, *Roman Provincial Administration* (1939). F. F. Abbott and A. C. Johnson, *Municipal Administration in the Roman Empire* (1926), and A. H. M. Jones, *The Cities of the Eastern Roman Provinces* (1937), both have valuable information on the municipal administrations that were the basis of the Roman provincial administration.

The standard introduction to Roman law is R. W. Buckland, *A Manual of Roman Law* (1925). See also J. A. Crook, *Law and Life of Rome* (1967). A good study of the army is G. Webster, *The Roman Imperial Army* (1969). See also R. MacMullen, *Soldier and Civilian in the Later Roman Empire* (1963).

Society, Literature, and Religion A comprehensive and interesting description of the society of the early Roman Empire may be found in S. Dill, *Roman Society from Nero to Marcus Aurelius** (1925). A more recent study is J. P. V. Balsdon, *Life and Leisure in Ancient Rome* (1968). Another very good book is R. MacMullen, *Roman Social Relations* (1974). Two good introductions to the literature of the era are M. Grant, *Roman Literature** (1954), and M. Hadas, *A History of Latin Literature* (1952). See also the two books by J. W. Duff, *A Literary History of Rome to the Close of the Golden Age,* 3rd ed. (1963) and *A Literary History of Rome in the Silver Age,* 3rd ed. (1964). For the arts, M. Wheeler, *Roman Art and Architecture* (1964), is excellent. The standard work on architecture is by A. Boëthius and J. B. Ward-Perkins, *Etruscan and Roman Architecture* (1970). The best discussion on the problems of Roman art is found in O. J. Brendel, *Study of Roman Art* (1979).

The most thorough treatment of Roman religion is F. Altheim, *A History of Roman Religion* (1938). The effect of the spread of Hellenistic religions is treated in T. R. Glover, *The Conflict of Religions in the Early Roman Empire** (1960), while the best study of eastern mystery religions in the era of the Roman Empire is F. Cumont, *Oriental Religions in Roman Paganism** (1956). R. MacMullen, *Paganism in the Roman Empire* (1981), is an excellent summary.

5 The Late Roman Empire 284–476

Even after the crisis of the third century, the Roman Empire still had two great assets: a formidable army and a well-organized bureaucracy. These two institutions proved strong enough to restore order and unity to the Roman world for another century. The revival of the Roman state had a profound effect on the history of civilization, for it was during the fourth century that Christianity became the official religion of the reunited Roman Empire. Christianity thereby won for itself a firm foothold in the western world.

THE RESTORATION OF ORDER: THE REIGN OF DIOCLETIAN, 284–305

The work of restoration was begun by Aurelian, who became emperor in 270. He checked the civil wars within the Empire and started the drive to push the Germans and the Persians back to their old frontiers. Aurelian might have been the founder of the Late Roman Empire, but he was assassinated in 275. His work was carried on by his successors, even though the army was still making and unmaking emperors at its usual rate. It was not until Diocletian became emperor in 284 that internal stability was fully restored.

Political and Military Reorganization

Diocletian's success was due first of all to his character. Shrewd, tough, and determined, he dominated rival generals as no emperor had been able to do for a century. He was able to keep most of the army on his side and to put down the few commanders who tried to rebel.

In an effort to improve the defense of the borders, Diocletian increased the size of the army and rebuilt the frontier fortifications. To prevent rebellions, he split large armies into smaller units and separated command from supply and payment of troops. To make his personal command over the troops effective, Diocletian abandoned Rome as his official residence and moved eastward to Nicomedia, nearer the frontiers. From this time on the city of Rome declined steadily in size and importance.

Just as ingenious, but less successful, were Diocletian's attempts to solve the problem of succession. He realized that the troubled Empire needed more than one high-ranking commander, and he realized that some potential revolts could be warded off by sharing power with able generals. Almost as soon as he was established as emperor, Diocletian named a fellow officer, Maximian, as coemperor. Later, each of the two emperors selected an assistant with the title of Caesar. It was understood that when the emperors retired or died, the Caesars would succeed as emperors and designate new Caesars in turn.

The system of divided authority was also helpful in Diocletian's reorganization of the imperial government. For purposes of administration, each emperor became responsible for half of the Empire: the western half, under Maximian, encompassed Italy, North Africa, Spain, Gaul, Britain, and northern Illyria. The eastern half, under Diocletian himself, consisted essentially of the provinces that were part of the Hellenistic world. Each half was divided into two prefectures, one of which was administered by the Caesar. Consequently, the administrative workload was shared among the emperors and their assistants, and decisions could be made rapidly and intelligently. Diocletian, however, did not give his corulers an entirely free hand; there was never any doubt that he was the senior emperor and that it was he who made the decisions that applied to the Empire as a whole.

In a further effort to increase stability and forestall rebellion, Diocletian emphasized the divine and autocratic nature of the emperor, completing a process that had been going on for generations. By the third century all pretense that the emperor was merely the First Citizen had long been abandoned; Diocletian became *dominus et deus,* lord and god. Everything that pertained to his household or administration was sacred, and he adopted many of the symbols and ceremonies of the eastern monarchies. Anyone granted an audience with Diocletian was required first to prostrate himself and then to kiss the hem of the emperor's garment.

Opposite: The declining creativity and technical skill of the artists of the late Roman Empire can be seen in the Arch of Constantine in Rome (312–315).

Economic Reform

Diocletian tried to stabilize the economy as well as the politics of the Empire. He was almost the only Roman emperor who realized the need for economic planning. Some of his reforms were successful, such as the issue of a new and much improved currency. Some were less successful, such as his attempt to stem inflation by freezing prices and wages. Because he lacked the means to enforce the new regulations, his edict soon became a dead letter.

The realization that something should be done about the Roman economy shows Diocletian's perceptiveness, but the means he used to carry out his ideas were harsh and often ineffective. Diocletian was a soldier who believed that a state could be run like an army. He was convinced that an unhealthy economy could be cured by edict; that men could be commanded to produce goods at fixed prices just as troops could be commanded to charge an enemy. Since most of Diocletian's successors were also military men with similar approaches to political and economic problems, almost all private activities came under the control of the state during the fourth century.

Diocletian and his coemperor stand in front, embracing each other; the two Caesars stand behind them (St. Mark's Cathedral, Venice).

RELIGION IN THE LATE ROMAN EMPIRE

One of the most baffling problems faced by Diocletian, and one he could not solve, was the growing popularity of Christianity and the many eastern mystery religions that had first appeared in the Hellenistic era (see p. 105). All these religions emphasized the afterlife and discouraged the vigorous participation in the affairs of this world on which Diocletian's program of restoration depended. The Christians were particularly offensive to Diocletian, for they continued to refuse to recognize the divine aspect of imperial authority and to make the sacrifices that were supposed to ensure the unity and security of the Roman world.

The Eastern Mystery Religions

During the first three centuries of the Roman Empire many people in the Mediterranean world had been seeking a faith by which to live. The appeal of the older Greco-Roman gods had been declining since the Hellenistic era; the rituals were still performed, but few people believed that Jupiter and his fellow gods were the only gods. The attempt to institute a state religion based on the worship of "the spirit of Rome and the genius of the emperor" had failed because the population lacked the intense patriotism that might have given the cult meaning. In the first and second centuries the upper classes had turned to Stoicism. But to the ordinary man Stoicism had little appeal. It was too intellectual and too impersonal; it valued eternal law, human brotherhood, and devotion to duty, but it elicited no strong emotional response. There was no individual salvation, no promise of a better life for the poor and the oppressed. Although the Stoics would have denied it, their main motivation was probably pride—pride in doing one's duty for duty's sake, pride in remaining unbroken by worldly problems. During the troubled third century even the upper classes began to abandon Stoicism, and by the end of the century a large part of the population had accepted one of the mystery cults.

Most of the mystery religions were based on very ancient beliefs, though they took on their characteristic forms during the Hellenistic era and the early years of the Roman Empire. Their gods were not the carefree deities of the Greek and Roman pantheons. Instead, they were semidivine heroes who had suffered as men suffer in the age-long struggle against darkness and evil. Most of them had been killed in the conflict but had returned to life, thus prefiguring victory over death and eternal life for the souls of their followers.

The worship of the Egyptian Isis was widespread throughout the Empire, especially in the more peaceful provinces. Just as widespread was Mithraism, a popular form of the Zoroastrian religion of Persia. Mithra was a warrior-god who had been killed by the god of darkness but who rose again and was thus able to bestow immortality on converts who would join him in the eternal war against evil. Mithraism was popular among soldiers and became almost the official religion of the Roman armies. It remained a competitor of Christianity all through the fourth century, and its dualistic theology (a god of good fighting a god of evil) was picked up again by the Manichean heresy that was to trouble medieval Christendom.

A person could join one of these mystic brotherhoods by participating in rituals that cleansed him of the contaminations of the physical world and ensured that his unstained soul would become a part of the eternal world of the spirit. An Isis-worshiper was purged of his earthly weaknesses and prepared for his reception by the pure and loving mother-goddess by being immersed in water that symbolized the sacred Nile.

The young boy in this painting (*ca.* 300–350) is an acolyte of the Isis cult. The cup and garland are emblems of his religious belief; the side hairlock was long associated with the child-god Horus.

THE ADMINISTRATIVE DIVISIONS OF DIOCLETIAN Third and fourth centuries

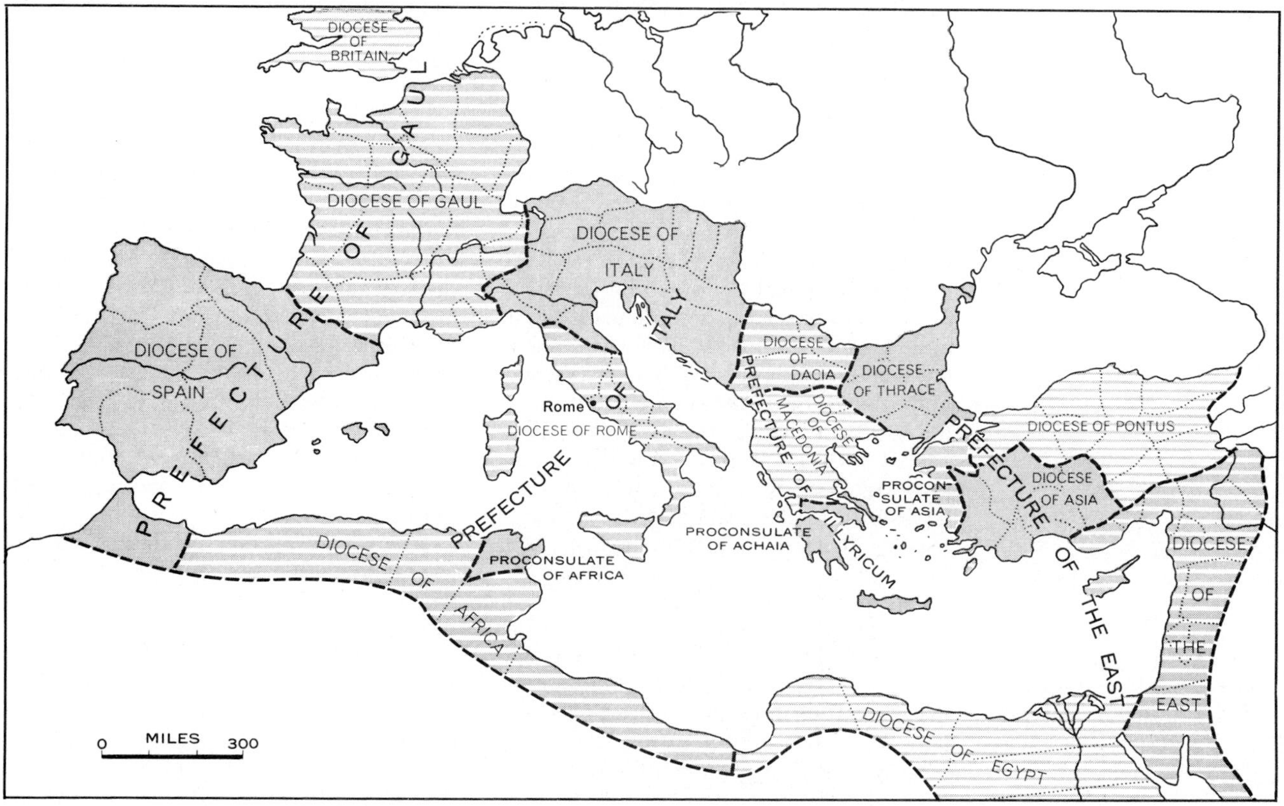

An initiate into the religion of Mithra took part in the ritual sacrifice of a bull, and worked upward to deeper knowledge and greater purity by passing through seven grades of instruction. Christian baptism wiped out all previous sins and prepared the recipient to receive the other sacraments.

For many people these religions satisfied a genuine need. The individual felt helpless and insecure in a society over which he had no control, in which his economic and political welfare was determined by remote and unapproachable authorities. He often felt a deep sense of isolation, not so much because of personal misconduct but because he was convinced that the misery of the human condition could be explained only by a fundamental blemish on the soul of each man. The eastern religions assured men of their importance as individuals, made them part of a closely knit fellowship, and promised them forgiveness of sin and a happy future life. It is not surprising that these religions won adherents in every part of the Roman world, and that many people joined more than one of these cults.

The Triumph of Christianity

Another religion that gained large numbers of adherents in the third century was Christianity. Although the Christian refusal to worship "the spirit of Rome and the genius of the emperor" was technically the equivalent of treason, the imperial government paid only intermittent attention to the sect in the first and second centuries. Few Christians belonged to the upper classes during this period, and the government took note of them only when there was political or social unrest (as in Rome under Nero or in Bithynia under Trajan). Even then, it persecuted Christians largely for political reasons; it made no attempt to wipe out the religion.

As a result the early Church had been able to develop its theology and to create a remarkable administrative system, modeled more or less on the administrative system of the Empire. It was important for the scattered members of the new faith to keep in touch with one another and to preserve uniformity of doctrine. In a polytheistic society where one man could belong to many cults heresy was a constant problem; therefore, a tight organization was necessary. The most respected members of each congregation became priests ("elders"), and in each city one priest was designated as bishop ("overseer"). The bishop was responsible for supervising all the Christian congregations in his city and in the surrounding villages. By the end of the second century some bishops (precursors of the later archbishops) were recognized as leaders in their provinces. The systematic organization of the early Church was an innovation in the ancient world and helped establish the supremacy of Christianity over the many other religions of the Empire. No similar system existed for the pagan or mystery cults; the priests of Jupiter or Mithra in one city, for example, were entirely independent of those in other cities.

During the third century Christianity began to attract members from all classes. Earlier, the educated classes of the Empire, broadminded by tradition, had been offended by the exclusiveness of the Christians, by their unwillingness to admit that there might be truth in other religions. Many people preferred to hedge their bets, so that devotees of the Great Mother (the goddess Cybele) might also join the Isis cult just to play it safe. But in the troubled third century—when economic decline, civil war, barbarian raids, and plague affected nearly every family and signaled confusion and decay in almost every aspect of civilized life—the very firmness of Christian beliefs began to make them attractive. Similarly, the unswerving morality of the Christians, their charity to the poor, and their belief in the fatherly love of God offered security in a time of confusion. Finally, the extreme other-worldliness of the Christians, which had seemed mere foolishness to all but the slaves and the poor in the affluent second century, fitted well with the intense desire in the chaotic third century for future happiness.

Christianity grew rapidly enough during the third century to alarm some of the emperors. They were annoyed by Christian lack of patriotism; these zealots would neither sacrifice to the emperor nor serve the state. This disregard of religion (it was even called "atheism") was sure to rouse the anger of the gods. There were some severe and prolonged periods of persecution during the century. The worst and longest began under Diocletian, who hated any kind of disobedience, and reached a peak with Galerius. But this persecution does not seem to have reduced the number of Christians greatly, even in the East, where it was most intense. It did cause a schism, however, (especially in Africa) between those who were willing to placate the emperor and those who refused to make any concessions (the Donatists).

THE REIGN OF CONSTANTINE, 307–337

Diocletian, an innovator to the end, abdicated in 305 and became one of the few Roman emperors to die peacefully. But his elaborate provisions for an orderly succession were soon disregarded, and a series of civil wars put five different generals in control of various parts of the Empire. One of these generals was Constantine, who completely reversed Diocletian's policy of persecuting Christians.

The Conversion of Constantine

Scholars have long argued about the reasons for and the sincerity of Constantine's conversion to Christianity. His mother is said to have been a Christian, and there is some evidence for Christian beliefs in his father's house; certainly Constantine had some idea of the doctrines and the power of the religion before he became emperor. On the other hand, he had held command in Gaul, where Christians were neither numerous nor influential. Constantine cannot have believed that there were enough politically active Christians in his part of the Empire to make any difference in the struggle for power with rival generals. When he invoked the help of the Christian God, he must have been motivated by religious conviction, not by political expediency. Perhaps he thought that he was only tapping a new source of semimagical power, but he surely did not think that he was gaining thousands of Christian recruits for his army. The decisive moment in Constantine's religious life came when he was about to meet his strongest opponent for the imperial title at the battle of the Mulvian Bridge (near Rome) in 312. Before the battle Constantine is said to have had a vision of a cross in the sky surrounded by the words *hoc signo victor eris* ("by this sign you will be victorious"). Convinced that the Christian God had helped him to victory, he ordered his troops to carry Christian insignia from that time on. Soon, in 313, Constantine (and the remaining co-emperor who still ruled with him) issued the Edict of Toleration ending the persecution of Christians.

Although not a full member of the Church (Constantine received baptism only on his deathbed, a not uncommon precaution at the time), he supported it throughout his reign, thus enabling

Colossal head of Constantine, from his basilica in Rome (*ca.* 320).

Constantine's Religious Beliefs

The official policy of the Empire after 312 was toleration, as shown in a letter sent in the name of both Constantine and his coemperor to the governor of Bithynia in 313.

. . . we resolved to make such decrees as should secure respect and reverence for the Deity; namely, to grant both to the Christians and to all the free choice of following whatever form of worship they pleased, to the intent that all the divine and heavenly powers that be might be favorable to us and all those living under our authority.

◊ ◊ ◊

But Constantine showed stronger personal convictions in a letter written only a year later to the governor of Africa, dealing with the problem of schism in that province.

Since I am assured that you are also a worshipper of the supreme God, I confess to your Excellency that I consider it absolutely wrong that we should pass over in insincerity quarrels and altercations of this kind, whereby perhaps the supreme divinity may be moved not only against the human race, but even against me myself, to whose care He has entrusted rule over all earthly affairs. . . . For then, and only then, shall I be able truly and most fully to feel secure . . . when I shall see all men, in the proper cult of the Catholic religion, venerate the most holy God with hearts joined together like brothers in their worship.

From *Great Problems in European Civilization,* ed. by K. M. Setton and H. R. Winkler (Englewood Cliffs, N.J.: Prentice-Hall, 1954), pp. 75, 79.

Christianity to become the dominant religion of the Empire during the fourth century. He apparently hoped that the Empire would be strengthened by strengthening the position of Christianity. Certainly the Empire was stronger in the fourth century than it had been during much of the third century, but quarrels among theologians proved almost as dangerous as quarrels among generals.

In spite of persecution, the Christians had never succeeded in suppressing all of their differences. After the Edict of Toleration Christian leaders fell into such bitter doctrinal disputes that the unity of the Church was threatened. While Christianity was not incorporated into the state, Constantine expected it to promote unity, not destroy it. And since, like any good Roman, he was sure that there must be some single legal formula that would be acceptable to all reasonable men, he often used the force of his imperial office to bring the Church to agreement.

One of the earliest controversies concerned the doctrine of the Trinity. A priest named Arius taught that the Son and the Holy Spirit had been created by, and were therefore subordinate to, God the Father. Other theologians attacked his teachings, insisting that the three aspects of God must be equal. The quarrels that sprang up were so bitter that Constantine called a council of bishops at Nicaea (in Asia Minor) in 325 to settle the matter. After some argument, the Council of Nicaea produced a confession of faith that completely rejected the teachings of Arius. The Arians were not cowed by this action and remained a powerful force in the Empire (and later on among the Germans) for many generations. New doctrinal disputes continued to emerge so that councils of bishops had to meet at frequent intervals. The decisions of a majority of a general council were held to be binding on the whole Church. Those who would not accept them were excommunicated—that is, cast out from the Church and the communion of the faithful.

The Extension of Military Absolutism

After his victory at the Milvian Bridge in 312, Constantine established his rule over the western half of the Roman Empire. In 324 he defeated his coemperor and thus gained full control over the entire Empire. Constantine, like Diocletian, was a tough-minded soldier who maintained the order and stability of the Empire with military discipline. Experience, however, had taught him the dangers of sharing the imperial power with other generals. So, although Constantine retained most of Diocletian's reforms, he did not revive the practice of dividing his authority among coemperors.

Realizing, as had many earlier emperors, that the economic and military strength of the ancient world lay in the East—the former Hellenistic world—Constantine sought a new capital that would be easy to defend, that would have access by sea to the commercial routes of the Aegean and the Mediterranean, and that would be near enough to endangered frontiers for the emperor never to be too far from either his administration or his armies. He chose the site of the ancient Greek city of Byzantium on the Bosporus. He named his capital New Rome, but after his death it became known as Constantinople (and after its occupation by the Turks in 1453, as Istanbul).

Constantine's efforts to make his new city prosper were successful. He had picked an excellent location, he coerced wealthy men to build there, and he plundered much of the Empire to embellish his new capital. Constantinople soon became one of the leading commercial and cultural centers of the Greco-Roman world. But this move to the East was one more step in downgrading the importance of the western provinces (including Italy) and in leading to a separation between the two sections of the Empire.

THE EMPIRE IN THE FOURTH CENTURY

So towering was Constantine's prestige that for several decades after his death members of his family retained the imperial throne. Except for the brief reign of Julian (361–363), all of Constantine's descendants were Christians. Therefore Christianity came to be more and more the official religion of the Empire. But imperial protection meant imperial intervention in the affairs of the Church. Thus, caesaropapism—the control of the Church by the emperor rather than by the bishops—developed. It was to cause many conflicts between Church and state in later periods. Though Constantine's successors quarreled bitterly among themselves over both politics and religion, most of them were men of military ability, a quality that was badly needed in the fourth century. They succeeded in holding the Empire together and protecting its frontiers.

The Barbarian Threat

Trouble was brewing almost everywhere along the eastern and northern frontiers. The Persians, the oldest and most dangerous of the enemies of the Empire, once more moved to attack the eastern provinces, and the best Roman troops had to be used to repel them. At the same time the Germanic tribes were in turmoil along the Rhine and the Danube. Large groups were migrating in search of better lands or more secure homes, and each migration touched off a series of tribal wars. The victors often raided Roman territory; the vanquished begged permission to settle in Roman frontier zones (as they had done since the time of Marcus Aurelius). Moreover, individual tribes banded together in more or less permanent confederations with such huge reserves of manpower that they could eventually challenge the Roman defenses.

Meanwhile, the Roman army was running short of manpower just when it needed to expand. There was never a time when the inhabitants of the Empire did not outnumber all their barbarian enemies put together. But more and more Roman citizens were being excluded from military service. Senators were barred from army posts because they were needed for civilian jobs; members of the urban aristocracies, because they were needed for local administration. Landlords (and tax collectors) felt that peasants could not be spared from the land, and the city proletariat was useless for military purposes. The frontier provinces still supplied troops, but, since those troops were used almost entirely as border guards, they could not be used as mobile armies to ward off sudden attacks. The need for cavalry became evident, but the Romans were not very effective on horseback.

To overcome this lack of officers and men, the Empire drew recruits from among the barbarians themselves. The barbarian soldiers acted as the shock troops of the Empire, and for the first time in the long history of Rome armies composed of foreigners were valued more highly than armies composed of Roman citizens. But except for a better-organized top command, these barbarian troops were very like the armies of the enemies they were opposing. Consequently, in a battle between armies of equal size it was by no means certain that the barbarized Roman army would prevail. The process that had created this

Roman soldier and barbarian warrior (detail from a third-century Roman sarcophagus).

Head of a barbarian found in Gaul, probably representing one of the Helvetian (Swiss) peoples.

Silver-gilt spear mount made for a barbarian warrior, found in a tomb in northern France (*ca.* fourth century).

dangerous situation was irreversible, for by the fourth century it was too late to rebuild an army composed only of Roman citizens. There were no mass levies of inhabitants of the Empire and no spontaneous organizations for defense. If barbarian armies could not defend the Empire, then there was no one left to defend it.

Economic and Social Problems

The growing apathy of the people of the Empire was even more dangerous than the barbarizing of the army. Even the upper classes seem to have assumed that the Empire would survive without any great effort on their part. Citizens obeyed orders and paid taxes when they could not evade them, but they showed no readiness to sacrifice life or property to save the state.

As if to reinforce this political apathy, the Roman economy continued to slump. Some parts of the Empire were reasonably prosperous in the fourth century, but in many provinces the depression that had begun in the third century persisted without relief. Population declined in many regions. The towns became less able to discharge their economic functions. Large amounts of arable land were permitted to slip out of cultivation, and many peasants tried to avoid the crushing burden of taxation by yielding their farms to great landowners, who could simply defy the tax collector. These peasants lost their freedom and became dependents of their landlords, and in so doing took one of the first steps toward serfdom (see p. 193).

Least affected by the depression were the great landlords, especially those of the western provinces. These men were able to ignore the world around them by operating their estates as independent social and economic units. By using the simple home manufactures of their peasants to supply the needs of the estate, they reduced contacts between town and countryside. This was especially disruptive in the West, where the cities were not very strong to begin with. As the cities declined, the landlords became more independent of local government, a practice that weakened the authority of imperial officials and eventually led to the autonomous lordships of the early Middle Ages.

Most citizens had long ago given up hope of controlling their political future. During the fourth century they began to give up hope for their economic future as well. They saw no prospect of rising in the world, nor even any assurance that they would be able to hold on to what little they had. This feeling of discouragement was especially strong in the West, and it is not surprising that in that region devotion to the Roman state and to the principles of the Greco-Roman civilization tended to decline.

A State-Controlled Economy

From the time of Diocletian the emperors had been aware of these problems, but they could not trace back through five centuries of history to find the roots of the people's indifference. They could deal only with the current symptoms. And since many of them were military men and all of them were occupied with military affairs, they tried to solve their problems by running the Empire like an army. If the people failed to do their duty voluntarily, they would have to do it under compulsion. If self-interested economic motivations were no longer enough to get essential work done, then it must be done under state control.

The emperors' treatment of municipal governments offers a good example of their attitude. One of the chief functions of municipal government was to collect taxes for the imperial government. These taxes were a heavy burden on the poor and the middle class, especially in a period of declining economy. The city officials who were responsible for collecting the taxes were in a precarious position; if some inhabitants failed to pay, then the officials had to make up the deficit. Since the income of these officials came from landholdings and many rural estates had been ruined by invaders and brigands, they were now less well-to-do, and, predictably, they tried to avoid municipal office. But the central government, instead of easing their burden, simply ruled that all municipal officials had to stay in office and that their sons had to succeed them when they died. Thus the government attempted to keep the municipalities operating through sheer compulsion. Such a policy alienated this class of officials, who had formerly been generous contributors to civic projects. It did nothing to halt the decline of commerce. Many western cities were dwindling away by the end of the fourth century.

At the same time the government passed laws to bind the peasants to the soil. Rural slaves had not been a major part of the labor force for centuries, and transplanted barbarians filled the gap only partially and only in the northern frontier zones. Elsewhere the supply of agricultural labor was declining, and land was passing out of cultivation. To avoid the consequent loss of tax revenues, the central government forbade tenant farmers to leave the estates they were working on. In the end, tenant farmers were more than slaves but something less than freemen; they became *coloni,* bound to the soil as serfs were in later centuries. Though not bound to personal service, the farmer was tied to a particular piece of land, and he and his heirs were bound to cultivate that land forever.

Some groups of artisans suffered a similar fate. Bakers in Rome and Constantinople, for instance, were bound to remain in their trade and to furnish a son to succeed them. In fact, by the middle of the fourth century a large part of the population of the Empire was probably frozen in permanent hereditary occupations. The laws could be evaded, but economic decline reduced opportunities and so reinforced the effects of legislation.

The Church

We are apt to exaggerate the number of Christians in the Empire during the fourth century. There were wide areas, especially in the West, where Christianity

THE LATE ROMAN EMPIRE *ca.* 395 A.D.

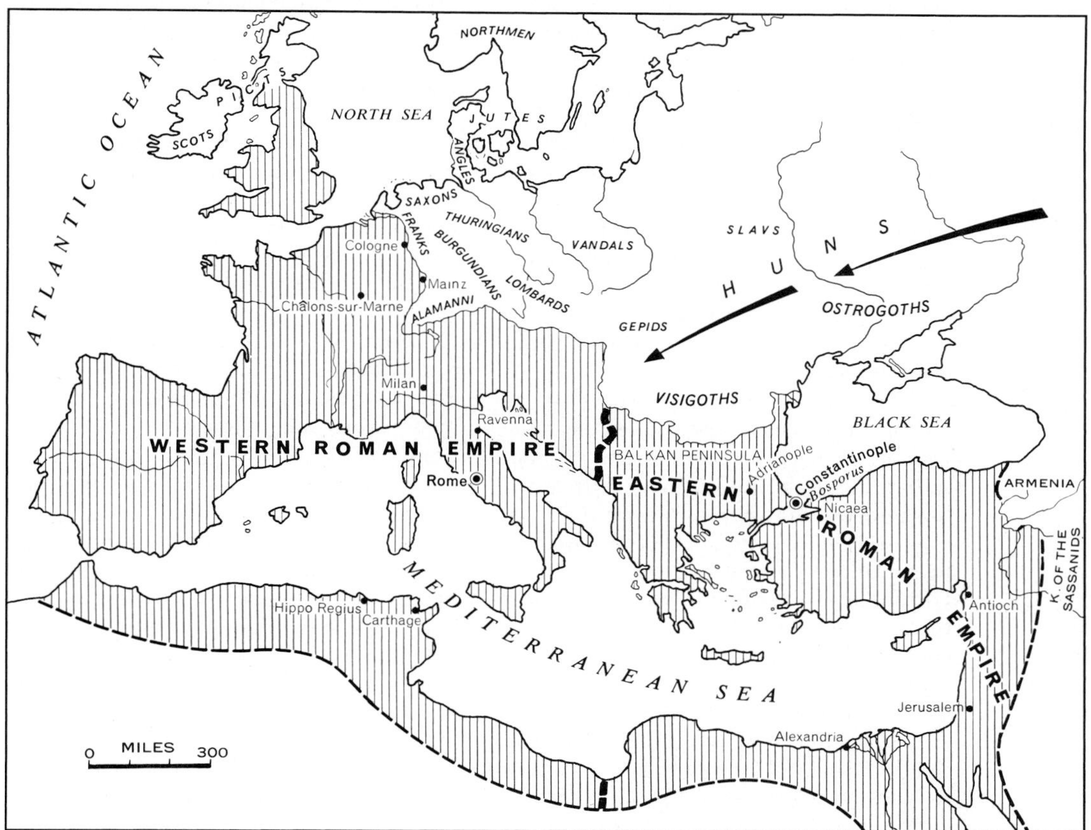

Symbol of Christianity, incorporating the Greek letters chi and rho (the monogram for Christ that forms the shape of the cross) and alpha and omega (meaning beginning and end).

had scarcely penetrated. Christianity was at first a city religion; it had yet to develop the parish organization that was later to make it successful in rural areas. The cities of the predominantly rural West were smaller, fewer, and weaker than those of the East. Thus hundreds of thousands of country dwellers had little contact with the new religion. As late as the early sixth century, missionaries could still make numerous converts in Italy and southern Gaul.

At the same time, to the detriment of both literature and politics, theological controversies absorbed the energies of the best thinkers and the ablest writers of the more urban and urbane East. Good Christians might, and did, say that this was only right, that it was better to study the things of God than the problems of the world, but concentration on theological disputes stirred up passions that injured both the Church and the Empire. This was especially true in the East, where there was strong rivalry among the patriarchs (religious leaders) of Constantinople, Antioch, and Alexandria. Antioch and Alexandria claimed apostolic origin; Constantinople was the capital of the Empire. The people of these cities supported their own clergy and argued vehemently over disputed doctrines. The Syrians of Antioch and the Egyptians of Alexandria voiced their resentment against centuries of Greek domination by adopting theologies that infuriated the Greeks. Religious separatism and local patriotism went hand in hand, and during the next two centuries the loyalty of the eastern provinces to Constantinople diminished steadily.

The West, with the exception of North Africa, was less shaken by religious controversy. Beginning with Tertullian in the second century, Latin theologians had shown a tendency to make clear and simple definitions rather than to speculate on fine points of doctrine. Fortunately, the definitions they made proved acceptable to the Church councils. The bishop of Rome, now regularly called the pope, was the heir to this Latin tradition and was therefore always on the side of orthodoxy. Since the pope was the successor of St. Peter (who, according to old tradition was founder of the church in Rome), no other bishop in the West had anything like the pope's authority. His interpretation of doctrine was usually accepted in the Latin-speaking provinces. The eastern provinces, attached to their own definitions of orthodox belief, were much less ready to accept papal pronouncements. Thus in religious matters, as in many others, East and West were drifting apart.

THE END OF THE EMPIRE IN THE WEST

In the last quarter of the fourth century the threat to the Rhine and Danube frontiers of the Empire reached a new intensity. To the familiar German raids was added a fresh menace: the advance of the Huns from Central Asia.

The Huns

The Huns were typical of the Asian nomads who for centuries threatened the civilized peoples of the Eurasian continent. These nomads lived in a harsh land of scant rainfall and great extremes of temperature. Often the distance between their summer and winter pastures was over a thousand miles, so they had to become expert horsemen. Living in the saddle, they invented most of the equipment that made cavalry an effective fighting force. For example, they used horseshoes and stirrups long before these devices were known in the West. If one imagines riding a horse into battle without stirrups, one can see why the Asian nomads long had supremacy in cavalry fighting. But even after their equipment was adopted by other peoples, the nomads were still almost unbeatable as horse soldiers; they were unafraid of death and as pitiless as the land in which they lived.

Fortunately for their neighbors, the nomads usually lived in small bands of no great striking force. But every now and then bands threatened by a common danger would join together, or a leader of genius would manage to unite several groups. Once this process started, it was almost irreversible. The ruler of some thousands of nomads could force all the smaller groups in an area of thousands of square miles either to join him or perish.

Thus were built up the great human avalanches that thundered down from the high plateaus of Central Asia onto the coasts of China, Europe, and India.

The Huns who attacked Europe were a part of one of these avalanches. As they moved west across the steppes their army snowballed until at last they broke out onto the Russian plain in the second half of the fourth century. No Germanic people could withstand them. Some of the resident population joined the Huns as satellite troops; others fled in terror to the shelter of the Empire.

The Goths

The first Germanic people to be struck by the Huns were the Goths, who had come from the north and had settled around the Black Sea. Since they were on reasonably good terms with the Romans, they turned to Rome for aid. The East Goths (Ostrogoths) were overrun by the Huns, but the West Goths (Visigoths) managed to cross the Danube and take refuge in the Empire. Unfortunately, some imperial officials regarded the West Goths as a new source of forced labor, and mistreatment soon led to revolt. After routing a hastily gathered Roman army in the battle of Adrianople (378), the Goths occupied a large part of the Balkan Peninsula.

This was not the first time that Germans had defeated a Roman army and occupied Roman territory. The time-honored tactic in such a case was to settle the invaders in a frontier province, and to integrate them gradually into Roman society. This was the policy adopted by the emperor Theodosius (378–395), and it very nearly succeeded. He concentrated the Goths in a small strip of land south of the Danube in the Balkans, where they lived as Roman allies under their own kings. Their most promising young men were sent to Constantinople for educa-

THE GERMANIC MIGRATIONS Fourth to sixth centuries

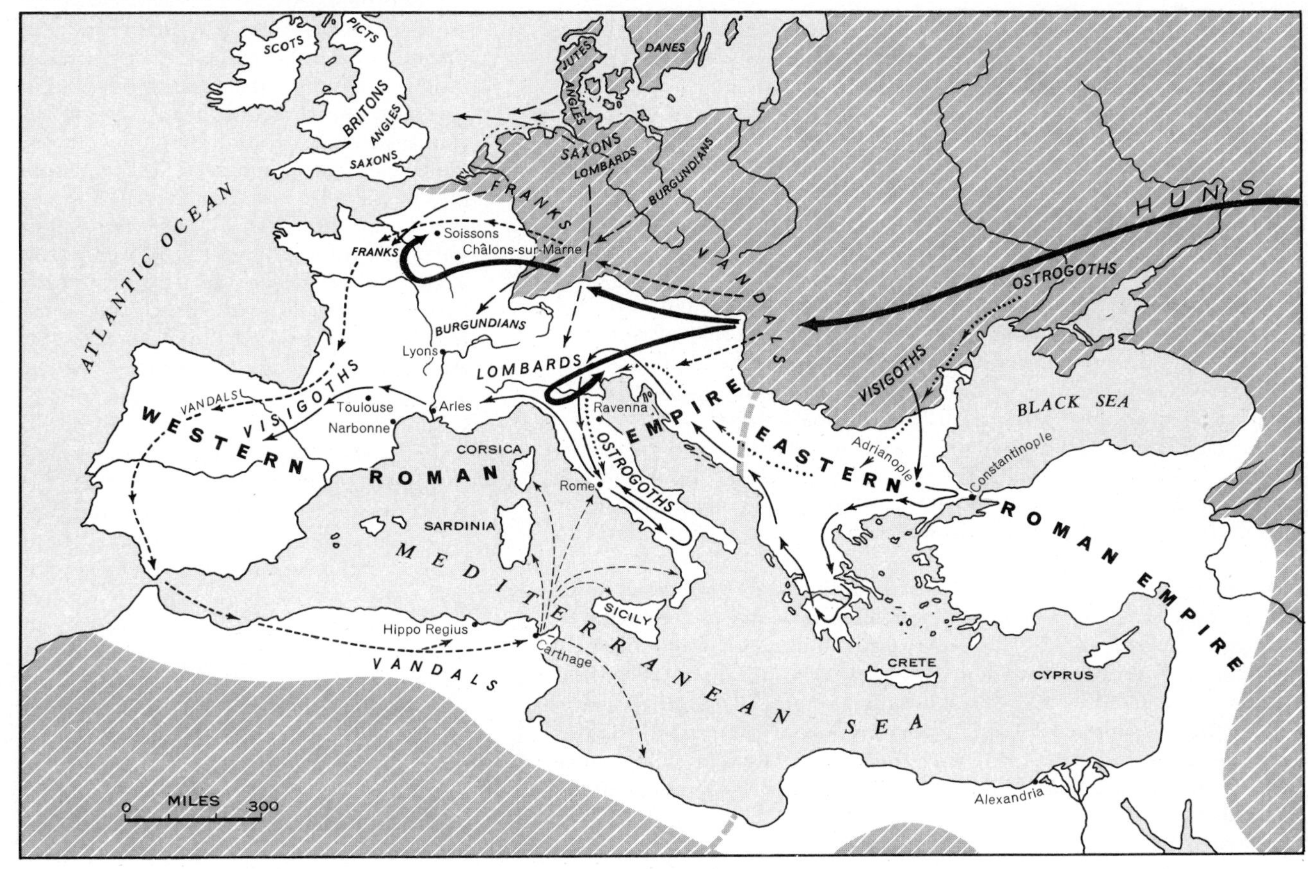

Silver commemorative plate depicting Theodosius and his two sons (*ca.* 390).

A Christian Priest on Social Conditions in the Late Empire

Salvian was a priest who lived in southern Gaul in the fifth century A.D. The passage is not entirely sincere—Salvian really disliked the barbarians—but praise of the barbarians ("noble savages") was an old theme in Latin literature and gave Salvian an excuse to criticize the government.

But as for the way of life among the Goths and the Vandals, how can we consider ourselves superior to them, or even worthy of comparison? To speak first of affection and charity . . . almost all barbarians, at least those who belong to one tribe . . . love one another, while almost all the Romans are at strife with one another. What citizen does not envy his fellows? Who shows complete charity to his neighbors? . . . Worse, the many are persecuted by the few, who use public taxes for their own individual gain. . . . Where can one find cities or even villages in which there are not as many tyrants as officials? . . .

The poor are robbed, widows groan, orphans are oppressed until many, even persons of good birth and education, flee to the enemy to escape . . . persecution. They seek Roman humanity among the barbarians since they cannot endure the barbarian inhumanity they find among the Romans. . . . They do not regret their exile, for they would rather live as free men, though seeming to be in captivity, than as captives in seeming liberty. Hence the name of Roman citizen, once highly valued and dearly bought, is now voluntarily repudiated and shunned.

From Salvian, *On the Government of God,* trans. by Eva M. Sanford (New York: Columbia University Press, 1930), pp. 138–42.

tion; some of them received posts in the army. For the remainder of Theodosius' reign the Goths remained quiet.

Theodosius tried to preserve the religious as well as the political unity of the Roman state, but here again he ran into the problem of the barbarians. After a half-century of conflict, Arius and his followers had been crushed by the authorities of the Empire, but before their final defeat Arian bishops had converted some of the Goths. One of these Goths, Ulfila, translated the Scriptures into Gothic and so gave the Arians an advantage in missionary work among the Germans. By the time of Theodosius most of the Goths, and an increasingly large number of other Germans, had accepted the Arian form of Christianity. Theodosius tried to suppress Arianism among his own subjects, but he could not interfere with the religious beliefs of his allies. Most German settlers and most German soldiers were Arians. Their heretical belief offended the Romans and was one of the factors that delayed the merging of the two peoples.

Theodosius was a defender of the orthodox faith; he made Christianity the official religion of the Empire in 390. He was also the first European ruler to do public penance for offending the Church. He had ordered a massacre of the people of Thessalonica because they had killed one of his officers. By this time Milan was the center of imperial power in the West, and the bishop of Milan, St. Ambrose, refused to give Theodosius communion until he had done penance. St. Ambrose was a greatly respected leader, and in spite of imperial threats, finally forced the emperor to admit his fault. Theodosius' submission demonstrated the growing power of the Church. St. Ambrose wrote some notable letters on this event, which medieval popes were to use as a precedent in their struggles with lay rulers.

Theodosius was the last emperor to control the whole Roman world and the last to keep the frontiers reasonably intact. He achieved this success, however, only by strengthening the barbarian element in the army and in the border regions. Theodosius himself was strong enough to control his generals, but his weak successors were puppets of the army commanders, most of whom were of Germanic origin.

The Division of the Empire

When Theodosius died in 395, he was succeeded by his two sons, Arcadius in the East and Honorius in the West. This division of the Empire was not meant to be permanent; during the last century there had usually been more than one emperor. While each ruler had been primarily responsible for one part of the Empire, the coemperors had always cooperated to some extent and in emergencies had acted in each other's territories. But the division between Arcadius and Honorius proved to be rather different. The army commanders who held real power under the two young emperors were suspicious of each other and would not cooperate. The Germans (both those in the army and those pushing across the frontiers) grew so strong in the West that the eastern ruler could not step in and reunite the two halves of the Empire when his western colleague died.

Theoretically, the Empire remained one state, but in fact it was permanently divided after 395, and each half had a different fate. The West fell completely under the power of the Germans and for centuries remained backward in political organization and economic activity. In the East the Empire continued, and, though it gradually became quite un-Roman, it was far more stable and prosperous than the barbarian kingdoms of the West.

The Sack of Rome

When Theodosius died, the Visigoths left their Balkan reservation and began raiding again. They might have been crushed if the western and eastern army commanders had cooperated, but each was afraid the other might gain an advantage. In fact, it seems likely that the eastern government persuaded the Goths to move west in order to spare the Balkans from further looting. When the Visigoths stormed down into the Italian peninsula, the emperor Honorius shut himself up in the fortified city of Ravenna and made no move to stop them. The Goths occupied Rome in 410—a catastrophe that sent a last feeble impulse of patriotism through the Empire.

Alaric, "King of the Goths," depicted in a seal contemporary with the sack of Rome in 410.

True, Rome had not been the real capital for many years, but it was still the symbol of the Empire. No enemy had touched it for almost eight centuries, and its fall shocked men who otherwise cared little about imperial affairs. Adherents of pagan religions said bitterly that this disaster occurred only after the Empire had forsaken its old, protecting deities for the powerless Christian God. St. Augustine, the ablest Christian writer of the period, was spurred into writing his most famous book, *The City of God* (see p. 119), in order to refute this argument. He insisted that the eternal City of God inhabited by the saints was far more important than any earthly city of sinners. Yet even St. Augustine admitted that the Romans had created the best secular government that had ever existed, and less devout Christians must surely have been worried by signs that this government was failing.

The Visigoths, perhaps seeking more fertile land, abandoned Italy and moved to southwestern Gaul. Here they settled permanently, gradually occupying Spain as well. They remained allies of the Empire and helped the Romans repel a dangerous Hun invasion in 451. But as the western Empire weakened, the Goths grew more independent; by 500 they were entirely free from imperial control. The Visigothic king ruled his own realm, and the authority of Rome was only a distant memory.

Other Germanic Migrations

Shortly after the Visigoths started their long march to the west, other Germanic groups pushed across the frontiers. The Romans had neither the troops nor the will to stop the invaders, but they were able, in most cases, to reach an accommodation with them. They granted the Germans the status of allies, and gave their kings Roman titles when they set up kingdoms in Roman territory. By thus regularizing the occupation, the Romans avoided much violence. The Germans, who were not very numerous, had no desire to destroy the Romans and their cities, or their political and economic

A Vandal general in the service of Rome. Although he is a barbarian, he wears Roman clothing (panel of an ivory diptych, *ca.* 400).

system; all they wanted was a reasonable share of the land. The Romans, with a declining population, had land to spare; so long as they could keep some of their property, they could tolerate the rule of barbarian kings. Thus in most of the western Empire there was no catastrophic loss of life or property as the Germans moved in. The one great exception was Britain, where the imperial government had collapsed so completely that no peaceful settlement could be worked out with the invading Anglo-Saxons.

One of the longest, and in the end the most unsuccessful, of the Germanic migrations was that of the Vandals. This coalition of peoples moved from north Germany through Gaul into Spain. Attacked by the Visigoths, they abandoned Spain and finally settled in North Africa. Here they built a fleet with which they dominated the western Mediterranean for half a century. They even managed to seize Rome briefly in 455; but although they plundered the city, they were not guilty of the kind of wanton destruction that has become associated with their name. The Vandals did not try to hold Italy, and even in North Africa they grew so weak that they were easily crushed by the Eastern Roman Empire in the sixth century.

More typical of the German migrants were the Franks and the Burgundians. They made a shorter journey and established successful and permanent settlements. Until the death of Theodosius both peoples had been confined to border territories along the Rhine and in northeastern Gaul. The Franks then began to move south and west, while the Burgundians settled in the Rhône valley. Neither people was ever again brought under control of the imperial government.

About this time, the Angles and the Saxons began to raid Britain from their homes along the North Sea. Rome had withdrawn its army and its officials from Britain, and the invaders, crossing the sea in small flotillas, were unable to concentrate their forces. With no unified command on either side, negotiations were almost impossible. Small groups of native Britons fought small groups of Anglo-Saxons in a bloody war that lasted for over a century. In the process Roman civilization was wiped out. Cities and villas were destroyed, and the Britons, driven back into Wales or Cornwall, gave up the use of Latin and reverted to their native Celtic. The larger part of Britain became England, a land of Germanic speech and customs.

By the middle of the fifth century all that was left of the Empire in the West was Italy and a fragment of Gaul. Even this remnant was threatened by a new advance of the Huns under their famous king Attila, the "Scourge of God." A first attack on Gaul was defeated in 451 by Aëtius, the "last general of the Empire," with the help of Visigothic and Frankish allies. Attila invaded Italy the next year, but he found the peninsula too barren to support his army. He was persuaded to withdraw by an embassy led by Pope Leo I, an episode that gave great prestige to the papacy. With Attila's death in 453 his empire disintegrated, and the Huns no longer menaced the West.

Aëtius' victory gained him only the jealous suspicion, not the thanks, of the emperor. The general was put to death; his followers retaliated by assassinating the emperor. For a while German army commanders governed Italy behind a façade of puppet emperors. At last, in 476, Odovacar, the leader of a band of German mercenaries, tired of the pretense. He deposed the last emperor and became king of Italy. All Roman territories west of the Adriatic were now under barbarian rulers.

Zeno, the emperor in Constantinople, promptly regularized the situation by naming Odovacar his representative in Italy. Thus the fiction of imperial unity was preserved, though Zeno had no real authority in the West. A decade later the imperial government tried to turn fiction into fact by sending a new group of Germans to attack Odovacar. These Germans were the Ostrogoths, who had finally escaped Hunnish domination after the death of Attila. Like the Visigoths, they had settled in the Balkans; and like the Visigoths, they were so unruly that the emperor was delighted to speed their way to Italy. After several years of fighting, the Ostrogoths defeated and killed Odovacar and by 493 had full control of Italy.

The Ostrogothic king, Theodoric, was one of the ablest of the Germanic rulers. Having lived several years at the court of Constantinople, he made a greater effort than most barbarian kings to preserve the forms of Roman government. He always acknowledged the formal sovereignty of the emperor, but in fact he was just as independent as Odovacar. Theodoric had no intention of restoring imperial rule in the West.

The "Fall of the Roman Empire"

The deposition of the last western emperor in 476 is often referred to as the "Fall of the Roman Empire." Taken literally, this is a meaningless phrase. There was almost nothing left to fall in the West, and in the East the Empire survived as a powerful state. No inhabitant of the Mediterranean world could believe that the Empire had "fallen" in 476, though he might have good reason to feel that the western part of it was decrepit.

Still, the passing of the Latin-speaking part of the Empire under Germanic rule was a watershed in history. Basic ideas of government and law had come from the Latin West; an Empire that was largely Greek could not remain a Roman Empire, even though it kept the name. The Latins became barbarized under Germanic rulers; the Greeks became Orientalized as their contacts with the West decreased. Thus the two halves of the Roman world drifted apart, preparing the way for the later split between eastern and western Europe.

This divergence between the two parts of the Empire raises a question that has puzzled generations of historians. Why did the Empire and the civilization it embodied collapse in the West and survive in the East? The East suffered the same social illnesses as the West; why did they do less damage? About all that can be said is that the East was favored by geography and that it had more economic and spiritual vitality than the West. As long as Persia remained neutral the rich eastern provinces of Asia Minor, Syria, and Egypt could not be attacked. They were protected by impregnable Constantinople, where the main strength of the defense forces could be concentrated. The Balkan provinces were more exposed, but they did not attract permanent German settlement. In the West it was easy to attack and occupy the rich farmlands of Gaul and the Po Valley. Furthermore, commerce and industry were concentrated in the East; the wealth of eastern cities could be used to hire armies and bribe enemies. The West had no such resources.

Finally, Christianity had cut deeper and spread more widely in the East than in the West, and zeal for the faith often led to support of the state that protected the faith. This identification of religion with patriotism was not universal—nor was it always helpful. Heretics often bitterly opposed the imperial authorities. But at least in the East some people felt strongly enough about their beliefs to fight for them; in the West, Christians were as apathetic as pagans. Western bishops disliked the Arian Goths, but they did not fight them, either to preserve the true faith or to save the eternal Empire. During the fifth century the eastern emperor was able to recruit soldiers from among his subjects, while in the West the Roman population hardly lifted a finger to protect itself.

But these were differences in degree and not in kind. The East was only a little

Capella on Geographic Zones

Martianus Capella's *Satyricon,* from which the following was taken, was written in the early fifth century. It was one of the typical encyclopedic digests of the late Empire. Note that Capella, and the scholars he quoted, knew that the world was round.

The round world may be divided into five zones or bands of different characteristics. Of these, great excesses of heat or cold force three to be abandoned. The two zones which touch either end of the earth's axis, dominated by terrible cold, are deserted because of frost and snow, while the middle zone, baked by flames and breath-taking heat, scorches all living things that come near. The two other zones, tempered by the breath of life-sustaining air, offer a habitation to living things. These zones, curving around the sphere of the earth, go around both the upper and the lower hemisphere. . . . Those who live opposite us are called "antipodes." . . . For when we roast in summer, they shiver with cold; when spring here begins to cover the fields with flowers, there worn-out summer is passing into sleepy autumn.

From Martianus Capella, *De nuptiis philologiae et Mercurii* (Leipzig: Teubner, 1866), Book VI (on Geometry), p. 252.

more stable than the West; it saved itself from the Germans but could not repel the next great attack, that of the Arabs (see p. 167). The basic trouble was that very few inhabitants of the Empire believed that the old civilization was worth saving. As we have seen, there never was a time when the Romans did not greatly outnumber the invaders. A reasonably trustworthy source numbers the entire Vandal people—men, women, and children—at about eighty thousand when they crossed the Straits of Gibraltar. Yet this small group overran all North Africa. The "Fall of the Empire" was not a political episode of the year 476; it was a deadly crisis in the history of a civilization.

ART AND LITERATURE DURING THE MIGRATIONS

Secular Art and Literature

Officially sponsored literature, education, and art were as decadent as imperial politics during the time of the Germanic migrations. The blight of imitation lay heavily on all secular thought and literature. Overrefinement of earlier techniques had produced a style that was involved, ornate, and often deliberately obscure. Greek was seldom studied in the West—another sign of the drawing apart of the two halves of the Empire—and the Greek scientific tradition was scarcely known to men of Latin speech. A final sign of the degeneration of secular studies was the making of digests—handy collections of familiar quotations, one-volume encyclopedias, and summaries of the rules of grammar in a few pages. Scholars studied these digests more than the original works from which they were drawn; they were to become the basic textbooks of the Middle Ages.

Official art, like secular literature, was heavy and imitative. Few new buildings or monuments were constructed. Those that were built often were decorated with materials taken from earlier works. For example, on the Arch of Constantine there is a striking contrast between the crude work of the fourth century and the elegant sculptures borrowed from a second-century monument. The same decline is evident in the coins of the period. The Romans had been masters of realism, if not of the higher forms of art, and the coins of the emperors of the first and second centuries carry striking portraits. By the end of the fourth century the coins were less well made and the portrait became a symbol—the emperor as a type rather than as an individual. The shift to symbolism from realism marked a change in attitude, but it also marked a change in skill. The symbolism of medieval sculptors resulted in great works of art; this can hardly be said of the symbolism of the Late Roman Empire.

Thus wherever one turns in the fourth and early fifth centuries one sees apathy on the part of the multitude and a lack of creativeness among the upper classes. The framework of imperial government held the Roman world together long after Roman civilization was dead, but it could not support a corpse indefinitely. New forms of organization and new beliefs were needed before civilization could revive.

Christian Art and Literature

The new beliefs and many of the new forms of organization were developed by the Christian Church, the only segment of late Roman society that still had any vitality and originality. Christian literature and Christian art of the fourth century stood at the beginning of a new tradition rather than at the end of the old classical tradition. But the old tradition had to die before the new tradition could reveal its full potential. Christians could no more preserve classical literary and artistic forms than they could preserve the political organization of the Empire.

Art of the fourth and fifth centuries declined from the elegant work of the first and second centuries. Contrast the fine modeling of the coin of Tiberius (14–37 A.D.) with the crude portrait of Honorius (395–423) beside it.

The career of St. Augustine, the greatest Christian theologian of the period, illustrates this point. Augustine (354–430) was born in what is now Tunisia, the only son of a well-to-do family. He received a good classical education and could have had a profitable career as a lawyer or as a member of the imperial bureaucracy. But Augustine, like many of his contemporaries, was concerned about religion and salvation. He was not at first a Christian—one more proof of the slow spread of the faith into the West. As a young man he turned to Neoplatonism and then to Manicheanism to satisfy his spiritual interests. When he finally accepted Christianity he abandoned public life entirely and dedicated his remarkable intellectual gifts to the service of the Church.

Augustine was not greatly concerned by the troubles of the Empire, though at the time of his death the Goths had seized Rome and the Vandals were attacking Hippo, the city where he was bishop. Pagan charges that neglect of their gods had caused the sack of Rome did inspire him to write *The City of God,* but only to prove that the fate of Rome was unimportant compared with the preservation of the holy community of saints and angels. His real concern was with God's ways toward man, and especially with the problems of free will and predestination, of evil and sin. If God is all-wise and all-powerful, does man really have free will? How can such a God allow man to sin and condemn himself to endless suffering? How can a merciful God countenance the existence of evil? These were the questions Augustine wrestled with in his *Confessions,* one of the most remarkable autobiographies of all time. He dealt with them again in *The City of God* and in the innumerable treatises that made him the most influential theologian of the West.

By avoiding extreme answers Augustine found solutions that have appealed to Christian scholars of all times and all sects. Thus he argued that evil is not an independent power (as the Manicheans taught) nor yet the creation of God; it is merely the absence of good. Man has free will, but this free will is ineffective without the assistance of divine grace.

St. Augustine on the City of God

Accordingly, two cities have been formed by two loves: the earthly by the love of self, even to the contempt of God; the heavenly by the love of God, even to contempt of self. The former glories in itself, the latter in the Lord. For the one seeks glory from men, but the greatest glory of the other is God, the witness of conscience. . . . In the one, the princes and the nations it subdues are ruled by the love of ruling; in the other, the princes and the subjects serve one another in love, the latter obeying, while the former take thought for all. The one delights in its own strength, represented in the persons of its rulers; the other says to its God: "I will love Thee, O Lord, my strength." And therefore the wise men of the one city, living according to man, have sought for profit to their own bodies or souls, or both, and those who have known God "glorified him not as God, neither were thankful, but became vain in their imaginations, and their foolish heart was darkened. . . ." For they were either leaders or followers of the people in adoring images, "and worshipped and served the creature more than the Creator." But in the other city there is no human wisdom, but only godliness, which offers due worship to the true God, and looks for its reward in the society of the saints, of holy angels as well as holy men, that God may be all in all.

From St. Augustine, *City of God,* in *Basic Writings of St. Augustine,* ed. by Whitney J. Oates, Vol. II, p. 274. Copyright 1948 by Random House, Inc. Reprinted by permission.

Augustine made his points emphatically, sometimes too emotionally, but he was writing about subjects that were important to him.

The other chief Latin Christian authors of the fourth century were St. Jerome and St. Ambrose. Jerome (335–420) was a better scholar than Augustine; he knew both Greek and Hebrew. He spent much of his life translating the Bible into Latin, a translation on which the Vulgate—the official Catholic text—was based. Ambrose (d. 397) was an administrator and preacher rather than a scholar. He had had a successful career in the imperial civil service before he became bishop of Milan. He was involved in a long quarrel with Arian heretics, and, as we have seen, he forced the emperor Theodosius to do public penance for his sins. During these disputes he encouraged his flock by writing sermons, and even more by writing hymns for them to sing. This was a rather new idea; Ambrose did much to popularize of the Late Empire are sometimes crude, but never flaccid.

It was also during this period that the basic patterns for church architecture were developed. In the West, the model was the Roman law court, or basilica, a long rectangular room with two sets of pillars dividing the room into a central hall, or nave, flanked by two side aisles. The roof over the nave was elevated to admit light through windows set above the side aisles. Eventually the far end of the nave was rounded into an apse that held the altar and seats for the clergy. Later a transept was inserted between nave and apse. This was a hall that crossed the nave at right angles and protruded beyond the aisle walls, thus giving the church the form of a cross. There were basilicas in the East as well, but the most typical form for eastern churches was a round or polygonal structure with a dome over the central portion. This pattern still characterizes churches of the Greek rite.

Christian art and Christian literature were to have their fullest development in later centuries. But even before 500 two things had been demonstrated: first, that under the inspiration of Christian doctrine new styles were arising to replace those that had dominated the Mediterranean world for centuries; second, that the people of the Greco-Roman world, despite all their troubles, were still capable of creative activity.

The church of Santa Sabina, built in 425, incorporates the characteristics of a Roman basilica—a long, rectangular nave divided from two side aisles by rows of pillars.

hymn singing in the West, and his hymns are still sung in the Catholic Church.

Christian art of the late Empire showed the same vigor as Christian literature. The trend away from realism to symbolism was entirely appropriate for religious art. During this period some of the most persistent symbols for representing Christian ideas were developed, such as the dove to represent the Holy Spirit. Christian painting and sculpture

Suggestions for Further Reading

Note: Asterisk denotes a book available in paperback edition.

The Late Empire There are many fine histories of the late Roman Empire. One that was used by many later scholars is the synthesis by F. Lot, *The End of the Ancient World** (1931). An excellent survey is A. H. M. Jones, *The Later Roman Empire,* 3 vols. (1964); an abridged version was published in 1966. Both S. Dill, *Roman Society in the Last Century of the Empire** (1910), and M. I. Rostovtzeff, *The Social and Economic History of the Roman Empire,** rev. ed. (1957), discuss the reforms of Diocletian. Rostovtzeff is more thorough and is useful as a reference, but Dill is more readable. P. Brown, *The World of Late Antiquity** (1971), is a brilliant study. See also J. Vogt, *The Decline of Rome* (1967), an excellent book. The most recent work is R. MacMullen, *The Roman Government's Response to Crisis* (1976). See also J. Matthews, *Western Aristocracies and the Imperial Court,* A.D. *364–425* (1975).

The Spread of Christianity

One of the great problems in European history is that of the conversion of the emperor Constantine. R. MacMullen, *Constantine* (1969), in his good, short biography of the emperor, is inclined to see a semimagical, semireligious impulse. The Swiss historian J. Burckhardt, in his influential book *The Age of Constantine the Great,** trans. by M. Hadas (1952), sees Constantine's conversion as completely an act of political expediency. A. H. M. Jones, *Constantine and the Conversion of Europe* (1948), interprets the conversion as religious in motivation. Both Burckhardt and Jones base their arguments on the writings of the court bishop Eusebius and the scholar Lactantius, significant parts of which are in K. Setton and H. R. Winkler, eds., *Great Problems in European Civilization* (1954). This book has excellent source material on the spread of Christianity. Other views can be found in J. W. Eadie (ed.), *The Conversion of Constantine** (1971). The latest, and a very good biography of Constantine is T. D. Barnes, *Constantine and Eusebius* (1981). J. Lebreton and J. Zeiller, *The Emergence of the Church in the Roman Empire* (1962), discuss the spread of Christianity. The short monograph of E. R. Goodenough, *The Church in the Roman Empire* (1931), presents Christianity as a summation of various religious ideas of the Roman environment. Goodenough is a useful introduction to the study of Christianity in this period. On the persecutions, see W. H. C. Frend, *Martyrdom and Persecution in the Early Church** (1967).

The Goths and the Huns

H. Mattingly, *Tacitus on Britain and Germany** (1952), is a rich mine of information about the political, social, and economic conditions of the Germanic peoples at the time when they first came in contact with the Roman Empire. There is a good picture of the Germanic migrations and warlike spirit in Jordanes, *Origins and Deeds of the Goths,* trans. by C. C. Mierow (1908). J. B. Bury's *The Invasions of Europe by the Barbarians** (1928) has valuable material on the barbarian impact on Europe, while L. Halphen, *Les Barbares* (1930), traces the beginnings and spread of the Germanic peoples down to the eleventh century. Halphen has good bibliographic material. Another good book in French is E. Demougeot, *La formation de l'Europe et les invasions barbares* (1969). The old study of P. Villari, *The Barbarian Invasions of Italy,* 2 vols. (1902), is still valuable. See also E. A. Thompson, *The Visigoths in Spain* (1969).

The Fall of the Empire in the West

E. Gibbon's monumental work, *The History of the Decline and Fall of the Roman Empire,* ed. by J. B. Bury (1896–1900), presents an answer to this problem in a book that has stood as a classic in English literature since 1776. A leading French medievalist, F. Lot, in *The End of the Ancient World** (1931), attributes the decline largely to economic causes, while C. Dawson, *The Making of Europe** (1934), shows the importance of religious developments. See also W. C. Bark, *Origins of the Medieval World** (1960), a good, short account of the transition from the late Empire to the early Middle Ages. Varying views can be found in M. H. Chambers (ed.), *The Fall of Rome** (1970).

Art and Literature

From its beginnings Christianity has inspired art in the pictorial form. C. R. Morey, *Early Christian Art** (1942), is an interesting introduction. W. Lowrie, *Art in the Early Church* (1947), is an excellent study of early Christian art, with fine reproductions and a critical bibliography. The broad survey of W. R. Lethaby, *Medieval Art from the Peace of the Church to the Eve of the Renaissance, 313–1350,* rev. by D. Talbot-Rice (1947), covers all art forms and has considerable material on the early Church. Also of interest is P. du Bourguet, *Early Christian Painting** (1965).

Perhaps the greatest thinker the western Church produced in the Middle Ages was St. Augustine of Hippo. *The Confessions of St. Augustine** (many editions) is one of the most remarkable accounts of a spiritual pilgrimage ever written. St. Augustine's *City of God** (many editions), which deals with such basic theological questions as the nature of God, free will, sin, and salvation, played a large part in the evolution of Roman Catholic and Protestant thinking. P. Brown, *Augustine of Hippo** (1967), is the best work in English. The writings of most of the early Church Fathers have been collected and translated in *The Fathers of the Church* series, ed. by R. J. Deferrari (1947 ff.).

H. Marrou, *History of Education in Antiquity** (1948), which carries the reader down to 700 A.D., has good material on Christian literature. A. Alföldi, *A Conflict of Ideas in the Later Roman Empire* (1932), is a short and brilliant book.

6 India and China in Antiquity

Civilization in South and East Asia developed later than in Mesopotamia and Egypt but well before Greece and Rome. India and China resemble each other in their antiquity, their duration, and the vast geographical extent of their cultural influence, but in many essential respects they represent a study in contrast. Furthermore, even though India, unlike China, did share in a broad and diffuse Indo-European heritage, it developed a civilization as distinct from those to the West as it was from that of China. Contact between the various civilizations is a fascinating and occasionally important historical theme, but the primary interest of Indian and Chinese civilizations, as of their western counterparts, lies in their intrinsic importance in the past and present history of the globe, the enduring value of their cultural achievements, and in the wealth of material they offer for the study of the comparative history of civilization.

INDIA

The Indian subcontinent, stretching from the frosty Himalayan Mountains to the tropical beaches of the south, is a vast area inhabited by peoples with strong regional and local traditions. In the course of time, sufficient unity developed so that we can speak of an Indian civilization, but within that civilization there has always been great diversity. The interplay of the factors making for one or the other is a major theme of Indian history.

As we have seen, civilization in India dates to the third millenium B.C. when a sophisticated culture flourished, centered in the Indus River Valley. Over a territory of half a million square miles, some 300 sites have been investigated, most of them near rivers whose waters sustained agriculture and provided transportation. The most impressive sites are those of Mohenjo-Daro and Harappa, the former a city of 25,000–30,000 inhabitants. Laid out on grids and capped by citadels, these two cities were complete with granaries and advanced drainage systems, and the presence of separate industrial areas points to class differentiation. Small square seals found as far away as Sumerian Mesopotamia attest to a flourishing commerce. These seals were probably used by merchants to mark their wares. Some are decorated with real or imaginary animals; others bear abstract symbols, including the Greek cross and the swastika. Written inscriptions on the seals have not been deciphered, although the script is generally considered to be in a Dravidian language. The technological repertoire of the cities included wheel-made pottery, cotton spinning, and metallurgy. The impressive bath at Mohenjo-Daro, similar to water tanks in later Hindu temples, may attest to the

Capital on a column erected by Asoka to commemorate the Buddha's preaching of the First Sermon in Sarnath.

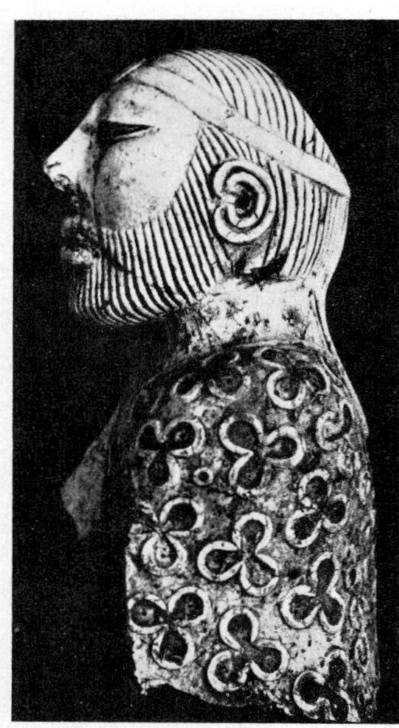

Statuette of a man, perhaps a priest, wearing an ornamental robe, from Mohenjo-Daro (*ca.* 2500 B.C.).

importance of religion, but no actual temples have been uncovered from this period.

Environmental factors such as devastating floods, a shift in the course of the Indus River, and exhaustion of soil fertility may have accounted for the demise of this civilization. A decline in social organization followed, as mirrored in later city planning. By the time the crude Aryan tribal peoples entered the subcontinent, the old civilization was gone, leaving in its wake impoverished localized cultures.

Early Aryan–Indian Society

The Aryans began to enter India in substantial numbers through the Hindu-Kush mountains around 1500 B.C. They were tribal peoples related to the inhabitants of Iran, and they spoke Sanskrit, an Indo-European language which became the classic language of India. They were a vigorous, indeed tumultuous and warlike people, not unlike the Greeks. Originally pastoral, as time passed they also turned to agriculture. They gradually achieved dominance first in the Indus Plain, then in North India. After 1000 B.C. there were also Aryan incursions into the region beyond the Vindhaya Mountain Range, which separates North from South India. Although ultimately North Indian culture profoundly influenced the South, the various southern regions never lost their cultural or linguistic identity. Today, South India continues to be dominated by peoples speaking Dravidian languages belonging to a different linguistic family from that of the Indo-European tongues of the North.

In the beginning the Aryans were divided into warriors, priests, and commoners, but as they settled down their social organization became more complex. There developed what became India's classic division of society into four social orders (*varnas*). Most likely, the warriors (*kshatriyas*) originally had pride of place, but the classic order ranks priests (*brahmans*) first with warriors second. Other Aryans were included in the third varna, that of the *vaishyas,* a term later used for merchants and cultivators. Members of these three orders were entitled to full membership in society as symbolized by the sacred thread granted to boys in an induction ceremony. This status was denied to the dark-skinned conquered people who formed the fourth order, the *shudras,* who were reduced to serfdom and forced to perform menial tasks. Still further down in social status were those whose work was considered polluting: attendants at cremation grounds, those who worked with animal carcasses, leather workers, and others. Later they were known as "untouchables," beyond the pale of Aryan society.

As political integration proceeded and Aryan influences spread, the interaction between India's various communities grew in complexity and extent. The process by which major components of North Indian culture were spread is frequently termed "Aryanization," but the influence was not all one way. The varna system did not operate everywhere in the same way, and another institution, the *jati* (caste) made for a diversity of life-styles and beliefs even within the same locality. The jatis were endogamous (inter-marrying) groups which shared a common religious heritage, traditional values, dietary rules, and, characteristically, a common occupation. It was the jati to which they belonged that gave men and women their basic sense of community and determined the essential pattern of their lives. Like membership in a family, membership in a jati was a matter of birth; a person could no more change his jati than he could his family. To be expelled from one's jati and become an outcast was the worst possible fate, for no other jati would accept such a person.

Although the tendency was for the jati to be grouped under the major varna, the fit was often imperfect. By preserving the traditions and identities of numerous groups, the jati system contributed to Indian pluralism while, at the same time, it reinforced social differentiation. Although much has changed in the long course of history, the existence of over three thousand jatis attests to the continuing significance of this institution in India today.

Religious Developments

The success of the brahmans (priests) in gaining first place in the social hierarchy suggests the importance of religion in early India. Like other Indo-European peoples, the Aryans worshipped a number of gods—some being more important than others. As the civilization grew in complexity and sophistication, the old rituals and formulas no longer met everyone's religious needs, and there appeared a tendency toward abstract thought and a posing of such ultimate questions as those concerning the nature of being and nonbeing, questions which were to be central to India's loftiest religious and philosophical discourses.

These religious concerns were expressed in the *Upanishads,* a group of religious treatises of the eighth and seventh centuries B.C. The *Upanishads* contain the religious speculations of teachers working in the traditions of the *Rig Veda,* an ancient collection of hymns handed down orally from generation to generation and written down in its present form around 600 B.C. Since the *Upanishads* do not stem from a single source, they contain diverse ideas, but they do agree on one central theme: that the invisible but essential "soul" within each of us (*Atman*) is identical with the world-soul (*Brahman*), the underlying reality of the world. Failure to realize this truth condemns people to be prisoners of their illusions and chains them to an unending cycle of birth and rebirth. Death provides no relief, for it is merely a stage, an interlude between lives. Release comes only when the individual Atman is rejoined with the Brahman, attainable only after comprehension is achieved through disciplined effort, meditation, and/or various spiritual and yogic exercises.

The individual fate of those who do not attain release is governed by the law of *karma,* according to which every action brings forth a reaction, not only in this life but also in the next. Thus a person who has led a good life but still falls short of the perfection needed for release will at least enjoy a favorable rebirth, but a wicked person might come back as a pig, a goat, or even an insect. In later Indian thought various theories were advanced to account for the operation of karma. Different behavioral conclusions were drawn (for instance, it reinforced a tendency toward vegetarianism), but the concept of karma itself was accepted as a basic truth not only by ordinary folk but by all traditional Indian thinkers and holy men.

The Buddha was at first not pictured in human form; his presence here is indicated by the tree in the upper left corner (detail from a pillar at Sanchi, first century B.C.).

Most of the era's men of religion stayed within the Vedic tradition, but there were some important exceptions. One was Vardhamana Mahavira (*ca.* 540–468 B.C.), the founder of Jainism, a religion that teaches nonviolence and is centered on the belief that everything is animated. Even more influential was Gautama Siddharta (*ca.* 563–483 B.C.), also known as Sakyamuni, who achieved religious illumination and became the Buddha, the "Enlightened One." He then spent the remainder of his life sharing his insights with others. His disciples renounced the world, took vows of chastity and poverty, and formed communities of monks and nuns. The idea of monasticism had such deep appeal to people of religious vocation that it spread not only to regions east of India but also west to the Near East.

Vedic Hymns

ORIGINS OF CASTE

When they [the gods] divided the Man,
into how many parts did they divide him?
What were his mouth, what were his arms,
what were his thighs and feet called?

The brahman [priest] was his mouth,
of his arms were made the warrior.
His thighs became the vaisya [merchants and cultivators],
of his feet the sudra [servants] was born.

The moon arose from his mind,
from his eye was born the sun,
from his mouth Indra and Agni [the war god and the fire god],
from his breath the wind was born. . . .

HYMN OF CREATION

Then even nothingness was not, nor existence,
There was no air then, nor the heavens beyond it.
What covered it? Where was it? In whose keeping?
Was there then cosmic water, in depths unfathomed?

Then there was neither death nor immortality,
nor was there then the torch of night and day.
The One breathed windlessly and self-sustaining.
There was that One then, and there was no other. . . .

But, after all, who knows and who can say
whence it all came, and how creation happened?
The gods themselves are later than creation,
so who knows truly whence it has arisen?

Quoted in A. L. Basham, *The Wonder That Was India* (London: Sidgwick and Jackson, 1954; New York: Macmillan, 1968), pp. 241, 247–48.

At the core of the Buddha's teachings were the Four Nobel Truths: that life is suffering; that the cause of suffering is craving or desire; that to stop the suffering the desire must be stopped; that this is accomplished through the Eightfold Path (right views, right intention, right speech, right action, right livelihood, right effort, right mindfulness, and right concentration). Like his contemporaries the Buddha taught that salvation lay in release from reincarnation, but he denied the existence of a soul and taught that what we think of as the self is merely a temporary aggregate of the material body, the sensations, perception, predisposition, and consciousness. It is a momentary cluster of qualities lacking any underlying unity. Transmigration, in this view, does not involve a substance but rather it is like the passing of a flame from one lamp to another until it is finally extinguished. The state of Nirvana, which literally means "extinguished," was the ultimate goal.

Another major difference between the orthodox Vedic traditions and Buddhism was that Buddhism rejected the hereditary claims of the brahmans. For Buddhists, birth did not determine worth. This attitude naturally appealed to merchants, warriors, and others offended by the pretensions of the priesthood. As Buddhism developed it acquired other features which enhanced its appeal and won it patronage. Its greatest Indian patron was the third emperor of the Mauryan Empire.

The Mauryan Empire 321–181 B.C.

In a gradual process over many centuries, tribes and tribal confederations were formed into more complex political organizations. By mid-sixth century B.C. there were sixteen kingdoms that we know by name. The largest of these was the Magadhan state, which from its base in the eastern Gagnetic Plain expanded to create an empire in North India. In the meantime, India's northwest became part of the great Achaemeneid Empire of Persia, which was destroyed by Alexander the Great in the fourth century B.C. When the power of Alexander's empire receded, the Magadhan state, under the Mauryan dynasty, took its place. The Mauryans then expanded until they ruled over the entire Indian subcontinent, except for the extreme south.

The empire had a complex administrative structure. It built public works (especially roads and irrigation facilities), maintained an army, and collected taxes. Theoretically, all land belonged to the emperor. Cultivators paid about a third of their crop in taxes, and were charged for the use of government water. There were also numerous levies on merchants

THE MAURYAN EMPIRE *ca.* 250 B.C.

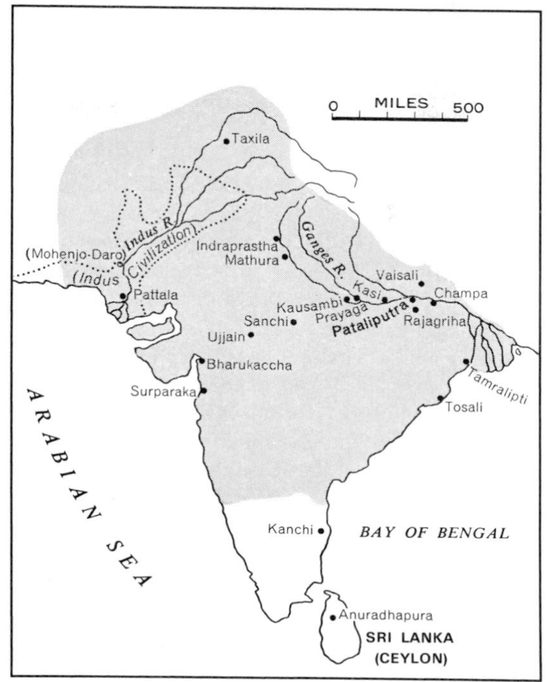

and craftsmen, many of whom lived in Pataliputra (modern Patna), a cosmopolitan city whose bazaars offered goods from places as far away as China, Mesopotamia, and Asia Minor.

Much of the empire's success has traditionally been ascribed to Kautilya, the author of the *Arthashastra* (Treatise on Material Gain), India's prime text on practical politics and administration. It contains a good deal of sound, practical advice (for instance, that officials should be selected on the basis of merit and that the king should devote himself to his tasks), but it also offers frank counsels of expediency. A notorious example is its advice to the ruler that he employ spies to inform him of what is happening in the state and also to spread propaganda for him.

Emperor Ashoka (r. 269–232 B.C.) is perhaps India's most famous ruler. Converted to Buddhism, Ashoka did much to advance the religion. He sponsored a great Buddhist council, sent out missionaries, and erected numerous stupas, Buddhist reliquary mounds. The largest of these, that at Sanchi, stands fifty-six feet tall and was later encased in sandstone and supplied with a beautifully carved railing and gateways. The lion column he erected to commemorate the Buddha's first sermon has become a symbol of India, adopted in the twentieth century to decorate the state seal of the Republic of India. In his patronage of Buddhism, Ashoka has been compared to Emperor Constantine and his support of Christianity in Rome, but the Indian monarch also maintained religious tolerance throughout his far-flung empire. In the edicts he had inscribed on rocks and special pillars, he displayed the imperial paternalism appropriate to a universal ruler. "I consider my work to be the welfare of the whole world," he proclaimed in one edict.

A half century after Ashoka's death, the Mauryan Empire was in collapse. Its last ruler was assassinated by a general who had to content himself with ruling over a much diminished state in central India. It would have taken an exceptionally strong ruler to organize a political machine and inspire the wide loyalty needed to maintain as huge and disparate a domain as that of the Mauryas, a domain with few economic or institutionalized political bonds that might have made for a more permanent union.

Political Division 180 B.C.–320 A.D.

The next five hundred years in India were complicated politically, but it was a period of cultural brilliance, economic growth, and increased contacts with other cultures.

A succession of many foreign peoples into India was a major source of the period's instability. We have already noted the invasion of Alexander the Great; the ultimate legacy of Greek interest in India was the formation of a number of Indo-Greek states, some of which issued bilingual coins. However, the most successful people to inhabit India during this period were the Kushans, who entered the subcontinent from Central Asia in the first century A.D. and created an empire that lasted until 240. The Kushan empire was the only one ever to straddle the Hindu-Kush and Baluchi Hills and become a major power in both Central Asia and India. Most of the lucrative trade along the silk route passed through the

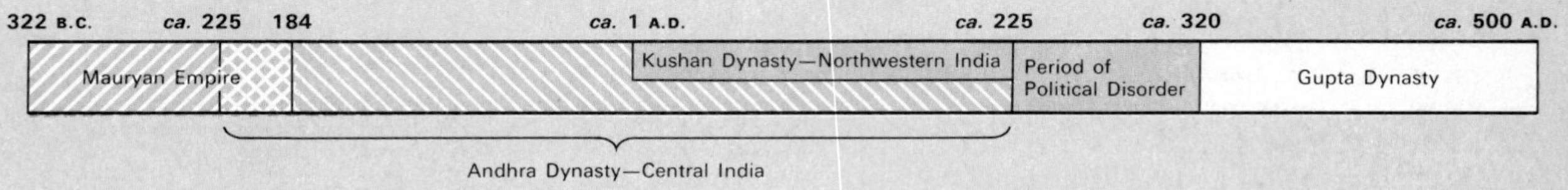

322 B.C. | ca. 225 | 184 | ca. 1 A.D. | ca. 225 | ca. 320 | ca. 500 A.D.

Mauryan Empire
Kushan Dynasty—Northwestern India
Period of Political Disorder
Gupta Dynasty
Andhra Dynasty—Central India

Kushan empire in the north while, at the same time, maritime trade flourished in the south. Hordes of Roman coins found in South India, beyond the borders of the Kushan empire, substantiate the complaint of Pliny the Elder that the trade was causing a gold drain in Rome.

The Kushans were converted to Buddhism and they eventually spread their new faith to Central Asia and to China. It was under the Kushans that the first statues of the Buddha appeared, executed in an Indo-Roman style that spread to the east. The growth of Buddhist art was only one of a number of ways in which Buddhism was gradually transformed and its appeal broadened. Another major development was the growth of devotionalism, with the recognition of a number of Buddhas and *bodhisattvas,* beings who, on the threshold of Nirvana, postpone their own salvation in order to help others. Such figures attracted the pious veneration of the common folk even as Buddhist theorists developed subtle and profound doctrines that supplied spiritual and intellectual nourishment to those who dedicated their lives to the religious quest. These developments coalesced to constitute Mahayana Buddhism, and it was largely in this form that the religion spread from the Kushan empire to East Asia, while the older Theraveda (or Hinayana) form prevailed to the south.

Running parallel to the changes in Buddhism were changes that transformed the traditional Vedic religion into Hinduism. With Hinduism, as in Buddhism, worshipers felt the need for divine beings that were accessible to them, and there developed a rich pantheon of gods and deities even as Hindu saints and philosophers pointed to an ultimate unity underlying all diversity. Of the three main Hindu deities—Brahma (The Creator), Vishnu (The Preserver), and Siva (The Destroyer but also a Creator)—the latter two became the main wings of Hinduism, inspiring sects which gained a vast number of devoted adherents who regarded their god as representative of the Absolute. Vishnu was believed to have appeared in nine incarnations. His ninth incarnation was as the Buddha suggesting that Buddhism was simply part of a greater Hindu whole. Vishnu was also incarnated as Rama, hero of India's great epic, the *Ramayana,* and as Krishna, an important figure in the Hindu pantheon.

It is as Krishna that Vishnu appears in the *Bhagavad Gita* (*The Song of the Lord*), which was inserted into the great and much older epic, *The Mahabharata.* In the *Gita* Krishna appears as the charioteer and friend of a warrior named Arjuna, who, greatly distressed to see some of his friends and relatives lined up in the enemy ranks as a battle is about to begin, lays down his bow. But Krishna urges him to perform his sacred duty (*dharma*) as a warrior, telling him that everyone has a social role that must be fulfilled, and as long as one fulfills his dharma without attachment, he will not incur bad karma.

There are other subtle and profound concepts in the *Gita,* the most widely studied Hindu text. One that fits in well with India's system of castes and social orders is the concept that people's *dharma* differs according to their social group, and that salvation lies in everyone's following his *dharma* without regard for self-benefit. The basic idea that different duties and lifestyles pertain to different groups of people was also involved in the theory of the four stages of life, which were prescribed as the ideal for members of the upper three varnas. First came the stage of the earnest student, diligently following the instructions of his teacher. Next came the phase of the householder, with all the joys and responsibilities of an active secular life. Love and pleasure (*kama*), as well as material gain (*artha*), were among the accepted goals of life. However, there came a time to retire from the active life of the householder and to partially withdraw into the forest to meditate. This was followed by the final stage, that of the ascetic wandering free from all human bonds, concerned only with the soul's liberation. Many, indeed most, householders did not actually end their lives in this manner, but it had its attractions in a land which honored ascetics and respected the religious quest.

The Guptas, ca. *325–550*

Like the Mauryan Empire, that of the Guptas was based in the Gangetic Plain. From there they expanded west to the Punjab, northwest to Kashmir, east to Bengal, and established themselves as a presence in the south. However, the south was not fully incorporated into the empire; defeated rulers were largely reinstated in their lands as tributaries. There were also rulers in distant places such as Sri Lanka who, in theory, accepted Gupta as an overlordship and sent the emperor gifts, but who were well beyond the range of its authority.

The dynasty reached its greatest height of well-being under Chandra Gupta II (*ca.* 375–415), even though it had not attained its greatest geographical extent. The account of Fa Hsien (Faxian), a Chinese monk who visited India at this time, testifies to the safety of travel and the general prosperity of the realm. He tells of cities with fine mansions, and that in Pataliputra (Patna) there were "houses for dispensing charities and medicine." He also reports, optimistically, that no one in the kingdom killed animals, drank intoxicating liquor, or ate onion or garlic—no one except "wicked men" who had to warn others of their approach by striking a piece of wood so they could avoid contamination.

It was a time of prosperity and, at least at court, luxury, for there were great feasts with drink served in ruby cups or cups in the shape of dancing peacocks. The quantity and quality of Gupta coins attest to the importance of commerce. India's trade with China and Southeast Asia was on the increase and trade with the West remained significant. Merchant and artisan guilds prospered. The fiscal basis of the state included a land tax and various supplemental levies. There was also a government monopoly on salt and metal mines. Once again, as under the Mauryans, there was a complex administrative hierarchy and a strong network of government agents and spies.

The last great Gupta emperor was Skandagupta (455–67), who repelled the Hunas (Huns) who invaded India from Central Asia. After his reign, however, the dynasty went into decline. The throne was weakened by succession disputes, a recurrent problem in India where there were no clear rules of primogeniture (succession by the eldest son). In the end, the state was unable to withstand repeated attacks from the Huns.

The Gupta period is celebrated less for its political achievements than for its cultural brilliance. India's greatest playwright, Kalidasa, most probably served at the court of Chandra Gupta II. There were notable advances in mathematics and astronomy. The numerals later introduced into Europe by the Arabs and consequently known as Arabic numerals were actually Indian in origin, as was the decimal system. In 499 an Indian astronomer calculated the value of *pi,* determined that there are 365.3586805 days in a year, and argued that the earth is

THE GUPTA EMPIRE *ca.* 400 A.D.

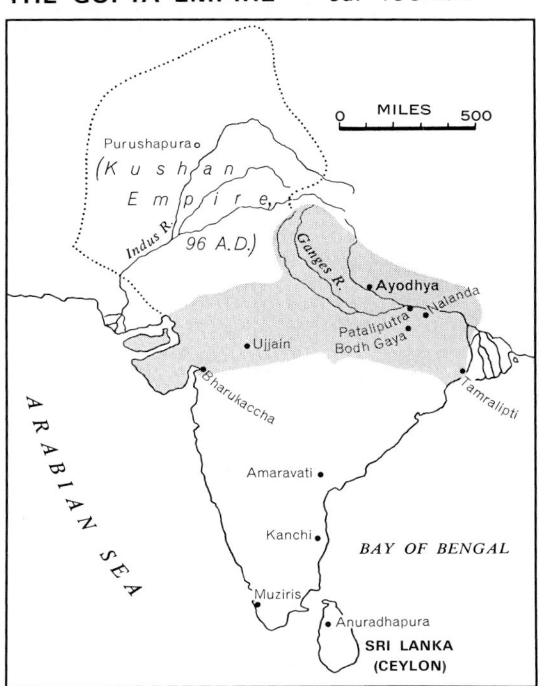

The Buddha (detail of a relief from Gandhara, second century A.D.).

round, that it revolves around its own axis, and that lunar eclipses occur when the earth's shadow falls on the moon. However, these theories were disputed by other astronomers. As elsewhere, astronomy itself remained firmly wedded to astrology.

The Ends of Man

Some say that dharma [virtue] and material gain are good, others that pleasure and material gain are good, and still others that dharma alone or pleasure alone is good, but the correct position is that the three should coexist without harming each other.

From *Sources of Indian Tradition*, ed. by Wm. Theodore de Bary and others (New York: Columbia University Press, 1958), p. 213.

Along with a flourishing literary and intellectual culture, the visual arts also reached new excellence. The most lasting achievements were made under religious auspices. Although the Gupta rulers generally favored Hinduism, it was in Buddhist sculpture that Gupta artists created their masterpieces. They achieved a classic style not only in the sense that it served as a touchstone for later artists, but also in that it achieved a perfect balance between the transcendental and the human in idealized figures representing the Buddha. India's finest wall paintings also date from this period, although they were produced in the south, beyond the bounds of the empire. These are the world famous Buddhist caves at Ajanta, which are decorated with secular as well as religious scenes and constitute a narrative art of the highest quality.

South India

The fact that both of India's great empires were based in the north should not obscure the contributions of the south to the development of Indian civilization. Inscriptions began to appear in South India in the second century B.C. and a century earlier in Sri Lanka. During the first three centuries A.D. anthologies of poetry were compiled in Tamil, a major Dravidian language. The nucleus of the culture which produced this literature was a little south of modern Madras. The early Tamil poems describe a complex culture of farmers and townspeople—over a hundred towns are mentioned, as are numerous occupations. Politically the Tamil-speaking area was long divided between three competing states until the Pallavas (roughly 315–800), with their highpoint around 600) achieved dominance. Over the centuries the Tamil and other southern cultures were deeply influenced by Sanskrit culture without, however, loosing their identities. The interaction between the southern cultures and those of the north forms a major theme in the study of South India.

The Spread of Indian Culture

By the middle of the sixth century, Indian influence had spread far beyond

A stone relief of an amorous couple from a sculptured cave temple at Karli, 100 A.D..

the subcontinent. It was a gradual and selective process of cultural diffusion. The peoples of Southeast Asia did not have Indian culture forced upon them. Local rulers, impressed by the achievements of Indian civilization and valuing the power of Indian knowledge and religion, selected and adapted certain Indian institutions to their own distinct cultural patterns.

The influence of India was deep and permanent in all regions of Southeast Asia, with the exception of the Philippines and North Vietnam. The figures of Borobudur, the great eighth-century Buddhist monument in Indonesia, clearly show the influence of Gupta sculpture, and elsewhere South Indian influences were also much in evidence. In later centuries, the temples at Pagan in Burma and the magnificent structures in the jungles of Kampuchea (Cambodia) were to attest to the appeal of Hinduism, as well as Buddhism. The largest religious building in the world is Angkor Wat in Kampuchea. Dedicated to Vishnu, this Hindu temple was built in the first half of the twelfth century. It is a walled complex measuring some 1500 by 1300 meters and is surrounded by a moat 200 meters wide—just as the world, in Indian eyes, is surrounded by the ocean. The

A view of the temple of Angkor Wat, built in the twelfth century by the king of Cambodia.

balustrades in the first interior section are in the shape of nine-headed snakes, referring both to an ancient snake cult and to Vishnu's rainbow, the magic bridge which leads to heaven. Relief carvings on the wall portray stories of Rama and Krishna, the two most prominent incarnations of Vishnu.

Although Angkor Wat was built much later than the period we are concerned with here, it symbolizes the enormous influence of Hinduism in the lands to India's east. Yet it was the influence of Buddhism that was to be the more lasting; to this day it is the dominant religion of the Southeast Asian mainland and Sri Lanka. As a proselytizing religion of great force, Buddhism also spread from India through Central Asia to China, where it eventually made a great impact.

CHINA

Archeologists have uncovered a number of Neolithic cultures in China, but it was in the Shang period (*ca.* 1600–1027 B.C.) that the first real civilization emerged. As in India, the first substantial cities appeared in the north from which the first states grew. A good indication of Shang organizational power was its ability to mobilize the manpower needed to build a wall surrounding an early capital city. Estimated at 2385 feet long, 60 feet wide, and 30 feet high, it has been calculated that this wall took 10,000 laborers working 330 days a year, 18 years to complete.

With the Shang, China entered the bronze age. The finest products of the period are bronze vessels unsurpassed in their artistry, as befitted their use in solemn sacred rites. Many such vessels have been found, along with jades and other precious objects, in Shang tombs of the rich and powerful. The remains of people buried alive have also been found in these tombs. In one case, a chariot was discovered, complete with horse and driver; in others, entire entourages accompanied the deceased in death. The victims were non-Shang barbarians, captured in war and reduced to slavery, who were believed to accompany the dead on a journey to the afterworld.

Of more permanent influence was the development of the Chinese system of writing during this period. The earliest Chinese characters were pictograms (stylistic pictorial representations) and ideograms (visual representations of a thing or concept), but most characters were more complex, consisting of an element that indicated a category of meaning and another that functioned as a phonetic indicator. Unfortunately, the pronunciation of the language later changed so that today the phonetic element is not neces-

A ceremonial vessel in the form of an elephant (Shang dynasty).

THE SPREAD OF BUDDHISM Sixth century B.C. to sixteenth century A.D.

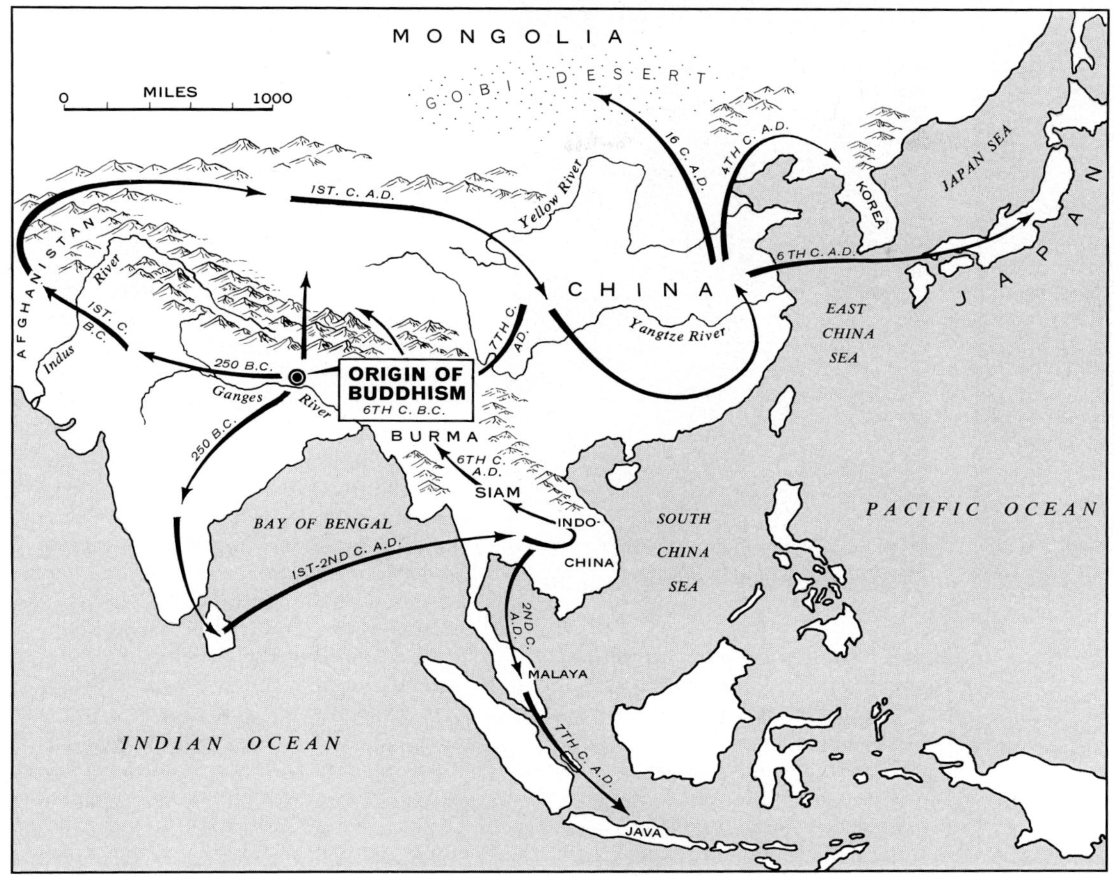

sarily a reliable guide to pronunciation. The early characters were used to inscribe oracle bones and tortoise shells used for divination. Command of the written language was the prized possession of a privileged group, and full literacy, until modern times, remained the possession of an elite minority who prided themselves in working with their brains rather than with their hands.

While the written language was associated with the perpetuation of social distinctions, it helped to overcome geographical barriers, for people who spoke mutually unintelligible languages could still communicate with each other in writing, particularly after the form of characters was standardized in 221 B.C. Thus today, even though Cantonese and Mandarin speakers cannot converse with each other, they can communicate in writing and they can read the same books and journals. Similarly, scholars in Korea, Japan, and Vietnam acquired a command over China's literary culture even though they were unable to speak Chinese.

When the Shang were overthrown by the Chou (Zhou*) around 1027 B.C., at first there was no break in cultural continuity since the Chou themselves represented a variant of Shang culture. They even produced bronze vessels very similar to those of their predecessors. However, the inscriptions on the vessels, as well as the decorations and artisitic effects gradually changed, indicating a process of secularization which transformed them into treasured family heir-

*This text uses the standard Wade-Giles system of romanization, followed in parentheses by *pinyin*. An exception to this is geographical names which appear in their earlier customary forms, followed by *pinyin*.

Chinese calligraphy. Left: a rubbing from one of the ten "Stone Drums," an example of the Great Seal style of writing, which evolved in the latter part of the Chou dynasty. Right: a rubbing from a stone inscription of the Han dynasty, inscribed in the Official Style.

Bronze wrestlers (Chou dynasty).

looms. At the same time, burial practices changed, and the immolation of humans and animals in the tombs of the powerful became increasingly rare.

The Chou did not attempt to govern the area they conquered directly, but invested members of the royal house, favored adherents, and allies with the authority to rule over more than a hundred separate territories, which these men were free to administer without interference from the Chou king. These subordinate rulers received ranks later systematized into a hierarchical order. They were obliged to render military service and tribute. In practice these positions were hereditary under a system of primogeniture, but with each generation the succession to a local lordship had to be legitimized by formal royal investiture. Some of these Chou arrangements resembled those of the feudal system which later developed in Europe and Japan.

We are inadequately informed about the political structure of local village life or the economic relations between those who cultivated the soil and their rulers. However, we can learn something from the folk poetry included in the *Book of Songs,* which was compiled around 600 B.C. and was later accepted as one of the classics of Confucianism. Some songs show ordinary people at work: the men clearing weeds from the fields, plowing, planting, and harvesting; the girls and women gathering mulberry leaves to feed the silkworms, making thread, carrying food out to the fields for their men. There is much about the staple crop, millet—both the eating variety and that used for brewing. We hear about wheat, barley, and rice, and men building a house, stamping down the earth between planks to make the walls. There are joyful celebrations of granaries full of grain and references to men gathering thatch for their roofs. Mention is made of lords' fields and private fields, and a "bailiff" is referred to, but the details of the system remain hidden. There are also poems of complaint against the government. One compares tax collectors to big rats. Another tells of the hardships of military service, men constantly on the march, day and night without rest, living like rhinoceroses and tigers. Sometimes a soldier survives the dangers of war and returns home only to find that his wife has given him up for dead and married another. Among the most appealing in their freshness and the innocence of their language are the love poems, for this was a time when girls and young women were not yet restricted by the rules of etiquette from free expression of their longing for their sweetheart or their wish to be married.

The Age of Philosophers

As the bonds which tied the lords to the Chou king weakened, there was an erosion of power so that by the ninth century B.C. the Chou kings were unable to prevent the local rulers from fighting each other. Nor could they check the incursions of non-Chinese barbarians from beyond the pale. It was to evade the latter that in 771 B.C. the capital was moved from Shensi (Shenxi) east to the Loyang region. After this move the Chou "king" nominally continued to reign for another five hundred years, until 256 B.C., but actually he exercised no military, political, or economic power. China was now divided among competing states. During the aptly named "Warring States Period" (403–221 B.C.) the competition between the states became increasingly more desperate and ruthless. With strong states subduing and annexing the weaker, the number of states diminished. The successful states grew ever bigger and more formidable until the process reached its logical conclusion and only one huge state remained.

Confucius (*ca.* 551–*ca.* 479 B.C.), a contemporary of the Buddha, lived relatively early in this period of accelerating change. Distressed by the disintegration of the political and moral order, he sought to put the world back together again and hoped to find a ruler who would implement his ideas. When this failed, he turned to teaching. Confucius saw himself not as a creator but as one who merely transmitted the traditional wisdom and values of civilization. He was a creative transmitter who understood the tradition in terms suitable for his own age and thereby revitalized and transformed old values. A good example is his redefinition of nobility as a quality acquired through virtue and wisdom, not through birth. For Confucius, the ideal man is humane, wise, and courageous. He is motivated by virtue, and the ultimate virtue is *jen* (*ren*), a term sometimes translated as "benevolence" or "humaneness," but for which there is no exact English equivalent. *Jen* is the ground for all other virtues, the condition of being fully human in dealing with others. The written Chinese character for *jen* consists of the symbols for "man" and "two."

Morality and the achievement of social harmony were at the core of Confucius' concerns. He urged the need for people to observe the *li*, a term meaning sacred ritual, ceremonial, and propriety, as well as good manners. The *li* were part of the precious heritage of antiquity, imbued with an aura of sacred reverence. When performed with true sincerity, life is truly human and civilized. When everyone follows the *li* and carries out his social role with genuine devotion, harmony will ensue. There will then be no need for coercion, no need for laws or punishments. Of crucial importance to achieve this was the initiative of the ruler who, by following the advice of a perfectly virtuous minister, could make government benevolent and win over the people.

Among the virtues and *li* emphasized by Confucius were those related to the family. He placed special importance on filial piety, the wholehearted obedience a child owes a parent. The obligations toward a father have priority over those owed a state: a son should not turn in his father for stealing a sheep. The relationship between father and son formed one of the classic Five Relationships of Confucianism. The others were ruler/minister, husband/wife, elder/younger brother, friend/friend. They entail reciprocal obligations between people of superior and inferior status and illustrate the importance of the family. Even the two which are not familial were thought of in family terms: the ruler/minister relationship was compared to that between father and son, while that between friends is analogous to that between elder and younger brother. The Confucian view of society was thus paternal and hierarchical.

Confucius and his followers also believed there was only one valid and true, eternal way. The Way was open to all, but only the morally and intellectually cultivated could understand it. The idea that there might be a number of legitimate ways to live one's life and conduct

Ancient symbol *Yi,* which stands for "changes." One of the five Confucian classics is the *Book of Changes.*

THE CHINESE STATES AT THE TIME OF CONFUCIUS *ca.* 500 B.C.

Confucius on Government

Tzu-kung asked about government. Confucius said, "Sufficient food, sufficient armament, and sufficient confidence of the people." Tzu-kung said, "Forced to give up one of these, which would you abandon first?" Confucius said, "I would abandon the armament." Tzu-kung said, "Forced to give up one of the remaining two, which would you abandon first?" Confucius said, "I would abandon food. There have been deaths from time immemorial, but no state can exist without the confidence of the people."

Analects 12:7. From *A Source Book in Chinese Philosophy* by Wing-tsit Chan (Princeton, N.J.: Princeton University Press, 1963), p. 39.

affairs was foreign to the Chinese who, at that time, had no contact with other highly developed and literate civilizations that were radically different from their own.

Confucius' ideas were not widely accepted for many centuries, but ultimately he proved to be one of the world's truly seminal thinkers. His person became a model to be emulated by later Confucians. As he appears in the *Analects,* discourses written by his disciples, he was a man of moderation: gentle but firm, dignified but not harsh, respectful but at ease. One passage gives an account of his intellectual and spiritual progression, culminating at the age of seventy when he was able to follow his heart's desires without transgressing against morality. The Confucian sage personified these characteristics and perfected his moral wisdom to the point that he automatically did what was right.

Confucius was only the beginning of Confucianism. There were many issues he left unsettled, and his philosophy permitted various interpretations. His later followers, such as Mencius and Hsün Tzu, further developed his teachings, partly in response to challenges from other schools, such as that founded by Mo Tzu (Mo Zi, *ca.* 470–391 B.C.), who taught the practicality of universal love. Mencius (371–289 B.C.) is famed for his view that human nature is fundamentally good but that this goodness has to be cultivated and nourished. Hsün Tzu (Xun Zi, 298–238 B.C.) is associated with the opposite view, that people are naturally selfish but nevertheless have the potential to become good. Although for different reasons, education was of essential importance for both men. Consistent with these positions, Mensius stressed the need for benevolence in government, while Hsün Tzu more readily accepted the need for laws and punishment. Mencius is also famous for developing the older idea of the mandate of Heaven, according to which a dynasty ruled only as long as it ruled properly. When a regime lost the mandate, rebellion was justified, and an evil ruler forfeited the right to rule.

Divine seal of Lao-Tzu, used in Taoist magic.

While Confucians put a premium on social harmony, the thinkers known as Taoists (Daoists) sought to understand the eternal order of the universe. Taoism deals with the unconditioned, unnameable source of all reality that transcends being and nonbeing by standing above and beyond all distinctions. The first great Taoist classic, the *Tao Te Ching* (*Dao De Jing*), or *Lao Tzu* (*Lao Zi*), is cryptic, paradoxical, and highly suggestive. Among its themes there is a preference for the negative over the positive, nothing over something, weak over strong, nonaction over action. It teaches silence is more meaningful than words and ignorance is superior to knowledge; in sum, "Those who know do not speak; those who speak do not know." This view of the limitation of language is shared by Chuang Tzu (Zhuang Zi), author of the second great Taoist classic which bears his name. Chuang Tzu had a keenly developed sense of paradox, as when he argues for the usefulness of the useless: when the able-bodied young men of the village are marched off to war, it is the hopelessly deformed hunchback who stands by the side of the road waving them off. Another theme he pursues is the relativity of everything.

The Unification of China

During the period from 771 B.C. to 221 B.C., momentous and rapid changes took place in all areas of human activity. Warfare is a good example. No longer were battles fought by gentlemen in chariots; now most of the fighting was done by foot-soldiers, peasant conscripts commanded by professional officers. Armies grew enormously. Some are said to have numbered a million men, although that may be an exaggeration.

Armies had to be fed and supplied. To support the forces, an increase in agricultural production was achieved by reclamation projects, irrigation, and technological changes, including the introduction of iron. There were also changes in management and administration as states adopted systems of taxation and labor services. Land became a commodity to be bought and sold. Commerce increased along with the size of states and the development of roads. Metallic currencies appeared, replacing the cowrie shells used earlier. Among the items of trade were various kinds of textiles, metals, woods, bamboo, jade, and regional specialties. Urban centers grew and expanded until they required new city walls.

Social change was inseparably linked to military, economic, and political change. Merchants and generals were not the only new professionals. It took a skilled diplomat to steer a state through the treacherous waters of international relations, someone with an eloquent voice to win a debate. Faced with internal and external challenges, rulers tended to pay more attention to a man's competence than to his pedigree. Old families declined and new ones grew in importance.

Faced with a world of disturbing and baffling change, many Chinese turned for guidance to what they perceived to have been a much better past, but some, such as Han Fei Tzu (Han Fei Zi, d. 233 B.C.), held that new problems demanded new and drastic solutions. These so-called Legalists stressed the rationalization of administration, the improvement of managerial techniques, and the strict enforcement of punitive laws. Their theories which were applied by the state of Ch'in (Qin) unified China in 221 B.C.

The Ch'in was located in the west of North China, the same region from which the Chou had conquered North China. This area was economically able to support a strong military and political apparatus, and it was well situated strategically, protected by mountains whose passes were easy to defend and yet provided access to the east. It was something of a buffer region between the Chinese and various warlike tribal peoples. Making the best of this situation, the Ch'in toughened its armies by fighting the tribesmen. At the same time it drew on the administrative and technological expertise developed in the more sophisticated, centrally located states. Under Legalist influence the state was divided into districts governed by a centralized bureaucracy and financed by a direct tax on the peasantry. A system of mutual responsibility was introduced, with harsh

Chuang Tzu (also called Chuang Chou)

Once Chuang Chou dreamt he was a butterfly, a butterfly flitting and fluttering around, happy with himself and doing as he pleased. He didn't know he was Chuang Chou. Suddenly he woke up and there he was, solid and unmistakable Chuang Chou. But he didn't know if he was Chuang Chou who had dreamt he was a butterfly, or a butterfly dreaming he was Chuang Chou. Between Chuang Chou and a butterfly there must be *some* distinction! This is called the Transformation of Things.

The fish trap exists because of the fish; once you've gotten the fish, you can forget about the trap. The rabbit snare exists because of the rabbit; once you've gotten the rabbit, you can forget the snare. Words exist because of meaning; once you've gotten the meaning, you can forget the words. Where can I find a man who has forgotten words so I can have a word with him?

From *Chuang Tzu: Basic Writings,* trans. by Burton Watson (New York: Columbia University Press, 1946). p. 45 and p. 140, respectively.

penalties for criminals and those who failed to report a criminal. Everything was designed to make the state wealthy, strong, and disciplined.

The First Empire: Ch'in and Han

The unification of China by the Ch'in was the beginning of some four hundred years of imperial rule even though the Ch'in Dynasty (221–207 B.C.) itself barely survived the first emperor, Ch'in Shih Huang-ti (Qin Shihuangdi). He and his Legalist advisor, Li Ssu, (Li Si) applied to the whole domain the policies first enacted in the state of Ch'in, including the division of the state into administrative districts governed by a bureaucracy. The integration of the realm was also furthered by a program of road building, the issuance of a standard official coinage, the standardization of weights and measurements and of the script, and the suppression of scholars and writings critical of the new order. The Ch'in hostility toward Confucianism was reciprocated by Confucian hatred for the dynasty, which acquired a negative reputation in traditional China.

A life-size terracotta figure of an armored archer of the Ch'in dynasty. This is one of over 7,000 such figures unearthed from the tomb of the first emperor of China.

Vast building projects and military campaigns were a heavy burden on the people. The most famous Ch'in project was the creation of the Great Wall, built to protect and separate China from barbarism. It was constructed by linking segments of walls previously erected by individual states. Although the present wall dates from the fifth century, the Ch'in wall was its ancestor.

After Ch'in Shih Huang-ti's death, the Ch'in quickly disintegrated and massive peasant uprisings put an end to the dynasty. The Ch'in system was repudiated, but the dynasty left foundations on which the Former Han (202 B.C.–8 A.D.) and the Later Han (25–220) were able to erect less severe and more lasting edifices.

In many respects Han China was comparable to Imperial Rome. Both were great empires with powerful armies ranging far beyond the heartland: Han forces even crossed the Pamir Mountains to the West. Both are celebrated for their practical accomplishments, as in civil engineering: The Han maintained some 20,000–25,000 miles of highway radiating out from the capital. They also made advances in shipbuilding (the axial rudder), medicine, astronomy, and agriculture. Intellectually, both empires built on the achievements of their predecessors and were noted more for the synthesis of old philosophies rather than for producing strikingly new ones. Both also excelled in the writing of history. China's greatest historian was Ssu-ma Ch'ien (Sima Qian, *ca.* 145 B.C.–*ca.* 90 B.C.) whose *Records of the Grand Historian* is a literary masterpiece as well as a work of careful scholarship.

In China, as in Rome, it took great political ability to create and maintain a huge empire over a long period of time. But there was no counterpart in the Han to the Roman development of law. Instead, the Chinese relied on a bureaucracy staffed by men who shared a common education, a common fund of historical references, and a common set of largely Confucian values. To help mold these men there was an imperial university where, under the Later Han,

THE HAN EMPIRE 100 B.C.

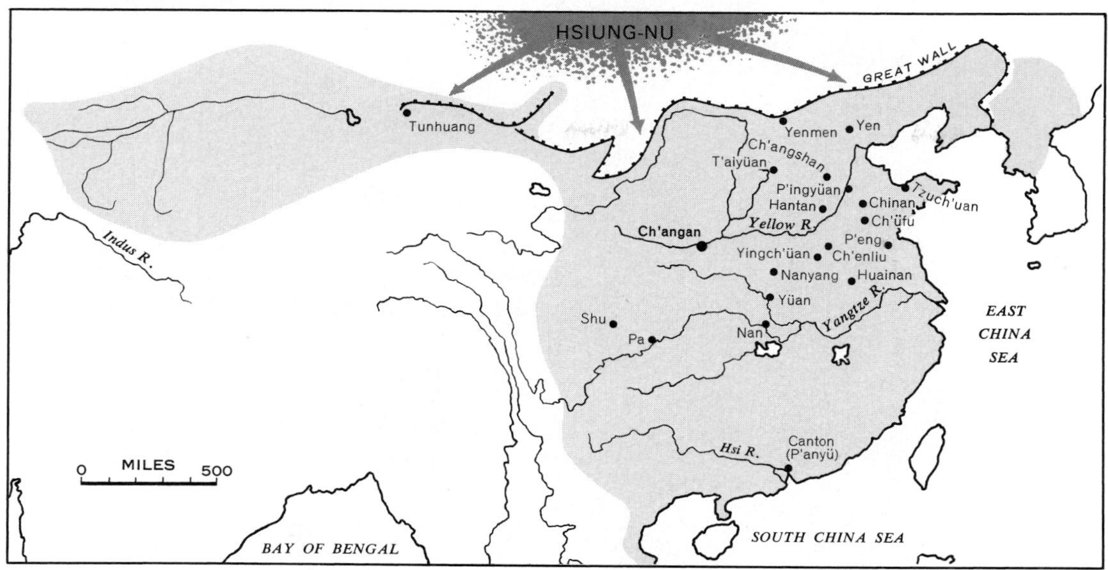

some 30,000 students were studying mostly Confucian texts. Imperial Confucianism did not preclude the employment of pragmatic Legalist military and political policies, but it did provide the dynasty with legitimacy and could prompt ministers to faithful service. The Confucian ideal was one of unselfish public service, not unthinking compliance with the whims or policies of a ruler. Intellectual and political independence from the throne was also made possible because most officials came from families of notables that dominated the local power stucture.

The system operated best when there was a balance between central and local power. Since the wealthy and powerful were also the most apt to evade taxes, the state had a stake in preventing an undue concentration of landownership, but attempts to limit the size of landholdings failed, as did the attempt to stabilize the price of grain through government purchases when it was plentiful and inexpensive and reselling it when grain became scarce. For its own finances, the government drew heavily on agriculture but also collected commercial taxes and operated salt and iron monopolies.

As in Rome, in weak hands the throne itself became a source of political instability as various groups maneuvered for influence and control. In the Han the families of imperial consorts became exceedingly powerful, and it was a member of one such family who, after serving as regent for a child emperor, overthrew the Former Han but did not succeed in establishing a lasting dynasty of his own. Instead, after a period of turmoil and fighting, a member of the imperial Han family established the Later Han in 25 A.D.

The Han established a Chinese presence in North Korea and North Vietnam, but the most challenging foreign policy problem was how to deal with the nomads who lived beyond the northern and northwestern frontiers. Nomadic peoples, like the Altaic speaking Hsiung-nu (Xiongnu), were formidable opponents because of their skill in warfare. For them war was merely a special application of the skills of horsemanship and archery they practiced every day in guarding their flocks. Their mobility was an asset in defense as well as attack, for, traveling lightly with their flocks and tents, they could elude Chinese military expeditions and avoid destruction or control. Chinese measures to deal with these troublesome neighbors ranged from military suppression to conciliation by means of gifts and marriage alliances, so that the nomads would accept tributary status. Tributaries had to acknowledge Han supremacy but profited by an exchange of presents and

Pottery tile rubbing depicting hunters and peasants (Han dynasty).

the opportunity to trade. Much of this trade was conducted in markets along the borders. Chinese exports included lacquerware, ironware, bronze mirrors, and silk, which first reached Europe over the famous Silk Road. The Chinese also did whatever they could to foster disunity among the tribal peoples; "using barbarians against barbarians" became a permanent part of their foreign policy.

China in Disunity, 220–589

Disrupted by internal strife, in fiscal trouble because of a shrinking tax base, and beset by foreign challenges, the Han came to an end in 220. Beginning early in the next century, a succession of nomadic peoples carved out states in North China. Some of these, notably the Northern Wei (386–534), attained a good measure of success, but none matched the Han in duration or extent. To enjoy their Chinese conquests, the nomads required a more sophisticated political system than the tribal organization they brought from the steppes. They had to rely on Chinese administrators who knew how to operate a tax system, keep records, and run a government. There was also a tendency for the nomads themselves to become more like the Chinese. This not only jeopardized their cultural heritage but also tended to alienate those nomads who had remained on the steppe.

Warfare and devastation in the north stimulated vast migrations to south China, especially into the Yangtze region, which underwent great economic development, foreshadowing the time when it would become China's rice bowl. Politically the south remained under Chinese control, but the southern states were unstable and weak. When reunification came, it was, as always, from the north.

When the Han fell, a whole civilization seemed to have collapsed. A spiritual and intellectual, as well as political vacuum was created. Some of China's most brilliant and talented men responded by turning to Taoism or to discovering new meaning in poetry, calligraphy, and painting. Others, both humble people and aristocrats, were attracted to Buddhism, which addressed itself more directly to human suffering than did any of the components of the native Chinese tradition. In the north, Buddhism also benefitted from the patronage of rulers who, as foreigners themselves, could sympathize with a foreign religion.

It took many long years for Buddhism to overcome its foreigness in China, years during which Buddhist missionaries patiently labored to translate and explain the Buddhist teachings. It was a formidable task to render the highly inflected Indian languages and discursive Indian writings into uninflected and terse Chinese, to find Chinese equivalents for concepts such as karma or Nirvana, and to bridge the gulf which separated Indian and Chinese perceptions of the meaning of life and the nature of the universe.

The greatest of the translators was a Central Asian, Kumārajīva, who, early in the fifth century, directed a staff of about one thousand monks. In a vivid comment on the translator's predicament, he once compared his work to that of a man who chews rice and then gives it to another to swallow. By the end of the period of disunity, the labors of such men had made Buddhism palatable to the Chinese, but it was not until after reunification in 591 that they felt sufficiently familiar with the faith to develop it in ways of their own.

For a time Buddhism provided a link between China and India, yet there remained distinct differences between the historical-minded Chinese tradition and the focus in India on the ultimate. The contrast between the two civilizations is also apparent in their different political histories. At the end of the sixth century, India was again politically fragmented, whereas China had entered one of its great ages of imperial unification.

Suggestions for Further Reading

Note: Asterisk denotes a book available in paperback edition.

India A gold mine of authoritative information is *A Historical Atlas of South Asia* (1978), edited by Joseph E. Schwartzberg, which contains historical essays and bibliographies. A. L. Basham, *The Wonder that Was India** (1954), is a lucid and balanced account of Indian civilization. Stanley Wolpert, *A New History of India,* 2nd ed.* (1982), is a good survey, although stronger on modern India. A good compedium for intellectual history is *Sources of Indian Tradition** (1958), edited by Wm. Theodore de Bary *et. al.*

China The following are up-to-date and authoritative: Kwang-chih Chang, *Shang Civilization* (1980); Burton Watson, *Early Chinese Literature* (1962) and *Ssu-ma Ch'ien: Grand Historian of China* (1958); and Cho-yun Hsu, *Han Agriculture* (1980). There are three valuable anthologies: *Sources of Chinese Tradition** (1960) by Wm. Theodore de Bary *et. al;* Wing-tsit Chan, ed., *A Source Book in Chinese Philosophy** (1963); and Patricia B. Ebrey, *Chinese Civilization and Society: A Sourcebook** (1981). A general survey is provided by Conrad Schirokauer, *A Brief History of Chinese and Japanese Civilizations** (1978), which includes suggestions for further reading.

Buddhism A straightforward introduction to Buddhism written in simple language and presuming no background is Kenneth Chen, *Buddhism: The Light of Asia** (1968). Another fine introduction is *Buddhism: Its Essence and Development** by Edward Conze (1951). For China, see *Buddhism in Chinese History** (1959) by Arthur F. Wright. Buddhist materials are also included in the source books listed above.

Reference For recent studies see the *Bibliography of Asian Studies,* published annually by the Association for Asian Studies, Inc.

7 The Germanic Kingdoms in the West

The great empires of the Eurasian continent had all been destroyed by internal struggles and foreign invasions during the third, fourth, and fifth centuries. They had all suffered a decline in economic and cultural activity. Everywhere men faced the problems of adapting the remains of an old civilization to new conditions, of rebuilding political organization and stimulating economic growth. The people of western Europe had perhaps the most difficult task of all. Disintegration and barbarization had gone further there than in most other areas, and religious disputes were more divisive. The period during which western Europe slowly rebuilt its civilization is known as the "Middle Ages," and it is to the early centuries of the medieval period that we now turn.

During the fifth century all the Roman territories of the West fell under

This fragment from the crown of the Lombard king Agilulf shows the king being greeted in the cities he conquered (early seventh century).

the control of Germanic peoples. The Vandals ruled North Africa; the Visigoths held the Iberian Peninsula; Italy itself was occupied by the Ostrogoths. Gaul was split among the Visigoths in the southwest, the Burgundians and Ostrogoths in the southeast, and the Franks in the north and center. The Angles and Saxons gradually took over most of Britain, although the Celts preserved fiercely independent kingdoms in Scotland and Wales.

THE NORTHERN AND SOUTHERN KINGDOMS

The Germanic kingdoms that emerged from this welter of migration and conquest had very different fates. The Mediterranean group—the Vandals, the Visigoths, the Ostrogoths, and the Burgundians—absorbed Roman civilization readily and preserved much of the Roman way of life. But though they seemed to be more advanced than the northerners, the Germanic kingdoms of the Mediterranean had no staying power. During the sixth century the Vandals and Ostrogoths were crushed by the Eastern Roman Empire, and the Burgundians were conquered by the Franks. The Visigoths weakened and finally, in the eighth century, came under the rule of Moslem invaders. In contrast, the northern invaders—the Franks and the Anglo-Saxons—learned much less from the Romans and at first had a lower level of civilization. But their kingdoms endured and became the strongest states of medieval Europe.

This difference in the history of the northern and southern kingdoms can be explained largely by geographic and

THE GERMANIC KINGDOMS *ca.* 500

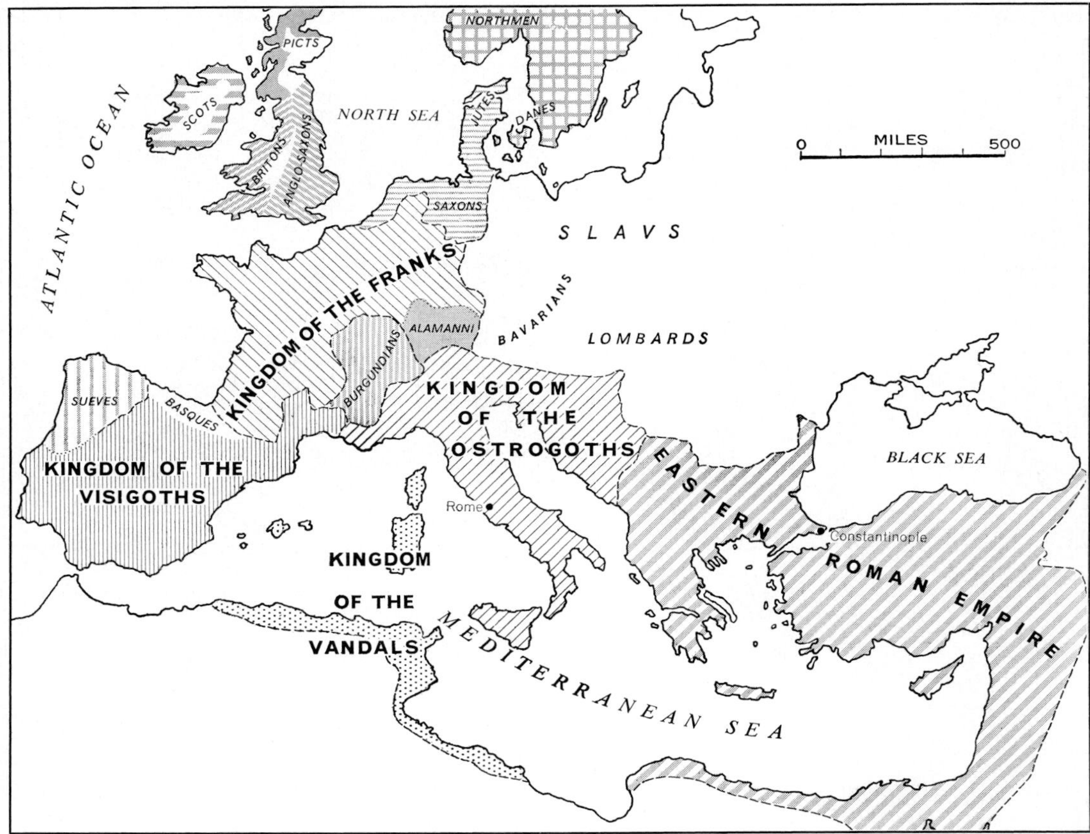

demographic factors. The Germanic groups that reached the Mediterranean were entirely cut off from their old homes and could not be reinforced by new migrants. They found themselves in the most densely populated and most thoroughly Latinized area of the Empire. They were not traders, nor did they understand the Mediterranean style of farming. Thus, their economic situation was poor and they could not afford to build an army, which left them vulnerable to attack from the strong states of the eastern Mediterranean—first the Eastern Roman Empire and then the Moslem caliphate. The Goths, Vandals, and Burgundians also suffered from having been converted to the heretical Arian form of Christianity. This made it extremely difficult for their rulers to win the loyalty of the orthodox Roman population. Thus the Germanic kingdoms that had the greatest need for strength were actually the weakest. The number of their fighting men dwindled, and the apathetic Roman population gave little support to the new rulers.

The northern invaders, on the other hand, remained in constant contact with their homelands, and for several generations their ranks were strengthened by new bands of migrants. In the sparsely settled lands they entered, they had an opportunity to preserve their old customs and to maintain effective armies. Since they were eventually converted to orthodox Christianity, they gained the support of the Church. The Eastern Roman Empire never touched Gaul, and the Moslems, even at the height of their power, could only send raiding parties toward the Loire. Thus the northern invaders had time to develop new institutions strong enough to enable them to survive during the troubled centuries of the early Middle Ages.

A glance at a modern map will illustrate this difference between the northern and southern Germanic kingdoms. Italy and Spain have retained their old Roman names; they did not become East Gothia and West Gothia. But the Franks imposed their name on Gaul, which became France, just as the Angles imposed theirs on the largest part of Britain, which became known as England.

And yet the southern kingdoms, even though they were politically short-lived, aided the difficult transition to a new age by making a conscious effort to adapt Roman culture to the needs of a simpler, semibarbaric society. Latin literature and Roman law survived in the south, but not in the north. The Burgundian and Visigothic kings, for example, issued brief codes of Roman law for the use of their Roman subjects. These codes would have seemed crude and incomplete to the great lawyers of the Roman Empire, but they covered most of the cases that were likely to arise and they preserved some of the basic principles of Roman law. Moreover, the existence of Roman law codes encouraged Germanic kings to put some of their own legal customs in writing.

The Ostrogothic Kingdom of Italy

The most important work in assimilating Roman culture was done in Ostrogothic Italy. Theodoric, king of the Ostrogoths, had been closely associated with the court at Constantinople and understood Roman ways very well. During his reign in Italy (493–526) he safeguarded the elements of Roman civilization and ensured the continuation of the Roman administrative system. The fact that the Ostrogothic army had its own law meant no more to the ordinary citizen than does the existence of military law in a modern society. Theodoric also named eminent Roman scholars to the highest official posts. Two of these men, Boethius and Cassiodorus, eager to preserve the learning of the past, made a deliberate effort to put it into a form that could be used by future generations.

Boethius (*ca.* 480–524) was especially disturbed by the gap that had opened between Greek and Latin learning. Since the fourth century few inhabitants of the West had studied Greek, and even so eminent a writer as St. Augustine was not able to read it easily. This ignorance of Greek was particularly serious in mathematics, science, logic, and philosophy, where Latin scholars had done little original work and where all the advanced texts were in Greek. Boethius hoped to preserve this precious heritage by writing elementary treatises on mathematics and translating the major works of Aristotle and Plato. Unfortunately, Boethius did not live to complete his ambitious project, and some of the translations he did make were neglected by later scholars. But his basic mathematical texts and his translations of two of Aristotle's introductory treatises on logic were used throughout the Middle Ages. Until the twelfth century these treatises supplied medieval scholars with most of their philosophical vocabulary and ideas about logic. By showing, in his theological *Tractates,* how logic could be applied to problems of Christian theology, Boethius ensured the survival of logic as a branch of medieval learning.

Boethius' career was cut short when he fell into political difficulties. Theodoric, in spite of his admiration for Roman culture, was always a little uneasy about the loyalty of the upper-class Romans. The Arianism of the Ostrogoths offended the Catholic Romans, and the emperor at Constantinople, who still claimed authority over the West, encouraged intrigues against Theodoric. It is possible that Boethius entered into these plots against his king; at any rate, he was accused of treason, jailed for a year, and then executed. While he was still in prison he wrote the work for which he is best remembered, the *Consolation of Philosophy,* a long dialogue, partly in prose and partly in verse, between the prisoner and Philosophy. Philosophy argues that all worldly honors and pleasures are vain and that external misfortunes are unimportant. The only thing worth striving for is the good of the soul, expressed in virtue and in reason. This idea was at least as old as Plato, but the conviction with which Boethius stated it made his work a real consolation to many troubled men in years to come.

Cassiodorus (*ca.* 490–580) was more skillful in riding out political storms. Though he had been secretary to Theodoric, he survived both court intrigues and the long wars between the Eastern

Gold coin of Theodoric, Ostrogothic king of Italy in the early sixth century.

Religious carving from Niederdollendorf, probably depicting the symbols of Thor.

Bust of a young German warrior, of the type the Romans fought. The soldier wears a necklace believed to have magic power.

Romans and the Goths and died peacefully at the age of ninety in his ancestral home in southern Italy. He was something of a pedant; the letters he wrote for Theodoric are tricked out with far-fetched allusions to classical literature and mythology. But he saw, perhaps more clearly than Boethius, that ancient learning could be saved only with the aid of the Church. In his last years he founded a monastery to preserve the secular learning that he felt was necessary for true understanding of Christian writings. Cassiodorus preserved as many classical texts as he could and, in his *Introduction to Divine and Secular Literature,* outlined the basic reading that was necessary for an educated clergyman.

Digests such as that of Cassiodorus, and elementary treatises such as those of Boethius, made up the basic educational materials of the early Middle Ages. Many classical works had been lost, and those that survived were seldom studied because they were too long or too difficult. The digests and handbooks were no real substitute for the originals, for they stressed what was obvious and omitted or oversimplified what was complicated. Nevertheless, they preserved useful knowledge. Even more important, they suggested that better sources might be available. A quotation from Virgil might make a reader eager to ferret out the whole *Aeneid;* a reference to Aristotle might encourage a scholar to seek the original work. It was a long time before any large-scale efforts were made to recover and study the basic works of the classical period, but at least the scholars of the early Middle Ages were aware that their knowledge was incomplete.

Compurgation

When Chilperic I was assassinated, he left a young son who was to hold his father's share of the Frankish kingdom under the guardianship of his uncle, King Guntram. There were doubts about the boy's legitimacy, doubts that Guntram apparently shared.

After this King Guntram went to Paris [in 585] and openly addressed all the people, saying, "My brother Chilperic on his death is said to have left a son . . . but the boy is concealed, he is not shown to me. Therefore I feel certain that matters are not as they have been represented, but that the child is, as I believe, the son of one of our nobles. For if it had been of our blood, it would have been brought to me. Know therefore, that I will not acknowledge it until I receive satisfactory proofs of its paternity." When Queen Fredegonda [the mother of the boy] heard this she summoned the chief men of her kingdom, namely three bishops and three hundred nobles, and with them made oath that Chilperic was the father of the child. By this means suspicion was removed from the king's mind.

From Gregory of Tours, *History of the Franks,* trans. by Arthur C. Howland, *Translations and Reprints* (Philadelphia: University of Pennsylvania Press, 1897), Vol. IV, No. 4, p. 3.

GERMANIC SOCIETY

Since the early Germans had lived in rather small groups given over to agriculture and cattle raising, they had felt no need to create elaborate political institutions. The family was their basic social unit—not the small family of father mother, and children, but the large family that included grandparents, uncles, cousins out to the second or third degree, and even the servants. The family protected the lives and property of its members, sometimes waging blood-feuds with other families. Above the family was the neighborhood, a group of family heads who cooperated in local defense, in settling disputes, and in performing difficult agricultural tasks. The folk, or people, which was made up of many neighborhoods, was supposedly a blood-group descended from a few common ancestors. It had almost no function except to make war on or defend itself against neighboring peoples.

Early Germanic society was not democratic; it was very conscious of differences in class and rank. Certain families, which claimed descent from the gods, had great wealth and supplied leaders in time of war. But these leaders—the kings and the nobles—had little to do in time of peace. Their wealth and ancestry won them respect, and their bands of armed retainers commanded fear. Although their advice was often sought when trouble arose, they did not administer a state or govern a people. Most of the ordinary business of the people was conducted by the family and neighborhood groups.

Germanic Courts

The difference between Germanic and Roman political organization is seen most clearly in the administration of justice. A Roman who had a grievance against a neighbor went to a court established by imperial authority. His case was judged according to laws promulgated by the emperors, and the court's decision was enforced by local administrative officials.

A German who felt that he had been wronged, however, had to rely first and foremost on his own strength and that of his family. The most common remedy was reprisal, which easily developed into the blood-feud. Only if the injured family felt that reprisal and feud were unnecessary or dangerous would the case go to a court. The usual court was an assembly of neighbors that, lacking coercive power, relied largely on public opinion and religious sanctions. It had no power to force a defendant to come to court. If he did appear and denied his deed, the court had no means of establishing the facts in the case. A defendant with a bad reputation was usually sent to the ordeal. This meant that he was obliged to expose himself to a test and let the gods indicate whether or not he was lying. He might, for example, be thrown into a pond to see if he would float or sink. Floating was a sign of guilt, for it meant that the pure element of water had rejected the accused. A man of good reputation, however, could clear himself by compurgation—that is, he would swear that the charge against him was baseless, and a fixed number of friends and relatives would swear that his oath was "clean." These oath-helpers were not giving testimony in behalf of the accused, for they might know nothing at all about the facts in the case. They were simply swearing that the accused was not a perjurer, and by so doing they automatically cleared him of the charges against him.

If the plaintiff won his case, he received compensation from the defendant, either in money or in kind. This was true even for crimes of violence, such as homicide or mayhem. There was no idea that crime was an offense to the community as a whole, and no attempt was made to inflict physical punishment on the wrongdoer. Tables of compensation made up the largest part of the laws of every Germanic people. It cost more to kill a man of high birth than an ordinary freeman, more to kill a woman of childbearing age than a grandmother. The penalties were substantial; the compensation for killing a man of high birth would ruin a poor family. However, no provision was made for collecting the penalties, other than the threats of the injured family and the pressure of public opinion.

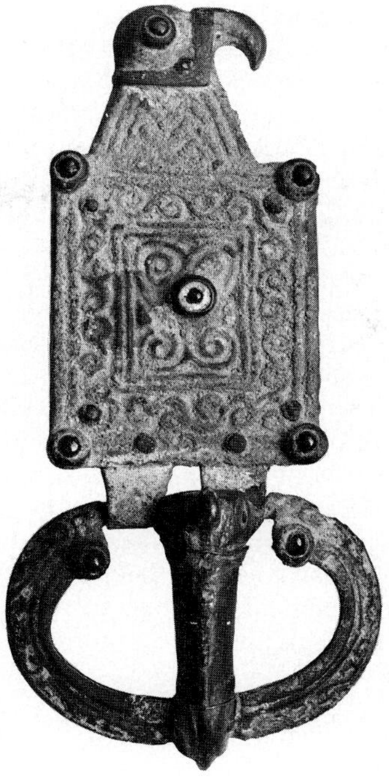

An artifact of the migration period. Ostrogothic gilt bronze buckle with jewels (sixth century). The style is Germanic.

These courts were probably more effective than we might think in dispensing a rough kind of justice. The most common offenses among the early Germans were acts of physical violence, of which no one was ashamed and which no one sought to conceal. To quarrel, fight, wound, and kill was the natural behavior of a self-respecting man. Thus in many cases the facts were not denied, and the sole function of the court was to prevent a feud by determining the compensation to be offered to the injured party. When the facts were in dispute, ordeal and compurgation, though they might not reveal the truth, at least provided quarreling families with an excuse not to launch a feud. Once the gods had spoken, it was unnecessary to prove one's manhood by fighting. Like many other legal systems, the system dictated by Germanic custom was more concerned with stopping fights than with administering abstract justice. Any solution, so long as it was peaceful, was better than a grievous outbreak of blood-feuds.

Nevertheless, this Germanic legal system had serious defects, and no civilized life was possible until they had been remedied. It gave no place to public authority and set loyalty to the family far above loyalty to any larger group. It accepted as natural a state of violence in which no one's life was secure. Effective only in dealing with open wrongdoing, it could not easily be applied to commercial transactions. From the fifth to the twelfth century western European rulers struggled to create effective courts of justice; only when they had succeeded in this difficult task could the people they ruled advance beyond the stage of small, self-sufficient agricultural communities.

Germanic Kingship

The loyalties of a German were personal. He was loyal first of all to his family—and understandably so, for he could scarcely hope to exist without family backing. Men who had no families or whose families were weak had to become dependents or even slaves of some strong man. Next, the German showed loyalty to the leaders of the local community. Finally, he might show some loyalty to the king, if that king was known and respected for his prowess in war. But the king could not count on the unanimous support of his peoples; his real strength lay in his bands of armed retainers. These retainers lived with the king, were bound to him by personal oaths of loyalty, shared in the spoils of conquest, and were usually faithful to him unto death. A king seldom had more than a few hundred of these devoted retainers. The rest of his subjects were not ready to die to protect him from usurpers or outside enemies. So long as there was a king to lead them in times of emergency, they cared little who he was.

It was difficult enough for kings to exercise authority when they ruled small groups in limited territories and when they were personally acquainted with most of the fighting men of the folk. The task became far more difficult when they tried to rule large populations, composed of different races, scattered over wide areas of the old Empire. The king could not be present in all parts of his realm, nor could he know more than a few of the leading men in each district. He could neither preserve the old Roman administrative system nor create a new Germanic one. The idea of a civil service was foreign to Germanic custom, and the Germans did not know how to delegate authority. Either they ignored the king's delegate and tried to deal directly with the king, or else they transferred their loyalty to the delegate himself and enabled him to become an almost independent ruler in his administrative district. Until kings were able to delegate authority without losing control—and it took them centuries to find out how—European kingdoms remained loose federations of local communities.

Given the primitive state of the Germanic economy and the structure of Germanic society, the local community was almost self-sufficient. The ordinary German might like to hear stories of adventures in distant lands, but otherwise he was not particularly interested in anything that happened more than a day's journey from his home. He drew almost everything he required from his own land and he produced nothing to sell in distant markets. He relied on the great men of his community for local defense and followed them to war without worrying about causes or objectives. Thus

Archbishop Hincmar on the Ordeal by Cold Water

Ninth century

Now the one about to be tested is bound by a rope and cast into the water, because, as it is written, each one shall be holden with the cords of his iniquity. And it is evident that he is bound for two reasons; to wit, that he may not be able to practice any fraud in connection with the judgment, and that he may be drawn out at the right time if the water should receive him as innocent, so that he perish not. . . . And in this ordeal of cold water whoever, after the invocation of God, who is the Truth, seeks to hide the truth by a lie, cannot be submerged in the waters above which the voice of the Lord God has thundered; for the pure nature of the water recognizes as impure and therefore rejects . . . such human nature as has once been regenerated by the waters of baptism and is again infected by falsehood.

From Archbishop Hincmar, trans. by Arthur C. Howland, *Translations and Reprints* (Philadelphia: University of Pennsylvania Press, 1897), Vol. IV, No. 4, p. 11.

the establishment of a large kingdom did little to aid the ordinary German, nor did the division of a large kingdom into little principalities hurt or shock him.

Although settlement in the Western Empire posed puzzling new problems for the Germanic kings, it also gave them some help in solving those problems. Royal authority was always greatest in time of war, and the period of migration was a period of almost constant war. And, though they did not fully understand the Roman concept of the state and of public authority, the kings learned enough from contact with Romans to make them eager to be more than mere tribal war leaders. Most important, the Church, which had taken over many of the Roman traditions of government, sooner or later gained great influence in all the Germanic kingdoms. Not all churchmen were good administrators or enlightened statesmen; in fact, many were only one degree less barbarous than the flocks they tended. But most of them realized that Christianity could not flourish in an area broken up into isolated small communities and that, bad as the kings might be, there was more to be hoped for from them than from the even less enlightened lords of petty provinces. Many bishops served as advisors to the kings and helped to create a rudimentary central government. Others preserved a certain degree of unity by meeting together in local church councils. Prominent laymen frequently attended these meetings, which often dealt with such secular matters as the suppression of violence or declarations of loyalty to a king.

THE CHURCH IN THE GERMANIC KINGDOMS

Though the Church had a privileged place, it suffered severely during the chaotic years following the Germanic ascendancy. The old Roman population was far from being completely Christian in the fifth century, and the new Germanic population was either pagan or Arian. Even when they had been converted to Catholic Christianity, the Germans often tried to use the Church for their own purposes. A good many bishops of doubtful character, for example, were foisted on the Church by kings anxious to reward their friends and supporters.

The Church at this time was not yet the self-sufficient, highly organized institution it was to become in later centuries. Formerly it had relied on the imperial government for support and protection, and it had not yet perfected its own administrative system or established clear lines of authority. Theoretically, the kingdoms should have been divided into dioceses, each administered by a single bishop. North of the Alps this division was far from complete; many bishops had dioceses that were too large or whose boundaries had not been defined. The division of the dioceses into parishes had gone even less far. This meant that there were no churches at all in many rural areas and that many nominal Christians had little opportunity to attend Christian services. Finally, while the pope's authority to determine questions of faith and morals was generally acknowledged, his power to remove inefficient or corrupt bishops was not yet fully established. Thus the influence of the Church varied from diocese to diocese with the character of the bishop and the amount of aid he could get from his king.

Fortunately for the Church, the growth of monastic communities provided a new, disciplined force at a time when it was badly needed. In the Late Empire many Christians, feeling that they could not live a truly religious life while absorbed in secular activities, had withdrawn from the world to live as hermits in the wilderness or desert and passed their lives in contemplation and prayer. But it was not easy for the hermit to endure the rigors of an isolated existence; his devotion might falter or he might be unable to provide himself with food and clothing. Thus there was a tendency for hermits to come together in communities in order to obtain spiritual and physical assistance from their fellows. This was especially true in the Middle East, where the hot, dry climate and scarcity of water almost dictated communal life. By the end of the third century, some of these communities had become formally organized as monasteries under the headship of abbots.

Monasteries and monastic rules had

A German king (above) and his bishop. From an early manuscript copy of Alaric's code of law.

St. Benedict giving his Rule to his monks. This eighth-century drawing is the oldest known representation of St. Benedict.

existed in the East for several generations and were spreading to the West at the time of the Germanic migrations. But the eastern rules were not entirely suitable for western conditions; they were both too harsh and too soft. They were too harsh in physical matters, for the scanty food and clothing that would support life in the Egyptian desert were completely inadequate in the colder northern countries. They were too soft in matters of authority, for many eastern monks were completely undisciplined and wandered about from place to place as they saw fit. Yet the monastic life was becoming steadily more attractive to men in the West; it offered both spiritual and physical security in an age of increasing violence and instability. Many abbots in Italy and Gaul tried to develop rules suited to western conditions, but none had more than local influence.

St. Benedict and Monasticism

It was St. Benedict of Nursia (480–543) who was most successful in adapting monasticism to the needs of the Western Church. He was born into a well-to-do Roman family, but like many other men of his time he had fled in disgust from a world that seemed hopelessly corrupt. At first he lived as a hermit in the hills near Rome. As his reputation for holiness attracted others to him, he found himself forced to organize a regular monastic community. He built a monastery on the commanding height of Monte Cassino,* near the main route from Naples to Rome, and established a rule that gradually became the basic constitution for all western monks.

The great strength of the Benedictine Rule lay in its combination of firmness and reasonableness. The abbot's authority was absolute. Monks were not to leave their monastery or transfer to another monastery without permission. They were to keep themselves occupied all day. Their first and most important duty was to do the "work of God"—that is, to take part in religious services that filled many hours of the day. But they were also to perform any manual labor that was necessary for the welfare of the house, including such activities as copying manuscripts. The primary purpose of the Rule, however, was not to make the monastery an intellectual center but to keep the monks from extremes of idleness or asceticism. Most monks were neither writers nor scholars, and most monasteries never distinguished themselves by their literary productions. They did, however, distinguish themselves as centers of prayer and worship, as dramatic examples of the Christian way of life. Most monasteries also performed certain social services, such as extending hospitality to travelers or giving food to the poor, and a few operated important schools.

The earliest monasteries in the Germanic kingdoms were Irish in origin, and though they did not follow the Benedictine Rule in detail, they did offer pure Christian doctrine to people who were pagans, heretics, or at most only nominal Catholics. Very early these monasteries became centers of missionary activity and reform. Benedictine monasteries

*A great battle of the Second World War was fought for the strategic position of Monte Cassino. The mountain had long been occupied by a Benedictine monastery, though the buildings destroyed in the battle were not the original ones.

gradually became established north of the Alps and eventually were far more numerous than the Irish houses. Many of the latter group were taken over by the Benedictines. Their emphasis on obedience to higher authority helped to hold the Church together during a period when any sort of centralization was hard to achieve. The Benedictines emphasized papal authority and a well-organized Church; they opposed local autonomy and lack of discipline. Benedictine monasteries often served as nuclei for the growth of towns, for they were almost always more prosperous than the neighboring countryside. In many parts of Europe the Benedictines introduced valuable new techniques, such as building with stone and organizing agriculture around their large estates.

In view of these benefits, many kings and wealthy landowners decided that founding a monastery was a good investment. The founder and his family gained both spiritual and material rewards. It was obviously good for the donor's soul to have holy men praying for him; it was also good to know that the monastery might furnish grain in time of famine and lend its gold and silver ornaments when its benefactor ran short of money. By attracting settlers to waste lands, it might increase productivity and enhance the ruler's authority in remote areas. Thus monasteries spread rapidly throughout most of the Germanic kingdoms, often more rapidly than organized dioceses and parishes.

The Conversion of the Anglo-Saxons

England offers a good example of the importance of monasteries under the Germanic kingdoms. The Anglo-Saxon conquest of Britain was slow, piecemeal, and bloody. Faced with a stubborn enemy, the Angles and Saxons had to be more destructive than, for example, the Franks were in the Seine Valley. Abandoned by Rome, the Britons had reverted to their Celtic traditions, and they put up a stiffer resistance than any other group in the western part of the Empire. Very little of Latin civilization remained in Britain: the language was abandoned, the

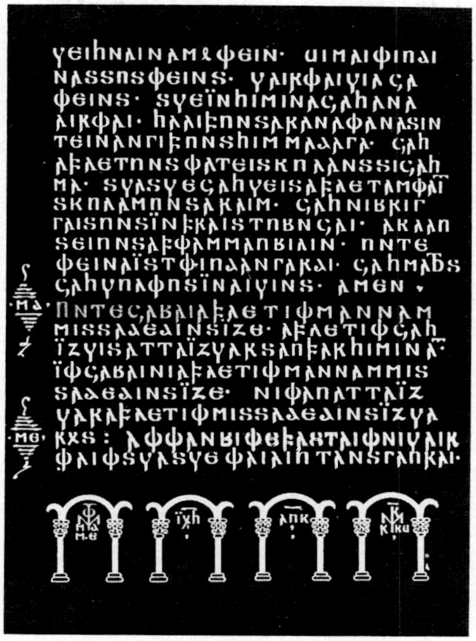

Page from a Gothic Bible (*ca.* 500). This translation, by the Arian bishop Ulfila, helps explain the success of the Arians in converting the Germans. Orthodox Catholics did not translate religious works into German until much later. Ulfila's Bible is one of the earliest specimens of a Germanic dialect and is the basis of most scholarly work on early German. Notice that some new letters, not in the Greek or Latin alphabets, had to be devised to accommodate unusual sounds in the Gothic language.

St. Benedict on the Authority of the Abbot

This excerpt illustrates the firm yet reasonable discipline that St. Benedict sought to instill in western monasteries.

Whenever any weighty matters have to be transacted in the monastery let the abbot call together all the community and himself propose the matter for discussion. After hearing the advice of the brethren let him consider it in his own mind, and then do what he shall judge most expedient. We ordain that all must be called to council, because the Lord often reveals to a younger member what is best. And let the brethren give their advice with all humble subjection, and presume not stiffly to defend their own opinion. Let them rather leave the matter to the abbot's discretion, so that all submit to what he shall deem best. As it becometh disciples to obey their master, so doth it behove the master to dispose of all things with forethought and justice.

In all things, therefore, every one shall follow the Rule as their master, and let no one rashly depart from it. In the monastery no one is to be led by the desires of his own heart, neither shall any one within or without the monastery presume to argue wantonly with his abbot. If he presume to do so let him be subjected to punishment according to the Rule.

From the *Rule of St. Benedict*, trans. by Cardinal Gasquet (London: Chatto and Windus, 1925), pp. 15–16.

The helmet (reconstructed from fragments) of a seventh-century Anglian king. From the Sutton Hoo treasure, one of the great archeological discoveries of this century, found under the untouched funeral mound of an early Anglian king.

towns were deserted, and much of the cultivated area sank back into wilderness. Christianity survived only among the native Britons in Wales; from Wales it spread into Ireland. The Christians of Wales and Ireland, cut off from the rest of the western world, were developing peculiar ideas and usages. They celebrated Easter at a different time; they gave abbots authority over bishops; they did not follow the Roman ritual. Irish missionaries had considerable influence in Scotland and on the Continent, but little in England, except in the north. Thus the basic ingredients that were to produce early medieval civilization—the Latin, Germanic, and Christian traditions—had not yet begun to fuse in Anglo-Saxon England.

The picture began to change during the pontificate of Gregory the Great (590–604). Gregory had been a monk and then an abbot; in fact, he had been most unwilling to leave his monastic life to take on the responsibility of governing the Church. He realized more fully than his predecessors the value of the monks as a disciplined force obedient to the orders of Rome. Gregory also realized how hard it was to maintain unity and decent conduct among the clergy of the Western Church. His correspondence shows how diligently he worked at this task and how difficult it was to make any impression on bishops and priests protected by Germanic kings. Gregory kept some measure of control in Italy, but beyond the Alps he could do little more than register his complaints. And beyond the Frankish area, where at least a form of Christianity existed, though corrupt and unsatisfactory, stretched a great expanse of heathen territory, from the North Cape down to the middle Danube, from England across Frisia and north Germany into the limitless lands of the Slavs.

Gregory probably prepared no master plan for the reform and conversion of the West. But he was quite ready to take advantage of special opportunities, and he turned to the monks for help. Britain seemed to be a promising field for conversion, since the king of Kent, in southern England, had married a Christian Frankish princess. So in 597 Gregory sent a group of monks to Kent, led by an abbot named Augustine.*

A self-sufficient monastery. Its produce included fish bred in the *vivarium* shown in the foreground. A *vivarium* was often taken as a symbol of a monastery. The fish represented the monks—note their faces.

*This Augustine also became a saint, but he should not be confused with the great theologian St. Augustine of Hippo, who died more than a century and a half before the mission to England (see p. 119).

THE ANGLO-SAXON KINGDOMS OF ENGLAND Seventh century

Augustine converted the king of Kent without much difficulty and established the first English bishopric, at Canterbury. But after this promising start the Roman version of Christianity spread only slowly through the island, partly because Augustine was not a very good organizer, partly because Irish missionaries were influential in the north, and partly because the Anglo-Saxons were divided and quarrelsome. It was only late in the seventh century that these obstacles were overcome. Most of the north abandoned Irish forms, and in 669 a great organizer, Theodore of Tarsus, became Archbishop of Canterbury. Theodore gave the Anglo-Saxon Church a firm institutional base by dividing the country into regular dioceses and made the Church an integral part of Anglo-Saxon society.

From this time on the Anglo-Saxons were loyal and energetic supporters of the Roman Church. The most successful missionaries of the eighth century were Anglo-Saxon monks, who not only converted the remaining pockets of heathen Germans on the Continent but even succeeded in reforming and making obedient to the pope the corrupt and anarchical churches of the Frankish kingdom. Gregory's decision to support monasticism and missionary activities produced remarkable results, for the missionary monks both increased the number of Christians and greatly strengthened the pope's authority in western Europe.

THE RISE OF THE FRANKS

During this period of missionary activity, the Franks were rising to political dominance in western Europe. They occupied a favored position. They had penetrated deep enough into the Empire to profit from its wealth but not deep enough to jeopardize the sources of their military power. They held northern Gaul, which was Roman, but they also held the solidly Germanic regions of the middle and lower Rhine. Their first great king, Clovis, a member of the Merovingian* family, came to power in about 480. He was king of only one group of Franks, and at first he held only a small corner of Gaul. But Clovis was both a good fighter and a skillful intriguer: he rapidly increased the size of his realm by assassinating or defeating his rivals. Clovis had married a Catholic Burgundian princess, and through her he gained the idea that the Christian God might be a powerful help in war. He is supposed to have tested this idea in a battle with the Alamanni (a Germanic people who held lands around the upper Rhine) about 506, in which he gained a hard-fought victory. It is still uncertain how much credit he gave to divine intervention, but soon after the battle, Clovis sought baptism from the Catholic bishop of Reims.

The conversion of Clovis, even more than that of Constantine, which it resembled so closely, was based on expediency. Clovis remained a bloody and treacherous barbarian; all he wanted was to exploit the power of the Christian God

*This family was named for an early and almost unknown Frankish king, Meroweg.

A Northumbrian cross (*ca.* 700).

Caesar Conquers Gaul 56 B.C.	ca. 486 A.D.	751	987	1328
Roman Gaul	Merovingian Dynasty	Carolingian Dynasty	Capetian Dynasty	

Childeric, father of Clovis and an early king of the Franks, from a signet ring found in his tomb. His long hair and his spear are signs of royal authority.

and gain the support of Catholic bishops and the old Roman population against Arian Germans. He used his newly acquired orthodoxy as an excuse to attack the Visigoths, who still held southwestern Gaul as well as Spain. Proclaiming that he could not endure the presence of heretics in Gaul, Clovis drove the Visigoths back across the Pyrenees and annexed their territories on the French side of the mountains. This victory almost completed the task of unifying Gaul. Only the Burgundian kingdom in the Rhone Valley escaped Clovis' domination, thanks to the aid it received from the Ostrogoths of Italy.

The Frankish kingdom remained strong for a century after Clovis' death in 511. His sons finally succeeded in conquering the Burgundians and added their territories to the Frankish realm. They also began to extend their authority over the Bavarians and other Germanic peoples east of the Rhine. Although the Frankish kings quarreled bitterly among themselves, the Franks still had the best army in the West, and none of their neighbors could profit from their disunity.

The Frankish kings also profited from the fact that their orthodoxy was seldom questioned, whatever might be said of their morals. Orthodoxy gained them the steady support of the bishops, most of whom came from old aristocratic families and had great influence with both Frankish warriors and Gallo-Roman landholders. Bishops could be very useful to kings, since they did not insist on impossibly high standards of conduct. Thus Bishop Gregory of Tours (538–594), who wrote the famous *History of the Franks,* was rather gentle in his judgment of the Frankish kings. Gregory admits that Clovis was treacherous and that on one occasion Clovis bewailed his lack of relatives "not because he grieved at their death but with the cunning thought that he might perhaps find one still alive whom he could kill." But Gregory could still sum up Clovis' career by saying: "God was laying low his enemies every day under his hand, and was increasing his kingdom, because he walked with an upright heart before Him, and did what was pleasing to His eyes." Gregory was equally favorable to King Guntram (561–593), of whom the best that could be said was that he murdered somewhat fewer people than his rivals did. "One would have taken him," says Gregory, "not only for a king, but for a priest of the Lord."

Nevertheless, the bishops did make an effort to mitigate the cruelty and selfishness of their rulers. They protected men unjustly accused; they did their best to prevent civil wars among members of the royal family. They were aided by the monasteries, which were just beginning to appear in the Frankish realm. Monks who had already abandoned the world

The Morals and Faith of the Early Franks

ca. 575

Ragnachar was then king at Cambrai, a man so unrestrained in his wantonness that he scarcely had mercy for his own near relatives. . . . Clovis came and made war on him, and he saw that his army was beaten and prepared to slip away in flight, but was seized by his army, and with his hands tied behind his back, he was taken with Ricchar his brother before Clovis. And Clovis said to him: "Why have you humiliated our family in permitting yourself to be bound? It would have been better for you to die." And raising his ax he dashed it against his head, and he turned to the brother and said: "If you had aided your brother he would not have been bound." And in the same way he smote him with his ax and killed him. . . . These kings were kinsmen of Clovis, and their brother, Rignomer by name, was slain by Clovis's order at the city of Mans. When they were dead Clovis received all their kingdom and treasures. And having killed many other kings and his nearest relatives, of whom he was jealous lest they take the kingdom away from him, he extended his rule over all the Gauls. . . . For God was laying low his enemies every day under his hand, and was increasing his kingdom, because he walked with an upright heart before Him, and did what was pleasing to His eyes.

From Gregory of Tours, *History of the Franks,* trans. and annot. by E. Brehaut (New York: Columbia University Press, 1916), pp. 48–50.

were not easily terrified by the threats of kings. St. Columban, the founder of Luxeuil, denounced King Thierry (595–613) to his face as a sinner and predicted that his sons would never be kings. The saint was exiled, but he soon returned and saw Thierry's family wiped out in a civil war. Yet in spite of all the efforts of bishops and monks, the Franks were Christians only in externals; it took a long time for the faith to sink into their hearts.

The Collapse of the Gothic Kingdoms

While the Franks were gaining control of Gaul and western Germany, their only possible rivals were being eliminated. After Theodoric's death, Justinian, the Roman emperor at Constantinople (see pp. 159–60), was determined to conquer the Ostrogothic kingdom in Italy. It took years of hard fighting, but by 552 the desperate resistance of the Ostrogoths had been snuffed out, and a devastated Italy was restored to imperial control. But Italians did not have any great loyalty to an empire that had ruined them, and they were too weak to defend themselves. As a result, when a new Germanic people, the Lombards, began to push into Italy from the Danube in the latter part of the sixth century, a large part of the peninsula lay open to conquest. The imperial forces held onto the south and some outposts in the north, such as Ravenna and Venice; the Lombards took the rest (although Rome retained some autonomy). The Lombards extended their conquests somewhat during the next century, but they never subdued the whole peninsula; in fact, no one was able to unite Italy again until 1870. The Lombard kingdom—weak, divided, and far less influenced by Roman civilization than the Ostrogothic kingdom had been—posed no threat to the Franks, who conquered it in the eighth century.

The Visigothic kingdom of Spain lasted a little longer than the Ostrogothic. The Visigothic kings strengthened themselves by abandoning their Arian heresy and accepting Catholic Christianity. Justinian struck them only a glancing blow; he regained some of the southeast coast of Spain but never had enough resources to reconquer the whole peninsula. But for more than 150 years the Visigoths suffered all the usual troubles of Germanic kingdoms—disputed successions, quarrels among the great men, and dwindling military strength. Thus when a Moslem army crossed the Straits of Gibraltar in 711 (see p. 175) and crushed the royal army, there was no effective resistance, and the Visigothic kingdom collapsed at once. A few Christians took refuge in the northern hills of Asturias and Galicia and established a petty kingdom there. The rest of the peninsula was drawn into an Arab empire and remained under Moslem control for centuries.

Two Ostrogothic brooches. The one above is made of gold inlaid with emerald and garnet and marks the zenith of the Ostrogothic style; the one below, made after the defeats of 552–553, is poor in quality and crudely decorated.

The Decline of the Merovingian Kings

After the sixth century only one power was left in Western Europe—the Frankish kingdom. The Anglo-Saxons were divided into petty kingdoms; the Scandinavian monarchies were just beginning to take form; the Germans of the north and east, such as the Frisians and the Old Saxons, had almost no organization; and the Visigoths and the Lombards were weakened by internal quarrels. But the apparent strength and solidity of the Frankish kingdom were deceptive. The

THE EUROPEAN KINGDOMS
ca. 700

Franks soon began to suffer from the same political ills as the other Germanic peoples; their kingdom survived only because it was not seriously threatened by outside enemies. In Frankland, as elsewhere, the kings had found it difficult to establish any sort of central control, and political power was passing rapidly into the hands of the great noble families.

In addition to holding large amounts of land, these families were the local representatives of royal authority. The Frankish kingdom was divided into counties, each ruled by a count who collected the revenues, presided over the courts, and controlled the military forces of his district. The king supposedly could name counts as he saw fit, and in the sixth century men of poor families sometimes achieved the position. But this was always distasteful to the great families, and as the kings weakened, the nobles gained a virtual monopoly of all important offices. By the eighth century counts could be selected only from a small group of aristocrats. Many countships were, if not strictly hereditary, usually held within the same family.

Frequent outbreaks of civil war strengthened aristocratic control over local government. The Frankish kings treated their state as private property and regularly divided the kingdom among their sons. Just as regularly, one or more of the rival kings tried to eliminate his brothers and cousins and acquire their territories and treasuries. To gain support, he rewarded his own men and bribed the retainers of his rivals with grants of land and concessions of governmental power. These grants further weakened royal authority. Whatever central power remained passed more and more into the hands of an official known as the mayor of the palace.

The Mayors of the Palace

Originally the mayor was merely the head of the royal household, the man who managed the king's private affairs. But the Germans made little distinction between public and private affairs and used any official for any business. Thus the mayor of the palace, who was always at court, gradually became a viceroy who acted for the king in all important matters. The mayor was usually a member of one of the great Frankish families, supported by a coalition of local magnates. In order to keep his place, he had to grant favors to these magnates just as the king had done.

To make things worse, by 700 the Frankish lands had been split into an eastern, largely Germanic kingdom called Austrasia, a western, more Latinized kingdom named Neustria, and a much weaker southern kingdom of Burgundy. Southwest Gaul (Aquitaine) and southeast Germany (Bavaria) were practically autonomous. In each of the major kingdoms there was a mayor of the palace who was constantly threatened by rebellion among his own supporters and who constantly threatened his rival mayors with direct attacks and underhanded intrigues. Wars among the mayors were as bad as wars among the kings, and there seemed to be little hope that the Frankish kingdom could survive this turmoil.

Yet by 700 a remarkable family had appeared that was to reunite the Frankish kingdom and strengthen it so that within its shelter a new western European civilization could begin to take shape. This family—called Carolingian, from its most famous member, Charlemagne, or Charles the Great (Carolus Magnus)—came from the eastern Frankish kingdom of Austrasia. It gave strong support to the Church and especially to missionary and reform activities. It also showed remarkable skill in gaining and keeping the loyalty of the counts and great landowners. With their support the head of the family, Pippin, made himself mayor of the palace in both Neustria and Austrasia late in the seventh century. When Pippin died there was a rebellion, but his illegitimate son, Charles Martel (714–741), was eventually accepted as mayor of all the Frankish kingdoms. With Charles Martel all power in the Frankish kingdoms was caught up by the Carolingian family. Although the Merovingian kings kept their empty title a few more years, they had no further influence on the course of events.

Suggestions for Further Reading

Note: Asterisk denotes a book available in paperback edition.

Theodoric, Boethius, and Cassiodorus

The life of one of the striking figures of the early Middle Ages is portrayed by T. Hodgkin, *Theodoric the Goth* (1891). Hodgkin writes in the "grand manner" of the nineteenth-century historian, and the book is still fresh. His *The Letters of Cassiodorus* (1886) contains the extensive correspondence of Cassiodorus and good biographical sketches of Cassiodorus and Boethius. A superior study of Cassiodorus and his monastic writings is *Introduction to Divine and Human Readings,* trans. by L. W. Jones (1946). Boethius' works are available in numerous translations. The most scholarly is in the *Loeb Classical Library,* trans. by E. K. Rand and H. F. Stewart (1918), but the Modern Library edition of Boethius' most famous work, *The Consolation of Philosophy,** trans. by W. V. Cooper (1942), or R. Green (1962), are more readable. Both E. K. Rand, *Founders of the Middle Ages** (1928), and H. O. Taylor, *The Emergence of Christian Culture in the West** (1901), discuss Cassiodorus and Boethius as "transmitters" of the Greco-Roman legacy. M. L. W. Laistner, *Thought and Letters in Western Europe, 500–900** (1966), combines fine scholarship with good style. Paul the Deacon's *History of the Langobards,* trans. by D. Foulke (1907), is our chief source for the Lombard kingdom of northern Italy.

St. Benedict and the Monasteries

The cornerstone of monasticism in the West is the short *Rule of St. Benedict,* trans. by J. McCann (1952). The best scholarly study of the Rule is P. Delatte, *Commentary on the Rule of St. Benedict* (1908), but the more recent study by H. van Zeller, *The Holy Rule* (1958), is more interesting and more understandable to the modern student. C. Butler, *Benedictine Monachism* (1923), and D. Knowles, *Christian Monasticism* (1969), are valuable for an understanding of the spirit and meaning of the monastic life. J. McCann, *St. Benedict** (1952), gives a good account of St. Benedict and Benedictines through the centuries. A fascinating and provocative picture of monastic life today, in the form of a diary, is T. Merton, *The Sign of Jonas** (1956). The classic work of W. James, *Varieties of Religious Experience** (1902), does a great deal to explain the "phenomenon" of monasticism in the perspective of modern civilization.

The Franks and Gregory of Tours

A shockingly vivid picture of the chaotic society of sixth-century Gaul is presented by the contemporary Gregory of Tours, *History of the Franks,** trans. by E. Brehaut (1916), or, in a fuller version, by O. M. Dalton (1927). This is our best evidence for the political and social condition of Merovingian Gaul. There is an excellent study of Gregory's language and its reflection of the decline of learning in the West in E. Auerbach, *Mimesis** (1946). *The Life of St. Columban,* trans. by D. C. Munro (1921), reinforces Gregory of Tours' picture of moral decadence. F. Lot, *The End of the Ancient World** (1931), contains a scholarly study of Gaul under the Merovingians, with emphasis on political conditions. The older work of S. Dill, *Roman Society in Gaul in the Merovingian Age* (1926), emphasizes economic and social aspects. A good overall survey is J. M. Wallace-Hadrill, *The Barbarian West: 400–1000** (1966); see also his excellent book on the Franks, *The Long-Haired Kings* (1962).

The Conversion of the Anglo-Saxons

The Venerable Bede of Jarrow's *The Ecclesiastical History of the English Nation** is incomparably the greatest authority we have for the early centuries of the English settlements. For the life and works of Bede, see the scholarly collection of essays edited by A. H. Thompson, *Bede: His Life, Times, and Writings* (1935), and P. H. Blair, *The World of Bede* (1970). The classic poem *Beowulf,** trans. by D. Wright (1957), is a mine of information about Anglo-Saxon society in the seventh and eighth centuries. D. Whitelock, *The Beginnings of English Society** (1952), is a very good introductory treatment of the period, and G. O. Sayles, *The Medieval Foundations of England,** Chapters 1–3 (1948), is a "history of ideas in action" with an excellent and detailed critical bibliography. See also S. J. Crawford, *Anglo-Saxon Influence on Western Christendom* (1933), and J. M. Wallace-Hadrill, *Early Germanic Kingship in England and in the Continent* (1971).

Gregory the Great

F. H. Dudden, *Gregory the Great,* 2 vols. (1905), the standard study of Gregory's pontificate, gives a good account of conditions in Italy at the time. Dudden pays special attention to the conversion of England. The increasing activities of the papacy under Gregory are shown in his letters in *Library of Nicene and Post Nicene Fathers,* Vols. XII and XIII (1895). *The Dialogues of St. Gregory the Great,* trans. by E. G. Gardner (1911), and, more recently, by M. Uhlfelder (1967), illustrates the religious and intellectual climate of the times. *The Dialogues* is our chief source for the life of St. Benedict.

8 Byzantium and Islam

The East was the first region of the Empire to be threatened by the barbarian inroads of the fourth and fifth centuries. Before moving west, the Visigoths and the Ostrogoths had held the Balkans for a time. But their presence, which was to alter profoundly the political and social pattern of the West, was only a passing episode in the history of the East. By 500 the Roman Empire in the West had vanished, whereas the Empire in the East was beginning a revival that was once more to give it a strong government, a highly developed economy, and an active intellectual and artistic life.

THE EASTERN ROMAN EMPIRE

This contrast shows once more that internal weaknesses rather than external attacks were the real cause of the collapse of the Roman Empire. In the West, where the internal weaknesses were more serious and more pervasive, nothing could be done to save the Empire. But in the East there were strengths as well as weaknesses. There the cities were economic assets rather than parasites, as they were in the West. Christianity was both more widespread and more deeply felt in the East than in the West, and it served as a substitute for patriotism. The excellent defensive positions of the East, especially Constantinople, made it impossible for the Germans to touch the richest cities and provinces. Moreover, the Eastern emperors and their advisers were somewhat more skillful—or at least more successful—politicians than their colleagues in the West. They prevented the Goths from making any permanent settlement in the Balkan Peninsula, and they freed themselves from dependence on Germanic soldiers by recruiting troops in Asia Minor. Because they retained control of the great trading cities of Constantinople, Antioch, and Alexandria, the Eastern emperors could always collect enough taxes to support their administration and their army. With the departure of the Ostrogoths for Italy and the weakening of the Huns, the Eastern Empire was freed from immediate danger. During the sixth century it was able to start the difficult task of recovery.

Justinian

The leader of this first revival of the Eastern Empire was the emperor Justinian (527–565), a man of ambition, energy, and imagination. In spite of his abilities, however, his stubborn determination in pursuing mistaken policies led him to waste resources, miss opportunities, and plunge the Empire into useless wars. He was successful in most of his projects, but a less successful ruler might have done less harm. Every success encour-

Opposite: View of the interior of Hagia Sophia in Constantinople (532–537).

Byzantine gold wedding ring (*ca.* fifth century).

aged him to extend his commitments, so that by the time of his death both the loyalty and the resources of his subjects had been nearly exhausted.

Justinian was not the sort of ruler one would expect to find in a state composed largely of Greeks, Syrians, and Egyptians. His family came from the extreme west of what was left of the Empire, from a district near the Adriatic, where Latin was still spoken. This Latin background may explain some of Justinian's policies. Fascinated by the idea of recovering the West, he was willing to sacrifice the people of the East in order to regain the old heart of the Empire. In a sense, Justinian was the last of the Roman emperors. After his death the Latin tradition died out, Greek became the official language of the Empire, and the ties between East and West slackened.

Justinian was lucky in that his immediate predecessors had rebuilt the army, set the Empire's finances in order, and repaired its administrative system. He was even luckier in what seemed at first a disastrous marriage. While he was still a young man, he had fallen in love with a woman named Theodora, who had been the sixth-century equivalent of a strip-teaser. She had had many lovers, and to marry her seemed socially impossible and politically unwise. But Justinian insisted on marrying his mistress, and he never had cause to regret it. Theodora was a courageous woman who kept Justinian from fleeing early in his reign when he was threatened by a rebellion of the people of Constantinople. She also understood the people of the East far better than her husband did; after her death he found it hard to retain their loyalty. Theodora secured important positions for many of her friends; through these supporters and through her own personal influence she was able to modify and even to reverse imperial policy, especially in the field of religion.

Nevertheless, the basic objectives of the reign were set by Justinian. He was determined to restore the Empire, to regain its lost territories, and to rebuild its cities. He always aimed high, reaching for the utmost in power and magnificence. Unfortunately, his resources were inadequate, and his plans were often contradictory.

Justinian's determination to reconquer the West was strengthened by the weakness of the Germanic kingdoms on

EXPANSION OF THE BYZANTINE EMPIRE UNDER JUSTINIAN 527–565

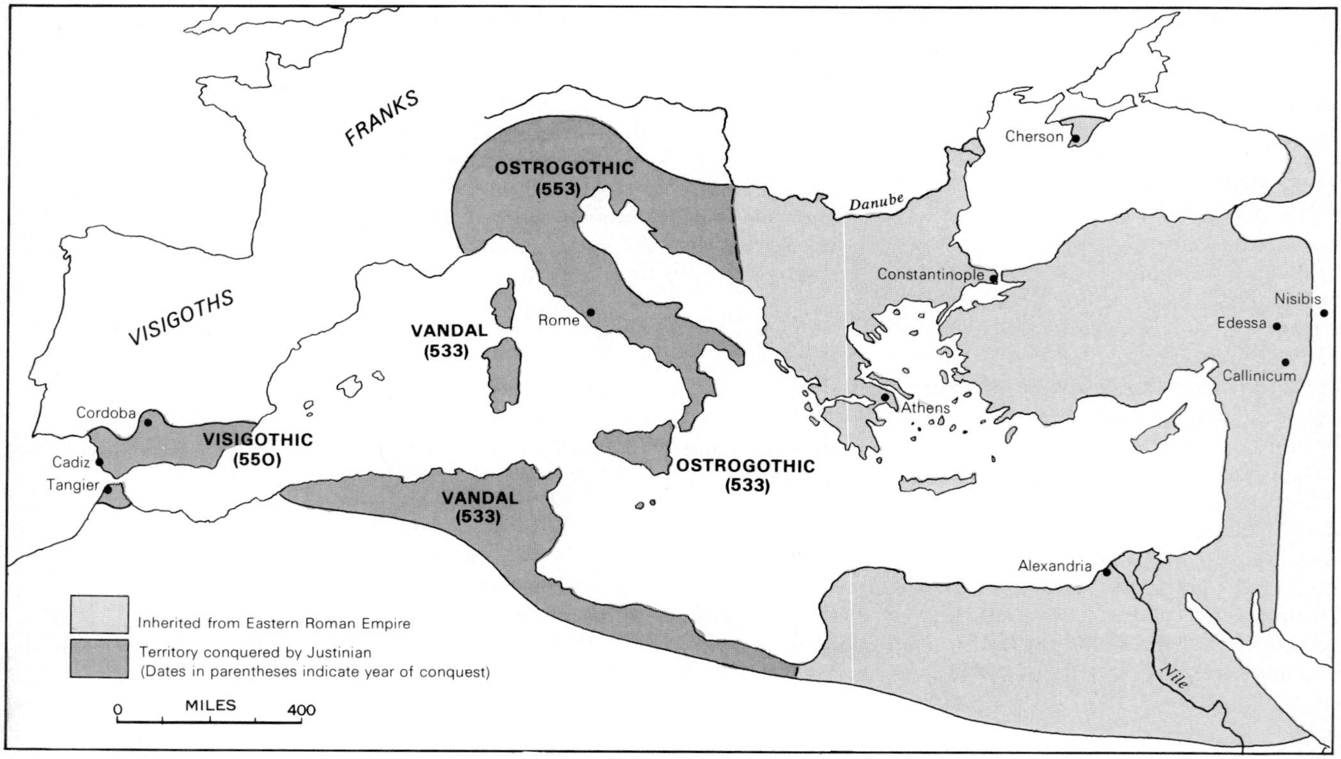

the Mediterranean. His first campaigns were encouragingly successful. The Vandal kingdom of Africa fell after a short war in 533. The Ostrogoths in Italy, left without a capable leader after the death of Theodoric, at first offered little resistance to the imperial army. In the end, the tide of reconquest even reached far-off Spain, where Justinian seized a strip of the southeastern coast with very little difficulty.

But it was easier to gain provinces in the West than to keep them. The Roman population of Italy, Spain, and Africa experienced no patriotic thrill on being reunited with the Empire. In fact, the reintroduction of the imperial tax system made many people long for the easier rule of the barbarians. Justinian tried to gain their loyalty by accepting Roman religious dogmas and rejecting the views of a large part of the clergy of Syria and Egypt. But he succeeded only in alienating many of his eastern subjects without gaining solid support in Italy. Soon the West lapsed into its old apathy. Justinian's rule was based on a small group of soldiers and bureaucrats; the bulk of the population was passive, taking part in neither politics nor war.

The barbarians were quick to take advantage of the situation. The Vandals had been thoroughly crushed, but the Berbers, fierce tribesmen living on the fringes of the civilized area, took up the fight for Roman Africa. After many years of conflict, the Berbers were pushed back from the coastal towns, but they continued to hold most of what is now Morocco and western Algeria.

Justinian had even more trouble in Italy. There the Ostrogoths, who had been defeated but not broken, elected a new king who nearly drove the imperial forces from the peninsula. Justinian never gave his Italian commanders enough troops, partly because so many other demands were being made on his resources and partly because he feared, like many a Roman emperor before him, that a too successful general might seek the throne for himself. As a result, the war dragged on for eighteen years, from 535 to 553. In the end the Goths were almost exterminated, but Italy had been devastated. Although Justinian retained Italy for the rest of his reign, it contributed nothing to the strength or wealth of the Empire.

In the long run Justinian's policy of reconquest was a failure. None of the western provinces he regained was secure, either in a political or a military sense; most of them were lost within a generation or two after his death. The Lombards, who had migrated from the north into what is now Austria, pushed through the mountain passes and settled in the Po Valley, to which they gave their name, Lombardy. Then they drove down past Rome, and in the end all that was left of Justinian's Italian conquest was a large part of the south and the districts of Venice, Ravenna, and Rome. The Spanish reconquest proved just as ephemeral; by 624 the Visigoths had regained all the

Procopius on Justinian's Wars

Procopius served for many years on the staff of one of Justinian's generals, and was later an official in Constantinople. He was well informed, but he exaggerated and was spiteful and envious, so that he must be read with caution. Nevertheless, there is much truth in his criticism of Justinian's military policies.

In estimating the territory that he depopulated, I should say that millions perished. For Libya [the Vandal kingdom] . . . was so thoroughly ruined that for a traveller who makes a long journey there it is no easy matter to meet a human being. . . . Immediately after the defeat of the Vandals Justinian did not concern himself with strengthening his dominion over the country nor make provision that its wealth should be safeguarded through the good-will of its inhabitants. . . . He sent out assessors of the land and imposed certain very heavy taxes. . . . As for Italy, it has become everywhere even more empty of men than Libya. Indeed, all the errors that he made in Libya were repeated. . . . By adding to the administrative staff oppressive financial agents he upset and ruined everything. . . . Meanwhile the Arabs were overrunning the Romans of the East . . . and the Persians under Chosroes four times made inroads into the Roman domain . . . leaving the land bare of inhabitants. . . . [Justinian] in time of war would grow lax for no good reason and carried on preparations for military operations too deliberately, all because of his parsimony. . . . [This last criticism is not entirely fair; Justinian often had trouble raising enough money for his armies.]

From Procopius, *The Anecdota or Secret History*, trans. by H. B. Dewing (London, 1954), pp. 215, 217, 219, 221.

Mosaic portraits of Justinian and Theodora, San Vitale, Ravenna (*ca.* 547).

coastal territories they had lost. North Africa stayed longer with the Empire, but fell to the Moslems at the end of the seventh century.

Though Justinian waged an offensive campaign in the West, he was kept on the defensive in the East. The Persian kingdom, the ancient enemy of Rome, was once more growing in strength and pressing hard on the eastern frontiers. On several occasions the Persians broke through the Roman defenses and plundered much of Syria and Asia Minor. With a large part of his army tied up in the West, Justinian was never able to defeat the Persians decisively, but through force of arms, diplomacy, and bribery he did manage to retain Syria and western Asia Minor. In the Balkans, Hunnic groups, aided by Slavic allies, staged raids that at times came very close to Constantinople. Justinian held on to most of the Balkan Peninsula, but he had to allow some of the Slavs to settle there. This was the beginning of Slavic predominance in the Balkans.

Justinian's policy in the East was not only cautious, which may have been sensible, it was also expensive. Diplomacy, bribes, and occasional payments of tribute to exceptionally dangerous enemies cost huge sums of money, but they did not end the necessity for maintaining an army and building fortifications. At the same time, many eastern provinces that were devastated by raids and invasions failed to pay their share of taxes.

Burdened though he was by wars of conquest in the West and by wars of defense in the East, Justinian did not spend the Empire's entire income on military operations. Restoration of the Empire meant more to him than territorial expansion; he was determined to recreate the magnificence of Rome at the height of its power. The New Rome of Constantinople was to be even more splendid than Old Rome, and provincial capitals were to reflect this splendor. Justinian put as much energy into this program as he did into his wars, and the results were somewhat more lasting.

They were more lasting because he accepted eastern standards instead of trying to impose his own western, Latin prejudices. Classical Roman art and architecture had simply decayed in the West, but in the East they had been transformed under the joint impact of Christianity and the revival of Oriental cultures. A new style was already emerging when Justinian gained the throne, and he gave it a chance to express itself through his great building program. All through the Empire, from Mount Sinai in the Egyptian desert to Ravenna in reconquered Italy, magnificent churches rose, rich with mosaics, goldsmiths' work, and many-colored marble.

The architects of these churches, so far as we know their names, came from the Asiatic provinces, and the decoration was largely inspired by Oriental examples. The new churches emphasized the interior, which blazed with light and color, rather than the exterior, which was often left rough and unadorned. In the famous church of St. Sophia in Constantinople, Justinian's architects built a great dome pierced with many windows high over the central part of the building. By solving the problem of setting a circular dome firmly atop a rectangular opening, they made the dome a far more effective element than it had been before, both esthetically and as a source of light. Earlier Roman architects had bolstered their domes with high walls that concealed them from view and blocked out much of the light. Even when Justinian's architects did not use the dome, they raised the walls of their churches and enlarged the window spaces in order to admit more light. And everywhere there were brilliant mosaics, gold and silver ornaments, richly woven textiles, polished stones of every hue. The decoration was stylized, symbolic, and not at all realistic; for this very reason it had a greater impact on the beholder. The endless ranks of saints and angels along the walls were clearly not human beings; rigid, solemn, and intense, these figures were unmistakably inhabitants of another world. And with the saints and angels appeared the figures of Justinian and Theodora, humble before their God, but haloed like saints and immeasurably superior to all other human beings. One of the emperor's most cherished titles was "Equal of the Apostles," and his churches gave visible support to this claim.

Procession of saints and martyrs, Sant' Apollinare Nuovo, Ravenna (*ca.* 574).

Religious Disputes

Justinian was certainly a sincere and pious Christian. But he was also something of a scholar with a dangerous taste for theology, and he ruled over subjects who would fight for religious dogmas when they would fight for nothing else. There had already been serious quarrels over basic articles of the faith before Justinian became emperor; he probably could not have avoided interfering in religious matters even if he had so desired. But he did not so desire. Instead, he wanted to use religion to unify the restored Empire. His efforts failed, although he bullied popes, deposed patriarchs, and imprisoned monks and priests. At his death the Empire was still badly divided in its religious beliefs.

The basis of the controversy was the old argument about the union of the human and the divine in Jesus Christ. If Jesus was not fully divine, then the Redemption was impossible; if Christ was not fully human, then he did not suffer for us, and so the Crucifixion lost its meaning. Few people any longer took the extreme positions of "fully divine" or "fully human," but in trying to describe the way in which divine and human were joined together it was easy to overstress one or the other and thus fall into heresy.

When Justinian took over the imperial government the most dangerous heresy was that of the Monophysites, a group that recognized the existence of a human nature in Christ but subordinated it to the divine nature to such an extent that it became meaningless. Those who supported and those who opposed the Monophysites were stirred by something more than a desire for precise theological definitions. Monophysitism had become the national religion of Egypt, and in Syria it probably had more adherents than any other sect. It gave the inhabitants of these lands a chance to voice their long-suppressed desire for cultural and spiritual independence. It was anti-Greek, anti-Roman, antipapal, and anti-West.

Justinian's own beliefs were opposed to Monophysitism, and his political aims intensified his opposition. As we have seen, he wanted to recover the West, and the West, led by the pope, was almost unanimous in its rejection of Monophysite doctrine. Early in his reign, therefore, Justinian persecuted the Monophysites and tried to suppress their teachings.

But in religion as in war, Justinian found that he could not concentrate exclusively on the West. Theodora, always far more understanding of eastern view-

Gold coin portraying Justinian on horseback. The coin was struck to commemorate the defeat of the Vandals in 535.

points than her husband, realized that his flat opposition to Monophysitism was endangering imperial control of Egypt and Syria. She probably had some personal inclinations toward the doctrine as well. Under her influence, Justinian became somewhat more tolerant and finally settled for an interpretation that was technically orthodox but that leaned toward the Monophysite position.

No one was pleased with this solution. Pope Vigilius, who had come to Constantinople against his better judgment to confer with the emperor, refused at first to accept the compromise formula. He yielded only after a long period of house arrest and threats. The orthodox clergy of Constantinople were equally indignant, although easier to deal with; Justinian simply dismissed them from their posts. The Monophysites themselves, whom Justinian was trying to conciliate, found the new orthodox doctrine just as unacceptable as the old. Almost all Egyptians, and many Syrians, seceded from the official Church and formed their own religious organizations, which were bitterly hostile to the government and to the orthodox, Greek-speaking clergy. This sharp division in religion helps explain the ease with which the Arabs took over most of the East in the next century (see p. 173). Syrians and Egyptians saw no reason to fight the Arabs to preserve the rule of intolerant and orthodox Greeks. The Moslems had nothing to gain by forcing religious uniformity on the inhabitants of the lands they conquered, so there was more toleration of different Christian sects under their government than under the Byzantine emperors.

Justinian's Summary of Roman Law

Justinian's love of precise definition, which led him into dangerous religious policies, found happier expression in the field of law. Perhaps his only two completely successful achievements were the building of St. Sophia and the codification of Roman law. The most impressive intellectual achievement of the Romans had been in law, and the keenest minds of the Empire had worked on legal problems. But this was the very reason that codification was needed; Roman law had developed over so many centuries that its basic rules had to be sought in the voluminous works of generations of lawyers and officials. There had been earlier attempts to codify and digest Roman law, but no one had had the energy or the determination to survey the entire mass of legal literature and reduce it to manageable proportions.

Justinian attacked the problem of codifying the law with the same energy and ruthlessness with which he planned the reconquest of the West. At the very beginning of his reign he picked a group of capable men, led by the great jurist Tribonian, and gave them a free hand to produce a statement of the law that would be brief, clear, and consistent. He must have put heavy pressure on them, for they completed the task with incredible speed. The essential work was done between 528 and 534, and little was added after 546, the year of Tribonian's death.

The books produced by this effort came to be known collectively as the *Corpus Juris.* The first and most important unit was the *Digest,* a collection of extracts from the works of leading Roman lawyers, especially those of the second century, the golden age of Roman law. These extracts dealt with such basic problems of jurisprudence as the nature of law and justice, and the relation between law and custom. But they also included brief statements on the guiding principles of Roman law in, for example, such matters as property, contract, and inheritance. The next book of the *Corpus Juris* was the *Code*, a restatement and simplification of statute law. These two major works were followed by the *Institutes*, a textbook of Roman law for students, and the *Novels*, laws promulgated after 534 to amend or supplement the *Code*.

The speed with which the *Corpus Juris* was compiled led to some unfortunate results. Important material was omitted, while insignificant and even contradictory statements were included. Moreover, because the *Corpus Juris* was the only authorized version of Roman law, earlier works on the subject were neglected and lost. Almost none of the thousands of volumes on Roman law written under the Empire have survived. On the other hand, judging by what happened to Latin literary works, most of the legal writings would have been lost in any case, and the *Digest* did at least preserve quotations from the ablest Roman lawyers.

Curiously, although the *Corpus Juris* was never applied as actual law in the West, it had a far greater effect on western countries than it did on the East. In the East the emperors continued to revise the laws, treating Justinian's work not as a final summary of legal thinking but only as a foundation for their own efforts. In the West the *Corpus Juris* was regarded as the final and perfect expression of Roman law. For many generations the *Corpus Juris* was neglected in the West, but when the revival of medieval civilization began in the late eleventh century (see Chapter 10), Justinian's work seemed a treasure beyond price. It gave men who were struggling with primitive and confused notions of social relationships the precise concepts of a highly developed legal system. It had a tremendous impact on both the state and the Church, on both private and public institutions. The *Corpus Juris* became an essential part of the western intellectual tradition and affected the law of every western European country. Justinian's real reconquest of the West came many centuries after his death, not through his armies but through his law.

From Eastern Roman to Byzantine Empire

It is well to remember this ultimate triumph of Justinian, for the immediate results of his reign were disastrous. His successors ranged from mediocre to despicable, but even able emperors would have found it difficult to cope with the legacy of bankruptcy, internal discontent, and external enmity that Justinian had left. Repeated rebellions made it impossible to guard the frontiers. The western conquests were lost, while in the East the Persians again attacked the Asian provinces of the Empire. And a new danger arose in the north: the Avars, a nomad people akin to the Huns, pillaged the Balkan provinces and threatened Constantinople itself. The Slavs again assisted the invaders and occupied large areas of the Balkans.

Early in the seventh century the plight of the Eastern Empire seemed hopeless. The Persians had taken Syria and Egypt, and the Avars had set up permanent camps close to Constantinople. But the Eastern Empire clung to life with amazing tenacity and showed marvelous powers of recuperation. Beneath the appearance of luxury and decadence, behind the intrigues and the factional quarrels, was a very hard core of administrative competence, diplomatic skill, military capacity, and a passionate loyalty among the people of Constantinople to their state and their religion. In the seventh century, as it would again and again in the future, the Empire rallied and beat off its enemies.

Heraclius, who became emperor in 610, slowly worked out a policy of avoiding conflict with the Avars through bribes and diplomacy, while throwing the bulk of his army against the Persians. This was a long and terribly expensive operation. The first attacks were failures, but after many years Heraclius finally ended the war with a raid deep into Persian territory that forced the Persians to make peace in 628.

The half-century of civil and foreign war that followed the death of Justinian wrought profound changes in the character of the Eastern Roman Empire. In the first place, the Latin element in the Empire, which had long been weakening, almost vanished. Early in his reign Justinian had used Latin for the *Corpus Juris*, but by the time of his death Greek was the only language that could be used for administrative and legal purposes. In the second place, religious dissent grew in Syria and Egypt, and the long period of Persian occupation and raiding did nothing to strengthen loyalty to Constantinople. The heart of the Empire was now the Greek-speaking, religiously orthodox region centering around Constantinople. The city itself supplied the wealth, the educated classes supplied the administrative personnel, and the poorer part of the population the politico-religious fervor that kept the Empire going. Only one more thing was needed—an army—and the best recruiting ground for soldiers was Asia Minor. Therefore a successful emperor had to hold Constantinople and enough of Asia Minor to maintain his military strength. If an emperor could keep this core area, the Empire would stand virtually unbeatable. Heraclius seems to have had some understanding of this principle; at least he made little effort to hold the northern and western Balkans and postponed the reconquest of Syria until he had gained access to the old recruiting grounds in eastern Asia Minor.

But an empire based on Constantinople and Asia Minor was no longer a Roman Empire, even though the name continued in official use. To mark the change, most historians have called the continuation of the Roman Empire in the East the Byzantine Empire. This term, derived from the old Greek name for Constantinople (Byzantium), emphasizes the importance of the capital city and the Greek-speaking element in the Empire. It should not be used, therefore, for the sixth-century Empire, which was still Mediterranean in outlook and largely non-Greek in population. It becomes increasingly appropriate during the seventh century, however, when Syria, Egypt, and North Africa were lost, and when the Empire was restricted to the eastern Balkans, Asia Minor, and a few districts in Italy.

The Byzantine Empire gradually developed patterns of behavior and organization that made it very different from western Europe. In religion, for example, slight differences in creed, organization, and ritual between the Christians of the West and those of Constantinople were

Greek fire, a mixture of quicklime, petroleum, and sulfur that ignited when it came in contact with water, was introduced into the Byzantine navy after 675. It was a very effective weapon against the Arabs (detail from a fourteenth-century manuscript).

magnified by quarreling theologians, ambitious rulers, and subjects who feared everything foreign. The Roman Catholic Church and the Greek Orthodox Church slowly drifted apart, a divergence that encouraged divergences in other fields.

But religion alone does not account for all the profound differences between the Byzantine Empire and its neighbors. More than any other state, it preserved the cultural traditions of Greece and the political techniques of the old Roman Empire. Not that the Byzantine Empire was a stagnant society. It showed marvelous skill and flexibility in adapting itself to new conditions, and this is precisely why it was able to preserve so much of its heritage. The Byzantine Empire never had to make an entirely fresh start, for it was always able to modify and thus retain its old ideas and institutions. It always possessed a highly trained bureaucracy, skillful diplomats, and a professional army. Economic activity and church administration were manipulated for the benefit of the government. Art, literature, and scholarship were encouraged, so that there was no break in the Greek literary and artistic tradition.

In short, the Byzantine Empire stood forth as a highly centralized and autocratic state at a time when the very concept of the state had been almost forgotten in western Europe. This state had a great urban center, an active commercial life, and a sophisticated literary and artistic tradition in contrast to the agricultural and largely illiterate society of western Europe. Both Augustus and Louis XIV would have understood and sympathized with many of the ideas and practices of the Byzantine Empire, but few western Europeans between 700 and 1400 could fathom the Byzantine way of life.

The differences between the Byzantines and the Arabs, who conquered Syria, Egypt, Armenia, and Palestine in the seventh century, were not so great as those between Byzantines and western Europeans. The Arabs took over much of the administrative system and many of the intellectual traditions of the old Eastern Empire. But religious hostility hampered intellectual contacts, since the Arabs had accepted the new religion of Mohammed. Moreover, while both the Greeks and the Arabs revered Plato, Aristotle, and other early philosophers, the Arabs put more emphasis on the Greek scientific tradition than did Byzantine scholars. There were interesting similarities between the Arab Empire and the Byzantine Empire, but these similarities became less apparent when the Arab Empire broke up into warring and short-lived states. No Moslem state endured as long as Byzantium or created such a permanent bureaucracy. Thus the Byzantine Empire gradually became unique, and it soon began to glory in its uniqueness. The Greeks of Constantinople, like their remote ancestors of the fifth century B.C., believed that they were the only civilized people and that their neighbors—especially their European neighbors—were barbarians. Caught between the barbarous West and the infidel East, the Byzantines clung with increasing tenacity to their government, their culture, and their religion.

MOHAMMED AND THE RISE OF THE ARAB EMPIRE

A few years after the death of Justinian in 565, a child was born in Arabia who was to found a religion that spread more rapidly than Christianity and an empire that was larger than that of Rome at the height of its power. Few men have had more impact on history than Mohammed. His religion split the old Mediterranean world and transformed the civilization of the Middle East; his influence is felt today in a broad belt of territory stretching from West Africa to the East Indies. Islam was the last of the three great world religions to emerge, and for many centuries it was more vigorous than either of its rivals—Christianity in the West and Buddhism in the East.

The Early Arabs

Arabia had played no important role in history before the time of Mohammed. The huge peninsula, about one-third the size of the United States, was like an arid wedge driven into the fertile lands of the

A Byzantine lady of rank (late fifth or early sixth century). Note her elegantly draped mantle and the snoodlike bonnet of the imperial type.

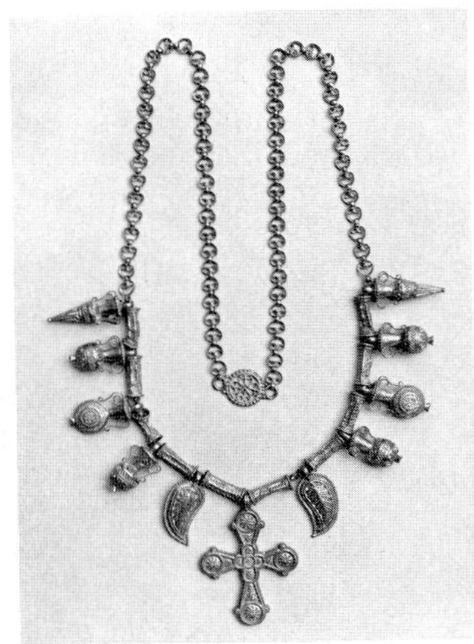

Early Byzantine jewelry contained Hellenistic and Roman features. The clasp of this late-sixth-century necklace, for example, is of a Hellenistic type, while the cylindrical slides between the pendants are a late Roman feature.

Middle East. Most Arabs were nomads, driving their herds from one scanty patch of vegetation to another. A much smaller, but very influential, group was made up of traders who dealt in products from the southern part of the peninsula, notably frankincense, and in goods imported from India and the Far East. Overland trade through Arabia was not extensive, but there was enough to support a few small towns along the southern and western sides of the peninsula.

The early Arabs were thus in touch with all the civilizations of the East and had learned something from all of them. Since they themselves spoke a Semitic language, they had been most influenced by other peoples of this language group who lived in the Fertile Crescent north of the peninsula. The Arabs developed a system of writing related, at least indirectly, to the Phoenician alphabet. They had the usual Semitic interest in religion, although it was expressed in almost indiscriminate polytheism. They had numerous tribal deities, and they had had contacts with the Christians and Jews who inhabited the northern part of the Arabian Peninsula. They honored poets, and the ideal Arab leader was as ready to make verses as he was to make war. They knew a good deal about astronomy, for knowledge of the stars is as helpful in crossing the desert as it is in navigating the seas. At their best, the Arabs were imaginative and eager to absorb new knowledge. They assimilated and profited from Greco-Roman civilization far more rapidly than did the Germans who took over the western part of the Roman Empire.

And yet there were grave defects in the social and political organization of the early Arabs. The nature of the country forced them to live in small, scattered tribes, and each tribe was almost constantly at war with its neighbors. The leading families within each tribe were often jealous of one another, so that blood-feuds were frequent and persistent. Weaker members of each tribe, and indeed of each family, were harshly treated by their stronger relatives. Sickly children were often killed, and orphans had little hope of receiving their parents' property. Women had almost no rights; their fathers or their husbands controlled their lives and their property. Men who could afford it had many wives and could divorce any of them whenever they wished. The divorced woman was usually left without any property or regular income.

In spite of all this disunity, certain strong ties bound the Arabs together. They were great genealogists; the leaders of many tribes could trace their ancestry back to the same ancient families—families that were known and respected throughout Arabia. Most of the tribes accepted a few common religious observances. There was a sacred period in each year, for example, when fighting was suspended and when many Arabs made a pilgrimage to the religious center of Mecca, a trading town near the west coast. In Mecca was the Kaaba, an ancient building full of images, including one of Christ. Here almost every god known to the Arabs could be worshiped. Here, too, was the most venerated object in the Arab world, the sacred Black Stone that had come from heaven. This habit of worshiping together at Mecca was the strongest unifying force in Arabia and one that was carefully preserved by Mohammed.

Mohammed's Teaching

Mohammed was born about 570 in Mecca. We know little about his early years, except that he was a poor orphan (although his grandfather had been a successful merchant). When he reached adolescence he began to work for a woman named Khadija, the widow of a rich merchant. In her service he made many caravan trips, during which he may have accumulated his information about the Jewish and Christian religions and his knowledge of the legends and traditions of other Arab tribes. He eventually married his employer, though she was considerably older than he, and the marriage gave him the wealth and leisure to meditate on religious problems.

Like many other Arabs, Mohammed had a sensitive mind, a deep appreciation of the wonders of nature, and a strong interest in religion. These qualities were enhanced by mysterious seizures, to which he had been subject since childhood. During these attacks he seemed to be struggling to express ideas that were not yet fully formed in his own mind. He gradually came to believe that this was God's way of trying to communicate with him, but until he was about forty he had no clear idea of what he was meant to do. Then he had his first revelation: a vision of the angel Gabriel, who commanded him to speak "in the name of the Lord, the Creator . . . the Lord who taught man what he did not know."

Mohammed was still doubtful about his mission, but as revelation succeeded revelation he became filled with the vision of the one, eternal God, the Lord of the world. He began to appeal to his fellow citizens of Mecca to abandon their host of false deities and to worship the one, true God. These early revelations bear some resemblance to the Psalms, both in their poetic quality and in their appeal to the wonders of nature as proofs of God's greatness and mercy. The stars in the heavens, sunshine and rain, the fruits of the earth—"all are signs of God's power if you would only understand."

By now Mohammed was convinced that he was a prophet, the last and greatest in the succession of prophets whom God had sent to enlighten and save mankind. He never claimed to be more than a prophet and even denied that he could work miracles, although he admitted that some of his predecessors had had this gift. He also admitted the divine mission of the Jewish prophets and of Jesus, but he claimed that their teachings had been distorted or misinterpreted. He was quite certain that the revelations he received superseded everything that had come before. The earlier prophets had had glimpses of the true religion, but he

The holy Kaaba in modern Mecca is the most sacred Islamic shrine.

An Early Revelation to Mohammed

By the white forenoon
and the brooding night!
Thy Lord has neither forsaken thee nor hates thee
and the Last shall be better for thee than the First.
Thy Lord shall give thee, and thou shalt be satisfied.

Did He not find thee an orphan, and shelter thee?
Did He not find thee erring, and guide thee?
Did He not find thee needy, and suffice thee?

As for the orphan, do not oppress him,
and as for the beggar, scold him not;
and as for thy Lord's blessing, declare it.

From A. J. Arberry, *The Koran Interpreted* (London: George Allen and Unwin, 1955), Vol. II, p. 342, Ch. 93.

alone had received the full message. Their teachings were to be accepted only when they agreed with the final word of God, which had been revealed to him.

Mohammed at first made little progress in converting his countrymen. His wife, Khadija, believed in him and comforted him when he was despondent, and his cousin Ali was one of his first converts. But most Meccans of good family were hostile; most of his early followers were from poor and uninfluential families. Mohammed's attacks on idols angered those who believed that the prosperity of Mecca as a center of trade depended also on its being the center of worship of all the known gods. Mohammed's followers were persecuted, and his own life was threatened. Finally he fled with his supporters to the city of Yathrib, some distance north of Mecca. The Mohammedan era begins with this flight, or Hegira, which took place in 622 A.D.*

Mohammed was welcomed as an arbitrator of local disputes in Yathrib. The town was renamed Medinet-en-Nabi (Medina), the City of the Prophet. Jewish influence was strong there, and the Arabs of Medina found nothing strange in the doctrine of a single, all-powerful God. Mohammed soon gained many converts among the pagan and half-Jewish Arabs and became virtually the ruler of the community. He now became involved in political problems, and the revelations he received during this period dealt largely with law and government. For example, it was at Medina that the rules about marriage, inheritance, and the punishment of criminals were laid down.

During the stay at Medina, Mohammed's reputation and power increased steadily. A desultory war between Medina and Mecca gradually became more serious, and by 630 Mohammed had gained so many supporters that he was able to capture Mecca with little difficulty. He immediately destroyed the idols in the Kaaba, except for the Black Stone, and made the temple the center of his religion. He had long asserted that the Kaaba had been built by Abraham and that Abraham had placed the heavenly Stone there as a sign of God's power. Thus he was able to preserve Mecca as the religious center of Arabia.

The fall of Mecca convinced many Arabs that Mohammed really was a prophet or at least that he was too strong to oppose. During his last years, most of the tribes of the peninsula acknowledged his spiritual and political leadership. Nevertheless, when Mohammed died in 632 Arabia was far from being a unified state, and many Arabs had only vague ideas about the religion they had accepted.

The Koran

Mohammed, however, had left a collection of his revelations, which became known as the Koran. He had taught that the Koran was God's guide for the human race, that it had always existed in heaven, but that no one had been worthy of receiving it before his own appearance on earth. Although he had received the Koran piece by piece, as circumstances made its teachings applicable, it formed a consistent and coherent whole. It contained all that man needed to know, and it was to be followed without question.

*This does not mean that dates of the Moslem era can be converted to our reckoning simply by adding 622 years. The Moslem year is based on a lunar calendar, and so does not coincide with ours. Our year 1978 was 1398 A.H.

Mohammed said: "Let the Koran always be your guide. Do what it commands or permits; shun what it forbids."

From the very start of Mohammed's mission, his followers had carefully written down his revelations on parchment, palm leaves, or whatever else was available. The task of sorting out and arranging this mass of sayings was begun soon after Mohammed's death by Abu-Bekr, but his version was not universally accepted. Othman, who ruled the Arab Empire from 644 to 656, ended the disputes that arose by compiling an authoritative version and banning all other collections. Othman's version has remained almost unchanged down to the present.

In no other major religion was there such early agreement on the official version of the founder's teachings. In fact, the Koran was put together so hurriedly that it seems somewhat confused and illogical to a non-Moslem. The basic rule was to put the longer passages first. Thus the earliest revelation, in which Mohammed was ordered to begin his mission, comes in Chapter 96, after many of the long, prosaic Medina passages. Seemingly repetitious and even contradictory statements were never harmonized. But these flaws are not admitted by orthodox Moslems, who consider the Koran a masterpiece of Arabic literature as well as the ultimate word of God to man.

The religion taught in the Koran was easy to understand and easy to follow. The basic creed was simple: "There is no God but Allah and Mohammed is his prophet." The faithful must also believe in the resurrection and the day of judgment, when every man will be rewarded according to his merits. The Mohammedan hell is very like the Christian one, but the Mohammedan paradise is unmistakably Arabian—a green garden full of running water and fruit trees with beautiful damsels to wait on the souls in bliss. Finally, the Koran teaches predestination: "Every man's fate have We bound around his neck"—that is, all human events have been determined, once and for all, by the will of God. Mohammed's own name for his religion was Islam—"submission to the will of God"—and his followers were called Moslems—"those who submit."

Leaf from a manuscript of the Koran, Egypt (eighth or ninth century).

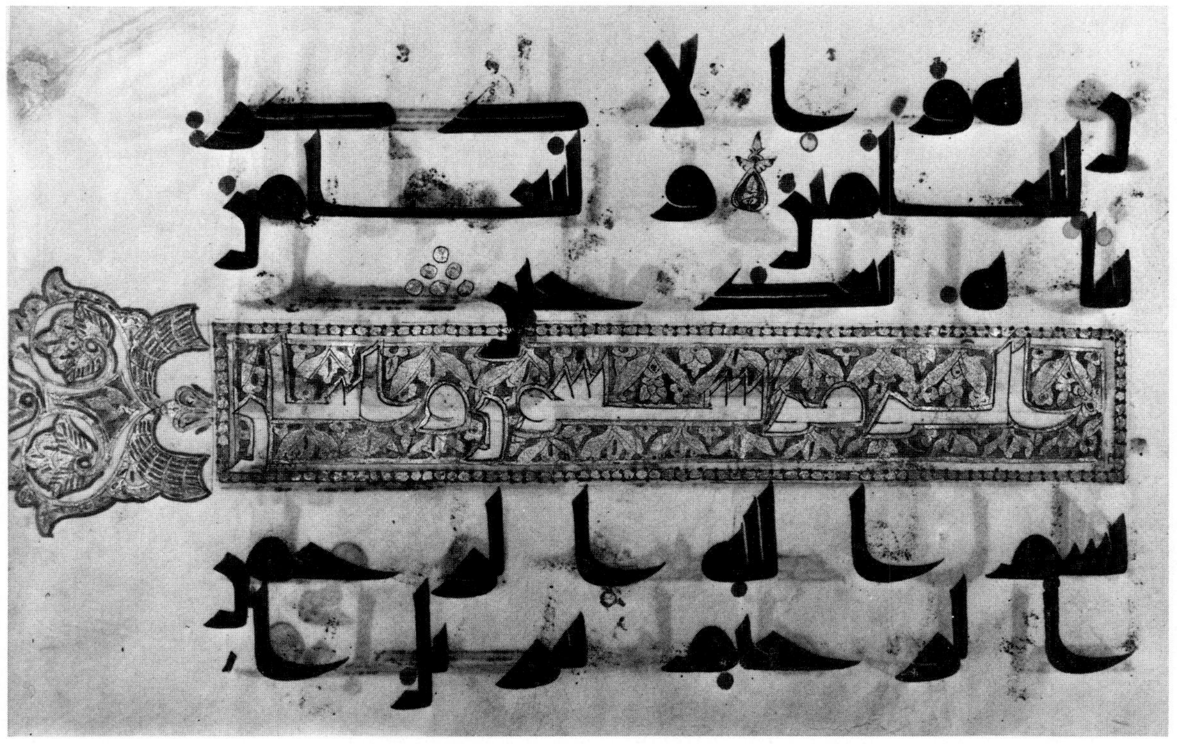

The principal religious practices of Islam were as simple as its theology. Every Moslem was to pray five times a day and to fast during the daylight hours of the month of Ramadan. Alms giving was a religious duty. Finally, every believer was to make a pilgrimage, if possible, to Mecca. But "only he shall visit the Mosque of God who believes in God and the Last Day, and is constant in prayer, and gives alms and fears God alone."

The Koran forbade wine drinking, usury, and gambling, and a dietary law, somewhat like that of the Jews, banned certain foods, especially pork. There was also a rudimentary code of law designed to check the selfishness and violence that had prevailed among the Arabs. Arbitration was to take the place of the blood-feud, infanticide was condemned, and elaborate rules of inheritance safeguarded the rights of orphans and widows. Mohammed also made an effort to limit polygamy by ruling that no man might have more than four wives simultaneously. Divorce was still easy, but the divorced wife could no longer be sent away penniless. These and other provisions were enough to furnish a framework for a judicial system.

There were obvious resemblances between Islam and Christianity, especially between Islam and the Christian heresies that denied or minimized the divinity of Christ. Since Mohammed admitted that Jesus was a major prophet, many heretics could accept Islam without feeling that they had greatly changed their beliefs. Other unorthodox Christians in Asia and Africa were so angered by their persecution by the Greek Church that they accepted Islam as a lesser evil. And in the competition for the loyalty of groups with little knowledge of either religion, Islam had a great advantage. It needed no organized church, for it had neither a priesthood nor a sacramental system. Each individual had to assure his salvation by his own right belief and good conduct. Every essential act of the religion could be accomplished by a man living quite by himself. It was customary for the faithful to meet together for prayers, especially on Friday, and from the earliest period certain men devoted themselves to explaining the Koran. But none of this was essential; anyone could accept Islam without waiting for the organization of a religious community, and any believer could make

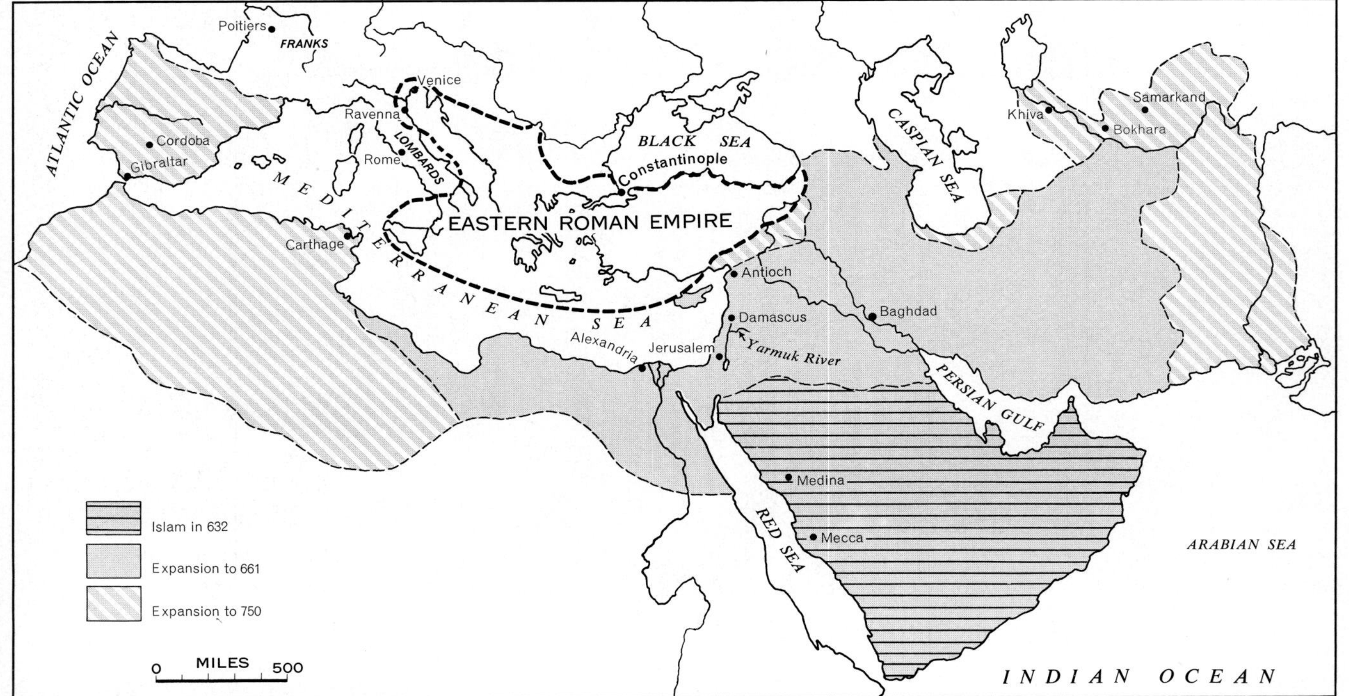

converts without waiting for an ordained priest to come and validate his action. Simple and uncomplicated monotheism was easier to explain than the doctrine of the Trinity.

These advantages often gave Islam the victory in competition with Christianity. On several occasions in the Middle Ages the Moslems were able to move in and convert a pagan people while the Christians were still trying to recruit a troop of missionary priests. And even today Islam is spreading more rapidly among the peoples of Asia and Africa than is Christianity.

An Islamic coin (698–699), the first silver coinage struck of purely Islamic type. The inscription in the center of the coin reads: "There is no God but God alone; no one is associated with him." The insistence on God's oneness and the denial of an associate to him is directed against the Christians and their doctrine of the Trinity.

The Caliphate

Mohammed left no very clear instructions about how his successor should be chosen. At his death there was confusion in the ranks of his followers and rebellion on the part of recently converted tribes. The faithful finally decided to choose a caliph, or successor to the prophet, who would act as both spiritual and political leader of Islam. The first caliph was Abu-Bekr, one of the earliest and most pious of Mohammed's converts. Though he ruled only two years (632–634), he succeeded in suppressing the revolts and in completing the unification of Arabia. Under his successor, Omar (634–644), the great conquests began. The Arabs had long been in the habit of raiding their wealthier neighbors to the north. Now they found themselves united for the first time, while both the Byzantine and the Persian states had been weakened by disastrous wars. In their first probing attacks, the Arabs met such slight resistance that they soon turned to wars of conquest. Their defeat of a Byzantine army at the Yarmuk River in 636 determined the fate of all the eastern provinces. Some fortified towns held out for a few years, but by 649 the Arabs had conquered Syria, Armenia, Palestine, and Egypt. Persia gave even less trouble and was completely in Arab hands by 642. Only the outbreak of civil war in Arabia slowed this first wave of conquest.

The civil war was caused by bad feeling between the early converts and some of the leading Arab families who had accepted Islam only after Mohammed's triumph was assured. The trouble began under the caliph Othman (644–656), who was an early convert himself but who was not so opposed to the latecomers as were some of the prophet's other companions. He was accused of favoring recent converts and of pushing forward his kinsmen, the Ommiads, who had at one time led the Meccan opposition to Mohammed. The accusation was largely true, but it is hard to see what else Othman could have done. He now had an empire to govern, and he needed the help of every man who displayed qualities of leadership, whatever his past religious behavior had been.

Quarrels between the two factions led to the assassination of Othman in 656. He was succeeded by an old believer, Ali, the son-in-law and adopted son of Mohammed. But since Ali was accused of condoning Othman's murder, the Ommiads soon revolted and secured the nomination of one of their family as caliph. Ali held Persia and Mesopotamia for a while but was assassinated in 661 by a member of a small, fanatical sect that believed the office of caliph was unnecessary. After Ali's death, the Ommiad caliph, who had taken no part in the assassination, was accepted as ruler by the entire Moslem world.

The Ommiad Dynasty

The first Ommiad caliph transferred the capital of the Arab Empire from Mecca to Damascus. This act was typical of the family, which put far more em-

Islamic door with ivory panel (eighth century).

phasis on politics than on religion. Damascus was not the prophet's city, but it had public buildings, a large group of educated and experienced civil servants, and a central location. It was far more satisfactory as a capital than Mecca, and it had the additional advantage of containing few of the prophet's early companions. The Ommiads bestowed key positions on members of the Arab aristocracy rather than on the early converts, and they filled the government bureaus with Christian Syrians and Egyptians. Thus the Arab Empire began to change from a loosely organized tribal theocracy into a centralized state employing many Byzantine administrative techniques. Finally, the office of caliph ceased to be elective and was made hereditary in the Ommiad family.

The Dome of the Rock in Jerusalem. This mosque was built on the spot from which Mohammed was believed to have ascended to heaven.

The policy of the Ommiads toward conquered peoples was also based on purely political considerations. The Arabs, like most tribal peoples, had never paid taxes, and they had no intention of doing so now that they were lords of a large part of the civilized world. In any case, the Arabs were not in actual possession of farms and businesses; they were administrators, not property owners. Thus the government was financed by tribute exacted from unbelievers, which meant that mass conversions would be a threat to its financial stability. So, instead of forcing Islam on their subjects, the Ommiad caliphs did not encourage conversion. New converts had to pay a heavy land tax, from which Arabs were exempt, and they were seldom given responsible positions in the government.

This policy caused little trouble in Syria, where the Arab aristocracy was satisfied with its special privileges and where Christians were numerous. But in both Persia and Mesopotamia, where Ommiad control was less secure, most of the population became converted to Islam. The new converts resented their inferior position and often revolted against the rule of Ommiad officials. They were encouraged in their resistance by the more pious Arabs, who felt that the Ommiads were far too worldly, and by survivors of the faction that had supported Ali.

In spite of hidden weaknesses in their state, the Ommiad caliphs profited more from the late Roman civilization they had taken over than did the Germanic kings of the West. Syria, the heart of the Ommiad state, had always been more advanced intellectually and economically than Gaul, the heart of the strongest Germanic kingdom. The Ommiads began to draw on their heritage from the older civilization almost as soon as they gained power. They organized their administrative services on Roman and Persian models. They welcomed scholars of all nationalities to their court and urged them to undertake the task of translating philosophical, scientific, and medical works into Arabic. They built impressive mosques at Damascus and Jerusalem, adapting Syrian architecture to the needs of the Mohammedan religion. A new civilization began to grow up around the Ommiad court, a civilization based on Greek, Syrian, Egyptian, and Persian traditions and yet with a style and a spirit of its own. This new civilization reached its peak only after the Ommiads had lost the throne and the capital had been moved from Damascus to Baghdad. Much of the work of the Ommiads was either absorbed in or surpassed by the accomplishments of their successors. But the Ommiads laid the foundations, and they did so at a time when western kings had almost no administrative services, when western scholars had almost no books but compendia and epitomes, and when western architects showed almost no skill in designing large buildings.

New Conquests

The stability and prosperity assured by the early Ommiads soon made it possible for the Arabs to undertake further conquests. In the East the Ommiads took Khiva, Bokhara, and Samarkand, thus gaining control of one of the oldest and most important trade routes in Eurasia—the silk road from China. These conquests in turn opened the way to the occupation of Afghanistan and the valley of the Indus. The strong Moslem position on the northwest frontier was a permanent threat to India, as the invasions of the next thousand years were to demonstrate.

In the West the Arabs advanced steadily along the southern shore of the Mediterranean. North Africa was their first objective, and here, as often before, the invaders profited from the fact that the native population hated Byzantine government. Justinian's reconquest of the Vandal kingdom had been followed by heavy taxation and persecution of heretics. Many of the Romanized Africans had fled the country; the Berbers, who remained, were neither Romanized nor obedient to the orders of Byzantine officials. When the Arab attack came, both the Roman cities and the Berber countryside resisted bravely, but there was little cooperation between them. The Arabs quickly defeated their divided enemies, taking Carthage in 697 and winning control of the entire North African coast by 708.

Although the Berbers had fought fiercely to preserve their independence, they felt no particular antipathy to Islam. Many of them became converts and joined the victorious army in the hope of sharing in the spoils of the next conquest. This addition to their strength enabled the Arabs to pass over into Spain. The Visigothic rulers of Spain had been weakened by quarrels over the succession and had not been able (or willing) to build up strong local forces. A single victory over the royal army in 711 was enough to open the whole country to Tarik, who commanded the invading forces, and from whom Gibraltar takes its name.* The largest part of his army was probably composed of recently converted Berbers, and now many Visigothic nobles joined the victors—an illustration of the Arabs' ability to gain the cooperation of conquered peoples in a remarkably short time. Only the support of thousands of non-Arabs made possible Islam's rapid conquests.

The Moslem army quickly overran the entire Iberian Peninsula except for the extreme northwest, where a few Christians maintained their independence. The Moslems then pushed on across the Pyrenees into the Frankish kingdom, which was not quite so helpless as Spain. The Franks could not de-

*Gebel Tarik—Tarik's hill.

fend the south, but when the raiders pushed north the Frankish leader, Charles Martel, assembled an effective army that checked the invasion. Charles' victory at Poitiers in 732 was not very decisive, for the Moslems withdrew in good order and held towns in southern Gaul for another thirty years. But they made no more raids on the north.

During the early years of the eighth century the Ommiads reached the height of their power. They had created the largest Moslem state that ever existed, and in less than a hundred years they had built an empire larger than that of Rome. But they had reached their limit; their setback at Poitiers in 732 had its counterpart in an earlier failure to take Constantinople in a great siege in 716 to 717. Although the Byzantine Empire had lost almost all of its outlying provinces, it had preserved the most important part of its territories. Like the Frankish kingdom, Byzantium grew stronger after the early eighth century, and the Moslems were long unable to make any headway against these two bulwarks of Europe.

The Rise of the Abbasids

The Ommiad state had also begun to weaken internally. It was difficult to rule a vast empire that stretched from Spain to India and that embraced dozens of different peoples. Moreover, many Moslems continued to distrust and oppose the Ommiads. There was still a party that honored the memory of Ali and considered the Ommiads usurpers; there were also puritanical Moslems who loathed Ommiad luxury and worldliness; and there were recent converts, especially in Mesopotamia and Persia, who resented the domination of the Arab aristocracy.

All these groups were united by Abu'l Abbas, who was to found the Abbasid dynasty. By claiming one of Mohammed's uncles as an ancestor, he satisfied most of the legitimists; by making himself appear more devout than the Ommiads, he gained the support of most of the inhabitants of Mesopotamia and Persia. By 750 Abu'l Abbas was strong enough to risk rebellion. He decisively defeated the Ommiad caliph and almost exterminated the family. One Ommiad escaped to Spain, where he founded an independent state in 756, but the rest of the Moslem world accepted Abu'l Abbas as caliph.

Since the Abbasid caliph's primary strength was in Mesopotamia and Persia, he moved his capital to Baghdad, a new city built on the banks of the Tigris. This move symbolized a turning point in the history of civilization. The old unity of the Mediterranean world, shaken by earlier events, was now forever destroyed. The Ommiad caliphs at Damascus had drawn heavily on Greco-Roman civilization, but the Abbasids at Baghdad were increasingly influenced by the ancient traditions of Mesopotamia and Persia. The Moslem world on the southern and eastern shores of the Mediterranean became more and more unlike the Christian world on the northern shores. At the same time, Moslem pressure was forcing Byzantium in on itself and accentuating the peculiarities of the Byzantine way of life.

A citizen of the Roman Empire had been equally at home in Rome and Constantinople, in Alexandria and Antioch. Now these centers of civilization were drifting apart and becoming more and more strange to one another. By the tenth century a westerner, merely by crossing the Mediterranean, entered a completely different world. Egypt was as strange as China, and even Christian Byzantium seemed remote and Oriental.

Thus the world of the Romans had broken into three fragments of unequal size and wealth. The largest and richest area was held by the Moslems, who also controlled the key trade routes to India and China and all but one of the great cities of the Middle East. Next came the Byzantine Empire, anchored on impregnable Constantinople, rich from its own industry and from the trade that flowed through its lands to the West. Far behind was western Europe, poverty-stricken and ill-governed, no match for the great civilizations centered in Constantinople and Baghdad. For centuries western Europe had depended on the East in trade and industry, in art and religion. It remained to be seen what the Europeans could do now that they were on their own.

Suggestions for Further Reading

Note: Asterisk denotes a book available in paperback edition.

The Age of Justinian P. N. Ure, *Justinian and His Age** (1951), is lively reading. The contemporary accounts by Procopius, *History of the Wars,* trans. by H. B. Dewing (1935) and *Secret History,** trans. by G. A. Williamson (1969), are also lively, but not entirely trustworthy. For this and the next section, A. H. M. Jones, *The Later Roman Empire,* 3 vols. (1964), is extremely valuable.

Byzantium A wealth of literature is available on the life and thought of Byzantine civilization. P. N. Ure, *Justinian and His Age** (1951), which discusses many facets of Byzantine history and civilization, is a good starting point. J. W. Barker, *Justinian and the Later Roman Empire* (1966), is even better. S. Runciman, *Byzantine Civilization** (1933), combines deep knowledge of the subject with a superb prose style in a very sympathetic treatment. The old theory that the Byzantine Empire was perpetually moribund is severely attacked in N. H. Baynes, *The Byzantine Empire* (1926), which stresses the vitality of the Empire's history. N. H. Baynes and H. L. B. Moss, *Byzantium** (1948), is a collection of essays on Byzantine history and culture written by leading scholars in the field. The most thorough and scholarly treatment of Byzantine history is G. Ostrogorsky, *History of the Byzantine State,* trans. by J. M. Hussey (1956). The older work of A. A. Vasiliev, *History of the Byzantine Empire,* 2 vols. (2nd ed., 1952), is more readable than Ostrogorsky but lacks recent bibliographic material. Two works by the French scholar C. Diehl, *History of the Byzantine Empire* (1901) and *Byzantium: Greatness and Decline** (1957), are valuable for the facts but are considerably dated in historical interpretation.

The beauty of Byzantine art has fascinated many who have come in contact with it. C. R. Morey, *Early Christian Art** (1942), which has good plates, describes the influence of Byzantine iconography on western art in the early Middle Ages. But for the magnificence of its reproductions and the general excellence of its text, no survey of Byzantine art can compare with the fine Skira edition, *Byzantine Painting,* ed. by A. Grabar (1953). The brief study of D. Talbot-Rice, *Byzantine Art** (1935), is worthwhile and perhaps more accessible.

Islam The best introduction to the world of Islam is the Koran,* of which there are many translations. Perhaps the best is that of A. J. Arberry, *The Koran Interpreted** (1955). H. A. R. Gibb, *Mohammedanism** (1949), is a good historical survey of the Moslem religion, while B. Lewis, *The Arabs in History** (1966), emphasizes the political and social aspects of Moslem history. See also his *Islam,* 2 vols. (1974). The foremost American historian of Islam, P. K. Hitti, has written a number of fine studies. His *The Arabs** (many editions) is a scholarly treatment of the rise and spread of Mohammedanism; his translation of *The Origins of the Islamic State* (1916) traces the growth of Islam and is excellent for an understanding of the Moslem world view. Even more thorough is M. G. Hodgson, *The Venture of Islam,* 3 vols. (1974). The now classic study by H. Pirenne, *Mohammed and Charlemagne** (1936), advances a significant theory about the impact of Islam on western Europe in the early Middle Ages. H. A. R. Gibb and H. Bowen, *Islamic Society and the West,* 2 vols. (1950), explores the impact of the West on Islam in later times. G. von Grunebaum, in his *Classical Islam, 600–1258* (1970) and in *Medieval Islam** (1946), traces the temper and flavor of the Moslem Middle Ages and gives a fine account of the Moslem influence on western Europe in the Middle Ages. Both R. P. A. Dozy, *Spanish Islam* (1913), and S. Lane-Poole, *The Story of the Moors in Spain* (1886), give exciting accounts of the Arabs in Spain. Washington Irving's *The Alhambra** (many editions) gives a vivid and unforgettable picture of Moslem culture in Spain. There is interesting material on the Ommiads in W. Muir, *The Caliphate: Its Rise, Decline and Fall* (1915), and in T. W. Arnold, *The Caliphate* (1963), but neither is so thorough in historical interpretation as is the research of Hitti. D. S. Richards, *Islam and the Trade of Asia* (1971), shows the shift in interest toward the East under the Abbasids.

H. A. R. Gibb, *Arabic Literature* (1926), is a brief survey of Arabic literature with an appendix of Arabic works in English and other modern languages. T. W. Arnold, *Painting in Islam** (1965), is a readable study of the place of art in Moslem culture, with very good reproductions. See also R. Ettinghausen, *Arab Painting* (1962). T. W. Arnold and A. Guillaume, *The Legacy of Islam* (2nd ed. by J. Schacht and C. E. Bosworth, 1972), an account of the elements in European culture that are derived from the Islamic world, is the best one-volume study of Moslem culture and thought.

9 The Emergence of a Western European Civilization

Not all contacts were lost when the Mediterranean world broke into three distinct cultural units—a German-Latin bloc in the West, a Greek-Slavic bloc in the East, and an Arab-Syrian-Persian bloc in the South. Merchants still traveled back and forth across the Mediterranean; ideas, art forms, and scientific and industrial techniques passed from the Byzantine Empire and the Moslem Caliphate to Italy, France, and Germany. And yet contacts among the West, the East, and the South of the Mediterranean world were less frequent and less intimate than they once had been. This was due in part to the endless wars between Byzantium and Islam, which discouraged Mediterranean commerce. It was due even more to the poverty and backwardness of western Europe, whose stocks of precious metals had been seriously depleted, making it difficult for westerners to purchase eastern goods. The western commodities most useful to the Greeks and Arabs were timber, iron, and slaves—all of which could be considered contraband of war in times of conflict. As a result, the West could not earn enough foreign exchange to trade extensively with either Byzantines or Arabs. Nor did the West have adequate intellectual capital for a rewarding exchange of ideas with Greek or Arab scholars. There were relatively few educated men in western Europe, and most of them were painfully at work trying to understand the writings of the Latin Church Fathers and fragments of the Latin classics. Until the West had fully assimilated its Latin heritage, it was to have little interest in the learning of the East.

Thus the people of western Europe were more dependent on their own resources than they had been for centuries. They had to create their own civilization. Several favorable factors allowed them to do so. Although western Europe seemed poor and backward in comparison with the East, it actually possessed great potential for growth. It had plenty of good agricultural land and virtually untouched resources of raw materials. Trade in the Mediterranean had fallen off, but trade in the northern seas was flourishing. The Scandinavians, who traded with the western kingdoms, were also beginning to import eastern goods through the Russian river system. The Church had preserved the rudiments of an educational system and some ideas about political and social organization. Finally, the new line of Frankish rulers that had emerged in the eighth century brought political stability and laid the foundations for a new civilization.

KING PIPPIN AND THE CHURCH

This new line of rulers descended from Pippin and Charles Martel, the mayors of the palace who had put an end to the disorders of the seventh century. These men had been content with the title of mayor, but the son of Charles Martel, another Pippin, decided in 751 to seek the kingship itself. This was a dangerous move; the king might be powerless, but he still had a sacral position. His family had been set apart from all others by a long tradition of both secular and religious recognition. Pippin won over most of the nobles, and to overcome the scruples of those who were still attached to the old dynasty asked the pope for an opinion on the legitimacy of his bid. Pope Zacharias declared that the man who bore the responsibilities of the king deserved the title; his successor actually journeyed to France and anointed Pippin in the manner in which the Old Testament kings had been anointed. This was probably the first use of this ritual in the West, and it is hard for us to realize the impression it must have made on public opinion. As God's anointed, Pippin became a semisacred personage, far above all ordinary lay dignitaries. It was God's will that he and his family should rule the Franks.

These acts of the papacy had serious consequences for future European kings. The pope had not initiated the change of dynasty, but the very fact that he had been consulted enabled later pontiffs to claim that Zacharias had deposed an unworthy king and had chosen a suitable successor. Therefore the Church could remove other unworthy rulers. Equally significant was Pippin's consecration, for it was soon believed that a king did not enjoy full authority until he had been

Opposite: Charlemagne presents a model of his church at Aix-la-Chapelle to the Virgin (detail from a panel of the shrine at Aix).

anointed by the Church. It could then be claimed that church officials were superior to lay rulers, since no layman could consecrate a bishop but a bishop could consecrate a king. The obvious conclusion was that royal power, in some fashion, was dependent on the sanction of the Church.

The Alliance of the Papacy with the Franks

Probably none of this had been foreseen by either Pippin or Zacharias. Their cooperation was based on the realization that each could gain some practical advantage by supporting the other. The pope, who received little support from the Byzantine emperor, was constantly harassed in Italy by Lombard attacks. He was also distressed by the condition of the Church in the Frankish realm. Many of the Frankish clergy were ill educated and corrupt, and the Church had little influence on a large part of the population. A strong Frankish king might be willing to protect the pope against the Lombards and aid in the administrative and moral reform of the Church.

As for Pippin, he had inherited a family tradition of cooperating with the Church. One of his ancestors had been a bishop and a saint, and his father, Charles Martel, had had the support of the Church in his struggle with the Frankish aristocracy. In return, Charles had supported the work of missionaries and reformers in the Frankish kingdoms. The family was undoubtedly pious, but it also had political reasons for aiding church reform. Educated and reformed bishops were likely to support strong government and resist aristocratic factionalism, and they would make useful advisers and administrative agents for the king. Moreover, a reformed Church that emphasized the principles of Christian morality could assist the king in his task of preserving public order.

The alliance between Pippin and the pope changed the political fate of western Europe. First, and perhaps most important of all, it removed Italy from the Byzantine sphere of influence and attached it to the Germanic north. The popes had long found the Byzantine emperors unsatisfactory suzerains. It was bad enough when they failed to push back the Lombards; it was even worse when they stirred up an unnecessary theological controversy by forbidding images of sacred personages in churches. It is true that eastern Christians had begun to pay extravagant respect to sacred images and that certain monasteries had gained enormous political influence by possessing images that were especially revered. But excessive devotion to images had not been particularly troublesome in the West, and the popes felt that the drastic remedy of iconoclasm (the destruction of images) was unnecessary. The largely illiterate western population needed images as illustrations of Christian doctrine, and the popes had no intention of abandoning them.

Dislike of iconoclasm, combined with concern over the Lombard threat, prompted the pope to look to the Franks for support. Charles Martel had refused to intervene in Italy, but Pippin was more willing to aid the papacy. In 753 he invaded Italy and forced the Lombards to withdraw from the environs of Rome. The campaign closed with two significant acts: Pippin gave Pope Stephen II a large strip of territory in central Italy which had formerly been held by the Byzantine

An iconoclast whitewashing an image in a Byzantine church (from a ninth-century psalter). In 730 Leo III issued an edict forbidding the veneration of images. For a hundred years thereafter, icons, mosaics, and frescoes in churches were destroyed or whitewashed.

Empire. The pope gave Pippin the title of *patricius Romanorum*, which had formerly been held by the chief Byzantine representative in Italy.

To ignore Byzantium's centuries-old claim to Italy was a bold act. It needed justification, which may be why an unknown churchman (probably a Frank) forged the famous *Donation of Constantine* at about this time. According to the forger, Constantine, as an act of gratitude after his conversion, had given all Italy and the western part of the Empire to the pope. After withdrawing to the East, the emperor was supposed to have left the pope as the supreme authority in the West. This was a clumsy falsehood, but no one disproved its authenticity for 700 years. Meanwhile it supported papal claims to lordship over a large part of central Italy and vaguer rights of intervention in the political affairs in the West.

North of the Alps, Pippin and the pope helped each other to gain control over peoples who were only nominally their subjects. Pippin had little authority in such outlying districts as Bavaria and Aquitaine; the backing of the Church aided him in gaining some measure of obedience from the rulers of these provinces. The Church had little influence over the people of Gaul and Germany; Pippin gave full support to the work of one of the greatest missionaries and organizers the Church has ever known, an Anglo-Saxon monk named Boniface.

St. Boniface

Boniface came to Frankland as a young man hoping to convert the still-heathen Germans of Frisia and Saxony. He soon realized that an even graver problem was posed by the state of Christianity among the Frankish people, many of whom were called Christians only because they had no other faith. They seldom saw an orthodox priest, and the visits of wandering Irish monks did little to strengthen their belief. Boniface realized that thorough reform and reorganization of the Frankish Church were essential, and he spent most of his life at this task. In 748 the pope made him archbishop with full powers over the German clergy. He used this authority to create the basic structure of the German Church. In Gaul he summoned local councils to improve the morality of Frankish churchmen and to make them more obedient to the pope. As the years passed, the Church north of the Alps became an effective force in the lives of the people, and its increased centralization and improved administration gave the Church strength enough to influence the ruling classes. At the end of his life Boniface returned to missionary work and found the martyrdom he had long desired. He was killed by heathen Frisians in 754.

The Establishment of Parishes and Tithes

Boniface's work was made more effective by the development of rural parishes in the Frankish kingdom—a development that had begun earlier but that received its greatest impetus from the descendants of Charles Martel. So long as churches existed only in the cities, as they did at first, country dwellers found it impossible to maintain regular contact

The Donation of Constantine

Constantine tells how Pope Sylvester I cured him of leprosy. In gratitude Constantine accepts baptism and decrees

that the sacred see of blessed Peter shall be gloriously exalted above our empire and earthly throne. . . . And the pontiff who presides over the most holy Roman Church shall be the highest and chief of all priests . . . and according to his decision shall all matters be settled . . . for the worship of God or the confirmation of the faith.

We convey to the most blessed pontiff, our father Silvester, universal pope, both our palace [the Lateran] and likewise all provinces, places and districts of the City of Rome and Italy and of the regions of the West, . . . bequeathing them to the power and sway of him and his successors.

Wherefore we have perceived that our empire and the power of our government should be transferred to the regions of the East . . . for it is not right that an earthly emperor should have authority . . . where the head of the Christian religion has been established by the Emperor of heaven.

From the Donation of Constantine, as quoted in *Select Documents of European History*, ed. by R. G. D. Laffan (London: Methuen, 1930), Vol. I, pp. 4–5.

with the clergy and hence Christianity had little influence on them. A rural parish with a resident priest was the obvious solution to this problem, but priests were not likely to stay resident until their churches had an adequate income. North of the Alps the landlords and counts were the only men wealthy enough to build and endow rural churches. They began to do so on a large scale only in the eighth century, prompted by Boniface's reforms and by the example and persuasion of the ruling family.

The ultimate step in giving parish churches an adequate income was taken when Pippin's son Charles made tithing compulsory. The clergy had long taught that the faithful should give 10 percent of their income to the Church, but they had permitted tithing to remain a purely voluntary act. By ruling that all Christians had to pay the tithe, the king assured the Church sufficient income to support an extensive network of rural parishes. Not all tithes went to parish priests, however; in fact, their share tended to diminish as time went on. Nevertheless, they always received enough so that the rural churches could function.

These were revolutionary changes. For the first time the ordinary inhabitant of the Frankish realm was in regular and frequent contact with Christian priests. The rapid growth of the parish system gave the Church more opportunities to impress Christian doctrine and morality on the people. There had always been sincere believers, but in the Merovingian period many men had acted as if Christianity were only a superior form of magic. Although they venerated relics that were alleged to bring good luck, they had no strong convictions about either faith or morals. Now Christianity began to be a matter of internal concern rather than one of exterior behavior. The eighth century is the first period in which one can be sure that all western Europe was hearing and beginning to understand the Christian message.

This improvement in the position of the Church had begun before Pippin's time and continued under his descendants. But Pippin's reign was the crucial period. He accelerated the pace of the reform movement, and he made the binding alliance with the papacy that ensured the cooperation of religious and secular authorities in building a new civilization. Pippin's work was overshadowed by that of his son Charles, but Charles built on the solid foundation left by his father.

CHARLEMAGNE

Pippin died in 768 and was succeeded by his two sons, Charles and Carloman. Fate saved the Franks from the dangerous consequences of divided authority, however, for Carloman died after three years, and Charles assumed sole control of the government.

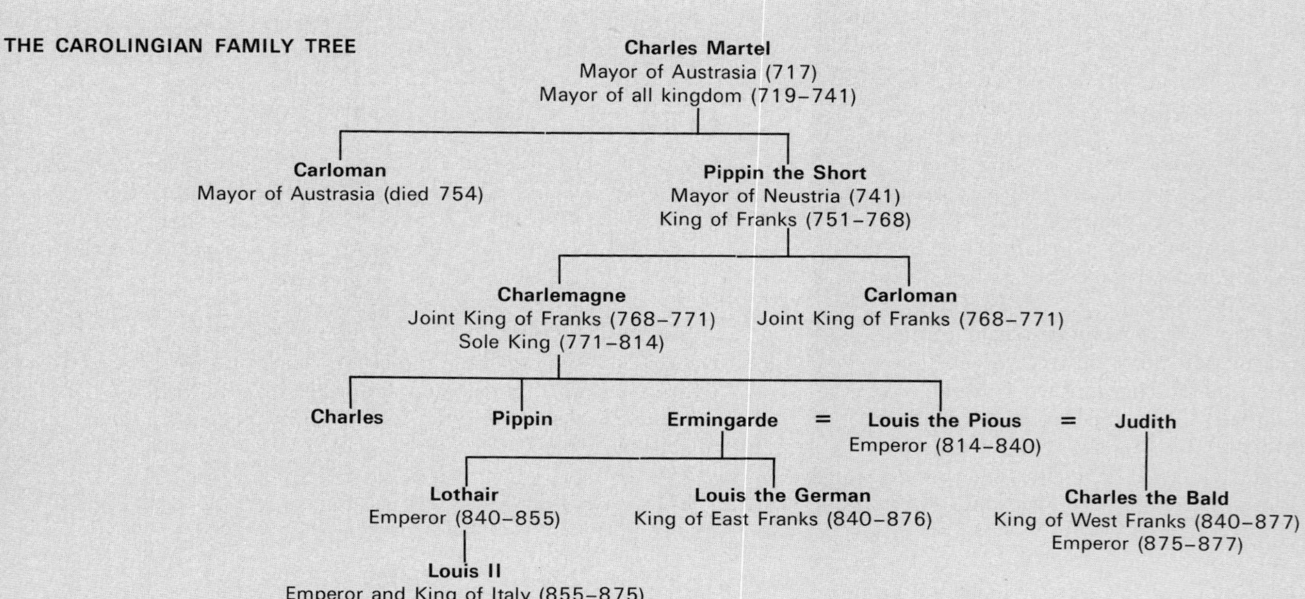

in patria pax inuiolata in regno·
& dignitaſ glorioſa regaliſ palatii·maxi
mo ſplendore regiae poteſtatiſ· oculiſ
omnium luce clariſſima coruſcare
atq; ſplendeſcere · qua ſplendidiſſi
mi fulgoriſ maximo pfuſa lumine

The elegant Carolingian handwriting was characterized by small letters and bold, rounded design. It is the basis of modern type (detail from a ninth-century manuscript).

Charles' reign was so successful that even in his own lifetime he was known as Charlemagne, or Charles the Great. To his contemporaries he was great first and foremost because he was a persistent and victorious warrior. He solved the Lombard problem by defeating the Lombard king and annexing the Lombard lands in northern and central Italy. He eased the Moslem threat by crossing the Pyrenees and annexing a small strip of Spanish territory to the Frankish kingdom. When the nomadic Avars, who had established themselves on the middle Danube, became troublesome, his army almost annihilated them in a single campaign. His longest and hardest war was with the Saxons of northeastern Germany, the last large group of German heathens. The Saxons resisted Frankish domination and Christianity with equal bitterness, and only after thirty years did Charlemagne finally manage to conquer and convert them.

Charlemagne's Educational Reforms

Charlemagne was more than a successful general, as many of his contemporaries realized. He wanted a strong kingdom, but he also wanted it to be a Christian kingdom, and his efforts to make it so left an indelible impression on western civilization. Even more than his father, Charlemagne realized that an untrained and uneducated clergy was an unorganized and uninfluential clergy. Both by decree and by his own example he tried to improve the character and the education of the clergy in the Frankish realm. He imported scholars from every country of western Europe and either kept them with him in his Palace Academy or gave them high positions in the Frankish Church. The most famous of these scholars was the Anglo-Saxon Alcuin, head of the Palace Academy and eventually abbot of St. Martin's of Tours, but there were also Franks, Lombards, Visigoths, and even newly converted Saxons among them.

The work of these scholars was not very original or imaginative, but originality and imagination were not the chief needs of the eighth century. What was needed were men who could preserve and assimilate the intellectual heritage left by Rome and the early Church. Even preservation was no easy task, for much of Latin literature had already been lost and there were few copies of the works that had survived. The Scriptures and the works of the Church Fathers were in less danger of being lost, but Charlemagne complained that copies of the Bible were full of serious errors. By encouraging the making of new and accurate copies of ancient texts, Charlemagne saved many classical works from oblivion; we have few manuscripts of Latin authors from before his time. The acceleration of manuscript production in turn led to a reform in handwriting, a reform in which Alcuin and his monastery at Tours played a leading role. The scribes of Tours developed a beautiful, clear script that was a notable improvement on earlier handwriting. The Romans had used only capital letters, which were hard to read when they filled a solid line, especially since the Romans did not separate words. Later writers separated words and developed small letters, but the letters were badly shaped and easily confused. It was the Carolingians who gave small letters almost the form they have today.

Charlemagne's educational revival gave Europe a common cultural tradition. As we have seen, scholars of all nations mingled at the Frankish court and worked with the same materials—the Bible, the Church Fathers, the encyclopedias of the Late Empire, and some of the Latin classics. When they became bishops or abbots, they carried this common stock of learning to various regions and taught it to their own students. All students used Latin, whatever their native tongue, so there was no problem of translation. Thus scholars everywhere were reading the same books and commenting on them in the same language, and western Europe developed a common stock of ideas and a common vocabulary in which to express them. If western Europe has any unity at all today, that unity lies in its ideas, in its way of looking at the world, and for this unity it owes much to the work of Charles the Great.

CHARLEMAGNE'S CONQUESTS AND EMPIRE 814

Revival of the Empire in the West

By annexing the Lombard kingdom, Charlemagne had made himself directly responsible for the security of the pope and the government of Rome. He also felt it his personal duty to make Christianity a more effective force in his kingdom. His laws dealt as often with ecclesiastical matters as with secular affairs. He laid down rules of proper conduct for monks and priests; he ordered schools to be established for the training of the clergy; he intervened in theological disputes; and, as we have seen, he gave the Church a solid financial basis by making the payment of tithes compulsory. He was the head of a Christian people, and he expected clergy as well as laity to follow his leadership.

This close relationship between king and Church reached its climax in the year 800. Pope Leo III, driven from Rome by his enemies in the city, had appealed to Charlemagne for aid. Charlemagne reinstated the pope in December and stayed on in Rome to make sure there would be no further trouble. On Christmas Day, 800, the pope placed the imperial crown on Charlemagne's head and hailed him as Augustus. The West once more had an emperor.

In one sense, the coronation merely symbolized existing facts. As ruler of France, Germany, and most of Italy, Charlemagne already had more power than the last western Roman emperors. The emperor had been the traditional protector of the Church, and Charlemagne was clearly performing this function. There seems to be no doubt that he wanted to be emperor, for the pope was in no position to impose undesired titles on his powerful protector.

Nevertheless, a man who knew Charlemagne well said that the king grumbled that he never would have gone to church that Christmas Day had he known what the pope had in mind. If the report has any substance it may reflect Charlemagne's misgivings about receiving his title from the pope, misgivings that proved well founded. Later popes claimed that Leo III, by his own authority, had transferred imperial power from the Greeks to the Franks, and that Charlemagne's coronation was one more proof of the superiority of ecclesiastical rulers over secular rulers. But whatever his doubts, Charlemagne accepted the situation. He referred to himself as emperor in public documents, and, before his death, he was careful to see that his son was crowned emperor. The pope took no part in this coronation, which suggests again that Charlemagne did not want to admit that the pope could make an emperor.

Charlemagne's Government

The essential unit of government under Charlemagne, as under his Merovingian predecessors, was the county. Each county was headed by a count, who was almost always a member of a noble and wealthy family. The count had to share his power with various subordinates; he had to respect the position of the other noble families of his county and of the neighboring bishops and abbots. Nevertheless, an energetic count could build up a strong position in his county. He presided over the local courts and kept a third of the fines that were collected there. He led the freemen of his district to war; he collected tolls; he built and garrisoned forts. Clearly, the king's chief problem was to keep his counts under control.

Charlemagne tried to meet this problem by two devices. First, in order to keep the counts from abusing their judicial power, he created independent groups of local judges to decide cases. Second, he sent out royal envoys—called *missi dominici*—to see that the counts obeyed his orders and observed reasonable standards of justice and honesty. The *missi* were chosen from men of the highest standing at court and had the full support of the emperor. Their admonitions and reports helped immeasurably

Ninth-century statue of Charlemagne on horseback. He wears a crown and carries an orb, symbol of royal power.

The Coronation of Charlemagne — 800

Now when the king upon the most holy day of the Lord's birth was rising to the mass after praying before the tomb of the blessed Peter the Apostle, Leo the Pope, with the consent of all the bishops and priests and of the senate of the Franks and likewise of the Romans, set a golden crown upon his head, the Roman people also shouting aloud. And when the people had made an end of chanting praises, he was adored by the pope after the manner of the emperors of old. For this was also done by the will of God. For while the said Emperor abode at Rome certain men were brought to him who said that the name of Emperor had ceased among the Greeks, and that there the Empire was held by a woman called Irene, who had by guile laid hold on her son the Emperor and put out his eyes and taken the Empire to herself. . . . Which when Leo the Pope and all the assembly of the bishops and priests and abbots heard, and the senate of the Franks and all the elders of the Romans, they took counsel with the rest of the Christian people, that they should name Charles king of the Franks to be Emperor, seeing that he held Rome the mother of empire where the Caesars and Emperors always used to sit.

From *Chronicle of Moissac,* trans. by J. Bryce, *The Holy Roman Empire* (New York: Macmillan and St. Martin's Press, 1911), p. 54.

Gold coin bearing the likeness of Irene, empress in Constantinople from 797 to 802. She was the first woman to assume sole rule over the Empire (and she took the title of emperor, not empress). Her rule provided the pope with an excuse to crown Charlemagne emperor in 800 to fill the allegedly vacant throne.

to improve the conduct of local government. Nevertheless, even the *missi* did not give the emperor full control over his counts. Abuses of power continued, and there were cases of flat disobedience to Charlemagne's orders.

The central government was not organized well enough to direct and coordinate the work of local authorities. The secretarial staff was very small—barely able to handle correspondence and keep records. It is worth noting that under Charlemagne these men were all members of the clergy,* whereas the Merovingians had had no difficulty in finding laymen capable of keeping records and writing letters. This change demonstrates the decline of education among laymen and the political as well as the religious importance of an educated clergy. In addition to the secretaries there were a few lay judges to hear the rare cases that were brought to the emperor's court, and a large and undifferentiated group of household officials and counselors. Any of these men could be used for any task, but no one had permanent responsibility for overseeing local courts or centralizing local revenues.

In directing and controlling local officials Charlemagne issued many capitularies (ordinances made up of various *capitula,* or chapters). Most of these were administrative directives that told the local officials what to do. For example, one capitulary contained rules for the education of the clergy, and another one regulated the powers and behavior of the counts. Charlemagne seldom attempted to make law, since he, like most men of his time, believed that law consisted of eternal and unchanging principles. Nevertheless, some capitularies interpreted, and thus changed, the law. And by laying down rules that were applicable to all subjects, Charlemagne did a good deal to wipe out earlier distinctions between Roman and German, or Frank and Burgundian law. There was never complete uniformity of law among his subjects, but the differences that remained were regional rather than racial. As long as local custom was observed, a competent ruler could control people of many different origins.

Charlemagne, working against great obstacles, had united the West and given it common ideals and common institutions. But he had succeeded only because

Louis the Pious, son of Charlemagne. The words in the poem written across the portrait can also be read as a crossword puzzle, so that the letters in the cross and halo also form verses (*ca.* 840).

*This is reflected in the similarity of the English words *clerk* and *cleric.* From the time of Charlemagne to the end of the Middle Ages, all "clerks" were members of the clergy.

he was a man of boundless energy, unusual perseverance, and strong personality, who had impressed himself on his contemporaries. It was too much to expect his descendants to be men of equal stature, and the Carolingian Empire was too large, too loosely administered, and too imperfectly unified for lesser men to hold it together. There were few economic ties among the far-flung regions. Bavarians, for example, had no reason to care about what happened in Aquitaine. Western Europeans could satisfy their common ideals simply by sharing in the life of the Church. Their common institutions, which were most effective at the county level, seemed to work equally well whether there was one empire or many kingdoms. Charlemagne himself apparently was not particularly concerned about preserving the unity of the Empire, for he followed the old Frankish tradition and divided his holdings among his sons. It was only the premature death of two of his heirs that gave an undivided realm to his son Louis.

THE COLLAPSE OF THE CAROLINGIAN EMPIRE

Louis had increasing difficulty in holding the Frankish state together. He was a well-meaning but weak man, easily swayed by his family and friends. In order to gain the aid of the Church, the only institution that was really concerned with western unity, he humbled himself as Charlemagne never would have done. Thus Louis allowed himself to be crowned emperor a second time by ecclesiastical authority and did public penance for mutilating a nephew who had rebelled against him. The greatest danger to the Empire sprang from the jealousies among his three sons—Lothair, the younger Louis, and Charles. Louis drew up several plans for partitioning the Empire, but none of them satisfied all his heirs. They fought with him and they fought with one another. When Louis died in 840, he left the Empire in a state of civil war.

Louis' sons finally settled their quarrels by dividing the Empire (and the imperial estates) in the Treaty of Verdun (843)—a division that had a lasting effect on European history. Charles received the western part of the Empire, a kingdom that corresponded roughly to modern France. Louis took eastern Frankland, including Saxony, Bavaria, and the counties along the Rhine. The eldest son, Lothair, became emperor and received the largest part of the family estates. This gave him a long, narrow strip of territory between the eastern and western kingdoms embracing the Low Countries, Alsace-Lorraine, Switzerland, Savoy, Provence, and northern Italy. Lothair's kingdom turned out to be a buffer state, and like many buffers it was ground to

THE DIVISION OF CHARLEMAGNE'S EMPIRE

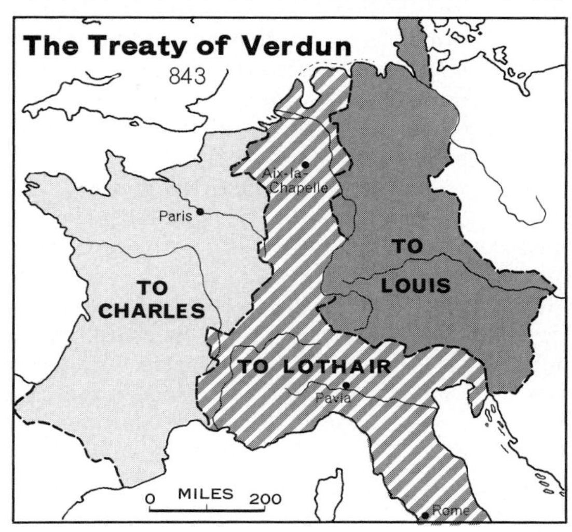

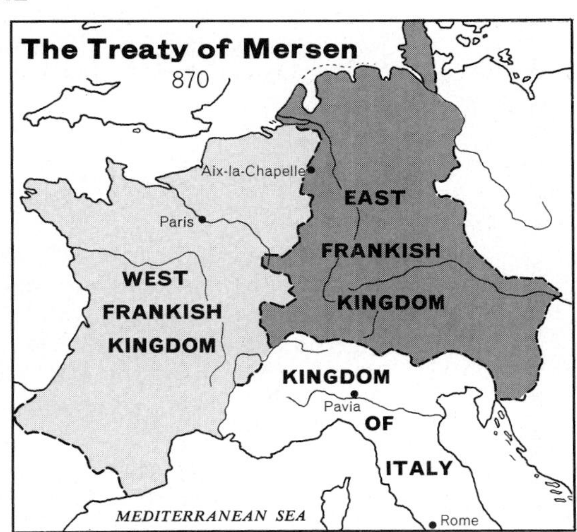

Section from the Strasburg Oaths, earliest examples of the dialects that became French and German. The oath was taken by Louis the German and Charles the Bald in 842, when they agreed to oppose their brother Lothair. The first paragraph gives the oath in French, taken by Louis, the second the same oath in German, taken by Charles. *The oath of Louis:* "For the love of God and the salvation of the Christian people and our common salvation, from this day forward, in so far as God gives me knowledge and power, I will succour this my brother Charles in aid and in everything, as one ought by right to succour one's brother, provided that he does likewise by me, and I will never undertake any engagement with Lothair which, by my consent, may be of harm to this my brother Charles."

Pro dõ amur & p xpian poblo & nrõ cõmun
saluament. dist di en auant. in quant dš
sauir & podir me dunat. si saluarai eo.
cist meon fradre karlo. & in ad iudha.
& in cad huna cosa. sicũ om p dreit son
fradra saluar dist. In o quid il mi altre
si fazet. Et ab ludher nul plaid nũquã
prindrai qui meon uol cist. meon fradre
Karle in damno sit. Quod cũ lodhuuuic
explesset. karolus teudisca lingua sic ec
eadẽ uerba testatus est.
Ingo des minna indu thes xpanes folches.
indunser bedhero gealtnissi. fon thesemo
moda ge frammordesso framso mir got
geuuizci indi madh furgibit so hald ih tes
an minan bruodher soso man mit rehtu
sinan bruher scal inthi utha zermigsoso
maduo. indi mit luheren in nohheiniu
thing nege ganga. zhe minan uuillon imo
ces cadhen uuerhen.

ernments and threw the burden of defense on local leaders.

The most dangerous and persistent of these new invaders were the Scandinavians of the north. Though related to the Germans, and just as fond of fighting, the Scandinavians had taken no part in the early migrations and conquests. By the ninth century, however, many of them had begun to venture overseas. They were expert seamen and traders, and they had perfected a type of long, shallow-draft ship that was very effective for raiding. These vessels used a sail when the wind was astern, but they were usually propelled by oars. Equipped with such craft, the Scandinavians could swoop down from the sea and loot a whole river valley before the local troops, moving slowly over bad roads, could be mobilized to repel them.

No one knows why the Scandinavians became so aggressive during the ninth century. It may be that improved metallurgical techniques enabled them to construct better weapons, such as their famous war axes. It may be that frequent civil wars forced defeated bands of warriors to flee the country. It may be that some families had a surplus of younger sons who sought adventure abroad. In any case, the political weakness of Europe and the relative wealth of the Frankish and English kingdoms would have tempted anyone. The Frankish Empire was disintegrating; the British Isles were split up into small, warring kingdoms; and the Slavs who now held eastern Europe were politically disorganized. The Scandinavians had been trading with all these areas for many generations; they realized that the Continent lay open to any group of determined men bent on marauding, on looting, and even, perhaps, on founding new states.

Although the Scandinavian raiders called themselves vikings, the rest of Europe usually referred to them as Northmen. In their first serious raids against Ireland early in the ninth century they rapidly occupied the east coast. They met somewhat stiffer resistance from the Anglo-Saxons in England, but by 870 they had subdued all the Anglo-Saxon kingdoms except the southern state of Wessex. They had already begun to at-

pieces in conflicts between its neighbors. After Lothair's death in 855 the kings of West Frankland and East Frankland began to contend for possession of parts of the Middle Kingdom. In the end the Treaty of Mersen (870) gave the king of East Frankland the provinces that lay north of the Alps, but the dispute has continued even to our own day. In 1870, 1914, and 1939, France and Germany were still fighting for Alsace and Lorraine, fragments of the old kingdom of Lothair.*

The New Invasions: The Northmen

The Frankish state, gravely weakened by civil wars, now was threatened by a series of new invasions with which the later Carolingians simply could not cope. Attacks from the north, east, and south strained the resources of the central gov-

* *Lorraine* is simply a French form of *Lotharingia*—Lothair's kingdom. The German *Lothringen* shows the connection even more clearly.

tack the Frankish lands. Year after year the Northmen pushed their long ships up the Rhine, the Seine, and the Loire to collect tribute and loot from towns and monasteries. Finally, an especially strong band of raiders forced the West Frankish king to cede them the land at the mouth of the Seine. This outpost, founded about 911, became the nucleus of Normandy, the most famous of the viking states.

In a show of bravado, the Northmen even sailed their ships into the Mediterranean and plundered a few coastal cities in Spain, southern France, and Italy. Their move west across the Atlantic had more permanent results, for they had settled Iceland before the year 900, and from Iceland a few adventurous leaders moved on to Greenland. Along the west coast of the island they established colonies that endured to the fourteenth century. And from Greenland some ships reached the North American continent, although it is still not known just where the Northmen landed or how long they stayed.

The viking raids and settlements in the West were largely the work of Danes and Norwegians. In the East the Swedes began to push down the Russian river valleys toward Constantinople. They had known this route for a long time; eastern goods and eastern coins had been common in Scandinavia long before the great raids began. In the late ninth and tenth centuries, however, the Swedes began to settle in Russia and to bring the scattered Slavic population under their control. The fortified trading posts where the

INVASIONS OF THE NORTHMEN, THE MOSLEMS, AND THE MAGYARS
Eighth to tenth centuries

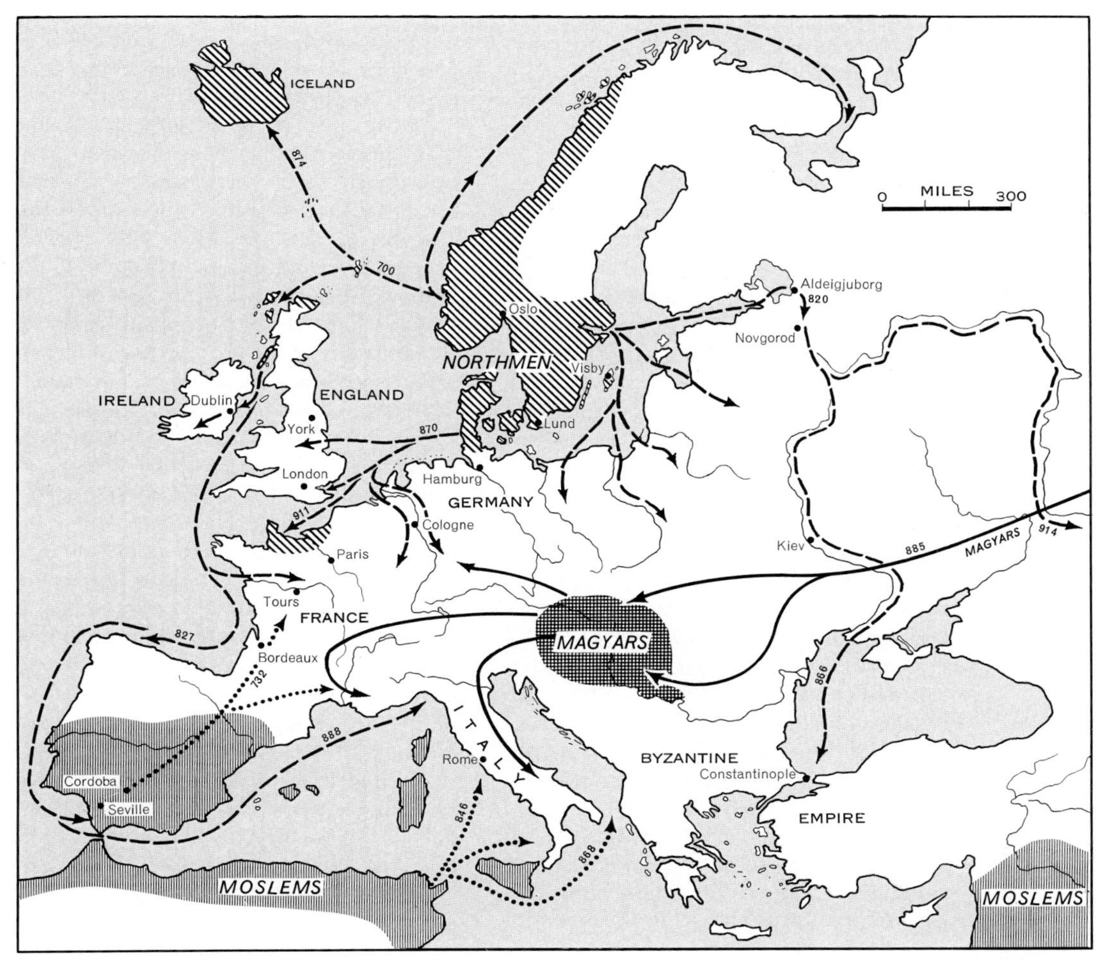

A rune stone (*ca.* ninth century) found in Scandinavia. The carving is distinctly viking: within an elaborate border are two panels, one showing a chieftain on a horse and the other, a viking ship on a voyage.

Swedish drinking horn (*ca.* eighth century).

vikings settled soon burgeoned into towns; the most famous of them was Kiev, which became the capital of a large principality. Once they had gained a footing in Russia, the vikings, with typical boldness, turned their eyes south to Constantinople. Their attacks on the imperial city were unsuccessful, but they did manage to wrest a favorable commercial treaty from the emperor. These early viking princes and warriors gave the eastern Slavs their first effective political organization; in fact, the word *Russia* itself probably comes from *Rus*, the name of a Swedish tribe.

The New Invasions: The Moslems and the Magyars

Compared with the Northmen, who settled from Greenland to the Ukraine and raided from Northumberland to north Italy, the other invaders of the ninth and tenth centuries seem almost provincial. But they covered enough ground to cause suffering in many parts of southern and central Europe. The Moslems already held Spain. Now, operating mainly from North Africa, they seized Sicily and the other islands of the western Mediterranean, thus endangering navigation in that part of the sea. They also established fortified outposts near Rome and on the coastal road from France to Italy, from which they molested land travelers as well.

Even worse were the Hungarians, or Magyars, who belonged to the nomadic stock of central Asia that had launched earlier raids against the coastal civilizations of China, India, and Europe. The Magyars were as great horsemen as the vikings were seamen, and their skill gave them the same advantages of surprise and mobility. They drove into the Danube Valley in the ninth century and established headquarters in what is now Hungary. From this base they raided Germany and Italy regularly and eastern France occasionally. The Magyar occupation of the middle Danube basin split the western Slavs into two groups. The Slavs were politically backward in any case, but this division made it even harder for them to form kingdoms strong enough to resist subjugation. And the weakness of the states of the western Slavs has continually tempted their neighbors to fight with and dominate them, as the history of Czechoslovakia in the period from the Thirty Years' War to the invasion by Hitler (1618–1939) demonstrates.

The End of the New Invasions

The people of western Europe suffered grievously at the hands of the new invaders. Large areas were depopulated and impoverished, and the plundering of monasteries dissipated many of the benefits of the Carolingian reforms. Yet western Europe resisted the new invasions far more successfully than Rome had resisted the earlier invasions of the Germans and Huns. Instead of a whole continent, only a few small territories, such as Normandy and Hungary, were permanently relinquished to the invaders. The Northmen and Magyars were converted to Christianity and accepted western traditions fairly quickly; the Moslems were pushed back from their advanced positions.

How was it that western Europe managed to weather these disastrous new invasions? There were several reasons. First, the new invaders were not so numerous as the Germanic and Hunnic groups that had overrun Europe at the end of the Roman Empire. Second, the Church took an active role in opposing the invaders. Finally, and most important, there was effective local resistance. The people of the Roman Empire had depended almost entirely on the imperial government for protection; when its armies failed, they had accepted barbarian rule without protest. But when the Carolingian kings failed to defend Europe during the ninth-century invasions, local leaders appeared who had enough military power to defend their territories.

This growth of new leadership was especially noticeable in England, Germany, and France. In England the collapse of all the other Anglo-Saxon kingdoms had left Wessex alone to face the Danish invaders. The king of Wessex, Alfred the Great (870–899), proved to be a brave and stubborn fighter. Though he was defeated again and again, he never gave up. He eventually forced the Danes to accept a peace that gave him control of about half of England. His son and grandson carried on the fight until they had seized the rest of the Danish-occupied territories. By 950 all England was united under the Wessex dynasty. In Germany, the new Saxon dynasty that replaced the Carolingians first checked and then, in 955, thoroughly defeated the Magyars.

France is the most instructive example of the development of new leadership. So long as the Carolingian kings were able to raise armies to fight the Northmen, they kept the loyalty of most of the country. But when, at the end of the ninth century, they failed completely in their efforts to defend northern France, local leaders took over most of the responsibility for defense. The counts of the Ile de France, the district around Paris and the richest part of the kingdom, were especially active in resisting the invaders. Eventually, in 987, Hugh Capet, the Count of Paris, seized the throne from the helpless Carolingians.

In short, the inhabitants of western Europe showed a will to resist that had been lacking in the fourth and fifth centuries. The resistance was strongest at the local level, among the counts who governed local districts and among the professional fighting men whom they controlled. When the kings proved that they could defend their countries, as they did in England and eventually in Germany, the local nobles supported them and a certain degree of unity was preserved. But when the kings failed, as they did in France, the counts became virtually independent rulers and gained the loyalty of most of the people in their districts.

FEUDALISM

Out of the ninth-century invasions emerged a new type of government, which we call feudalism. The invasions were only a contributing factor to this development, however, for the civil wars among the last Carolingians and the lack of strong economic ties among districts also played a part. Nevertheless, the fact that feudalism first appeared in northern France and only gradually spread to other countries suggests that the invasions gave the final push toward the development of this new form of political organization. France had suffered more severely from the invasions than any other country, and its kings had been less successful than other monarchs in coping with the danger.

The Ingredients of Feudalism

Feudalism may be defined by three characteristics: fragmentation of political authority, public power in private hands, and the lord–vassal relationship. The typical feudal state was a county, or a fraction of a county, and the typical feudal lord was a count, or a custodian of a castle, who had turned his office into a private, hereditary possession that he exploited for his own benefit. Rights of government were treated just as if they were rights to land; they could be given away, exchanged, or divided among heirs. The lord kept control over his district through his vassals, or retainers, many of whom lived with him in his

Twelfth-century seal depicting a vassal giving homage to his lord.

The Ceremony of Becoming a Vassal

1127

This description comes from the period when feudalism was fully developed. It is very full because the leading men of Flanders had just accepted a new count after a disputed succession. Homage (the specific obligation of the vassal) is carefully distinguished from the more general obligation of fidelity. By the twelfth century it was assumed that most vassals had fiefs.

On Thursday, homages were done to the count. First, they did homage in this way. The count asked [the vassal] if he wished to become his man without reserve, and the latter answered: "I do." Then, joining his hands together, he placed them in the hands of the count, and they bound themselves to each other by a kiss. Then the man who had just done homage pledged fidelity . . . to the count in these words: "I promise on my faith to be faithful from now on to count William and to observe [the obligations of] my homage completely, in good faith, and without deceit." This he swore on the relics of the saints. . . . Finally, with a little stick that he held in his hand, the count gave investiture of fiefs to all those who had . . . promised security, done homage, and taken the oath.

From Galbert of Bruges, *De Multro Karoli comitis Flandriarum,* ed. by H. Pirenne (Paris, 1891), p. 89.

fortified dwelling. Some vassals were local administrators, such as the viscounts (deputies of a count), or well-to-do landholders who needed the protection of someone more powerful. These men lived on their own estates and could have their own vassals.

The lands and rights held by a vassal from a lord were called at first benefices and later, fiefs.* All vassals were supposed to aid their lord in war, but they were also supposed to help him in the work of government. They attended his courts, witnessed his acts, and often administered small districts within the lands that he controlled. This was feudalism in its earliest form: a county or a group of counties ruled by a lord with the aid of his vassals.

*Our word *feudalism* comes from the medieval Latin *feudum*, which meant "fief." No medieval writer ever spoke of "feudalism"; he was more apt to say "vassalage," which stressed the personal relationship between the lord and his "men."

The Church and Feudalism

At the height of feudalism, churches needed protection against raiders but feared that they would lose much of their wealth to their protectors. This charter was an attempt to avoid both dangers.

I, Baldwin, by the grace of God count of Flanders, acknowledge and testify before all my barons that the abbey of Marchiennes was always free from obligations to an advocate. . . . However, because of the present evil state of the world, it needs an advocate for its defense. That I may be the faithful advocate and defender of the church, the abbot gave me two mills and two ploughlands in the town of Nesle. I, however, have given the mills and the land with the consent of the abbot to Hugh Havet of Aubigny, so that he may be a ready defender of the church in all things.

And this is what he receives in the abbey's lordship. He shall have one-third of all fines in cases where the church has asked his assistance and has gained something by his justice. If he is not called in he shall have nothing. In time of war he shall have from each ploughteam two shillings, from half a team one, and from each laborer three pennies. He shall not give orders to the men of the abbey, nor hold courts of his own, nor take money from peasants. He is not permitted to buy lands of the abbey, or to give its serfs in fiefs to his knights, nor to extort anything from them by violence. . . . Done at Arras in the year of our Lord 1038.

From *Polyptyque de l'Abbé Irminion*, ed. by B. Guerard (Paris, 1844), Vol. II, pp. 356–57.

Some of the ingredients of feudalism had come into existence in the last years of the Merovingian kingdom, but it was almost two centuries before these ingredients began to form a consistent pattern. The lord–vassal relationship, for example, emerged clearly in the eighth century, possibly because of a change in military techniques. During their wars, Charles Martel and Pippin discovered that heavily armed cavalrymen gave them increased striking power. They wanted large numbers of these soldiers, but ordinary freemen, with at best a small farm, could not afford to provide themselves with specially bred horses, mail shirts and swords. No ordinary horse could carry a fully-armed soldier, nor could an ordinary village blacksmith make armor or forge a sword. Only the wealthy lords could provide such equipment, and they naturally expected special loyalty from the men who received it. These men became vassals of the king or of the lords and were the most effective element in the army.

At about the same time, the ordinary freeman was beginning to find that participating in local government was something of a burden. Local courts not only dispensed justice, they were also charged with administrative duties. All freemen were supposed to attend these courts, but they were not annoyed when only a few of their number were required to come. These specially designated men were naturally selected from the wealthier groups of freemen, and many of their descendants later appeared as vassals.

Personal relationships had always been more important in Germanic society than the abstract idea of public authority. So the Frankish kings found that vassalage would strengthen their political as well as their military power. Pippin, Charlemagne and Louis the Pious tried to create personal ties with important men by using some of the forms of the lord–vassal relationship. Thus they granted public offices, such as countships, as benefices to lords, just as these lords might grant an estate to a vassal. But there was a great difference between an ordinary vassal, who had little individual power, and a count, whose retainers, relatives, and dependents could give him almost complete control over a large area.

Lesser vassals were usually obedient to their lords and could scarcely hope to become independent. But the great counts bargained with the king when asked for service, and often demanded new offices and lands in return for their aid. They recognized the nominal superiority of the king, especially when they could use it to confirm their acquisition of new holdings. But by the tenth century, since the king could not please everybody, they were just as apt to turn against him and depose him. This was especially true in France, where the real rulers were the lords who had succeeded in building little principalities out of fragments of the old West Frankish kingdom.

Feudalism was primarily a political system that developed out of the desire of great lords for power and wealth and the concomitant need to give a minimum degree of security to the lands that they controlled. But counts, lords of castles, and their vassals had to have adequate incomes, and the scanty public revenues that remained—mainly tolls, market dues, and fines from courts—were inadequate to meet the needs of the governing class. In the end everyone in authority (including bishops and abbots as well as laymen) was dependent on dues squeezed out of the peasants, who constituted the majority of the population.

The burden on the peasants varied greatly, according to the region in which they lived and the degree of freedom that they enjoyed. In some areas (for example, Normandy) most peasants were free and owed relatively little to their superiors—a few pennies or small amounts of grain per acre for the use and protection of the land they cultivated, presents (which soon became compulsory) of hens and eggs at Christmas and Easter, three or four days' work a year on the lord's land at harvest time. At the other extreme were the unfree serfs (numerous in eastern France) who owed heavy payments, worked several days a week for the lord, and could not even marry a subject of another lord without buying permission. Economic considerations, however, cut across these lines. A serf with a large holding might be better off than a freeman who had only four or five acres; a man who had oxen was far more

FEUDAL FRANCE Late eleventh century

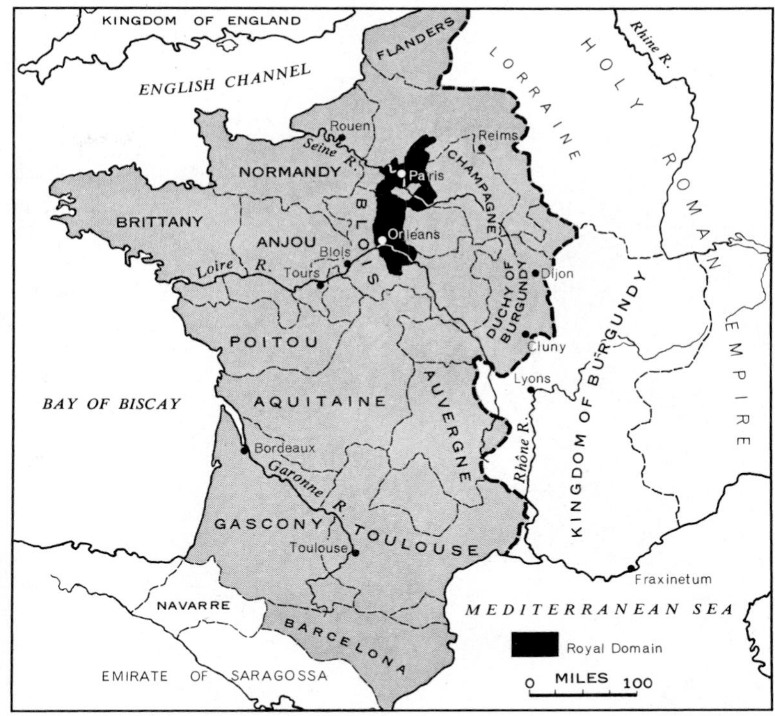

prosperous than a man who had no draft animals. But everywhere crop yields per acre were low, and even in a good year the average peasant did not rise for above a subsistence level of living.

From the point of view of the governing classes, the neatest arrangement was to possess a village in which all the peasants were under one lord and in which the lord's land, intermingled with that of the peasants, could be cultivated by the village as a whole. Such villages were relatively easy to exploit and usually produced a fairly regular income. But many villages were divided among several lords, and not all peasants lived in well-organized villages. Dues from scattered holdings and hamlets were difficult to keep track of and to collect. Moreover, a considerable number of small landholders, especially in southern France and in Spain, had full rights of ownership and owed very little to the lords. Eventually most (but not all) of these men did become dependents of a lord, but they still were far better off than serfs and many free peasants.

It is easy to see why the greater lords eventually granted some of their estates,

The life of a feudal knight: carrying a standard into battle, feasting, and accompanying a traveling king.

especially their smaller and more remote lands, to their vassals. The vassal had to be supported in any case; by giving him an estate the lord lost little income and saved himself the trouble of collecting peasant dues. The vassal who received and lived on a small estate might exploit it more efficiently than a distant lord. Thus in the long run large numbers of peasants became either tenants or serfs of lesser vassals.

This did not mean, especially in the ninth and tenth centuries, that the knight or other minor vassal had much political power over the peasants whose dues he received. He had to be given enough authority to force peasants to pay what they owed, and eventually most knights acquired a sort of police-court jurisdiction. They could judge cases of disorderly conduct; they could settle minor squabbles among peasants over the boundaries of fields and the division of family holdings. But they could not judge serious criminal cases or disputes over the possession of fiefs; such matters were referred to counts and other great lords. In short, the fragmentation of political authority never went down to the lowest level of the feudal hierarchy. The smallest effective political unit was the area ruled by the lord of a castle, not the estate held by a knight.

A Changing Institution

During the centuries when feudalism was at its height—from about 900 to about 1100—the institution underwent several striking changes. First, some lords succeeded in subduing their neighbors and building up relatively large and powerful states. This was especially true of the Count of Flanders and the Duke of Normandy, who added many counties to their original holdings and kept them under fairly effective control. Other lords in France, west Germany, the Spanish March, and north Italy were almost as successful, and their wars and alliances determined the political history of the area for two centuries. Second, since these new states were too large to be governed through the informal and personal decisions of their rulers, various new legal and financial institutions were created, which produced a body of feudal law. Third, the benefice, or fief, became more important. In the early years of feudalism many vassals had been primarily household retainers; they had no fiefs or only small holdings, and spent much of their time with their lord or in garrisoning his forts. But, as we have seen, lords often found it convenient to assign estates to their vassals, and by 1100 it was customary to give fiefs even to lesser vassals. It also became customary for the vassal to spend most of his time on his fief and to serve his lord only on special occasions or in time of war. Moreover, the fief, which originally had been only a loan to the vassal, gradually became hereditary, to be held by the vassal and his heirs as long as they gave service.

In short, the relationship between vassal and lord was changing, with the vassal becoming more of a country gentleman and less of an armed retainer. This was especially true of castellans (vassals who held a castle of their lord) and holders of large fiefs. They began to begrudge the time spent in the lord's service and tried to reduce it as much as they could. The lord countered by defining the service owed by vassals more and more precisely and by developing legal procedures for confiscating the fiefs of defaulting vassals. What had at first been a close personal relationship began to assume the form of a contractual obligation.

Feudalism was an inadequate and limited form of government; it did little for the mass of the people except to protect them against external and internal enemies. Even this protection was not always effective. In the endemic wars between neighboring lords, a favorite tactic was to ravage the peasants' fields and drive off their animals. Lords held local courts from time to time, and this helped to prevent neighborhood feuds, but they were more interested in pocketing fines than in administering justice. They made little effort to maintain roads and other public facilities. At its best, feudal government was inefficient paternalism; at its worst, it was pure exploitation of the peasants.

Yet with all its disadvantages, feudalism had vitality and real capability for growth. It spread from France throughout most of western Europe, and the countries that were most thoroughly feudalized, France and England, were the first medieval states to develop effective political institutions. Moreover, many feudal rulers managed to gain the loyalty of their subjects, something that neither the late Roman emperors nor the Germanic kings had achieved. There was personal devotion to the ruling dynasty; there was also a feeling that each man had an interest in preserving the customs and institutions of his little state. With this loyalty it was possible to build stronger states and to give more protection and better justice to the people.

Feudalism was almost perfectly adapted to conditions in early medieval Europe. The working political unit, the area dependent on a castle, matched the working economic unit, the local neighborhood. The struggle to base a large political organization on what was essentially a local economy—a struggle that had weakened both the Roman and the Carolingian empires—was abandoned. The exploitation of the peasants by an aristocracy was nothing new, and at least the feudal aristocracy had duties as well as privileges. Lords had to defend and govern their lands in person—no one else would do it for them—and if they did their job badly they would lose their lands to more efficient neighbors.

Even the fact that feudal government was rudimentary was an advantage. Europe at this time could not support a complex government; it had to concentrate on essentials. And precisely because early feudalism was highly informal and personal, change was easy and experimentation common. In the end the ablest feudal lords devised more effective forms of government than Europe had had for many centuries, and their methods were copied by their less imaginative colleagues.

GERMANY

It took several centuries for feudalism to reveal all its possibilities. At first it seemed to do as much harm in encouraging local wars as it did good in warding off outside raiders. During the tenth century, feudal France was weak and divided. Germany and England, still unfeudalized and united under their kings, were far stronger. Germany, in fact, was the dominant country in Europe from the early tenth century down through the eleventh century.

In the period after the breakup of the Carolingian Empire, Germany had remained more united than France. It had suffered less from invasion and civil war, which meant that the lords had had fewer opportunities to usurp power. Even the transition to a new ruling family was made more easily in Germany than in France. The last able German Carolingian died in 899; by 919 King Henry I had established the new Saxon dynasty on the throne.

In spite of these advantages, however, the German king had lost much of his authority by 919. During the troubles of the ninth century most of the country had come under the control of five great lords, the dukes of Saxony, Franconia, Swabia, Bavaria, and, after its final annexation to Germany in 925, Lorraine. Each of these dukes ruled a wider territory than that of any French feudal lord, and each exercised reasonably effective control over the counts and other nobles of his duchy. The dukes were willing to have a king as a sort of president of their club, but they expected to be virtually independent within their own duchies. Henry I, for example, was strong only in his own duchy of Saxony; elsewhere he had to negotiate with the other dukes to carry out his policies. Sons had begun to succeed their fathers as a matter of course in both duchies and counties.

GERMANY AND ITALY AT THE TIME OF OTTO THE GREAT 962

Nevertheless, Germany was not yet feudalized, although feudal ideas were creeping in through Lorraine, the duchy that lay closest to France. Counts and dukes were not completely independent of the king; they were public officers who could be removed if they failed to show obedience. Lords had not yet gained a monopoly of power; ordinary freemen had a voice in the courts and still served in the armies. Strong regional loyalties, especially in Saxony and Bavaria, held the duchies together. In short, Germany had not fragmented as France had, and the king still had a chance to establish his authority throughout the realm.

Otto the Great and the German-Roman Empire

Otto the Great (936–973) made the most of this opportunity. He held Saxony in his own right, and he gradually brought the other duchies under control by forcing out disobedient dukes and bestowing their offices on members of his own family. This policy was not wholly successful, for Otto's own sons rebelled against him. But there was still the Church, which had great wealth and cherished the idea of unity. Most of the bishops and abbots owed their positions to Otto; they supplied him with money and troops from their estates, and they provided him with administrative officers. The support of the Church made Otto supreme in central Europe; he was able to put down all rebellions and inflict a crushing defeat on the Magyars in 955.

Otto's position was so strong that he was able to intervene in Italian affairs and eventually to annex northern Italy. He has often been blamed for this action, since in the long run involvement in Italian politics weakened the German monarchy. But, given the situation in the tenth century, it would have been difficult for Otto to avoid involvement. The Italian kingdom was small—it included only the northern half of the peninsula—and its kings were weak. Tempted by this weakness, French feudal lords had already tried to establish themselves as kings of Italy, and the Duke of Bavaria also had thoughts of crossing the Alps. Members of Otto's own family had also used Italy as a base for rebellions. Otto, anxious to preserve his position as the strongest ruler in western Europe, could hardly allow Italy to pass to a potential rival, much less to one of his own subjects.

Otto's close relations with the Church in Germany also impelled him to intervene in Italy. He was not a mere exploiter of the Church; he felt, as Charlemagne had, that it was his duty to preserve and strengthen ecclesiastical institutions. The papacy was in miserable condition; deprived of the support of the Carolingians, it had fallen under the control of corrupt and self-seeking Roman nobles. So little authority and prestige did it enjoy that a tenth-century German archbishop actually refused to become pope. Otto may have hoped that intervention in Italy would free the papacy from domination by Roman nobles and that he could ensure his continued use of church resources by gaining a voice in papal elections.

Otto at least had a romantic as well as a political excuse for his invasion of Italy. Adelaide, widow of an Italian king, was being annoyed by her husband's successor. Otto came to the rescue of the queen, married her, and then claimed the Italian kingdom. A ruler backed by the German Church and in control of northern Italy could hardly be ignored by the pope, who recognized Otto's position by crowning him emperor in 962.

Ivory plaque showing Otto the Great offering a model of Magdeburg Cathedral to Christ (late tenth century).

Since there had been no emperor with real power since Louis, Charlemagne's son, and not even a nominal emperor since 924, Otto's coronation constituted a refounding of the medieval Empire. He was quite aware of this; he stressed the idea of renewal in his coinage and in his acts. After Otto there was no break; the imperial title and the German kingship were to remain indissolubly united for the rest of the Middle Ages. This Roman Empire of the German Nation, as it was called by some contemporaries, was the strongest state in Europe until about 1100, and an important force in European politics for two hundred years after that. Especially significant were the relations between the German-Roman Empire and the popes. Otto, as successor to Charlemagne, thought of himself as leader of the Christian West and protector of the papacy. He took this second responsibility so seriously that by the end of his life he dominated papal elections. The Church eventually reacted violently against imperial control, but for almost a hundred years the emperors named and deposed popes. And on the whole they strengthened the Church; popes chosen by the emperors were abler and better men than those selected by Roman nobles.

Gerbert

Having revived the Carolingian tradition of an alliance between emperor and Church, an alliance in which the emperor was unquestionably the dominant partner, Otto proceeded to revive the Carolingian interest in scholarship. One of the most famous of the scholars he encouraged was Gerbert, who was born in southwestern France about the middle of the tenth century but who spent much of his life in the service of Otto's son and grandson. Gerbert had studied in Spain, where contact with the Moslems had revived interest in mathematics and astronomy. He learned what he could of these subjects—very little by later standards but enough to give him a reputation for profound, even magical, knowledge in his own day. He also tried to teach elementary ideas about astronomy and devised some simple apparatus to demonstrate his points.

Although few westerners had paid much attention to mathematics or astronomy during the ninth and tenth centuries, these scientific interests were not unprecedented. What made them significant was the fact that Gerbert was more than a secluded scholar; he was one of the most influential churchmen of his time. The emperors he served made him first the abbot of a great monastery, then Archbishop of Reims, and eventually pope. As Pope Sylvester II (999–1003) he was the chief adviser of the emperor Otto III (983–1002), whose tutor he had been. The two men dreamed of an empire that would be much more like the old Roman Empire than Charlemagne's had been, an empire in which emperor and pope would act as the joint heads of a unified western state.

This was a hopeless dream, though both pope and emperor died before they realized quite how hopeless it was. But the fact that they could conceive of such a plan shows how strong Roman ideas were in the Ottonian court. And Gerbert might be excused for overestimating imperial power. After all, his spectacular career had been largely due to the emperor's support.

Gerbert's political program was a failure, but his scholarly work marked a turning point in European intellectual history. The fact that such an influential man was interested in mathematics and science attracted younger students who carried on his work. Other scholars took the road to Spain and prepared the way for the intellectual revival of the twelfth century, a revival in which western Europeans, for the first time, took a real interest in science.

Gerbert had also become absorbed in the study of logic, partly because logic and science were closely related in the Greek scientific tradition he was trying to revive, partly because he felt that he needed this tool in order to comprehend

The four provinces of Slavinia, Germania, Gallia, and Roma (left) paying homage to Otto III (right), from the Reichenau Gospels (tenth century). Note that Otto wears a Roman imperial costume, not a Germanic one.

the new knowledge he had acquired. Logic, like Latin, was essential in assimilating ancient knowledge, and Gerbert's use of logic, simple as it was, greatly impressed his contemporaries. Here again his example was not forgotten. The study of logic continued throughout the eleventh century and was one of the most important forces in the intellectual revival that came at the end of that century.

The direct line of Otto I ended in 1002 with the death of Otto III, but collateral branches of the family retained the throne and kept the Ottonian system of government going. Compared with France, which was splitting up into feudal states, Germany seemed to be flourishing. The German emperors stood unchallenged in their realm. They had wealth and prestige, and the greatest scholars of Europe came flocking to their courts. But the German state had serious weaknesses that had been masked by the remarkable ability of the emperors and the relatively slow development of feudal elements in German society. Imperial power depended on the support of the Church, and it was by no means certain that the Church would always be willing to remain subordinate to a secular ruler. The power of the local lord was growing in Germany as it had earlier in France, and there was no assurance that local lords would not some day seek independence. The emperor had to rely on churchmen and nobles to carry out his plans, for he had no bureaucracy. In short, the Ottonian Empire was little more than a slightly modified Carolingian Empire, an empire that had long been out of date. The emperor's position rested on a precarious balance of forces—clergy versus laymen, one group of lords versus another group—and the crises that arose in the last half of the eleventh century were to show just how precarious that balance was.

ANGLO-SAXON ENGLAND

England, like Germany and unlike France, was not feudalized in the tenth century. Like Germany again, it developed a relatively strong monarchy and an active intellectual life during that century. As the descendants of Alfred drove back the Danes, they had to develop new institutions with which to hold and govern the territories they reconquered. These institutions were especially effective at the local level—so effective that they survived the Anglo-Saxon monarchy for centuries and even formed the basic pattern of local government in the United States.

New Institutions

The Anglo-Saxon kings of the tenth century divided the country into shires, or counties, and then subdivided the shires into smaller units called hundreds. Shires and hundreds were judicial as well as administrative units; there was a shire court that met twice a year and a hundred court that met about once a month. Fortified towns, which were both military and trading centers, were called boroughs; the borough also had a court of its own.

This system was not unlike that of the Carolingian Empire and the states that succeeded it. But there was one striking difference: in England the nobles never gained control of shire, hundred, and borough government, whereas in France the count was the ultimate authority within his county. In England the highest royal official was the alderman, later called the earl. The alderman was usually responsible for many shires, and he could not handle all problems of local administration. An official was needed in each shire to collect revenue, muster troops, and preside over the courts. After a long period of experimentation the Anglo-Saxon kings eventually developed a very effective local official, the shire-reeve, or sheriff.

At first the shire-reeve was only one of a group of reeves, or agents, who managed the king's estates. It was logical to ask one of these men in each shire to supervise the others and to see that all the king's revenue in that district was brought together in one place. Eventually the chief reeve became the king's representative in all affairs, with wide administrative and executive powers. Just as the sheriff of a western county in the United

ENGLAND AFTER THE NORMAN CONQUEST
Late eleventh century

States in the nineteenth century was the key official in his district, so the Anglo-Saxon sheriff by the eleventh century was the most important official in his shire.

Powerful as the sheriff was, he never became independent of the king. He ranked beneath the really great men, the aldermen, or earls, and he could always be replaced if he failed to do his job loyally and efficiently. With a few exceptions, the office of sheriff never became hereditary. From 1000 on, the king of England always had a local official in every part of his realm who would carry out his orders with reasonable efficiency and collect his revenues with reasonable honesty. Kings on the Continent grew weak and poor because they had lost control of local government and revenues. But the king of England gained power and wealth, even though his country was small and thinly populated, because he could use the resources of all his counties.

Law and Literature

The Anglo-Saxon kings of the tenth and eleventh centuries also improved internal security by discouraging blood-feuds and by insisting that certain serious crimes, such as murder, arson, and rape, were offenses against the king. Since he received a substantial fine when a defendant was convicted of such crimes, the king had an added incentive to strengthen and support the courts in which these cases were tried. Much of the legislation of the Anglo-Saxon kings deals with the arrest and punishment of criminals. And it is a sign of their power that they could issue general laws; the great period of Anglo-Saxon legislation was between 950 and 1050, a time when the king of France could hardly make rules even for his own private estates.

Like the German kings, the Anglo-Saxon rulers encouraged ecclesiastical reform and sponsored literature and scholarship. But they were interested in writings in the vernacular as well as in Latin. Alfred the Great had translated Latin works into Anglo-Saxon, and under Alfred's successors, Anglo-Saxon literature reached its peak. The epic of *Beowulf* was put into its final form about 1000; the two great battle poems *Maldon* and *Brunanburh* came about the same time. Even more important for the historian is the *Anglo-Saxon Chronicle,* which was probably begun in the days of Alfred and was continued into the twelfth century. It is mainly a history of kings and bishops, of wars and rebellions, but it tells us much about Anglo-Saxon customs and beliefs.

Military Weakness

With all its achievements, the Anglo-Saxon monarchy was not exempt from the difficulties that had weakened the continental kingdoms. Most of the peasants had put themselves under the protection of lords, and most of the lesser landlords had placed themselves under

43 A.D.	ca. 400	ca. 900	Norman Conquest 1066
Roman Britain	Small Anglo-Saxon Kingdoms	House of Wessex	

the patronage of the king or an earl. Everywhere the bond between lord and follower was becoming stronger than the old ties of kinship and community. But, though the followers of the king and the great men had honorable status and were entrusted with important missions, they were not primarily a class of specially trained military retainers. Thus there were weaknesses in England's military posture. As the lords interposed themselves between people and king, the folk-army became less effective, and no one was developing the bands of heavy-armed cavalrymen that were proving so effective on the Continent. King and lords depended largely on their household retainers—good fighters, but probably not as well armed nor as versatile as French vassals.

This military weakness became evident soon after 1000 when the Danes renewed their attacks on England. King Ethelred the Ill-Counseled, after failing to defeat the Danes in battle, resorted to the hopeless expedient of buying them off with the proceeds of a national tax, the Danegeld. This gesture only encouraged the Danes, and by 1016 their king, Canute (or Knut), had completed the conquest of England.

England did not suffer greatly under Danish rule (1016–42), although some Anglo-Saxon lords lost their lands and official positions to Danes. Canute preserved, and even strengthened, Anglo-Saxon institutions; in fact, the last Anglo-Saxon laws were promulgated during his reign. But he did not entirely solve England's military problem. He increased the body of royal house-carls, or retainers, to several thousand; however, they were warriors of the old Germanic type, not mounted knights. A heavy-armed cavalry was essential; England still could not match the new type of force that was developing in France.

Edward the Confessor

When Canute's sons died without leaving direct heirs, the Anglo-Saxons had no trouble in restoring the old line of kings descended from the House of Wessex. But Edward the Confessor (1042–66) was strong only in his piety; in all other things he was easily swayed by his relatives and advisers. Having spent long years of exile in Normandy, he wanted to bring Norman ways into England and give Normans high positions in both ecclesiastical and secular administration. At the same time he was influenced by the earl Godwin, who was half Danish and wholly anti-French. Edward married Godwin's daughter and gave earldoms to Godwin's sons. Other Anglo-Saxon earls were naturally jealous of Godwin, and quarrels among the various factions at times reached the level of civil war.

Edward's situation was not unlike that of the last French Carolingians. Like them, he strove to preserve a precarious balance among aristocratic factions. Like them, he had to accept a notable transfer of political power into private hands. Bishops, abbots, and great lay lords assumed control of the courts of many hundreds, and even lesser lords acquired police-court jurisdiction over their men. Moreover, many of the powerful lords built up bodyguards large enough to constitute private armies.

Here we have some of the ingredients of feudalism, and it is possible that even without the Norman Conquest England might have developed its own kind of feudalism. The Anglo-Saxons, however, had not gone very far in this direction. The followers of the lords did not have the special military training of French vassals. Many of them were not even permanently bound to their lord; as the records say, they "could go with their

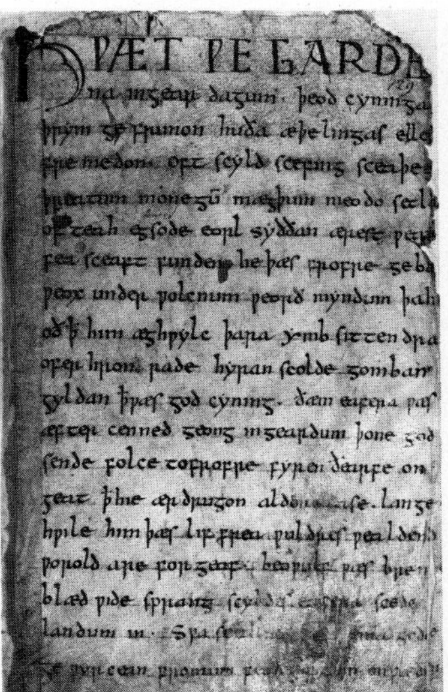

Page from the earliest manuscript of *Beowulf* (tenth century).

land" to any lord they chose. This meant in turn that there were no fiefs, that the followers of a lord did not hold land and offices in return for service. And this was even truer of the earls than it was of ordinary retainers. They were not vassals of the king, and they owed him no service for the lands they possessed. They expected, of course, to be consulted by the king, and they also expected to receive the chief offices of government, such as the earldoms. On his side, the king expected the earls and their relatives to assist him in the work of governing and defending the realm. But there were no permanent and binding obligations on either king or lord. The king could take an earldom from one lord and give it to another, and a lord who failed to serve the king in an emergency did not thereby forfeit his land.

England, in fact, was facing the same problem that Germany was facing in the eleventh century. In both countries the king still acted on the theory that the great men were his obedient subjects, that he could use them as public officials and dismiss them at will. But in both countries this theory was becoming unrealistic; the great men had acquired independent strength, and it was increasingly difficult for the king to control them. But while in Germany the tendency toward disintegration proved irreversible, in England it was checked at the end of the eleventh century. A disputed succession and quarrels among the earls exposed the Anglo-Saxon kingdom to conquest by a French feudal army. The leader of this army, William the Conqueror, introduced into England the most rigorous type of feudalism that Europe had yet seen. He imposed heavy and precise obligations on the lords and seized their lands if they failed to give the service they owed. Thus William corrected the chief weakness of the old Anglo-Saxon state. At the same time, he preserved all the really effective Anglo-Saxon institutions, especially the remarkable system of local government. The work of the Anglo-Saxon kings had not been wasted; the combination of their institutions with Norman feudalism was to make England for many generations the strongest state in Europe.

Suggestions for Further Reading

Note: Asterisk denotes a book available in paperback edition.

Pippin and St. Boniface

"The evolution of monarchical institutions and the idea of kingship during the Dark Ages from 400 to 1000 provides one of the most instructive examples of the complex process by which different social and religious elements became interwoven in a culture," writes C. Dawson in *Religion and the Rise of Western Culture** (1950), a very good introduction to this period. See also his *Making of Europe** (1934). C. H. Talbot, *Anglo-Saxon Missionaries in Germany* (1954), gives the correspondence of Pippin and St. Boniface and provides a cross section of the religious life of the eighth century difficult to parallel elsewhere. E. Emerton, *Letters of St. Boniface** (1932), is also very useful.

Charlemagne and the Revival of the Empire

The best biography that we have of the man who was at the center of this epoch is the contemporary Einhard's *Life of Charlemagne,** foreword by S. Painter (1960). Another edition, which also includes Notker's account of Charlemagne, was published by L. G. Thorpe (1969). See also B. W. Scholz, *Carolingian Chronicles** (1970). J. H. Robinson, ed., *Readings in European History,* Vol. I (1904), has excellent source material on the administration of the Carolingian Empire. There are several good studies of the man and the age: H. Kleinclausz, *Charlemagne* (1934), is a scholarly work that concentrates on political conditions, while the more recent and very readable study by H. Fichtenau, *The Carolingian Empire** (1957), gives greater attention to social conditions. D. Bullough, *The Age of Charlemagne* (1966), is a good and well-illustrated study. F. L. Ganshof, *The Imperial Coronation of Charlemagne* (1949), focuses on a problem that has interested many historians. Ganshof's collection of essays, *Frankish Institutions under Charlemagne* (1968), is also useful. The best study of the rise and decline of the Carolingian Empire is L. Halphen, *Charlemagne et l'Empire Carolingien* (1949). Halphen, however, is not as interesting reading as Fichtenau.

The Carolingian Renaissance

Most of the general works cited above have material on the Carolingian Renaissance. M. L. W. Laistner, *Thought and Letters in Western Europe, 500–900** (1966), devotes considerable attention to the prose and poetry of the period. E. S. Duckett, *Alcuin, Friend of Charlemagne* (1951), gives a somewhat romantic picture of the Frankish court and the Palace Academy. The influence of political and social factors on Carolingian art is brought out in A. Hauser, *Social History of Art,** Vol. I (1957). W. Levison, *England and the Continent in the Eighth Century* (1948), combines great knowledge of the literature of the age with a fine prose style. J. Boussard, *The Civilization of Charlemagne* (1969), is very helpful.

Collapse of the Empire and the New Invasions

For an overall view of this period drawn from the sources, see R. S. Lopez, *The Tenth Century* (1959). P. Sawyer, *The Age of the Vikings,* 2nd ed. (1971), gives a good description of the Northmen. J. Brønsted, *The Vikings** (1960), presents a fascinating account of viking art and civilization. T. D. Kendrick, *A History of the Vikings* (1930), shows the impact of the viking invasions on Britain, western Europe, Russia, and even America. A. Olrik, *Viking Civilization* (1930), and G. Turville-Petre, *The Heroic Age of Scandinavia* (1951), interpret the age of the vikings from the legends and sagas of individual Norsemen; of the two, Turville-Petre is the more readable. The great poem *Beowulf,** trans. by D. Wright (1957), provides information about viking civilization that has been documented by archeological findings. Gwyn Jones, *A History of the Vikings** (1968), is especially good. C. A. Macartney, *The Magyars in the Ninth Century* (1930), is a scholarly study of the origins and wanderings of the Magyars.

Feudalism

Both *Raoul de Cambrai,* trans. by J. Crosland (1926), and *The Song of Roland,** trans. by D. L. Sayers (1957), present excellent pictures of the ideals and attitudes of the feudal class in the first age of western feudalism. F. L. Ganshof, *Feudalism** 3rd English ed. (1964), shows the development of "classical feudalism" from its Carolingian origins. M. Bloch, *Feudal Society** (1961), is an outstanding study from a more social and economic point of view, while J. R. Strayer, *Feudalism** (1965), gives a brief account emphasizing political factors. G. Duby, *Rural Economy and Country Life in the Medieval West* (1968), is very helpful; see also his *Guerriers et Paysans* (1973). G. Fourquin, *Lordship and Feudalism in the Middle Ages* (1976), is the best up-dated study. R. Boutrouche, *Seigneurie et Féodalité,* 2 vols. (1968–1970), is very thorough, and has the special merit of comparing European feudalism with eastern forms. Boutrouche has a thorough bibliography. F. Kern, *Kingship and Law in the Middle Ages* (1939), is a historical essay that is invaluable for an understanding of the nature and development of the idea of kingship in early medieval Europe.

Otto I and the Saxon Dynasty

Medieval Germany, Vol. I, articles trans. by G. Barraclough (1938), has as its theme the internal development of the German state in the obscure period from the tenth to the thirteenth century. See also the materials published by B. H. Hill, Jr., *The Rise of the First Reich: Germany in the Tenth Century* (1969). There is information on Otto I and the Saxon dynasty in H. A. L. Fisher, *The Medieval Empire,* Vol. I (1898), but G. Barraclough's chapters in *The Origins of Modern Germany* (1947) are more up-to-date. Luitprand of Cremona, *Chronicle of the Reign of Otto I, Embassy to Constantinople,* trans. by F. A. Wright (1930), presents a picture of Church–state cooperation under the Saxons and an insight into the western attitude toward Byzantium in the eleventh century.

The Anglo-Saxon Monarchy to 1066

The Anglo-Saxon Chronicle (Everyman's Library) is the indispensable framework for developments in England before 1066. There is interesting source material in *Six Old English Chronicles,* trans. by J. Giles (1875), and *English Historical Documents,* Vol. I, *500–1042,* ed. by D. Whitelock (1955); Vol. II, *1042–1189,* ed. by D. C. Douglas and G. W. Greenaway (1953–55). F. Barlow, *The Feudal Kingdom of England, 1042–1216* (1953), has a good account of the reign of Edward the Confessor. The best scholarly treatment of the entire period is F. M. Stenton, *Anglo-Saxon England* (1943), but G. O. Sayles, *The Medieval Foundations of England,** Chapters 5–16 (1948), is much more readable and has a good critical bibliography. D. Whitelock, *The Beginnings of English Society** (1952), is a good brief account. P. H. Blair, *An Introduction to Anglo-Saxon England* (1959),* is very useful.

Anglo-Saxon Art

Most of the works cited above have information on the artistic achievements of the period. T. D. Kendrick, *Anglo-Saxon Art* (1938), is a good survey. D. Talbot-Rice, *English Art, 950–1100* (1952), traces the development of architecture, sculpture, and manuscript illumination. It has good plates and an excellent bibliography. A. W. Clapham, *English Architecture before the Norman Conquest* (1930), is a first-rate introduction to early Anglo-Saxon architecture. A more recent work is H. M. Taylor and J. Taylor, *Anglo-Saxon Architecture,* 2 vols. (1965).

10 Revival and Reform in Western Europe

Battered and torn by invasions and civil wars during the tenth century, western Europe began to recover after 1000. The worst of the invasions were over; France was achieving some degree of stability under its feudal lords; England and Germany were relatively peaceful under their kings. Italy was more turbulent, and Spain was still being devastated by Christian-Moslem wars. But the heart of western Europe, the great stretch of land running from Rome to London and from Bremen to Venice, had survived its worst difficulties.

Although the increase in security in the eleventh century was slight, western Europe had the resources and the vitality to profit from even slight improvement. Beginning in the last half of the eleventh century and continuing throughout the twelfth, there was a surge forward in all forms of human activity. Production and trade increased; political, legal, and religious institutions grew stronger; religious feeling became deeper and more meaningful. Along with these advances, remarkable work was done both in art and in scholarship.

THE ECONOMIC REVIVAL

The first and most obvious result of increased stability was a rise in population. The evidence for this rise—indirect, but convincing—is simply that during the late eleventh and twelfth centuries men could always be found to undertake new occupations and activities. There were enough men to clear forests and drain swamps, to enlarge old towns and build new ones, to establish new farms and villages in the half-deserted Slavic lands beyond the Elbe. There were enough men for conquests and crusades, for William's seizure of England, for the expansion of Christian holdings in Spain, for expeditions overseas to regain the Holy Land. And there were enough men, too, to furnish a striking increase in the number of students and teachers, of writers and artists, of clergymen, lawyers, and doctors.

Agriculture

The increase in population would have been a burden on society, rather than a stimulus, if production had not increased at the same time. The most important, and most difficult, increase to achieve was in the production of food. Clearing new land helped, since soil that had lain uncultivated for centuries was often very fertile. But new land came into production slowly, not nearly fast enough to keep up with the growing population. Production from old land had to be increased by acquiring more and better tools, by better organization of labor, and by better farming techniques.

Where soil and terrain permitted, the peasants developed a tightly integrated village community whose resources they

Tympanum of the church of St. Ursin at Bourges (twelfth century). This tympanum is unusual in its depiction of secular themes—the hunt and the labors of the months.

used with considerable efficiency. The arable land was divided into large fields, each of which was in turn divided into long, narrow strips. Each peasant held strips in each field, and some strips were cultivated for the benefit of the landlord. All the heavy work was done in common; the peasants pooled their work animals to form plow teams, and all joined together to harvest the big fields when the grain was ripe. Since farm animals were few and scrawny and tools were dull-edged and heavy, this was the best way to handle a hard job in a reasonable length of time.

One of the most bothersome problems was to find enough feed for the work animals. The yield of grain was low, at best only about four times the amount of seed sown, and almost all of it had to be saved for human consumption and for seed for the coming year. Since grass grew only in natural meadows along the streams, few villages produced enough hay to feed their animals during the winter months. To solve this problem, the peasants reserved the poorer lands exclusively for pasture and allowed the animals to graze on the cultivated fields after the crops had been harvested. Here again, through community organization the peasants saved themselves trouble and time, for a few herdsmen could take care of all the animals of the village.

Finally, the village had to have a common woodland. Wood was needed for fuel, for the frames of peasant huts, and for tools, which were made with as much wood and as little iron as possible. Forests were also used for pasturing large herds of half-wild pigs. These pigs supplied the peasants with most of their meat, since other animals were too scarce to serve as a regular source of food. The wild game of the forests was reserved for the lords, though there was a good deal of poaching.

The agricultural system had obvious advantages and equally obvious drawbacks. It left little room for individual initiative: everyone had to follow customary routines of planting and harvesting, and the work pace was set by the slowest oxen driven by the most stupid villager. Moreover, it provided no chance to improve the breed of animals or the stock of seed, since the animals ran together in common pastures and the seed on one strip was inevitably mixed with that of neighboring strips.

The medieval village, however, was less hostile to innovation than is sometimes believed. In the obscure years between the breakup of the Carolingian Empire and the end of the eleventh century, improved agricultural techniques spread widely throughout much of Europe. The heavy wheeled plow with a moldboard to turn the soil had been used in a few Germanic regions even before the collapse of the Roman Empire. It was far more effective than the light Mediterranean plow in cultivating the heavy, wet clay soils of northern Europe, but it required a large team to draw it. The ordinary peasant had at most one or two oxen, but those who lived in integrated villages could pool their animals to form a plow-team. By 1100 the heavy plow had been adopted in Germany, northern France, and southern and central England. Its use increased food production, for the peasants could now cultivate lands the Romans had never touched.

Another innovation, also closely connected with the integrated village, was the three-field system. Since artificial fertilizers were unknown and manure was scarce, the usual method of preserving the fertility of the soil was to let half the land lie fallow each year. In northern Europe farmers discovered that they could get equally good results by dividing the land into three large blocks (hence the term three-field system) and rotating their crops. During the first year of the cycle, they planted one block in winter wheat, which they harvested in July; then they let the winter-wheat field rest until the following spring, when they sowed it with spring grains. This crop they harvested in the fall, and then let the land rest once more until the following fall, when it was sown with winter wheat. Thus in any year, one-third of the land produced winter wheat, one-third produced spring grain, and one-third was left uncultivated. And yet, over the three-year cycle, each field could lie fallow for at least a year and a half. This system could not be used in the Mediterranean basin, where there is not enough summer rain for spring grain to mature. And it was hard to use in regions where there were no well-organized villages. But where it was used, it increased production by a third.

Only about half of western Europe was organized in integrated villages. Where the soil was thin or the rainfall scant there were only small, loosely organized hamlets and individual farms, as in northern England, Brittany, and Mediterranean France. Except for wine-growing areas, these districts produced less per acre and per man than the integrated villages, though they were normally self-sufficient in food. Overall, western Europe had a food surplus by the middle of the twelfth century. Nevertheless, bad roads, a shortage of draft animals, and local wars and brigandage meant that

THE THREE-FIELD SYSTEM	Field A	Field B	Field C
First Year	FALLOW until the fall Sow wheat in the fall	Harvest wheat in July FALLOW from July until the spring	Sow oats in the spring Harvest oats in the fall FALLOW until the next fall
Second Year	Harvest wheat in July FALLOW from July until the spring	Sow oats in the spring Harvest oats in the fall FALLOW until the next fall	FALLOW until the fall Sow wheat in the fall
Third Year	Sow oats in the spring Harvest oats in the fall FALLOW until the next fall	FALLOW until the fall Sow wheat in the fall	Harvest wheat in July FALLOW from July until the spring

there might be severe local famines even in a year of general surplus.

Commerce and Industry

During this same period, the towns of western Europe were experiencing a striking growth in size and number. They absorbed some of the surplus population and furnished a steadily growing market for agricultural products. They also intensified trade among all parts of Europe and increased the production of textiles and metalware. The growth of towns was especially conspicuous throughout Italy and Flanders.

The Italian towns depended almost entirely on international trade, particularly in Oriental goods such as silk and spices. During the eleventh century, Italian shipping in the Mediterranean increased steadily. With the Byzantine Empire weakening and the Moslem Caliphate breaking up, the Italian merchants had little competition. As if to aid the Italians in their new-found prosperity, nomadic invaders were strangling the alternate trade route from the East along the Russian rivers to the Baltic. Thus the Italians almost monopolized the trade in Oriental goods for western markets. And these markets were becoming steadily more profitable, thanks to the general increase in prosperity and security throughout the West. The great seaports of Venice, Pisa, and Genoa flourished most brilliantly, but the towns of the Po Valley, especially Milan, were not far behind. As the Italian merchants carried their wares north through France and Germany, they stimulated the growth of other trading centers along the routes they traveled.

The towns of Flanders found their nourishment in industry rather than in trade. The flat, marshy lands along the sea seemed to be good only for sheep raising, so that Flanders had a surplus of wool from a very early date. Moreover, since Flanders was one of the first feudal states to achieve a relatively high level of stability and internal security, there was soon a surplus population, both native born and immigrant, that could be used to process the surplus wool. Wool was the basic clothing material in western Europe, for cotton was scarce (it grew only in Mediterranean regions) and both linen and silk were terribly expensive. But to transform raw wool into good cloth took a great deal of time and energy. The wool had to be cleaned and carded, spun into thread, woven, smoothed by shearing off the knots and rough places, and finally dyed. All these tasks could be performed after a fashion by village workers, but the rough cloth they turned out was neither comfortable nor attractive. Anyone who had an income above the subsistence level wanted better cloth produced by skilled craftsmen. For many people, a good suit of clothes was the only luxury they possessed. This is why, from the early Middle Ages into the nineteenth century, the textile industry was the most important industry in western Europe.

Perhaps as early as the time of Charlemagne, and certainly by the eleventh century, Flanders had become the textile center of Europe. It had the wool, it had the labor, and soon Flemish cloth was famous near and far. It was bought by well-to-do people throughout Europe and even found markets in the Middle East. The first European manufactured product with much appeal for non-Europeans, it helped to balance European trade with the Orient. By the twelfth century the Flemish textile towns of Ghent, Bruges, and Ypres rivaled the flourishing seaports of Italy in wealth and population.

Outside Italy and Flanders the towns were smaller, and the growth of commerce and industry was less spectacular. But everywhere old towns were expanding and new towns were springing up. Some served as distribution centers along the trade routes; others specialized in manufacturing goods for local consumption. Thus western Europe began to enjoy a more rational division of labor

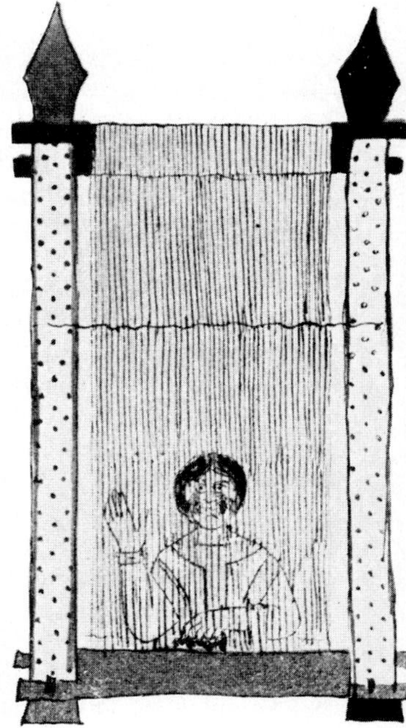

Weaving became an important industry in the eleventh and twelfth centuries. Note that the upright loom was used instead of the horizontal loom, which was developed a century later (detail of a miniature painting from the eleventh-century encyclopedia of Rabanus Maurus).

Illustration from an eleventh-century calendar depicting plowing and sowing.

An Early Medieval Merchant

When the boy had passed his childish years quietly at home [in Norfolk, England], he began to follow more prudent ways of life, and to learn carefully and persistently the teachings of worldly forethought. He chose not to follow the life of a husbandman but . . . aspiring to the merchant's trade, he began to follow the peddler's way of life, first learning how to gain in small bargains and things of insignificant price and thence . . . to buy and sell and gain from things of greater expense. For in his beginnings he was wont to wander with small wares around the villages and farmsteads of his own neighborhood, but in process of time he gradually associated himself by compact with city merchants. . . . At first he lived for four years as a peddler in Lincolnshire, going on foot and carrying the cheapest wares; then he traveled abroad, first to St. Andrews in Scotland and then to Rome. On his return . . . he began to launch on bolder courses and to coast frequently by sea to the foreign lands that lay about him. . . . At length his great labors and cares bore much fruit of worldly gain. For he labored not only as a merchant but also as a shipman . . . to Denmark and Flanders and Scotland; in all which lands he found certain rare wares, which he carried to other parts wherein he knew them to be less familiar and coveted by the inhabitants. . . . Hence he made great profit in all his bargains, and gathered much wealth in the sweat of his brow, for he sold dear in one place the wares which he had bought elsewhere at a small price.

From *Life of St. Godric of Finchale,* trans. by G. G. Coulton, *Social Life in Britain from the Conquest to the Reformation* (Cambridge: Cambridge University Press, 1925), pp. 415–17.

A peddler offering silver beakers (detail from a thirteenth-century manuscript).

and a better use of human resources. Peasants and landlords began to specialize in producing food for the market, while skilled craftsmen in the towns concentrated on manufacturing. This development may seem so elementary that it is hardly worth mentioning. But it was precisely this division of labor between town and country that had been lacking in the late Roman Empire and the early Germanic kingdoms.

The growth of towns stimulated the economy of Europe, but it put serious strains on the social and economic system. The ruling classes, feudal lords and churchmen, knew how to control and exploit peasants, but they were not so sure of themselves in dealing with merchants and artisans. Obviously, townspeople needed personal freedom and some local self-government. A serf could not function as a merchant, and feudal courts were poorly equipped to deal with lawsuits among businessmen. But if the townsmen became too free they might escape completely from the control of the ruling classes. It became a fairly common practice for kings and lords to offer charters to new towns, granting them special privileges in order to attract settlers. Older towns were given some of the same rights so they could match the growth of the new ones. The rulers gave the towns enough freedom to become prosperous but retained enough control to share in that prosperity, through taxes, tolls, and payments for market rights. It was not always easy to strike this balance, however, and all through the eleventh and twelfth centuries lords and towns haggled over the terms of their relationship. The Church had an especially difficult time. Like all landlords, it hated to surrender any of its rights, and it had little sympathy with the businessman's way of life. In eastern France there were bloody conflicts between bishops and their towns, and Rome itself staged frequent rebellions against the pope throughout the thirteenth century.

In the end, the towns gained personal freedom for their people and a separate system of municipal government. But the extent of self-government varied with the strength of the country's kings and nobles. In England and in the feudal states of France, for example, the towns never became independent. Towns in Spain enjoyed considerable liberty at first, but it was gradually whittled away as the kings became stronger. In Germany the process went the other way: so long as the emperors were strong, the towns had little independence; but after the collapse of the Empire in the thirteenth century many, though not all, of the cities became free. In Italy no medieval ruler managed to control the towns for any length of time, and most of them became independent city-states. These differences in the autonomy of towns from one country to another were to have a significant effect on the political structure of Europe. Rulers who could not tap the wealth of their towns found it difficult to build strong centralized states; this is one reason why Italy and Germany remained disunited for so long. Conversely, rulers who could draw on the resources of their towns were able to build powerful administrative and military organizations; this is one reason why France and England had centralized governments at such an early date.

THE POLITICAL REVIVAL

The economic revival of Europe was accompanied by a political revival, which was most noticeable in northern France and in England. In northern France the Count of Flanders and the Duke of Normandy had built up relatively well-governed states. The counts of Flanders were fortunate in having neither dangerous neighbors nor powerful vassals. They enlarged the boundaries of their original holdings without ever losing personal control over the county. They named their own men to occupy the fortified castles; they suppressed private wars; and they kept the higher law courts firmly in their own hands. Warfare often broke out along the borders, but the heart of Flanders was relatively peaceful and Flemish industry grew apace.

The vikings had received Normandy in 911, but it took some time for the wild sea rovers to settle down on the land. Only after 950 could the dukes of Normandy begin to organize their government. Given the environment, this had to be a feudal government, but the dukes stressed those elements in the feudal relationship that kept them strong and minimized those that reduced their power. They had the advantage of starting with a clean slate; there were no old, well-entrenched noble families to hamper them. Thus they could build a simpler, neater system than their rivals. They avoided the fragmentation of political authority that occurred elsewhere and kept full control over barons and lesser vassals. The Duke of Normandy could raise a larger army in proportion to the size of his holdings than could any other French feudal lord. At the same time, to ensure that no vassal became too powerful, he discouraged private war, ordered that no new castle could be built except by special license, and reserved to himself the administration of justice over serious crimes throughout Normandy. His firm control over most of the towns assured him a good income from their growing commerce. And, since he named all the bishops and most of the abbots, he dominated the Norman Church. In order to keep their lands, churchmen had to supply the duke with a large part of his army and much of his administrative staff. Normandy, like Flanders, was a relatively peaceful and prosperous state, and its population soon began to expand.

The energies of Normandy and Flanders were directed into different channels, however. The Flemings concentrated on industry and agriculture. Many of them settled in the towns and became textile workers; others began the centuries-long struggle to reclaim from the sea the flooded land of the coast. They became so skillful in the arts of diking and draining that they were sought by rulers of other provinces. In the twelfth century thousands of Flemish peasants moved across Germany to clear and drain the lands that German lords had won from the Slavs. In Normandy, on the other hand, though some new land was cleared, there was none of the intensive agricultural and industrial activity that marked Flanders. Instead, the Normans turned toward military and political expansion.

The Duke of Normandy and the Norman Church

1172

Although this document comes from the twelfth century, it repeats obligations laid on the Norman Church in the time of William the Conqueror.

The bishop of Avranches owes 5 knights, and another five from the fief of St. Philibert.

The bishop of Coutances, 5 knights

The bishop of Bayeux, 20 knights

The bishop of Sées, 6 knights

The bishop of Lisieux, the service of 20 knights

The abbot of Fécamp, the service of 10 knights

The abbot of Mont St. Michel, the service of 6 knights in the Avranchin and Cotentin and 1 knight in the Bessin

The abbot of St. Ouen of Rouen, the service of 6 knights [other abbots owe a total of 25 knights].

From Charles H. Haskins, *Norman Institutions* (Cambridge, Mass.: Harvard University Press, 1925), p. 8.

The Normans in Italy

The first Norman conquest was in southern Italy, where only the wreckage of earlier political systems survived. The Byzantine Empire held the mainland coasts; the interior was divided among Lombard princes; and the island of Sicily was ruled by rapidly shifting Moslem dynasties. The first Normans came to Italy in the early eleventh century as mercenary soldiers, but soon they were fighting for themselves instead of for their employers. Under Robert Guiscard the Normans had conquered almost all of the mainland by 1071. Meanwhile Robert's younger brother Roger had launched the conquest of Sicily. In this slow and bloody operation, the Moslem strongholds had to be reduced one by one, but by 1091 Sicily was firmly in Roger's possession. His son, Roger II, eventually inherited the mainland conquests as well and in 1130 took the title of King of Sicily.

This conquest of southern Italy and Sicily was in many ways a more remarkable feat than the Norman conquest of England. There were fewer Normans in southern Italy than there were in England, and their first leaders had little authority. But in Italy, as in Normandy earlier and in England later, the Normans showed an uncanny ability to build a strong government out of whatever institutions they found ready at hand. They introduced Norman feudalism in order to guarantee the ruler a strong army, but they preserved much of the Byzantine and Moslem bureaucratic apparatus. The Norman kingdom of Sicily, when it finally took shape in the twelfth century, was one of the wonders of the medieval world. Norman barons and knights, Greek secretaries, and Moslem financial experts all worked together to make the king strong. He had full control over justice and administration; he regulated the commerce of the entire kingdom; he enjoyed a steady income collected by a centralized financial bureau. Only the king of England could rival him in these matters, and during most of the twelfth century even the king of England probably had less authority.

THE NORMAN CONQUEST OF SOUTHERN ITALY 1130

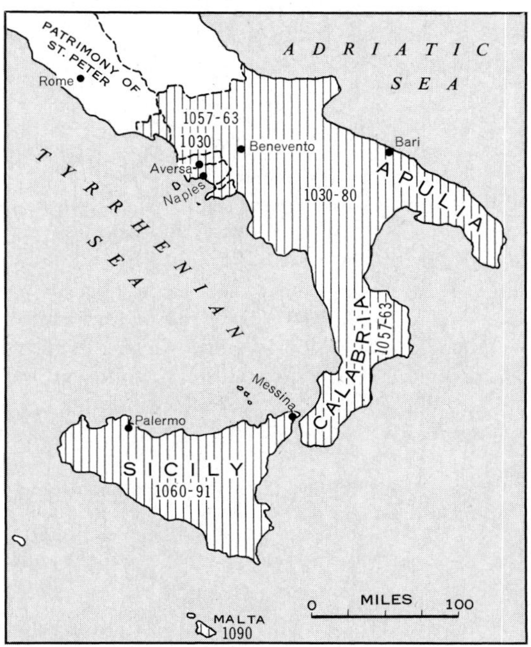

The Norman Conquest of England

In the long run, however, it was the Norman conquest of England that had the more important consequences. The brilliant Sicilian state fell on evil days in the thirteenth century when it was conquered by a French prince. Only in England did the Norman genius for government have an opportunity to produce lasting results.

As we have seen, in the years just before 1066, Anglo-Saxon England was torn by dissension. King Edward the Confessor could not control his quarreling earls, and he had no direct heir. At one time he had thought of naming his mother's cousin William, Duke of Normandy, to succeed him. But William was not descended from the Anglo-Saxon kings, and the English disliked the Normans. Later Earl Godwin and his son, Earl Harold, became so strong that William's claims were set aside. Harold gained the dominant voice in the government, and when Edward finally died in 1066 Harold was unanimously chosen king by the leading men of the country.

But William was determined not to lose the inheritance to which he thought himself entitled. As Duke of Normandy he already had a powerful army, and he reinforced it by recruiting soldiers from

Norman troops on horseback engaging Anglo-Saxon foot soldiers in battle (detail from the Bayeux tapestry, late eleventh century).

all the neighboring feudal states. The pope was annoyed with the Anglo-Saxons because they had driven out a French Archbishop of Canterbury during one of their anti-Norman demonstrations and had replaced him with a disreputable and unreformed Englishman. He gave his blessing to William's enterprise, an act that helped William's recruiting efforts. By the summer of 1066 William had assembled an army of over five thousand men.

Harold, aware that the attack was coming, massed his forces in southern England. But just as William was ready to sail, Harold was called north to face the last great invasion of the Northmen. Harold defeated the invaders in a hard battle and hurried back to the south in time to take up a strong position on a hill near Hastings. He might have been better advised to stay back of the Thames and let William's army waste away, as invading armies usually did in the Middle Ages. Forced marches had exhausted the Anglo-Saxon army, and heavy battle casualties had thinned its ranks; moreover, expected support from the northern earls failed to materialize. Harold made a heroic defensive stand, but in the end he was killed and the English shield-wall broke. William marched on London and was accepted as king.

William's victory owed much to chance, but his subsequent consolidation of power in England demonstrated his real ability as a ruler. He had to deal with a bewildered and disoriented native population and with an unreliable group of conquerors, more than half of whom were not Normans. There were some Anglo-Saxon risings; there were even more cases of disobedience and rebellion on the part of his French barons. But he rode them all down: "The rich complained and the poor lamented," says the *Anglo-Saxon Chronicle,* "but he was so sturdy that he cared not for their bitterness; they had to follow his will entirely if they wished to live or to keep their lands."

William's power rested on two basic principles. First, he insisted that he was the lawful heir of Edward the Confessor and so had inherited all the rights of the Anglo-Saxon kings. The Anglo-Saxon aristocracy, by opposing their rightful ruler, had forfeited their lands and rights. This led to the second principle: the new Norman aristocracy now held all lands and rights as fiefs of the king. No lord *owned* anything; he merely had a right to hold it so long as he obeyed and rendered service to the king. This arrangement overcame the chief weakness of the Anglo-Saxon monarchy—namely, its failure to control or discipline the earls and great landlords. A Norman baron who resisted the king knew that he would lose part or all of his land.

William gave his barons and knights extensive powers in local government.

The death of Harold, as portrayed in the Bayeux tapestry.

Silver penny bearing the likeness of William the Conqueror.

He transferred most of the hundred courts to private hands and named Norman barons as sheriffs. This put the peasants at the mercy of the new aristocracy, and many freemen became serfs. But men above the peasant level were protected by the king. The county courts were still the king's courts, and any baronial sheriff who showed signs of trying to build up independent power could be summarily removed. The king kept the peace so well that, to quote the *Chronicle* again, "a man might travel through the kingdom unmolested with a bosomful of gold."

Norman Government in England

The most striking result of the Norman conquest was a steady growth in the power of the king's central court. This court had a solid core of household officials and clerks, and a fluctuating population of bishops and barons who happened to be with the king at any given moment. The court assisted the king in any business he laid before it; it could advise on policy, audit accounts, or try cases involving the barons. William kept it very busy, and he himself traveled incessantly up and down England settling local quarrels. When he could not be present himself, he sometimes sent a delegation from his court to represent him. These delegations, with the full authority of the king, could try suits involving land disputes among the king's vassals. They often used a new and very effective procedure that William had imported from Normandy: trial by inquest. In an inquest, neighbors of the litigants were sworn to give true answers to questions concerning the matters in dispute. Procedure by inquest was a much better way of getting at the facts than trial by battle (the procedure favored by the Norman barons), and it enabled the king to settle disputes peacefully and to protect both his own rights and those of his vassals.

The most famous example of the inquest was the Domesday Survey. Faced with the confusion caused by the rapid redistribution of land after the conquest, William wanted to know what each district owed him and what estates were held by his vassals; he probably also wanted to settle a number of boundary disputes among his barons. In 1086 he sent delegations from his court to every county in England with orders to obtain inventories of the possessions of the great landholders. These inventories were checked by swearing in a group of men to make an inquest in each village. The village inquests told the king's men how much land there was in the village, how many men, who had held the land before the conquest, who held it now, and what it owed the king. The results of all these inquiries were summarized by the king's clerks in Domesday Book, a nearly complete survey (London and the northern counties are missing) of the kingdom of England. This amazing feat shows both William's power and his administrative skill. No other eleventh-century king could have done it; no later medieval king had vision enough to attempt it. Domesday stands alone between the tax

William the Conqueror

This description of William, in version E of the *Anglo-Saxon Chronicle,* was written by a man, who, as he says, "once lived at his court."

King William was a very wise man and more honored and stronger than any of his predecessors. He was mild to those good men who loved God but severe beyond measure towards those who resisted his will. . . . He kept in prison earls who acted against his pleasure . . . and at length he spared not his own brother Odo. . . . Among other things the good order that William established is not to be forgotten; it was such that any honest man might travel over the kingdom with his bosom full of gold unmolested and no one dared kill another, whatever injury he had received. . . . Being careful of his own interest he surveyed the kingdom so thoroughly that he knew the possessor of every hide* of land and how much it was worth. . . . [Domesday Book]

He caused castles to be built and oppressed the poor. He took from his subjects many marks of gold and many hundred pounds of silver. . . . He made great forests for game and ordered that anyone who killed a deer should be blinded [for] he loved the stags as if he were their father. . . . The rich complained and the poor lamented, but he was so sturdy that he cared not for their bitterness; they had to follow his will entirely if they wished to live or to keep their lands.

*hide: 120 acres.

There are many translations of this passage; this one is adapted from J. A. Giles, *The Anglo-Saxon Chronicle* (London: Bell and Daldy, 1868), pp. 461–63. Easier to find is the version in *English Historical Documents, 1042–1189,* ed. by D. C. Douglas and G. W. Greenaway (London: Eyre and Spottiswoode, 1953), pp. 163–64.

surveys of the Roman Empire and the censuses of the modern period.

William died in 1087 and was followed by his sons William Rufus (1087–1100) and Henry I (1100–35). Rufus exploited his rights over bishops and barons until he brought them to the point of rebellion, but he made no permanent innovations in government. Henry, on the other hand, made the central government much more efficient. Following earlier precedents, he segregated the financial work of the court in a separate department, the Exchequer, to which the sheriffs had to give an accounting twice a year for every penny of income and expenditure. All these reports were copied out each year in a long document called a Pipe Roll. By consulting earlier Pipe Rolls the Exchequer could make sure that the sheriffs had not overlooked or embezzled royal revenues and that they were paying their arrears. Though England was still thinly inhabited—Domesday figures suggest a population of not much over 1 million—Henry's efficient administration gave him an income larger than that of the king of France, who nominally ruled a much larger country.

Henry also improved the administration of justice. He sent out delegates from his court so often that they came to be more like circuit judges than special commissioners. Few important cases were any longer heard by the sheriffs—a precaution that, added to the strict financial accounting imposed on them, removed any danger of their becoming too independent. Henry also used inquests frequently and kept the peace as his father had done. At his death in 1135 England was a unified kingdom, far more peaceful than most of western Europe, far more powerful than its size and population seemed to warrant.

THE RELIGIOUS REVIVAL

The perfecting of the parish system and the elimination of paganism west of the Elbe during the Carolingian period meant that for generations everyone in western Europe had been exposed to Christianity. By the eleventh century the cumulative effects of this exposure began to make themselves felt. True, the strength of Christian ideals was diluted by the corruption or ignorance of many members of the clergy, but the ideals were powerful enough to survive. Slowly Christianity became less and less a matter of external observance, more and more a matter of strong internal conviction. A great wave of popular piety swept through Europe in the eleventh and twelfth centuries, changing the whole character of European society.

The Peace Movement

The Peace Movement was one of the earliest manifestations of the growing influence of Christian ideals. Feudal warfare was waged by lords and kings, largely at the expense of noncombatants; the usual tactic was a raid on enemy lands in which crops were destroyed, cattle driven off, and churches plundered. During the late tenth century, bishops in central France and commoners began to form associations to protect themselves against the violence of the military class. This movement was considered dangerous in many places, but was welcomed by most of the population, including some of the lesser lords. Under the leadership of churchmen peace associations were formed in which each member swore not to attack peasants, merchants,

The Domesday Survey 1086

The monks of Ely added this note to their copy of Domesday returns for their lands.

Here is written down the inquest of the lands [of Ely] as the king's barons inquired about them: namely, by the oaths of the sheriff of the shire and of all the barons and their French soldiers, and of the whole hundred [court], and of the priest, the reeve and six villeins of each vill. Then, how the manor is called, who held it in the time of King Edward [the Confessor] and who holds it now, how many hides, how many plows on the demesne, how many men, how many villeins, how many serfs, how much woods, how much meadow, how much pasture, how many mills . . . how much it was worth altogether and how much now. . . . All this three times over, once for the time of King Edward, once for the time when King William gave it out, and once as it now is—and whether more can be had from it than is now being given.

Translated from W. Stubbs, *Select Charters* (Oxford: Clarendon Press, 1921), p. 101.

or churchmen. The associations raised armies to punish violators and often levied an annual assessment to support their operations. The movement to protect noncombatants was known as the Peace of God. Leaders of the Peace Movement also tried to forbid fighting on certain holy days, such as Sunday and the Christmas and Easter seasons. This attempt, known as the Truce of God, was far less effective than the Peace of God and did little to curb feudal warfare.

So long as the Peace of God depended on diocesan armies led by churchmen, it had only limited success. But in the eleventh century the idea was taken up by powerful lords in northern France and western Germany as a means of restraining unruly vassals. With no hope of plunder, feudal war seemed less enticing; and with no chance to make war on his neighbors, a minor lord could seldom become strong enough to challenge his lord. The Count of Flanders and the Duke of Normandy, along with many other rulers, enforced the Peace of God in their lands. Thus the Peace Movement gave added security to peasants and merchants and helped increase agricultural production and trade.

Bronze figure of a monk writing on the tail of a monster, on which he is seated (from a cross or candlestick base, north German or English, *ca.* 1150).

Monastic Reform

Another sign of the growing strength of Christian ideals was the movement toward monastic reform. The older monasteries, rich in endowments and resigned to the demands of kings and nobles, were no longer centers of piety or learning. Reform was clearly necessary; the movement began in Germany and France in the tenth century and reached its peak in the eleventh. Reforming abbots, after they had improved the discipline and the administration of their own monastery, were often asked to help reorganize neighboring establishments. Thus groups of monasteries, inspired by the same ideals and governed by the same methods, were formed. The most famous of these groups was the one headed by Cluny, a monastery in eastern France, and the abbot of Cluny was often as influential as the pope.

Many people were attracted by the opportunity to enter one of the reformed monasteries, so that by the end of the eleventh century there were more monasteries and more monks than ever before. And, without exactly intending it, the reformed monks stirred up such enthusiasm for strict adherence to Christian ideals that it spilled over into other areas and caused drastic changes in the Church.

The Problem of Secular Control

The most dramatic manifestation of popular piety and the desire for reform was a struggle, in the late eleventh century, to free the Church from secular control and to make it the final authority in western society. The early monastic reformers had worried little about this problem. So long as kings and lords let them restore discipline within their orders, they were quite willing to give service to the ruler and even to accept his candidates as abbots. What happened outside the monastery was the king's business, not theirs. But so long as laymen controlled the appointment of bishops and abbots, and in Germany, even talked of owning the churches, there was no hope of creating a truly Christian society outside the monasteries. At best, kings and great lords appointed good administrators who spent most of their time on secular affairs. At worst, they sold abbacies and bishoprics or gave them as a sort of pension to incompetent relatives. In either case prelates appointed in this way were likely to be poor spiritual leaders. Some reformers were reluctant to break entirely with the kings, who after all were semisacred personages, but as the eleventh century went on, more and more of them came to believe that the Church could not accomplish its mission until it was independent of lay authority.

They also came to believe that the only way to gain independence and authority for the Church was to strengthen the position of the pope. There had been earlier attempts to do this: in the Carolingian period the pseudo-Isidorean decretals had magnified papal power. Unfortunately, these decretals were not authentic, as some contemporaries had suspected, and they had had little influence. But by the eleventh century it was clear that an isolated bishop or group of clergymen could not resist the pressure of secular rulers. If, however, the Church were tightly organized under the pope's leadership, then the moral influence of the entire Church could be brought to bear on all the problems of European society. By 1050 the reformers began to proclaim that the pope should be completely independent of all laymen, even the emperor, and that he should have complete administrative jurisdiction over all churchmen, even those who were officials and vassals of kings.

The man who did most to formulate and execute this program was the monk Hildebrand, who later became Pope Gregory VII. He had served in the papal court since the 1040s, and in 1059 he inspired a famous decree that placed the election of the pope in the hands of the cardinals. The cardinals were the leading clergymen of the Roman region—priests of the major Roman churches and bishops of the dioceses around the city. This decree, designed to eliminate the influence of both the Roman nobility and the emperor, proved remarkably successful; after 1059 no pope owed his position to direct lay appointment.

The Investiture Conflict

Hildebrand soon became pope. As Gregory VII (1073–85) he tried to gain the same independence for the Church as a whole that he had already won for the papacy. He concentrated his attack on the appointment of bishops by laymen. Eventually, this controversy became focused on lay investiture, the practice by which a secular ruler bestowed the symbols of spiritual authority, such as the ring and staff, on the bishops he had appointed. The target was well chosen; the practice had already been forbidden by

Detail of a manuscript illustration of Gregory VII.

Principles of Gregory VII — *ca.* 1075

This document was certainly drawn up in Gregory's circle, and probably by the pope himself. It expresses the views of those who were trying to increase papal power in both Church and state.

1. That the Roman church was founded by the Lord alone.
2. That only the Roman pontiff is rightly called universal.
3. That he alone can depose or reestablish bishops.
4. That his legate, even if of inferior rank, is above all bishops in council; and he can give sentence of deposition against them. . . .
12. That it is permitted to him to depose emperors. . . .
18. That his decision ought to be reviewed by no one, and that he alone can review the decisions of everyone.
19. That he ought to be judged by no one.
20. That no one may dare condemn a man who is appealing to the apostolic see.
21. That the greater cases of every church ought to be referred to him.
22. That the Roman church has never erred nor will ever err, as the Scripture bears witness.
23. That the Roman pontiff, if he has been canonically ordained, is indubitably made holy by the merits of the blessed Peter. . . .
24. That by his precept and license subjects are permitted to accuse their lords. . . .
27. That he can absolve the subjects of the unjust from their fealty.

From *Dictatus Papae Gregorii VII,* trans. by E. Lewis, *Medieval Political Ideas* (New York: Knopf, 1954), Vol. II, pp. 380–81.

Gregory's decree in 1059. A king might legitimately claim that he should have some influence in the choice of bishops, since they had secular as well as religious duties. But he could hardly justify a ceremony that suggested that he was bestowing spiritual authority on officials of the Church. Gregory, however, was seeking more than the abolition of an obnoxious ceremony. He was trying to end all forms of lay control over ecclesiastical appointments and so free the Church to exert its influence directly on all people in western Europe.

The attack on lay interference with ecclesiastical appointments plunged Gregory into a bitter struggle with the emperor Henry IV (1056–1106). Henry had had a difficult time asserting his authority in Germany; he had succeeded only because he controlled the resources of most of the bishoprics and abbeys of the country. Thus Gregory, by forbidding lay investiture, was in effect depriving Henry of the only means he had to preserve the unity and strengthen the central government of Germany.

Henry's reaction was violent and ill advised. He had just defeated a dangerous group of rebels in Saxony and was feeling both belligerent and overconfident. He denounced Gregory as an illegally elected pope and summoned a council of German bishops to depose him from the papal see. In a bitter letter announcing this decision to Gregory, Henry ended with the curse: "Down, down, to be damned through all the ages!" Gregory countered by excommunicating Henry and freeing his subjects from their oath of allegiance to him. "It is right," said Gregory, "that he who attempts to diminish the honor of the Church, shall himself lose the honor which he seems to have."

The issue was fairly joined. Now everything depended on the reaction of the bishops and princes of the Empire. Many of the German princes were delighted to have an excuse to resist Henry; the bishops, who owed their jobs to the king, were more loyal. The religious issue, in the end, brought the waverers over to Gregory's side, and an assembly of bishops and princes at Oppenheim in 1076 decided to depose Henry unless he was absolved by the pope.

Henry, headstrong but no fool, saw that he must make his peace with the pope. In wintry weather, he journeyed to Italy and came to Gregory at the castle of Canossa in 1077. This posed a difficult problem for Gregory; he had to wrestle with the conflict between his political aims and his spiritual duties. If he absolved Henry he would wreck the coalition supporting his German policies, but the head of the Church could scarcely reject a repentant sinner. In the end Gregory admitted Henry, accepted his promise to obey papal orders, and then granted him absolution.

In the short run Henry gained a political victory by his act of submission. As both he and Gregory had foreseen, the German princes felt that the pope had failed them; they could no longer oppose a king who had been reconciled with the Church. Henry regained much of his authority; he even became strong enough to invade Italy and force Gregory to take

Henry IV before journeying to Canossa. Miniature from an early–twelfth-century manuscript of the life of Countess Matilda of Tuscany. Henry, kneeling, asks Abbot Hugh of Cluny and Countess Matilda to intercede for him with Pope Gregory VII.

refuge with the Normans in the south. But in the long run the victory went to the papacy. The pope had demonstrated that he could force the most powerful ruler in the West to yield and that he could stir up rebellion against an anointed king. The lesson was not lost on western rulers; for two hundred years after Canossa few of them were willing to risk prolonged defiance of the pope.

The struggle over lay investiture persisted for a generation after Gregory's death in 1085. Henry was plagued by rebellions for the rest of his reign, through which his son, Henry V (1106–25), eventually came to power. Trouble continued under the younger Henry until at last a compromise was reached in the Concordat of Worms (1122) by which lay investiture in the strict sense was abandoned. The emperor could still nominate bishops, but the pope could refuse approval to men who were clearly unqualified and suspend or remove bishops who proved unworthy. In practice, this meant that the German bishops had to show a certain amount of obedience to the pope if they wanted to keep their positions. The German ruler, deprived of full control over the Church in his own country, lost his chief source of power and the independence of the German princes increased accordingly. Many of them had been sincere supporters of the reform movement, and most of them got along well with the bishops in their lands, so they were able to strengthen their governments as imperial authority waned.

Similar but less acute struggles took place in France and England. In neither country was the king as dependent on control over the Church as the German emperor had been, so it was easier to reach a settlement. The outcome was about the same: the pope admitted royal influence over appointments, but he remained the final judge of the qualifications of bishops. No one who offended the pope could hope to become or remain a bishop. Assured of administrative control of the Church, the pope could now insist that his policies be accepted throughout Europe. Acceptance was slow and grudging in some places, but it could never be entirely denied. The Church, far stronger and more independent than it had ever been before, had an unprecedented opportunity to guide and control European society.

The First Crusade

During the Investiture Conflict many barons and knights had supported the pope. The influence of the Church over the military class was further demonstrated by the First Crusade. A crusade was a military expedition organized by the pope to attack enemies of the Church. Earlier expeditions against the western Moslems had been encouraged by the pope in Italy and in Spain but these campaigns included only small groups of knights and were not fully under the control of the Church. By the end of the eleventh century, however, the papacy was stronger, and the military class was eager to prove its devotion to the faith.

The First Crusade was proclaimed by Pope Urban II at the Council of Clermont in 1095. He had many reasons for his action, and it is impossible to decide which was dominant. Urban had just reaffirmed the principles of the Peace of God, and he certainly believed that Europe would be more tranquil if the military classes turned their weapons against an outside foe instead of fighting one another. Moreover, the investiture struggle was still going on; if the pope could enlist large numbers of fighting men

Urban's Speech at Clermont 1095

I exhort you . . . to strive to expel that wicked race [the Turks] from our Christian lands. . . . Christ commands it. Remission of sins will be granted for those going thither. . . . Let those who are accustomed to wage private war wastefully even against believers go forth against the infidels. . . . Let those who have lived by plundering be soldiers of Christ; let those who formerly contended against brothers and relations rightly fight barbarians; let those who were recently hired for a few pieces of silver win their eternal reward. . . . The sorrowful here will be glad there, the poor here will be rich there, and the enemies of the Lord here will be His friends there. Let no delay postpone the journey . . . when winter has ended and spring has come . . . enter the highways courageously with the Lord going on before.

Adapted from Fulcher of Chartres, *History of Jerusalem,* trans. by M. E. McGinty (Philadelphia: University of Pennsylvania Press, 1941), p. 16. Fulcher was at Clermont and went on the First Crusade.

Capital in the Cathedral of St. Lazarus at Autun showing the flight into Egypt.

under his banner, it would demonstrate that he and not the emperor was the real leader of the West. Finally, the situation in the Near East seemed ripe for intervention. The Turks, who had come into Mesopotamia as mercenary soldiers of the caliphs, had crushed the Byzantine army at Manzikert (1071) and had occupied most of Asia Minor. The Byzantine Empire, in mortal peril, turned to the West for aid. At the same time Jerusalem had fallen to a fanatical Moslem dynasty that ruled from Cairo. Pilgrimage to the Holy City was now more difficult than it had been when Jerusalem was held by the tolerant Abbasid caliphs. A western army could strengthen Byzantium, and gratitude for its assistance might close the breach that had opened up between the Roman and Greek Churches since the controversy over iconoclasm and differences over the wording of the creed and the form of communion, which led to the mutual excommunication of pope and patriarch in 1054. The capture of Jerusalem would also make it easier for Christians to accomplish the most salutary of all pilgrimages, the visit to the Holy Sepulchre.

Urban's appeal for an army to fight the Turks and regain Jerusalem met with an astonishing response. The Count of Toulouse was the first to take the Cross, and he was soon joined by the Duke of Lorraine, four great lords from northern France, two Norman princes from southern Italy, and thousands of lesser men. The largest number of crusaders came from France and the German provinces near France, but all the countries of western Europe were represented in the undertaking. Nothing shows more clearly the strength of religious conviction and the effectiveness of the leadership of the Church. Some of the greater nobles may have thought of the crusade as an opportunity to acquire new lands; some knights may merely have been seeking adventure. But the majority of crusaders had purely religious motives. Urban had promised them full absolution for their sins and immediate entrance to heaven if they died fighting the infidels. So numerous were the volunteers that it took a year to organize the main armies; meanwhile thousands of noncombatant pilgrims, escorted by a few knights, set off for the East. Most of them were massacred by the Turks; only a few survived to join the armies that followed.

The crusaders' slogan was "God wills it!" Certainly it was a near miracle that they succeeded. Almost everything was against them: they knew nothing of the geography or politics of the East; they had little money and no supply services; they had no single commanding officer, and bitter feuds broke out among their leaders even before they entered Moslem lands. The Byzantine emperor, as soon as he found that he could not use them as mercenaries, grew suspicious of them; he wanted to reconquer Asia Minor, not go off on a harebrained raid on Jerusalem. That the crusaders overcame all these obstacles was due partly to their enthusiasm, and partly to the fact that the Turks were divided into many small principalities and were disliked by other Moslems. Moreover, the heavy-armed western cavalry was one of the best fighting forces on the Eurasian continent. The crusaders suffered severely from disease and starvation; they were battered in two hard-fought battles; they were weakened by continuing dissension among their leaders. But somehow they kept going. In 1099 they took Jerusalem and set up a series of crusading states stretching from Antioch in the north down through Tripoli and Jerusalem to the Dead Sea.

The dramatic success of the First Crusade reinforced the influence of the Church and strengthened the self-confidence of the peoples of western Europe. The many chronicles that describe the great campaign, though ascribing victory to God's protection, nevertheless show obvious pride in the crusaders' heroic deeds. But it would be a mistake to overemphasize the effects of the crusade; it was a result, not a cause, of the great medieval revival.

THE "RENAISSANCE OF THE TWELFTH CENTURY"

That revival continued without break into the twelfth century. Few periods in the history of the West have shown as much energy and originality. The men of the twelfth century not only continued the reform of ecclesiastical and secular government but also laid the foundations for a new architecture, a new literature, and a new system of education. All these activities drew on the Church for intellectual inspiration and material support, and in many of them churchmen played a leading role.

St. Bernard

The most powerful churchman of the early twelfth century was St. Bernard of Clairvaux (1090–1153). He was the first outstanding leader produced by the Cistercian Order, one of the very strict monastic groups founded toward the end of the eleventh century. Earlier reformers, such as the monks of Cluny, had aimed only at honest observance of the Benedictine Rule, but this was not enough for the new generation of religious leaders. The strong religious feeling that made possible the First Crusade also found expression in more ascetic forms of monastic life. The Cistercians refused to own serfs or revenue-producing properties and insisted on living in the wilderness by the labor of their own hands. In the end this uncompromising attitude gained them considerable wealth, for they had to develop new agricultural techniques, such as large-scale sheep raising, to make up for their lack of serfs. But in the early, heroic days the Cistercians attracted many able and zealous men by the example of their rigorous life.

St. Bernard, who entered the Cistercian order as a young man, was soon sent to found a new monastery at Clairvaux. Under his direction Clairvaux became a center of piety and asceticism. St. Bernard sought only to be a worthy abbot of this model monastery, but while he had no ambitions for himself, he had great zeal for the Church. Whenever he saw its unity threatened by schism or heresy, or its ideals menaced by worldly pressures and interests, he could not rest. Therefore this abbot, who wanted only a narrow cell in a secluded monastery, spent most of his life in public business, advising popes, giving lectures to kings, preaching to crowds, and writing letters to every prominent man in Europe.

From 1125 to the year of his death in 1153, St. Bernard dominated the West through his eloquence, his piety, and his boundless energy. His support saved causes that were tottering to failure; his opposition damned men who seemed born for success. In a disputed papal election in 1130, St. Bernard convinced the rulers of Europe that Innocent II should be recognized as the rightful pope, even though he had received fewer votes in the College of Cardinals than an opposing candidate. Innocent II was naturally influenced by St. Bernard, as was Pope Eugenius III (1145–53), who had been a monk at Clairvaux himself. When Eugenius inaugurated the Second Crusade in 1147 to regain some lost territories in Syria, he turned to St. Bernard for help in recruiting leaders for the campaign. St. Bernard did not disappoint the pope; he persuaded both the king of France and the emperor of Germany to take the Cross. When the Second Crusade failed, St. Bernard wrote the official apology ascribing the debacle to the sins of the Christians.

St. Bernard was in many ways a conservative man. He disliked the new architecture of the twelfth century; costly churches seemed to him unnecessary for the worship of God and a waste of money that might better be given to the poor. He disliked the new learning, which exalted human reason and led men to think that they could approach God through logic rather than through faith. He worried about the growing bureaucracy at the papal court, even though he realized it was essential to the unity of the Church and the authority of the pope.

Cistercian monks shown living by their own labor. Detail from a manuscript of St. Gregory's *Moralia in Job,* written at the motherhouse of Cîteaux in the twelfth century.

But although he was a conservative in worldly matters, St. Bernard was an innovator in religion. He was a leader of the new piety, the movement to humanize Christianity and Christianize human life. He emphasized devotion to the Virgin and dwelt on the life of Jesus on earth. As Dante was to point out, the central theme in St. Bernard's teaching was love, the love of God for man and the love that man should have for God. He talked more of the joys of heaven than of the pains of hell. He was saddened and angered by those who rejected the love and mercy of God, but he always hoped to save the sinners he de-

Left: barrel vault, church of St. Savin (eleventh century). Although no light could be admitted in the upper part of the nave, the vault could be covered with fine Romanesque painting. Center: groin vault, formed by the intersection of two barrel vaults, Mont-Saint-Michel (twelfth century). The walls could now be pierced with windows. Right: rib vault, Mont-Saint-Michel (late Romanesque). Ribs made it easier to design and build a groin vault, but the effect is still heavy.

nounced. In all this he gave a lead to his contemporaries. The number of churches dedicated to the Virgin increased sharply, more emphasis was placed on the Nativity and the childhood of Jesus, and hope of salvation began to outweigh fear of damnation. In many ways the twelfth century was an age of optimism, an optimism that was reflected in its religion as well as in its secular activities.

Abbot Suger and Gothic Architecture

Another great abbot, second only to St. Bernard in influence, was Suger of St. Denis (*ca.* 1091–1152). The son of poor peasants, he had been given to the monastery by his parents when only a child. Sheer ability carried him to the position of abbot, an outstanding example of the opportunities the Church offered to men of low birth. St. Denis was one of the wealthiest monasteries in France as well as the burial place of the French kings. Suger was thus closely associated with the royal house, and his administrative ability made him a close adviser of two kings, Louis VI and Louis VII. During the absence of Louis VII on the Second Crusade, Suger acted as regent of France; he was remarkably successful in preserving both the stability and the solvency of the realm.

Suger was more than a successful administrator, however. He wrote several books, including an interesting biography of Louis VI. But his overwhelming interest was the rebuilding of the church of St. Denis, which he was determined to make the most beautiful church in France, the "crown of the kingdom." St. Bernard was suspicious of this desire for magnificence, as he was of Suger's involvement in worldly business, but the abbot of St. Denis had tact as well as energy. By giving his full support to the Cistercian's reform policy, he conciliated St. Bernard and gained a free hand for his own activities.

Suger wanted his church to be full of light and color. He had enough money to do as he wished and a remarkable willingness to experiment with new ideas. Workmen flocked to St. Denis from all over France, bringing with them solutions to problems of church architecture that had been worked out in the last half-century. The result was a church that, for the first time, incorporated all the essential elements of the Gothic style.

From 1000 on there had been a great wave of church building in western Europe. The basic plan was still that of the old basilica, a long nave with lower side aisles and a transept crossing the nave before the altar. At first the churches were low and dark, with strong emphasis on horizontal lines. Then experiments

St. Bernard on Love

First, then, a man loves his own self for self's sake, since he is flesh, and he cannot have any taste except for things in relation with him; but when he sees that he is not able to subsist by himself, that God is, as it were, necessary to him, he begins to inquire and to love God by faith. Thus he loves God in the second place, but because of his own interest, and not for the sake of God Himself. But when, on account of his own necessity, he has begun to worship Him and to approach Him by meditation, by reading, by prayer, by obedience, he comes little by little to know God with a certain familiarity, and in consequence to find Him sweet and kind; and thus having tasted how sweet the Lord is, he passes to the third stage, and thus loves God no longer on account of his own interest, but for the sake of God himself. Once arrived there, he remains stationary, and I know not if in this life man is truly able to rise to the fourth degree, which is, no longer to love himself except for the sake of God. . . .

From *Some Letters of Saint Bernard,* trans. by S. J. Eales (London: Hodges, 1904), pp. 202–03.

were made in raising the walls and enlarging the windows. For example, architects discovered that a pointed arch over a window increased the area that could be glazed. There had also been some use of stained glass.

But the most important innovations had to do with the vaulting of the interior roof of churches. The flat wooden roofs of the early Roman churches were not very satisfactory in the wet, cold climate of the north. A stone vault covered by a steep-sloped roof would be far more satisfactory in keeping out the weather and reducing the danger of fire. But it took generations for architects to devise the best way of covering the great open spaces of a church with a stone vault. The first and easiest solution was the barrel vault, a continuous semicircular arch extending the entire length of the church. But this scheme was not particu-

Left: early Gothic rib vault, Mont-Saint-Michel. Greater height and light are now being exploited. Right: rib vaulting on a grand scale, the nave of Chartres Cathedral (1194–1220). Great height and light have been achieved; the upper (clerestory) windows are larger and more useful than those at floor level.

larly safe when used for very wide areas. Moreover, because the barrel vault put an equal strain on every part of the side walls, it made the use of large windows impossible, since any substantial cutting into the walls would weaken the whole structure. Then architects hit on the idea of designing a roof as if it were the intersection of two barrel vaults, in that way concentrating the downward and outward thrust of the roof at a few points along the wall, which in turn could be strengthened by pillars, or piers, and buttresses. Now the walls could be pierced with large, high windows, flooding the church with light. The final refinement was to mark the lines of the intersecting vaults with stone ribs, thus both strengthening and improving the appearance of the roof.

The churches of the eleventh and early twelfth centuries were larger and more beautiful than any that had been built before in the north, but no single church embodied all these innovations. They still adhered more or less to the old, or Romanesque, style. But the massive Romanesque churches, impressive and beautiful as they were, did not satisfy many churchmen of the twelfth century. They wanted a style that reflected their new aspirations, something less practical and earthbound, something that symbolized the mystery and splendor of heaven.

Suger felt these longings with particular keenness, and it was under his direction in the church of St. Denis that the decisive step was taken in the evolution of the new style. Suger used almost all the new ideas: pointed arches, rib vaults, larger and higher windows, and stained glass. He described the result in one of his verses: "Bright is the noble building which is pervaded by the new light." Churches were built near Paris along the same principles, and the new Gothic style soon became the standard for church architecture. Southern France, Germany, and Italy clung for some time to Romanesque, but by the early years of the thirteenth century, Gothic was triumphing in those areas as well.

Abelard

A third great figure of the early twelfth-century revival, Abelard (*ca.* 1079–1142), was also an abbot, but an unwilling and unhappy one. The son of a minor vassal in Brittany, he had, like many other men of the twelfth century, become inflamed with the love of learning. About 1100, he renounced his inheritance and went to study at Paris.

Paris was full of famous teachers, though there was as yet no formal curriculum. The growing horde of students had overflowed the old cathedral school on the Île de la Cité, and lectures were already being given on the Left Bank in what was to become the Latin Quarter. This new enthusiasm for learning resembled in some ways the new piety; scholars were examining old texts that had been known for centuries and were discovering in them fresh meanings and personal applications. The learning of the Moslem-Byzantine world had not yet entered Europe, but students were finding a new excitement in the old books.

Abelard's first love, like that of many of his contemporaries, was logic. He mastered all the available material in a remarkably short time and immediately set himself up as a teacher, much to the annoyance of some of his former professors. Abelard thoroughly enjoyed teaching logic, but, again like many of his contemporaries, he saw in it more than a formal intellectual exercise. He was convinced that it was a universal tool (somewhat like mathematics today) that could be used to solve old problems and acquire new knowledge. To a man of his time, the most important problems were theological, so he decided to become a master of theology as well as logic. Again he completed his studies in record time and began to steal students from, and contradict, his old teachers.

Abelard was a great teacher and scholar; he was also a very brash young man. For example, he produced an exercise book for his students called *Sic et Non* (*Yes and No*), in which he marshaled opinions from the Bible and the Church Fathers on both sides of controversial questions. It took considerable ingenuity to find support for some of his statements—for example, that God is threefold and the contrary; that sin is pleasing to God and the contrary—and his cleverness added to the jealousy of some of his contemporaries. The prologue to the book made it seem even more dangerous, for here Abelard announced: "The first key to wisdom is this . . . industrious and repeated inquiry. . . . For through doubting we come to inquiry and through inquiry we discover the truth." Abelard also wrote a treatise on the Trinity in which he tried to define the attributes of each Person by a rigorous use of logic. This meddling with the central mystery of the faith shocked St. Bernard, who in one of his angriest letters denounced Abelard as a writer who sought to place "degrees in the Trinity, modes in the Majesty, numbers in the Eternity." St. Bernard felt that God was too great to be defined by the human mind and that all the virtue went out of faith when it was made to seem too rational.

Abelard's personal life increased his reputation for vanity and presumption. His downfall began when he seduced Héloïse, the niece of a canon of the cathedral of Paris. The affair could not be hushed up, for his love poems had been circulated throughout the city, and Héloïse had a child. The girl's uncle was, naturally, furious and put such pressure on Abelard that he agreed to marry Héloïse, provided that the marriage were kept secret. This was not one of Abelard's most brilliant ideas; there had to be witnesses to the marriage, and the witnesses talked. Héloïse had argued against the marriage because it would block Abelard's chance of promotion in the Church and would lessen his reputation as a philosopher, a man who should be above earthly pleasures and cares. When rumors about the marriage spread, Héloïse denied that they were true. Abelard was even more perturbed, and considerably less self-sacrificing. He persuaded Héloïse to take refuge in a nunnery, an act that looked suspiciously like an attempt to dissolve the marriage. The uncle, angrier than ever, hired a gang of thugs to castrate the scholar. The scandal was so enormous that Abelard temporarily retired from teaching and became a monk in St. Denis.

St. Denis was not a very lively place (this was just before Suger became abbot), but Abelard managed to stir things up. He criticized some of the legends about the monastery's patron saint and denounced the scandalous life of the monks. He was right on both points, as he often was, but he was thoroughly disliked by his companions. At the same time he wrote a treatise on the Trinity that was condemned and burned at the Council of Soissons (1120). It was clearly impossible for Abelard to stay at St. Denis; Suger (now abbot) gave him permission to live elsewhere. He established an oratory in the wilderness (later given to Héloïse as the foundation of a new nunnery), and then became abbot of a remote Breton monastery. He found the monks there brutal (they threatened his life), ignorant and entirely unwilling to follow any monastic rule. Abelard finally

Abelard on Scholarship

. . . Investigation is the first key to wisdom: it is the kind of industrious and repeated inquiry which Aristotle, the wisest of all philosophers recommended to his students in saying: "It is difficult to solve problems with confidence unless they have been frequently discussed. It is not useless to express doubts about some matters." For through doubting we come to inquiry and through inquiry we discover the truth, as Truth Himself said: "Seek and you will find, knock and the door will be opened to you."

St. Bernard on Abelard

We have in France an old teacher turned into a new theologian, who in his early days amused himself with logic and who now gives utterance to wild imaginations upon the Holy Scriptures. . . .

There is nothing in heaven above nor in the earth below which he deigns to confess ignorance of: he raises his eyes to heaven and searches the deep things of God and . . . brings back unspeakable words which it is not lawful for a man to utter. He is ready to give a reason for everything, even for those things that are above reason. Thus he presumes against reason and against faith. For what is more unreasonable than to attempt to go beyond the limits of reason? And what is more against faith than to be unwilling to believe what cannot be proved by reason? . . .

And so he promises understanding to his hearers, even on those most sublime and sacred truths that are hidden in the very bosom of our holy faith. He places degrees in the Trinity, modes in the Majesty, numbers in the Eternity. . . . Who can endure this? . . . Who does not shudder at such new-fangled profanities?

Translated from *Sic et Non,* ed. by V. Cousin, *Ouvrages inédits d'Abélard* (Paris: Imprimerie royale, 1836), p. 104; translated from *Patrologia latina,* Vol. 182, cols. 1055–56.

abandoned his post and returned to the neighborhood of Paris, where he began to teach again. As usual, he drew crowds of students, but he had changed neither his methods nor his opinions. His enemies, led by St. Bernard, found his success unendurable. His writings on the Trinity were again condemned by a local council (Sens, 1140). Abelard appealed to the pope, but fell ill on his way to Rome. He took refuge at Cluny, where Peter the Venerable let him live in peace until his death in 1142.

Abelard's real fault was vanity, not impiety; he had sought to make Christian doctrine more precise, but not to contradict it. He was only the most conspicuous of many scholars who were trying to combine logic, philosophy, and theology in an effort to give Christian doctrine a more rigorous intellectual structure. St. Bernard, who was a mystic rather than a scholar, was perhaps right in feeling that excessive rationalism would weaken the appeal of religion. But he was fighting a losing battle; the future belonged to men who followed Abelard's methods. For the rest of the Middle Ages, theology was studied according to the rules of formal logic, and authorities were cited on both sides of every question in order to reach a final, and orthodox, answer. The most popular theological book of the twelfth century, Peter Lombard's *Sentences,* resembled Abelard's work far more than it did that of St. Bernard. The system used by Abelard, Peter Lombard, and others eventually became known as "scholasticism," and scholastic methods dominated European thought for the next three centuries.

The Beginnings of Universities

Exciting as theology was, it did not monopolize the attention of twelfth-century scholars. A revival of interest in the Latin classics, especially noticeable in the scholars who congregated at Chartres, led to a marked improvement in Latin style. John of Salisbury (d. 1180), who wrote one of the first medieval treatises on political theory, had had some connection with these scholars and eventually became bishop of Chartres. A growing interest in medicine, centered at Salerno in southern Italy, prompted the study of old Roman textbooks and the new observations of Arab doctors. But theology's real rival was law, and in the long run students of law became far more numerous than students of theology.

Although Roman law had not been completely forgotten during the early Middle Ages, it had been little studied, and most of the copies of Justinian's *Corpus Juris* had disappeared. At the end of the eleventh century there was a revival of interest in Roman law, especially in Italy and southern France. The first great teacher, Irnerius, attracted so many students to his school at Bologna that the city became, and remained for centuries, the chief center of legal studies in Europe. Roman law appealed to students for many reasons: it was a fine example of logical and precise reasoning; it was part of the intellectual legacy of Rome; it gave intelligent answers to problems of human relations that the unsophisticated customary law of medieval Europe had scarcely considered. The Romans had been the most legal-minded people of antiquity, and western Europeans had inherited their fondness for law. The *Corpus Juris,* which summed up the work of generations of Roman lawyers in fairly compact form, could be mastered by students within a reasonable length of time. And a young man soundly trained in

Roman law could look forward to a brilliant career; by the middle of the century legal training had become the surest route to promotion in the service of popes and kings. The number of law students who flocked to Bologna from the most distant parts of the Continent increased steadily during the twelfth century.

A special branch of legal studies was canon law, the law of the Church. The Church, of course, had relied heavily on Roman law in formulating its basic rules and procedures, but it had to cope with many problems that Roman law had never touched—for example, the forms to be followed in choosing a bishop, or the requirements for a valid Christian marriage. In deciding these questions the Church relied on the writings of the Fathers, decrees of councils, and administrative and judicial rulings of the popes. Some collections of this scattered material had been made, but none of them enjoyed unquestioned authority. Then about 1140 the monk Gratian produced his *Decretum,* or *Concordance of Discordant Canons,* which was rapidly accepted as the definitive treatise on canon law. Gratian, following the pattern already set by earlier students of canon law, quoted the authorities on both sides of each question and then (quite compatible with the methods of Abelard and other theologians) gave what seemed to him the approved solution. Since Gratian taught at Bologna, students went there to study canon law as well as Roman law, and soon there was a large group of experts on the subject. Canon law, even more than Roman law, opened the road to high office, in this case high office in the Church. Many bishops and almost all the popes from 1159 to the end of the fourteenth century were students of canon law.

These groupings of students and teachers at centers like Paris and Bologna eventually coalesced into universities, one of the most significant institutional legacies of the Middle Ages. The best of the cathedral schools, such as Paris, had some degree of organization before 1150, but not all schools were cathedral schools, and even the cathedral schools needed a stronger structure and more powers of regulation. The many foreign students at Bologna, for example, felt that they were being cheated by the Italian boardinghouse keepers, and sometimes by their professors as well. They formed a union to keep down the price of food and lodging and to make sure that teachers covered an adequate amount of material in their lecture courses. At Paris the chief problem, illustrated by Abelard's career, was to determine at what point a student was entitled to set himself up as a teacher. The bishops, or their chancellors, who were supposed to license teachers, had neither the knowledge nor the time to deal with the growing number of applicants. So in Paris the teachers themselves formed a union, to which they admitted only students who had passed a rigorous examination. It was out of these unions of students and teachers that the university was to emerge.

The intellectual interests that created the first universities were the most striking manifestations of the new vigor of western European society. The people of western Europe had not yet equaled the Romans in the arts of government, and they perhaps had done no more than equal the Romans in total economic production. But they had an intellectual curiosity, an urge to acquire new ideas, that the Romans of the Empire had never possessed. And in the long run this curiosity and drive were to lead to the revival of science and the transformation of European society.

The Revival of Roman Law

Three times has Rome given her laws to the world, three times has she bound different peoples together: first, by the unity of the state, when the Roman people stood at the height of their strength, second, by the unity of the Church after the Empire had fallen, and third, by the unity of law when Roman Law was accepted during the Middle Ages. The first victory was won by force of arms, but the other two by the power of the mind. . . . Roman Law, like Christianity, has become an essential element of modern civilization.

From Rudolph von Jhering, *Geist des römischen Rechts* (Leipzig: Breitkopf und Härtel, 1907), Vol. I, p. 1.

Suggestions for Further Reading

Note: Asterisk denotes a book available in paperback edition.

Economic Revival

Carlo Cipolla, *Before the Industrial Revolution,** is the best overall survey. N. Neilson, *Medieval Agrarian Economy* (1976), and Marc Bloch, *French Rural Society* (1966), are good brief accounts. The first three volumes of the *Cambridge Economic History of Europe,* ed. by M. M. Postan (1952–66), contain excellent articles on medieval agriculture, commerce, and industry. (Be sure to get the second, much improved, edition of Vol. I.) There is good source material on the revival of medieval trade in R. S. Lopez and I. W. Raymond, *Medieval Trade in the Mediterranean World** (1955). A useful short survey is R. Latouche, *The Birth of the Western Economy** (1961). Frederic Lane, *Venice, A Maritime Republic* (1973), is the best account of the rise of a great trading city. For England, see R. Lennard, *Rural England* (1959). The effect of the Moslem control of the Mediterranean on European economy is discussed by H. Pirenne, *Economic and Social History of Medieval Europe** (1937), with special attention to the economic activity of Italy and the Low Countries. H. F. Brown, *Venice: An Historical Sketch of the Republic* (1895), is the best one-volume study in English of that important commercial center. G. Duby, *Rural Economy and Country Life in the Medieval West* (1968), is the best overall study of rural life. E. Power, *Medieval People** (1954), gives a vivid picture of social and manorial life from the point of view of individuals. F. Rörig, *The Medieval Town** (1967), and M. M. Postan, *The Medieval Economy** (1972), are very good on towns. Both C. Stephenson, *Borough and Town* (1933), and J. Tait, *The Medieval English Borough* (1936), are scholarly studies of town development in England with opposing interpretations on the origins of towns. For source material, see J. H. Mundy and P. Riesenberg, *The Medieval Town* (1958).

Political Revival

There are many valuable works on the political history of this period. C. Petit-Dutaillis, *Feudal Monarchy in France and England* * (1936), discusses the preservation and development of the monarchy in France and England from the tenth to the thirteenth century. An excellent brief study of the growth of royal power in France is R. Fawtier, *The Capetian Kings of France,** trans. by L. Butler (1960). The older study of E. Lavisse, ed., *Histoire de France,* Vol. II, Part 2 (1901), which reviews economic, social, and cultural phenomena as well as political, has not been surpassed for comprehensiveness.

Medieval Germany, Vol. I, articles trans. by G. Barraclough (1938), has good material on Germany in this period, and G. Barraclough, *The Origins of Modern Germany* (1947), analyzes the reasons why Germany lagged behind the rest of Europe in the development of political institutions.

We have interesting evidence on England at this time in the contemporary Ordericus Vitalis, *History of England and Normandy,* trans. by Marjorie Chibnall (1969), and in William of Malmesbury, *Chronicle,* trans. by J. A. Giles (1847), which gives attention to both political and religious developments. Both histories go up to 1154. F. W. Maitland, *Domesday Book and Beyond** (1897), is a monument in historical prose writing. The best scholarly treatment of the establishment of Norman feudalism in England is F. M. Stenton, *First Century of English Feudalism* (1932). D. C. Douglas, *William the Conqueror* (1964), is an excellent biography.

C. H. Haskins, *The Normans in European History** (1915), shows the Normans as founders and organizers of states. More recent works on this subject are D. C. Douglas, *The Norman Achievement* (1969) and *The Norman Fate* (1976). See also J. Le Patourel, *The Norman Empire* (1976). Political developments in Italy are discussed by P. Villari, *Medieval Italy from Charlemagne to Henry VII* (1910), a broad readable survey. C. Cahen, *Le Régime féodal de l'Italie normande* (1940), is a critical study of Norman institutions in Italy. An older but still useful book is E. Curtis, *Roger of Sicily and the Normans in Italy* (1912).

Religious Revival

Since the impetus for the religious revival of the eleventh century was the monastery at Cluny, J. Evans, *Monastic Life at Cluny* (1931), is a good starting point for study. L. M. Smith, *Cluny in the Eleventh and Twelfth Centuries* (1930), is a valuable if somewhat disjointed study of the influence of Cluny on the religious life of Europe, while D. Knowles, *The Monastic Order in England* (1951), is a thorough and readable study of almost every facet of English monastic life from 900 to 1215.

A good overall account is R. W. Southern, *Western Society and the Church** (1976). There is interesting source material on the Investiture Conflict in B. Tierney, *The Crisis of Church and State** (1964), and in K. Morrison, *The Investiture Controversy* (1971). A. J. Macdonald, *Hildebrand: A Life of Gregory VII* (1932), is a good brief biography. The *Correspondence of Gregory VII,* trans. by E. Emerton (1932), contains information not only on the problem of investiture but on the increase in papal activities under Gregory. The excellent book by G. Tellenbach, *Church, State, and Christian Society at the Time of the Investiture Controversy* (1940), shows the conflict as a papal attempt to revalue Christian society in the light of canon law. The consequences for the Church and the state are carefully analyzed by N. F. Cantor, *Church, Kingship and Lay Investiture in England, 1089–1135* (1959), a very scholarly study. W. Ullmann, *Growth of Papal Power in the Middle Ages* (1955), treats the effect of the controversy on the growth of the papal government.

The First Crusade

A. C. Krey, *The First Crusade* (1921), gives a very good picture of the crusade from the accounts of eyewitnesses and participants. One of the best chronicles of the crusade is Fulcher of Chartres' *History of the Expedition to Jerusalem,** ed. by H. S. Fink (1973). *The Alexiad of Anna Comnena,* trans. by E. A. S. Dawes (1928) and by E. R. A. Sewter (1969), contains the Byzantine attitude toward the crusade, and Usāmah ibn Munqhid, *An Arab-Syrian Gentleman and Warrior in the Period of the Crusades,* trans. by P. K. Hitti (1929), gives the Moslem point of view. A better, updated book on the crusade is the fascinating account of S. Runciman, *A History of the Crusades,** Vol. I (1951). Runciman includes a thorough bibliography. M. L. W. Baldwin, ed., *The First Hundred Years* (1955) (Vol. I of *A History of the Crusades,* ed. by K. M. Setton), is a collection of essays by leading historians of the crusades. The establishment of feudalism in the conquered East is treated by J. L. La Monte, *Feudal Monarchy in the Latin Kingdom of Jerusalem* (1932). H. E. Mayer, *The Crusades* (1972), is a good short synthesis of the whole movement.

The Renaissance of the Twelfth Century

The best general study of the revival of learning in the West is C. H. Haskins, *The Renaissance of the Twelfth Century** (1927), which discusses scholarship, Roman law, and philosophy, and has a good critical bibliography. Another excellent book is C. Brooke, *The Twelfth Century Renaissance** (1969). H. O. Taylor, *The Medieval Mind,* Vol. I (1953), has good material on intellectual developments in the twelfth century, and R. W. Southern, *The Making of the Middle Ages** (1953), presents an excellent account of the influence of the new piety on cultural growth. His *Medieval Humanism and Other Studies* (1976) is even more useful. There is a good cross section of the poetry of the period from 900 to 1160 in H. Waddell, *Medieval Latin Lyrics** (1929). C. J. Webb, *John of Salisbury* (1932), deals with the leading humanist of the period.

St. Bernard, Suger, and Abelard

There is a wealth of material on these three men, who to a great extent dominated the intellectual life of the first half of the twelfth century. *St. Bernard of Clairvaux,* trans. by G. Webb and A. Walker (1960), is an interesting biography written by Bernard's friend William of St. Thierry. Bernard's relations with political and intellectual leaders of his time are presented in *The Letters of St. Bernard,* trans. by S. J. Eales (1904). E. Gilson, *The Mystical Theology of St. Bernard* (1940), stresses Bernard's thought. B. S. James, *St. Bernard of Clairvaux* (1957), focuses attention on Bernard the man.

Suger on the Abbey of St. Denis, trans. by E. Panofsky (1946), is a mine of information about the beginnings of Gothic architecture and about monastic government and life. Panofsky's introduction has a good brief biography of Suger. K. J. Conant, *Carolingian and Romanesque Architecture** (1959), gives the background out of which the new architecture developed.

The best serious study of Abelard is E. Gilson, *Heloise and Abelard** (1948). H. Waddell's novel *Peter Abelard** (1959) gives a good picture of twelfth-century intellectual activity based on sound scholarship. *Abelard's Letters* were translated by C. K. Scott-Moncrieff (1926). B. Radice, *The Letters of Abelard and Héloïse* (1976), is a more recent and in some ways a more satisfactory version.

11 Medieval Civilization at Its Height

After 1150 western Europe began to cash in on the pioneer work of the tenth and eleventh centuries. The steady increase in population, production, and trade brought increasing prosperity. The peasants embarked on a great migration to new lands, comparable only to the nineteenth-century movement to the New World. Forests were cleared in England, France, and western Germany; marshes were drained and walled off from the sea in the Netherlands. In the biggest shift of all, migration toward the East, the Germans filled up the land between the Elbe and the Oder and settled large areas of western Poland, eastern Prussia, and Bohemia. This drive to the East almost doubled the size of medieval Germany. It also set the stage for the contending nationalisms of modern times, for the Slavs remained numerous in Bohemia and the lands beyond the Oder, which meant that many German settlements were surrounded by Slavic populations.

TOWNS AND TRADE

Atlantic and Baltic trade grew steadily during the twelfth century. German merchants, who dominated Baltic commerce, pushed their outposts to Riga and to Novgorod in Russia. They dealt in furs, timber, and other bulky commodities that returned only a small profit per ton. Atlantic trade, in wool from England and in salt and wine from ports in the Bay of Biscay, was also only moderately profitable. Most of these goods were carried by German and French vessels; the English had little shipping and could not even move their own wool overseas. This northern trade brought modest prosperity to such towns as Lübeck in Germany and Bordeaux in France.

The really profitable trade, however, was still the trade in Oriental goods. Italian towns, especially Venice, Genoa, and Pisa, had by far the largest share of this lucrative business. Their fleets made regular voyages each year to Constantinople, Alexandria, and Acre to bring back incense, spices, and silk. By the end of the twelfth century these fleets were large enough to move whole armies. Crusaders no longer had to take the long and dangerous overland route; they simply hired ships.

It was not until the second half of the thirteenth century that the Genoese and the Venetians began to make regular voyages through the Strait of Gibraltar to England and the Netherlands. Even then, most of their goods were sent north across the Alps by pack-train. The steady stream of merchants along this route stimulated the growth of the towns of the Po Valley, southern France, and southern Germany. It also stimulated the development of the fairs of Champagne, which became the central market for all western Europe. Champagne lay across the river valleys leading south to the Mediterranean and north to Paris, the English Channel, and western Germany. The counts of Champagne were wise enough to encourage commerce and strong enough to protect the wandering merchants. At the fairs of Champagne, textiles and wool from the north were exchanged for Oriental goods from the south. Merchants gradually developed the practice of settling their yearly accounts when they met in Champagne, thus making the fairs the money market as well as the commodity market of the West.

By the end of the twelfth century no one could deny any longer that businessmen were entitled to special status. Personal freedom and some degree of local autonomy made the townsmen a privileged class—not so privileged as the clergy and nobles, but still well above the peasants. As a privileged class they began to be accorded a special name—*bürger* in Germany, *burgesses* in England, and *bourgeois* in France, whence the collective term, *bourgeoisie.** Most townsmen were satisfied with this special status; only in the greatest cities could they dream of full independence, and only in Italy did they have much hope of getting it. But the old hostilities still ran deep. The bourgeoisie still distrusted the nobility and criticized the clergy, who in turn still suspected the bourgeoisie of harboring

*All these terms are derived from the German word *burg,* which meant first "fort" and then "walled town." Walls were the symbol of a town's autonomy.

Opposite: The rose window of Amiens Cathedral (thirteenth century).

GERMAN EXPANSION TO THE EAST 800–1400

dangerous ideas about religion and the social order. A twelfth-century clergyman could still speak of free towns as *tumor plebis, timor regis*—a cancer of the people, a threat to the king.

Bankers and Moneylenders

The growth of banking and moneylending strengthened this hostility. The great international merchants, and the money changers who served them, had become expert at transferring funds from one region to another and had also accumulated surplus capital. They gradually began to act as bankers who received deposits, paid out money on order, and made loans. Kings and popes called on them when, for example, they wanted to transfer money to the East to pay for crusades. And bishops and abbots, lords and knights, all borrowed money from the bankers to pay for their steadily rising living standards. But as a result of all these transactions the bourgeoisie seemed to be profiting at the expense of the clergy and the nobility. Even kings had to pay a high rate of interest on loans—8 to 10 percent for a ruler with as good a reputation for financial integrity as Saint Louis of France—and lesser folk paid more. When the day of reckoning came, the borrowers often had a hard time repaying their loans: kings had to impose new taxes on their subjects; barons had to sell their lands; churches had to melt down their altar vessels. Bankers were generally unpopular, for they seemed to be thriving on the misfortunes of their fellow Christians.

Artisans, Gilds, and the Proletariat

Most townsmen were not bankers or international merchants but small shopkeepers with purely local trade. Butchers, bakers, and the like profited little from the growth of international commerce. The same was true of many artisans in the metal industries. And even artisans who produced goods for a wider market had to rely on international merchants to distribute their wares to get a share of the profits. Many workers in the textile industry were only subcontractors, dependent on merchants for raw materials and for markets. A Flemish weaver in Ghent, for example, could not import his raw wool directly from England; he had to obtain it from a merchant. When his cloth was finished, he could not carry it to the fairs of Champagne or the ports of Italy; he had to sell it at a low price to a merchant who knew the markets and the trade routes and who was willing to assume the risks of distribution. The position of such workers was precarious and they often suffered prolonged unemployment. For the first time since the fall of the Roman Empire an urban proletariat began to appear in the countries of western Europe.

It was during the twelfth century that townsmen began to organize themselves into occupational groups. The men within each trade or craft naturally saw a good deal of one another and felt that they had common interests to defend against outsiders. They often had a code prescribing standards of good workmanship, and they were determined to see that these standards were maintained. And so they formed associations, called gilds in England, to pursue their common objectives. The gild contributed to the local church that honored its patron saint, and it acted as a mutual benefit society for the families of its members. Often, all the members of a gild lived in the same quarter of the town. Gilds also tried to enforce regulations barring strangers and untrained men from their craft and forbidding careless or dishonest production. The gild was usually dominated by its most experienced members, the master workmen, who owned their own shops and equipment. Under them were the journeymen, who worked for daily wages, and under them the apprentices, who were boys learning the trade. In the thirteenth century, when most journeymen could hope to become masters themselves one day, there was little friction among these groups.

There was considerably more friction among the gilds themselves, including all the jurisdictional disputes that we find among trade unions today. For example, the harness of a horse contains both metal and leather: should it be made by leather workers, metal workers, or both? There was also a good deal of jockeying for political advantage. Strong gilds tended to take over the control of town governments, and often the larger gilds would line up against the smaller ones, or the wealthy gilds against the poor.

To escape such controversies and to protect themselves from the excessive power of the gilds, many lords refused to allow gilds to be established in their towns. But the advantages of some sort of trade organization were so obvious that the lords usually created similar, but looser, associations under their own control, keeping the same regulations on production and the same division of workers into the three groups of masters, journeymen, and apprentices.

In the long run, the division between the urban rich and the urban poor sharpened into political conflict and even armed rebellion. But during the first part of the thirteenth century the people of most towns remained fairly well united. Still rather insecure in a society that originally had had no place for them, they feared outside oppressors more than internal exploiters. Only when the bourgeoisie began to feel reasonably secure did internal differences break out into open feuds.

LITERATURE AND ART

The general prosperity of the period was reflected in a burst of artistic and literary activity. Wealth does not necessarily produce great art, but it certainly increases the opportunities open to artists. Vast sums of money were needed to build a Gothic cathedral, and more cathedrals were built in the late twelfth and thirteenth centuries than at any other time in European history. This money did not all come from the Church; kings and feudal lords made large contributions, as did the people of cathedral cities. In fact, there seems to have been a good deal of civic rivalry: if one town

Money changers are portrayed in this stained-glass window at Le Mans Cathedral (thirteenth century).

erected a handsome new cathedral, its neighbors strove to surpass it. The classic example is Beauvais, whose residents decided that they would build the loftiest cathedral in France. The technical difficulties were great—the vaults collapsed twice—and by the time they were overcome, money and enthusiasm were running out. So the cathedral of Beauvais stands today still unfinished, with almost no nave. But it does have the greatest interior height of any church built during the period.

Gothic Art

As the example of Beauvais shows, the architects of the day were trying to exploit all the possibilities of the new Gothic style. They strove for greater height and more light by emphasizing vertical lines and making their windows larger and larger. In a small church like the Sainte-Chapelle in Paris they were able to build the walls almost entirely of magnificent stained glass, supported by a few slender pillars. Even in the larger churches there was far more glass than stone at the upper (clerestory) level.

The portals of Gothic churches were filled with hundreds of statues of Christ, the Virgin, the apostles, and the saints. The windows all had a story to tell or a moral to point. There was a strong tendency toward allegory and symbolism; thus at Chartres the continuity between the Old and New Testaments is illustrated by windows in which a prophet carries an evangelist on his shoulders. But there was also a tendency toward realism in Gothic art, a tendency that appears even in the twelfth century in some of the floral decorations. This tendency grew stronger during the thirteenth century, preparing the way for the very realistic art of northern Europe in the fifteenth century.

Technically, Amiens is perhaps the most perfect Gothic cathedral of all—the cathedral in which all problems were solved successfully. But many critics prefer the massive solidity of Notre Dame of Paris or the less uniform but more interesting cathedral of Chartres,

Two representations of the Visitation. Left: Romanesque façade of the abbey church of St. Pierre at Moissac (twelfth century). Right: Gothic façade of Reims Cathedral (late thirteenth century). The Romanesque work is linear and heavily stylized, like a manuscript illustration. The Gothic sculpture is more naturalistic.

with its glorious stained glass. As the Gothic style spread to England, Germany, and other countries, it produced remarkable buildings, not entirely like the French, but beautiful in their own right. Only in Italy was Gothic a relative failure. The commercially minded Italians were less willing to spend money on their churches, and they were so imbued with Roman traditions that they never really understood the basic principles of the Gothic style.

Histories and Vernacular Literature

The great period of cathedral building was also a period of intense literary activity. We shall return to the work of scholars writing in Latin and mention only one of their activities here—the writing of history. Western Europeans had always been interested in historical narratives, partly because they had inherited this tradition from Rome, partly because the Christian religion puts strong emphasis on the way in which God's plans are worked out through history. There had always been chronicles, but never before had they been as numerous or as well written as they were after 1150. Kings began to patronize writers who would glorify their deeds and justify their policies—writers like Otto of Freising in Germany, Guillaume le Breton in France, and the St. Albans group of historians in England. Counts and bishops also sought to have their acts recorded in local histories. Western Europeans were proud of their recent achievements and wanted them to be remembered.

An even more striking change was the rapid development of vernacular literature. Minstrels had been composing songs and epic poems long before 1100, but very few of their compositions had been written down. During the twelfth century the practice arose of recording their poems in more or less permanent form, and by the early years of the thirteenth century there was a respectable body of literature in French, German, and Provençal (a southern French dialect). Italy lagged somewhat, perhaps because the Italian dialects were still so close to Latin that they were scarcely recognized as separate languages. England was even further behind because of the Norman conquest. The upper classes in England spoke French and patronized French poets well into the thirteenth century, and without their support the Anglo-Saxon literary tradition could not survive. Left to the peasants, Anglo-Saxon gradually became what we call Middle English; it was only toward the end of the thirteenth century that the ruling classes began to use this language

William of Poitou: A Song of Nothing

These verses from a poem by William, Count of Poitou and Duke of Aquitaine (1071–1127), are not typical of the lyric poetry that was developing in southern France in the late twelfth century—most troubadours took themselves and their loves more seriously. But it illustrates the emerging modernism of the lyric poem, which dealt with personal and emotional themes that were unknown to the epic tradition. William, who was reputed to have been the first troubadour, was, through Eleanor of Aquitaine, the great-grandfather of Richard Lion-Heart, who also wrote songs.

I'll make some verses just for fun
Not about me nor any one,
Nor deeds that noble knights have done
Nor love's ado:
I made them riding in the sun.
(My horse helped, too.)
When I was born I cannot say.
I am not sad, I am not gay,
I am not stiff nor dégagé;
What can I do?
Long since enchanted by a fay
Star-touched I grew.
I have a lady, who or where
I cannot tell you, but I swear
She treats me neither ill nor fair.
But I'm not blue,
Just so those Normans stay up there
Out of Poitou.
I have not seen, yet I adore
This distant love; she sets no store
By what I think and furthermore
('Tis sad but true)
Others there are, some three or four,
I'm faithful to.

"A Song of Nothing," trans. by T. G. Bergin, in C. W. Jones, ed., *Medieval Literature in Translation* (New York: McKay, 1950), p. 668.

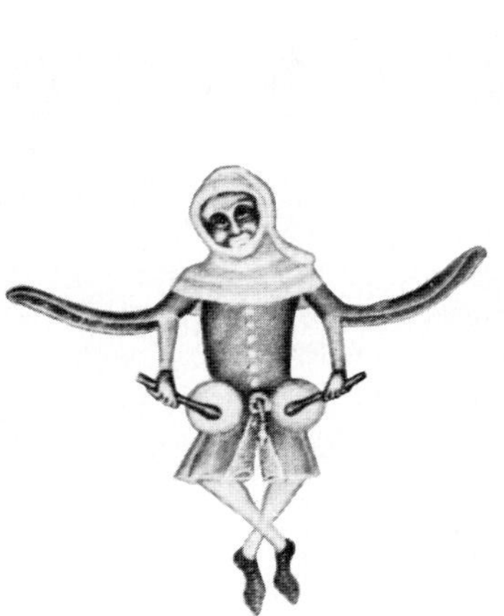

Medieval English minstrels, as depicted in marginal drawings in the Luttrell Psalter (*ca.* 1340).

and that English came to be a literary language.

Most works in the vernacular were written for the aristocracy. The *chansons de geste*, for example, are long narrative poems celebrating the courage and fortitude of feudal warriors. The most famous, the *Song of Roland*, tells of the heroic death of a handful of Charlemagne's knights ambushed by a Moslem army; others describe conflicts between unreasonable lords and long-suffering vassals. At about the same time the short lyric poems appeared, which seem to have originated in southern France but quickly spread to Germany and Italy. Some of these lyrics describe the joys of battle, others are political satires, but many of them are love poems. They show a high degree of skill in versification; the sonnet, for example, was to develop out of this type of poem.

Lays, simple ballads based on Celtic legends about King Arthur and his court, appeared a little later. They introduced an element of the marvelous—Merlin and his magic, the knights of the Round Table, the search for the Holy Grail—and the theme of romantic love—King Arthur and his queen, Guinevere. Both the Charlemagne and Arthurian legends had political implications. If the king of France was the heir of Charlemagne, the king of England was the successor of Arthur. Historians in both countries stressed this connection, so that if kings were patrons of literature, writers were propagandists for kings.

One might say that medieval vernacular literature began with the masterpieces, such as the *Song of Roland*, though perhaps only the masterpieces survived. But besides its intrinsic interest, this literature had long-lasting consequences. First, it introduced themes, such as the tragic love story of Tristan and Isolde, that are still common in our literature today, and in expressing these themes medieval poets developed most of our traditional poetic forms. Second, it helped to weaken Latin as the universal language. Not all early vernacular literature was written for amusement; portions of the Bible were translated into French in the twelfth century, and several histories had been written in French by the early thirteenth century. If French could be used for these purposes, it could also be used for official documents, and during the thirteenth century an increasing number of royal letters and government records were written in French. This same pattern developed in other countries. The growing use of the vernacular language was one, though only one, of the forces that gave each kingdom a sense of its own identity and contributed to the rise of nationalism.

Finally, the new literature was one of the forces that helped soften the manners of the upper classes. Even the poems about warfare were often a substitute for violence. The lords and knights who listened to the *Song of Roland* were likely to be less belligerent than the heroes they admired. Love poems and religious works were even further removed from the old tradition of violence. The new ideas of courtesy and chivalry were expressed in many romances. It is easy to exaggerate this development; many members of the feudal class were still ignorant and brutal. But in some circles and at some levels ignorance and brutality were being softened by the desire for a little learning and for rudimentary good manners. Vernacular literature both reflected and helped to spread this new pattern of courtly life.

THE WESTERN MONARCHIES

It is in this context of a more prosperous and more peaceful western Europe that political developments must be placed. There was a general desire for more gov-

1066	1135	1154	1189	1199	1216	1272	1307
Norman Kings	Disputed Succession	Henry II	Richard I	John	Henry III	Edward I	

ernment and better government to help preserve the gains of the last hundred years—a desire that eased the task of the leaders who were reorganizing secular government during the late twelfth and early thirteenth centuries. The greatest progress was made in England and France, but everywhere there was a tendency to create new institutions and to make laws that were more exact and more inclusive.

England Under Henry II

Royal government in England had been weakened by a dispute over the successor to Henry I. A prolonged civil war (1135–1152) made it difficult to consider changes in the legal and administrative systems. But in 1154 Henry II, the grandson of Henry I, came to the throne with a clear title. He was already lord of all western France, for he had inherited Anjou and Normandy from his parents and had acquired Aquitaine by marrying Eleanor, the only child of the last duke. Henry spent more than two-thirds of his reign in France—naturally enough, since he held more land there than the French king. Nevertheless, he made a greater impression on England than many kings who spent their entire lives there. He needed a strong government in England both to keep the country quiet while he was abroad and to obtain men and money to protect his French possessions against jealous neighbors. In his attempts to strengthen the English government, he enlarged the activities of the royal courts and created the English common law.

Henry invented no new procedures; he simply used old devices, such as the circuit judge and the jury, more intensively. But by making regular and habitual procedures that his predecessors had employed only on exceptional occasions, Henry changed the whole nature of royal government. Whereas William the Conqueror had used inquests or juries on a large scale only once in his reign (to obtain the information recorded in Domesday Book), Henry's circuit judges summoned juries in county after county, year after year. These juries were somewhat like our grand juries today, but they not only indicted criminals; they also had to answer questions about the state of the royal domain and the behavior of local

The Death of Roland

This passage comes from the *Song of Roland.* Roland, commander of the rear guard of Charlemagne's army, has been cut off by a greatly superior Moslem force. He beats off their attacks repeatedly, but finally all his men are killed and he himself is mortally wounded. He hears the horns of Charlemagne's army as it advances to avenge him, and prepares for death.

Then Roland feels that death is seizing him;
Down from the head upon the heart it falls.
Beneath a pine he staggers, lays him down
On the green grass, and hides beneath his heart
His famous sword and his great ivory horn.
He turns his face toward the infidel
For greatly he desires that Charles should say,
With all his men: "Roland, the noble count,
Roland the brave has died a conqueror."

Then Roland feels that his last hour has come.
Facing toward Spain he lies upon the hill. . . .
And many memories flood into his mind
Of all the conquests he, the brave, had made.
Of gentle France, of heroes of his House,
Of Charlemagne, his lord, who fostered him. . . .

He cries his Culpe, he prays to God for grace:
"O God the Father who has never lied,
Who called the holy Lazarus back to life,
And Daniel from the lions' jaws preserved,
Protect my soul, and pardon all my sins!"

His right-hand glove he proffered unto God;
Saint Gabriel took it from his faltering hand. . . .
God sent to him his angel cherubim
And the count's soul they bore to Paradise.

Translated from *La Chanson de Roland,* ed. by T. A. Jenkins (Boston: Heath, 1924), ll. 2355–95.

officials. Again, William the Conqueror and Henry I had occasionally allowed prelates or barons to use juries to determine disputes over the possession of land and rights annexed to land. Henry II made this procedure available to every free man and established the rule that no one need answer suits involving land without the king's writ and except in the king's court.

The early jury was by no means an ideal instrument of justice, for it based its decisions on common knowledge and neighborhood gossip rather than on the carefully tested evidence of sworn witnesses. But imperfect as it was, it was far better than trial by ordeal or combat. Litigants began to flock to the king's courts, and by the end of Henry's reign all disputes over land were being settled by juries in royal courts. By the middle of the thirteenth century all cases of any importance, both criminal and civil, were decided by juries.

This great increase in the amount of work done by the king's court naturally strengthened the royal government and weakened the control of feudal lords over their vassals. Important cases no longer came to the courts of the lords, and if the lords tried to resort to extralegal means their vassals could always turn to the king's courts for protection. The circuit judges rode regularly through the counties, and a royal court at Westminster heard cases that came up when circuit judges were not available (although this court did not become permanent until the early thirteenth century). Everyone in the country was subject to the king's justice, and most men, sooner or later, appeared in royal courts as jurors or litigants.

This constant exposure to royal justice enhanced the people's respect for royal power and indoctrinated generation after generation in the principles of English law. By applying the same rules in all parts of the country, the king's judges gradually created a common law for the whole realm. The first textbook on the English common law was written at the end of Henry's reign, and others followed in the thirteenth and fourteenth centuries. A powerful unifying force, the common law eventually became a symbol of English nationalism. Englishmen were proud of it, regarding it as a guarantee of their liberties rather than as a manifestation of royal power. And this pride is one reason that English common law survived when all the other countries of Europe were abandoning their medieval legal systems in favor of codes based on Roman law.

Henry II also increased royal revenue. Following a precedent of his grandfather, he regularly accepted money from his vassals in lieu of military service they owed him. He also imposed a general tax on the country in 1188 in order to pay for a crusade he had promised to join. A tax of this sort was not easy to make stick,

ENGLAND AND FRANCE AT THE TIME OF HENRY II
1154–89

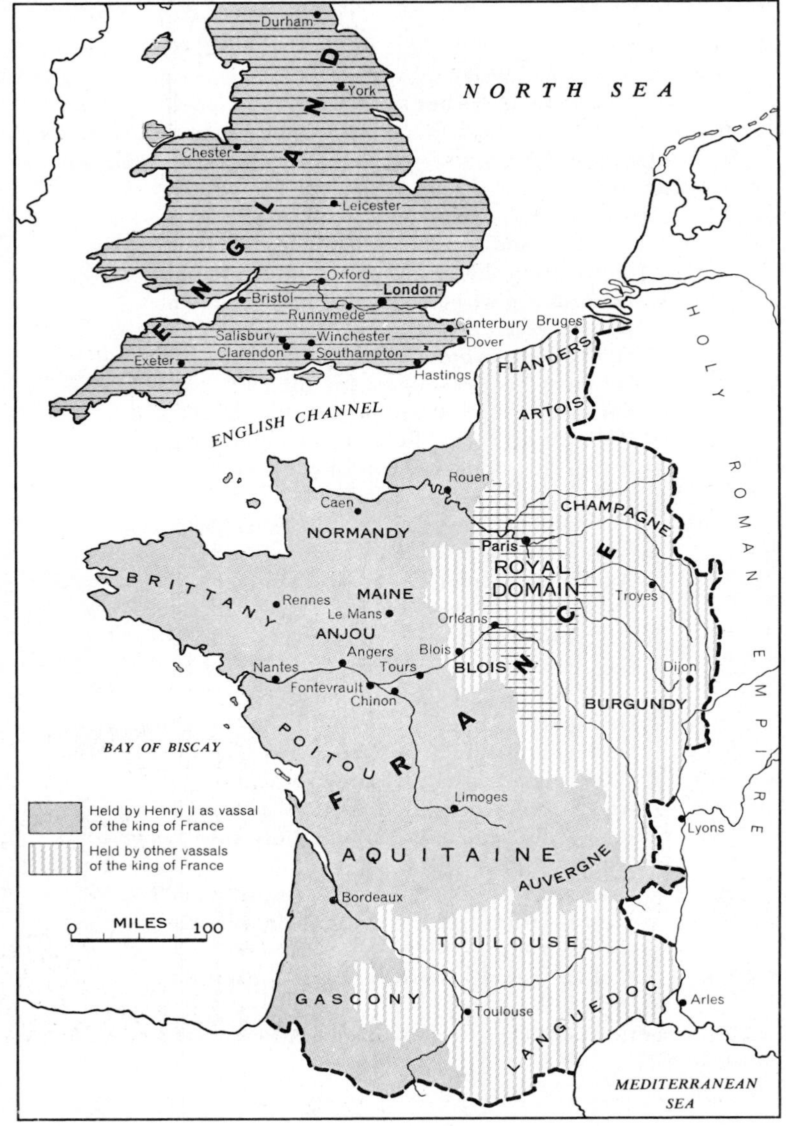

for medieval opinion was strongly set against taxation, even for a worthy cause. But, while the king of France had to abandon his efforts to impose a tax for the same crusade, Henry's tax was collected and set a precedent for additional taxes in the years ahead.

Although the English barons offered no effective opposition to Henry's reforms, Henry did have one dangerous opponent: Thomas Becket, Archbishop of Canterbury, who resisted Henry's efforts to subject clergymen accused of crimes to the jurisdiction of royal courts. The quarrel grew bitter, and at last the archbishop was murdered in his own cathedral by four of Henry's knights, who thought they would please their king by ridding him of a troublesome foe. Henry swore, probably quite truthfully, that he had not planned the assassination, but he abandoned his attempts to bring clergymen under the jurisdiction of royal courts. This concession did little harm in the long run. It did define more precisely relationships between Church and State and forced later kings to find ways to control the clergy without trying them in royal courts. But Thomas was canonized and became one of the most popular saints in England. His stand against injustice (as he saw it) was invoked by later opponents of powerful kings, not only in England, but throughout Europe.

The murder of Archbishop Thomas Becket in his cathedral at Canterbury in 1170. This representation was made shortly before 1200.

Magna Carta

Henry's sons, Richard (1189–99) and John (1199–1216), lacked his political ability. Richard was a good general and nothing more; he spent his entire reign either on the Third Crusade or in fighting Philip Augustus of France. Richard was feared for his strength and admired for his bravery, but he gave little attention to the government of England. He spent less than ten months during a reign of ten years in his island kingdom; all he wanted from England was men and money. It says much for Henry II's political institutions that the government continued to function despite Richard's neglect and his repeated demands for taxes to pay for his wars.

John was not even a good general. Richard had been winning the war with the king of France, but John lost it. Intelligent but neurotic, he suspected his most loyal supporters of treason and thus forced them into neutrality or opposition. William Marshal, Earl of Pembroke, was famous throughout Europe as a model of knightly behavior; John exiled him to Ireland because he did not trust him. This kind of behavior explains why, in the long war with Philip Augustus of France, John's vassals either deserted or fought with little enthusiasm. As a result, John

Richard I spent much of his reign fighting in the Third Crusade or against Philip Augustus of France (detail from the effigy on his tomb, 1199).

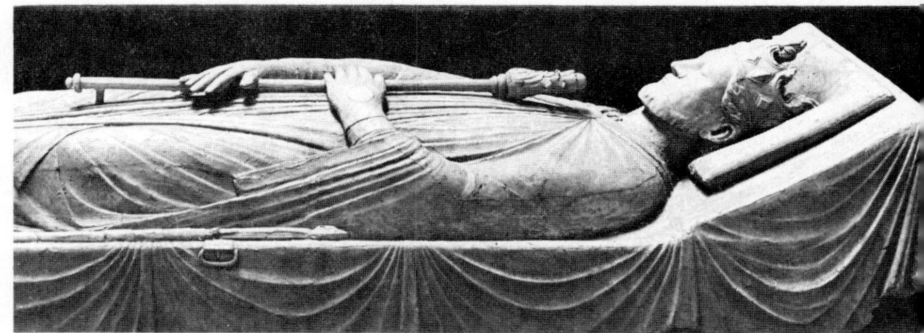

lost Normandy, Anjou, and the northern part of Aquitaine to the French king. He also suffered a serious defeat by the Church; after resisting for five years, John finally was forced to accept an Archbishop of Canterbury he did not want but who had been chosen by the pope. John also became a vassal of the pope. His service was only a small monetary payment, but it was humiliating. Eventually this was disavowed by later kings.

John had taken large sums of money from his vassals for his wars in France; he had also punished without trial many of the men he distrusted. These actions might have been tolerated if he had been successful, but his repeated failures made him vulnerable. The barons of England were outraged by the loss of Normandy, where they or their relatives had had extensive holdings. Many of them had been unjustly punished by heavy fines or confiscation of their lands. In 1215 a large group of barons revolted. The Archbishop of Canterbury advised them, and the merchants of London supported them. This coalition was too powerful for John to resist; on June 15 at Runnymede he put his seal to a charter that embodied the barons' demands for reform.

This document, which soon became known as "Magna Carta"—the Great Charter of Liberties—was reasonable and workable. It shows how well John's predecessors had accomplished their task of unifying England and instilling a respect for law even among the feudal lords. The barons made no attempt to break England into autonomous feudal states or to preserve local laws and institutions. They accepted the new legal system and the institutions of central government created by Henry II almost without question. The barons simply wanted to restrain the abuses of the central government, not to destroy it. They insisted that the king, like everyone else, was bound by law and that he was not to tax them without their consent. They demanded that he observe due process of law and forgo punishing an alleged offender before he had been convicted in the king's courts. If the king broke these promises, the barons warned, his subjects were free to rebel against him.

The purpose of Magna Carta was to protect the rights of the barons, not to establish constitutional government. But the English barons were more advanced politically than the feudal lords of other countries, for powerful kings had forced them to work together and to think in terms of laws that affected the whole kingdom. Consequently, they stated the liberties they claimed for themselves in such a way that those liberties could easily be extended to other classes. Thus before the end of the century the right to consent to taxes, originally restricted to the barons, was gained by lesser landholders and merchants, and the right to a fair trial was appropriated even by unpropertied classes. Magna Carta symbolized the supremacy of law, the conviction that even the king was bound by law and must respect the limits it set on his power. Since it was invoked again and again in protests against the arbitrary use of royal power, it served as a foundation stone in the English system of constitutional government.

Excerpts from Magna Carta 1215

We [John] have conceded to all free men of our kingdom, for us and our heirs forever, all the liberties written below, to be held by them and their heirs from us and our heirs: . . .

12. No scutage [redemption of military service] or aid [grant to the king] shall be taken in our kingdom except by the common counsel of our kingdom. . . .

14. And for obtaining the common counsel of the kingdom, for assessing an aid . . . or a scutage, we will cause to be summoned by our sealed letters the archbishops, bishops, abbots, earls and greater barons, moreover we will cause to be summoned generally by the sheriffs . . . all those who hold of us in chief [the other vassals] for a certain day . . . and place . . . and once the summons has been made the business shall proceed on the assigned day according to the advice of those who are present, even if all those summoned have not come. . . .

39. No free man may be seized, or imprisoned, or disposessed, or outlawed, or exiled . . . nor will we go against him or send against him except by the legal judgment of his peers and by the law of the land.

40. To no one will we sell, to no one will we deny or delay right and justice.

Translated from W. Stubbs, *Select Charters* (Oxford: Clarendon Press, 1921), pp. 294 ff.

The Growth of Royal Power in France

In England, which had achieved unity at a very early date, the chief political problem was how to restrain an overpowerful sovereign. In France, which had been divided into autonomous feudal states since the tenth century, the chief political problem was how to build larger and more effective units of government. The first solutions to this problem had been reached in the feudal states themselves, and by the end of the twelfth century such provinces as Normandy, Flanders, and Champagne had well-developed legal, financial, and administrative systems. There were as yet no similar institutions for the kingdom as a whole, however. Even in the region stretching from Paris to Orléans, which the king ruled directly, political institutions were less advanced and less specialized than in some of the great feudal states.

As the king of France gained power and prestige during the twelfth century, however, he gradually became master of his own domain; no longer could petty lords defy him from castles only a few miles from Paris. A series of legends grew up about the king that transformed him into a semisacred personage far above any ordinary feudal lord—in the end, far above any other European king. According to these legends, at his coronation he was anointed with holy oil that had miraculously descended from heaven; he healed the sick; he carried the sword and banner of Charlemagne. This increased prestige was reinforced by the growing desire for law and order that appeared everywhere in the twelfth century. More men sought the judgment of the royal law courts, and the king was occasionally able to impose his decisions even on lords outside his own domains. In short, a real opportunity existed for a great expansion of royal power. And at the end of the twelfth century a king appeared who made the most of that opportunity.

This king was Philip Augustus (1180–1223), the first really able ruler of the Capetian dynasty. Because Philip could not be strong so long as the kings of England held all of western France, he spent much of his reign trying to pull them down. Richard withstood his attacks, but John was more vulnerable. John had made himself even more unpopular in France than in England by murdering one of his nephews, who was heir to the county of Brittany. He exposed himself even more by marrying an heiress who was engaged to one of his own most powerful vassals in Aquitaine. This was a clear breach of feudal law. John had dishonored his vassal, and the aggrieved man promptly appealed to the king of France, from whom John held all his French lands. Philip Augustus seized on this excuse joyfully. He was already planning to attack John; now he could do so in a way that would give him the support of many feudal lords. Philip summoned John to his court, and John, by failing to appear, again put himself in the wrong. Philip ordered all John's French fiefs confiscated for default and carried out the sentence by force of arms. John's English vassals fought badly, and many of his French vassals refused to fight at all. So Philip annexed Normandy, Anjou, and Poitou with little difficulty.

By this conquest of northwestern France, Philip more than tripled the royal domain. For the first time in centuries the king of France was stronger than any of his vassals. And in order to hold and exploit the territory he had gained, Philip went on to devise new institutions that set a pattern for all his successors. Because he created a territorial base from which the king could dominate the rest of the country and provided an institutional base with which to control the enlarged domain, Philip was the real founder of the French monarchy.

Philip seems to have been guided by two principles. One was to use local institutions whenever he could, thus preserving the earlier work of the feudal lords and at the same time conciliating his new subjects. The other was to divide the new provinces into small administrative districts and to give full powers in each district to men sent out from his own court. Thus Normandy, for example, retained its Norman law and its Norman court system and was never subjected to the law and customs of Paris. But it was divided into thirteen districts, in each of which a bailiff appointed by the king presided over the courts, collected the king's revenues, and

THE EXPANSION OF THE ROYAL DOMAIN IN FRANCE 1180–1314

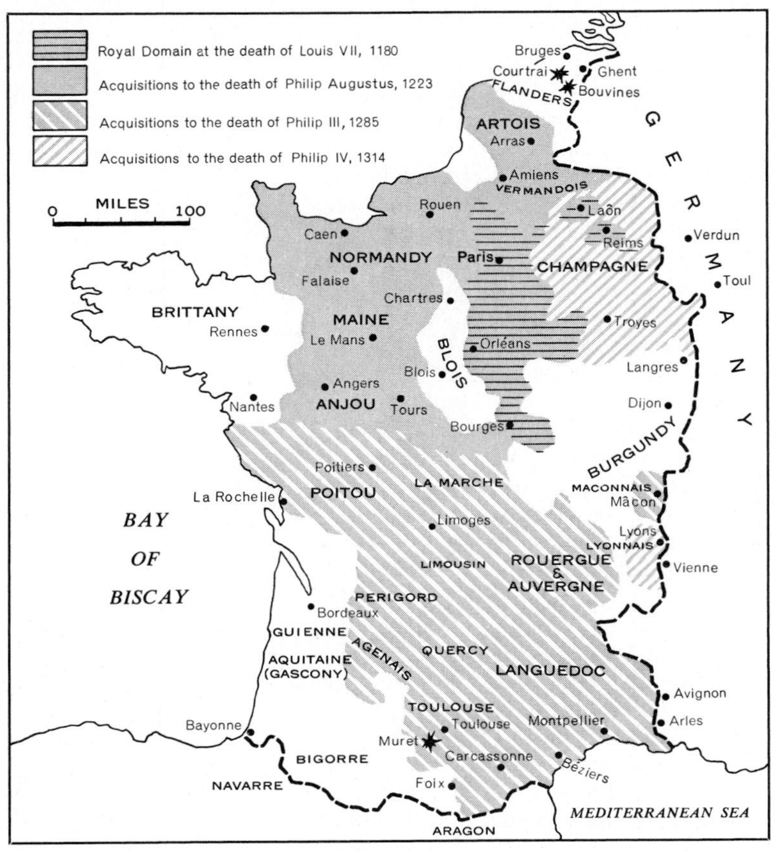

commanded the castles and the military forces. No Norman was named as bailiff until much later in the century, and even then most of the bailiffs still came from the old royal domain around Paris.

Philip's principles of government served him well. His respect for local institutions and customs induced the conquered provinces to accept his control with little protest. The bailiffs, who depended on him for their high office, were loyal and reasonably efficient. Philip made sure that his bailiffs were always strangers to the district they ruled, and he moved them frequently from one district to another to keep them from forming local attachments. He paid them well and made it clear that they could expect better jobs if they gave him faithful service. Some of them were unnecessarily harsh, and some were dishonest. But on the whole their behavior convinced Philip's new subjects that royal government was, for the most part, better than the government of the feudal lords had been.

All Philip's successors followed his practice of permitting local diversity within a centralized bureaucratic framework. They enlarged the administrative districts, reducing the thirteen original districts in Normandy to five, for example, and they sent out more and more officials to help the bailiffs in their work. But they did not alter Philip's basic system. In the end, France became a very different sort of country from England. With no common law, most Frenchmen remained attached to their local rights and customs. This meant, in turn, that local leaders were uninterested in the problems of the central government; their loyalties were primarily to their provinces. France was held together by the king and his officials; it was a much more bureaucratic state than England. Moreover, as France grew into the most powerful state in Europe, its example was followed by others. The bureaucracies of the continental countries today are all descended from the model set by Philip Augustus.

Spain

To the south of France, Spain was having its own unification problems. While the Moors had overrun most of the Spanish peninsula in the eighth century, some small Christian principalities in the mountainous regions of the North remained independent, such as Asturias in the northwest and the Basque country of Navarre in the central Pyrenees. Charlemagne created another Christian principality when he invaded and conquered the extreme northeastern corner of Spain—the Spanish March, which eventually became the County of Barcelona. From these outposts new conquests were made—Leon and Castile in the west and Aragon in the east. Asturias, Leon, and Castile were more or less unified, and Navarre sometimes joined, and for a brief period, controlled them. In the east, Aragon and Barcelona were eventually united. These larger and stronger kingdoms were able to nibble away at Moorish territory to the south, especially since the Moslems had ceased to be united politically and had broken up into small

962	1073	1122	1152	1254
Ottonian Emperors	Investiture Conflict	Period of Imperial Weakness	Hohenstaufen Emperors	

quarreling kingdoms. Some of these Moslem kingdoms sought the help of Christian rulers and nobles against enemies of their own faith. For example, the Cid—the hero of Spanish epic poetry—was as apt to be fighting for a Moslem ruler as for a Christian. Thus, little by little, the Christian kingdoms expanded, and finally, in the decisive battle of Las Navas de Tolosa (1212), Moorish power was broken. By the end of the thirteenth century the Moors held only the little kingdom of Granada on the southeastern coast, which they kept until 1492.

This long, slow reconquest caused many problems for the Spaniards. Because it was difficult to coordinate their efforts there was a tendency to set up separate kingdoms and principalities that might become independent states. Even Castile and Leon were not always united, and Portugal, which was originally only a county, became an independent kingdom. In the uncertainty as to what was united and what was not, no firm rule of hereditary succession could be developed. Wicked uncles took the throne from young nephews; bastards had as good a claim as legitimate heirs, and, as opposed to northern Europe, women could assert a right to, or at least a right to transmit, the throne. Thus Spain, throughout the Middle Ages, was plagued by quarrels over succession. Because fighting between claimants to the various kingdoms and war against the Moors were incessant, Spain attached special value to military virtues. Often, the great lords were practically independent (again the Cid is a good example), and even in the towns there was a class of urban knights—a concept that would have seemed ludicrous in northern Europe. Finally, after the First Crusade, military orders were established in Spain—more or less in imitation of the orders of the Temple and the Hospital in the crusading kingdom of Jerusalem. These military orders were richly endowed and politically powerful, and their quarrels added to the latent instability of the Spanish kingdoms.

As a result of the long struggle with the Moors, the kingdoms of Aragon and Castile-Leon profited from an increase in the area they controlled and in the income that their kings received. Their kings were not mere military commanders; they had clear ideas of what was needed to create effective administrative systems. Some of the earliest financial records from any western European kingdom came from Barcelona, and some of the earliest town charters were issued by kings of Castile in order to persuade people to settle newly conquered lands. Law codes appeared in Spain earlier than in France, and Alfonso X of Castile (1252–1284) produced the *Siete Partidas,* which gave precision and sanction to the laws enforced in his courts.

Germany and Italy Under the Hohenstaufen

Germany and Italy, meanwhile, were still nominally united under the emperor. But the emperor's power, which was based on his control of the Church, had been seriously weakened by the struggle over lay investiture. The German princes, profiting from the emperor's predicament, had seized local rights for themselves and had begun to insist on their right to elect the emperor. The towns in Italy were becoming almost as independent as the German princes. Thus the old institutions of the Empire were falling into decline, and there were no new institutions to replace them.

In spite of these difficulties, Frederick Barbarossa (1152–90) of the new Hohenstaufen dynasty* made a heroic and al-

*The Hohenstaufen descended, in the female line, from Henry V. They took their name from their ancestral castle in Swabia.

Late-twelfth-century gilded reliquary bearing the features of Frederick Barbarossa.

most successful effort to unify the Empire once again. Apparently impressed by the achievements of the kings of France and England, he modeled much of his program on their example. Imitating the king of France, he tried to build a secure royal domain in the Hohenstaufen lands in the southwest corner of Germany. Imitating the king of England, he tried to make all vassals take an oath of allegiance directly to the king, no matter who their immediate lord was. Most important, however, was his attempt to transform German feudalism into a coherent and all-embracing system of government. Many of the most powerful men in Germany owed him no allegiance, and many of those who did held part of their lands as private property exempt from feudal obligations. Frederick seems to have hoped that by bringing all men and all lands into a feudal system he could check the disintegration of the Empire. Thus by making the leading churchmen vassals of the king, as they were in England, he could regain his control over the resources of the Church; and by making the princes of the Empire his vassals, he could curtail their growing independence and punish them for disobedience by confiscating their fiefs.

Frederick had some success in these attempts, but his own version of feudalism proved inadequate. Both points are illustrated by his conflict with Henry the Lion, Duke of Saxony and Bavaria. Henry was the head of the Welf family, which had long had hopes of gaining the imperial throne, and his two duchies made him the most powerful man in Germany. When Henry failed to give Frederick the military support he owed during an imperial war, Frederick decided to eliminate this dangerous enemy once and for all. He had Henry condemned by a feudal court in 1180, just as Philip Augustus of France was to have John of England condemned by a feudal court some twenty years later. But while Philip was able to seize John's lands and incorporate them into the royal domain, Frederick was immediately obliged to grant Henry's duchies to other princes. Moreover, Henry still held extensive lands that were not fiefs (Brunswick, for example) and thus remained wealthy and powerful. Frederick seems to have been seduced by the idea of a perfect feudal pyramid, in which all lesser lords held their lands and powers from the princes, who in turn held them from the emperor. Thus when one prince was dispossessed, his place had to be filled by another, or else the pyramid would lose its symmetry. For obvious reasons the princes were delighted with this rule, and for reasons of his own the emperor seems to have accepted it as well. In the long run this peculiar form of feudalism tended to build up the power of the princes rather than that of the emperor.

Frederick also tried to reassert his imperial rights in Italy, for he knew that if he could gain control of the Italian towns he would be the richest ruler in western Europe. The incessant quarrels among the Italian towns enabled him to establish himself in the Lombard plain and take control of many of its cities. But the Italians, frightened by his success, suddenly called a halt to their feuding and formed a coalition—the Lombard League—to oppose him. Pope Alexander III, who feared that any increase in imperial power in Italy would threaten his independence, supported the League. Frederick tried to overcome this opposition by supporting an antipope and by destroying Milan, the chief Lombard town. But the hostile coalition proved too strong for him. The towns of the Lombard League defeated Frederick at Legnano in 1176 and with the pope's backing forced him to accept a peace that assured them virtual independence.

Frederick, still hoping to make something of his Italian claims, moved his base of operations farther south to Tuscany, where the towns were weaker and less hostile. Though he had some success in Tuscany, his advance there created new problems for himself and his successors. Tuscany was closer to Rome than Lombardy; the imperial base there frightened the pope and involved Frederick even more deeply in Italian affairs.

The involvement increased when Frederick's son married the heiress of the Norman kingdom of Sicily. When Frederick was drowned in 1190 while leading a crusading army through Asia Minor, his son, Henry VI (1190–97), was accepted as emperor by the German princes. But Henry spent almost all his time in Italy, first making good his claim to Sicily and then opening a corridor along the east coast of Italy to connect his south Italian kingdom with Germany. Henry secured his corridor by taking lands claimed by the papacy by virtue of the donations of Pippin and Charlemagne. With Rome now encircled by lands held by the emperor, the popes' old fears of imperial domination became stronger than ever.

THE CHURCH AT THE HEIGHT OF ITS POWER

The late twelfth century was a bad time in which to alarm popes, for they were steadily increasing their power. They were gaining administrative control of the Church, and in a fervently Christian Europe this meant that they could control public opinion. While kings, lords, or local clergy might nominate bishops, the pope had to approve all appointments and could quash those he felt to be irregular. In the event of a dispute over the choice of a bishop, the pope frequently set aside both candidates and imposed a man of his own choice, as he did at Canterbury in 1207. At the same time he kept close watch over the bishops by sending out legates to enforce papal orders and by encouraging appeals from bishops to the papal court. The bishops in turn strengthened their control over the clergy of their dioceses by making frequent tours of inspection and appointing men trained in canon law to preside over the ecclesiastical courts. Thus the Church became a highly centralized organization, with the bishops responsible to the pope and with all lesser clergy responsible in turn to the bishops.

This centralization created new problems. As the popes and bishops spent more and more of their time on administrative and judicial details, they ran the danger of abdicating their role as spiritual leaders. St. Bernard had worried about this problem in the middle of the twelfth century, and later reformers shared his concern. Moreover, papal and episcopal courts had to demand heavy fees from those who did business with them. But these fees were not enough to cover extraordinary expenses, and in 1199 Pope Innocent III imposed an income tax on the clergy, an example that was followed by all his successors. The higher clergy shifted these expenses to the parish priests, who in turn began to exact fixed fees for such services as marriage and burial. Soon the complaint arose that the Church was selling its spiritual benefits.

Contemporary mosaic portrait of Innocent III, from the old basilica of St. Peter in Rome.

Innocent III

The Church reached the height of its power at the end of the twelfth century, during the pontificate of Innocent III (1198–1216). Innocent, who felt responsible for the moral and spiritual welfare of all western Europe, once said, "Nothing

Detail from a page of Innocent's Register showing two wolves, one in friar's clothing, probably assisting in a heretical mass. The page deals with the Church's power to punish sinners.

in the world should escape the attention and control of the Sovereign Pontiff." The Vicar of Christ, "less than God but more than man," could reprove and punish kings who broke the divine law. A man of remarkable energy (he was only thirty-seven years old when he became pope), Innocent came very close to making the papal court a supreme court for all of Europe. He kept the clergy under tight control and intervened repeatedly in secular affairs whenever he felt a moral issue was involved. Thus he threatened to support a French invasion of England in order to make John accept his own choice as Archbishop of Canterbury. But when John yielded and became a vassal of the pope, Innocent granted him papal protection and forbade the French to carry out their planned attack.

Innocent III and the Empire

Innocent's most striking intervention, however, was in the affairs of the Empire. The premature death of Henry VI in 1197 created a complicated problem of succession. Henry's heir, Frederick II, was only three years old, and, though Frederick's claim to Sicily was undeniable, the princes of the Empire had never accepted the rule of hereditary succession. They split into two factions, one supporting Philip of Hohenstaufen, the brother of Henry VI, the other supporting Otto, the son of Henry the Lion and head of the Welf family. Innocent took advantage of this dissension by driving the German troops and the governors out of central Italy and resuming control of all the Papal States, including the territory on the east coast. Alleging that since the pope crowned the emperor he had a right to reject unworthy candidates, he postponed the solution of the German problem for ten years. Finally, in 1208, after Philip had been assassinated, Innocent recognized Otto as emperor on condition that Otto renounce all claims to the lands in central Italy that had been seized by Frederick Barbarossa and Henry VI. When Otto broke his agreement, Innocent turned against him and persuaded the German princes to accept Frederick II as their ruler. By 1215 the young Frederick was in full control of Germany, and Innocent felt that he had an emperor who would be a dutiful subordinate of the Church instead of a dangerous rival.

Actually, Innocent had made a series of disastrous mistakes. By prolonging the dispute over the succession in Germany, he had given the German princes a chance to increase their power at home; after 1215 the position of the emperor north of the Alps was very shaky indeed. Frederick II, soon deciding that he could make nothing of Germany, turned his eyes toward Italy, thus reviving the danger of encirclement that Innocent thought he had ended by putting Frederick on the German throne. Instead of showing gratitude for the pope's support, Frederick renewed the old attempt to annex a corridor along the east coast and to assert imperial power in Tuscany and Lombardy. But Innocent had committed the papacy to the propositions that the Papal States must stretch from coast to coast and that the emperor must not gain control of central and northern Italy. The result was a long struggle that badly damaged the prestige of the Church. It also destroyed the last chance of unifying Germany, or of bringing Italy under a single government, leaving two dangerous problems for the nineteenth century.

Innocent III and Heresy

Innocent also found that, for the first time in centuries, the Church was seriously threatened by heresy. Dangerous ideas were creeping in from the East along the busy trade routes; others were being formulated by the leaders of towns in Italy and southern France. Many people charged that priests were ignorant and prelates were greedy and immoral. Some of these critics remained Christian but felt that they were as capable as the clergy of interpreting the Bible. Laymen organized themselves into groups to read the Scriptures together and to try to apply Christian standards in their daily life. The Waldensians, who still exist, were typical of these groups; they had adherents throughout the Rhone Valley and in many northern Italian towns. Other groups accepted a new and only partly Christian faith that had originated in the Balkan provinces of the Byzantine Empire. Based on very early Christian heresies, it taught that all material things had been created by an evil god, who was engaged in a constant struggle with the God of good. It rejected the Old Testament as the work of the evil god and thought of Jesus as simply an emanation of the good God and so denied His humanity. The believers in this doctrine called themselves "Cathari" (the purified) because they had rejected the evil world. They organized a church of their own, with a very simple ritual and with leaders who were admired even by Catholics for their piety and goodness. Because they were especially numerous in the region of Albi in southern France, they were often called Albigensians.

By 1200 the heretics had the support of thousands of people and dominated whole communities. Innocent tried at first to convert them by peaceful means, but he soon became convinced that he would have to use force. He proclaimed a crusade against the Albigensians in 1207 and enlisted an army of knights from northern France to invade the south. The conflict was as much a civil war as a religious war; since the northerners aimed at the conquest of the south, many Catholic nobles of the region aided the Albigensians. An old legend reports that at the sack of Béziers the exasperated northerners cried: "Kill them all, God will know his own!" In spite of stubborn resistance, the southerners were crushed, and the lords of northern France now ruled the entire land.

The victory over heresy was still not complete. Repeated revolts against northern domination could be suppressed only by a new crusade led by the king of France himself. He took over all the conquests of the northern lords; thus one unforeseen result of the Albigensian war was a marked increase in the power of the French king. The king's victory ended open manifestations of heresy, but many heretics continued to practice their rites in secret. In order to unearth them the Church had to develop a new court, the Inquisition. Any contact with heretics was ground for suspicion. The court accepted neighborhood rumors as a basis for accusations and used torture to secure confessions. The Church justified this procedure on the grounds that the heretic, who caused the loss of an immortal soul, was far worse than the murderer, who merely killed the body. In the end the Inquisition wiped out the Albigensian heresy, but it had an evil effect on European society. It often corrupted communities by encouraging fanatics and talebearers, and it provided a regrettable example for secular courts to follow. The only major areas to escape the Inquisition were England and Scandinavia, where there were not enough heretics to bother about.

Thirteenth-Century Arguments About the Crusade

Should the Crusade never be preached against schismatics and the disobedient and rebels? This is not expressly stated in the law and therefore certain people in Germany have doubts about it, saying that it does not seem right or honest to take up the cross against Christians. . . . However, the Son of God did not come into the world, nor did He die on the cross to gain land, but to call sinners to penitence. There is greater danger in permitting sin than in losing land because the soul is more precious than material things. Thus if we consider the degree of the offense, no one can doubt that disobedient and schismatic Christians are greater offenders than the Saracens. . . . And although the overseas Crusade may seem more desirable to the simple, the Crusade against disobedient Christians will seem more just and reasonable to anyone who considers the problem intelligently. . . .

Rome should not, I think, if one of her sons has fallen into error . . . send upon him an elder brother to destroy him. Rather should she summon, talk gently, and admonish him than waste his country. When the French go against the people of Toulouse, whom they consider heretics, and when a papal legate leads and guides them, that is not at all right in my opinion.

The first quotation is from Hostiensis (a cardinal and a famous canon lawyer), *Summa aurea* III, 34 (de voto), 19 (in quo casu). The second is from Guillaume le Clerc (a French poet), as cited by Palmer A. Throop, *Criticism of the Crusade* (Amsterdam, 1940), p. 43.

The Revival of Science

By the middle of the twelfth century the scholars of the West had absorbed the Latin classics and Roman law. Searching about for new materials, they seized on the rich store of learning in the East that had never been translated into Latin. Though Aristotelian logic had greatly stimulated the revival of scholarship, the West had only Aristotle's introductory treatises on logic. Scholars were deeply interested in astronomy and astrology, but they had only a few brief texts on these subjects, while the Greeks and Arabs had scores of volumes. The same problem existed in medicine and biology, in mathematics and physics. All the really advanced works were in the eastern languages; in Latin there were only elementary texts.

To correct this deficiency, the scholars of the West began the task of translating into Latin the works of Aristotle and the scientific writings of the Greeks and Arabs. The difficulties were formidable. First, and easiest to overcome, was the problem of distance. The Arabs had been very interested in Greek science and had made many valuable contributions of their own in mathematics, physics and astronomy, but to acquire the learning of the Arabs it was necessary to go to Spain (as Gerbert had done), or to Sicily where Arabic scholarship had survived the Norman conquest. The Greeks had been less interested in science than the Arabs but they had preserved many fundamental texts, often in more accurate versions than the Arabic translations. To use the Greek material a journey to Constantinople was necessary. When western scholars arrived in Spain or Byzantium the real trouble began. There were no grammars, no lexicons, none of the scholarly apparatus we take for granted in learning foreign languages. The Romans had never been particularly interested in science and had never developed a scientific vocabulary; consequently, even when a translator knew the meaning of a Greek or an Arabic word he had trouble finding a Latin equivalent. Moreover, many of the important texts had been corrupted by repeated translation.

Nevertheless, western scholars completed the task they had set for themselves. By the middle of the thirteenth century they had translated into Latin almost all the works of Aristotle and a great mass of other material. The West had acquired the philosophy and the science of the East—and just in the nick of time, for during the thirteenth century both Byzantium and the Arab world were shattered by civil wars and foreign invasions. Though they made a partial recovery later on, they were never again the intellectual centers they had been in the early Middle Ages. The scientific tradition that the Greeks had originated and the Arabs had preserved might have vanished had it not been for the efforts of the translators of the twelfth and thirteenth centuries.

Medieval science was not the science of our own day. It was based on authority rather than direct observation; it developed its ideas through formal logic rather than through experimentation; and it was contaminated by the wishful thinking of philosophers and magicians. But at least it was an attempt to explain the physical world, to find ways of summing up seemingly unrelated phenomena in general laws. The important thing was not the accuracy of the results, but the fact that meaningful questions were asked about the nature of the universe. The questioning, once it began in the twelfth century, never stopped, and from that questioning our modern science has developed.

Understandably, the Church was suspicious of this new learning, which had been derived from pagan Greeks and handed on by Moslems and Jews. It carried with it many dangerous ideas—remnants of old religions disguised as magic, and philosophical doctrines that denied basic articles of faith. For example, some of the Arabic commentators on Aristotle had advanced the idea that the

A university lecture, as portrayed in a fourteenth-century Italian miniature. Attention to the lecturer is not undivided; several students are talking, and one is certainly asleep.

world was eternal and by so doing denied the Creation and the Last Judgment. By 1200 western scholars were teaching these ideas to eager young students, especially in the great center of learning at Paris.

The First Organized Universities

The Church wanted to control the new learning, and it found a means of doing so in the universities. As we have seen, twelfth-century professors and students had formed associations to protect their respective interests. Both groups found it to their advantage to insist on prescribed courses of study and examinations as prerequisites to obtaining a license to teach, or, as we would say, a degree. This system enabled the students to know what their obligations were and permitted teachers to bar unqualified men from their profession. It was not unlike the system that prevailed in the gilds, where a journeyman had to demonstrate his knowledge of his craft to a board of masters before he could become a master himself. In fact, the word *university* originally meant an association of any sort and not just an organization of accredited teachers and their students.

But any corporate group had to be recognized by some higher authority, and the natural authority for scholars was the Church. The Church saw obvious advantages in patronizing associations of scholars: it could more easily control the new learning, and it could use the professors as experts to examine suspect doctrines. The University of Paris, for example, began to denounce dangerous ideas derived from Aristotle and the Arabs almost as soon as it received official recognition from the pope.

Innocent III, who had been a student at both Paris and Bologna, favored university organization and bestowed valuable privileges on both his old schools. His patronage was matched by secular rulers, who needed educated men to staff their rapidly growing bureaucracies. By the end of the thirteenth century there were universities at Oxford and Cambridge in England, at Paris, Montpellier, Toulouse, and Orléans in France, at Coïmbra and Salamanca in the Iberian Peninsula, and at Bologna and Padua in Italy. There was no university in Germany until the fourteenth century. Paris remained the unquestioned leader in theology and liberal arts, and Bologna in law, but many men studied at more than one university. The famous scholars of the thirteenth century were university professors, and university graduates filled high offices in the Church and important positions in secular governments. In short, during the thirteenth century the universities took over the intellectual leadership of western Europe.

The idea of the university was one of the most important medieval contributions to modern civilization. Most civilized peoples have had schools of one kind or another, but they have usually concerned themselves with the private instruction of novices by priests, or the

Church Regulation of the University of Paris 1215

Robert [de Courçon] by the divine mercy cardinal priest . . . and legate of the apostolic see, to all the masters and scholars at Paris, eternal safety in the Lord.

Let all know, that having been especially commanded by the lord pope . . . to better the condition of the students at Paris, and wishing . . . to provide for the tranquility of the students in the future, we have prescribed the following rules:

No one is to lecture at Paris in arts before he is twenty years old. He is to study in arts at least six years before he begins to lecture. . . . He must not be smirched with any infamy. When he is ready to lecture, each one is to be examined according to the form contained in the letter of the bishop of Paris. . . .

The treatises of Aristotle on logic, both the old and the new, are to be read in the schools in the regular and not in the extraordinary courses. The two Priscians [on grammar] . . . are also to be read in the schools in the regular courses. On the feastdays [there were nearly one hundred of these] nothing is to be read except philosophy, rhetoric, books on the *quadrivium* [arithmetic, geometry, music, and astronomy], the Ethics [of Aristotle] and the fourth book of the Topics [of Boethius on logic]. The book of Aristotle on Metaphysics or Natural Philosophy, or the abridgements of these works, are not to be read, nor the doctrines of [certain contemporary teachers accused of heresy].

From Robert de Courçon, *Statutes,* trans. by D. C. Munro, *Translations and Reprints* (Philadelphia: University of Pennsylvania Press, 1899), Vol. II, No. 3, p. 12.

St. Francis strips off the garments he wore as a well-to-do young man and renounces all worldly goods. Painting by Giotto (1266?–1337), in the church of St. Francis at Assisi.

private tutoring of wealthy young men by individual teachers. True, the Roman Empire established professorships for scholars to lecture to anyone who cared to listen, but it never developed the university or an examination system. China, during the European Middle Ages, had a prescribed course of study, with an examination system and something very like our system of scholarly degrees, but it lacked an autonomous, self-perpetuating faculty. Only in medieval Europe does one find all the elements that make a modern university—a faculty constituting an organized and privileged community of scholars, a regular course of study, and final examinations leading to the degree as a certificate of scholarly competence. This type of educational organization has its disadvantages—it tends to become overly conservative and tradition-bound—but by and large it has proved the most successful form of higher education ever devised, and it has spread throughout the world.

The Mendicant Orders: Franciscans and Dominicans

The heresies mentioned above were only the most obvious manifestations of a threatened decline in the Church's influence over the population of western Europe. Even those who were not heretics criticized the character of the clergy and the administrative system of the Church. They felt that the Church was not doing its job, that it was failing to meet the challenge of changing times. They feared that it was yielding to the temptations created by a more prosperous and better-organized society—the love of wealth and the love of power—instead of finding ways to combat them. A society that had been oriented toward the future life was now finding far too much satisfaction in the pleasures of this world.

It was in response to these criticisms that the medieval Church, with the establishment of the Franciscan and Dominican Orders, embarked on its last great wave of reform. St. Francis (*ca.* 1182–1226), the son of a well-to-do Italian merchant, was particularly sensitive to the problem of wealth. His own conversion began with his renunciation of all claim to his family's property, and throughout his career he insisted on absolute poverty for himself and his followers. He also demanded literal and unquestioning observance of the precepts given in the Gospels to the disciples of Christ. His ideal was the *vita apostolica* (the apostolic life), and probably no other group of Christians has ever come closer to imitating the life of Jesus and the Apostles than did St. Francis and the early Franciscans. Their example of holy living impressed laymen who had become weary of routine religious services and encouraged them to make a new effort to apply Christian principles in their daily life.

The other leader of the new religious movement was St. Dominic (*ca.* 1170–1221), a Spanish priest who had begun his career by trying to convert the heretics of southern France. He was primarily concerned with the instruction of the faithful through preaching and teaching. Like St. Francis, he emphasized the ideal of absolute poverty, not only as good in itself but also because the leaders of the heretics he was combating had gained great influence by renouncing all worldly goods. Even more than St. Francis, he wanted his order to be an order of preachers. Realizing that perfunctory sermons and routine services were scorned by the more sophisticated groups of western Europe, St. Dominic spent his life training men who would be subject to the rigorous discipline of a religious order but who would also be well enough educated to hold their own in arguments with scholars, townsmen, and secular officials. The Dominicans established excellent schools to train

Women and Religious Reform

The impulse toward lay devotion and voluntary poverty was not confined to the Mendicant Orders. It was especially strong among women who founded private associations to satisfy their religious aspirations. These women were called "beguines" in the Low Countries, where they were numerous. Jacques de Vitry, a famous crusade preacher and historian (and later a cardinal), described them in 1213.

You have seen and you have rejoiced to see . . . great crowds of holy women in many places who despising the charms of the flesh for Christ and scorning the riches of this world for the heavenly kingdom . . . seek by the labor of their hands their meager nourishment, although their relatives have an abundance of riches. They abandon their families and the homes of their fathers, preferring to endure poverty rather than to enjoy wealth wrongly acquired or to stay with danger among the proud men of this world.

From Jacques de Vitry, *Vita B. Marae Orgniciacensis* in *Acta sanctorum,* for 4 June (Antwerp, 1717).

St. Francis Gives a Lesson in Poverty

Once when the blessed Francis had visited the Cardinal of Ostia [who was afterward Pope Gregory IX] at the hour of dinner he went as if by stealth from door to door begging food. And when he had returned, the Cardinal had already sat down at table, with many knights and nobles. But blessed Francis placed those alms which he had received on the table beside him. . . . And the Cardinal was a little ashamed . . . but he said nothing. . . . And when blessed Francis had eaten a little he took of his alms and sent a little to each of the knights and chaplains of the Cardinal on behalf of the Lord God. And they all received them with great joy and devotion. . . . [The Cardinal later rebuked him gently, but Francis answered:] "I will not be ashamed to beg alms, nay, I hold this a very great nobility and royal dignity before God and a means of honoring Him Who, when He was Lord of all, wished for our sakes to become servant of all, and when He was rich and glorious in His majesty became poor and despised in our humility."

From "The Mirror of Perfection," *The Little Flowers of St. Francis* (New York and London: Everyman's Library, 1910), Ch. 23, p. 203.

members of the order, and the graduates of these schools soon dominated the faculties of theology of European universities.

Both the Franciscan and the Dominican Orders met with immediate success. Thousands of men joined their ranks during the thirteenth century, and these friars, as they were called, became the most influential group among the clergy. Unlike the monks, who secluded themselves in their cloisters, the friars wandered about as missionaries, preaching and talking to laymen. They brought religion to the very centers of thirteenth-century society—to the courts, the universities, and the towns. At first there was some tendency for the Franciscans to appeal more to emotion and the Dominicans to reason, but by the middle of the century this difference had almost vanished. Each order produced a famous teacher of theology—the Dominicans, St. Thomas Aquinas; the Franciscans, St. Bonaventura. And each order carried on revivals among the people of the towns. The fact that the Church managed to preserve its leadership throughout most of the thirteenth century, in spite of the growing prosperity and worldliness of society, was due largely to the work of the friars.

Suggestions for Further Reading

Note: Asterisk denotes a book available in paperback edition.

Towns and Trade

The articles in the *Cambridge Economic History of Europe* remain the best guide for this period. Older and still useful works are W. Cunningham, *The Growth of English Industry and Commerce* (1910), and P. Boissonade, *Life and Work in Medieval Europe** (1929). R. de Roover, *Money, Banking and Credit in Medieval Bruges* (1948), is a readable study of the operations of the Italian merchant-bankers in Flanders. A. Sapori, *The Italian Merchant in the Middle Ages** (1970), is excellent. L. White, *Medieval Technology and Social Change* (1962), is a good introduction to the fascinating subject of medieval technology.

Gothic Art

There are many beautiful and exciting books on Gothic art. A. Temko, *Notre-Dame of Paris** (1955), is a charming study of this cathedral written as a biography. A. E. M. Katzenellenbogen, *The Sculptural Program of Chartres Cathedral** (1959), is a detailed study of Chartres, with the latest and most plausible historical interpretation. The best treatment of Gothic art in the High Middle Ages is P. Frankl, *Gothic Architecture** (1963), which traces the development of this architecture in all regions of Europe and stresses the slow perfection of the art. Frankl includes the most up-to-date bibliography. O. von Simson, *The Gothic Cathedral** (1956), is another first-rate book. The old work of T. G. Jackson, *Gothic Architecture* (1915), is sound and still valuable. Every student of medieval history should become familiar with one of the great monuments of American scholarship, Henry Adams' *Mont-Saint-Michel and Chartres** (1905). This is a great appreciation not only of the art but of the entirety of medieval civilization. In the same way, E. Mâle, *Religious Art in France in the Thirteenth Century* (1913) (published in paperback edition as *The Gothic Image*), is a study of the thought of the thirteenth century as expressed in art. J. Gimpel, *The Cathedral Builders* (1961), describes the techniques of cathedral building.

Vernacular Literature

A general introduction is W. T. H. Jackson, *Medieval Literature* (1966). Both C. C. Abbott, *Early Medieval French Lyrics* (1932), and J. A. Symonds, *Wine, Women and Song* (1899), have selections of typical lyric poetry of the twelfth century; the translation of Symonds, although somewhat more romantic, is superior. P. Dronke, *Medieval Latin and the Rise of the European Love-lyric* (1968), is very useful. *French Medieval Romances,* trans. by E. Mason (1911), is a collection of short novels probably dating from the reign of Henry II. The best critical study of the vernacular literature of the twelfth and thirteenth centuries is E. Curtius, *European Literature and the Latin Middle Ages** (1963), which has excellent bibliographic materials. For France, see U. T. Holmes, *A History of Old French Literature,* and for Germany, J. G. Robertson, *A History of German Literature* (1947). R. S. Loomis, *The Development of Arthurian Romance* (1963), is interesting.

Scholarship and the Rise of the Universities

Perhaps the central figure of the Christian humanism of the twelfth century was John of Salisbury, most of whose works have now been translated. *The Statesman's Book,* trans. by J. Dickinson (1927), a work of political theory, had a great influence on the development of twelfth-century humanism.

John of Salisbury's *Historia Pontificalis,* trans. by M. Chibnall (1956), describes western Europe during and after the Second Crusade as seen through the eyes of an Englishman in the papal Curia. An excellent penetration into John's thought and personality and his close association with Canterbury and Rome is given in *Letters of John of Salisbury,* 2 vols., ed. by W. J. Millor and H. E. Butler (1955). C. J. Webb, *John of Salisbury* (1932), presents him as a great medieval churchman and plays down his role as scholar and humanist.

There is very good source material on university life in L. Thorndike, *University Records and Life in the Middle Ages* (1944). L. Thorndike, *History of Magic and Experimental Science,* Vol. II (1923), traces the origins of modern science in the medieval universities. C. H. Haskins, *The Rise of the Universities** (1923), is a good general survey of the beginnings of the universities. Another useful short account is by H. Wieruszowski, *The Medieval University** (1966). The standard scholarly study is H. Rashdall, *The Universities of Europe in the Middle Ages,* 3 vols., rev. and ed. by F. M. Powicke and A. B. Emden (1936). H. Waddell, *The Wandering Scholars* (1927), gives a good picture of student life in the period of the formation of universities.

Henry II, Richard, and John

The English practice of preserving records has provided us with a vast amount of evidence for this period. Both Roger of Hoveden, *The Annals,* 2 vols., trans. by H. T. Riley (1853), and Roger of Wendover, *Chronicle,* 2 vols., trans. by J. A. Giles (1849), are interesting contemporary histories. There is valuable material in *English Historical Documents,* Vols. II and III, ed. by D. C. Douglas and G. W. Greenaway (1953–55). For the study of the growth of English law there are representative documents in C. Stephenson and F. G. Marcham, *Sources of English Constitutional History* (1937). J. E. A. Jolliffe's *Constitutional History of Medieval England** (1937) is a readable and scholarly study with a good critical bibliography, and F. Pollock and F. W. Maitland, *History of English Law,** Vol. I (1923), is fundamental. J. E. A. Jolliffe's *Angevin Kingship* (1955) traces the character and growth of royal power and the development of the organs of government through the twelfth century. S. Painter, *The Reign of King John** (1949), gives an excellent account of the political and administrative history of this reign. See also W. L. Warren, *Henry II* (1973) and his *King John* (1961). Painter's *William Marshal: Knight-Errant, Baron, and Regent of England** (1933) is an exciting biography that presents a vivid picture of the thoughts and attitudes of the English feudal class. The most thorough treatment of Magna Carta is that of W. S. McKechnie, *Magna Carta* (1914), a chapter-by-chapter analysis. See also J. C. Holt, *Magna Carta** (1965). A. L. Poole, *Domesday Book to Magna Carta* (1951), is the most comprehensive one-volume history of this period; although it is sometimes dull reading (on a fascinating period), there is an excellent critical bibliography.

Philip Augustus

Both J. Evans, *Life in Medieval France* (1925), and A. A. Tilley, *Medieval France* (1922), are very good surveys arranged in topical fashion. There is a good account of French society in A. Luchaire, *Social France at the Time of Philip Augustus,** trans. by E. B. Krehbiel (1912). The works by Petit-Dutaillis, Fawtier, and Lavisse listed at the end of Chapter 10, in the second section, also contain material on this subject.

Innocent III

The best study of this important pope is that of the great French historian, A. Luchaire, *Innocent III,* 6 vols. (1904–08). *Selected Letters of Innocent III Concerning England,* ed. by C. R. Cheney and W. H. Semple (1953), provides us with considerable information on English-papal relations in the stormy period from 1198 to 1216. There is a very readable interpretation of Innocent's remarkable ascendancy in S. R. Packard, *Europe and the Church under Innocent III* (1927). Another useful book is C. Edwards, *Innocent III, Church Defender* (1951). J. M. Powell, *Innocent III* (1963), is a collection of articles on Innocent's policies.

Heresy and the Friars

H. C. Lea, *A History of the Inquisition of the Middle Ages,* 3 vols. (1888), has considerable material on the Albigensian heresy, but the reader would do well to take Lea's judgments with some reservations and to read in conjunction with it E. Vacandard, *The Inquisition* (1908), which sees this terrible institution more in the light of its time. S. Runciman, *The Medieval Menichee* (1947), follows the history of the Dualist tradition in Christianity. This is a sound and urbane book. For the crusade against heretics, see J. R. Strayer, *The Albigensian Crusades* (1971), and W. L. Wakefield, *Heresy, Crusade and Inquisition in Southern France* (1974).

The best one-volume collection of the lives and writings of St. Francis is in *The Little Flowers of St. Francis** (Everyman's Library). P. Sabatier, *The Life of St. Francis of Assisi* (1894), is a scholarly book with good bibliographic material, but J. Jorgensen, *St. Francis,** trans. by T. O. Sloane (1955), is more interesting. B. Jarrett's *Life of St. Dominic** (1924) gives a good, if adulatory, picture of the man, and P. Mandonnet, *St. Dominic and His Work* (1944), emphasizes the spirit and work of the Order. Another very good collection of the same material is M. A. Habig, *St. Francis* (1973).

super infernu & contristat e valde &
laxate sunt o s aie q erant i iferno &
clamabant voce magna dicentes vn
dicimus te xpe fili dei vivi q dignat
es nob refrigeriu dare h diei & h noc
tis quam totum temp q vivimus
i terra. Vir ergo qui custodivit die dnica
qm ipi habebit pte cu scis i scla sclor.

12 The Rise of the Secular State

The popes and the mendicant orders had combined to check the spread of heresy in the thirteenth century. By organizing the Albigensian Crusades and the Inquisition the popes ended the threat of popular heresy. A remarkable group of theologians (mostly Dominicans and Franciscans) succeeded in reconciling the new Greco-Arabic learning with the Christian faith and thus reduced the danger of intellectual heresy. By the middle of the thirteenth century there was little open dissent from orthodox doctrine in western Europe. Most people were honestly and sincerely Catholic in belief; the few who were not found it expedient to pretend that they were.

THE IMPACT OF ECONOMIC CHANGE

Yet the position of the Church was less secure than it seemed. The Church could deal with the heretic, who was an open enemy; dealing with the lukewarm friend was a more difficult problem. Men had to make a living and obey their rulers. But at what point did a normal desire to make a decent living turn into an immoderate lust for wealth? At what point did obedience to authority turn into a loyalty that subordinated the interests of the Church to those of the state? It was easier to sense this gradual growth of worldliness than to do anything about it, and the Church itself was infected by the ills it sought to cure. Some clergymen sought to accumulate offices in order to augment their income. Even more of them entered the service of secular rulers. The first group exposed the Church to criticism; the second often failed to defend its interests.

It has always been hard for a religion to deal with the problem of prosperity. Wealth creates pride and self-assurance, neither of which is entirely compatible with devoutness. The thirteenth-century Church strove, with some success, to give the wealthy a sense of social responsibility. It condemned flagrant profiteering and callous neglect of the poor. It accepted the idea that a man who invested in a commercial enterprise was entitled to interest on the money he risked, but it denounced the small moneylenders who charged high rates for personal loans. Many of these loansharks in the end left large sums to charities to atone for their profits from usury. But while the Church

Opposite: Manuscript illumination of the coronation ceremony from a Coronation Order (text of the ceremony) written between 1272 and 1325. The king may be Edward II.

Medieval coins. Top to bottom: Florentine gold florin (thirteenth century); Venetian gold ducat (thirteenth century); obverse and reverse of a silver penny of Henry III of England (thirteenth century); gold agnel of Philip VI of France (fourteenth century). The gold coins were used for large-scale transactions; the silver, for wages and household purchases.

could mitigate some of the consequences, it could not alter the fact that western Europe was shifting to an economic system in which money was becoming more important than inherited status. Concern over money made it hard for men to follow the teachings of the Church or to put the interests of the Church ahead of their own.

The growth of a money economy involved the landed classes, including most churchmen, in an economic squeeze. Increasing demand caused a steady rise in prices, while income from land lagged behind. Ancient custom or fixed agreements determined what peasants paid. On many estates lords had commuted labor services and payments in kind for rents of a few pennies an acre. It was not easy to change customary payments or contractual agreements, for peasants who were pushed too hard could flee to the towns or to the new lands that were still being cleared in the East. Thus the real income of landlords tended to decrease during the thirteenth century.

Some landlords saved themselves by leasing their domain lands for short times. This gave them an income related to the market value of their produce rather than an income tied to a customary rent. In some regions landlords turned as much land as they could into pasture, since wool brought in more profit than grain. But these devices could not satisfy the financial needs of kings and princes, of popes and bishops, who had to govern as well as live comfortably. Sooner or later they had to supplement their ordinary income by taxes and fees. When they did, however, they stirred up bitter resentment among their subjects and conflicts among themselves over who had the right to tax.

The Church was especially vulnerable to criticism of its financial policies. The income tax on the clergy, first imposed by Innocent III, was levied more and more frequently, and at higher rates—10 percent or even 20 percent. Fees were imposed or increased for papal letters, legal documents, and confirmation of appointments to high offices in the Church. Both taxes and fees were derived, in the last analysis, from payments by laymen. As a result the Church was criticized for being too eager to raise money, too ready to give spiritual benefits in return for cash payments. The more zealous wing of the Franciscans urged that clergymen abandon all their property and lead lives of apostolic poverty, but this solution was hardly realistic. The Franciscan Order itself was acquiring property, even though it tried to disguise the fact by vesting title in trustees. When reformers—Franciscans and others—became bishops and popes, they found that in the existing economic situation they could make no important changes in the Church's financial system. Since not even the most zealous reformers could find inoffensive ways of raising money, there was a loss of respect for the Church as an organization, even among men who were completely orthodox in doctrine.

THE FRENCH AND ENGLISH MONARCHIES

At the very time that respect for the Church was declining, the prestige of secular governments was rising. These governments were not hostile to the Church, but they were consciously or unconsciously competing with the Church for the loyalty of the people. And just as the Church was becoming more worldly and more like a secular government, so secular rulers were reasserting their old claim to be God's lieutenants on earth and were taking on responsibilities hitherto reserved for the Church. Kings claimed to be protectors of the common welfare, agents of divine justice, defenders of the faith. None of the great thirteenth-century popes became a saint, but several kings were canonized. And one of these saintly kings, Louis IX of France, probably exercised greater moral authority over the Europe of his day than did any churchman.

St. Louis

Louis IX (1226–70) was the grandson of Philip Augustus, the first really strong French king. Philip had conquered the northwestern part of France in his war with John, and Philip's son, Louis VIII, had acquired large holdings in the south by his timely participation in the crusade against the Albigensians. As a result, Louis IX was far more powerful than any combination of hostile French lords. He put down a few halfhearted rebellions early in his reign, and for the rest of his life his authority was never challenged. No one could oppose Louis' claim to rights or land. An arrogant man might have abused this power, but Louis was determined to follow the ideals of a Christian ruler. He settled the longstanding dispute with England by a generous treaty that gave the English king many border districts in Aquitaine. He kept faith with all men, even with Moslems. In France he submitted all disputed questions to the decisions of his courts and did his best to restrain the zeal of his administrative agents, who tended to exaggerate the extent of royal rights. No other medieval king had such a reputation for honesty and fair dealing.

Louis was pious and generous, but he was not soft. His loyalty to the faith did not keep him from exercising independent judgment about the policies of the Church. He refused to join Pope Innocent IV in the attack on the emperor Frederick II; he rejected demands of the French bishops that he punish all men who remained excommunicated for more than a year. He felt that, as a Christian king, he knew better than anyone else how to provide for the spiritual and material welfare of his people.

Louis' concern for law and justice led, naturally enough, to a strengthening of the royal judicial system. During his reign one of the great institutions of the French monarchy was created—the Parlement of Paris. This was the king's own court, staffed with his closest advisers. It heard appeals from the decisions of his local administrative agents and, even more important, it heard appeals from the courts of the great feudal lords. By reviewing, and often reversing, the decisions of feudal courts, it established a legal basis for royal claims to supremacy over all subjects.

The king's local courts, headed by bailiffs and other administrative agents, were even more zealous than the Parlement in upholding royal rights. Since

Statue of Louis IX, in the church of Mainville in Normandy.

St. Louis as Described by Joinville

Jean de Joinville, a noble of Champagne, was a friend of St. Louis and went with him on his crusade of 1248.

This holy man loved God with all his heart, and imitated his works. For example, just as God died because he loved his people, so the king risked his life many times for the love of his people. . . . He said once to his eldest son: . . . "I beg you that you make yourself loved by the people of your realm, for truly, I would rather that a Scot came from Scotland and governed the people of the kingdom justly and well than that you should govern them badly. . . ." The holy king loved the truth so much that he kept his promises even to the Saracens.

A friar told the king . . . that he had never read that a kingdom was destroyed or changed rulers except through lack of justice. . . . The king did not forget this lesson but governed his land justly and well, according to the will of God. . . . Often in summer he went to sit down under an oak-tree in the wood of Vincennes, after hearing mass, and made us sit around him. And all those who had suits to bring him came up, without being hindered by ushers or other people. And he would ask them: "Does anyone here have a suit?" And those who had requests would get up. . . . And then he would call Lord Pierre de Fontaines and Lord Geoffroi de Villette [two of his legal experts] and say to one of them: "Settle this affair for me." And if he saw anything to correct in what they said on his behalf, he would do so.

From Jean de Joinville, *Histoire de Saint Louis,* ed. by N. de Wailly (Paris: Firmin Didot, 1874), pp. 11, 34.

earlier kings had been too weak to enforce their theoretical claims, no exact boundary between the privileges of local lords and the rights of the monarch had ever been drawn. Thus on issues for which there were no clear precedents it was only natural that the bailiffs should rule in favor of the king. Louis did not take undue advantage of this situation; in fact, he and his Parlement often modified the more extreme claims of the bailiffs. But the net result was an increase in royal power, an increase that was cheerfully accepted by most of the people in the country. After all, Louis had suppressed disorder, and his courts, though not perfect, dispensed a better brand of justice than those of most feudal lords.

A just and powerful king, Louis was also a zealous crusader. Jerusalem had been lost to the Moslems in 1187, and all efforts to recover it had failed. Armed expeditions had gained nothing, and a treaty arranged by Frederick II of Germany had given the Christians only a few years of occupancy of the city before it fell again to the Moslems. These successive failures had somewhat dampened enthusiasm for overseas expeditions, but Louis felt that his responsibilities as a Christian ruler extended beyond the limits of his realm. In 1248 and again in 1270 he led crusades to recover Jerusalem. The earlier expedition had some chance of success, but after a first victory Louis' army was cut off from its supplies and was forced to surrender. The second expedition was hopeless from the beginning, for Louis let himself be talked into attacking the outlying Moslem state of Tunis. Even if he had conquered the country, it would have done his cause little good; as it was, he and many of his followers died of fever soon after landing.

Louis IX was made a saint within a generation after his death. His canonization was more than a personal tribute to a pious crusader; it completed the work of sanctifying the French monarchy. Louis' grandson, who insisted on the canonization as part of a general settlement of disputes with the papacy, was quite aware of the political value of the act. Louis' long search for justice and order had been officially recognized by the Church, and it had created an almost inexhaustible reservoir of support for his dynasty. Some of his successors were evil and some were weak, but for centuries loyalty to the king was the strongest political force in France. The king stood as the symbol of unity and good government; he alone could override provincial differences and selfish local ambitions. France remained Catholic, but loyalty to the Church began to take second place to loyalty to the state.

Henry III of England (1216–72) discusses the progress of a building (perhaps Westminster Abbey) with his architects. The workmen are raising materials to the masons with a windlass.

1066	1135	1154	1189	1199	1216	1272	1307
Norman Kings	Disputed Succession	Henry II	Richard I	John	Henry III	Edward I	

Henry III of England

France was united only through its king and his bureaucracy. The provinces retained their own customs and privileges; no one could have spoken of a French common law or the "rights of Frenchmen." But in England the monarchy, in its long years of ascendancy, had created a common law and common institutions. The propertied classes in England had become attached to the laws and institutions that protected their rights. Thus the growing loyalty to the English state was loyalty to a system of government as much as it was loyalty to a dynasty. The king could not claim that he alone was working for the common welfare, for his opponents could assert that they too were seeking the good of the "community of the realm." Thus in England even bitter struggles between king and aristocracy could not destroy the unity of the country.

This unusual political situation in England explains certain apparent contradictions in the reign of Henry III (1216–72). On the one hand, royal officials strengthened the administrative and judicial institutions of the country. They created new types of general taxation and devised new writs for bringing more cases into royal courts. Most important of all, the Lateran Council of 1215 had forbidden the use of ordeals to settle criminal cases. In other countries, decisions on such cases were turned over to lay judges, but in England trial by jury, already used to settle most land disputes, became the normal procedure for all criminal offenses too. Thus almost all lawsuits of any significance were now tried by royal judges, and private courts began to die out. These developments were summed up in a remarkable treatise on English law based on a work by Henry de Bracton, a royal judge. The final version, written in the 1250s, gave a clear, logical, and thorough explanation of the common law, citing precedents and stating general principles. This made the common law so coherent and self-sufficient that it was invulnerable to all outside influences for many centuries, and the book became the basic text for the training of English lawyers.

On the other hand, during Henry's reign there was constant friction between the king and his barons. The barons were not trying to destroy the central government; they were trying to use it to protect their status and their views of what English policy should be. And they often found it expedient to claim that they were defending the realm against a foolish and spendthrift monarch.

When Henry came of age in 1225, the barons persuaded him to confirm Magna Carta by granting him a tax. There was no rebellion, as there had been in 1215, but a fair bargain. Henry III gave his consent without coercion, and the 1225 version of the Charter was accepted by everyone as the law of the land. What is more, the king made his officials enforce it, thereby satisfying the barons for some time. But by the 1240s they were once more in open opposition to the king. They could not hate him as they had John—Henry was a likable, honest man, almost as pious as St. Louis—but they did dislike his policies. He wasted money in vain attempts to reconquer lost territories in France. He filled bishoprics and secular offices with his French relatives and friends. Moreover, he allowed the pope to draw large sums of money from England for the papal war against the Hohenstaufen rulers of Italy. Modern nationalism did not exist in the thirteenth century, but we can see the beginnings of nationalism in the attitude of the barons: they were not interested in Henry's French lands; they resented his French friends; they saw no reason for England to help the pope. They wanted English jobs to be filled by Englishmen, and they

The shield of Simon de Montfort (1208?–65).

wanted English money to be spent in England. The barons' opposition to foreign intruders and foreign entanglements were supported by most lesser landholders and by a surprising number of English clergymen.

Henry III's chronic shortage of money enhanced the power of the barons. Ordinary income from the royal domain was barely adequate for peacetime needs, and Magna Carta made it difficult to gain new revenues without the consent of the barons. If Henry wanted to wage war he had to levy taxes. But after 1240 the barons steadily refused to grant any taxes. Henry nevertheless went ahead with an ambitious project to help the pope conquer Sicily. The English clergy, under papal pressure, gave him some money but not enough. By 1258 Henry was hopelessly in debt, and his foreign policy was a complete failure. In desperation, he appointed a committee of barons to reform the government.

The baronial committee soon forgot reform and concentrated on making policy and appointing high officials. Naturally, it soon split into factions. The barons had found it easy to agree in their opposition to Henry's policies; they found it more difficult to agree on a positive policy of their own. Though the barons clearly needed someone to act as leader, they felt that they were all equal, and they were jealous of the ablest man in their group, Simon de Montfort. In the end, Simon gained control of the government, but he lost most of his baronial support in doing so. Henry's eldest son, Edward, managed to raise an army with which he defeated and killed Simon in 1265, and Henry's authority was fully restored.

This episode is significant for two reasons. First, it set a pattern that was to be repeated in England many times during the next two centuries. Again and again the barons, annoyed by royal policy, took over the central government; and again and again factionalism and jealousy kept them from maintaining their position. Second, the struggle between Henry and the barons for control of the central government speeded up the development of a representative assembly in England. The two sides were so evenly matched that they both sought support from men of lesser rank—the knights and other free landholders in the rural areas and the burgesses of the towns. The easiest way to win the support of these men was to invite them to send representatives to the full meetings of the king's court, which, from the 1240s on, were beginning to be given the name Parliaments.

Early Parliaments

A Parliament, in the middle years of the thirteenth century, was a meeting of the king with his chief officials, his bishops, and his barons. *Parliament* was a slang term at first; it meant "talk-fest" and could be used for any sort of discussion. Gradually it came to mean a meeting at which difficult cases were heard that could not be decided by ordinary law courts. The English Parliament, like the French *parlement,* was a high court of justice. Even today the House of Lords is the highest court in England, though cases are actually heard only by specially appointed "law lords." But the English Parliament was also a Great Council that advised the king on matters of policy and granted taxes. It was in Parliament, for example, that the English barons criticized Henry III's plans and refused to give him money. A meeting of parliament, with all the great men of the realm assembled to deliberate and make important decisions, was truly an impressive occasion.

Representatives from the countryside and the towns who were summoned before Parliament were naturally influenced by its authority and prestige, and they in turn influenced their constituents when they went back home to report what had taken place. It was useful to impress these people because local government in England was still largely controlled by local notables. The king of England, unlike the king of France, had never had to establish a provincial bureaucracy. With no conquered provinces to hold down and no strong loyalty to provincial institutions to fear, it was perfectly safe, and much cheaper, for the central government to pass on its orders to local notables, who served without pay. Thus in the counties the sheriffs, the tax collectors, and the custodians of royal property were usually knights of the shire—that is, country gentlemen resident in the district they governed. In the towns the mayors and aldermen were well-to-do businessmen. These local officials proved reasonably loyal, but they found their government jobs burdensome and annoyingly unprofitable. When they did not like government orders they could drag their feet with no fear of reprisal. It was no great punishment to be removed from office, and those removed had to be replaced with men of the same sort. Thus when the king or his barons wanted to introduce any innovation in government, such as a new law or a new tax, it was clearly advisable to gain the goodwill of the knights and burgesses. And a good way of doing so was to invite them to send representatives to Parliament, where they could hear and discuss the reasons for the shift in policy. Since Parliament was a court, these representatives were, in a sense, attorneys for their community. They were bound by the decisions of the court, but they could bring petitions to it. When they returned home, they would explain the court's acts to their fellow landholders or businessmen.

Both Henry III and the baronial leader, Simon de Montfort, had tried to justify their policies by asking the counties to send knights to parliament. In 1265 Simon de Montfort, in an effort to compensate for his loss of baronial support, took the additional step of asking the towns to send representatives. These precedents were not forgotten. In 1268 Henry III summoned both knights and burgesses to Parliament, and Edward I called the same groups to the first great assembly of his reign in 1275. These early representatives had little power and always accepted the propositions laid before them by king and barons, but the very fact that they were being summoned at frequent intervals was to be significant in the future.

Parliament was not the first or the only representative assembly. During the Middle Ages most governments found it expedient to summon local leaders to hear explanations of policy. Innocent III, for example, had called representatives of the towns when he was establishing his government in the Papal States, and the Spanish kings held similar assemblies during the reconquest of the peninsula from the Moslems. In the end, the English Parliament was to prove unique, but there was nothing unusual in the experiments conducted by Simon de Montfort and Henry III.

Portrait of Emperor Frederick II, from a manuscript of his treatise, *The Art of Hunting with Falcons.*

THE PAPAL–HOHENSTAUFEN FEUD

In Germany and Italy the central government was far weaker than in England and France—a situation that Frederick II, whom Innocent III had made emperor, spent his life trying to correct. Though he failed in this effort, he came close enough to success in Italy to precipitate the last great struggle between Empire and papacy.

Frederick II was by birth and education an Italian, although he was descended from the Hohenstaufen of Germany. He spent a few years in Germany after becoming emperor, but he never felt at home there and never had much power over the Germans. Apparently deciding that he could do nothing with Germany, at least until he had brought Italy fully under control, he abandoned almost all authority to the princes of the Empire. All he expected from Germany was a supply of soldiers for his Italian wars.

In Italy he followed exactly the opposite course. First he eliminated all opposition in his hereditary kingdom of Sicily, transforming it into a nearly absolute monarchy, and then he began to revive the old imperial claims to central and northern Italy. Thanks to the factional quarrels within and among the Italian towns, he was able to make substantial acquisitions of territory. Some of the northern Italians became so frightened that they revived the Lombard League, but Frederick crushed them at Cortenuova in 1237. For the moment he seemed to be in control of the entire Italian peninsula.

The papacy, however, was still determined to keep Italy from falling into the hands of one master. The independence of the Church seemed bound up with the independence of the Papal States, and Frederick's victories were threatening that independence. No pope could believe that an emperor who ruled all Italy except the region around Rome would long respect Rome itself. Innocent III had kept the Empire in turmoil for years rather than risk this danger; the precedents he laid down were hard to forget.

Moreover, Frederick II's orthodoxy was somewhat doubtful. No one was ever sure what this brilliant and inquisitive man really believed. He exchanged friendly letters with Moslem rulers; he dabbled in science and magic; he was accused of writing a book called *The Three Impostors: Moses, Jesus, and Mohammed.* This charge was completely false, but the fact that it could be made tells something of Frederick's reputation. He tried hard to convince people that he was an orthodox ruler, even going on a crusade and persecuting heretics, but these actions raised more doubts than they settled. He succeeded in regaining Jerusalem for a few years, not by fighting the Moslems but by making a treaty with the sultan of Egypt, and his persecution of heretics seemed prompted only by a desire to improve his political position.

When it became apparent that Frederick was going to insist on full control of both northern and southern Italy, the

GERMANY AND ITALY AT THE TIME OF FREDERICK II
ca. 1250

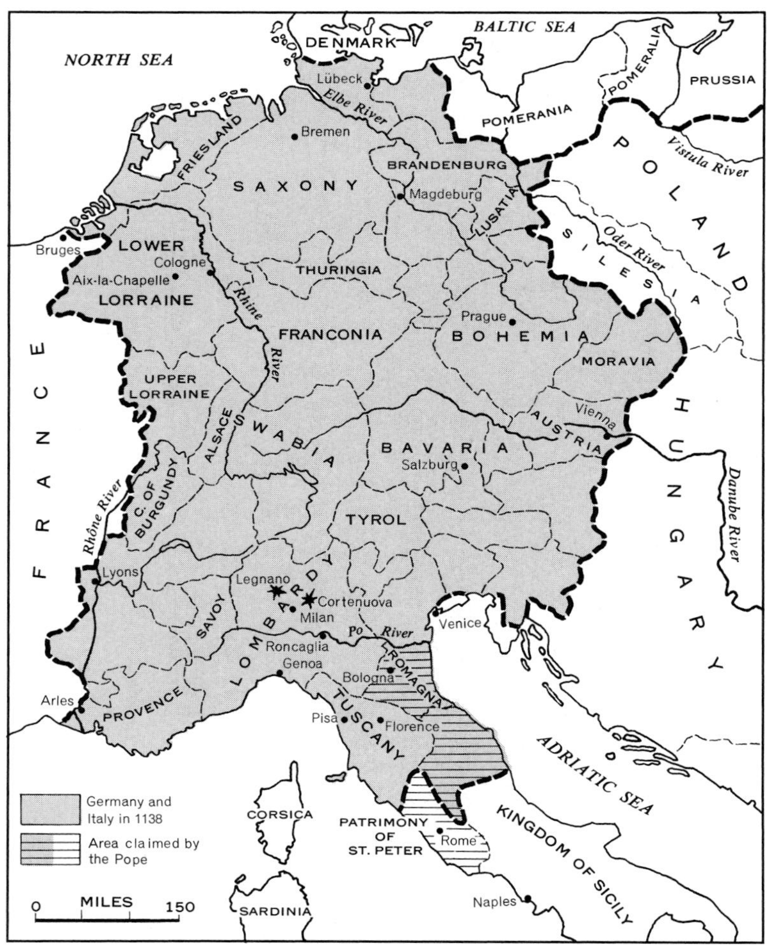

In 1241 Frederick's fleet captured (or drowned) two cardinals and a hundred bishops who were on their way to a council summoned by Gregory IX to depose the emperor. This manuscript illustration shows Frederick in the ship on the left, though actually he was not present. On the right, his soldiers attack the prelates in a ship bearing the papal ensign of the keys of St. Peter.

pope decided that drastic measures were necessary. Pope Gregory IX tried to hold a council in Rome to discuss the problem, but Frederick intercepted the fleet bearing many of the prelates and captured or drowned most of them. This direct attack on the Church did not improve Frederick's reputation. The next pope, Innocent IV, just as determined and almost as able as his great namesake, Innocent III, called a council at Lyons in 1245. The council declared that Frederick had forfeited all his possessions, and that neither he nor any member of his family should ever be allowed to rule in Germany or Italy. Innocent IV proclaimed a crusade against Frederick and imposed a tax on the clergy to pay for armies to carry it out.

The papal attack destroyed the last remnants of imperial power in Germany. Turning the conflict to their own advantage, the princes refused to obey either Frederick or an opposition line of rulers elected by propapal factions. Germany became a loose confederation of states under the control of princes who were free to accept or reject the policies suggested by the nominal ruler. No German emperor after Frederick exercised any real authority except in his own family possessions.

In Italy the issue was not decided so quickly. Frederick held on to most of the territory he had gained, but he never managed to build up a strong government in the north. After his death in 1250 the towns of northern and central Italy became independent, though the Kingdom of Sicily remained loyal to his sons. The papacy might have been satisfied with this state of affairs—after all, the danger of encirclement had been dispelled forever—but it had been too badly frightened by Frederick to take any chances. So the popes carried on the war against the "viper brood" of the Hohenstaufen, refusing to rest until the hated family had been ejected from Sicily and Naples. They preached crusades, collected taxes from the clergy to cover their expenses, and sent cardinals out with armies to do battle with Frederick's heirs. And when all these efforts proved ineffectual, they turned for help to England and France. The attempt to involve England led only to the rebellion of the English barons against Henry III, but the approach to France met with greater success. St. Louis reluctantly permitted his brother, Charles of Anjou, to attempt the conquest of the Kingdom of Sicily. Charles, aided by crusade privileges (including remission of sins for his soldiers) and crusade taxes, defeated the last Hohenstaufen ruler of Sicily in a lightning campaign in 1266. A grandson of Frederick II made a desperate attempt to regain the kingdom, but his forces were crushed in 1268 and the young Hohenstaufen was executed in cold blood. The papacy, aided by the French, had won a complete victory over its enemies.

Loss of Prestige by the Church

But in winning this political victory, the papacy had lost moral prestige. There had been some doubts about the deposition of Frederick II—St. Louis had preserved a careful neutrality in this struggle—although the Church clearly had a case against him. Frederick was threatening the independence of the Papal States, and he was certainly unconventional and possibly unorthodox in his ideas. But Frederick's heirs were much less powerful and much less dangerous to the Church; it seemed pure vindictiveness to harry them for two decades. The Church was using its spiritual authority to gain a political end. The pope was acting very much like a secular prince, assembling armies, making alliances, carrying on political intrigues. The distinction between ecclesiastical government and secular government was no longer clear. One could argue that if it was proper for the pope to tax the clergy for a war in Italy, it was equally proper for a king to tax the clergy to defend his kingdom. This claim was to cause the next great conflict between the papacy and secular rulers.

Moreover, the popes had won their victory over the Hohenstaufen only by creating political instability in both Germany and Italy, and this instability in the long run weakened the Church. No one in Germany was strong enough to protect the bishops, so they had to fight and intrigue to protect themselves. No one in Germany was strong enough to wipe out the heresies that erupted in the fifteenth century and laid a foundation for Luther's revolt against the papacy in the sixteenth century. In northern and central Italy the absence of any central government encouraged the growth of powerful city-states that dominated the rural districts around them. Genoa and Venice, the towns that controlled the lucrative trade with the East, remained fairly stable and used their energy to establish colonies in the Aegean and, even (for Genoa) on the northern shores of the Black Sea. But the inland towns, even wealthy trading centers such as Florence and Pisa, were constantly plagued by factionalism, rebellions, and wars among themselves. The situation was no better in the Kingdom of Sicily (which included both the Island of Sicily and Southern Italy). Peter III of Aragon, who had married the daughter of the last Hohenstaufen king of Sicily, took advantage of a rebellion against

St. Thomas Aquinas, detail from the Crucifixion, by Fra Angelico (1387–1455). Although this representation was made two centuries after Thomas lived, it seems accurately to depict his large head and bearlike appearance.

the French ruler who had been made ruler of the kingdom by the Church. He seized Sicily in 1282, but never acquired Naples and the mainland, which remained in the hands of a younger branch of the French royal family. This kingdom of Naples, torn by quarrels over the succession, was unable to help the papacy.

The situation around Rome was especially precarious. The Roman nobility was trying to build up petty lordships in the region around the city, the small towns around Rome were striving for independence and territory, and Rome itself was torn by quarrels among the great families. The Pope's position was almost impossible. He could either flee Italy and lose the prestige that was associated with Rome, or stay and play the petty politics of a minor prince. Neither course would strengthen the papacy.

SCHOLARSHIP AND THE ARTS

It took a generation for the Church to feel the full consequences of the new political situation; meanwhile it enjoyed its last years of unquestioned leadership in Europe (1250–98). The kings of the West were at peace with one another and obedient to the pope. Both the education and the behavior of the clergy had steadily improved. This last period of Church leadership saw the building of the most perfect Gothic cathedrals and the culmination of medieval Christian philosophy in the work of Thomas Aquinas (1225–74).

It was probably no accident that these two forms of expression reached their peak at about the same time. There was a strong logical element in the perfected Gothic cathedral, just as there was a strong architectonic quality in Thomas Aquinas' thought. In both, the basic structural plan is clearly revealed, uncluttered by architectural or literary embellishment. Just as the cross section of a pillar of a Gothic church shows exactly what the superstructure will be, so the first paragraph of a chapter by Thomas Aquinas reveals exactly how his argument will proceed. But while we still appreciate the qualities of Gothic architecture—the emphasis on height and light, the clean expression of the function of each architectural member—we are less at home with the methods and ideas of medieval scholastic philosophy.

The Reconciliation of Christian and Classical Philosophy

This extract from the *Summa Contra Gentiles* by St. Thomas Aquinas shows how a thirteenth-century scholar was able to use the ideas of Aristotle.

We have now shown that the effort to demonstrate the existence of God is not a vain one. We shall therefore proceed to set forth the arguments by which both philosophers and Catholic teachers have proved that God exists.

We shall first set forth the arguments by which Aristotle proceeds to prove that God exists. The aim of Aristotle is to do this in two ways, beginning with motion.

Of these ways the first is as follows. Everything that is moved is moved by another. That some things are in motion—for example, the sun—is evident from sense. Therefore, it is moved by something else that moves it. This mover is itself either moved or not moved. If it is not, we have reached our conclusion—namely, that we must posit some unmoved mover. This we call God. If it is moved, it is moved by another mover. We must, consequently, either proceed to infinity, or we must arrive at some unmoved mover. Now, it is not possible to proceed to infinity. Hence we must posit some prime unmoved mover.

From *On the Truth of the Catholic Faith. Summa Contra Gentiles,* trans. by A. C. Pegis (New York: Doubleday, 1955), p. 85.

St. Thomas Aquinas

Thomas Aquinas, unlike some other Christian thinkers, feared neither the world nor the new knowledge about the world that scholars had acquired from the Greeks and the Arabs. God had put man in the world not to punish him but to enlighten his feeble understanding through concrete examples. Man could rely on his reason, which was the gift of God; the truths discovered by the ancient philosophers were perfectly valid truths, though they might be incomplete. Thus a pagan philosopher could give an acceptable proof of the existence of God even though he knew nothing of the doctrine of the Trinity. Reason needed to be enlightened by faith, but there was no conflict between the two.

In the same way, there should be no conflict between the Church and secular governments. Secular government was necessary and good in itself, for it gave men an opportunity to manifest social virtues. Even among the pagans, secular governments were divinely established and should be obeyed. Thomas admitted that it was proper to resist a king who was openly violating the law of God, but he felt that resistance to a secular ruler should be resorted to only after everything else had failed.

As for the new wealth, here again there was no danger if men used their reason properly. God had given man dominion over the world, and it was part of the divine plan to make full use of the world's natural resources. Land did not fulfill its function unless it was cultivated; a tree was of no use unless it was used for construction. Men should remember their Christian duty to the poor, and they should never allow their desire for wealth to become immoderate. But there was nothing wrong in an honest effort to earn a decent living.

Thomas Aquinas believed that in the light of true reason everything made sense, that the world was a harmonious whole. Wisdom was the greatest earthly good, and the felicity of the afterlife consisted in the contemplation of the eternal Wisdom which is God. It was this serene conviction of the unity and rationality of all experience that made Thomas Aquinas' work so persuasive, that led to his early canonization and to his present reputation as the leading philosopher of Catholicism.

Even in his own day, not all scholars shared the views of Thomas Aquinas. Doubtless there was some professional jealousy involved; Aquinas was a Dominican, and scholars in other orders resented the influence the Dominicans had acquired in theological studies. But there was also honest concern, both about the extreme rationalism of his approach and about the reliance he placed on Aristotle and other Greek philosophers. The most eminent Franciscan theologian, St. Bonaventura, emphasized will rather than reason. And a group of Franciscan scholars at Oxford undermined the philosophy of Aquinas by proving that his chief authority, Aristotle, had made certain mistakes about natural phenomena. In correcting these mistakes they helped start a new trend in physics, which, advanced by obscure scholars of the fourteenth and fifteenth centuries, culminated in the work of Galileo. Roger Bacon was a member of this Oxford

Dante's Divine Comedy

THE INSCRIPTION ON THE ENTRANCE TO HELL

Through me you pass into the woeful city
Through me you pass into eternal pain
Through me you go amid those lost forever.
Justice it was that moved my Great Creator;
Power divine and highest wisdom made me
Together with God's own primeval love.
Before me there was nothing save those things
Eternal, and eternal I endure.
All hope abandon, ye who enter here.

THE ATTACK AT ANAGNI

Dante disliked Boniface VIII, whom he consigned to hell, but still felt that the attack at Anagni, which he describes below through the lips of Hugh Capet, was an outrage.

O avarice, what worse canst thou now do
Since thou dost so completely rule my race
That they care nothing for their flesh and blood?
Past wrongs and future they will now compound.
Into Anagni storms the lilied flag;
Christ is a captive in his Vicar's form,
And the old mockery again renewed
With vinegar and gall. I see him bleed
Amid the living robbers; Pilate too,
I see, so cruel that even this dreadful deed,
Is not enough.

THE FINAL VISION

O grace abundant, through which I presumed
To fix my gaze on the eternal light
Which near consumes who dares to look thereon.
And in those depths I saw, bound up by love
Into one volume, all the universe. . . .
Here vigor failed the lofty vision, but
The will moved ever onward, like a wheel
In even motion, by the love impelled
Which moves the sun in heaven and all the stars.

From Dante, *Inferno,* canto 3; *Purgatory,* canto 20; *Paradise,* canto 33, trans. by H. F. Cary (London: Bell, 1877).

group, but he has received more credit than he deserves; his vague predictions about automotive vehicles and the like had no scientific basis. The real leader of the Oxford school was Bacon's teacher, Robert Grosseteste. Grosseteste realized that theory needed to be verified and refined by experiment. His own work on optics was not entirely successful, but it led to a better understanding of the field, notably in an explanation of the rainbow (*ca.* 1300) that was almost the one accepted today.

These scholarly disputes shook the confidence of scholars. More important was the fact that Thomas' arguments were too rational to have much influence on laymen. He might see no conflict between reason and faith, no opposition between secular interests and those of the Church, but for most people these contradictions did exist and could not be exorcised by words. They were faced with hard choices between the teachings of the Church and the demands of secular life, and they did not always choose the side of the Church.

Dante

The greatest medieval poet—one of the greatest poets of all time—was Dante Alighieri (1265–1321). One of the first men to write in the vernacular in Italy, he helped establish the Tuscan dialect as the standard form of the Italian language. He wrote graceful lyrics in Italian and two notable treatises in Latin, one defending his use of the vernacular, the other a strong plea for strengthening and preserving the Empire. But the work for which Dante will always be remembered is the *Divine Comedy,* a vision of Hell, Purgatory, and Heaven written in magnificent Italian verse.

Dante had a troubled and unhappy life. Deeply involved in Florentine politics, he was permanently exiled from the city he loved in 1302. In spite of these troubles Dante, like Thomas Aquinas, remained convinced of the unity and meaningfulness of all human experience. Unlike many of his contemporaries, he did not sink into pessimism or seek out partial truths. He was almost the last representative of the confident, optimistic, all-embracing spirit of the great period of medieval civilization.

Dante was well read in both secular and religious literature. His guide through Hell and Purgatory was the Roman poet Virgil, and this part of his poem is full of allusions to classical mythology. But he also knew scholastic philosophy; the *Paradise* in many places reads like a verse translation of Thomas Aquinas. Like Thomas Aquinas, Dante saw no contradiction between the truths worked out by human reason and the truths revealed to the Church; all knowledge led to God if it was rightly used.

But to Dante knowledge was not enough; even good conduct was not enough. Faith in God and love of God and of one's fellow man were the essentials. In Hell the most lightly punished sins were those against oneself, such as gluttony. The lower depths were reserved for those who hurt others, and the

Dante and his guide, Virgil, visiting the circle of Hell to which usurers have been relegated (illustration from a fourteenth-century Italian manuscript).

worst sinners were Judas, who betrayed Christ, and Brutus and Cassius, who betrayed Caesar. In Purgatory sins were purged through suffering, and angels sang Beatitudes at each step of the ascent. In Paradise Dante came closer and closer to the eternal Light until he finally had his great vision of God—"the love which moves the sun and all the stars."

The *Divine Comedy* was recognized as a classic almost as soon as it was written, but admiration for the poem did not mean wide acceptance of its point of view. Few of Dante's contemporaries had his serenity or his breadth of vision; few could accept any longer his dream of a harmonious world in which men could seek both happiness on earth and eternal rewards in heaven. By the end of the thirteenth century secular and religious goals were coming into conflict, and more and more attention was being given to the secular.

Secularism in Art and Literature

The gradual growth of secular interests may be seen clearly in art and literature. For example, after 1270 there is a striking change in statues of the Virgin. In early Gothic sculpture she is the Queen of Heaven, majestic and dignified. In late Gothic sculpture she is girlish and human, with none of the semidivine characteristics of the earlier period. In literature the break is shown by the difference between the two parts of a famous poem, *Romance of the Rose.* The first part, written by Guillaume de Lorris in the 1230s, is an allegory of courtly love; the second part, written forty years later by Jean de Meung, is a satiric encyclopedia. The first part respects the ethics and conventions of upper-class society; the second part attacks the fickleness of women and the greed of the clergy and gives brief summaries of the knowledge that every educated man was supposed to possess. The discrepancy between the two parts is obvious today, but apparently it was not obvious to men of the late thirteenth century. No other poem was so popular during the later Middle Ages. It was copied and recopied in hundreds of manuscripts, and at the end of the fourteenth century Chaucer began an English translation of it. Nothing illustrates better the rise of a class of educated laymen, eager for wordly knowledge, suspicious of the clergy, and a little cynical about ideals of any kind. Such men could no longer be counted on to support the policies of the Church if those policies interfered with their interests, or even with their convenience.

The Courtly Lover *ca.* 1237

But be thou careful to possess
Thy soul in gentleness and grace
Kindly of heart and bright of face
Towards all men, be they great or small. . . .
Watch well thy lips, that they may be
Ne'er stained with ill-timed ribaldry. . . .

Have special care
To honor dames as thou dost fare
Thy worldly ways, and shouldst thou hear
Calumnious speech of them, no fear
Have thou to bid men hold their peace. . . .
Above all else beware of pride. . . .
Let him who would in love succeed
To courteous word wed noble deed.

And next remember that, above
All else, gay heart inspireth love.
If thou shouldst know some cheerful play
Or game to wile dull hours away
My counsel is, neglect it not. . . .
And much with ladies 'twill advance
Thy suit, if well thou break a lance
For who in arms his own doth hold
Winneth acceptance manifold.
And if a voice strong, sweet and clear
Thou hast, and dames desire to hear
Thee sing, seek not to make excuse.

From Guillaume de Lorris, *Romance of the Rose,* Part I, trans. by F. S. Ellis (London: Dent, 1900), Vol. I, ll. 2184–2291.

ENGLAND, FRANCE, AND THE PAPACY

In England and France the central government grew stronger than ever in the last quarter of the thirteenth century. Edward I of England (1272–1307) was determined to increase his power but clever enough to retain the support of

Scene from a manuscript of *Romance of the Rose.* The lover enters the garden in which he will catch his first glimpse of the Rose.

most members of the propertied classes. He seems to have had two main objectives: first, to restore royal authority after the weak reign of his father, Henry III; and second, to make himself supreme ruler of the British Isles. He achieved his first goal through sheer force of personality, hard work, and intelligent selection of officials. Edward's royal rages were terrifying—the dean of St. Paul's dropped dead of fright during a dispute with him—and few men dared to contradict him openly. There was less reason to contradict him than there had been to oppose his father. Edward's policies were on the whole successful, especially during the first part of his reign. His avoidance of continental entanglements and his concentration on the conquest of Wales and Scotland harmonized with the desires of the aristocracy. As a result, Edward controlled his administration and, unlike his father, was not dominated by a baronial council.

He was less successful in attaining his second objective. He did complete the conquest of Wales, which had been begun long ago by the barons of William the Conqueror. He replaced the last native prince of Wales with his own infant son, thereby creating a precedent that has endured to the present day. But Scotland proved more troublesome. Edward first tried to install a puppet king, but when his candidate proved less subservient than he had hoped he deposed him and tried to rule the country directly. But Edward could not keep a big enough army in Scotland to suppress all dissent, and the Scots rebelled, first under William Wallace and then under Robert Bruce. The rebellion was still raging when Edward died, and the Scots won their independence at Bannockburn in 1314.

Edward I and Parliament

Outside his own island, Edward had to resist an attempt by the king of France to take over the duchy of Aquitaine, the last French holding of the English royal family. Edward's wars cost huge sums of money and kept him very busy—two reasons why he made greater use of Parliament than any of his predecessors. With all the important men in the kingdom present at meetings of Parliament, Edward could get their advice on policy, settle difficult legal cases, make statutes, and obtain grants of taxes. He could probably have done all this outside Parliament, but it was more efficient to take care of everything at one time and in one place. Moreover, Parliament had great prestige; it was the highest court in the kingdom, and it spoke for the community of the realm. England, unlike other countries, was so thoroughly united that decisions made in a single central assembly were accepted as binding on all men. Thus it was clearly advantageous to obtain the sanction of Parliament for as many decisions as possible. Edward lost nothing by following this policy, for he controlled Parliament as effectively as he did every other branch of government. He could not have foreseen that he was building up a powerful institution that might some day develop a will of its own.

Edward I of England (1272–1307) on his throne (illustration from a fourteenth-century manuscript).

Representatives of counties and towns came before the king in 1275, but for the next twenty years Edward summoned such representatives only sporadically. The essential element in Parliament was still the Council, composed of high officials, bishops, and barons. But in 1295 Edward summoned representatives to a very full meeting (the "Model Parliament"), and from that time on they were frequently present. Again, Edward's decision seems to have been prompted by the desire to save time and trouble. Legally, baronial approval was probably enough to validate his new laws and new taxes, but in practice it was necessary to win the support of the knights and burgesses as well. They were the men who, as sheriffs and mayors, would have to enforce the new laws, and they were the men from whose ranks tax collectors would have to be appointed. There were obvious advantages in bringing representatives of all the counties and towns together at a meeting of Parliament where they could listen to the great men of the realm discuss the king's needs.

These representatives had not yet joined together in an organized body, and their role seems to have been largely passive: "to hear and to obey," as some of the early summonses put it. Such opposition as there was in Parliament came from the barons. On one notable occasion in 1297, when Edward had pushed a new tax through at a very small meeting of the Council, the barons protested and forced the king to promise that in the future he would levy taxes only "with the common assent of the whole kingdom." This was not quite an admission that only Parliament could grant taxes, but it certainly implied that the assent of a large number of people was needed; and clearly the easiest way to obtain such assent was in Parliament. The barons hesitated to grant taxes on their own and were usually anxious to get the endorsement of at least the county representatives. And when, in the last years of Edward's reign, the barons sent him petitions asking for government reform, they invited the representatives of both counties and towns to join them. Finally, Edward was a great legislator. The common law needed additions and revisions to adjust to the new economic and political situation of the late thirteenth century. For example, it no longer made sense to transfer freehold land by granting it as a fief to the new owner; it was much simpler to rule that the purchaser merely took over all the rights and duties of the seller. Statutes such as this were discussed by the Council and often announced to the other members of Parliament. In all these ways the representatives gradually became caught up in the work of Parliament, though their position was still much inferior to that of the barons.

France Under Philip the Fair

In France, which was less unified politically than England, the growth of royal power followed a different course. The French barons were still struggling to preserve their local rights of government and their exemptions from the authority of royal officials. Not particularly interested in controlling the central government in Paris, they simply wanted to keep it from interfering with their lands and their subjects. The chief problem of the French king was not to keep the barons from dominating his council but to see that his orders were enforced in their lands.

This problem came to a head in the reign of Philip the Fair (Philip IV, 1285–1314), the grandson of St. Louis. Like his grandfather, Philip was pious, upright in his private life, and imbued with a sense of the divine mission of the French monarchy. But he was narrow-minded where St. Louis had been magnanimous, and grasping where St. Louis had been merely firm. The number of bureaucrats grew enormously during his reign, and Philip encouraged them in their efforts to expand royal authority. He was willing to condone any expedient to break the power of a local ruler who tried to retain a semi-independent status. Lesser vassals could not resist, but the more powerful men were indignant. It is not surprising that Philip spent a large part of his reign warring with his greatest vassals, including the king of England (as Duke of Aquitaine) and the Count of Flanders. He gained some land from both, but he never took the rich textile cities of Bruges and Ghent from Flanders, or the flourishing port of Bordeaux from Aquitaine.

Philip the Fair had a harder time than Edward I in raising money to pay for his wars. The French had never been subjected to a general tax, whereas the English had been afflicted with national taxes since the end of the twelfth century. Moreover, France was so divided that no central assembly like the English Parliament could impose a uniform tax on the whole country. Instead, royal agents had to negotiate with each region, and often with each lord or each town within each region. This cumbersome system consumed a great deal of time and reduced the yield. France was at least four times larger than England in both area and population, but it is doubtful whether Philip enjoyed any larger tax revenue than did Edward I.

These difficulties in collecting taxes explain some of the military weakness of France during the next hundred years. They also explain why the French representative assembly, the Estates General, never became as powerful as the English Parliament. Philip, as we shall see, was the first French king to call representatives to meetings at Paris. But he never asked them for a grant of taxes, for he knew that the country at large would pay little attention to the decision of a central assembly. This lack of any real power over taxation remained one of the chief weaknesses of the Estates General. Conversely, tax negotiations with local leaders and assemblies, though tedious, in the long run gave the ruler a free hand in imposing levies. It was easy to play one region off against another, or to threaten isolated areas that could not count on outside support. The royal bureaucracy was so persistent and skillful in conducting these negotiations that sooner or later it succeeded in breaking down most of the regional resistance to taxation.

Thus England was a strongly united country in which the king and the propertied classes cooperated in carrying out policies that they both approved. France was united more by the royal bureaucracy than by common interests, but the propertied classes in France were on the whole ready to trust the king on policy matters. And in both England and France some of the ideas that distinguish the modern sovereign state were beginning to appear: the welfare of the state was the greatest good; the defense of the realm was the greatest necessity; opposition to duly constituted authority was the greatest evil. As one of Philip's lawyers put it: "All men, clergy and laity alike, are bound to contribute to the defense of the realm." People who were beginning to think in these terms were not likely to be impressed by papal appeals and exhortations.

The Struggle with Boniface VIII

The pope at this time was Boniface VIII (1294-1303), an able canon lawyer and a veteran of the political conflicts endemic to Italy. Sensing that the new type of secular authority developing in the West would be more dangerous to the Church than the medieval Empire had ever been, he tried to reassert the superiority of ecclesiastical interests and the independence of the Church. He made no claim that had not already been made by his predecessors, but the climate of opinion had changed since the days of Gregory VII and Innocent III. With the shift in basic loyalties from the Church to the state, many people now believed that their chief duty was to support their king rather than to obey the pope. As a result, Boniface was defeated in a head-on clash with the kings of England and France—a blow from which the medieval Church never recovered.

The issue was clear-cut: were the clergy to be treated as ordinary subjects of secular rulers, or were they responsible only to the pope? Specifically, could they be taxed for defense of the realm without the pope's consent? As we have seen, thirteenth-century rulers could not run their governments without taxes, and it was always a temptation to tap the resources of the Church. By imposing taxes on the Church for political crusades, the popes had suggested that the clergy might also be taxed for purely secular conflicts. And so, when Edward I and Philip the Fair drifted into a war over Aquitaine in 1294, they both asked their clergy for a grant of taxes. They were outraged when Boniface prohibited these grants in 1296. Both Edward and Philip succeeded in stirring up public opinion against the clergy as disloyal members of the community. Both kings seized ecclesiastical property and forbade the transfer of money to Rome. Edward went further and virtually outlawed the English clergy. In the end, the harassed churchmen of both countries begged the pope to reconsider and remove his ban. Boniface did so, grudgingly but effectively, in 1298.

This was bad enough, but worse was to follow. In 1301 Philip the Fair imprisoned a French bishop on a flimsy charge of treason and refused to obey a papal order to free him immediately. When Boniface threatened to punish the king and his agents, Philip countered by calling a great assembly at Paris in 1302. This assembly contained representatives of the three Estates, or classes, of clergy, nobility, and bourgeoisie; it was the prototype of the French Estates General. The assembly gave its full support to the king and emphatically rejected any papal authority over France. When the dispute continued, Philip, through his minister, Guillaume de Nogaret, accused Boniface of immorality and heresy and appealed to a general council to condemn him. Local assemblies throughout France endorsed Philip's plan—the nobility and townsmen enthusiastically, the clergy reluctantly but almost unanimously. Philip undoubtedly resorted to pressure to ensure this response, but he clearly had the backing of his people, as subsequent events were to show. The people may not have believed all the accusations, but they felt that a worldly Church was probably corrupt and that the pope should not interfere with French internal affairs.

Assured of support at home, Philip now launched a very risky venture. In 1303 he sent Nogaret to Italy with a small force to join some of the pope's Italian enemies. Together they staged a surprise attack on Boniface's summer home at Anagni and succeeded in capturing the pope. They probably hoped to take him back to France as a prisoner to await trial by a church council, but they had no chance to put their plan into effect. The Italians had no great love for the pope, but they cared even less for the French. A

The Issue Between State and Church 1302

Boniface VIII says in the Bull Unam Sanctam:

Both the spiritual sword and the material sword are in the power of the Church. But the latter is to be used for the Church, the former by her; the former by the priest, the latter by kings and captains, but by the assent and permission of the priest. The one sword, then, should be under the other, and temporal authority subject to spiritual power. . . . If, therefore, the earthly power err, it shall be judged by the spiritual power. . . . Finally, we declare, state, define and pronounce that it is altogether necessary to salvation for every human creature to be subject to the Roman pontiff.

One of Philip's ministers, speaking for the king, says:

The pope pretends that we are subject to him in the temporal government of our states and that we hold the crown from the Apostolic See. Yes, this kingdom of France which, with the help of God, our ancestors . . . created—this kingdom which they have until now so wisely governed—it appears that it is not from God alone, as everyone has always believed, that we hold it, but from the pope!

From *Select Documents of European History,* ed. by R. G. D. Laffan (London: Methuen, 1930), p. 117; from C. V. Langlois, *St. Louis, Philippe le Bel, et les derniers Capetiens directs* (Paris: Hachette, 1911), pp. 149–50.

counterattack by the people of Anagni and neighboring regions freed Boniface from his captors. He took refuge in Rome and began to prepare bulls of excommunication against the French. But Boniface was an elderly man, and the shock of capture had proved too much for him. He died before he could act.

Force had been used against earlier popes, but for the last two centuries the Church had always been able to retaliate and put the aggressor in a worse position than before. After the assault at Anagni, however, the Church did not dare to react strongly. No one, either inside or outside France, seemed disturbed by what had happened, and Nogaret remained one of Philip's favored ministers. Boniface's successor was not a strong man, and when he died within a year the cardinals surrendered completely. They elected a French archbishop as pope, a man who was not even a member of their group and a man who was clearly agreeable to Philip, if not suggested by him. This new pope, Clement V, yielded at every turn to the king of France. He absolved Nogaret and declared that Philip had been prompted by laudable motives in his attack on Boniface. By failing to defend itself—indeed, by praising the aggressor—the papacy revealed that it had surrendered its leadership and its control over public opinion. From this time on the pope could influence and advise, but he could no longer command as Innocent III had done.

The Popes at Avignon

The pliability of Clement V soon led him to an even more momentous decision. After he was elected pope, he set off for Rome, but, ill and dismayed by the disorder in Italy, he paused in the Rhône Valley. The papacy was now paying for its stubborn opposition to the establishment of a strong Italian kingdom; the warring city-states had made even the Papal States unsafe. Somehow Clement never got started again. France was pleasant, and Italy was dangerous; moreover, the French king and the French cardinals

Pope Boniface VIII receives St. Louis of Toulouse, a grandnephew of St. Louis of France and son of Charles II of Naples. The representation of the pope corresponds to other pictures of him. Fresco by Ambrogio Lorenzetti, Siena (*ca.* 1330).

were urging him to stay on. And so Clement settled down at Avignon on the Rhône, where he and his successors were to reside for over seventy years. Avignon was not in France; as boundaries then ran, it was in the Holy Roman (German) Empire and France was just across the river. But neither the emperor nor any prince of the Empire had any power in Avignon.

This long period of exile is known in church history as the Babylonian Captivity.* From 1305 to 1378 all the popes and a majority of the cardinals were French, and Avignon remained the seat of the papacy and the surrounding country, papal territory. And yet, though the papacy did not lose its independence, it did lose its reputation. Many people, especially the English, were convinced that the pope was a servant of the French king, in spite of the fact that no later Avignonese pope was as subservient to the king as Clement V had been; most of them were able, even forceful, administrators of the affairs of the Church. Many others believed that no true successor of Peter would abandon Rome for the "sinful city of Avignon." A spiritual leader was not supposed to be swayed by motives of expediency or fear of discomfort. Charges of worldliness and corruption leveled against the Church seemed more justified than ever.

Actually, although the Avignonese popes were not especially corrupt, they were primarily administrators rather than religious leaders. Their chief accomplishments were to perfect the Church's legal system and its financial organization. To men who were already critical, this very success looked like a proliferation of red tape and a perfection of methods of extortion. No one could obtain anything from the papacy without engaging in long and expensive lawsuits or paying heavy fees to everyone from doorkeeper to cardinal. So drastically did the prestige of the pope sink that during the Hundred Years' War mutinous mercenary troops did not hesitate to threaten him and force him to buy them off. Leadership in Europe had clearly passed from the papacy to secular rulers; what they would do with it remained to be seen.

*This is an allusion to the exile of the Jews to Babylon under Nebuchadnezzar in the sixth century B.C. The original Babylonian Captivity lasted only fifty years.

Suggestions for Further Reading

Note: Asterisk denotes a book available in paperback edition.

St. Louis

The royal councilor Joinville's *Life of St. Louis** (Everyman's and other editions) is one of our chief sources for the life of King Louis IX of France and for an understanding of the spirit of the thirteenth century. There is excellent material on the growth of monarchical power and the development of institutions under St. Louis in C. Petit-Dutaillis, *Feudal Monarchy in France and England** (1936), and in E. Lavisse, ed., *Histoire de France,* Vol. III, Part 2 (1901). J. R. Strayer, *The Administration of Normandy under St. Louis* (1932), is a study of one of the most important provinces of the French monarchy and the Norman influence on that monarchy. W. C. Jordan, *Louis IX and the Challenge of the Crusade* (1979), gives a convincing picture of the development of the French system of government.

Henry III and England

There is a vast amount of significant detail in the contemporary Matthew of Paris, *Chronicle,* trans. by J. A. Giles (1852), a valuable framework for events in the period from 1235 to 1273. F. M. Powicke, *King Henry III and the Lord Edward,* 2 vols. (1947), is an excellent study of the political and social history of England at the time and the best biography of a medieval king. There is documentary material on early representative assemblies in C. Stephenson and F. G. Marcham, *Sources of English Constitutional History* (1937); the best commentary is F. Pollock and F. W. Maitland, *History of English Law,* Vol. II (1923). R. F. Treharne, *The Baronial Plan of Reform, 1258–1263* (1932), has a good account of the aristocratic reaction to royal rule presented as a great constitutional revolution. F. M. Powicke, *The Thirteenth Century* (1953), is a fine study of the period, with a critical bibliography.

The Papal–Hohenstaufen Feud

Philippe of Novara's *The Wars of Frederick II Against the Ibelins,* trans. by J. L. La Monte (1936), has primary material on the career and imperialism of Frederick II and presents a vivid picture of the life and ideas of the thirteenth-century knights who settled in the Latin Orient. E. Kantorowicz, *Frederick II* (1931), encompassing the broad and complex field of papal–Hohenstaufen relations, is a classic study in historical biography. There is a broad survey of politics, religion, literature, and art in H. D. Sedgwick, *Italy in the Thirteenth Century,* 2 vols. (1912). W. F. Butler, *The Lombard Communes* (1906), has information on the Lombard Communes in the Hohenstaufen wars. T. C. Van Cleve, *The Emperor Frederick II* (1972), can also be highly recommended.

Scholasticism: St. Thomas Aquinas

The most useful edition of St. Thomas' writings is *Basic Writings of St. Thomas Aquinas,* ed. by A. C. Pegis (1944), which contains a good selection of the most significant and widely read treatises. F. C. Copleston, *Aquinas** (1955), is a very good introduction to Aquinas' ideas, and G. Leff, *Medieval Thought** (1958), shows the influence of Aquinas' thought on the thirteenth century. M. De Wulf, *Philosophy and Civilization in the Middle Ages** (1922), describes how the thought of the period was intimately connected with the whole of medieval civilization. The best scholarly treatment of scholastic philosophy is in E. Gilson, *History of Christian Philosophy in the Middle Ages* (1954), which has valuable bibliographic material. E. Panofsky brilliantly shows the parallel development of art and philosophy in the thirteenth century in *Gothic Architecture and Scholasticism** (1954).

Edward I and Parliament

T. F. Tout, *Edward the First* (1893), is an old but sound biography of Edward with a good account of the beginnings of legislation and the English Parliament. A good introduction to the development of Parliament is G. L. Haskins, *Growth of English Representative Government** (1948). D. Pasquet, *Essay on the Origins of the House of Commons* (1925), is an excellent study of the evolution of Parliament from the king's court. There is much useful material on Parliament in B. Wilkinson, *Constitutional History of Medieval England,* Vol. III (1958). See also the titles by Stephenson and Marcham, and Pollock and Maitland mentioned above, and P. Spufford, *Origins of the English Parliament* (1967). For Edward's lawmaking, see T. F. Plucknett, *The Legislation of Edward III* (1949).

Philip the Fair and Boniface VIII

There is valuable material on the reign of Philip the Fair in E. Lavisse, ed., *Histoire de France,* Vol. III, Part 2 (1901). J. R. Strayer and C. H. Taylor, *Studies in Early French Taxation* (1939), explore the relationship between finances and early representative assemblies under Philip the Fair and Philip V. There is material on the reign of Philip the Fair in the books by Fawtier and Petit-Dutaillis cited in the bibliography at the end of Chapter 10. C. T. Wood, *Philip the Fair and Boniface VIII* (1967), has interesting extracts on the conflict between king and pope. See also J. R. Strayer, *The Reign of Philip the Fair* (1980).

H. K. Mann, *Lives of the Popes in the Middle Ages,* Vol. XVIII (1932), is a lengthy study of Boniface VIII and his pontificate from a Catholic point of view. A. C. Flick, *The Decline of the Medieval Church,* Vol. I (1930), has material on Boniface from a Protestant point of view. Though interesting reading, both are rather provincial in interpretation. The best study of this pope is T. S. R. Boase, *Boniface VIII* (1933), which is a sympathetic but far more critical treatment.

Clement V and the Babylonian Captivity

W. E. Lunt, *Papal Revenues in the Middle Ages,* 2 vols. (1934), contains considerable source material on the bureaucracy and finances of the papal Curia. An amusing, if infuriating, study of the period of the Babylonian Captivity is L. E. Binns, *The Decline and Fall of the Medieval Papacy* (1934), which was written as a supplement to the great history of E. Gibbon. See also G. Mollat, *The Popes at Avignon** (1965). A serious introduction to this period, M. Creighton, *A History of the Papacy from the Great Schism to the Sack of Rome,* Vol. I (1919), traces the reasons for the decline of papal power. G. Barraclough, *The Medieval Papacy** (1968), explores the historical background of the papacy. His *Papal Provisions* (1935) explains the system of papal appointments to offices in the Church.

13 The End of the Middle Ages

The fourteenth and early fifteenth centuries were a time of confusion and chaos in the West. Decade after decade everything seemed to go wrong: economic depression, war, rebellion, and plague harried the people, and neither ecclesiastical nor secular governments seemed capable of easing their distress. At times the whole structure of European society seemed to be crumbling, as it had at the end of the Roman Empire. Yet the Europe that emerged from this time of troubles went on to conquer the world. The science and technology, the navies and the armies, the governments and the business organizations that were to give Europe unquestioned supremacy for four centuries—all were taking shape in the fourteenth and fifteenth centuries. The dire stretch of history marked by the Hundred Years' War, the Black Death, and the Great Schism seems an unlikely seedbed for these great accomplishments. We are struck by the decay of the medieval way of life rather than by the almost imperceptible emergence of new ideas and new forms of organization. But we should not forget that the new ideas were there, that the people of western Europe never quite lost faith in their destiny, never quite gave up striving for a more orderly and prosperous society. There was confusion and uncertainty, but not the complete disintegration that had followed the collapse of the Roman Empire.

ECONOMIC WEAKNESS AND POLITICAL FAILURE

The most obvious cause of the troubles of the last medieval centuries was economic depression. Given the techniques then prevalent, by 1300 western Europe had about reached the limit of its capacity to produce food and manufactured goods, and, consequently, its ability to increase its trade. There were no more reserves of fertile land to bring into cultivation; in fact, a good deal of the land that was already being cultivated was marginal or submarginal in quality. For many years there was no significant increase in industrial output; production might shift from one center to another, but the total output remained about the same. Population ceased to grow, and after the Black Death (see p. 280), declined sharply. Most towns barely held their own, and many, especially in southern France, became smaller. The Italian towns fared better; they increased their share of Mediterranean trade and of the production of luxury textiles. But even Italy had economic difficulties. It, too, was ravaged by plague, and during the middle years of the fourteenth century northern rulers, like Edward III of England, repudiated the debts they owed Italian bankers. In short, until Europe found new sources of wealth and new markets, both governments and individuals were constantly on the verge of bankruptcy.

Economic stagnation created a climate of opinion that made it difficult for people to cooperate for the common welfare. Each individual, each community, each class was eager to preserve the monopolies and privileges that guaranteed it some share of the limited wealth available. It was during these years that the towns and gilds adopted their most restrictive regulations. Ordinary laborers found it difficult to become master workmen; master workmen were discouraged from devising new methods of production. Fortunately the attempt to preserve the status quo was thwarted by the weakness of government and by the ingenuity of enterprising businessmen. Some new techniques were introduced, and some new industries were established. But capital was limited, and it took many years before new techniques or new products had much impact on the economy.

Economic weakness helps explain the weakness of most governments. Rulers were always short of money, for the old taxes brought in less and less revenue and it was very difficult to impose new taxes. Salaries of government officials were insufficient, because of continuing inflation, and were often years in arrears. Most officials supported themselves by taking fees, gifts, and bribes from private citizens; they began to think of their offices as private possessions. Men with this attitude could keep up the routine, which was an important element of stability in a troubled society. But they showed much less zeal in perfecting their

Opposite: Manuscript illustration of the crucial point in the meeting of Richard II with the main body of the rebels during the Peasants' Rebellion of 1381. Wat Tyler is being struck down by one of Richard's men.

1305	1337 *ca.* 1340	*ca.* 1400	1417	1453

Black Death
Hundred Years' War
Babylonian Captivity and Great Schism

administrative techniques than had their thirteenth-century predecessors.

Financial difficulties were not the only cause of weakness in government. The assertion of sovereignty by secular rulers at the end of the thirteenth century had been somewhat premature. They had neither the ability to make realistic plans for the welfare of their people nor the authority to impose such remedies as they did devise. Most secular rulers could think only of increasing their revenues by conquering new lands. Such a policy solved no problems; it merely postponed them for the victor and aggravated them for the vanquished. With governments discredited by futile and costly wars, many men lost faith in their political leaders and turned to rebellion and civil war.

The leaders of revolt, however, showed no more ability than the kings and princes against whom they were rebelling. Many of the leaders were members of the landed nobility who still had wealth and influence even though they had lost their old rights of feudal government. But while they found it easy enough to gain power, they did not know how to exercise the power that they gained. Their main purpose was to preserve their own privileges or to direct government revenues to their own pockets—again, policies that solved no basic problems. Impatient with the routine tasks of administration, the aristocracy usually split into quarreling factions. The upper classes sometimes used parliamentary forms to justify their acts, but this only made representative assemblies appear to be vehicles of factionalism and disorder. When the desire for stronger government finally arose again, the kings found it easy to abolish or suspend assemblies; only in England did representative assemblies retain any vitality.

Other classes performed no better than the nobles. The bourgeoisie thought in terms of local or, at most, regional interests, and they were inept in running their own municipal governments. The townsmen split into factions—old families against new families, international traders against local merchants, rich against poor—and the faction in power tried to ruin its opponents by unequal taxation or discriminatory economic legislation. The result was that local self-government collapsed in town after town.

Lawlessness in Fifteenth-Century England

John Paston was the son of a royal judge and well-to-do landowner in Norfolk. His father had bought the manor of Gresham, but in 1448 Lord Molyns claimed it, though he had no right to it. John Paston tried to settle the claim peacefully, but Molyns' men seized the manor house and Paston moved to another "mansion." While he was seeking help from his friends, Paston's wife was left to defend their home. She wrote her husband this letter late in 1448.

Right worshipful husband, I recommend me to you and pray you to get some cross-bows and windlasses to wind them with and arrows, for your house here is so low that no one could shoot out of it with a long-bow, even if we had great need. I suppose you could get these things from Sir John Falstoff [a friend of the Pastons]. And also I would like you to get two or three short pole-axes to guard the doors and as many jacks [padded leather jackets] as you can.

Partridge [leader of Molyns' men] and his fellows are sore afraid that you will attack them again, and they have made great preparations, as I am told. They have made bars to bar the doors cross-wise, and they have made loop-holes on every side of the house to shoot out of both with bows and with hand-guns. The holes made for hand-guns are scarcely knee-high from the floor and no one can shoot out of them with a hand bow.

[Margaret Paston apparently took all this as a matter of course; she then turned to an ordinary shopping list.] I pray you to buy me a pound of almonds and a pound of sugar and some cloth to make clothes for your children and a yard of black broad-cloth for a hood for me.

The Trinity have you in His keeping and send you Godspeed in all your affairs.

Put into modern English from Norman Davis, ed., *Paston Letters* (Oxford: Clarendon Press, 1958), pp. 9–10.

Venice remained powerful and independent under a merchant oligarchy, as did many of the German trading towns. But more often a tyrant seized power, as in the towns of northern and central Italy, or else the officials of a king or a powerful noble took over control of the towns.

As for the peasants, they were far more restive and unhappy than they had been in the thirteenth century. With no new lands to clear and no new jobs to be had in the towns, they had little hope of improving their lot. Some of them managed to ease the burden of taxes and of payments to landlords by renegotiating their leases or by moving from one estate to another, but for most of them this road to advancement was too tedious and uncertain. The peasants rebelled in country after country, killing landlords, burning records, and demanding that payments for their land be lowered or abolished altogether. These rebellions were hopeless; untrained and poorly armed peasants were no match for an aristocracy with a strong military tradition. But the fact that the peasants did rebel reveals the despair and the tendency to violence that marked the end of the Middle Ages.

THE TROUBLES OF THE CHURCH

The failure of secular government would not have been so serious had the Church been able to regain its old leadership. The people of western Europe were still Christians, and they knew that they were not living up to the precepts of their faith. They multiplied religious ceremonies and appeals for the intercession of the saints; they flocked to revival meetings to repent their sins with tears and trembling. But the Church failed to remedy the disorders of western society; in fact, the Church was infected with the same evils that beset secular government. Repentant sinners returned to their careers of violence and fraud because no one could show them any other way to survive.

The Great Schism

The leadership of the Church was further impaired by the Great Schism that followed the Babylonian Captivity. The popes at Avignon, realizing that their exile was impairing their authority, had made several halfhearted efforts to return to Rome. Finally, in 1377, Gregory XI actually moved back to Italy, but he was

Miniature paintings of a fourteenth-century pewterer turning a jug on a lathe (left), and a locksmith (right), from the Guild Book of the Twelve Brothers' Foundation in Nuremberg.

THE GREAT SCHISM 1378–1417

appalled by the disorder in Rome and the Papal States. He was about to return to Avignon when he died, in 1378. The Romans, with the papacy once more within their grasp, had no intention of again losing the income from pilgrims and visitors to the papal court. When the cardinals met to elect Gregory's successor, they were besieged by a howling mob demanding that they choose a Roman, or at least an Italian, pope. It is hard to estimate how effective this pressure was; certainly it had some influence. In the end the cardinals elected an Italian archbishop who took the title of Urban VI.

The cardinals may have hoped that Urban would be a pliant and cooperative pope; instead he bullied them, rejected their advice, and denounced their behavior. The majority of the cardinals were French, but even the non-French were outraged by Urban's behavior. The whole group soon fled from Rome and declared that Urban's election was void because it had taken place under duress. They proceeded to choose a new pope, a French-speaking cardinal of the family of the counts of Geneva. He took the title of Clement VII, set up his court at Avignon, and denounced Urban as a usurper.

Emperors such as Henry IV and Frederick Barbarossa had tried to set up antipopes, but they had never deceived secular and religious leaders. Everyone knew who the true pope was, even if the emperor supported an opponent. But this time there was no such consensus, and most of Europe was honestly bewildered. Both popes had been elected by a majority of duly appointed cardinals; if Urban had the advantage of being the first named, he also had the disadvantage of being repudiated by the very men who had elected him. Rulers could decide which pope to follow only on the basis of political expediency. France, and its ally Scotland, naturally accepted the Avignonese pope; England just as naturally supported Urban at Rome. The Spanish kingdoms backed Clement, while most of Germany and Italy held to the Roman pontiff. Both popes intrigued to gain support in hostile areas, and both created new cardinals. When Urban and Clement died, in 1389 and 1394, respectively, the rival groups of cardinals each elected a new pope, thus prolonging the Great Schism into the next century.

Though the people of western Europe were deeply distressed by the schism, they could see no way out of their troubles. Who could be sure which was the false pope and which the true one? This uncertainty weakened both the organization and the moral influence of the Church. The popes of the Captivity had at least been good administrators, but the schism made effective administration impossible. Reform in the Church's financial system was desperately needed, but a pope who controlled only half the Church could hardly afford to lose revenues or alienate supporters by abolishing profitable abuses. A divided and unreformed Church had little hope of guiding European society.

Reformers and Heretics

The state of the Church during the Captivity and the Great Schism seemed so hopeless that many men began to seek salvation through their own efforts. The mildest, and probably the most numerous, group of reformers did not break openly with the Church; they simply ceased to rely on it. They formed little associations, such as the Brethren of the Common Life, to encourage one another to lead devout Christian lives and to seek direct contact with God through mystical experiences. These groups, which were especially numerous in the Rhineland and the Low Countries, produced some remarkable works of devotion, such as the *Theologia Germanica,* which influenced later reformers. They also founded schools that were to play a great role in the educational revival of the fifteenth and sixteenth centuries; Erasmus (see pp. 376–77) was educated in such a school. These mystical and contemplative reformers were looked on with some suspicion by conservative churchmen, but most of them remained within the bounds of orthodoxy.

A more radical element was not content simply to withdraw into devout groups. These men wanted a thoroughgoing reform of the Church, and many of them felt that only laymen could do the job. An early example of this attitude can be seen in the *Defensor pacis,* written by Marsilius of Padua about 1324. Marsilius, who like many Italians had a completely secular point of view, believed that the state should control the Church just as it controlled other organizations. If the state could regulate the behavior of doctors, it could also regulate the behavior of priests. Marsilius' book was condemned, but his ideas inspired criticism of the Church throughout the fourteenth and fifteenth centuries.

Another dangerous critic of the Church was an Oxford professor, John Wiclif (*ca.* 1320–84). At first concerned mainly with the problem of private property, including the property of the Church, Wiclif decided that the Church was being corrupted by wealth and that it would be better for everyone if church lands were taken over by kings and nobles. This position naturally pleased influential laymen and may explain why Wiclif was never punished for his unorthodox doctrines. Wiclif went on to cast doubt on the Catholic doctrine that the bread and wine in the communion service are transformed into the Body and Blood of Christ. He wound up by attacking the whole administrative structure of the Church as corrupt and largely unauthorized by the Bible. He taught that the pope could err, that the hierarchy had no absolute authority, and that kings should protect and guide the Church in their own realms.

Though Wiclif had no intention of launching a popular movement, his ideas spread rapidly beyond the scholarly circles for which he had written. By emphasizing scriptural authority, he had encouraged his followers to produce an English translation of the Bible that could be used by wandering preachers. These preachers, taking advantage of social discontent, popularized Wiclif's most radical views and gained a considerable following among the lower and middle classes in England. Some of them became social as well as religious reformers: if the Church had no right to property because it misused it, did the barons and knights

A manuscript illumination showing an antipope receiving his crown from the Devil and in turn crowning an emperor as a pledge of mutual support against the true head of the Church.

have any more right? Such ideas may have helped to touch off the English Peasant's Rebellion of 1381. Fear of economic radicalism may have induced the English upper classes to join with the king in suppressing the religious radicals—or Lollards, as they were called—after 1400. But the suppression was not wholly effective; the Wiclifite translation of the Bible and memories of Lollard doctrines survived until the time of the English Reformation. And the writings of John Wiclif reached as far as Bohemia, where they influenced John Hus, the great fifteenth-century opponent of the Church (see pp. 360–61).

THE BLACK DEATH

The effects of economic depression, political confusion, and religious uncertainty were intensified by terrible outbursts of plague in the middle years of the fourteenth century. The Black Death (probably bubonic plague) first appeared in Italy in the 1340s and swept through Europe during the next two decades. The worst was over by 1360, but repeated, though less severe, outbreaks well into the fifteenth century kept the population from reaching its preplague numbers for many generations. Although no accurate estimate can be made of the mortality, it was especially severe in thickly populated areas. Some towns lost more than two-fifths of their inhabitants, and some monasteries almost ceased to function. Since doctors were helpless, the only way to avoid the plague was to take refuge in isolated country districts.

The panic caused by the Black Death drove the sorely tried peoples of western Europe into emotional instability. It is no accident that the bloodiest peasant rebellions and the most senseless civil wars took place after the plague, and that the witchcraft delusion, almost unknown in the early Middle Ages, then reached its height. This was a double delusion. Innocent men and women were falsely accused of practicing black magic, but there were people, including men of high position, who genuinely believed that they could gain their desires by making a compact with the Devil. More than anything else, the witchcraft delusion demonstrated the state of shock in which western Europe found itself at the end of the fourteenth century. The rationalism and confidence in the future that had been so apparent at the height of medieval civilization had vanished.

The Black Death in England

Then that most grievous pestilence penetrated the coastal regions by way of Southampton and came to Bristol, and people died as if the whole strength of the city were seized by sudden death. For there were few who lay in their beds more than three days or two and a half days; then that savage death snatched them about the second day. In Leicester, in the little parish of St. Leonard, more than three hundred and eighty died; in the parish of the Holy Cross, more than four hundred, and in the parish of St. Margaret, more than seven hundred. . . .

And the price of everything was cheap, because of the fear of death, there were very few who took any care for their wealth, or for anything else. For a man could buy a horse for half a mark [about 7 shillings] which before was worth forty shillings, a large fat ox for four shillings, a cow for twelve pence, a heifer for sixpence, a large fat sheep for four pence. . . . And the sheep and cattle wandered about through the fields and among the crops, and there was no one to go after them or collect them. They perished in countless numbers everywhere, for lack of watching . . . since there was such a lack of serfs and servants, that no one knew what he should do. For there is no memory of a mortality so severe and so savage. . . . In the following autumn, one could not hire a reaper for less than eight pence [per day] with food, or a mower at less than twelve pence with food.

From Henry Knighton, *Chronicle*, in *The Portable Medieval Reader*, ed. by J. B. Ross and M. M. McLaughlin (New York: Viking, 1949), pp. 218–19.

ENGLAND IN THE LATER MIDDLE AGES

Even France and England, the two strongest states in the West, were shaken by the events of the fourteenth century. They had enough momentum and solid enough administrative structures to survive as political units, but there were times when neither country had a government capable of preserving law and order. While the bureaucrats were able to keep the machinery of government running, they could not hold back the

1066	1154	1399	1461	1485
Norman Kings	House of Plantagenet	House of Lancaster	House of York	

rising tide of lawlessness. Under these circumstances, the nobles regained much of the power they had lost in the thirteenth century. They tried to control policy and direct revenues to their own pockets; in England they even deposed their kings.

The expansionist policies of Edward I (see p. 266) had severely strained English resources. A reaction would have taken place in any case; it was made more acute by the character of Edward II (1307–27). So incompetent that no one respected him, Edward turned over the business of government to a series of favorites who were hated by the great lords. The barons tried the old expedient of setting up a committee to control the government, but it worked no better than it had under Henry III. Finally Edward's own wife and her lover, Mortimer, one of the lords of the turbulent lands of the Welsh frontier, led a rebellion against him. Edward was deposed in 1327 and quietly murdered a few weeks later; his young son, Edward III (1327–77), became king.

The Hundred Years' War: The First Phase

Edward III shared his barons' fondness for courtly magnificence and chivalric warfare. More popular with the aristocracy than his father had been, he was also more susceptible to their influence. Never quite willing to risk his popularity by forcing a showdown with the barons, he allowed them to retain a strong position in Parliament and in the Council. This is probably why he drifted into the Hundred Years' War with France. War was a policy on which he and his barons could agree, and so long as the war was successful he could avoid domestic controversies.

There were, of course, other reasons for the war. France was still trying to annex the English holdings in Aquitaine and gain full control of Flanders, which was the best market for English wool. France was aiding Scotland, which had regained its independence in the battle of Bannockburn (1314) and was in a state of almost permanent hostility with England. French and English sailors were intermittently plundering each other's ships. These frictions were enough to cause a war, but they do not quite explain why the war lasted for generations. The king persisted because he gained new and valuable territories; the barons, because they acquired booty and profitable military commands.

After a bad start, caused largely by financial difficulties, Edward came up with an amazing string of victories. He gained control of the Channel in a naval battle at Sluys (1340) and nearly annihilated the French army at Crécy (1346). Then he went on to take Calais, which remained a port of entry for English armies for two centuries. Ten years later, Edward's son, the Black Prince (also

The Later Middle Ages

So violent and motley was life, that it bore the mixed smell of blood and of roses. The men of that time always oscillated between the fear of hell and the most naïve joy, between cruelty and tenderness, between harsh asceticism and insane attachment to the delights of this world . . . always running to extremes. . . .

Bad government, the cupidity and violence of the great, wars and brigandage, scarcity, misery, and pestilence—to this is contemporary history nearly reduced in the eyes of the people. The feeling of general insecurity . . . was further aggravated by the fear of hell, of sorcerers and of devils. Everywhere the flames of hatred arise and injustice reigns. Satan covers a gloomy earth with his sombre wings.

From J. Huizinga, *The Waning of the Middle Ages* (London: Arnold, 1924), pp. 18, 21.

THE HUNDRED YEARS' WAR 1337–1453

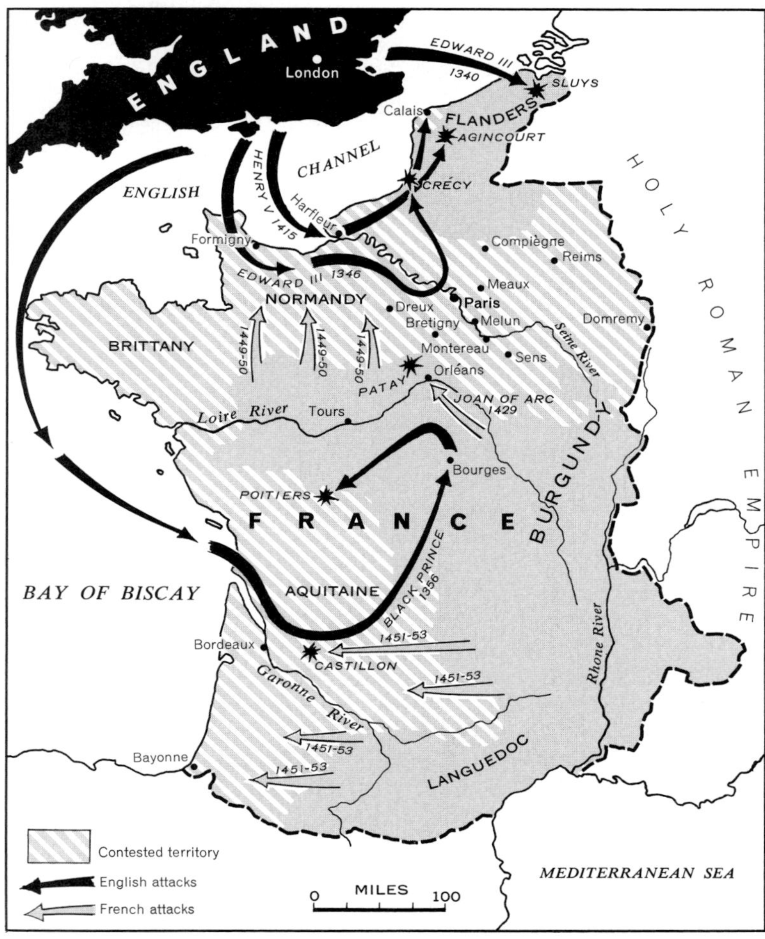

named Edward), crushed another French army at Poitiers and took the French king prisoner. In the treaty that followed this victory the French agreed to pay a huge ransom for their king and to cede about two-fifths of their country to the English.

Edward had succeeded because his country was more united than France and gave him more consistent financial support, and also because he had developed new tactics for his army. He mixed companies of archers, armed with the famous English longbow, with companies of dismounted cavalry in heavy armor. A charge, by either mounted or foot soldiers, would be thrown into confusion by showers of arrows. The few men who broke through to the main line could be easily dealt with by the troops in heavy armor. The only weakness in Edward's formation was that it was essentially defensive; it could not be used for a charge. Only when portable firearms were invented at the end of the fifteenth century was it possible to use missile weapons for an attack.

Like many other generals, Edward found it easier to win victories than to profit from them. The French, with no intention of fulfilling the terms of the treaty they had signed, launched a war of attrition that gradually exhausted their enemies. England simply did not have enough men or enough resources to garrison territories larger than Edward's whole kingdom. The French learned to avoid headlong rushes at large English armies and concentrated instead on picking off isolated garrisons and small detachments. As a result, the English had lost a large part of their conquests by the time of Edward III's death in 1377.

Rebellion and Revolution

Military misfortunes abroad led to bickering at home. There was a complete failure of leadership during Edward's last years. The king was sinking into senility, and the Black Prince, crippled by disease, died a year before his father. One of Edward's younger sons, John of Gaunt, Duke of Lancaster, had more authority than anyone else, but he was disliked and distrusted by many members of the aristocracy. He was accused, with some justice, of associating with a group of corrupt officeholders and, with less justice, of coveting the throne. The duke's taste in art and literature was excellent—he gave a government job and a pension to Geoffrey Chaucer—but interest in the arts has seldom added to the stature of a politician in English public opinion.

The new king, Richard II (1377–99), the son of the Black Prince, was only a child when he inherited the throne. During the first part of his reign England was governed by successive groups of barons. These men did nothing to distinguish themselves; their inefficiency and bad judgment led directly to the Peasants' Rebellion of 1381. The war in France was

1066	1154	1399	1461	1485
Norman Kings	House of Plantagenet	House of Lancaster	House of York	

1454–1485: Wars of the Roses

still costing large sums of money, even though the English were now almost entirely on the defensive. Casting about for a new source of revenue, the government hit on the idea of a poll tax, a levy of a few pennies on each English subject. This brought to a peak all the smoldering resentment of the peasants and the poorer inhabitants of the towns. They were already suffering from economic stagnation; now they felt that they were being asked to carry an unfair share of the tax burden. All southern England exploded in rebellion. Peasants and artisans burned tax rolls and manorial records, killed unpopular officials and landlords, and finally marched on London. The barons, taken off guard, scurried about trying to raise an army. Meanwhile Richard had to stand by and watch the rebels occupy London, burn the palace of the Duke of Lancaster, and murder the chancellor and the treasurer of England. Forced into humiliating negotiations with the rebel leaders, he was obliged to promise complete forgiveness for all past offenses, the abolition of serfdom, and the remission of almost all manorial dues.

The rebellion was weakened when its leader, Wat Tyler, was killed during a conference with the king. It was suppressed as soon as the barons could get their troops together, for the poorly armed peasants and townsmen were no match for professional soldiers. The king repudiated his promises and apparently all was as before. Actually, the rebellion had two important results. The Black Death had caused a shortage of labor but the revolt had shown that the peasants would not make up for the shortage by accepting increased tax burdens or lower wages. As a result, they were given land for low rents, and serfdom declined steadily after 1381. By 1500 there were almost no serfs left in England. Second, Richard had seen a convincing demonstration of the inefficiency and clumsiness of baronial government. It is not surprising that when he came of age in 1386 he tried to increase royal authority and to concentrate all power in his own hands.

Richard showed considerable skill in his efforts to strengthen the monarchy, but he made two fatal mistakes. The barons might have tolerated the loss of

Richard II, from the portrait by Beauneven of Valenciennes (1398) in Westminster Abbey.

political power, but Richard threatened their economic position as well by confiscating the property of those he distrusted. Moreover, Richard failed to build up a powerful army under his own control. Most of the armed forces in the country were private companies paid by the king but recruited and commanded by barons and knights. This system had developed during the early years of the Hundred Years' War, when it had seemed easier to allow members of the aristocracy to raise troops than for the government to deal with the tedious problem of recruiting. Any lord with a taste for fighting could maintain his own little army at government expense, a situation that encouraged disorder and rebellion. The king's personal bodyguard was no match for the combined forces of several great barons. As a result, Richard was helpless when Henry of Lancaster, son of John of Gaunt and cousin of the king, rebelled in 1399. Henry himself had been driven into exile and stripped of his lands, and he was supported by many members of the aristocracy who feared the same fate. Richard was deposed and died in prison, and Henry of Lancaster mounted the throne as Henry IV (1399–1413).

The Hundred Years' War: The Second Phase

The Lancastrian kings, who ruled from 1399 to 1461, never quite lived down the violence by which they had come to power. Their title was faulty—there were other descendants of Edward III with a better claim—and they seldom had the unanimous support of the great lords. Henry IV had difficulty suppressing two serious rebellions, and Henry V (1413–22) tried to unite the country by the dangerous expedient of reviving the Hundred Years' War. He was a brilliant general, as he revealed in his victory at Agincourt (1415); he was the first commander of a European army to use siege artillery on a large scale. By securing the alliance of the Duke of Burgundy, a disgruntled French prince, he was able to force the French king, Charles VI, to accept a treaty in which Charles disinherited his son, married his daughter to Henry, and agreed that any son born of this union was to be king of France. The

The battle of Formigny, which was fought at the end of the Hundred Years' War. Notice that the English (right) are on foot and are flanked by bowmen, while the French are delivering a cavalry charge. Usually the English won in such circumstances, but this time they were defeated.

next year both Charles and Henry died, and a one-year-old baby, Henry VI, became king of England and France.

Henry V, with all his ability, would have found it hard to control two kingdoms; Henry VI never had a chance. His long minority was disastrous. In England his uncles and cousins, supported by baronial factions, quarreled bitterly. In France, the disinherited son of Charles VI claimed the throne as Charles VII and carried on the war from the unconquered country south of the Loire. The English pressed him hard, but just as his cause seemed hopeless he was saved by the appearance of Joan of Arc (see p. 288). To the English, Joan was "a limb of the devil." But she stirred the French to drive the English back from the Loire and to win an important victory at Patay (1429). After these successes it hardly mattered that Joan fell into English hands and was burned as a witch, for the courage and enthusiasm with which she had inspired the French survived her. The Burgundians abandoned the English alliance, and the English position in France deteriorated steadily. Forts and provinces fell one by one, until by 1453 only Calais was left. And so after twelve decades of fighting and plundering, the war at last came to an end.

The Wars of the Roses

When the English could no longer blame Joan of Arc for their defeats, they began to blame one another. Commanders were accused of treason and incompetence; some were executed and others exiled. Henry VI, even when he came of age, could do nothing to stop the feuds among the great lords. Humble in spirit and weak in mind, he was dominated by a French wife whom most of the aristocracy disliked. The English barons had acquired the habit of violence, and a decade after the end of the Hundred Years' War they plunged England into the series of civil conflicts known as the Wars of the Roses.* The ostensible reason for these wars was an attempt by some of the barons to replace the Lancastrian king with the Duke of York, who represented the oldest line of descent from Edward III. The attempt succeeded, but the Yorkist kings, who ruled from 1461 to 1485, had almost as much trouble with the barons as their Lancastrian predecessors. In fact, the Wars of the Roses were the last uprising of the barons, the last attempt of a small clique to take over the central government and use it for their own purpose. The wars destroyed everyone who took part in them—the House of Lancaster, the House of York, and many of the great noble families. It was left for the half-alien Tudors, indirect and illegitimate descendants of John of Gaunt, to restore order in England.

*Long after the wars, the legend arose that the Red Rose was the badge of Lancaster and the White Rose, of York. This error led to the name Wars of the Roses.

England made some economic gains toward the end of this period in spite of the failure of political leadership. The kings of the fourteenth and fifteenth centuries were no economists, but they were able to grasp one simple fact—that so long as England produced only raw materials, she would never grow very rich. From Edward III on, they encouraged the migration of textile workers to England and protected the growing English textile industry. They also encouraged the development of English shipping. The results should not be exaggerated, for even at the end of the fifteenth century England could not rival Flanders in textiles or Italy in shipping. But a good start had been made; England had come a long way from being a country whose chief economic function was to raise raw wool to be carried in foreign ships to Flemish looms.

The Development of Parliament

There were also two important institutional developments: the rise of the justices of the peace and the continuing growth of Parliament. The justices of the peace were created by Edward III in the fourteenth century to take over some of the work of local law enforcement that had formerly been the duty of sheriffs and feudal lords. The justices were men of position and leisure, not great lords but well-to-do local landholders of the class that had long carried heavy respon-

The only known contemporary portrait of Joan of Arc.

sibilities in local government. Like the sheriffs and the tax collectors, they served without pay; their reward was leadership in their own community. By the middle of the fifteenth century their powers had grown to a point where they controlled local government. They arrested criminals and tried minor offenses (major cases were reserved for the circuit judges). They were responsible for enforcing economic regulations and orders of the central government. They collected information for the Council and were supposed to inform it of plots against the government. In practice, the justices of the peace were often the creatures of the most powerful baron of their region. But when the Tudors reestablished royal authority, the justices of the peace, with their wide local knowledge and influ-

An English court in the later Middle Ages. This miniature is from a law treatise of the reign of Henry IV (early fifteenth century). At the top are the five judges of the Court of King's Bench; below them are the king's coroner and attorney. On the left is the jury, and in front, in the dock, is a prisoner in fetters, flanked by lawyers. In the foreground more prisoners in chains wait their turn. On the center table stand the ushers, one of whom seems to be swearing in the jury.

ence, became the key agents of the crown in the counties.

The century and a half of political instability, stretching from Edward II through Henry VI, gave Parliament a chance to make itself an indispensable part of the government. Weak rulers sought the appearance of public support, and usurpers sought the appearance of legitimacy. Both were eager for parliamentary ratification of important acts, since Parliament represented all the propertied classes of the country. Thus Edward III and Henry IV, after successful revolutions, asked Parliament to accept statements justifying the deposition of their predecessors. Similarly, all taxes and most legislative acts were submitted to Parliament for approval.

Equally important was the union (about 1340) of the county representatives (knights) and the town representatives (burgesses). These groups, which had acted separately under Edward I, now formed the House of Commons and made Parliament a far more effective assembly. Now there were only two houses (Lords and Commons) instead of three, or, as in some countries, even four. And the lower house included an element, the knights, which would have been considered noble in any other country. The knights were landlords, just as the barons were; they could intermarry with baronial families, and some of them became barons themselves. Their presence gave the House of Commons much more influence than a mere assembly of burgesses (such as the French Third Estate) could have. Through the leadership of the knights, cooperation with the lords could be assured. This situation sometimes enabled Parliament to effect significant changes in government, for when both houses attacked a minister of the king they could usually force him out of office.

By the fifteenth century Parliament had become an integral part of the machinery of government, and no important act was valid until it had received parliamentary approval. So well established had Parliament become that it survived even the period of strong kingship that began under the Tudors in 1485. But Parliament only gave legal validity to acts of government; it did not make policy, which was the province of the king or the great lords. For example, Edward II and Richard II were not deposed by the initiative of Parliament; Parliament was merely asked to ratify the results of a revolution engineered by a few great barons. Not until the seventeenth century did Parliament begin to formulate policies of its own.

FRANCE IN THE LATER MIDDLE AGES

The monarchy in France also had its troubles during the fourteenth and fifteenth centuries. The sons of Philip the Fair (see pp. 268–69) died in rapid succession, leaving only daughters to succeed them. The barons, afraid that one of their number might gain excessive power by marrying a reigning queen, invented a rule barring women from the succession. In 1328 they placed Philip of Valois, a cousin of the last king and a nephew of Philip the Fair, on the throne. But since Philip owed his position to the barons, he had to spend most of his reign bestowing favors on his supporters and keeping peace among factions of nobles. The widespread loyalty to the king that had marked the late thirteenth century weakened, and the rebellions and acts of treason plagued the country. These internal disorders help to account for the French defeats in the first few decades of the Hundred Years' War.

Philip's son, John (1350–64), had no better fortune. His capture by the English at Poitiers, with the subsequent loss of territory and the heavy taxes needed to raise his ransom, caused widespread dissatisfaction. In 1358 the peasants rose in a revolt that was no more successful than the English rebellion but much more bloody and destructive. In the same year the Estates General, led by the Paris bourgeoisie, tried to take over the government. The attempt failed, both because the Estates had had little experience in government and because their leaders had no support among the great nobles. John's son, Charles V (1364–80), regained much of the lost ground by suppressing his opponents at home and by driving the English from one stronghold after another. If his successor had been a more capable ruler, the French might have escaped another century of troubles.

Unfortunately, most of the brains and determination in the French royal family went to uncles and cousins of the new king rather than to the king himself. Charles VI (1380–1422) was never strong either in mind or in character, and after 1390 he suffered intermittent spells of insanity. The government was conducted largely by princes of the blood royal who quarreled bitterly among themselves over offices, pensions, and gifts of land. When the Duke of Burgundy was assassinated in 1419 by the followers of the Duke of Orléans, the quarrels turned into a civil war and the new Duke of Burgundy allied himself with the English. Since, in addition to Burgundy, he had acquired Flanders and other provinces of the Low Countries, he was the most powerful prince in France and his defection proved disastrous. It was during this period of civil war that Henry V made his rapid conquests and forced Charles VI to recognize Henry's son as heir to the French throne.

The Defeat of England

Charles VII (1422–61) faced an almost hopeless situation when his father died. He had been officially disinherited; the English and their Burgundian allies held the largest and richest part of France. Charles had little military strength, and he was not using what he did have very effectively. It was at this moment that Joan of Arc, a peasant girl from the extreme eastern frontier, appeared at court and announced that heavenly voices had ordered her to drive the English out of the country. Joan, self-confident and persuasive, shook Charles from his lethargy and talked him into the counteroffensive that turned the tide of the war. Joan's execution by the English scarcely checked the reconquest, for Charles soon had another stroke of good fortune. England under Henry VI was as torn by factional strife as France had been under Charles VI, and the leader of one faction, an uncle of the English king, mortally offended the Duke of Burgundy. The duke's return to the French cause in 1435 greatly weakened the English and facilitated Charles' recovery of northern France.

Joan of Arc was not unique in having visions, for in those troubled years many men and women were convinced that they had had divine revelations. But in the content of her visions we can see how deep were the roots that the religion of the French monarchy had struck among the people. Joan was convinced that Charles VII was the only rightful king of France and that it was her religious duty to restore him to his throne. She also believed that "to make war on the holy kingdom of France was to make war on the Lord Jesus." Her beliefs were shared by people of all classes. In spite of the misgovernment of the last century there was still a deep reservoir of loyalty to the French monarchy. And in spite of treachery and factionalism there was at least a beginning of national feeling among the French people. Under all the confusion and disorder of the early fifteenth century they clung to two basic beliefs: faith in the French monarchy and faith in the Christian religion. When the two beliefs were united as they were in Joan of Arc, they were irresistible. Joan foreshadowed that union of religion and monarchy on which the absolute states of the early modern period were to be built.

Restoration of Royal Power

France suffered more severely than England during the Hundred Years' War, since all the fighting took place on French soil. Wide areas were devastated by raiding armies and wandering companies of mercenary soldiers who found plundering more profitable than loyal service. But precisely because the French predicament was so much graver than the English, royal power was restored more rapidly and more completely in France. A king who showed any promise of putting an end to disorder could override most limitations on his power to levy taxes. Charles V began the work of freeing the monarchy from these restraints, and Charles VII finished the job. As soon as he had the English on the run he began to levy taxes at will, without asking consent from the Estates. His task was made easier by the fact that provincial feeling was so strong in France that a central parliamentary assembly was seldom called, and when it was called it had little authority. Real influence lay with the provincial and regional assemblies, with the local Estates of Normandy or of Languedoc rather than with the Estates General. And it was relatively easy for Charles to overcome the fragmented opposition of these local assemblies.

The same overwhelming interest in provincial affairs kept the great French nobles from entrenching themselves in the central government, which remained the preserve of the king and his bureaucrats. Thus in the long run the Hundred Years' War reinforced tendencies that had been apparent in France prior to the end of the thirteenth century—tendencies toward a bureaucratic state in which the king was strong and all other political forces were weak and divided. This French pattern became a model for the rest of Europe during the early modern period.

SPAIN IN THE LATER MIDDLE AGES

Spain, like the rest of western Europe, was wracked by civil wars during the fourteenth and fifteenth centuries. The Spanish kingdoms were especially vulnerable because there was no fixed rule of succession in either Castile or Aragon, and because, with Moorish power reduced to the little kingdom of Granada, the Spanish tradition of military prowess could be demonstrated only by fighting fellow Spaniards. Far too many kings came to the throne as minors, which meant quarrels over the regency at best, and attempts by other members of the royal family to supplant the legitimate king at worst. There were few peaceful reigns and almost no opportunities to influence European politics. At the lowest point, Castile became a pawn in the Anglo-French conflict. Pedro I was opposed by his illegitimate half-brother, Henry of Trastamara. Pedro was supported by the English, Henry by the French, and it was the victory of the French troops (led by their Constable) over English troops (led by the Black Prince) that gave Henry the throne.

Aragon had a little less trouble, because younger sons could be given small kingdoms such as Majorca (the Balearic islands) or Sicily (and eventually Naples) in Italy. Nevertheless, the disorder continued until John II of Aragon married his son Ferdinand to Isabella, the heiress of Castile. The union of the two crowns (1479) did not mean that the institutions of the two countries were merged, but it did bring a large increase in security for the people of Spain. On the whole, the Catholic Kings (as Ferdinand and Isabella were called) followed the French model; each province was allowed to keep its old customs, but was administered by officials sent out by the central government. Moreover, the Catholic Kings did not bear that name in vain; they made religion a test of loyalty. Jews and Moslems, even if officially converted, were suspected of secretly adhering to their old faiths, and even driven into exile. In the long run, this loss of skilled artisans and capable businessmen weakened Spain, but the loss was not immediately apparent. By 1500 Spain was the strongest kingdom in Europe. It could support both the exploration and the conquest of much of the New World (this was the area that Isabella and the Castilians controlled) and act as the arbiter of European politics (Ferdinand's specialty). Even far-off England found it advisable to ally itself with Ferdinand.

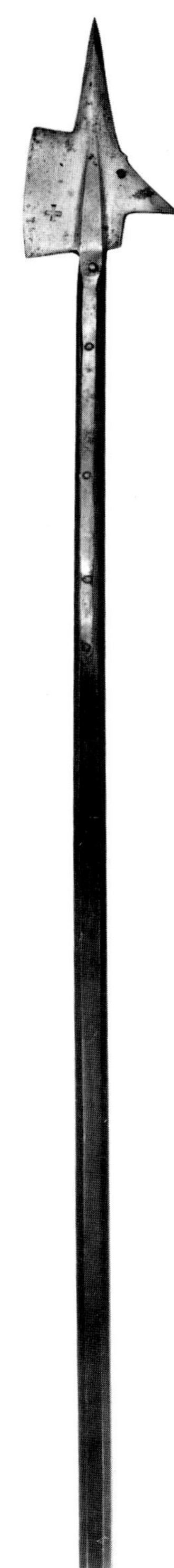

A fifteenth-century Swiss halberd.

GERMANY IN THE FOURTEENTH CENTURY

GERMANY IN THE LATER MIDDLE AGES

The political history of the rest of western Europe during the later Middle Ages resembled that of France and England. Everywhere there were rebellions, civil wars, and attempts to conquer neighboring territories. But all this furor produced surprisingly little change. A political map of Europe in 1450 looks very like a map of 1300, and the basic characteristics of most of the governments were similarly unchanged.

Certain developments in Germany deserve attention, however. First, during the fifteenth century the dukes of Burgundy gradually gained control over all the provinces of the Low Countries, roughly the equivalent of modern Belgium and the Netherlands. This was one of the richest and most productive regions of Europe. The union of the Low Countries under the House of Burgundy separated their fate from that of the rest of Germany and gradually gave them a distinct national identity. At the same time their wealth made them the object of a long series of European wars that began in the fifteenth century and have continued to our own day.

Second, during the fourteenth century the peasants and townsmen of Switzerland gradually gained their independence from the Habsburg family, which had dominated this part of Germany. In defeating the Habsburgs the Swiss developed well-disciplined infantry formations, armed with long pikes, that could beat off a charge of heavy cavalry. By the fifteenth century companies of Swiss infantry had acquired such a reputation that they were being hired by French kings and Italian princes. The Swiss were also demonstrating the possibility of republican government to a Europe that had had little confidence in this system. The faction-ridden Italian towns were losing their independence to tyrants and the German towns proved unable to form a permanent confederation, although for a while the Hanseatic League (a union of North German towns) controlled trade in the Baltic. But the Swiss Confederation, loosely knit though it was, endured. Each district, or canton, had its own institutions, and no canton was under a feudal lord. The towns were ruled by the wealthier burgesses, but the peasant cantons, where the movement for independence had begun, were almost pure democracies.

The third important development in Germany was the rise of a new power center on the middle Danube as a result of the peculiar electoral habits of the German princes. By the fourteenth century the number of princes taking part in imperial elections had been reduced to seven. These great men feared giving the title to any powerful prince, so for some time they regularly chose as emperors counts with small holdings. Though the title gave no real power, it did confer enough social prestige to enable such counts to marry well-endowed heiresses. Thus the Habsburgs, petty princes in West Germany who had served briefly as emperors around 1300, managed to acquire the duchy of Austria and nearby counties. A little later, the Count of Luxemburg, an equally undistinguished prince, became emperor and arranged a marriage through which his son received the kingdom of Bohemia. Later Luxemburg emperors acquired Silesia and eventually Hungary. When the last male Luxemburg leader died in 1438, his nearest heir was the Habsburg Duke of Austria. The union of the two sets of holdings marked the beginning of the vast Habsburg Empire, for five centuries one of the great powers of Europe.

ART, LITERATURE, AND SCIENCE

The art and literature, the scholarship and the technology of western Europe during this period showed the same uneven development as the politics. There was a considerable amount of sterile imitation, or mere elaboration of familiar themes. On the other hand, no essential skills or ideas were lost, and there were some promising innovations. For example, while many late Gothic churches were cold and uninspired copies of earlier work, in other churches some striking results were achieved by making windows higher and wider, by emphasizing perpendicular lines, and by devising intricate patterns of vaulting. Elaboration could be carried too far; one late Gothic style is rightly known as the Flamboyant, because spikes and gables,

Jan van Eyck, *Giovanni Arnolfini and His Bride* (1434).

traceries and canopies concealed the basic lines of the structure. Better results were achieved in manuscript illumination, because the richly ornamented borders did not hide the text or distract attention from the miniature illustrations, which were becoming more realistic.

In literature there were the same contradictions. Many of the old narrative poems became fantastic romances (such as those Cervantes mocked in *Don Quixote*), and the lyrics became society verse. On the other hand, there were significant gains—deeper psychological insights in describing human behavior, and a notable improvement in the writing of prose. It is much harder to write good prose (especially on technical subjects) than to write acceptable poetry, but a high level of prose writing was reached in all western countries in the later Middle Ages. To take only one example, Nicolas Oresme, a French scholar and bishop, translated Aristotle's *Politics.* He had to invent or redefine many words in accomplishing this task, and in doing so he greatly enriched the French language.

The scholars of the period could also be accused of thrashing old straw without producing much new intellectual grain. Some of their arguments were overrefined—elaborate games that interested only the players. But there were original thinkers, especially, as we shall see, in the fields of science and mathematics.

These contradictory developments in late medieval culture disgusted the Italians of the Renaissance. They damned most medieval work as "gothic," which to them meant barbarous. It took many generations to overcome this prejudice, and even now it has not entirely disappeared.

Literature

The medieval authors who are most widely read today all wrote in the fourteenth and fifteenth centuries. The best-known example is Geoffrey Chaucer (*ca.* 1340–1400), who began as a mere translator and adapter of French works and developed into one of England's greatest poets. His most famous work, the Prologue to the *Canterbury Tales,* reveals his skill in describing individual characters and his wit in depicting human foibles. His people range from the "perfect, gentle Knight" and the poor parson, who taught Christ's lore, "but first he followed it himself," through the earthy Wife of Bath, who had buried five husbands, down to scoundrels like the Miller and the Summoner. Perhaps his knowledge of all levels of English society was due to the fact that Chaucer worked for years in the customs service in the busy port of London. But his subtle portrayal of human behavior, shown also in *Troilus and Criseyde,* came only from his own genius. Chaucer was something of a psychologist as well as a poet, but while he saw through pretense and sham, he never became bitter. He rose fast in English society under the patronage of John of Gaunt; he accepted the world as he found it and rather liked what he found.

François Villon (b. 1431) was less fortunate. A friend of the thieves and prostitutes of Paris, and a convicted criminal himself, he shows how close French society came to breaking down under the strains of the early fifteenth century. He used the old poetic forms to describe with gusto life in taverns and thieves' dens. But his poems also express his bitterness over his wasted life and portray the hopes and fears of the poor and the outcast—the simple piety of an old woman, the last thoughts of men condemned to hang. The tendency toward realism, already evident in Chaucer, became even stronger in Villon.

Devotional works written for laymen were far more numerous after 1300 than they had ever been before. There was a tremendous desire among all classes for more intense and personal religious experience to supplement the conventional observances. Writers of the fourteenth and fifteenth centuries produced innumerable meditations, visions, and moral tracts. Some of the finest religious writings of any period were composed at this time, especially the *Imitation of Christ,* ascribed to Thomas à Kempis. In England there was *The Vision of Piers Plowman* by William Langland, one of the first important works written in English after the long eclipse following the Norman Conquest. We know little of Langland, except that he lived in the middle years of the fourteenth century and that he came of peasant stock. The English of *Piers Plowman* is archaic, but it is recognizably English and not, as Anglo-Saxon was, an early German dialect.

Piers Plowman also illustrates the widespread desire to transform religion into a strong social force. The poet criticizes every class for its worldliness and selfishness; only by a return to the pure principles of the Gospel can the world be saved. There was nothing anti-Catholic in Langland's program, but it did bear testimony to the continuing inability of ecclesiastical authorities to satisfy adequately the aspirations expressed in the poem and in many similar works.

Painting and Sculpture

The same tendency toward realism that we have noted in Chaucer and Villon is also evident in much of the sculpture and painting of the period. This tendency, which had already appeared in some of the details of thirteenth-century works, now began to be expressed in the principal figures. It sometimes took a macabre form: skeletons and corpses were depicted with loving care on funeral monuments and in the Dance of Death, a favorite subject of artists. But we also find at this time the first real portraits painted in western Europe and the first attempts to depict a landscape that is more than a conventional background. There were capable artists everywhere—English, French, and German sculptors, French and German painters. But the most interesting group were those who worked for the dukes of Burgundy. The Flemish school of painting, which developed in the late fourteenth and early fifteenth centuries, was a worthy rival of the Italians of the early Renaissance. In some techniques these painters were ahead of the Italians—the first painting in oils, for example, was done in Flanders. The best-known Flemish painters, such as the van Eycks, van der Weyden, and Memling, combined meticulous attention to detail with genuine religious feeling. And there is nothing in Italy that quite equals the Flemish portraits of this period, such as Jan van Eyck's picture of the Arnolfinis, or his *Léal Souvenir.*

Science

The scholarly work of the period is less well known, and in the nineteenth and early twentieth century it was often dismissed as unoriginal and unimportant. But even when it was unoriginal it was useful to men with ideas of their own. For example, Columbus based most of his ideas about geography on books written in the fourteenth and early fifteenth centuries. And not all the work was unoriginal. In philosophy there was

Death was a favorite subject for illustration in the late Middle Ages. Shown here is the Dance of Death from a manuscript of about 1400. Death, playing a trumpet decked with the papal banner of the keys of St. Peter, summons a pope.

A fifteenth-century representation of Chaucer from the Ellesmere manuscript of the *Canterbury Tales.*

a sharp attack on the system of Thomas Aquinas that freed scholars, to some extent, from their adherence to the Aristotelian ideas that had been incorporated into Thomas' theology. Once Aristotle's ideas had been challenged, there could be wider speculation on scientific questions, especially on explanations of motion. The problems through which Galileo revolutionized the science of physics had already been raised by fourteenth-century scholars. For example, mathematicians at Oxford came very close to a correct solution of the problem of accelerated motion; and the French scholar Oresme, who was interested in physics as well as in political theory and economics, was at least willing to discuss the possibility that the earth rotated.

More important than any specific achievement was the very fact that interest in scientific problems persisted. Up to the end of the Middle Ages, western scholars, relying largely on the work of the Greeks and Moslems, had made no outstanding contributions to scientific knowledge. But they were remarkably persistent and kept working on scientific problems after other peoples had given up. The Greeks and Moslems eventually lost interest in science, as did the Chinese, who had had their own independent scientific tradition. But from the twelfth century on, there were always some scholars in the West who were interested in science, and this long devotion led, in the end, to the great discoveries of the early modern period. Early modern astronomers like Copernicus and Galileo were trained in universities that used the methods and the books of the later Middle Ages.

No one has ever given a completely satisfactory explanation of this continuing interest in science. Certainly westerners were paying more attention to the things of this world during the later Middle Ages and less attention to the aims of the Church. But Chinese society was far more secular, and the Chinese, in the long run, fell behind the Europeans. Perhaps more important was the western tendency to be dissatisfied with the status quo, a tendency that was especially evident in the crucial years between 1300 and 1600. In China, a philosopher like Thomas Aquinas would have become an unchallenged authority; in Europe his system was questioned within a generation after his death. Europeans respected authority, but they always felt that authoritative treatises needed to be reinterpreted. Finally, there was a curious patience with details, a willingness and an enthusiasm to work very hard for very small gains.

An early gun, lighter and more portable than the first cannon. The gun was placed on a forked stand and was braced against the ground by its long tail (illustration from a German manuscript, *ca.* 1405).

Technology

These qualities also explain some of the advances in technology that were made in the last medieval centuries. Perhaps the most important was the development of firearms. Here, as in many other cases, the Europeans capitalized on a technique known to other peoples. The Chinese, for example, were probably the first to discover gunpowder, and they had cannon about as early as the Europeans. But Chinese guns were never very efficient, and the Chinese never developed an army that was primarily dependent on firearms. The Europeans carried their experiments with cannon much further than the Chinese. Although the first European guns were not very good—they were as apt to kill the men who fired them as those at whom they were aimed—they had become fairly reliable by the end of the fifteenth century. The military significance of this development is obvious. It reduced the power of local lords by making their castles untenable; conversely, it increased the power of kings and great princes like the Duke of Burgundy, for they were the only ones who could afford the expensive new weapons.

The development of firearms caused a rapid growth in other branches of technology. In order to make gun barrels that would not burst under the shock of an explosion, much had to be learned about metallurgy. And in order to make gun barrels that were truly round and hence could deliver the full effect of the charge, better metalworking tools and more precise measuring instruments had to be developed. Better techniques in using metals led to greater demands for metals, and this in turn stimulated the mining industry. The miners of Germany (including Bohemia and Austria), who were the chief suppliers of metals for Europe, learned to push their shafts deeper and to devise ways of draining off underground water. Increased use of metals and greater skill in mining in the long run transformed European industry. To take the most famous example, pumps operated by a piston traveling in a cylinder were developed in order to remove water from mines; it was this kind of pump that eventually furnished the model for the first steam engine.

The invention of printing in the fifteenth century (see p. 364) also owed much to developments in metallurgy. The essential element in printing was the use of movable type, and good type in turn depended on the availability of a metal that would take the exact shape of the mold into which it was poured. Thanks to their knowledge of metallurgy, the Germans succeeded in developing an alloy that expanded as it cooled, so that it fitted the mold exactly. Type faces molded from this alloy produced sharp, clear impressions.

Another technical advance of western Europe in the later Middle Ages was in ocean shipping. Here there was at first more patient experimentation than striking discoveries. By the end of the thirteenth century the sailors of western countries had ships that could tack against the wind and were seaworthy enough to survive the storms of the Atlantic. The navigators of the period could find their latitude, though not their longitude, by star and sun sights; they knew that the earth was round, and that the distance to the rich countries of the East was not impossibly great. Very little more was needed for the great voyages of discovery except practice, and during the fourteenth and fifteenth centuries daring men were mastering the art of oceanic navigation. French and Spanish seamen had reached the Canary Islands at least by the early fourteenth century, and the Portuguese by 1400 had pushed down to the bend in the African coast, claiming Madeira and the Cape Verde Islands along the way.

These voyages illustrate the point that was made earlier: Europeans were no more skillful or intelligent than other peoples; they were simply more persistent or more aggressive. During the same years in which the Europeans were making their first sorties into the Atlantic, the Chinese were sending expeditions into the Indian Ocean. There they found rich kingdoms, ancient civilizations, and profitable sources of trade. In contrast, the Europeans discovered only barren islands and the fever-stricken coast of Africa. Yet the Chinese abandoned their explorations because they, or at least their rulers, were satisfied with what they had at home. The Europeans persisted, though it was almost two centuries before they reached the thriving trading centers of the East or the treasures of Mexico and Peru.

Not as striking as the early voyages, but almost as significant, was the invention of the mechanical clock. The first clocks, which appeared in the fourteenth century, were not very accurate, but they were soon improved by the discovery of the principle of escapement—the system by which the train of gears moves only a precise distance before it is checked and then released to move the same distance again. Crude as the first clocks were, they modified, in the long run, the mental outlook of the western peoples. For several centuries one of the sharpest differences between the West and the rest of the world lay in attitudes toward precise measurement, especially the precise measurement of time. Western civilization has come to be dominated by the clock and the timetable, and westerners have had little sympathy with people who have managed to escape this domination.

Mechanical clock made in 1410. The first clocks had only one movable hand.

Suggestions for Further Reading

Note: Asterisk denotes a book available in paperback edition.

Economic Weakness H. A. Miskimin, *The Economy of Early Renaissance Europe, 1300–1460** (1969), is a good brief survey of the problem. J. W. Thompson's *Economic and Social History of Europe in the Later Middle Ages* (1931), which has excellent material on almost all aspects of European economic life in this period, is a good starting point for further study. There is a very thorough treatment of the methods for the enforcement of early economic legislation in England in B. H. Putnam, *The Enforcement of the Statutes of Labourers* (1908). B. N. Nelson, *The Idea of Usury* (1949), studies the development of a universal morality conducive to systematic capitalist enterprise. The second edition of Vol. I of the *Cambridge Economic History of Europe* is especially good on this period. See also E. E. Power and M. M. Postan, *Studies in English Trade in the Fifteenth Century* (1933), and S. L. Thrupp, *The Merchant Class of Medieval London* (1948).

Attacks on the Church: Marsilius, Wiclif, and Hus There is a wealth of material available in English on these men, who revolutionized the political and religious thinking of western Europe. A. Gewirth, *Marsilius of Padua,** Vol. I (1951), is a scholarly and readable treatment of the political philosophy of Marsilius. The great treatise of Marsilius, the *Defensor pacis,* trans. by A. Gewirth (1956), brings out the premises by which Marsilius overthrew the doctrines of the papal plenitude of power and the Gelasian theory of the parallelism between the spiritual and temporal powers.

G. Leff, *Heresy in the Later Middle Ages* (1967), is a good survey of the problem. A good introduction to the political, social, and religious climate on which the thought of Wiclif fell is G. M. Trevelyan, *England in the Age of Wycliff** (1899). Trevelyan was one of the great social historians of his century and a very good writer. H. B. Workman, *John Wyclif,* 2 vols. (1926), is a study of the impact of Wiclif's thought on his times and on the English Church. See also K. B. McFarlane, *John Wycliffe* (1952). D. S. Schaff, *John Huss* (1915), is an interesting biography of this Czech nationalist and precursor of reformation. The short monograph of M. Spinka, *John Huss and the Czech Reform* (1941), is a study of the influence of Wiclif on the thought of Hus. There is valuable material on the influence of Marsilius and Wiclif on the evolution of political thought in C. H. McIlwain, *Growth of Political Thought in the West* (1932). For an excellent account of the Hussite movement, see F. G. Heymann, *John Ziska and the Hussite Revolution* (1955) and *George of Bohemia* (1965). H. Kaminsky, *A History of the Hussite Revolution* (1967), is also very useful.

The Great Schism The best background for understanding the Great Schism of the West is W. Ullmann, *Origins of the Great Schism* (1948). W. E. Lunt, *Papal Revenues in the Middle Ages,* 2 vols. (1934), has source material on the finances of the papacy at this time. There is a full account of the Great Schism in M. Creighton, *A History of the Papacy from the Great Schism to the Sack of Rome,* Vols. I and II (1919), and in L. Pastor, *History of the Popes,* Vol. I (trans. 1891), but the interpretation of Creighton is more balanced.

The Black Death F. A. Gasquet, *The Black Death* (1893), is a good study of this epidemic, with detailed material on the consequences of the plague for the social and economic life of England in the later Middle Ages. The more recent work of A. E. Levett, *The Black Death on the Estates of the See of Winchester* (1916), rejects the older view that the Black Death seriously disrupted the economic development of England. Differing points of view on this problem are presented by W. M. Bowsky, ed., *The Black Death* (1971).

England from 1307 to 1485 A. R. Myers, *England in the Later Middle Ages** (1952), a broad survey of this period, is a good introduction. There is valuable source material on the reign of Edward II in *The Life of Edward II,* trans. by N. Denholm-Young (1957), which goes into considerable detail on the revival of baronial powers and the civil wars under Edward. T. F. Tout, *The Place of the Reign of Edward II in History* (1936), sees this reign as the period of marked transition from court administration to national administration.

J. Froissart, *Chronicles** (many translations), presents a vivid picture of the life and spirit of fourteenth-century England. Froissart is an invaluable source for the reign of Edward III. There is a wealth of primary information on the reigns of Henry VI, Edward IV, and Richard III in *The Paston Letters,* 3 vols., ed. by J. Gairdner (1895). H. L. Gray, *The Influence of the Commons on Early Legislation* (1932), is a scholarly study of the development of the House of Commons in the fourteenth and fifteenth centuries. S. Armitage-Smith, *John of Gaunt* (1904); A. Steel, *Richard II* (1941); and P. M. Kendall, *Richard the Third** (1955), are all interesting reading and based on sound scholarship.

For material on the development of the English constitution, see B. Wilkinson, *Constitutional History of Medieval England,* Vols. II and III (1958).

E. Perroy, *The Hundred Years' War,** trans. by W. B. Wells (1952), is an excellent account of the military history of this period, with a discussion of the implications of the war on the constitutional growth of England. R. B. Mowat, *The Wars of the Roses* (1914), and J. R. Lander, *The Wars of the Roses* (1965), are interesting, if somewhat romantic, treatments of this confusing struggle.

France from 1314 to 1461

H. Pirenne et al., *La fin du moyen age* (1931), is a thorough study of this period by outstanding French historians. The broad scholarly work of E. Lavisse, ed., *Histoire de France,* Vol. IV, Part 2 (1902), is invaluable for the political, economic, military, and cultural history of France in this period.

There is a full documentary account of the trials of Joan of Arc in *Jeanne d'Arc,* ed. by T. D. Murray (1920), a very readable translation. L. Fabre, *Joan of Arc,* trans. by G. Hopkins (1954), is a fine biography of Joan and presents a fascinating picture of France in the period of the Hundred Years' War. Another good biography is S. Stolpe, *The Maid of Orleans* (1956). R. Vaughn in *Philip the Bold* (1962), *John the Fearless* (1966), and *Philip the Good* (1970), gives a good picture of the growth of Burgundian power.

There are two very readable studies of the last Duke of Burgundy: J. F. Kirk, *Charles the Bold, Duke of Burgundy,* 3 vols. (1864–68), is a study of the man in relation to his times; R. Putnam, *Charles the Bold* (1908), concentrates on Charles the man. A good picture of the brilliant life of the Burgundian court is given in O. Cartellieri, *The Court of Burgundy* (1929). The outstanding achievement of J. Huizinga, *The Waning of the Middle Ages** (1924), is a study of the forms of life and thought in France and the Netherlands in the last days of the brilliant court of Burgundy.

Spain in the Later Middle Ages

R. Altimira, *A History of Spain* (1949), and H. J. Chaytor, *A History of Aragon* (1933), both provide information on Spain during this period.

Germany in the Later Middle Ages

Both J. Bryce, *The Holy Roman Empire* (many editions), and G. Barraclough, *The Origins of Modern Germany** (1947), contain information on Germany in the later Middle Ages. Barraclough presents a fresher historical interpretation. The old study of H. Zimmer, The *Hansa Towns* (1889), is still valuable. C. Bayley, *The Formation of the German College of Electors* (1949), and F. L. Carster, *Princes and Parliaments in Germany* (1959), are also useful.

The origins and development of Switzerland are carefully treated in W. D. McCracken, *Rise of the Swiss Republic* (1901).

The titles by Pirenne, Lavisse, and Vaughn in the section on France above contain information on the rise of the Habsburg dynasty and the Burgundian takeover of the Low Countries.

Art, Literature, Science, and Scholarship in the Later Middle Ages

E. Panofsky, *Early Netherlandish Painting* (1953), is a beautiful study of art in northern Europe at this time, and M. Meiss, *Painting in Florence and Siena after the Black Death** (1951), describes the impact the Black Death had on the art of southern Europe. Both volumes are by outstanding art historians and have good reproductions.

Some of the greatest literature of the western world was produced in the later Middle Ages. Chaucer's *Canterbury Tales** (many editions); Villon's *Poems,* trans. by H. D. Stacpoole (1926); and Dante's *Divine Comedy,** trans. by D. L. Sayers (1949–58), are all masterpieces. Each was written in the vernacular, each reflects the changing world view, and each gives a superb picture of the spirit and thought of the times. J. Gardner, *The Life and Times of Chaucer* (1977), is a lively reconstruction of the poet's career. The great English poem of Langland, *Piers the Ploughman,** trans. by J. E. Goodridge (1959), is a fourteenth-century inquiry into the good life as judged by contemporary criteria. G. Lagarde, *Naissance de l'esprit laïque,* 2 vols. (1956–58), a brilliant treatment of late medieval thought and scholarship, traces the development in western Europe of a distinctly secular spirit. There is interesting material on late medieval science in H. Butterfield, *Origins of Modern Science, 1300–1800** (1949), a broad survey. A. C. Crombie, *Medieval and Early Modern Science,** 2 vols. (1959), gives considerable attention to methods in physics in the late Middle Ages and stresses the continuity of the western scientific tradition from Greek times to the present. Crombie includes a good up-to-date bibliography. The thought of the fourteenth century is lucidly presented in G. Leff, *Medieval Thought** (1958), which discusses Occam, science, and political theories. E. Gilson, *History of Christian Philosophy in the Middle Ages* (1954), has information on Occam and the later Schoolmen. There is a wealth of material on the intellectual and spiritual life of the period from 1216 to 1485 in D. Knowles, *Religious Orders in England,* 2 vols. (1954–55).

14 Western Europe's Neighbors During the Middle Ages

At a time when the governments of western Europe were weak, its cities almost nonexistent, and its scholars limited to the study of encyclopedias and digests, both Byzantium and Islam had well-organized bureaucratic states, large commercial cities, and eminent scholars. Understandably, western Europeans felt awkward in dealing with their more fortunate neighbors, and their sense of inferiority often led them into suspicion and hostility. But neighbors they were, and contacts of some sort were inevitable.

THE BYZANTINE EMPIRE

The Byzantine Empire recovered only slowly from the external shock of the Arab conquests and the internal shock of the long religious controversy over the veneration of images. The Moslems remained a constant threat from the south, and the Bulgars, an Asiatic people who gradually mixed with the southern Slavs, menaced Constantinople from the north. But the Empire still had its wealth, its diplomatic skill, and its professional army, and with them it managed to limp through the eighth and early ninth centuries.

With the accession of Basil I (867–886), who founded the Macedonian dynasty, the Byzantine Empire began one of its marvelous recoveries. For a century and a half most of the emperors were first-rate generals. They took advantage of dissensions among their enemies to drive back the Moslems in the south and the Bulgars in the north. They recovered all of Asia Minor and gained control of the eastern Mediterranean, making possible the reconquest of Crete and Cyprus. The Byzantine Empire was never richer or more powerful than it was about the year 1000.

Byzantine Art and Literature

An intellectual and artistic revival accompanied and outlasted the political revival. The schools at Constantinople reached the peak of their activity soon after 1000, when a faculty of philosophy and a school of law were established. This was not quite a university of the western type, since standardized courses and degrees were lacking, but professors

Opposite: Interior of the mosque at Cordoba (*ca.* 785).

Byzantine art exhibited Christian influence and a love of ornamentation. Above: a tenth-century clasp bearing the image of a saint. Below: a reliquary cross (probably twelfth century).

were paid regular salaries and often held high positions at the imperial court. Byzantine scholars spent much of their energy copying and commenting on ancient texts, useful though not original work that preserved many books that otherwise would have been lost. Especially important was the Byzantine interest in Plato. The other great group of scholars of this period—those who wrote in Arabic—were much more concerned with Aristotle, and western Europe had inherited only a few fragments of Plato in Latin translation. When the Italians of the fifteenth century became interested in Plato, they had to obtain their texts, and scholars to expound them, from Constantinople and other areas of the collapsing Byzantine Empire.

Not all Byzantine writing, however, was based on ancient materials. The Byzantines produced some notable histories—works that were not impartial, since they were usually written to justify the actions of a ruler or a faction, but that were far superior to contemporary western chronicles. Another interesting genre that flourished during this period was the popular epic. Stories of heroic deeds performed against the enemies of the Empire were written in the language used by the people, and for this reason they were far more widely known than scholarly works written in correct classical Greek. The most famous of these poems, the epic of Digenis Akritas, was still remembered at the time of the Cypriote rebellion of 1957 to 1958.

Under the Macedonian emperors and their immediate successors, Byzantine art entered into its golden age. As in scholarship, so in art there was a revival of classical influence. Byzantine artists were far less imitative, however, than were Byzantine writers. While deriving a certain dignity and sobriety from ancient works, they retained the Byzantine love of color and ornamentation. Unlike the scholars, they had something to say to the people; they portrayed the truths of the Christian faith and the events of recent history. Every church and many private homes had their icons (paintings of sacred personages); every important manuscript was illustrated with miniatures. With hundreds of artists at work, it is not surprising that many of them were competent and a few great.

Byzantium and the West

Byzantine influence was felt throughout western Europe. Italian merchants came regularly to Constantinople and after 1100 took over most of the carrying trade of the Empire. Byzantine influence remained strong in southern Italy, even after the Norman conquest in the eleventh century of Byzantine holdings there, and in Venice, which had once been a Byzantine protectorate. Popes and German kings exchanged embassies with the emperor at Constantinople, and thousands of western pilgrims passed through the city on their way to the Holy Land. Easy access to the markets of Constantinople speeded up the growth of Italian cities, and the Italian cities in turn led the economic revival of the West. The use of Byzantine artists by Italians—as in the designing of the Venetian Cathedral of St. Mark's—left its mark on Italian art. The first native Italian painters were clearly influenced by Byzantine models.

Western scholars were not greatly interested in the theology or philosophy of the Byzantines. But after 1100 a few westerners journeyed to Constantinople to discover and translate ancient manuscripts. Their work was less appreciated than that of their contemporaries who were working on translations from the Arabic, and sometimes books that had passed from Greek to Syriac to Arabic to Latin were preferred to direct translations from the Greek. Because western translators were primarily interested in Aristotle, they overlooked the opportunity to increase the stock of Platonic works available in Latin. Nevertheless, some important texts, such as the advanced works of Euclid, would have been unknown to western medieval scholars had it not been for the efforts of the translators at Constantinople.

During the eleventh century the Latin and Greek Churches gradually drifted apart. There had long been friction between them, since the patriarch at Constantinople rejected the pope's claims to universal authority and the pope resented the patriarch's claim to indepen-

ca. 570	632	661	750	Mongols Take Baghdad 1258
Life of Mohammed	First Four Caliphs	Ommiad Dynasty	Abbasid Dynasty	

dence. There were theological disputes, such as the one over sacred images, and the question raised by Charlemagne about the relationship between the Holy Ghost and the other two Persons of the Trinity. But the basic reason for the split was that the West and Byzantium were becoming so different in institutions and culture that each was suspicious of the other's motives. Finally, in 1054, pope and patriarch excommunicated each other, and the two Churches broke off relations. The break was not taken too seriously at first; such splits had happened before and had always been repaired. But this time, in spite of repeated efforts, the breach could not be healed. Each Church went its own way, and cooperation between them became more and more difficult.

Byzantium and the Slavs

Byzantium's greatest influence was on the peoples of the Balkans and Russia. In spite of frequent wars and rebellions, there were long periods in which the Serbs and the Bulgars were either subject to, or allied with, the Eastern Empire. Byzantine princesses were frequently married to Slavic rulers in order to gain influence in neighboring courts. These ladies brought with them missionaries and teachers, artists and scholars, thus helping to spread the Greek Orthodox religion and Byzantine culture throughout the regions inhabited by the eastern Slavs. The conversion of the Bulgars began in the ninth century and that of the Russians in the tenth; both peoples were soon thoroughly Christianized. For a long time the leading clergymen in Bulgaria and Russia were appointed by the patriarch of Constantinople. Even with a growing tendency toward autonomy in the Slavic churches, Byzantine influence remained strong. Down to the fifteenth century all but two or three of the metropolitans (heads) of the Russian Church were Greeks.

The fact that the eastern Slavs received their religion and culture from Constantinople had lasting consequences for the history of modern Europe. Byzantine civilization and western European civilization had a common origin, but, as we have seen, they drifted apart during the Middle Ages. Byzantium remembered much that the West forgot, and it was always more strongly influenced by eastern ideas and customs. The West went through experiences, such as the Investiture Conflict, and developed institutions, such as feudalism, that scarcely touched Constantinople. Misunderstandings were inevitable, and they were especially bitter because each region expected better things of a related Christian civilization and because each felt that the other was betraying a common heritage. The eastern Slavs, especially the Russians, shared these tensions. The West both attracted and repulsed them, and the current Russian attitude toward the West is a new and intensified form of an old suspicion.

THE MOSLEM CALIPHATE

The Abbasid Caliphate, established in 750, achieved its golden age before the tenth-century revival set in at Constantinople. It reached its peak of power and wealth under Harun-al-Rashid (786–809). Harun, who exchanged letters and gifts with Charlemagne, ruled a far larger empire than his western contemporary. The lands of the caliph stretched from Morocco to the Indus River, from the steppes of central Asia to the Sudan. After 900, although the Caliphate began to break up into separate states, the Moslem world remained an economic and cultural unit. In this vast territory, which was traversed by all the important East–West trade routes, there were dozens of populous and prosperous cities, but Baghdad was the largest and richest.

Byzantine masons at work (miniature from a psalter, 1066).

Arabic Scholarship

The city of Baghdad attracted books and scholars just as it did merchandise and traders. The Abbasids did even more than the Ommiads to transform their empire into a center of scholarship. Hundreds of Greek works, especially on philosophy, science, and mathematics, were translated into Arabic, and much was learned from Persian and Jewish sources. Chinese scholarship had little influence, but the Abbasids borrowed many ideas from the Indians, notably the system of arithmetic notation that we call Arabic figures. By the ninth century Moslem scholars had assimilated the work of their predecessors and were beginning to make original contributions of their own. From 900 to 1200 the most important work done anywhere in the world in mathematics, astronomy, physics, medicine, and geography was done in Moslem countries.

Much Arabic scholarship merely added details to support established scientific theories—for example, accurate observations of star positions or clinical descriptions of certain diseases. More was done in geography because the Arabs knew more about the world than had the ancient writers. But their most remarkable contribution was in physics and mathematics. In physics they performed interesting experiments in reflection and refraction. In mathematics, besides greatly simplifying arithmetical operations through the use of the new Arabic figures, they carried trigonometry far beyond the Greek accomplishment. And their work in algebra was even more impressive, for they fashioned a whole mathematical discipline out of the few hints provided by their predecessors. Their contribution is recorded in the very word *algebra,* which is Arabic.

Two notable Moslem mathematicians were al-Khwarizmi (d. *ca.* 840) and the poet Omar Khayyám (d. *ca.* 1120). Al-Khwarizmi recognized, more clearly than many of his contemporaries, the value of the new Hindu-Arabic figures, especially the zero. Use of the zero made it possible to reckon by position and simplified all work in arithmetic. Al-Khwarizmi did much to popularize this new arithmetic; he also wrote a text on algebra that was used in both Moslem and Christian countries for centuries. Omar Khayyám calculated the length of a solar year with great accuracy and devised methods of solving algebraic equations that had been too complicated for his predecessors.

Arabic Influence on the West

Moslem interest in mathematics and the natural sciences had a decisive influence on the course of western civilization. The Byzantines tended to neglect these subjects, and little was known about them in western Europe. The Chinese had great technical skill—for example, they discovered the principle of the compass very early—but they developed few general theories. And the Indians, after a promising start, lost their interest in scientific problems. Thus the Moslem world was the only region that was both actively interested in science and close enough to western Europe to touch off a revival of scientific interest there. Western European scholars made their first attempts to recover ancient scientific texts by going to the Moslems of Spain and Sicily; only after the revival was well under way did they begin to seek manuscripts in Constantinople. Certainly the West would not have developed a scientific tradition of its own as rapidly as it did without the assistance of Moslem scholarship, and quite possibly it never would have developed the tradition at all.

It is somewhat anachronistic, however, to separate science so sharply from other studies. For Moslem scholars, as for medieval Christians, science was merely one aspect of philosophy. Aristotle, the great authority on science for both peoples, was thought of primarily as a philosopher, and one of the chief intellectual problems of the Middle Ages was to reconcile his philosophy with the revealed truths of religion. Here again, Moslem scholars led the way. Avicenna (ibn-Sina, 980–1037), who wrote a famous book in Arabic on medicine, also prepared commentaries on Aristotle that influenced western scholars during the twelfth and thirteenth centuries. Even more important was the Spanish Moslem Averroës (ibn-Rushd, 1126–98), some of whose assertions shocked both Islam and Christendom—for example, that the world is eternal, and that there is no personal immortality. But Averroës was no freethinker; one of his strongest convictions was that there can be no real conflict between the truths of philosophy and the truths of revealed religion. This doctrine, which was taken over by Christian scholars in the thirteenth century, made it easier for them to justify the assimilation of Greco-Arabic philosophy into the Christian tradition. Maimonides (Moses ben Maimon, 1135–1204), a Spanish Jew living under Moslem rule, was thoroughly familiar with the Arabic versions of Aristotelian philosophy and tried to reconcile them with the Jewish faith. His proofs of the existence of God are very like those advanced a half-century later by Thomas Aquinas.

Until the Moslems broke away from the Koran's strict ban on representing living beings, they could do nothing with sculpture and painting. They were, however, great builders and created a distinctive style out of such old forms as the dome, the arcade, and the tower. Moslem architectural styles made a deep impression on every country in which they appeared; their influence may still be seen in Spain and India. Moslem buildings were lavishly decorated with colored tiles and intricate geometric carvings—ideas that were imitated by neighboring countries.

THE DECLINE OF BYZANTIUM AND THE CALIPHATE

The Byzantine Empire and the countries controlled by the Abbasid Caliphate remained important centers of commerce and intellectual and artistic activity throughout the European Middle Ages. But after the tenth century they began to decline as political units. Some problems were common to both states—for example, the lack of a fixed rule of succession to the throne. Neither the emperor nor the caliph was necessarily the eldest son of his predecessor; he might be anyone connected with the ruling family who had been able to win the support of the bureaucracy and the army. Theoretically this practice might have assured the selection of the ablest man; actually it encouraged palace intrigues and civil wars. The western European tendency to insist on the rule of primogeniture was not an ideal way of picking a ruler, but in practice it gave greater stability and continuity to political institutions. Another problem common to both the Byzantine Empire and the Arab Caliphate was that of raising an army. It was easier to hire soldiers from among the neighboring barbarians than to disrupt civilian life by forcing city workers and peasant farmers into the army. But mercenaries were never entirely reliable, and the better they were as fighting men, the greater the danger that they might try to take over the government.

Each state also had problems of its own. In Byzantium there was a growing hostility between the bureaucracy of the capital city and the great landlords of the

A Moslem pharmacist concocting a medicinal wine (from a thirteenth-century manuscript of Dioscorides' *Materia Medica*). The text reads: "The making of a drink (*shirab*) for catarrhs, coughs, swelling of the belly, and loosening of the stomach." The recipe calls for wine mixed with myrrh, roots of licorice, and white pepper.

rural districts. The bureaucrats, quite rightly, felt that the landlords were trying to reduce the peasants to a state of serfdom and to make themselves independent rulers in the outlying provinces. The landlords felt, quite rightly in turn, that the bureaucracy was a nest of intrigue and corruption. Attempts to weaken the landlords or reform the bureaucrats merely intensified the bad feelings between the two groups. These disruptive tendencies were held in check during the tenth century, but after the death of the last great Macedonian emperor, Basil II, in 1025, they grew more virulent.

The problems peculiar to the Caliphate sprang from its size and from the peculiar nature of Moslem law, which emphasized ethical and religious duties, but left enforcement to the whims of the ruler. It was almost impossible to establish a centralized administrative system for such widely separated regions, each with its own traditions. Regional viceroys had to be given extensive powers, and there was always the danger that one of them would set himself up as an independent ruler. Moreover, though the caliphs had built up a bureaucracy on Roman and Persian models, and though they had developed a comprehensive legal system, Moslem government was always rather arbitrary and unpredictable. No one wanted to be bound by rules, least of all the caliph and his officials. Since everything depended on the whim of the man in power, it was better to catch his ear than it was to try to win a case at law. This lack of respect for legal principles encouraged intrigue and disobedience. Instability was increased by religious divisions among the Moslems. Minority groups that questioned the Abbasid ruler's claim to be the orthodox successor of Mohammed naturally felt very little respect for his government.

The first crack in the Caliphate showed itself in 756, when a member of the deposed Ommiad dynasty established an independent state in Spain. The loss of this outlying territory did little damage, but the next secessions were more serious, for they cost the Caliphate all of North Africa. In the tenth century much of this area was seized by the new Fatimid dynasty. This family claimed descent from Fatima, the daughter of Mohammed, a claim that gave it the support of the Shi-ites, the largest group of dissenters in Islam. The Shi-ites believed that Islam must always be led by a lineal descendant of Mohammed; they had rejected the Ommiad caliphs and were now ready to turn against the Abbasids. By taking the title of caliph in 909, the founder of the new dynasty directly challenged the claim of the Abbasid ruler to be leader of all the Moslems. In 969 the Fatimids conquered Egypt, thereby gaining one of the wealthiest Moslem provinces; they established their capital in the newly built city of Cairo in 973. The Fatimid domains now stretched from Morocco to the Red Sea and even included Jerusalem. At the height of their power the Fatimid caliphs of Cairo were far stronger than the Abbasid caliphs of Baghdad.

The Coming of the Turks

By the end of the eleventh century the Fatimid Caliphate was beginning to weaken. The Abbasids, however, profited little from the decline of their rivals. In an effort to hold on to their remaining provinces, they had come to rely more and more on mercenary soldiers, especially the Seljuk Turks. A branch of the nomadic stock of central Asia, the Turks had all the toughness, bravery, and love of conquest of their eastern relatives. They became devout Moslems and fought well for their new religion, but they also fought for themselves. Having become the dominant military power in the lands of the Abbasid Caliphate, they soon began to seek political power as well. By the eleventh century the Turkish sultans (kings) had become the real rulers of most of Syria and Mesopotamia. They preserved the caliph as a religious leader, but they did not allow him any real power in government.

The rise of the Turks had serious consequences for the Byzantine emperors as well. Disputes over the succession to the imperial throne and quarrels between the bureaucrats of Constantinople and the great landlords had seriously weakened the Eastern Empire. Suspecting that they would meet with little resistance, the Turks began to push into Asia Minor; when the emperor Romanus IV tried to drive them out he was defeated and captured at the battle of Manzikert in 1071.

The Byzantine Empire never fully recovered from this defeat. After Manzikert the Turks overran almost all of Asia Minor; they even took Nicaea, only fifty miles from Constantinople. Through heroic efforts a new Byzantine dynasty, the Comneni, regained some of the lost territory, but it could never eject the Turks from central and eastern Asia Minor. This was a serious loss to the Empire, for the provinces seized by the Turks had furnished large numbers of fighting men and had protected the wealthy coastal regions. Skillful diplomacy and the wise use of limited resources enabled Byzantium to survive, but the Eastern Empire under the Comneni never had the vigor it had displayed under the Macedonians.

Fortunately for the Byzantines, the first Turkish Empire began to disintegrate almost as soon as it was established. As might have been expected in this part of the world, the lack of a fixed rule of succession did most of the damage. Each sultan established little principalities for junior members of the family, and military commanders began to turn their governorships into independent states. Each ruler fought and intrigued with his neighbors in order to gain more land. In the end the old Abbasid Caliphate dissolved into a welter of petty states, only loosely associated by their theoretical allegiance to caliph and sultan.

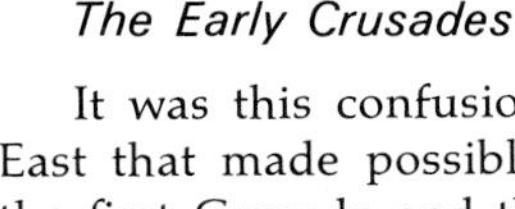

The Early Crusades

It was this confusion in the Middle East that made possible the success of the first Crusade and the establishment of the crusader Kingdom of Jerusalem in 1099. The Moslems were too divided to cooperate against the common enemy, and some of them even encouraged the Christians to attack their rivals. Only a part of the Turkish forces could be assembled to fight the crusaders at Antioch; once Antioch had been lost to the Christians, few of the Syrian Moslems cared about the fate of Jerusalem. Jerusalem, after all, was held by the Fatimid heretics, who were little better than the Christian infidels. The Fatimids, on their part, regarded Jerusalem as an outlying possession of little military or political value and made no great effort to regain the Holy City. A dynasty of Christian kings, descended from the crusader Baldwin of Lorraine, held Jerusalem and most of Palestine from 1099 to 1187.

The emperor Alexius Comnenus (1081–1118) must have looked on the First Crusade as a very successful piece of Byzantine diplomacy. He had shown remarkable skill in whisking unruly western armies through his lands with a minimum of friction and looting, and he had used the crusading forces to screen his reoccupation of much of western Asia Minor. The establishment in 1099 of the Kingdom of Jerusalem and the northern

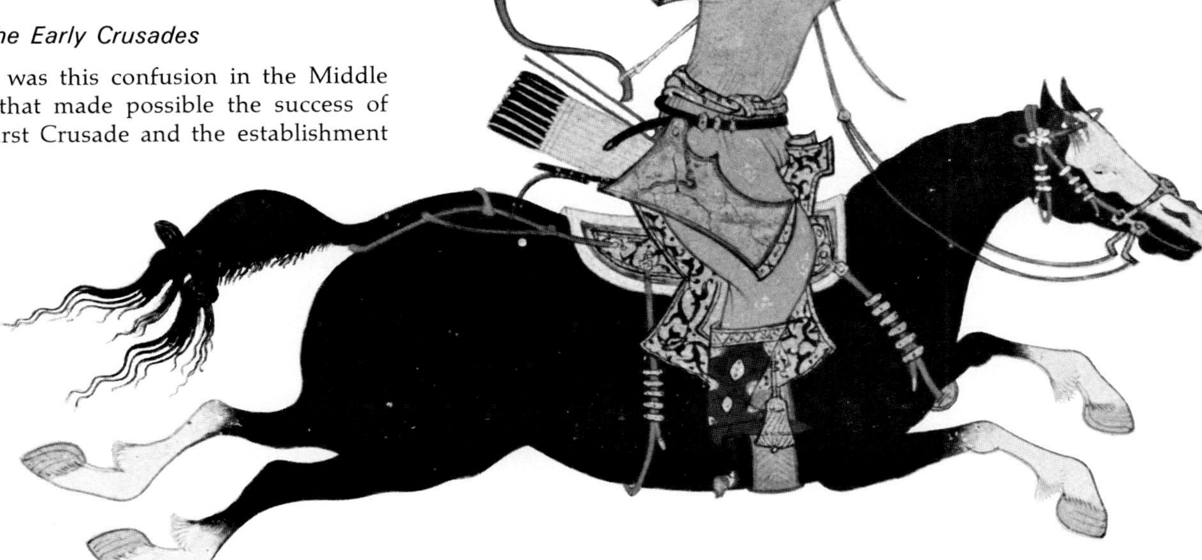

Turkish miniature depicting an Asiatic bowman. Unencumbered by armor, he could move swiftly on his small, strong horse.

CRUSADE ROUTES 1096–1270

crusading states of Tripoli, Antioch, and Edessa drove a wedge into the Moslem states of the Middle East and made cooperation among them more difficult than before. Moreover, by posing a threat to Islam, the crusading states also distracted Moslem attention from Byzantine expansion in Asia Minor.

The crusade was not all profit for the Byzantines, however, for it reinforced western suspicions of Byzantine morals and motives. The leaders of the crusade were sure that Alexius' failure to aid them in the siege of Antioch showed that he was more interested in recovering his lost provinces than in freeing the holy places from the Moslems. Western hostility to Byzantium was strengthened by the events of the Second and Third Crusades. The Byzantines were not really interested in fostering these movements; in fact, they twice withdrew into neutrality in return for advantageous treaties with the Turks. The westerners, dismayed by this subtle diplomacy, soon began to think that the Byzantines were almost as great a threat to Christendom as the Moslems. The sack of Constantinople by a crusading army in 1204 was the price Byzantium paid for arousing these suspicions.

The Moslems recovered only slowly from the shock of the Christian conquest of Jerusalem. Gradually a series of able army commanders began to reunite the scattered Moslem states. The first of these generals, Zangi, took the outlying Christian county of Edessa in 1144 and held it against the badly mismanaged Second Crusade. Even more decisive was the work of Zangi's son, Nureddin (Nūr-al-Dīn), who put an end to the decaying Fatimid Caliphate of Egypt in 1171. Nureddin was already master of most of Syria; by adding Egypt to his domain he became far stronger than the Christian kings of Jerusalem. He was succeeded by his ablest general, Saladin (Salāh-al-Dīn), who overran the Kingdom of Jerusalem and seized the Holy City itself in 1187. The Christians were left with only a few seacoast towns.

The loss of Jerusalem sent a shock of horror throughout Latin Christendom. The three greatest kings of the West—Frederick Barbarossa of Germany, Philip Augustus of France, and Richard Lionheart of England—agreed to unite their forces in an attack on Saladin. But this Third Crusade was only partially successful. Frederick was drowned while crossing Asia Minor with his army, and Philip Augustus, after helping to recapture Acre, rushed back to France to look after the affairs of his kingdom. Richard hung on, fighting so bravely that he became a legend among the Moslems, but he never had a large enough army to risk an attack on Jerusalem. He did reconquer a long strip of coastal territory, thus prolonging the life of the Kingdom of Jerusalem for a century. But the revived kingdom was never strong; it played a far less important role in the thirteenth century than it had in the twelfth.

The Later Crusades

Saladin's empire began to dissolve soon after his death in 1193. As so often happened in the Moslem world, his states were divided among members of his family, who promptly began intriguing against one another. The Christians could once more hope to regain Jerusalem, and they staged three major and several minor expeditions to the Middle East in the first half of the thirteenth century. None of these crusades was successful; when Frederick II briefly regained Jerusalem he did it through a treaty with the sultan of Egypt. On the other hand, the thirteenth-century crusades, by weakening both Saladin's dynasty and the Byzantine Empire, aided the rise of new powers in the Middle East.

The Byzantine Empire in 1200 was neither as rich nor as powerful as it once had been. Most of its commerce was in the hands of Italian merchants; the Byzantine navy had almost ceased to exist; and the army, composed largely of mercenaries, was too weak to guard all the frontiers. The Turks were threatening Asia Minor, and a revived Bulgarian kingdom was attacking Thrace. Internal dissension had reached a dangerous point, with many of the great families lined up against the emperor. More or less by accident, the first people to take advantage of this inviting situation were a group of crusaders.

The Fourth Crusade started in 1202 as a routine expedition against the Moslems of the East. But the army was heavily in debt to the Venetians, who had supplied ships to carry it to the East. The Venetians, who cared little about crusades but a great deal about profit, made the army work off part of its debt by capturing Zara, a rival trading town across the Adriatic. Then a pretender to the Byzantine throne turned up with a very tempting proposition: he would pay all the army's debts and augment its forces if the crusaders would make him emperor. The Venetians saw a chance to acquire a monopoly of trade with Byzantium, and under their urging, most, though not all, of the crusaders agreed to attack Constantinople. Aided by Byzantine weakness and disunity, the small western force—probably not more than twenty thousand fighting men—managed to seize one of the most strongly fortified positions in the world (1203).

They soon quarreled with their puppet emperor and took over the city for themselves (1204), sacking churches and stealing relics. Then they elected one of

A Byzantine View of the Crusaders

Anna Comnena, the author of this piece, was the daughter of the Emperor Alexius I.

Now he [the emperor] dreaded the arrival of the Crusaders, for he knew their irresistible manner of attack, their unstable and mobile character, and all the peculiar . . . characteristics which the Frank retains throughout; and he also knew that they were always agape for money, and seemed to disregard their truces readily for any reason that cropped up. . . . The simpler-minded Franks were urged on by the real desire of worshipping at our Lord's Sepulchre, but the more astute, especially men like Bohemund . . . had another secret reason, namely the hope that . . . they might by some means be able to seize the capital itself. . . . For the Frankish race . . . is always very hot-headed and eager, but when it has once espoused a cause, it is uncontrollable.

From Anna Comnena, *The Alexiad,* trans. by E. A. S. Dawes (London: Kegan Paul, 1928), pp. 248, 250.

A Crusader's View of Byzantium

Odo of Deuil, the author of this piece, was a historian of the Second Crusade.

And then the Greeks degenerated entirely into women; putting aside all manly vigor, both of words and of spirit, they lightly swore whatever they thought would please us, but they neither kept faith with us nor maintained respect for themselves. In general they really have the opinion that anything which is done for the holy empire cannot be considered perjury. . . . When the Greeks are afraid they become despicable in their excessive abasement, and when they have the upper hand they are arrogant. . . .

Constantinople itself is squalid and fetid. . . . People live lawlessly in this city, which has as many lords as rich men and almost as many thieves as poor men. . . . In every respect she exceeds moderation, for just as she surpasses other cities in wealth, so too does she surpass them in vice. . . .

[The bishop of Langres] added that Constantinople is Christian only in name and not in fact . . . and that her emperor had ventured a few years ago to attack the [Crusader] prince of Antioch. . . . "Though it was his [the emperor's] duty to ward off the near-by infidels by uniting the Christian forces, with the aid of the infidels he strove to destroy the Christians."

From Odo of Deuil, *De profectione Ludovici VII in orientem,* trans. by V. G. Berry (New York: Columbia University Press, 1948), pp. 57, 65, 69.

their own leaders, Baldwin, Count of Flanders, as emperor, and divided most of Greece and Thrace among the Venetians and western feudal lords. This Latin Empire of Constantinople lasted only a half-century (1204–61), but feudal principalities held by western lords survived in Greece to the end of the fourteenth century, and Venice held some of the Greek islands and ports in the Peloponnesus until the seventeenth century.

Innocent III, who was pope at this time, at first severely condemned the diversion of the Fourth Crusade. After 1204, however, he was seduced by the prospect of ending the schism with the Greek Church and gave full support to the Latin Empire. His first reaction was the sounder one; the capture of Constantinople was a disaster for western Christendom. Instead of healing the breach between the two Churches, it intensified Byzantine hatred of the Latins and convinced the Greeks that the independence of their Church was synonymous with national survival. Even when they were about to be conquered by the Turks, the Greeks refused to consider union with Rome. As one of them said: "Better the turban of the sultan than the tiara of the pope." Nor did the capture of Constantinople help the Kingdom of Jerusalem; instead, it meant that western money and fighting men had to be diverted to support the Latin Empire and the feudal principalities of Greece. By ruining the Byzantine Empire the crusaders exposed all southeastern Europe to Turkish conquest. Even though the Latins were driven out of Constantinople in 1261, the revived Byzantine Empire was only a shadow of what it had been. It held only a fragment of the Balkans and a small strip of Asia Minor; it could not check the Turkish advance into Europe in the fourteenth century.

Saladin's dynasty would have lost power in any case, but the thirteenth-century crusades speeded up the process. Louis IX of France precipitated a crisis by leading an army against Egypt in 1248. The sultan of Egypt by this time was almost entirely dependent on his household slaves, who formed the core of his army and held many high administrative posts. There were many able men among these slaves, or Mamelukes, as they were called, and they were weary of fighting to keep a decaying dynasty in power. The early successes of the crusading army led them to assassinate the sultan and to replace him with one of their own commanders. For centuries Egypt was to be ruled by Mameluke generals who rose from the ranks of a slave army. Only tough and brutal men could reach the top, and when one of them showed signs of softening, he was apt to be replaced by a younger and more vigorous fighter. But in spite of their internal quarrels, the Mamelukes were a first-rate military power. They were determined to drive the westerners out of the Middle East, and they rapidly accomplished their purpose. By 1271 they had occupied the entire area except for a few coastal towns, and in 1291 Acre, the last stronghold of the crusaders, was taken by the Mameluke sultan.

The fall of Acre did not end the crusades; there were some large-scale expeditions against the Turks in the fourteenth century, and popes talked of crusades as late as 1464. But none of the later crusades gained a permanent foothold in the East or did much to halt the Turkish advance. Whatever influence the crusades had on western civilization had been exerted by the end of the thirteenth century. And that influence was considerable: the crusades had helped to stimulate the growth of the Italian naval power that was to make the Mediterranean a Christian lake for three centuries. The fact that thousands of westerners lived in, or visited, Syria and Palestine encouraged the demand for eastern luxuries and thus changed western standards of living, although there would have been some increase in demand in any case.

On the other hand, the crusaders showed little evidence of intellectual or cultural interests. Armies of occupation are more likely to bring home material objects than ideas. Western scholars learned more from peaceful contacts with the Moors of Spain and the Greeks of Constantinople than they did from the inhabitants of the Kingdom of Jerusalem. In short, the significance of the crusades in East–West relationships was primarily political and economic. The crusades marked the first attempt of western Europe to expand into non-European areas, and they added to the difficulties of both the Byzantine Empire and the Moslem Caliphates. They did little to promote understanding or intellectual contacts among the three civilizations that bordered the shores of the Mediterranean Sea.

THE MONGOL EMPIRE

Far more important than the later crusades was the advance of the Mongols into Russia and the Middle East. The Mongols were another of those nomadic peoples of central Asia who from time to time developed great military power and burst into the lands of their civilized neighbors. The pattern was a familiar one: an able leader would organize his own tribe into an effective striking force and then subjugate other tribes belonging to the same racial stock. Once he had established himself as the predominant power in the vast steppes of central Asia, other nomadic peoples would join him either out of fear or in the hope of sharing in the loot. Finally, the united forces would become strong enough to strike out at China, India, or Europe. This had been the story of the Huns, and it was to be the story of the Mongols.

A small group originally, the Mongols became the dominant element in a great federation of nomadic tribes. But while the Mongols followed the old pattern, they expanded more widely and held their conquests longer than any of their predecessors. The leader who began the expansion of Mongol power, Genghis Khan (*ca.* 1160–1227), was the ablest of all the nomad rulers, and his immediate descendants were almost as competent. The Mongol khans were not only first-rate generals; they also knew how to organize and administer an empire. As a result, the Mongols became the dominant power in Asia and eastern Europe for a century and a half, and they remained a formidable force well into the fifteenth century.

The Mongols first concentrated their forces against China; they took Peking in 1215 and had occupied most of northern China by the death of Genghis in 1227. The Sung dynasty in the South held out longer, and the Mongols were not able to gain control of the whole country until the 1270s. Meanwhile they found easier conquests to the west. A strong army, under one of the ablest Mongol generals, set out against Persia and Mesopotamia. The Mongols overran Persia quickly, and in 1258 they took Baghdad, plundered the city, and put the caliph to death. This attack ended the Abbasid Caliphate, the last symbol of Moslem unity.

For a time it looked as if the Mongols were going to conquer all the Middle East. But when they attempted to take Syria, they were completely defeated by the Mameluke sultan of Egypt (1260). Since no one else from the Mediterranean to the Yellow Sea could claim to

Genghis Khan (detail from a manuscript illustration, *ca.* 1310).

Iron and silver helmet found at the site of a battle between the sons of a Russian prince (1216). The helmet bears the figure of the archangel Michael.

have defeated a Mongol army, this victory gave the Mamelukes great prestige. The Mongols made little effort to advance further, and the Mamelukes in Egypt and the Turks in Asia Minor remained independent.

Russia and the Mongols

Meanwhile another Mongol horde had attacked Russia, the chief outpost of Byzantine culture. The viking leaders, who had invaded Russia in the ninth century, had built a strong state around Kiev. This state controlled the trade route between the Black Sea and the Baltic, a route that in the early Middle Ages probably carried as many Oriental wares as the route across the Mediterranean. The princes of Kiev grew rich from their trade and were powerful enough to attack Constantinople itself on several occasions. But after the conversion of the Russians to Greek Orthodox Christianity at the end of the tenth century, relations between Kiev and Byzantium were generally friendly. The Russians accepted the civilization of the Eastern Empire along with its religion; they built their churches in the Byzantine style, and their scholars translated Byzantine texts into Russian. Although the Russians added ideas of their own, Kiev at the height of its power in the early eleventh century must have resembled Constantinople in many ways. It was certainly larger, wealthier, and more of an intellectual center than either the Paris of the first Capetian kings or the London of William the Conqueror.

In the twelfth century Kiev began to decline. It lost some of its trade to the Italians, who exploited the Mediterranean route and sent their ships into the Black Sea. It suffered even more from the Pechenegs, a nomadic people who pushed through the gap between the Urals and the Caspian and cut the trade

THE MONGOL EMPIRE AND ITS SUCCESSOR STATES Thirteenth century

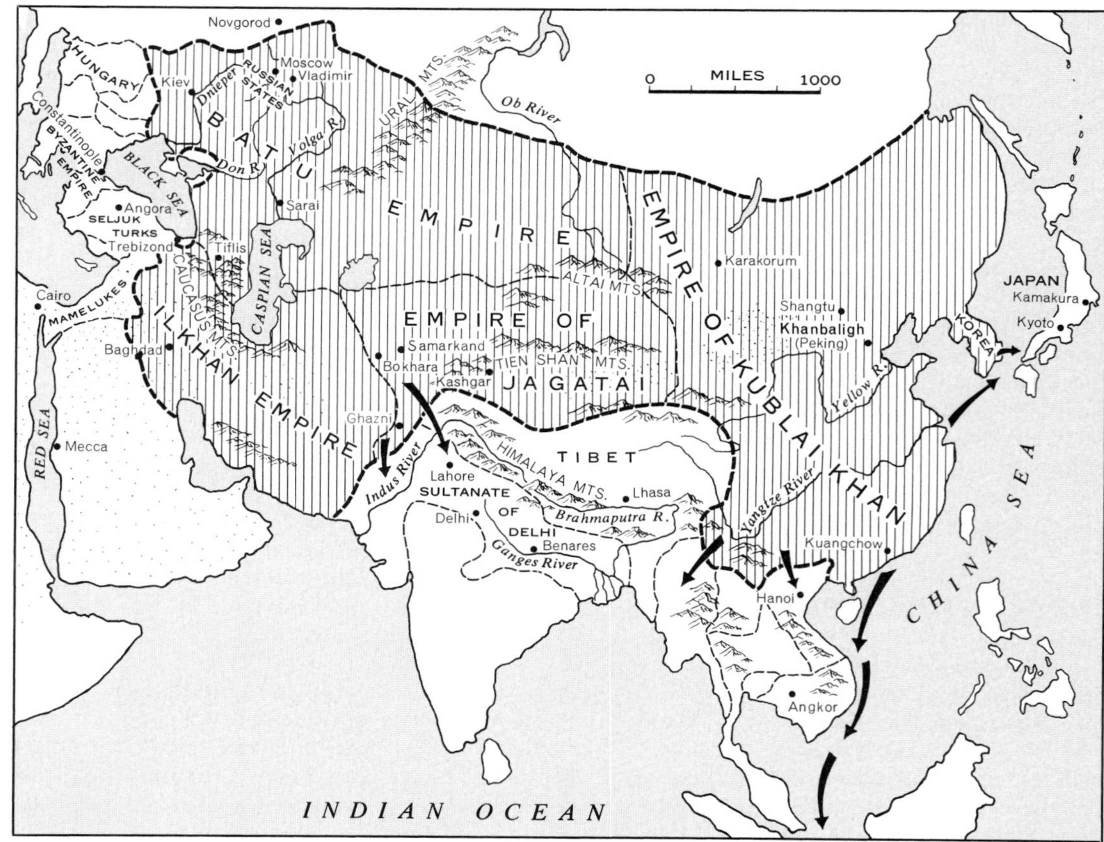

route between Constantinople and Kiev. Meanwhile other centers of power were developing in the upper Volga basin. The princes of Kiev had given outlying towns to younger members of their family to be ruled as dependent principalities. This practice worked well enough at first, but as Kiev declined and family ties weakened, the junior princes became greedy for power. They sacked Kiev itself in 1168, and this disaster, combined with commercial difficulties, put an end to the unity and prosperity of early Russia. The strongest ruler was now the prince of Suzdal, a region that included the newly founded town of Moscow, but his territories were poor and backward compared with Kiev in its great days. Once a land of cities and merchants, Russia was now becoming a land of peasants scratching out a bare living from the thin soils of the north. Declining prosperity, however, did not put an end to feuding among the princes, who found it almost impossible to take combined action against a common enemy such as the Mongols.

It is not surprising, then, that the Mongols conquered Russia so easily. Their first serious attack came in 1237; by 1241 they had overcome all resistance and were pushing across the Carpathians into Hungary. Hungarians resisted no more successfully than Russians—their armies were slaughtered near Budapest—but the death of the Great Khan ended the Mongol threat to central Europe. The commander of the Mongol army rushed home to influence the choice of a new ruler, and he never resumed his attack. The Mongols were at last satiated. They had every right to be, for they had created one of the largest empires the world has ever known.

The Mongols used terror as a means of conquest, wrecking cities and executing entire populations in order to convince their foes of the dangers of resistance. But once they had established their empire, they were willing to profit from the knowledge and skills of their subjects. In China and Persia, where they came in contact with relatively advanced civilizations, they soon became assimilated and carried on the old administrative and cultural traditions. In Russia, where they had less to learn, they held themselves apart and retained more of their own characteristics. They occupied only the steppes north of the Caspian, a region in which there never had been very many Slavs.

RUSSIA ABOUT 1200

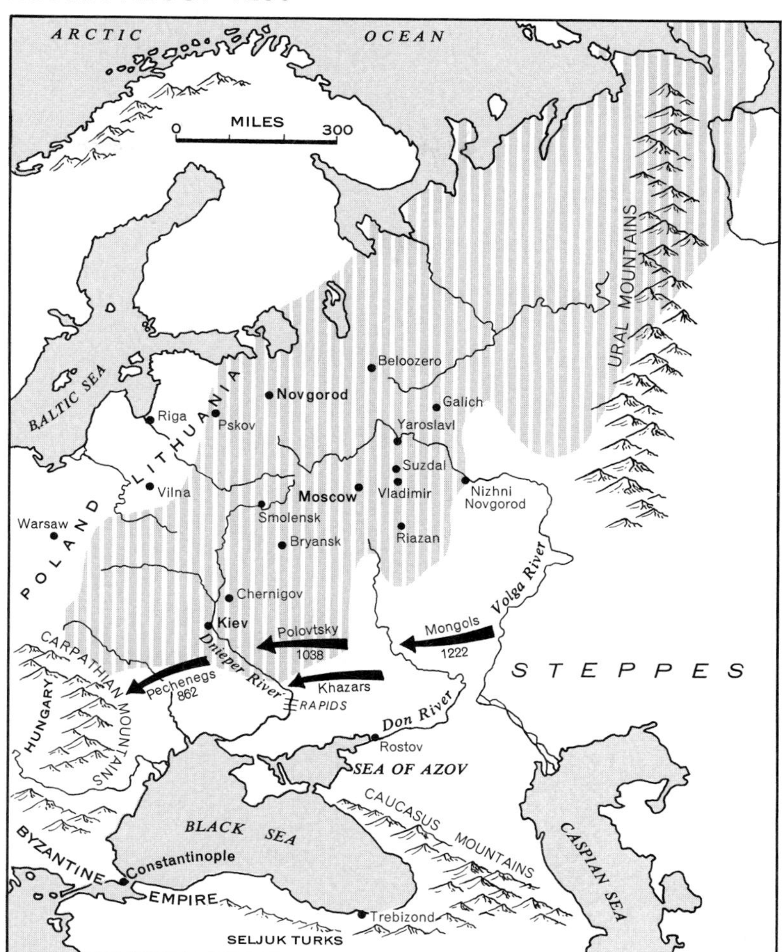

Western Europe and the Mongols

The coming of the Mongols might have changed the history of all Europe if western Europeans had been more alert. For several decades the most dangerous opponents of the Mongols were Mamelukes and Turks, and the Mongols repeatedly suggested to Christian rulers that they form an alliance against the common Moslem enemy. None of these suggestions was ever followed up very seriously, however, and an alliance may well have been impossible. Nevertheless, an alliance between Mongols and Christians might have checked the rising power of the Turks.

Europe also missed the opportunity to convert the Mongols. They were not greatly attached to their own primitive beliefs, and at times they seemed attracted to Christianity. The first Mongol viceroy of Persia had a Christian wife and favored her coreligionists, and the Mongol khan of China, Kublai, asked the pope several times to send him missionaries. Unfortunately, the thirteenth-century popes were occupied with matters nearer at hand, such as their feud with the Hohenstaufens and their efforts to preserve the crusading states. They sent a few envoys, but no solid corps of permanent missionaries. The popes of the early fourteenth century made a greater effort, but by that time it was too late. The western Mongols had already been converted to Islam, one more example of the advantage the simpler Moslem faith enjoyed in missionary competition. The Mongols of China were becoming submerged in the sea of Chinese culture and were soon to lose their power. The few missionaries who were sent from the West made thousands of converts, and a Catholic archbishop sat in Peking for a few years. But the whole effort was swept away when the Mongols were overthrown in 1368 and the strongly antiforeign Ming dynasty came to power.

Kublai Khan (1259–94), a descendant of Genghis Khan and ruler of China at the time of Marco Polo's visit.

Some Italian merchants took advantage of the opening of the overland route to China. The most famous of them was Marco Polo, who went to China in 1275 and spent many years in the country, part of the time as an official of the Mongol government. After he returned to Italy, Marco wrote a long and fairly accurate account of his travels, and his description of the wealth and splendor of the Far East did much to encourage the great explorations of the fifteenth century. But Marco had less influence on the people of his own time. He was accused of wild exaggeration and nicknamed "Marco Millions"; few other merchants followed in his footsteps. Here was another lost opportunity. At the end of the thirteenth century the European economy was grinding toward stagnation; it desperately needed the stimulus of new markets. But fourteenth-century Europe lacked the capital, the energy, and the technical skill needed to open direct trade with the Far East. It was not until the late fifteenth century that western merchants could again dream of reaching China.

RUSSIA: ISOLATION AND AUTOCRACY

During the Mongol occupation, the Russians were allowed to live under their own princes and had little direct contact with the Mongols. So long as the princes paid tribute and sought confirmation of their authority from the khan, they could have whatever laws and religion they pleased.

Loss of Contact with the West

Nevertheless, the period of Mongol domination was a difficult one for Russia. Contacts with the West were sharply reduced, for both in commerce and in diplomacy the Russians had to deal primarily with the Mongols. The Russians were also blocked off from the West by the growing power of Poland and Lithuania.

Poland had received its religion and much of its civilization from the West. It had been converted at the end of the tenth century by Roman Catholic missionaries, and for a long time it was a vassal state of the German Empire. Often weak and divided, the Poles gradually began to grow stronger in the fourteenth century, as the German Empire fell apart. Their trade was largely with the West; their official language, for government as well as for religious affairs, was Latin; and they were rather inclined to look down on the Russians as a backward people.

The Lithuanians were a very ancient people, of the Indo-European language group, who had struggled for centuries to maintain their independence in their home on the south Baltic coast. Both Russians and Germans had tried to convert them, but the bulk of the population remained pagan until well into the fourteenth century. Just as the Poles profited from German weakness, so the Lithuanians gained by the collapse of Kievan Russia. They expanded south and east, acquiring some of the most fertile Russian lands.

In 1386 the Poles and the Lithuanians united. The Poles accepted the Lithuanian grand duke as their king; in return the Lithuanians were supposed to become Latin Christians. Poland-Lithuania was oriented to the West and was usually hostile to the Russians. Down to the sixteenth century, Poland-Lithuania was larger and stronger than all the Russian principalities put together. It intervened again and again in Russian politics, and it acquired so much Russian land that Moscow, at times, was almost a frontier city. Except for the Russian republic of Novgorod, which in the fourteenth century held much of northern Russia and traded directly with merchants coming up the Baltic, Russia was cut off from the sea and had few dealings with any western states.

Russia's loss of contact with the West was at first compensated for by increased contacts with the East. As long as the Mongols remained relatively united, the long land route across the Eurasian plain to China was heavily traveled—more heavily than it was to be again until the nineteenth century. But the subordinate khans who governed outlying regions of the Mongol Empire gradually became independent of the Great Khan, who had his headquarters in Mongolia. Thus the Russians had little to do with the relatively civilized Mongols of China and Persia. They dealt primarily with the so-called Golden Horde, the Mongols of the lower Volga region, who were the least advanced of all the Mongol groups.

Thrown back on themselves, the Russians took refuge in their religion. Their faith differentiated them from the Mongols, but it separated them almost as sharply from the West. They became fiercely orthodox and even less willing than the Greeks to compromise with the Roman Church. This stubbornness, added to their fear of the Catholic Poles, made them suspicious of westerners and western influences that might change their way of life and endanger their faith.

The Rise of the Autocratic Russian State

Isolation, poverty, and constant wars were not ideal conditions for the growth of Russian society. Opportunities diminished for all classes, especially for the peasants. The most the peasants could hope for was to keep their freedom and a little piece of land, and often they found even these modest desires thwarted. Almost the only productive group in the country, the peasants had to support the Mongols, the princes, the nobles, and the Church. The easiest way for their overlords to make sure that they would meet all these obligations was to bind them to the soil; thus serfdom grew in Russia at

The Church of the Savior at Novgorod (twelfth century). This is an early example of what became a typical style of ecclesiastical architecture in Russia.

the very time it was declining in the West. In order to escape serfdom, some peasants moved off into the desolate forest regions of the northeast, but even there the princes caught up with them and assigned them as serfs to monasteries and nobles.

The government of the princes became increasingly arbitrary, though its arbitrariness was always tempered by administrative inefficiency. Economic pressure forced the princes into absolutism; their states were small, and the burdens of Mongol tribute and war expenses were great. The princes had inherited a tradition of autocracy from Byzantium, and Mongol demands encouraged the growth of absolutism. A prince who could not collect his tribute was sure to be in trouble; it did him no good to explain that he could not raise the money without violating the rights of his nobles and peasants.

During the fourteenth century the principality of Moscow became the strongest state in Russia. Its rise was due partly to chance; for several generations only one heir to the principality survived, and thus it was not weakened by constant divisions. Moreover, the metropolitan of Russia moved his seat to Moscow, thus bestowing on the Muscovite princes

THE GROWTH OF THE GRAND PRINCIPALITY OF MOSCOW 1300–1584

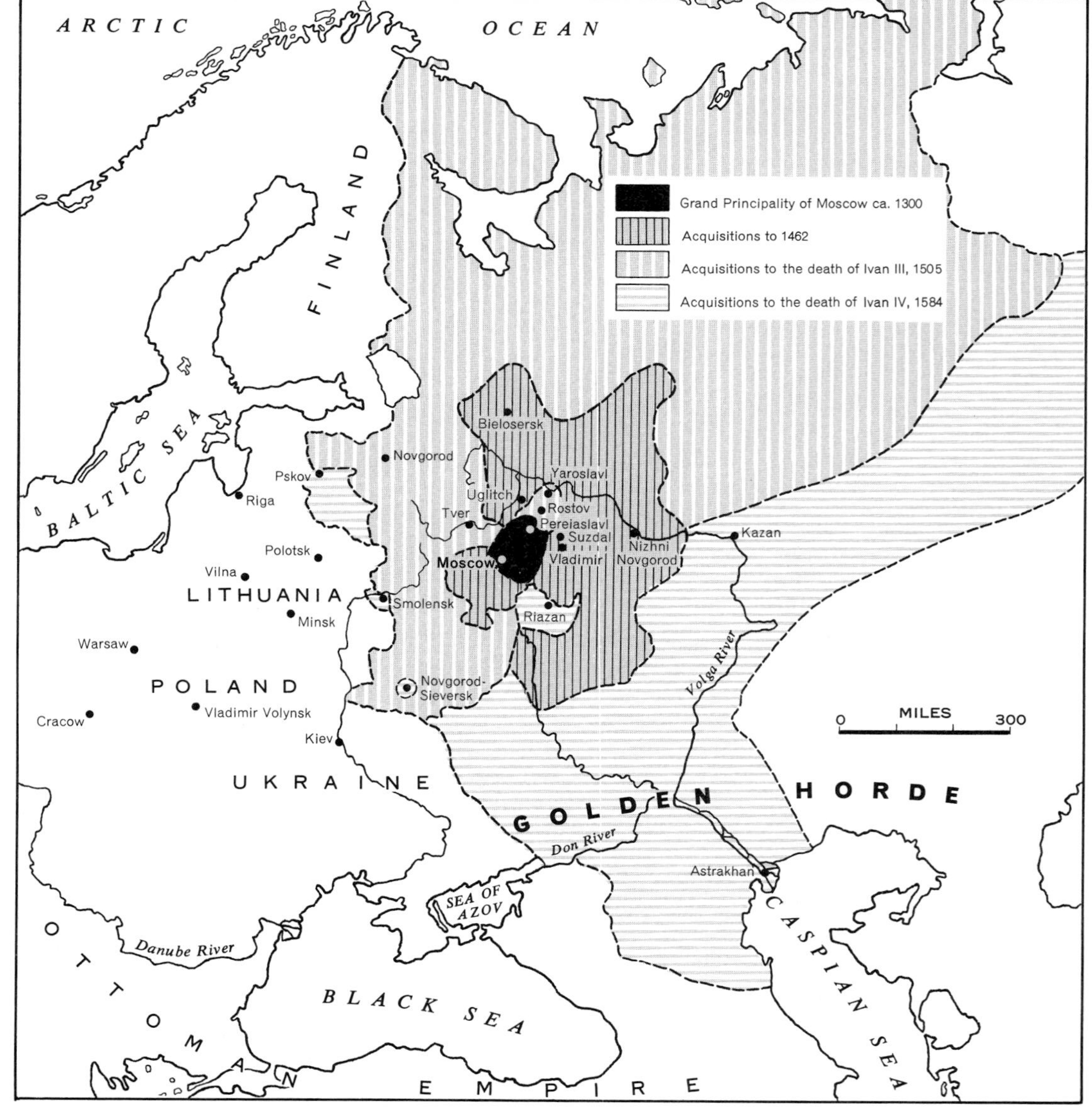

the support of the highest religious authority in the country. Many of the Muscovite princes were men of superior ability, both in diplomacy and in war. They managed to keep on relatively good terms with the Mongols and were given the title of Grand Prince, which meant that they were the chief tribute collectors for the entire country. This position gave them an excuse to intervene in the incessant quarrels of other principalities and an opportunity to annex surrounding territory. As the Mongols weakened, the Grand Princes of Moscow became bolder; one of them actually defeated a Mongol army in 1378. Their assertion of independence was premature, however, for the Mongols still had a strong enough army to defeat the Grand Prince and burn Moscow a few years later. Mongol suzerainty was reestablished and continued into the fifteenth century. Nevertheless, the Grand Prince had established himself as leader of the Russians, and his victory over the Mongols was better remembered than his subsequent submission.

During the fifteenth century a civil war broke out in Moscow, but it served to strengthen the principality. The legitimate heir won the final victory and established the principle that Moscow was not to be divided as other Russian states had been. From this point on, the growth of the Muscovite state was phenomenal. It quickly absorbed neighboring principalities and, under Ivan the Great (Ivan III, 1462–1505), annexed the Republic of Novgorod, which held all northern Russia to the White Sea and the Arctic. Ivan also rejected, once and for all, Mongol suzerainty, and the Russians soon began to annex Mongol lands along the lower Volga. By the end of the sixteenth century the Muscovite state had expanded into a Russian Empire, with territories stretching from the White Sea to the Caspian and from the Lithuanian frontier well into western Siberia. The original principality of Moscow had covered only about five hundred square miles; the Russian Empire of the sixteenth century was the largest state in Europe.

Absolutism grew with the growth of the Muscovite state. The peasants had lost their rights long before; now it was the turn of the nobles. They were not as independent as the nobles of the West. Most of them had become servants of the princes and held their estates only so long as they performed services for the ruler. They had no permanent power base, such as a duke of Lancaster or a duke of Burgundy had in the West. Soon their very life and property depended on the whim of the prince. By the sixteenth century the greatest men in the land could be put to death on the mere suspicion of disloyalty, and bishops and metropolitans who contradicted the wishes of the sovereign were sent into exile. The old title of Grand Prince no longer seemed sufficient to express this concentration of power. Ivan the Great, who married a niece of the last Byzantine emperor, soon began to think of himself as successor to the Caesars. Moscow was to be the "Third Rome" that would endure forever, and Ivan began to call himself Autocrat and Sovereign of All Russia. He also occasionally used the title of tsar (a Russian form of Caesar), but this did not become official until the reign of Ivan the Dread (Ivan IV, 1533–84). Ivan the Dread was a great conqueror and one of the bloodiest tyrants in history. He massacred nobles and townsmen with little reason and killed his own son in a fit of rage.

Russia, the Heir of the Byzantine Empire

Letter of Abbot Philotheus of Pskov to Tsar Vasily III in 1511.

The Church of ancient Rome fell because of the Apollinarian heresy; as for the second Rome, the Church of Constantinople, it has been cut down by the axes of the Hagarenes [Turks]. But in the third, new Rome, the Universal Apostolic Church under thy [Tsar Vasily III] mighty rule sends out the Orthodox Christian faith to the ends of the earth and shines more brightly than the sun. And may thy lordship realize, pious Tsar, that all Christian kingdoms have come together under thy sole empire; thou alone in all the earth art Tsar to the Christians. . . . Two Romes have fallen, but the third stands, and there will be no fourth.

Adapted from Thornton Anderson, *Russian Political Thought* (Ithaca, N.Y.: Cornell University Press, 1967), p. 72.

Part of the dowry of the marriage of Byzantine Princess Zoe to Ivan the Great (1462–1505) was the right to adopt the Byzantine two-headed eagle as the tsar's royal coat of arms.

In spite of its size and the authority of its ruler, sixteenth-century Muscovy was not yet a powerful state. Still cut off from the main trade routes, its only outlet to the ocean was in the far north, on the White Sea. It was thinly settled; probably there were more people in France than in all the territories of the tsar. It was poor; it had almost no industry, and agriculture was backward. It was still militarily weak, open to attack by Poles from the west and Turks and Tatars from the southeast. The bulk of the peasants were still farming the poor soils of the north by primitive methods, and there were few settlers in the rich black-earth districts of the south. It was far behind its neighbors in all intellectual activities, in science and technology as well as in scholarship and literature. Only after 1600 did the Russians begin to overcome these great handicaps.

THE ADVANCE OF THE TURKS

The problem for much of Europe was not the Mongols but the Turks. As we have seen, the Mongol advance left the Turks of Asia Minor relatively unharmed, and the Byzantine Empire had been fragmented by the Fourth Crusade. The Serbs and Bulgars dominated the back country, western feudal lords ruled most of Greece, and Venice held the islands. The Byzantine Empire, as revived in 1261, possessed only Constantinople and a narrow strip of land on each side of the Straits. The new Turkish dynasty of the Ottomans, founded in 1299, rapidly exploited the weakness of the Christians. As good at war as their predecessors, the Seljuks, the Ottomans showed far more ability in building a permanent state with a strong administrative system. After conquering most of western Asia Minor, they began, in the 1350s, to make permanent settlements on the European side of the Straits. The Christians offered no concerted resistance, and by 1365 the Turks had established their capital in Adrianople, not far from Constantinople. In 1389 they broke the power of the Serbs, who had the strongest state in the Balkans, at the battle of Kossovo. This victory brought the Turks to the borders of Hungary, and the West at last began to take alarm. The pope proclaimed a crusade, and a large army—mostly German and Hungarian with some French knights—advanced against the Turks. But bad generalship and poor discipline ruined whatever chance of success it had, and the crusaders were thoroughly defeated at the battle of Nicopolis in 1396.

The battle almost destroyed Christian power in the Balkans, but before the Turks could fully exploit their victory they were attacked from the east. Timur the Lame (Tamerlane), who claimed to be a descendant of Genghis Khan, had created a nomad army worthy of his supposed ancestor. The Mongols were once more on the march, and this time the Ottoman Turks were one of their chief enemies. In 1402 the two armies met at Ankara, where Timur won a complete victory. The Mongols captured the Turkish sultan and occupied most of his lands in Asia Minor.

Timur died soon after his victory, and his successors made little effort to hold the remote regions he had taken from the Turks. Nevertheless, the defeat at Ankara, followed by a generation of civil war, was a severe test of the Ottoman political system. The fact that the state was pulled together once again showed that the early sultans had done their work well. They had created a corps of disciplined and capable administrators, and it was with their assistance that one of the Ottoman princes was able to reestablish himself as sole ruler. By the 1440s the Turks were once more advancing in the Balkans. Their chief opponents this time were the Hungarians, commanded by John Hunyadi. Though a first-rate general, Hunyadi lost two major battles to the Turks.

The End of the Byzantine Empire

Now the road lay open to Constantinople. The last Byzantine emperor, Constantine XI, made a desperate appeal to the West for aid. Over the strong opposition of his subjects, he agreed to reunite the Greek and Latin Churches in return for western aid. But the union was never effective, and the popes of the fifteenth century lacked the prestige needed to rouse the West. Constantine received no real help and was left to fight the final battles alone. In 1453 the Turks made an all-out attack on the imperial city. The emperor was killed defending a breach in the walls, and the Turks poured into Constantinople. This was the end of the Byzantine Empire and of the emperors who claimed to be heirs of Caesar and Augustus. For many years there had been nothing Roman about them except their titles, but they were not unworthy of those titles in their last struggle.

Turkish advances in Europe continued after the fall of Constantinople, largely at the expense of Hungary. The Hungarians fought valiantly but were pushed back little by little until the Turks reached their high-water mark of conquest at the unsuccessful siege of Vienna in 1529.

As the Turkish advance slowed down in Europe, it speeded up in Asia and Africa. During the sixteenth century Syria, Mesopotamia, and Arabia were added to the Turkish Empire in Asia, and Egypt, Tunisia, and Algeria in North Africa. With this Turkish conquest of the southern and eastern coasts of the Mediterranean, Moslem naval power began to revive. The Turks never closed the Mediterranean to Christian shipping, but they and the semipiratical fleets of their subjects did interfere seriously with commerce from time to time. It was not until the 1800s that the Mediterranean became as safe for western merchants as it had been in the thirteenth century.

The Decline of Moslem Civilization

The rise of the Turks coincided with a decline in Moslem intellectual activity. Both the Turks and the Mongols have often been blamed for this decline, but neither people seems to have been entirely responsible. It is true that both Turks and Mongols were originally rough warriors from the steppes with little interest in intellectual matters, but both of them absorbed Moslem civilization with great rapidity. Art and literature flourished under the Mongol rulers of Persia. In fact, Persia was the leading cultural center of Islam in the fifteenth century, but its influence was felt more in the East, especially in India, than in the West. The Turks did some remarkable work in architecture and developed a highly literate corps of administrators. Moreover, one of the most eloquent laments over the decline of Moslem learning came from the historian ibn-Khaldun (1332–1406), who spent most of his life in North Africa, a region that was never touched by the Mongols and that fell under Turkish control only in the sixteenth century. There must have been more deep-seated causes, prevalent throughout the Moslem world, of the decline of Moslem civilization.

Ibn-Khaldun, probably the greatest of all Moslem historians, tried to work out a historical theory to explain the decline.

Mohammed II, ruler of the Turks when they took Constantinople in 1453.

His idea was that there had always been antagonism between the educated, open-minded, prosperous city dwellers and the ignorant, narrow-minded, poverty-stricken inhabitants of the desert and the steppes. When the city people became soft and decadent, as they had in his time, power passed to the crude but warlike tribes of the open country. This political shift in turn caused a shift in the climate of opinion. Rigid orthodoxy was favored, and science and philosophy were looked on with contempt and suspicion.

There is some truth in ibn-Khaldun's explanation. The dominant dynasties of the Moslem world in the fourteenth century were all nomad in origin, and some of them did emphasize strict Moslem orthodoxy. But this is only part of the story. Earlier nomadic conquerors, beginning with the Arabs themselves, had absorbed the intellectual heritage of the ancient world without difficulty, and fourteenth-century orthodoxy did not prevent the rise of mysticism in the Moslem world. Some leaders of the mystical movement, who had large followings, advanced ideas that went far beyond the early teachings of Islam, so that we cannot say that a sort of Islamic fundamentalism blocked all forms of speculation. It seems rather that Moslem science and philosophy had reached a dead end, and that the educated classes had become uninterested in them.

Perhaps Moslem learning had reached its peak too early and too rapidly. Few new ideas entered the world of Islam after the tenth century, and all the changes on the old themes had been rung by the thirteenth century. With nothing new to be done, there was naturally a loss of interest in academic subjects. In comparison, western scholarship, which was far inferior to that of the Moslem world in the tenth century, received a fresh stimulus every time it was about to reach a dead end. There were the translations from the Arabic in the twelfth century, the revival of Greek studies in the fifteenth, and the great scientific discoveries of the early modern period. Moreover, theology, philosophy, and science were so closely associated in Christian thought that activity in one field prompted activity in the others. Extraordinary interest in theology in the fourteenth century stimulated activity in philosophy and science. The theology of Islam, on the other hand, was much less complicated. Some Moslems took it for granted; others simply memorized the Koran, paying no attention to philosophy. Thus religious education in Moslem countries did not require corresponding activity in philosophy or science. Finally, as we have seen, western scholars were not quite so bound to authoritative, scholarly interpretations; more innovation was possible in fourteenth-century Paris than in fourteenth-century Cairo.

Whatever the value of these explanations, one basic fact is clear: for the first time in history, western Europe was to take the lead in certain types of scholarly investigation. Byzantine scholarship, never very original, was blighted by the Turkish conquest. Moslem scholarship was rapidly decaying in the fourteenth and fifteenth centuries. Of all the peoples who had inherited the great Greek tradition of philosophical and scientific inquiry, only the scholars of western Europe were still active. And their activity was to give the West an incalculable advantage in the next four centuries.

Suggestions for Further Reading

Note: Asterisk denotes a book available in paperback edition.

Byzantium 750–1453

S. Runciman, *Byzantine Civilization** (1933), gives a good general picture of Byzantine institutions and culture and is the best introduction. The most thorough and scholarly study is G. Ostrogorsky, *History of the Byzantine State,* trans. by J. M. Hussey (1956). The older work of A. A. Vasiliev, *History of the Byzantine Empire,* 2 vols. (1928), is more readable than Ostrogorsky but not as thorough nor as fresh in historical interpretation. There is valuable material on the commercial activities of the Italian city-states within the Byzantine Empire in E. H. Byrne, *Genoese Shipping in* *the Twelfth and Thirteenth Centuries* (1930). G. Every, *The Byzantine Patriarchate* (1947), compares the liturgical and doctrinal differences between the eastern and western Churches, and J. M. Hussey, *Church and Learning in the Byzantine Empire* (1937), is useful for understanding Byzantine intellectual activity. See also the titles by Baynes, Diehl, Grabar, and Talbot-Rice mentioned after Chapter 8. An interesting survey of Byzantine civilization and its influence on the West is S. Vryonis, *Byzantium and Europe** (1967). The best account of the Latin conquest of Constantinople is *Latin Conquest of Constantinople,* ed. by D. E. Queller (1971).

The Caliphate 750–1258 B. Lewis, *The Arabs in History** (1966), a broad, quick survey, is a good starting point for study. B. Spuler, *The Muslim World,* Vol. I, trans. by F. R. C. Bagley (1960), is an authoritative survey of the entire period and a useful handbook. The old account of T. W. Arnold, *The Caliphate* (1963), is still valuable for the theory and development of the Caliphate. There is considerable material in P. K. Hitti, *A History of the Arabs** (1956), the standard treatment of the subject, invaluable for the facts of the period but quite controversial in historical interpretation. For the Caliphate as an institution, see E. Tyan, *Le Califut* (1954), and E. I. J. Rosenthal, *Political Thought in Medieval Islam* (1958). The growth of Turkish power is well treated by P. Wittek, *The Rise of the Ottoman Empire* (1958).

The Crusades There are several accounts of the later crusades that give us real insight into the spirit and motivation of the crusaders. Both Geoffrey de Villhardouin, *The Conquest of Constantinople** (Everyman's Library), and Robert of Clari, *The Conquest of Constantinople,* trans. by E. H. McNeal (1936), are fascinating eyewitness accounts of the Fourth Crusade. Philippe of Novara, *The Wars of Frederick II Against the Ibelins,* trans. by J. L. La Monte (1936), contributes a great deal to our knowledge of Frederick II and his crusades. The counselor Joinville's *Life of St. Louis** (Everyman's Library) has exciting material on St. Louis' expeditions to Egypt and Tunis on the Sixth and Seventh Crusades.

E. Barker, *The Crusades* (1923), is old but still valuable. The best recent study is the beautifully written and highly urbane account by S. Runciman, *A History of the Crusades,** 3 vols. (1951–54). Runciman includes a thorough bibliography. There is good material on the crusades in the books by Setton, Hitti, and La Monte listed after Chapter 10, in the fourth section. For crusading efforts after 1300, see A. S. Atiya, *The Crusades in the Later Middle Ages* (1938).

East–West Relations See Deno J. Geankoplos, *Byzantine East and Latin West: Two Worlds of Christendom in Middle Ages and Renaissance* (1976) and *Medieval Western Civilization and the Byzantine and Islamic Worlds* (1979).

The Mongols in the Arab World and Russia B. Spuler, *The Muslim World,* Vol. II: *The Mongol Period,* trans. by F. R. C. Bagley (1960), is excellent. G. Le Strange, *The Lands of the Eastern Caliphate* (1905), a study of the historical geography of the Near East and central Asia in the Middle Ages, is an old treatment but very good reading. Juvaynī 'Alā' al-Din 'utā Malik, *The History of the World Conqueror,* trans. by J. A. Bayle (1952), is an important study, while V. V. Barthold, *Four Studies on the History of Central Asia* (1955), contains the authoritative history of central Asia and the Mongols. Probably the best treatment of the Mongol rule of Russia is G. Vernadsky, *The Monguls and Russia* (1953), a scholarly and readable work by a leading authority on Russian history.

Russia 1100–1600 There are several very good studies of this period of Russian history. M. T. Florinsky, *Russia: A History and Interpretation,* Vol. I (1955), has valuable material on this formative period of the Russian state. The old work of V. O. Kliuchevsky, *A History of Russia,* 2 vols. (1912), is very interesting reading and still important. Undoubtedly the best treatment of Russia from 1100 to 1600 is G. Vernadsky, *Russia at the Dawn of the Modern Age* (1959). Vernadsky includes excellent maps and genealogical tables and up-to-date bibliographic material. *A History of the U.S.S.R.,* ed. by A. M. Pankratova (1947), is a modern Marxist interpretation of the evolution of the Russian state. See also F. Nowak, *Medieval Slavdom and the Rise of Russia* (1930).

The Decline of Arabic Learning Most of the titles mentioned in the second section above contain information on Arabic learning. R. Landau, *Islam and the Arabs* (1958), devotes considerable attention to Moslem culture. T. W. Arnold and A. Guillaume, *The Legacy of Islam* (2nd ed. by J. Schacht and C. E. Bosworth, 1972), provide a good summary that traces those elements in European culture that have roots in the Islamic world.

Index

A

B

C

D

E

F

G

H

I

J

K

L

M

N

O

P

Q

S

T

U

V

A 3
B 4
C 5
D 6
E 7
F 8
G 9
H 0
I 1
J 2